# WHAT CRITICS SAID ABOUT
# FRANK SINATRA, THE BOUDOIR SINGER

*"Authors Darwin Porter and Danforth Prince prove once again that the major stars had sex lives —wild, crazy, dirty sex lives, and the Sinatra book is full of these stories. It's amazing how much they kept out of the gossip columns back in the day. There's so many astonishing tales, like the story that Frank carried suitcases full of cash from Havana as a favor to the Mob, or the whole chapter detailing the roller coaster ride that was his marriage to Ava Gardner. The chapter about Billie Holliday and her tragic death proves that the authors can depict moving, sad moments as well. And I just loved it every time Frank punched a member of the press, which was often. I like to think that if Frank were still alive, he'd be taking a swing at both Darwin and Danforth for spilling so many juicy, juicy secrets! A must-read if you love gossip, sex, Sinatra, or just a good story told well."*

**—Paul Bellini, *FAB magazine*, Toronto**

*"With this sizzling book, Blood Moon scores again—as did Frank Sinatra, the serial womanizer whose innumerable sexual conquests frame a lusty peephole account of the acclaimed crooner's life. More than a mere biography,* **Sinatra: The Boudoir Singer** *(and never was a title more apropos!) tracks the Hoboken-born performer's rise, fall, and rise again while serving up deep dish on scenes ranging from Manhattan's jazz clubs to Grace Kelly's Monaco, from Havana's pre-Castro sexual playground to the battleground that was Sinatra's tempestuous relationship with Ava Gardner."*

**—Richard Labonté, *Books to Watch Out For* and *Q-Syndicate***

*"Every page turn of this book is brimming over with shocking situations and scandalous stories. Authors Darwin Porter and Danforth Prince have excelled themselves with this their latest publication. This book is like a pressure cooker that's just blown its lid, answering in full many mysterious down and dirty questions that have been blurred about O'Blue Eyes for decades. It's hotter and spicier than the hottest Indian curry dish—reading this book is a tumultuous and amazing experience! Warning alert—this book is not for the faint hearted!"*

**—David W. Hartnell, MNZM**

*"A lot of the Hollywood in-crowd tell me things. I'm constantly amazed. They're always telling me things, so I do know where every body is buried. And I have to tell you this: The Truth is so much stranger than fiction. So many things I can't write because nobody would believe me. I'd be laughed off the page."*

**—Author Jackie Collins**

*"**For Criss-sake!** What a place Hollywood was back then. Women like Joan Crawford were sleeping with different partners at least four times a week. Bogart was in like Flynn before any-one ever heard of Errol. Hollywood was one giant bordello. Men with women, men with men, women with women. And the public never knew."*

**—Bette Davis**

*"The press was always rough on Frank Sinatra and me, plus a few others, but many of the whoring rats of Hollywood got by with a whitewash, especially those on the bottom of the orgy pile. If the public only knew the truth about those overhyped masculine men—Clark Gable, John Wayne, John Ford, Errol Flynn, Johnny Weissmuller, Gary Cooper, Tyrone Power, Robert Taylor. Those guys have sucked as many cocks as I have."*

**—Tallulah Bankhead**

*"L.A. was a smog-shrouded netherworld orbiting under a dark star and blinded by the glare of scandal-rag flashbulbs. Every third person was a peeper, a prowler, pederast, poon stalker, panty sniffer, prostitute, pillhead, pothead, or pimp. The other two-thirds of the population were tight-ass squares resisting the urge to peep, prowl, poon stalk, and pederastically indulge. This mass of self-denial created a seismic dislocation that skewed L.A. about six degrees off the cen-tral axis of planet Earth."*

**—Author James Ellroy**

*"Fifty years ago, to be a celebrity meant being presented—groomed and glittering—to the adoring public under carefully controlled circumstances. Tawdry behavior or unseemly habits were swept under the rug by savvy publicists and managers with cozy ties to the media. Very few people really knew what was being cooked up behind closed doors. Blood Moon Productions, a publishing house based in Staten Island, is on a quest to change all that."*

**—Marjorie Hack, *The Staten Island Advance***

# FRANK SINATRA

## THE BOUDOIR SINGER
### All the Gossip Unfit to Print

BLOOD
MOON
Productions, Ltd.

# OTHER BOOKS BY DARWIN PORTER

### BIOGRAPHIES
*The Kennedys, All the Gossip Unfit to Print*
*Humphrey Bogart, the Making of a Legend*
*Howard Hughes: Hell's Angel*
*Steve McQueen, King of Cool, Tales of a Lurid Life*
*Paul Newman, The Man Behind the Baby Blues*
*Merv Griffin, A Life in the Closet*
*Brando Unzipped*
*The Secret Life of Humphrey Bogart*
*Katharine the Great: Hepburn, Secrets of a Lifetime Revealed*
*Jacko, His Rise and Fall (The Social and Sexual History of Michael Jackson)*
and, co-authored with Roy Moseley
*Damn You, Scarlett O'Hara, The Private Lives of Vivien Leigh and Laurence Olivier*

### COMING SOON:
*J. Edgar Hoover and Clyde Tolson, Investigating the Sexual Secrets of America's Most Famous Men & Women*
and, in collaboration with Roy Moseley
*Olivia de Havilland and Joan Fontaine, Twisted Sisters: To Each Her Own*

### FILM CRITICISM
*50 Years of Queer Cinema--500 of the Best GLBTQ Films Ever Made (2010)*
*Blood Moon's Guide to Recent Gay & Lesbian Film--Volumes One (2006) and Two (2007)*
*Best Gay and Lesbian Films- The Glitter Awards, 2005*

### NON-FICTION
*Hollywood Babylon-It's Back!*
*Hollywood Babylon Strikes Again!*

### NOVELS
*Butterflies in Heat*
*Marika*
*Venus (a roman à clef based on the life of Anaïs Nin)*
*Razzle-Dazzle*
*Midnight in Savannah*
*Rhinestone Country*
*Blood Moon*
*Hollywood's Silent Closet*

### TRAVEL GUIDES
Many editions and many variations of *The Frommer Guides* to
Europe, the Caribbean, California, Georgia and the Carolinas, Bermuda, and The Bahamas

# FRANK SINATRA

## THE BOUDOIR SINGER

### All the Gossip Unfit to Print

DARWIN PORTER AND DANFORTH PRINCE

# FRANK SINATRA, THE BOUDOIR SINGER
## ALL THE GOSSIP UNFIT TO PRINT

Copyright © 2011, Blood Moon Productions, Ltd.

Manufactured in the United States of America

**ISBN 978-1-936003-19-8**
First printing November 2011

Cover designs by Richard Leeds (www.bigwigdesign.com)
Photo licenses courtesy of www.PhotofestNYC.com
Videography and publicity trailers by Piotr Kajstura

Distributed in North America and Australia
through the National Book Network (www.NBNbooks.com)
and in the U.K. through Turnaround (www.turnaround-uk.com)

Blood Moon acknowledges the **National Book Network**
for its savvy guidance in the presentation and marketing of this book.
Special thanks go to **Monica Dunn** for her tireless research, and to
Frank Sinatra devotee **Roy Moseley**, author of numerous celebrity biographies

# DEDICATION

This book is dedicated to Frank Sinatra,
Because of his charisma and his talent,
and because no other singer
has ever provided us with the possibility of
so much Entertainment.

# REST IN PEACE

*"Known affectionately as Ol'Blue Eyes, The Voice, the Greatest Roman of Them All, and the Chairman of the Board, Frank Sinatra is perhaps the greatest and most versatile performer of all time, enjoying a 40-year career as band singer, recording star, Academy Award actor, international concert artist, and humanitarian. He has always been a singer's singer, an entertainer who raised popular singing to the highest level of artistry."*

**—Arnold Shaw**
Musicologist, composer, author

# FRANK SINATRA
### An American Classic

1915-1998

# CONTENTS

# Frank Sinatra

## THE SKINNY KID FROM HOBOKEN

**Francis Albert Sinatra,** age three (on the left), poses for his first formal portrait, where he appears with a top hat and in tails for the first time. Up until then, he'd been dressed only in pink, since his mother, Dolly Sinatra, had wanted a girl and had purchased pink clothing in advance of the blessed event.

He was born in a tenement apartment in Hoboken, a birth so difficult it nearly cost the lives of both mother and son. Dolly, throughout her life, reminded her son that giving him life nearly cost her her own.

The doctor pronounced Baby Frank a stillborn, but his quick-thinking grandmother, Rosa, rushed him to the sink and held him under cold running water until he uttered his first cry. No, it was not a melodious sound, but a screeching cry for life, announcing that the little baby who would one day be known as Frank Sinatra had entered the world...just barely.

*[Right photo]* Even though only ten years old, Frank for the first time wore what was to become his trademark, a man's fedora. In time, he would become so associated with a hat that Bill Zehme once wrote a biography of him called *The Way You Wear Your Hat*. The photographer of this picture wanted him to take off the hat, but the cocky young boy said, "The hat stays on. No one tells Frank Sinatra what to do except *mamma mia*."

# "I'm Gonna Be a Singer"

Because Dolly was fond of dressing young Frank like a Little Lord Fauntleroy, he often got into fistfights every time he walked on the streets of Hoboken. He is seen here in his first Holy Communion portrait. "I was already called Scarface because of the injuries some quack doctor caused me at birth," Frank recalled. "but you could become Scarface by walking through the wrong neighborhood in Hoboken. Street gangs were lying in wait for you, especially if you looked like the little faggot that Dolly dressed me as. She wanted me to grow up to be a gentleman; Marty wanted me to learn how to use my fists. I acheived both of their dreams for me."

*"There are many rumors about why Frank abandoned his hometown of Hoboken, as there are mysterious middle-of-the-night Sinatra sightings. Some say he was booed at a performance; others that he was egged during a parade. Some say he turned his back on the town when he became famous; others say it was the town that resented his fame. Whatever. Frank won't be coming home anymore."*

—**Jenifer D. Braun**

*"My son is like me. You cross him, and he never forgets."*

—**Dolly Sinatra**

*"Some day, that's gonna be me up there."*
—**Frank Sinatra** looking up at a marquee in Jersey City (summer 1935) that starred Bing Crosby

*"My mother scared the shit outta me."*

—**Frank Sinatra** to Shirley MacLaine

When Giovanni ("John") and Rosa Sinatra left Sicily for America at the turn of the 20th Century, they had already given birth to a son, Marty. Unable to make a living in their native land, they landed in Hoboken, New Jersey, along with thousands of other immigrants, including not only Italians, but Scots, Scandinavians, British, Germans, French Huguenots, and the Irish who had fled the 1845 potato famine in their home country. New Jersey itself became known as "a foreign country" within the Greater American continent.

John Sinatra had been told that in America the streets were paved with gold. A very different world awaited his wife and child in Hoboken, which had long passed its heyday when in the late 19th century it was a fashionable resort for rich people wanting to escape from the torrid heat of Manhattan or Brooklyn.

John found a job making pencils for the American Pencil Company. He brought home eleven dollars a week, and cursed the day he ever left Sicily. At night he walked home, hearing the anti-Italian slurs from everyone from the Turks and Syrians to the Romanians and Russians. "No one likes Sicilians," he told Rosa. "They claim we're thieves."

Once he stopped in a *biergarten*, thirsty for a lager and drawn to the sound of a brass band. Two burly German bodyguards tossed him out of the hall on his ass.

John got revenge. During World War I, many of these Germans were arrested as spies. Hoboken was under military law for the duration of the war, and the large German population was rounded up and detained.

As Marty grew into manhood, John had no money to pass on to him. But he had some advice. "In Hoboken, walk with your eyes in the back of your head. Fuck any pretty girl you want to, but don't get her pregnant."

Even though he suffered from bouts of asthma, Marty became a prizefighter, billing himself as "Marty O'Brien." He figured if fans thought he was Irish, the virtual ruling class in Hoboken, they would cheer him on. [After a particularly gruesome fight in 1926, he broke his wrist and was forced to hire himself out as a boilermaker in a seedy, rat-infested shipyard.]

At a dance for Italian immigrants, Marty met "Dolly," actually Natalie Catherine Garavente, who came to Hoboken in 1898 with her immigrant parents when she was only two years old. Like him, she too had piercing blue eyes.

It was a scenario straight out of *Romeo and Juliet*. Her Genovese family detested Sicilians, considering them peasants. Marty's parents wanted him to marry a Sicilian gal. "But I won him over, although I was much better educated," Dolly said. "After all, I finished the sixth grade, and he couldn't read or write."

Dolly despaired of ever winning her parents' approval. Finally, this strong-willed woman told Marty, "Hell with them. We're eloping. You'd better tell me now. We've never gone to bed, and I've got to know something. Are you any good in the sack? If you're not, I'm wasting my time with you."

Marty told her he was an accomplished lover, as any number of beautiful women in Hoboken could tell her. "I met these gals when I was a boxer."

Marty and Dolly eloped and were married at City Hall on Valentine's Day, February 14, 1913.

After a brief honeymoon in Atlantic City, they moved back to Hoboken's Little Italy, sharing an address at 415 Monroe Street with eight other impoverished immigrant families.

As World War I raged in Europe, and in a dreary tenement bedroom, Francis Albert Sinatra entered the world on December 12, 1915. "That's my Christmas present to you," Dolly told Marty. "We can't afford anything else."

A quack doctor had to use forceps to pry the big

When Frank was broke, hungry, and looking for work in the 1930s in Manhattan, he agreed to appear as "The Masked Bandit" in a porno flick (referred to at the time as a "blue movie"). But in the upper photograph, he appears nude on camera for the first time.

The fat baby in this picture weighed 15 pounds. "He ripped my insides out," Dolly claimed, "and after Frank I could have no more children." The photographer took this picture from the right because the birth wounds caused on the other side of his face and neck had not healed.

In the lower photo, Dolly is all dolled up to pose with her husband Marty during the celebration of their second wedding anniversary. It was attended by members of both sides of their family, but each clan hated the other and stayed on different sides of the room. Marty's mother, Rosa Sinatra, told her son: "Your marriage won't last. In Sicily, it is the man who must wear the pants—never the woman."

3

baby, weighing 13 and a half pounds, from her body. Not really knowing what he was doing, he nearly killed the boy and injured his neck and left cheek. He also punctured an eardrum. After this difficult birth, Dolly would never be able to conceive again.

The doctor pronounced young Francis a stillborn, but Dolly's mother, Rosa, had been trained as a midwife in her native Sicily. She grabbed the child from the doctor and placed its head under cold running water. Thus, Francis came into the world kicking and screaming.

At the St. Francis Holy Roman Catholic Church on April 12, 1916, Francis Sinatra was baptized. The Albert was added to his name later.

Until he was nearly ten years old, Frank and Marty bathed in the same tub. He later told Dolly, "I think Frankie has inherited more from me than just my blue eyes."

When the United States entered World War I, Hoboken became a major port for ships heading for and returning from Europe. President Woodrow Wilson imposed Prohibition, the new law against alcohol first being recognized in Hoboken. However, most locals ignored it. Alcoholic beverages were plentiful, and local officials didn't enforce this new federal law.

In this picture from a summer interlude on the Jersey shore, Frank's first girlfriend, **Marie Roemer**, appears bigger than he is. Frank was befriended by a young boy, William Roemer, who came from a German family. Frank went home with Roemer, where he met his sister, Marie, who was six months older.

Frank fell hard for the pretty, bright, and beautiful German girl. He wooed her, but she wasn't particularly impressed, even when he gave her a birthstone ring on St. Valentine's day. He also bought for her the swimming suit she's wearing. For her Sweet Sixteen party, he purchased his first three-piece sharkskin suit for $29.

Soonafter, she met someone else and told him, "Get lost, Frankie."

Dolly opened a tavern at Fourth and Jefferson Streets, calling it Marty O'Brien's. "I wanted to attract the Irish because they drink more."

Wise cracking, full of laughter and spirit, Dolly became known as the best bartender in Hoboken. She mixed in with some of the toughest characters. "I had more balls than most of my patrons," she later bragged.

It was not Dolly's son who was the first to hang out with mobsters. He was following in his mother's footsteps. "This hell-raiser used to make her joint party night every night," claimed patron Giuseppe Friddi. "She could belt out songs in Italian, of course, but she also learned all the songs that would bring tears to an Irishman. Frank got his singing talent from his *mamma mia*."

When she found out her young son could sing, she had him entertain the patrons at her bar, mostly with Irish favorites.

While Dolly hawked the drinks, Marty drove as a security guard behind the trucks of bootleggers to prevent them from being hijacked.

"Marty left the business when a rival bootlegger nearly split his head open with an ax," Dolly said.

Frank learned to sing listening to the radio, especially to the singing of Bing Crosby and Rudy Vallee. "The radio was like a religion to me. If you've ever noticed, they were constructed in the shape of a church."

On the movie screen, he preferred more violent characters, and liked tough guys such as Edward G. Robinson or James Cagney.

Long before Paul Muni made a movie called *Scarface* (1932), Frank was called that by the neighborhood kids because of the birth marks that still showed, which were caused by those forceps.

Almost every day Frank had to face the older and bigger bullies at David E. Rue Junior High, which he attended in 1928. His

4

mother insisted on dressing him "real fancy like Little Lord Fauntleroy." She made his velvet suits herself.

"I dressed him in pink because I really wanted a girl but he came out of me as a boy with a thing between his legs that even some grown men don't possess," she confided to her jealous women friends on the block.

As Frank walked the streets of Hoboken, he was called "faggot WOP" or "a sissy little dago." One Irish bully learned the hard way not to do that. Frank broke a milk bottle and, with its jagged edge, sliced the right side of the boy's face, turning him into a Scarface.

"He was both violent to bullies and seductive to girls even though he was the skinniest boy on the block," said a boyhood acquaintance, Guido D'Orazio. "At the age of thirteen, he seemed to have developed his man's cock, and he didn't mind showing it to us. All the boys in the neighborhood had penis envy. He started screwing gals at that early age, taking them into back alleys and making them scream, their screeches competing with those of the stray cats."

Dolly and Marty were so engaged in other pursuits that neither of them had time for Frank. He more or less grew up by himself, with a little help from kindly women such as his grandmother Rosa.

A neighbor, Maurilla Santana, said "Frank was the wildest kid in Hoboken. He'd do anything. Take any dare. His favorite pastime was going up on the roof and pissing down on the people below."

He fought racial prejudice, as he would do for the rest of his life. When some Irish boys, usually much bigger, called him "a dirty little guinea," he took care of them. "I ended up breaking their fucking heads," he said.

Marty and Dolly kicked Frank out of their apartment, calling him "a no-good bum" because he could not hold down a steady job. But when he got a gig singing, they welcomed him back.

At some point, Dolly decided he might make some money singing, so she purchased a new suit for him.

She was the powerhouse of the family, and even got her husband a job as a fireman through her political cronies at Hoboken's City Hall.

He tried to avoid the horseshit as he walked the cobblestone streets of "Guinea Town," another name for Little Italy in Hoboken.

For years he had a cauliflower ear until he could afford plastic surgery to improve it somewhat in later years.

He would claim, "I was ripped from Dolly's entrails and put aside to die as the doctor tried to save her life. Fuck him. When I was older I went to his office with the intention of killing the son-of-a-bitch. Fortunately, he wasn't in that day, and I never went back again. Good thing. I would have grown up in jail if I had."

For one whole year, Frank was a truant, playing hooky from school, and Dolly never found out about it until much later. When she forced him to go back to school, he stood at the boys' urinal one day taking a piss. Standing next to him was a Jewish kid named "Herbie." He kept staring at Frank's penis. "You're so much bigger than I am," he told Frank.

"That's obvious," Frank shot back.

"If you'll go into one of the stalls and let me play with it and get it hard, I'll give you a dollar."

"Don't touch me, you faggot," Frank told Herbie. "I'll make a deal with you. I'll go into the stall with you and jerk up it real big and hard. I'll let you look at it, but don't touch or you're dead meat."

"It's a deal," said the eager Herbie. Frank lived up to his promise, and in so doing found a way of making money throughout the rest of his school term.

Herbie knew five or six other Jewish boys who were homosexuals. He'd invite Frank over to give a performance. The boys formed a circle around Frank and watched him masturbate. He never allowed one of the boys to touch him. But he masturbated to climax in front of their voyeuristic eyes. Years later, he told Sammy Davis Jr. and Peter Lawford, "One week I made more than fifty bucks from these little Jewish boys. That was a hell of a lot of money for a kid back then. I spent the faggot dollars on broads."

"I soon grew tired of Herbie and his friends," he said. "By the time I was fifteen, I was pumping it to young housewives whose husbands weren't satisfying them. I charged five bucks to each of the bitches. I always demanded money up front like a true hustler. I got stiffed a few times so I learned my lesson."

Ultimately Frank could not tolerate sitting in a boring classroom. "There was money to be made out there, and I wanted in on it," he said.

His decision to drop out of high school provoked violence in Dolly. "She nearly beat me to death with an iron skillet," he later admitted.

While Frank was showing off his large penis, which was overly developed for a boy of his

age, Dolly was working as an abortionist. Depending on the wishes of the woman or her family, she would deliver a baby or abort it. Local women called her "Hatpin Dolly."

The police arrested Dolly in November of 1937 and again in February of 1939, but she used her political influence to get off.

When not attending her bar, Dolly spent a lot of time getting in good with the local politicos at City Hall. She became a lifelong Democrat, unlike her son, who would later switch alliances to the Republicans, when he supported Richard Nixon.

Through her influence, Dolly came to dominate the political machine of Little Italy, currying favor with and garnering votes for the leading politicians.

"Dolly wanted to run for mayor of Hoboken, and she would have run too, had I not talked her out of it," Marty said. "I didn't want to be known as the 'wife' of the mayor."

"Dolly cursed louder and more violently than any longshoreman working the waterfront. Nearly every word was, "Fuck that, you son of a bitch! Talk like that to me, you shithead, and I'll cut off your dick."

She was a "ward-heeler," meaning a neighborhood political boss for the Democrats, and was in constant contact with Jersey City Mayor Frank Hague, who presided over Hudson County, of which Hoboken was a part. He was one of the most ruthless and most corrupt political bosses in American history. "I learned my lessons well," Dolly said later.

On Election Day, Dolly organized false arrests, ballot box stuffing, and even beatings of recalcitrant Republicans who refused to back the Democratic machine. Many of her opponents often found themselves bloody and in jail on Election Day.

In 1919, Dolly chained herself to the Hoboken City Hall as a protest for women's suffrage.

She used her political connections in Hoboken to get Marty a job in the local Fire Department. To supplement the family income, she made sticky Sicilian sweets and sold them to homesick immigrant families.

Dolly and Marty wanted their son to take a paper-bundling job at *The Jersey Observer*. His mother used her influence with Frank's godfather, Frank Garrick. But when Garrick chastised him one afternoon, the cocky little kid poured out every obscenity he'd heard his mother utter. A half century would go by before godfather and godson spoke again.

Marty laughed at Frank's ambition to become a singer. When he confided his ambition to Dolly, "She beat the shit out of me and got me a job plastering walls. I was later fired when I was caught sleeping on the job."

Jobless and lazy around the house, Frank was later kicked out of the apartment by Marty.

"I not only wanted to be a singer, I'm gonna be a singer, bigger and more famous than Bing Crosby."

"Yeah, right," Dolly said. "When pigs fly. Now get the fuck out of here."

At the tender age of seventeen, he was kicked out and on his own, having to make his own way in the world without any help at all from Dolly and Martin. He disappeared from the radar late in 1933, not emerging again until the fall of 1935. Biographers often call these "the lost years."

Long after they had passed, Frank refused to speak of them. He is believed to have earned almost no money singing during this long, lonely period. It is known that he made one porno film in Brooklyn, and he also hustled for a living. In spite of his skinny frame, he could entice homosexuals and horny woman to "sample Big Frankie," of which he constantly boasted. For a brief time, he was said to have been the kept boy of a Broadway producer, and later was reported living with a rich older widow. "Whatever I did is my own damn business," he once told Sammy Davis Jr. "I'm not proud of what I did. But it's called breaking into the music business."

When he finally did come back to Dolly and Marty—"still a singing fool making no money," in his words—they welcomed him back. He told Dolly, "There was many a night I got the hook. Some audiences didn't want to see a little dago boy from Hoboken take the mike."

At roadhouses, taverns, meeting houses of local unions, school proms, and bars, he sang. His pay was often a roast beef sandwich or a package of cigarettes.

Dolly was furious when she heard he was working for no money. She set up a regular gig for him at her local Union Club. She also got other gigs for him, including when he appeared in blackface in "The Big Minstrel Act." He imitated Al Jolson singing "My Mammy" from the film *The Jazz Singer*.

"Frank was the perfect singer to sing 'My Way' later in life," claimed D'Orazio. "In his early days in Hoboken, if he didn't get his way, he usually beat the shit out of you and robbed anything valuable on your body. Then he'd tell you to go fuck yourself."

Finally, Dolly succumbed to his desire to become a singer, and she saved up enough money, $65 in all, to buy him a mike and a public address system, which he carried around with him from club to club.

In the closing weeks of the autumn of 1935, he joined the Hoboken Four, appearing as the lead singer with "The Three Flashes." He toured with these jealous boys for three months, mostly imitating The Mills Brothers. But since all the women wanted to go to Frank's room, The Three Flashes said, "Bye bye, Frankie."

"He got all the woman," said one of the Flashes. "If a damn bitch had a choice of a big dick or a little dick, you know how a whore is gonna go."

As the year 1937 drifted on, Frank took whatever gig he could get, often for no money. He sang on the local radio station, and he could be seen lugging around his public address system. For a while, he billed himself as "Freddie Trent."

The following year, Dolly again swept in to take charge, getting him a gig as a singing waiter at a seedy roadhouse in New Jersey. The place was called The Rustic Cabin, and it lived up to its namesake. Frank's salary at The Rustic Cabin shot up to $25 a week. One night, Louise Tobin, a singer with Benny Goodman's band, noticed him when he was broadcasting "The WNEW Dance Parade" over a radio wire linked to WNEW in New York.

During the late 30s and early 40s, Tobin was a major singer in her own right, having introduced "I Didn't Know What Time It Was" with Benny Goodman's band in 1939. Her big hit was also with Goodman: "There'll Be Some Changes Made," which was number two on the "Hit Parade" in 1941 for fifteen weeks.

She was the first wife of the trumpeter Harry James. She invited James the following night to hear Frank sing.

James had left Benny Goodman to start his own band. He was impressed with Frank's singing "Begin the Beguine" and offered him a $75-a-week salary to join him on the road. "From this day forth, you're Frankie Satin," James told him.

"Like hell I am!" Frank shot back. "My mother would cut off my nuts." James gave in, and Frank was on his way to the big time.

Betty Grable lay in both of their futures.

White-suited **Frank Sinatra** (third from left) in a publicity still for **"The Three Flashes"** (aka **"The Hoboken Four"**). It was this experience that convinced Frank that he never wanted to be a singer in a group. "I'm a star. I want to perform solo."

A famous talent scout of his day, Major Bowes, heard the group and featured them on his popular radio show. The other members included "Patty" Principe, Fred Tamburro, and James Petrozelli. "We were rather ugly guys, and the gals didn't think we were sexy, but every time that horny little Sinatra kid opened his mouth to sing, the bitches creamed their bloomers," said Tamburro.

Frank's father, Marty, snapped this picture of his wife, **Dolly**, and his well-dressed young son, **Frank**. Dolly looks grim in this photograph. She warned people, "Don't mess with me—you'll regret it."

She was a woman of her word. When Marty's sisters spread the false rumor that she had a boyfriend stashed in Jersey City, she rushed over to their grocery store, overturned two barrels of olives, threw thier homemade pasta on the floor and stomped on it, and then "beat the shit outta them," she claimed.

# Frank Sinatra & Nancy Barbato

## HIS CHEATING HEART

"I'm not one of those complicated, mixed-up cats," **Frank Sinatra** told his fellow musicians in New Jersey before and after his marriage to **Nancy Barbato** (*pictured above*). "I'm not lookin' for the secret of life. I just go on from day to day, takin' what comes. If that includes a piece of ass, I'm buoyant. I feel about eight feet tall. I always make sure the broad enjoys it too. When I get bored, I go back home to Nancy. Don't get me wrong: My constant philandering ain't got anything to do with Nancy. She's a good woman. If I ever caught her with another man, I'd kill her."

For a while, Frank billed himself as "Frankie Trent," inspired by the name of his cousin, John Tredy, who had died of tuberculosis. Tredy played the banjo in a group and sang. "Everyone says Sinatra is just too Italian, that I'd be just another dago singer. But when Dolly leaned what I was doing, she kicked my ass. The next day I was Frank Sinatra, and so I have remained. Changing my name is the best thing I ever *didn't* do."

On February 4, 1939, as the world prepared to go to war, **Frank Sinatra** took as his bride **Nancy Barbato** at Our Lady of Sorrows Catholic Church in Jersey City. Nancy's wedding gift was a bag of rainbow-hued jellybeans with a diamond watch inside. For Nancy, it was "the happiest day of my life."

Heartbreak and sorrow lay in their future. Their honeymoon was spent in a dreary third-floor walkup on Garfield Avenue. The rent was $42 a month, and his nightly gig at the Rustic Cabin brought in only $25 a week. She took a job as a $25-a-week secretary at the American Type Founders in Elizabeth, New Jersey.

For the actual wedding Frank borrowed the cutaway tuxedo, and Nancy was lent the wedding dress of her sister.

## YOUNG FRANK INSPIRES HEADLINE:

## "SONGBIRD HELD IN MORALS CHARGE"

*"I can have every dame I want. I just can't help myself. I don't want to hurt Nancy. I just don't want to sleep with her no more."*

—**Frank Sinatra**

*"We're animals, fuckin' animals, each and every one of us, that's what we are, and we're damn proud of it, too. There's more to life than just Nancy, and I gotta have it. I'm just looking to make it with as many women as I can."*

—**Frank Sinatra**

*"It was just a romp in a rumble seat, where I must have scored a bull's eye on the first go round."*

—**Frank Sinatra**
responding to a 1938 charge that he made
Toni Della Penta pregnant.

*"In his early days as a singer, he had sex on the brain. He would make love to anyone who came along. There was something unusually intensive about his lovemaking when I crawled into the sack with him."*

—**Nancy Venturi**

*"I'd already seen it in action, but Frank was always bragging about the size of his dick. Some of the boys in my band accused him of exaggerating. He invited them to his dressing room where he whipped it out for them. 'Get a load of*

*Big Frankie,' he told my boys—and they did."*

—**Harry James**

*"One thing you've got to know about Frank and women. He is well equipped, if you know what I mean—hung like a horse, to be blunt—and the dames liked that. Soon the word got around that Sinatra had the equipment to satisfy."*

—**Joey D'Orazio,** 1930's Hoboken friend

*"I married one man for life, and with my luck it had to be your father."*

—**Nancy Sr.** to Nancy Jr.

*"In Nancy I found beauty, warmth, and understanding; being with her was my only escape from what seemed like a grim world."*

—**Frank Sinatra**

They were teenagers when they met, in that scorching summer of 1934 when air-conditioned homes were a dream of the future. The son of a former boxer and a mother who aborted children, Frank was a skinny little boy of eighteen, who looked fourteen. A virgin, Nancy Rose Barbato, daughter of Mike Barbato, a plasterer, was sweet seventeen, and had never been kissed.

He had first noticed her when he was visiting Mrs. Josephine Garaente Monaco (Aunt Josie, he called her) at her beach house in Long Branch along the Jersey shoreline.

Frank was playing a ukulele on his Aunt Josie's front porch when he spotted Nancy manicuring her nails across the street. He was immediately attracted to her, and soon he was across the street telling her that he needed a manicure, too. He was quite aggressive. "A little loving thrown in with the manicure couldn't be bad either. Not at all."

"Hold on a minute, buster," she is reported to have said. "You'll be lucky if I give you that manicure."

"While you take care of my toenails, I'll sing to you and play on my ukulele," he promised.

It was not a just a summer romance. Their love affair would continue for the next four years with him commuting on the bus from Hoboken to Jersey City where she lived. Sometimes she had to lend him the bus fare.

In the summer of 1934, a skinny eighteen-year-old met a seventeen-year-old virgin named **Nancy Barbato**. It happened between two world wars, when much of America was still mired in a depression.

There was little money to buy anything. But for their occasional flings in Jersey City, to which he commuted by bus from Hoboken, they learned how to do things on the cheap. Beach picnics with baloney sandwiches, walks along the boardwalk, listening to opera records at her home. On special occasions, they went dancing at the local casino.

She thought he might be just a summer romance, but even when the cold winds blew in from the Atlantic, he still came on that bus to see her. He also "sang for me all the time," she recalled.

"We ate a lot of Creamsicles in those days," he later recalled. "I was singing for two dollars a night. Even though she had to lend me money at times, I told her I was going places big-time."

When Frank started out, he lacked self-confidence, which Dolly Sinatra, his mother, did not provide with her frequent attacks. Close friends of the Sinatras claimed that Nancy did more than anyone else in Frank's life to bolster his self-esteem.

Sal Salvador, a boyhood friend from Hoboken, had a different point of view. "What really gave Frankie more self-confidence than anything began in junior high school when he realized he was different from other boys. He became known as the guy who had the biggest *schlong* in Hoboken."

Frank's first big singing gig had been at a roadside inn in New Jersey. At the Rustic Cabin one night he had met Antoinette (Toni) Della Penta, age 27, and began dating her. When he met Nancy, he became a two-timer, as it was called back then. Only Dolly knew of Frank's two girls, and his mother favored Nancy—"she's a good girl"—but denounced Toni as a "piece of Saturday night trash."

It took Frank many weeks of dating before Toni agreed to go to bed with him in a seedy motel where they registered as "Mr. and Mrs. Sinatra." Apparently, she found him rather unskilled in bed—"he was so skinny." But she fell for him, planning to divorce the husband from whom she was estranged.

After six weeks of these motel shack-ups, she found herself pregnant. At first, Toni feared that Frank would take her to Dolly for an abortion, but he didn't. The problem of an unwanted baby was solved when she had a miscarriage in her third month.

Frank was holding out the prospect of marriage to both Toni and Nancy, and had given each of them an engagement ring. Somehow Toni found out about Nancy. Toni showed up at the Rustic Cabin one night when musician Henry Beaver tipped her off that Nancy would be at the club.

"The shit hit the fan that night," said Beaver. "A real catfight. Toni ripped Nancy's dress and scratched her face. She was a streetfighter. Nancy wasn't. Frank broke up the two warring broads fighting over him. It must have flattered his ego. Two bouncers kicked out each gal. Toni through the front door, and Nancy out the back."

Nancy was furious and walked out on Frank, telling him she'd never speak to him again. But with his personal charm and magnetism, he won her back, promising "never to look at another woman as long as I live." Surely he had his fingers crossed behind his back when he took that fidelity oath.

Frank dumped Toni, his excuse being that, "You're standing in the way of my becoming a bigtime singer." He'd also delivered the same charge directly to

Frank first achieved recognition at a roadside dive in Englewood Cliffs, **The Rustic Cabin**, "on the Palisades" in New Jersey. A hamburger with coffee and dessert cost 60 cents, with Manhattans going for 35 cents each. The roadhouse stood on Route 9W near the town of Alpine.

Frank started out at "fifteen clams a week." His job: to sing, to wait tables, and to act as master of ceremonies. "I needed some extra dough, so I put a little dish on the piano where patrons could drop coins."

"The Rustic Cabin was just a stepping stone for me. I wanted to sign on with a big band, maybe Tommy Dorsey or else Harry James. As my night ended, there would be at least three or four broads waiting for me—maybe more."

Nancy's face, which brought a protest from her that she'd never do that.

On November 26, 1938, Toni filed charges against Frank, who was arrested and taken to the county jail where he was booked under the charge of "Seduction," a rarely enforced law.

A man could be charged for seducing a woman "under the promise of marriage whereby she became pregnant." The law also stated that the single female must be "of good repute for chastity."

Frank's mug shot as prisoner no. 42799 was taken the day after his arrest. For years it disappeared from Hoboken police files, but one day turned up. Souvenir stores from Hollywood Boulevard to Times Square continue to hawk the picture today to tourists.

Using her political influence, Dolly got the charge dismissed. She personally investigated the complainant and discovered that the girl was already married.

Toni came from a street-toughened family; her father was in the illegal alcohol trade. She, too, was a fighter and wasn't going to disappear gracefully into the night.

She came to Hoboken and appeared on Dolly's doorstep. Unlike the more demure Nancy, Dolly was a street brawler herself. The women got into a screaming catfight, and Dolly overpowered Toni. She dragged her into her cellar and locked her up while she called the police to take her away.

Two burly Irishmen, both friends of Dolly's, arrived to arrest Toni. At the local precinct, she was charged with disorderly conduct. She was found guilty and convicted of the charge, but a lenient judge gave her a suspended sentence.

Toni still wasn't ready to give up. On December 22, 1938, she swore out another warrant for Frank's arrest.

At the Rustic Cabin, Frank was singing for a Christmas audience when two constables from Hackensack, New Jersey, arrested him on a morals charge. They arrived armed with a warrant charging adultery. At the courthouse, he was able to post a bond of five-hundred dollars and was released on his own recognizance.

The Hoboken newspaper ran the story the following morning—SONGBIRD HELD IN MORALS CHARGE. Marty and Dolly couldn't complain too much, since Marty had once been arrested for receiving stolen goods, and she had been apprehended twice for performing illegal abortions.

Frank read the story in the morning paper and called the city editor. It would mark the first of his epic battles with journalists. "I'm coming down there and I'm gonna beat your brains out, you hear me? I'm gonna kill you and anyone else who

While still dating Nancy Barbato, Frank met another beautiful woman, Antoinette (Toni) Della Penta, at the Rustic Cabin. Long separated from her husband, Toni confessed, "I had the hots for Frankie the moment he came out on stage. We got off to a bad start. He claimed that my sucking a lemon from my scotch threw him off his mark. But when he asked me to dance, and rubbed his body tight against mine, I knew I had him."

During the months that followed, Frank secretly dated both Nancy and Toni until each woman learned of her competition. A fight ensued.

Frank promised Nancy he'd be faithful. But an angered and jealous Toni brought two charges against him—one for "Seduction" and a second charge for "Adultery," for which he was fingerprinted and had to pose for the mug shot above. The charges were later dropped, but the event marked the beginning of "the bum rap the press gave me and would continue to do so over the years," Frank charged.

had anything to do with that article. And I ain't no fucking songbird."

***

Right after New Year's Day, 1939, Dolly herself mailed out the wedding invitations, announcing that her son, Mr. Francis A. Sinatra, was going to marry Nancy Rose Barbato, a marriage which met her approval. "At least she's not another one of Frank's cheap whores," Dolly told not only her husband, Marty, but her friends in Hoboken.

At that point, Toni had not withdrawn her adultery charges against Frank. But two weeks before the wedding on February 4, the charges were dropped.

Rumors spread among their friends and neighbors that it was a shotgun wedding, but these turned out to be false. Nancy Sinatra Jr. wasn't born until June of 1940.

For the wedding, everything seemed borrowed. Nancy was married in a wedding dress that had belonged to her sister, and Frank borrowed a black tailcoat and ill-fitting striped pants from a friend. Dolly gave Frank the ring to give Nancy. He even had to borrow two-hundred dollars for his honeymoon expenses.

A family friend of the Sinatras, David Manners, attended Frank's wedding at Our Lady of Sorrows Church in Jersey City. "The bridegroom looked like it was the bleakest day of his life. I think Frankie thought he was attending a funeral. Nancy was the typical blushing bride. Although she'd had some warnings, I truly don't think the poor innocent gal had the slightest clue about what she was letting herself in for."

Frank's wedding present to Nancy was his first ever recording, a song called "Our Love."

Actually he got a gig and wasn't able to go on that honeymoon, but he never returned the two-hundred-dollar loan, even when he became rich.

He settled Nancy into a small apartment in Jersey City and hit the road again. Three nights after the wedding, Frank was shacked up with not one woman, but two. "They were very young," Manners said. "I drove them to Frank's motel. I think one was sixteen, the other not much older.

Nancy answered his fan mail, and many of the letters were very explicit from the bobby-soxers, or even older women, promising Frank what he could do to them in bed.

With all this sudden success and growing fame, Frank began to change before Nancy's eyes. His popularity was going to his head. He might be skin and bones with scars on his face, but he would make bobbysoxers and women scream.

When he was away from Nancy, which was most of the time, she knew that temptation faced him on a massive basis daily. "He's Italian," Dolly said. "What red-blooded Italian man ever resisted temptation? Adam was Italian. That's why the fucker ate that god damn apple Eve offered to him."

At one point, during a brief respite from his life on the road, Nancy accused Frank of "being seduced by your own celebrity." [Although Frank was an errant husband, he became a devoted father to his children-Nancy Sinatra Jr. born on June 8, 1940; Frank Sinatra Jr, born on January 10, 1944, and Christina (Tina) Sinatra, born June 20, 1948.]

14

# *Young Frank Meets Cole Porter*

## "JUST ONE OF THOSE THINGS"

Set in Paris, the breezy, lightweight Broadway show, *Can-Can,* became **Cole Porter**'s second longest-running musical, topped only by *Kiss Me, Kate.*

Its plot, such as it was, revolved around a Parisian constabulary trying to shut down a café because of its "indecent dancing," notably the Can-Can. The Broadway musical made a star of Gwen Verdon.

When Cole sold the property to Hollywood, he specifically requested Frank Sinatra for the lead. In spite of his troubled relationship with Cole, Frank agreed to join a cast that included his friend, Shirley MacLaine, show business veteran Maurice Chevalier, and Louis Jourdan, who had once been voted the handsomest man on the planet.

# "I'm Mad About the Boy, and I Mean that Two Ways."

—Cole Porter

Two musicians at work, **Frank Sinatra** (top photo) and **Cole Porter** (below) could not have been more different as personalities. They had many conflicts over the years, the loudest of which, a shouting match, involved a dispute over the film version of *Can-Can*. Frank demanded that Cole revise the lyrics for his number, "It's All Right with Me."

"It's perfect the way it is," Cole shouted before slamming down the phone.

With the cooperation of director Walter Lang, Ira Gershwin and Sammy Cahn were hired to write new lyrics. As author Tom Santopietro wrote, "Gershwin and Cahn rewriting Porter? It's as if Rembrandt painted over da Vinci—wrong on about twelve levels at once."

After viewing the finished film, Cole wrote Frank a letter criticizing him. "It was an offensive gesture when you raised your eyes to form narrow slits while singing, 'In old Japan, all the Japs do it.'"

Cole was referring to the song, "Let's Do It (Let's Fall in Love)."

Frank was still living on the $25-a-week salary from his gig at the Rustic Cabin. To make extra money, Nancy worked the first year of her marriage as a low-paid secretary.

Hank Sanicola, Frank's manager, said, "It was some marriage. Frank slept in the apartment during the day while Nancy worked. When she came home, Frank gave her a kiss and headed out for the Rustic Cabin where he was surrounded all night by gals. He could have his pick."

Less than a year into his marriage, Frank told Sanicola, "Getting married was the dumbest thing I've ever done. I get so much pussy backstage I don't want it when I finally get home. What to do?"

He later confessed, "Nancy and I are good friends. I wouldn't call it love. For that, I'll have to go to Hollywood one day and fuck that little number with the bouncy tits. Lana Turner."

He was a man of his word.

One night the manager told Frank that Cole Porter had come to the club to hear him sing. The famous composer had heard exciting reports about this skinny guy with the blue eyes and the big *schwanz*.

At an appearance at Yale University in 1986, Frank recalled the night he met Cole Porter, who had heard about his singing and showed up at the Rustic Cabin. "There were only seven people in the audience, and we had a six-piece orchestra. I had heard that Cole Porter was sitting out there. I tried to do one of his songs—'Night and Day.' I told the audience, 'Ladies and gentlemen, I'd like to sing this song and dedicate it to the greatly talented man who composed it and who is maybe one of the best contributors to American music at this particular time in our lives.' I then proceeded to forget all the words. I kept singing the words 'Night and Day' for fifteen bars."

"Backstage in Frank's dressing room, Porter had no comment on Frank's singing. He was obviously visiting for other purposes. He bluntly told Frank, "I hear you have the biggest cock in show business, and I want to suck it. There's a hundred dollars in it for you."

Frank turned down the offer but didn't want to pass up an easy hundred, since he desperately needed money.

"I'll make you a counter offer," he told Porter. "I'll strip down and sit in my chair. You sit in that other chair. I'll play with myself and make it big. You can play with yourself but only at a distance of a few feet. Is that a deal?"

"In your case, you're on," Porter said. "I'll take what I can get. *Showtime!*"

Porter related his involvement with Frank, such as it was, to author Truman Capote. The gossip maven later said, "Cole used to describe his sex life in great detail. I think it excited him."

Porter suggested that Frank might star as Porter in the ludicrous, highly sanitized Hollywood film biography, *Night and Day* (1946). Frank turned it down. "We settled for Cary Grant—not bad, not bad at all," Porter said of his former lover. "Of course, Cary has only half of what Frank does."

The composer, **Cole Porter**, first suggested that Frank Sinatra should play him in the filmed biography *Night and Day* (1946). But the producers nixed the idea, giving the role to Cary Grant instead.

After seeing the finished film, the composer said, "Oh well, they made me look like Cary Grant—and that was a bonus. The picture was so sanitized it was ludicrous. They say I'm a practicing homosexual. That's a damn lie. I'm perfect as a homosexual."

Cary Grant had been a lover of Cole Porter before he migrated to a career in Hollywood. His competition for Porter was "Black Jack" Bouvier, the father of Jacqueline Bouvier Kennedy.

When not seducing Black Jack or Cary, Cole patronized a notorious male brothel in Harlem staffed by young black men. On some nights, he preferred a chorus boy, but other nights he sought out sailors, soldiers, truck drivers, and his special favorite, longshoremen.

Like Black Jack, Cole was a Yale graduate of the class of 1914. "I'm mad about the boy," Cole told his homosexual friends about Jackie's father.

When Cole and Black Jack tired of each other, they attended secret "fucking parties." Even though their love affair was relatively brief, they remained intimate friends throughout the rest of their lives.

***

About a decade later, when Frank met with Cole Porter on the set of *High Society* (1956), Frank was not overly enthusiastic. "It's better not to wake up sleeping dogs," he told Porter, as if to remind him he didn't want any talk about their early days in show business.

Their relationship had not been friendly over the years. In the late 1940s Porter had sent Frank a telegram: "Why in hell do you sing my songs like you don't like the way they are written?" He got no answer from Frank.

Porter may have been referring to "What Is This Thing Called Love," "Begin the Beguine," or "Just One of Those Things." Porter claimed that Frank was giving a "Sinatrification" to his music.

In "I Get a Kick Out of You," whereas Porter had written, "I get a kick…" Frank sang "You give me a boot." In "It's All Right With Me," Porter had written, "They're not her lips, but such tempting lips." Frank sang, "They're not her chops, but they're such tempting chops." He rewrote the lyrics of other composers as well.

In spite of this, many Sinatra fans claim that his renditions of Porter's "I've Got You Under My Skin" are some of the greatest single recordings of his entire career.

# VERY LITTLE PRIDE AND NO PASSION

Cary Grant kept popping up in the lives of both Cole Porter and Frank Sinatra, but in very different ways. In spite of Grant's notorious bisexual past, which on occasion made Frank "a little nervous," the two men bonded and became friends for life when Frank signed for a role in *The Pride and the Passion (1957).*

Cary took top billing, with Frank in second position, followed by Sophia Loren in her American film debut. Each of the stars was miscast in this big-screen spectacle set in 19th century Spain. The plot involved the capture of a huge cannon by a British naval officer, as played by Grant. Based on the C.S. Forester novel, the film was ridiculous. Frank played Miguel, a Spanish peasant and *guerillero* leader with spit curl bangs and a put-on accent.

Writing in *The New York Times,* critic Bosley Crowther said, "This is what often happens when producers try to be Cecil B. DeMille."

In spite of the critical attacks, *The Pride and the Passion* was a box office success because of the drawing power of its stars.

Amazingly, Frank and Marlon Brando were often up for the same roles, although they were remarkably different in their styles of acting. Brando was sent the script for the role of Miguel, which eventually went to Frank. The Method actor wrote to the film's producer, Stanley Kramer, "It's a piece of shit. Overblown. Badly written, A pseudo epic. Total nonsense. If any-body's the star of this crap, it's the fucking cannon. Go shove this script where the sun don't shine."

When Kramer read Brando's note, he told his staff: "If only Brando would be more forceful in his opinion."

Frank later admitted that he accepted the role only because the film would be shot in Spain, where Ava Gardner had gone to live early in 1956. Just in case things didn't work out for a reunion with Ava, Frank brought along a live-in girlfriend, Peggy Connelly, a Texas-bred singer and actress.

Frank Sinatra, cast as a Spanish peasant

Peggy recalled that Frank was cantakerous throughout the entire 16-week shoot, practically coming to blows with Kramer. He hated the accommodations on location, opting instead to drive three hours each night back to his suite at the Castellano Hilton in Madrid.

Complaining about his thinning hair, he wore an improbable hairpiece. On a night shoot, Frank warned Kramer that if filming went beyond 11:30pm, he was going to urinate on him. True to his word, at midnight, thirty minutes after the deadline he had created, Frank emerged from his dressing room and approached Kramer, who was sitting in a director's chair. "Frank came over to him, pulled out his cock, and pissed all over

Kramer," Peggy said. "He remained in a black, angry mood, downing enitre bottles of Spanish Fundador. Living in Madrid, the same town as Ava, was more than he could handle."

From his hotel suite, Frank caused an international incident when he hung a banner from his window: FRANCO IS A FINK, a reference to Francisco Franco, Spain's brutal dictator.

Consumed with memories of Ava, and otherwise occupied with Peggy, Frank pretty much left Sophia Loren to Cary Grant. Cast as Juana, a Spanish peasant girl, Sophia seems immaculately groomed at all times, as if she'd just emerged from makeup. Right down to her false eyelashes, her makeup was exquisite, and so was her amply displayed bosom, which seems to take up most of the screen whenever she appears in the film. Grant told Frank, "I've proposed marriage to Sophia. I think I've fallen in love with her."

Frank looked astonished. "You've got to be kidding, Cary. I thought you only liked to suck dick."

One day, after Peggy returned from a sightseeing visit to Toledo, she entered their suite at the Hilton to catch Frank in bed with Ava. Peggy retreated from the scene, and Ava quickly dressed and left. When Peggy returned to the bedroom for a confrontation with Frank, she found him lying nude on the bed covers, drinking brandy. He looked up at her. All he said was, "Shit happens."

The following day, Frank was furious when he read in the press that Ava was referring to him as *"Mr. Sinada,"* a name that loosely translated from the Spanish as "Mr. Nothing." Ava also asserted in the press that she might marry Italian comedian Walter Chiari.

That afternoon, Frank ordered a white Thunderbird for Peggy. "It's the same model I gave this chick Ellie Graham," he said. "I made her pregnant, and she agreed to abort my child, so she deserves the wheels."

In retaliation for her unflattering remarks about him in the press, Frank telephoned Ava the following evening. "Sweetheart, I've got to tell you what I'm doing right now. I'm in bed in my suite at the Hilton. Peggy is under me. I'm fucking her real hard. She's squealing like a pig at castrating time."

Ava slammed down the phone.

Peggy herself would go on to enjoy a long career. She eventually married Dick Martin of *Rowan & Martin's Laugh-In.* During an interview shortly before her death, she said, "I was just a footnote in Frank's life, one of those post-Ava girls. He asked me to marry him, but how can you marry a man who screams "AVA" when he climaxes? Once in a restaurant in Madrid, I encountered Ava in the powder room. She looked very skeptically at me. 'When Frank had me he had the best. Choice sirloin, baby. It looks like it's hamburger for him from now on.'"

**Sophia Loren** and **Frank Sinatra** (*right*) had the Pride, **Cary Grant** (*left*) the Passion.

# Frank Sinatra & Pamela Harriman
## "The 20th Century's Last Great Courtesan"

At a party in New York during the late 1940s, Cole Porter introduced a young singer, Frank Sinatra, to the woman who would become known as Pamela Digby Churchill Hayward Harriman. The lady, once the daughter-in-law of Sir Winston Churchill, was the U.S. Ambassador to France at the time of her death in the swimming pool of Paris' Ritz Hotel. She was called "the last great courtesan of the 20th century."

In the years to come, Frank wined and dined with Pamela because his close friend, Leland Hayward, a famous Broadway producer, was married to her.

Pamela had ridden out Frank's marriage "to that darling child," Mia Farrow, a marriage which had ended in 1968. Pamela's own affair with Frank didn't begin until she flew with him aboard his private jet from London to New York. Their sexual link was formed thirty thousand feet over the Atlantic.

After Hayward's death in 1971, Frank arrived for a private viewing of the casket, at which event he encountered Jackie Kennedy, dressed all in white, even wearing white-rimmed dark glasses. After the viewing, a distraught Pamela called Frank into her library, where he held her as she sobbed, "The bastard left me penniless."

For some R&R, he invited her to his sprawling compound in Rancho Mirage, near Palm Springs. In 1971, she moved in, obviously earmarking him as her next husband. London's *Sunday Express* announced that she was "Frank's bride-to-be."

A woman of deep-seated taste and elegance, she found the place "utterly lacking in style." A world class art collector, she viewed his paintings as "more suited to a lower East Side Sicilian tenement."

Rosalind Russell and Claudette Colbert were frequent guests of Frank's at Rancho Mirage. Pamela referred to these former movie stars as "The Late Show."

He told Rosalind, "Pamela is not my kind of broad." To Colbert, he claimed that Pamela was invited for a weekend, but stayed for months. He had to eventually throw her out.

Leland's son, William Hayward, called Frank and asked him if he planned to marry his former stepmother. "Forget it!" Frank said. "She's too old for me. Besides, she's got no humor."

Pamela's close friend, Christopher Ogden, a correspondent for *Time* magazine, said, "Sinatra found her boring, arrogant, pompous, pretentious, and generally phony."

Two views of **Pamela Harriman.** *(Top photo)* with then-husband **Leland Hayward,** shortly before his death in 1971; and *(lower photo)* during her tenure (1993-1997) as then-president Bill Clinton's U.S. Ambassador to France.

# Frank & the Big Band Sounds of Harry James

**Harry James** (*left*) and young **Frank Sinatra** at the mike evoke the best of the Big Band era when swing was in vogue—Harry on his trumpet and Frank with "that voice." Before the war, it was a time of soaring trumpet solos and romantic hit tunes, and Frank and Harry could deliver both of them.

In 1939 and in the early 40s, Harry was called "an incubator for many pop music stars," and none became more famous than Frank himself. Two of the most glamorus women of the 1940s, Betty Grable and Ava Gardner, lay in their futures as wives, although both marriages would be turbulent.

When Harry noticed that Frank was having trouble breathing as he sang, the bandleader advised him to jump rope. "Keep the bottom filled up," Harry said, referring, of course, to Frank's lungs, encased in a very skinny frame. After the first time Harry and Frank, for reasons of economy, shared a bedroom together on the road, Harry later told his wife of the future, Betty Grable, "The kid's all dick, no man."

She snapped back, "That would be enough to satisfy most women, especially me. Betty Grable doesn't deal in trifles."

On the road, **Harry James** and **Frank Sinatra** *(top photo)* often read Frank's fan mail from love-starved young women. The girls were often quite explicit about what they wanted Frank to do to them.

**Betty Grable** *(lower photo)*, Harry's future wife, remembered one night when she went to see him. "Couples dancing on the floor stopped when Frank started to sing. Girls deserted their boy friends and crowded around the mike to hear him. On the bandstand, he was so skinny, the mike almost obscured him."

On a secret note, she told Carmen Miranda, "Whenever Harry wasn't around, Frank liked for me to give him blow-jobs."

### AND THE BEGINNINGS OF A LIFELONG FRIENDSHIP WITH A THEN-UNKNOWN ACROBAT,

# BURT LANCASTER

Before he hooked up with Harry James, Frank was desperate to sign on with a big band. One night at a club, he walked right up to band leader Glenn Miller. "Hey, guys, I hear you're good. I'm good too. The best singer in the business. Hire me."

"Don't call me," Miller told him. "I'll call you."

Through a friend, Frank got Tommy Dorsey to come and see him at the Rustic Cabin. Dorsey sat bored through two numbers before abruptly getting up and leaving the club. "Italian crooners like that guy are a dime a dozen."

Frank got another chance to try to hook up with the Tommy Dorsey Band. It was at a New Jersey roadhouse, Charlie's Grill, run by gangster Willie Moretti. "I don't get it," Tommy said. "Right in mid-song he forgets the fucking lyrics. There's no way I'm going to hire this fucker. He's just another Italian grease ball with swept-back hair."

At the Rustic Cabin, one door was slammed in his face as another door opened wide. Shortly after his arrival at the club that late afternoon, Frank was told by the manager that, "This is your last night. Clear out your stuff by midnight. You're through here."

But before that midnight curfew, a job offer paying three times his salary had come in from the rising young bandleader Harry James.

James, at the age of 23, had just broken from Benny Goodman and was starting up his own band. Like Dorsey, James wasn't bored with Frank's voice, but was thrilled by its sound. "Frank was really a singing waiter," James recalled. "He whipped off his apron, bounced up on the stage,

22

shook that big dick that was obvious in those pants of his, and belted out 'Night and Day.' I felt the hairs on the back of my neck rising. I knew this kid was going to become a big-time vocalist. I could just feel stardom around the corner."

Before that midnight curfew, Frank had agreed to go on tour with James's "Boys in the Band," for the grand sum of $75 a week, more money that he'd ever made before.

After the offer from James, Frank called Nancy. "Quit that fucking job as secretary. I've been hired as the boy singer with Harry James and his Music Makers."

Although Harry was a virtuoso musician, among the best in the business, Frank and the Music Makers often played to sparse audiences as they toured the country.

"Money was real tight," said singer Louise Tobin, who was married to James at the time.

Although Frank preferred to be a free agent on the road, where he was constantly meeting young women, Nancy sometimes went along.

"The kid's name is Sinatra, and the conceited little punk thinks he's the greatest vocalist in the world," James said. "No one's ever heard of the fucker. No hit record, nothing. He looks like a limp dishrag with protruding ears. But the kid's going places. Even if you like his singing, don't compliment him. He'd demand that I up his salary."

"Nancy was a great little housekeeper when she went on the road with me, Frank, and my boys," James said. "For just one dollar, she could make a decent supper for Frank, herself, me, and whatever broad I was with that night."

Frank found life too restrictive with Nancy on tour with him, so he told James, "I'm gonna make her pregnant. That way, she'll need to stay home and raise our kids."

On the first tour with James, Frank met the girl singer of the band, Connie Haines, when they appeared jointly at the Baltimore Hippodrome. "Frank didn't even get billing," Haines later recalled. "But that was about to change. The young girls in the audience screamed and pissed their pants when Frankie came out. We never knew why until much later."

In later life, as revealed by Frank's longtime valet, George Jacobs, he had special underwear made to conceal his genitals. But in his early days to get the bobbysoxers screaming, he wore no underwear.

A musician, Rodney Davis, said, "I once shared a dressing room with Frank. He wore no underwear but had this kind of G-string thing that hoisted him up. I didn't want to look too closely because I didn't want him to think I was a fucking queer. But once on stage, as he moved his legs—a little bit like Elvis in the 1950s—Frank's dick practically bounced out of his pants."

"In those days no newspaper would ever write shit like that. It just wasn't done. But Frank knew how to get those bobbysoxers creaming in their bloomers."

**Harry James** posed along the roadside with his first wife, singer **Louise Tobin**, to whom he was married between 1935 and 1943, when he fell for Betty Grable, the pinup queen of WWII.

Tobin knew that Grable was after her man long before the divorce. The singer told Frank, "I hear she sits in the audience alone, just staring at Harry as he blows that trumpet."

Harry once asked Betty if he married her, could she stand the adulation of his fans? But the dynamic of their star status soon changed: He was walking with Betty through Times Square and a sailor shouted, "It's Betty Grable!" A mob formed and the police had to be called in to rescue this famous pair.

In the hysteria, Betty told her future husband, "I'm the truck driver's delight."

23

"Frank used Harry James as a role model for his womanizing," Davis later said. "Both Harry and I smoked a lot of marijuana back then. Frank tried it but didn't like it. He preferred regular cigarettes and Jack Daniels as his drugs of choice. Those two horny guys shared woman. Between the two of them they took on five or six gals on many a night."

On July 13, 1939 Frank recorded "From the Bottom of My Heart" and "Melancholy Mood" with the Harry James band. That was followed on August 31 with a recording of "All or Nothing at All." Upon its release, it sold 8,000 copies. But when he recorded it again in 1943, it sold more than a million.

Tommy Dorsey finally came around and hired Frank in November of 1939, although he was still under contract to James. "Harry was a sweetheart and let me go," Frank recalled. "What a great guy. But my final weeks with him were the loneliest and dreariest of my life."

Christmas of 1939 found Frank alone in a hotel bed in Cleveland suffering with pneumonia. Nancy, staying with her parents in Jersey City, was pregnant with her first child.

Frank's last engagement with James and the Music Makers was in January of 1940 in Buffalo, New York, at the Shea Theater on a bill with Red Skelton, who was a big money-maker at the time.

On the same bill was an acrobat who would become one of Frank's greatest friends, a relationship that endured a lifetime. His name was Burt Lancaster.

Startling handsome, fanatically loyal, devilishly charming, and intensely sexual, Burt bonded with Frank on their first meeting. They met on New Year's Eve, 1940, when the Harry James Band appeared at Shea's Theater in Albany, New York. Right after this booking, the "boy singer," Frank himself, would join the Tommy Dorsey orchestra.

Frank first spotted Burt in white tights "swinging on those crazy bars," as he'd been booked as an acrobat. He was very physical, very athletic, and with a powerful, muscular build that was in vivid contrast to Frank's skinny physique.

At the time of their meeting, Frank could hardly imagine that he'd be co-starring with Burt in their most prestigious film, the 1953 *From Here To Eternity*.

The exact details of their private relationship are not known. They often met privately, sometimes in the years to come on long weekends at Frank's villa at Palm Springs where servants reported them swimming nude together.

Close friends speculated over the years that there was a romance of some sort. Burt, according to reports, fell in love with Frank. Although Frank may have loved Burt as a friend, he presumably was not "in love" with him. But he treasured their friendship.

Peter Lawford, after his split from Frank, often spoke more openly about

"The Boys in the Band"—Harry James's band, that is, with a young Frank seated on his left, and the band's "girl singer" on his right.

Harry recalled that when Frank joined the band, "He was always thinking of the lyrics. To him, the melody was secondary. If a word was a delicate one, he would try to phrase it with a prettier, softer type of voice. He would do that for the rest of his days. The feel he has for the words of a song is just beautiful. Even when he sings the wrong melody, the sound is still beautiful coming from him."

his former friend's secrets. He maintained that he suspected Frank was "the recipient of nonreciprocal fellatio from Burt on many a night."

Frank could not tolerate Montgomery Clift falling in love with him, but he gave Burt great leeway in their relationship and remained loyal to him in spite of the homosexual overtones on Burt's part.

After his departure from Harry James and his band, James replaced Frank with another singer, Dick Haymes, who would later marry the film goddess Rita Hayworth.

At the time he signed with Dorsey, Frank had seventeen months to go with his contract with James. "I didn't try to hold onto him even though I knew he was going to be a big-time star," James said. "At the time, I didn't even have enough bucks to pay him his seventy-five dollars a week."

It was snowing in Buffalo when a bus carrying the Music Makers pulled out for their next gig without Frank. "I stood in the snow, I hugged and kissed Harry and said goodbye to all the boys. I stood there until their red taillight disappeared down that snowy highway. Then I cried and cried some more until Burt came and rescued me."

"Soon I'd be on the road with Tommy Dorsey singing 'Marie.' But first I had to go back to Jersey City to see Nancy."

"It's a new life I'm heading to," he told Burt, whom he suspected had fallen in love with him, even though Frank had warned him, "I'm hopelessly heterosexual."

"Both Frank and Burt shared their mutual dream of going to Hollywood "to take over that fucking town."

During that cold winter in Buffalo, the dreams of both Frank and Burt seemed impossible. But before the end of the war, each of them would be together in Hollywood as movie stars. Each man would also be pursuing other lovers.

Ironically, Burt's first big affair with a Hollywood star, the first of many to come in the years ahead, would be with the sultry North Carolina beauty, Ava Gardner. Burt and Ava both gained fame in the 1946 *The Killers,* based on a short story by Ernest Hemingway.

While Burt was seducing Ava, Frank was also realizing his dream, which was not of Ava at the time,

**Ava Gardner** and **Burt Lancaster** heated up the screen in Hemingway's *The Killers.* "I love to go to bed with my leading ladies," Burt told Frank after he'd seduced Ava. Fortunately, for Burt's sake, Frank had not yet staked out Ava as his personal property.

Burt was also proud of his reviews, showing Frank what columnist Sheilah Graham had written about him: "Masculinity oozes from every pore." But to prick his balloon, Frank reminded Burt, "But you can be a lady on some nights."

"Only when politely asked by a gentleman," Burt snapped back, flashing his pearly white teeth.

After Ava had been seduced by both Burt and Frank, she reviewed their performances with Lana Turner. "Burt has only a third of what Frank has, but does he know how to drill home with it. I'll give him credit for that!"

In the most famous beach love scene in the history of cinema, **Deborah Kerr** and **Burt Lancaster** made love right before the Japanese attack on Pearl Harbor in *From Here to Eternity (1953).* Frank told Burt that he didn't think Kerr was whorish enough to pull off the role—"It should have gone to Joan Crawford."

But after seeing the rushes, he changed his mind. "You two guys burn up that beach," Frank told Burt.

but of Lana Turner. When he and Burt went bar hopping one night along Sunset Strip, Frank boastfully told Burt, "I've had her. Lana Turner. I set out to get her, and I got my gal. I think I'm in love. Of course, there's the problem of Nancy to get rid of."

"I've got you beat, big boy," Burt said. "I'm sleeping in Ava Gardner's bed."

"You're welcome to Ava," Frank said. "She's okay if you can put up with that Southern drawl. But I'm into the blonde goddess, Miss Lana."

Frank would obviously change his mind. In the years to come, he would kick Lana out of his bed in favor of Ava, whom he also married, of course.

Years later, Ava, aging, drinking heavily, and in retirement in London, said something enigmatically. "Burt and I had an affair when we made *The Killers*. That Papa Hemingway thing. But, to tell you the truth, Burt got Frank long before I did. Imagine that."

---

# *From Here to Eternity*

### "Too Much Macho" (Deborah Kerr)

In Hawaii, shooting *From Here to Eternity,* Deborah Kerr confided to Frank Sinatra and Merv Griffin, who was visiting Montgomery Clift at the time, "I'm surrounded by men. All of them are a bit macho for me. I find Burt very sexy, but so does everybody else. What woman in her right mind would say no to him?"

Frank responded quickly: "Are you sure you're not talking about me?"

They were interrupted by the appearance of Burt himself, dressed in military uniform. "Fred Zinnemann cast me in this film as the beefcake," Burt said. "Because you two guys [Frank and Monty Clift] look like you were just released from Auschwitz."

Later that night over drinks, Burt introduced Frank to James Jones, the author of the novel on which the film had been based. Like the male members of the cast, Jones exuded macho sexuality. "I wanted Eli Wallach to play Maggio," a drunken Jones said to Frank, "but I guess you'll do."

"Thanks for the compliment," Frank shot back.

"I wrote a scene into the screenplay that Zinnemann rejected," Jones said. "It's a scene you'd have played with your back to the camera, getting sucked off by an older man in a dark alleyway. That's what Maggio would have done when he was broke and needed a fiver."

"Too bad," Frank said. "Audiences would have really dug that. But I don't think cocksucking will be filmed on screen in our lifetime."

The next day, after Burt saw the rushes of his performance on the beach with Deborah, he told Frank, "When the world sees me making love to Deborah, no one will believe all those gay rumors about me ever again."

Back in Hollywood, Frank called Burt for a night of drinking. Over whiskey, Frank confessed " My vocal cords are hemorrhaged. And I just got a devastating blow from MCA. My agent told me, 'No one wants you, Frankie. No more movie deals, no more nightclub offers.'"

"Well," Burt said, "in a case like that, there's only one way to go—and that's up!"

# Frank & The Lady Who Sang The Blues

## Billie Holiday

Throughout his career, Frank Sinatra was often treated as a male chauvinist pig. He was called every name from a Mafia don to a child molester (i.e., his marriage to Mia Farrow). To Frank, at least according to the press, women journalists were $2-a-night hookers.

What was not exposed was the tender, supportive Frank, as best exemplified by the way he treated two African American entertainers, **Billie Holiday** (*pictured above with Frank*) and another singer, Mabel Mercer.

"The two singers I have admired most in life were women, Billie and Mabel," he said. "They were also black and had to fight prejudice all their lives. All my life, I, too, have fought against racial prejudice."

"When she sings, Billie comes across almost like an unwilling musical instrument," Frank said. "The words coming from her golden brown throat are wrung first from her gut with unbearable pain and emotion."

"If we'd been born and had lived in another day, maybe I would have married Billie," Frank admitted years later. "I might have saved her from herself, and I always regretted that I didn't. I saw drugs do her in. She told me if she had to live her life without the stuff, then life wouldn't be worth living."

# WITH "LIP SERVICE" FROM
## WWII PINUP QUEEN
# BETTY GRABLE

*"So many shadows in her eye . . .*
*Lady Day has too much pain."*
—**Frank Sinatra** singing "Lady Day"

*"Talent has always had a blindness to color."*
—**Frank Sinatra**

**Lady Day** was like no other woman Frank Sinatra ever went to bed with. He told Harry James, "Most broads scream, 'fuck me, fuck me.' But Billie always said, 'use me, use me.' She told me I didn't need a rubber. Something to do with a fucked-up abortion she had when she was just a kid. She could never have children."

Then Frank said something that caused James to ponder a bit: "When she was with a man, Lady Day dug all the holes she'd been given."

"When I was just a kid, Billie was my first black broad," Frank said. "I was a bit inexperienced the first time. She told me it was like a fourteen-year-old boy taking his matronly aunt to bed. But as the months went by, she taught me sexual technique like she taught me how to sing."

Nicknamed "Lady Day," Billie Holiday grew up in Harlem and became a legendary jazz singer. Inspired by jazz instrumentalists, she pioneered a new way of manipulating phrasing and tempo, and would in time have an enormous influence on a crooner from Hoboken.

Frank Sinatra also became her lover, and over pillow talk she confided in him some of the secrets of her past. Florence Williams ran a whorehouse at 151 West 140th Street in New York and hired young Billie as a prostitute. "I got my start in show business singing to the johns at that brothel," she once told Frank. "And then heading with one of them to one of the much-used beds in the back room."

The trauma of Frank's Hoboken days paled in comparison to Billie's life in Harlem. She had been "born a bastard child," as she called it, "to a thirteen-year-old mother who was raped by a sixteen-year-old banjo player." Following in her mother's footsteps, Billie was raped twice when she was only eleven years old.

When Billie wasn't whoring for a living, she scrubbed "white people's bathroom floors for fifteen cents a floor."

She once told Frank and others, including her autobiographer, that she might have fared better if she'd stayed in Harlem and not gone downtown where she encountered racial prejudice.

"I found out the main difference between uptown and downtown. Uptown a whore was a whore; a pimp was a pimp; a thief was a thief; a faggot was a faggot; a dike was a dike, a mother-hugger was a mother-hugger. Downtown it was different—more complicated. A whore was sometimes a socialite; a pimp could be a man about town; a thief could be an executive; a faggot could be a playboy; a dike might be called a deb; a mother-hugger was somebody who was not adjusted and had problems. I always had trouble keeping this double-talk straight."

She was only eighteen, and beautiful in her special way, when Frank first saw her in New York singing at the famous Door Night Club with pianist Teddy Wilson.

When he first heard her, he recalled that "Billie sang of love and loneliness with more power than any singer I'd ever heard—before or since."

Backstage, he went to her dressing room and asked her out. She looked him up and down rather skeptically. Provocatively, she said, "You're a pretty skinny white boy. I usually find that white boys aren't worth messing up your mouth with."

"Try me," he said. "I'm different. No complaints yet, only praise."

"Okay," she said. "You certainly sound cocky enough. I'll probably regret this, but you're on. I'm starving. I know this little club in Harlem where you can get ribs and collards all night long."

"Let's go," he said.

Four hours later she turned over in her bed and said something that "was music to my ears," he'd recall. "I'm not used to white boys having dicks like yours."

He beamed and couldn't wait to tell the musicians in Harry James' band. "I've been given the stamp of approval from Billie herself," he boasted.

Frank was without racial prejudice. In ordering hookers in the years to come, he often told the madam or the pimp, "Tonight I want two vanillas and one chocolate." He usually didn't talk about his affair with Billie Holiday, though he did confess it to his valet, George Jacobs, who revealed the link in his memoir, *Mr. S.*

"I kissed her like she needed to be kissed, and I fucked her like she needed to be fucked," Frank told Harry James. "She'll be coming back begging for more."

In later life, Frank would change his order for prostitutes, often preferring as many as three black hookers. He'd tell the pimp or madam, "Tonight I'm cutting back on vanilla, and going all chocolate. If one of the pussies looks like Billie Holiday as she did in 1939, then send her along. There's only one requirement. I want all of these 'hos' to wear a white gardenia in their hair."

It was at the Onyx Club on 52nd Street in Manhattan where Billie always came out with a white gardenia in her hair.

Frank was a frequent guest at this little club, which black musicians from Harlem defined as the place in New York "where we black dudes meet the white folks from downtown."

He was mesmerized by her voice and "The Lady Herself," he later recalled in an interview given to a reporter on *The New York Daily News*. He said he was influenced by "Billie's matters of shading, phrasing, dark tones, light tones, and bending

At the Onyx Club in 1945, seated from left to right are **Sarah Vaughan, Louis Armstrong**, a mink-clad **Billie Holiday**, and an unknown friend. The New York club on 52nd Street between Fifth and Sixth Avenues was the best known of what was called "thirty eight Judas-hole joints," where sex, drugs, and the best jazz music in Manhattan" could be heard.

These musicians, although they looked happy, were mourning the loss of the heyday of this jumping street, where post-war property speculators were tearing down the dives and turning them into dull office blocks. The few clubs that remained were holding on as strip joints.

"When I first came here," Billie remembered, "I couldn't sit outside with the downtown folks 'cause I was colored. But they let me sit by the toilets until it was time for me to go on again. Then a new club owner told me I could sit out front with the crowd from Park Avenue. 'Some of my best customers like a little nigger pussy from time to time,' he told me."

notes."

One night Billie invited Frank back to her apartment for some fried chicken. In later years, he claimed, "Only Ava Gardner fried chicken better than Billie."

Before hopping into bed with him, she played a song recorded in 1939. Called "Strange Fruit," it was her anti-lynching refrain. "It is so God damn hot Columbia won't release it."

Later in 1939, *Strange Fruit* was released for Commodore and became her best-selling record, rising to Number Sixteen on the pop charts of the 1930s.

Billie saw talent in Frank, but also recognized he had a long way to go before he became the singer he thought he was. "Honey," she said to him, "your voice is a little thin and a bit high-pitched. At times the notes get stuck in your throat. You've also got to get sexier. No one comes to hear a singing priest. You gotta shake your big dick at the audience. Let them know you've got something hot in your pants. That, baby, will really turn on the horny gals and the homos. They'll fill up your empty saloon if you make yourself hot to trot."

By the time he'd taken up with Billie, Frank had already met another one of her admirers, the bandleader Harry James. James had stopped in Hoboken one night to catch Frank's act and signed him up that very night. Frank's first successful record, "All or Nothing At All," was recorded with Harry before he moved on and hooked up with the Tommy Dorsey band.

James was as skinny as Frank, although he towered six feet. "My blue eyes are bluer than yours," the bandleader told Frank on the day they met.

The marijuana-smoking James was only twenty-three when he hired Frank to sing with his band.

Billie Holiday

This infamous photograph (right) was taken in 1930 in Marion, Indiana, showing the dead bodies of victims Abram Smith and Thomas Shipp, two black Americans hanging from the limbs of a tree, much to the amusement of the white observers. A pivotal moment in Billie's career occurred when she recorded the anti-lynching song, "Strange Fruit," which included the lyrics, "Southern trees bear a strange fruit."

She sang of "Bulging eyes and the twisted mouth, the scent of magnolias, sweet and fresh, then the sudden smell of burning flesh. Here is a fruit for the crows to pluck."

At first, Billie didn't understand the lyrics, but in time "it became my song. It was like I wrote it." Her audiences were mesmerized. *Time* came and photographed her singing it, and her picture ran in the magazine. marking the first time a picture of an African American appeared in that publication. Of course, dozens of white patrons walked out on her gig any time she sang "Strange Fruit."

Frank and Harry soon discovered they were "womanizers of the first rank." To save money, they often slept together on tour in a double room and seduced hookers on the same bed at the same time, sometimes trading partners.

"I loved Harry James," Frank recalled in later life. "Loved him for a long time." It's assumed he didn't mean sexual love, although they were blasting off only a foot from each other on many a night when they had two women in the same bed at the same time, or when cash was low and they were forced to share the same girl, taking turns before each mounted the prostitute for the finale.

Although married at the time, Harry was dating a struggling young blonde actress, Betty Grable. By 1943, when she was the top female box office attraction in America and the pin-up girl of WWII, he'd marry her. In the meantime, he dated her in secret. One night he told her, "You should catch Sinatra's act. He claims he's the greatest singer in the world, but no one's ever heard of him yet. He looks like a limp dishrag."

"Sounds enticing," Betty told her future husband.

Almost overnight, Frank became Grable's favorite male vocalist. She came backstage after he'd finished his act. Her date for later in the evening, Harry himself, was conducting dance music for patrons at The Panther, a Chicago nightclub.

Knocking on the door to Frank's dressing room, she opened it immediately before he'd given her permission to enter. She found Frank in his underwear.

"Hi, I'm Betty Grable," she said. "You are the greatest male vocalist in America." To his shock and amazement, she got down on her knees. "I've come to pay homage to your talent."

Almost before he knew what was happening, she reached into the flap of his underwear, pulled out his penis, and began fellating him. She didn't back off until he'd delivered a spectacular climax.

As biographer Mart Martin wrote, "Grable had a life-long affection for chorus boys and dancers, many of whom were homosexual. When she couldn't find other sex partners, she'd press her demands on them to service her. But she really preferred rough men of the truck driver and bartender type and especially liked to fellate them." Martin might also have added that she liked to fellate musicians like Harry James and singers like Frank Sinatra.

Grable had also been married to child star Jackie Coogan. She later said, "Honey, Coogan taught me more tricks than a whore learns in a whorehouse." With Frank, she'd demonstrated those lessons learned from Coogan.

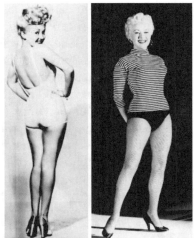

Three views of blonde-haired **Betty Grable.** The one on the upper left was the most famous pinup picture of World War II. The one on the right got her left leg voted "loveliest in the world," making her wonder about her right one.

The photo at the bottom was taken around the time she first met Frank Sinatra, and before her 1943 marriage to his former boss, bandleader Harry James. "Frankie and I in those days were pretty well acquainted with each other's anatomy," she told Carmen Miranda. "Of course, we never discussed marriage—it was just for the hell of it."

When Betty and Harry divorced on October 8, 1965, he'd been living on her savings, having lost all his money at the gambling tables.

Frank later told Sammy Davis Jr., "I went from vanilla at ten o'clock to chocolate at two in the morning." He was referring, of course, to Betty earlier in the evening and Billie, with whom he'd hook up later. She, too, was appearing in Chicago.

In the future, Betty continued to deliver those blow-jobs whenever she caught up with Frank, and he also continued his on-again, off-again affair with Billie. He was especially defensive of her if he heard of any ill treatment from whites.

In New York at the Onyx, he went to see her performance after his own show had ended. Two obnoxious men sat in front of him and kept making derogatory remarks about Billie. Finally, Frank had had it. Rising to the challenge, he punched out both of them with his fists trained on the tough streets of Hoboken years before.

When Frank left Harry James to join the band of Tommy Dorsey, he often linked up with Billie in the Los Angeles area. One such night occurred in the early 1940s. Lana Turner was dating his boss, Tommy.

Frank Sinatra's second great musical inspiration was the cabaret entertainer **Mabel Mercer**.

Critics hailed the British-born star for her "regal manner, rarefied repertoire, and crisp enunciation" Her fans included everyone from Cole Porter to Ernest Hemingway. Along with Tony Bennett, Frank was a frequent visitor to Mabel's concerts in the 1940s at such Manhattan clubs as Spivy's and The Blue Angel. "Everything I know, I learned from Mabel Mercer," he claimed. Those not in the loop claimed, "Mercer can't even sing for toffee."

She agreed, "I'm just a storyteller in words and music."

"She had the feel for a lyric and for the narrative at the heart of a song better than anyone in the business," Frank said.

Frank invited Lana and Tommy to drive with him to a club in San Fernando Valley to hear Billie sing. Frank had made a date with her after her late show, promising, as always, "I'll show you a good time, baby."

Frank had to drive because Tommy wanted to take advantage of Lana in the back seat. Frank obviously got a preview of coming attractions with Lana, although his sexual trysts with her lay in his future.

At Billie's late show, Lana, Frank, and Tommy gave the singer her most enthusiastic response of the evening. Tommy and Lana disappeared after the show, and Billie and Frank retreated to a nearby motel. Since blacks weren't accepted, he booked the room and slipped her in later.

She'd brought a bottle with her and over drinks told him that "some drunk called me a nigger during my first show."

"If I'd been there, I would have castrated the bastard," he boasted to her. "When I was growing up in Hoboken, I used to be called 'a dirty guinea.' My gang had a way of dealing with shits like that. We broke the head of the guy who yelled that slur. We did the same if they called us wops, Jews, or niggers."

In addition to Billie, Frank also owed a debt to another black diva, Mabel Mercer. They had a great friendship, but not a sexual one. Called a singer's singer, Mabel had a devoted following, every singer from Nat King Cole to Johnny Mathis.

Beginning at the famous Bricktop's in Paris in the early 1930s, Mabel gave each note and each syllable of the words she sang "an almost painful consideration" in the words of one critic. Frank discovered her when she came to New York in the late 1930s. Often sitting in the audience with him were Peggy Lee, Lena Horne, Sarah Vaughan, and even Dorothy Parker.

On reflection, Frank said, "Elvis Presley owed a lot to black musicians, and I did too, especially my beloved Billie and Mabel."

Yet in 1944, Billie told columnist Earl Wilson that "I didn't teach Frank anything. I just told him about notes at the end he should 'bend,' and later he said I inspired him." She was being far too modest, as Frank himself would later admit.

She had paid Frank the compliment of using many of his signature songs in her last albums. Leonard Mustazza, author of *Ol' Blue Eyes: A Frank Sinatra Encyclopedia*, called it a case of "the master learning a lesson or two from the pupil."

Mustazza articulated a defense of Billie's musical genius very well, each of his insights having been previously recognized by Frank, who loved her. "Unfortunately, Holiday's limited voice (which never could sustain a long vocal line) turned sour early, and her later, often self-conscious records, are accessible mainly to aficionados. Holiday's life of drugs and booze, abuse and ill health, limited her experiences and, sadly, ended just when the world was opening up for black entertainers like the prim and proper Nat Cole."

As regards her last and final album, Billie told a reporter, "I always wanted to be known as the female Sinatra." As a tribute to him, she sang, "All the Way" on that farewell album.

On May 31, she'd been taken to the Metropolitan Hospital in New York City, suffering from heart and liver disease. Because she'd been arrested for narcotics, her hospital room was raided by the police, who later stationed three guards at her door so she wouldn't have access to any more drugs.

Although she'd made fortunes for club owners, she'd been swindled out of her earnings. At the time of her death, she had only seventy cents in the bank. A total of $750 was found on her body, which she was afraid to deposit in the bank for fear of it being confiscated.

In July of 1959, Frank heard that Lady Day was near death.

On the way into the hospital Frank saw protesters carrying placards. LET LADY DAY LIVE, the signs proclaimed.

The police, who had arrested her, had cut off her supply of heroin, and the withdrawal from the drug was killing her. Her most ardent fans demanded that the hospital supply her with legal narcotics. If they did not, the fans warned, she would die from withdrawal symptoms.

Frank was shocked at the once beautiful woman he encountered in the hospital. As Gilbert Millstein of *The New York Times* described, "She was wasted physically to a small, grotesque caricature of herself. The worms of every excess—drugs were only one—had eaten her. This cynical, sentimental, profane, generous, and greatly talented woman was to be arraigned the following morning but death at the age of forty-four removed her from earthly jurisdiction."

When Frank walked in the door, she held up a yard-long telegram. It was from Gary Cooper. "What's got into Coop?" she asked him. "This is shit he's writing me. The man has converted to the Pope's religion and all he thinks about is the Holy Ghost. He used to have his mind on getting laid. This is the crap he's writing. Is this what religion does to you, Frankie?"

Although he tried to indulge in harmless chit-chat, she grabbed his arm when the nurse had gone. "Let's cut this shit, baby, and get down to business. Get me some dope, honey child. I know you can."

Knowing she was near death, Frank was in no mood to deny Lady Day anything. Although he despised drug use, he knew in her case if she didn't get a supply of heroin, she'd die. He went to her doctor and tried to bribe him with $10,000 under the table, a gift of cash. The doctor refused.

He even tried to intercede with Mayor Robert Wagner to get him to overrule the hospital and the police department, but the mayor didn't return his calls.

After the third call to the Mayor, Frank slammed down the phone. "Wagner hates my ass."

Finally, Frank turned to a dealer in Harlem who sold him an ample supply of heroin. But the dealer failed to get through the security guards at the door.

Billie still thanked Frank for his efforts to get her the heroin. The last time he was allowed into her room, she told him, "When I was a little gal, I was told if you wash the curtains, company won't come. They'll only show up when you and your house are a mess. If you expect nothing but a pile of shit, maybe a rose will bloom. Don't ever believe that happy days are around the corner. If you do that, they'll never come. Life gives us only a few good surprises, and it's a long waiting period before one of those days comes around."

"Even if you see the end coming around the corner, run from it," he told her. "When the body fails us, keep that will to live. Beat the God damn devil."

"I will, Frankie," she said weakly. "I will. I know I've been a bad gal, and I know I'm not gonna go to Heaven. So I'll fight for life. I don't want that Devil to get me."

"You'll always live in my heart, Billie, until they come for me, too."

"The other night I tried to relive my life. The first thing I remembered was getting raped. I was only eleven. That was the beginning. It seems I've been fucked every day of my life since then."

He leaned over and whispered in her ear. "That damn nurse says I have to go. But before I do, I want to sing you a little song." He selected "I'll Be Seeing You," which he sang softly in her ear. Tears ran down her face.

When he left the room, tears were also running down his own face, as he knew there would be no more songs from Billie, not even sad ones.

Frank didn't cry at the death of many of his celebrity friends, but he broke down and cried on that hot night on July 17, 1959 when he learned that Lady Day had died. Mortally ill, she'd died in the bed in which she'd been arrested for possession of narcotics a little less than a month before.

At his penthouse on Seventy-second Street, Frank wept for two days, endlessly playing her records, his favorite being "Autumn in New York." His other favorites were "Wishing on the Moon" and "The Very Thought of You."

Two years later when Frank ran into Harry James, the bandleader asked him, "You miss Billie, don't you?"

"Of course, I do," he said. "Her death causes me pain, but I listen to her music a lot. It's not just the music. I sometimes hear her words, the stories she told me, the things she said. I remember once, she said, 'I grew up in a whorehouse which was about the only place where black and white folks could meet in a natural way.'"

Frank Sinatra was in the audience when **Count Basie and Billie Holiday** performed together in 1948. Having been influenced by each of these African American performers, he was an ardent fan of both of them

Frank used to stroll down New York's 52nd Street in its heyday to hear his favorites, such as Count Basie but also Fats Waller and Louis Prima. He thrilled to Ethel Waters and listened to scat by Louis Armstrong. "The black bands of Count Basie were wildly swinging, real innovative," Frank said. "Peggy Lee and I danced to his music. People wanted to forget the Depression and get on with FDR's New Deal. It was a new day dawning."

# Julie Sinatra

## FRANK'S MYSTERIOUS DAUGHTER

**Frank Sinatra** may have had a number of illegitimate children, only two of which have surfaced. He would have had a lot more if he had not arranged for them to be aborted. As he later admitted, "I didn't believe in using a rubber back in the 40s and 50s." He learned about abortions while still a boy growing up in Hoboken.

His mother, Dolly Sinatra, was known as "Hat Pin Dolly," and she, even though a Catholic, saw no reason against performing an abortion to prevent an unwanted pregnancy. "A kid has three strikes against him if the mother is forced to give birth," Dolly claimed. "It's unfair to the kid to bring him into a world where he's not wanted. Life is rough enough even if you have a loving family."

One person with an excellent claim as Frank's offspring is **Julie Sinatra** *(depicted above)*, who certainly looks like him. A singer and songwriter herself, she wrote a very convincing book, *Under My Skin,* relating the story of how she learned she was Frank's daughter.

"On the night of February 10, 1943, at the moment I was born, my identity was sent into exile," Julie claimed. "At age 53, I learned for the first time what my mother had never before told me: I am Frank Sinatra's daughter."

# Under My Skin

## My Father, Frank Sinatra
### The Man Behind the Mystique

## Julie Sinatra

The 2003 publication of Julie Sinatra's memoirs, *Under My Skin, My Father, Frank Sinatra, The Man Behind the Mystique,* sent shock waves through the heirs to the Sinatra estate. She claimed that she met resistance from the Sinatra children "on all fronts," although she found Frank Sinatra Jr. the most sympathetic.

In this book, which is compelling, Julie writes of how she fought for years to establish herself as Frank's daughter.

Even though none of Frank's children would submit to a DNA test, when she faced the Sinatra heirs before a judge, she won a court settlement.

Basically, the book is self-styled as a "love mystery," a journey by Julie Sinatra to find her identity and come to terms with whom she really is.

## A BLUE-EYED DAUGHTER IN SEARCH OF OL' BLUE EYES

In the darkest days of World War II, on the night of February 10, 1943, Julie was born. But she was 53 years old before her mother told her, "You are Frank Sinatra's daughter."

Christened Julie Ann Maria Lyma, she changed her name to Julie Sinatra on June 1, 2000.

Her mother was Dorothy Lyma, who used the stage name of "Alora Gooding" when she first met Frank in 1940.

Dorothy caused the first rupture in Frank's marriage to Nancy. It occurred in October of 1940 when he went to Hollywood with Tommy Dorsey's band to open at the Palladium. During the day the band was making *Las Vegas Nights*, their first feature film, in which Frank appeared on screen as an anonymous band vocalist singing "I'll Never Smile Again."

Dorothy was working at the studio as an extra on the film. He met her on his first day on the Paramount lot. By the third day they were "shacked up" at the Hollywood Plaza, where the band was staying.

Actually sharp-eyed fans of Frank learned of his affair with Alora Gooding (alias Dorothy) when Kitty Kelley published her unauthorized biography of Frank called *His Way* in 1986.

In 1940 when he returned home to Jersey City and Nancy, she discovered a picture of a beautiful blonde in his wallet. He claimed it was of "just a fan." Actually, as Kelley revealed, he was "besotted with Alora at the time."

"This was Frank's first big love away from home," Nick Sevano, his long-time manager, told Kelley. "She was the first big love of his life after he married Nancy. He was crazy about Alora, really in love with her. She was his first brush with glamour, and he was made for her. The affair lasted a few years, and Frank even tried to leave Nancy because of it, but Dolly put the pressure on and wouldn't let him get a divorce."

Kelley, however, was apparently unaware that deep into the affair, the Frank/Dorothy liaison spawned a daughter. Dorothy never told him about her pregnancy. Since she was away from the singer for months at a time, she could conceal Julie from him.

By 1960, Julie was growing up and had developed a school-girl crush on a handsome young politician, John F. Kennedy, who was campaigning for president. As a coincidence, he happened to be a close pal of Frank Sinatra's.

At that time her mother, Dorothy, was married to yet a third husband, Carroll Hunter, her second husband having died of a heart attack in 1954.

Politically, Hunter was very conservative. When he learned of his stepdaughter's fascination with Kennedy, he shouted at her, "You're a pinko like your father. Tom Lyma wasn't your father. Your father's that pinko singer who's a friend of Kennedy."

Julie didn't know what singer her stepfather was referring to.

Then Hunter delivered a bombshell. "In fact, your whoring mother is off right now having an affair with that singer. He's been fucking her for years."

Julie did not make the Sinatra link that Hunter was suggesting, and her mother remained resolutely silent on the subject. At that point in her life, Julie wanted to be a folk singer and was more inspired by Bob Dylan than Frank.

In 1963 she met a fellow folk singer, Tom Brown, and they were soon married, giving birth to a son. Like her father, Julie would go through four marriages.

In June of 1996 while she was living in Cave Creek, Arizona, she saw a CBS biopic on Frank. The mini-series pictured Frank singing to a beautiful starlet against the backdrop

**Frank Sinatra** at the mike is shown in the 40s when he began an affair with an aspirant starlet who called herself "**Alora Gooding**." She was, in fact, Dorothy Lyma, whose dreams of stardom never came true.

Alora first met Sinatra in October of 1940 when he was "a twig of a man," the boy singer with Tommy Dorsey's band. Back in New Jersey, Nancy, Frank's wife, had recently given birth to Nancy Jr. Alora was working as an extra, hoping to break into films bigtime. Instead of fame on the silver screen, she was offered the roles of cigarette girl, waitress, and hat-check attendant.

She met Frank on the set of *Las Vegas Nights,* a film where he sang "I'll Never Smile Again." She also worked as a daytime greeter at the famous, celebrity-haunted Garden of Allah Hotel. Frank checked in one night. After work, Alora was on his doorstep. Within days, they were living together at the Plaza Hotel in Los Angeles.

Aspirant starlet **Alora Gooding** and an unknown hunk in 1940 were having fun in the water when Mickey Rooney, a reigning star of the time, invited them to a press party honoring June Preisser. That skilled acrobat actress had just appeared with Rooney and Judy Garland in *Strike Up the Band (1940),* having previously performed with them in the 1939 film *Babes in Arms.* Preisser would go on to film two Andy Hardy films with Rooney.

Alora was eventually hired as a stand-in for Preisser, even though she'd have preferred to appear before the camera herself. She joined hundreds of young women who flocked to Hollywood during the war, hoping to become the next Betty Grable, the next Veronica Lake, or the next Joan Crawford. But Alora never made it. Soon, she saw another of her dreams—marriage to Frank Sinatra—burst.

In spite of his promises, Frank eventually went back to his wife, Nancy.

of Dorsey's band. The setting was El Rancho in Las Vegas. Julie remembered that her mother had worked that lounge when Frank appeared there.

Could the starlet Alora actually be her mother, Dorothy?

Although she had not spoken to her mother in months, she called her the next day. Julie bluntly asked, "Is Frank Sinatra my father?"

After years of concealment, her mother bluntly said, "Yes."

"But why did you let me go on all these years thinking a man I didn't like was my real father?"

For most of her years, Julie thought her father was Tom Lyma, a womanizing traveling salesman who sold food and wine to joints along the Nevada/California border.

Dorothy explained that she had called Frank's home in Jersey City to tell him she was pregnant. But she got Nancy on the phone instead. His wife learned the shocking news.

Nancy then conspired with George Evans, his long-time manager, to prevent Frank from leaving her and going with "Alora." Of course, Nancy had Dolly in her corner as well. Frank gave up his dream and returned home to Nancy.

Evans called Alora and told her he could make a career for her in Hollywood if she kept her mouth shut. "Studios have moral clauses in contracts. Frank must not know of this. A child out of wedlock would not only ruin his career, but finish you off in your dream of stardom."

"If you don't cooperate with us, you'll end up selling cigarettes from a neon tray instead of having your own name up in lights," Evans claimed. "Alora" continued her affair with Frank, but never mentioned the birth of Julie.

Of course, in time her own dream of a career turned into a nightmare. As she lost her looks, she slowly descended into alcoholism. Her dream of stardom as Alora faded, and she became plain Dorothy again.

In looking back at old Sinatra movies, Julie discovered her mother performing as a background extra in some of them. In one faded photograph "Alora Gooding" (her stage name) was photographed sitting near Ava Gardner. Ava wore a set of jade earrings. Enraged, Dorothy removed a matching pendant from her jewelry box. "That skinny bastard gave Ava the rest of the set."

Julie admitted that she was in a state of shock when she found out that she was the daughter of Frank Sinatra. "I admire him so, and I'm proud that he gave life to me."

"The sadness is that I knew who my father was but was prevented from meeting him before he died," Julie claimed. "That still hurts. The money was never an issue with me. When I realized who I was, it explained so much about my life, gave me answers which were wealth in themselves. All my life I was lost. Now I feel like a proper person."

Julie decided she wanted to meet her father, but "I faced a stone wall of lawyers. I was trying to beat the clock to see my father before he died."

She also accused Tina of "firing the first shot" with a cease-and-desist order. "She in essence told me to buzz off," Julie said.

She hired lawyers and even wrote Tina, sending photographs showing her physical resemblance to Frank. The data was returned. Only Frank Sinatra Jr. returned Julie's calls. "He was the only one who treated me with a measure of compassion," she said.

He told her the pressure was upsetting his siblings. "The issue will have to be settled in court," he said. "I will not take a DNA test. Good luck with this identity thing."

In the midst of her battle for identity, Frank Sr. died on May 14, 1998. "I knew he was ill, and I knew I was in a race against time," Julie said. "All I wanted to do was talk to him, touch his hand, and tell him that I understood, that I had survived and was okay, and that I didn't blame him for anything that happened. But they wouldn't allow it. They seemed to be so terrified of me."

Julie even hired private investigators, who grilled Dorothy at the age of 82, but she refused to cooperate. She told her daughter, "I never benefited from knowing Frank. On the contrary, he brought me a lot of heartache. I don't want you to benefit either. Give this up for your own good. You'll never best the people around him. You should just think of him as a ditch-digger and move on with your life. Go ride your horses and be happy."

On September 30, 2002, Julie attended the Los Angeles Superior Court for a hearing. Frank's will was being probated.

Before entering the courtroom, she was plagued with fears. She'd changed into three different outfits before leaving the house. "Would the judge throw me out without any DNA proof? Would I be belittled by Sinatra's lawyers?" She asked herself so many questions.

"Your honor," Julie said to Judge Thomas W. Stoever. "I am Julie Sinatra. I am here to object to the final accounting because it does not include my fair share because I am an heir."

On November 21, 2002, Julie appeared for a second hearing, but it would take yet another hearing before a confidential contract was agreed upon by the estate.

At the end of the probate hearings, the Frank Sinatra estate awarded Julie a cash settlement of $100,000. A confidential contract was made between Julie and Frank's three

Even though Frank Sinatra returned home to Nancy, he continued his affair with Alora, which was conducted in Hollywood, Palm Springs, and Santa Barbara.

In her memoirs, **Julie Sinatra** *(depicted above)* said she believed that Dorothy (alias Alora) blamed her for a lifetime lived in the shadows rather than in the spotlight of a glamorous Hollywood career.

"I grew up frightened of my mother and thinking she hated me." Julie also claimed that her mother made several attempts to alter her appearance so she wouldn't look so much like Frank, but more like Tom Lyma, whom Dorothy was claiming was Julie's father.

Julie also said that her mother and Frank shared more in common than a daughter. "They both loved to drink Jack Daniels."

other children, Nancy Jr., Frank Jr., and Tina. Julie was granted total control of her career. She could do whatever she wanted under the name of Julie Sinatra.

She later billed herself as THE BLUE-EYED DAUGHTER OF OL' BLUE EYES.

Hearing her sing one night, a man in the audience shouted, "You look like Sinatra in drag."

In 2003, Julie published her memoirs called *Under My Skin* with the subtitle of *My Father, Frank Sinatra: The Man Behind the Mystique.*

To judge only by her face on the cover of this book, she looks like the daughter of Frank Sinatra.

Her story was a voyage to discover what her father was like, but it was also an attempt to find herself. "I missed all of this man who lived larger than life, and I am his daughter."

**Julie Sinatra** *(right)* missed out on all the glamorous Sinatra family events, such as the formal occasion of Frank's fiftieth birthday party. He went with his recognized daughters—**Tina Sinatra** *(left)* and **Nancy Jr.** *(right).*

To prove her claim as Frank's daughter, Julie knew she had to produce more than a mother's belated confession. When she attempted to contact her father, Tina Sinatra "fired the first shot with a 'cease and desist' order, essentially telling me to buzz off. That left me with no other option but to go to court."

Julie hired lawyers and private investigators who quizzed her then-82 year-old mother.

"You ruined my life when you were born," the mother told Julie. "I couldn't go to the resorts any more. They were even talking about making me a singer because I was Italian."

Nancy Sr. threw the 50th birthday party for Frank at the Beverly Wilshire Hotel. On the way there, Frank got pissed off at Nancy Jr. for teasing him about his baldness. At this point in his life, he owned 75 *toupées.*

Before the party, Gay Talese in *Esquire* had written: "In an age when the very young seem to be taking over, Frank Sinatra survives as a national phenomenon, one of the few pre-war products to stand the test of time. He does not feel old, he makes old men feel young."

That wasn't quite true. Frank was feeling old, admitting, "As a singer, I have only a few more years to go—as an actor, maybe a few more, but not many. I'm getting tired."

When he released his album, *September of My Years,* critic Arnold Shaw wrote: "The silken baritone of 1943 now sounds like torn velvet, the voice of a man who has smoked thousands of unfiltered Camels."

# Frank and Nancy

## BREAKING UP IS HARD TO DO

**Frank Sinatra** began his marriage to **Nancy Barbato** *(upper left photo)* by cheating on her, and he continued to do so during his musical road tours. Although he was attracted to many women, **Ava Gardner** *(upper center photo, in makeup for an MGM movie, Bhowani Junction, released in 1956)* became the passion of his life. He never got over her. She had the same cheating heart that he did, and he could not stand that. Their marriage evolved into a long-running disaster.

**Marilyn Maxwell,** seen lounging in the lower left cheesecake photo, was Frank's steady. "She was always there for me. When Nancy or Ava kicked me out of the house, Marilyn's door was always opened to me." This blonde MM type was eventually replaced by an even more famous blonde, Marilyn Monroe herself.

Throughout the late 40s, Frank had an on-again, off-again romance with another blonde bombshell, **Lana Turner** *(depicted in the heart-framed photo)*. Lana later confessed, "I was actually far more in love with Tyrone Power than I was with Frank, but Ty dumped me. Frank was there and available...and a lot of fun. He was terrific in bed. But I had to surrender him to my best gal pal, Ava herself."

Although Frank had not "officially" dumped Lana Turner, he had a public reconciliation with Nancy one night during March of 1947 at Slapsie Maxie's nightclub in Hollywood. It was a scene almost written for a movie, but it was real. Phil Silvers, the comedian, was performing there. He asked Frank to join him onstage for an impromptu skit and a song.

Nancy had showed up at the club alone and unannounced. Frank sang "Going Home," and cried throughout the number. At the end of the song, Phil took Frank's hand and guided him to Nancy's table. "These two kids belong together," Silver said.

Nancy was crying when Frank put his arms around her. It was a reconciliation of sorts.

The next day, Frank packed his luggage and moved back in with Nancy. But how long would it last?

# AND SO COSTLY

As World War II came to an end, and Frank and Nancy entered into the sometimes bitter post-war era of their marriage, she knew about the other women. And if she didn't know, "friends" kept her informed of Frank's various assignations, often with prostitutes of any color. He used his home like a hotel, coming and going as he wished, without telling where he was going or when he was coming back.

"He once told me he was going to divorce me to marry Lana Turner," Nancy confided to friends. "That love affair fell apart. I think the same thing will happen with his next screen goddess, perhaps Ava Gardner."

In 1948, Frank had turned thirty-two and was about to become a father again. The girl who was to be known as Tina Sinatra was born in June.

Although Nancy wanted her husband to be home with her, that was not the case. In California, he made only rare appearances at their Toluca Lake estate and seemed to come by more as a sense of duty than anything else.

He rented a bachelor pad at Sunset Towers in Hollywood where he entertained friends who included Burt Lancaster and Jimmy Van Heusen until the dawn broke through.

Ava Gardner lived in an apartment nearby. One night, a drunken Frank stood on his balcony in his underwear. He pulled out his penis and shook it in the wind. "Ava, can you see me?" he shouted. "Come and get some of this, babe." It is not known if Ava witnessed this vulgar display or not.

After his affair with Lana ended, Frank tried to repair his relationship with Nancy. As the repentant husband, he showered her with gifts, including an ermine coat. He took her to New York City, and they were seen around town. That Christmas he presented her with a super expensive three-strand pearl necklace. He even purchased her a new Cadillac.

In the glove compartment, Nancy found a diamond bracelet, which she just assumed was going to be another Christmas gift to her from her errant husband. But although he may have originally purchased the bauble for Lana, he had other plans for it now.

At a private Yuletide party at the Sinatra home, Frank's longtime girlfriend, Marilyn Maxwell, showed up wearing that same diamond bracelet. Recognizing it at once, Nancy demanded she remove it and give it to her.

"It's mine. God knows I've earned it. Now give it back. I'm the one who has put up with all Frank's crap for the past eight years."

Frank intervened and ushered Marilyn into the coatroom. Nancy had ordered her out of the house. In the hallway, having emerged from the coatroom, Marilyn appeared without the bracelet. "In show business," she said with a kind of gallows humor, "you must learn how to make a spectacular entrance, and a spectacular exit as well."

Soon Frank didn't have to display his genitalia to Ava from an apartment balcony. She could turn over in bed and feel it up close and personal.

"I'm caught between two capricious and unpredictable women," Frank told Jimmy Van Heusen, no doubt referring to Ava Gardner and Nancy. "They're impulsive, and they're crush-ing the life out of me, squeezing the last drop of blood. I should have been a god damn homosexual and accepted Burt Lancaster's invitation to come and live with him. At least if we broke up, it wouldn't be a matter of the larcenous courts and those scumbag newspaper reporters to decide."

Frank did not attempt to conceal his ongoing affair with Ava from the press. Nancy felt humiliated and finally arrived at the point where she could no longer tolerate such outrageous behavior on his part.

On the verge of a nervous breakdown, Nancy appeared in Santa Monica's Superior Court on September 28, 1950. Her testimony was interrupted by sobbing. She claimed that throughout the course of her marriage, Frank was often not at home when he was in town and not on the road. "He con-stantly stayed away. He spent weekends in Palm Springs with others—not me."

Judge Orlando Rhodes granted her $2,750 monthly in temporary support. It was revealed in court that Frank's income in 1949 had been $93,740.

Supported by her sister, Julie Barbato, Nancy was pho-tographed leaving the courtroom, having won her plea for legal separation and separate maintenance.

In her court plea for a separation, Nancy had claimed that her married life had become "unhappy and almost unbearable."

Nancy definitely had the public's sympathy, and Ava garnered all the bad press, at least at first. She was called "a hussy," a "Tarheel slut," and a "homewrecker."

"I was more than just 'The Other Woman,'" Ava told Lana Turner. "I was the daughter of the Devil sent directly up from Hell. Those assholes at the Legion of Decency called me indecent."

Nancy had sought a separation rather than a divorce. "That way he'll get Ava out of his system and come back to

"**Marilyn Maxwell** *(depicted above)* is a helluva broad," or so said Frank Sinatra, who dated her throughout the late 1940s. It was 1945 and he had set-tled in Hollywood. "I started seeing a dif-ferent type of woman, and I'd already said goodbye to my steady piece, Lips Luango, in Jersey City."

Now two Hollywood blondes, Marilyn Maxwell and Lana Turner, were moving in on him. Each beauty made her inten-tions clear. "I really believe I could have had any dame I wanted in Hollywood at the time. But I was in no rush. I planned to knock them off one by one—that's knock them off, not knock them up."

me."

She is also reported to have said, "Of all the women Frank has known, I'm the only one who presented him with children." If she did indeed say that remark attributed to her, she should probably have altered it somewhat. She remains the only woman who had "legitimate" children with Frank. So far as it's known, he did have two additional daughters, neither of whom were ever acknowledged. And if it weren't for the services of several abortionists during the course of his lifetime, he might have had a lot more.

In her memoirs, Tina Sinatra asserted, "The pressure against mom, meanwhile, kept mounting. The tabloid winds shifted—one columnist compared Frank and Ava to Romeo and Juliet—and suddenly my mother was an ogre for trying to hold her family together. Dolly was seduced by Ava's glamour, and her devout Catholicism took a backseat. She'd tell Mom: 'Better to let him go—better for you, better for the children. You can't keep a man if he doesn't want to be there.'"

After leaving Nancy once again, Frank Sinatra began making appearances with Ava Gardner whether the photographers snapped their pictures or not.

Ava later admitted, "I knew my running around with Frank might generate some bad publicity, but I had no idea the shit would hit the fan. Our affair outraged the public because Frank was still a family man with three children and a doting, loyal wife. I was the fucking homewrecker, although that home had been wrecked a long time ago—and not by me. My god, nuns at some Catholic schools were even asking the kids to pray for Nancy and condemn me to hell's fire. It was a time of McCarthy witch hunts and blacklists, and the press let me have it. Many friends told me I could say goodbye to my career. Look at what happened to Ingrid Bergman when her adulterous affair was exposed."

Finally accepting the fact that her husband was "gone from me forever," Nancy agreed to give in and let the divorce proceed.

Frank was not happy at the slow divorce proceedings. He established a six-week residency in Nevada and filed for divorce himself on September 19, 1951. His attorneys notified him that Nancy was going to contest the divorce. "She already filed for divorce in California," he shouted at his lawyers. "Why would she object to my filing? It makes no sense."

It made sense to Nancy's lawyers. A divorce in California would be more favorable to her financial interests than one granted in Nevada. After all, California had joint property rights.

A tougher, more belligerent Nancy fought back. Through her lawyers, she notified Frank's attorneys that the property settlement once agreed upon was no longer acceptable, citing that Frank was $50,000 behind in his alimony payments, She ordered her attorneys to obtain a levy on 177 S. Roberson Boulevard in Beverly Hills, an office building owned by Frank.

Then, to make matters worse, Frank's own lawyers turned on him, suing him to collect $12,250 in legal fees. They too filed a lien on that office building.

Almost suicidal, Frank said, "I can't fight Nancy any more. Give her all my god damn money. Agree to everything. Send me to the fucking cleaners. Just get this divorce over with. I want to be a free man. I'll start all over again."

At long last Frank got his divorce. It was granted on October 31, 1951 in Santa Monica, while Frank was in Manhattan in bed with Ava. "Regrettably, I am putting aside religious and personal considerations and agreeing to give Frank the freedom he has so earnestly requested," Nancy said. "This is what Frank wants, not what I want."

According to the terms of the divorce, Nancy would receive one third of his gross yearly income on the first $150,000. She'd then receive ten percent of the next $150,000. After that, she'd receive a smaller percentage. She retained custody of Nancy Jr., Frank Jr., and Tina and kept the home in Holmby Hills. In addition, she retained a partial interest in the Sinatra Music Corporation, and she was able to keep all their furnishings, plus a 1950 Cadillac. Frank kept his 1949 Cadillac along with his villa in Palm Springs.

"As if Frank weren't skinny enough, Nancy took a few more pounds of flesh he couldn't spare," Ava said when learning of the terms of the settlement. Even though Frank was appearing at such clubs as the Desert Inn in Las Vegas, all of his checks seemed to go to Nancy, leaving him less than $400 a week for living expenses. He was paying dearly for leaving home and hearth.

Nancy was emotionally shattered when the divorce came through. Beginning back in the 1930s in Hoboken, she'd come to realize that she'd have to share her husband with other women. "She always wanted to be known as Mrs. Frank Sinatra," said friend Esther Williams. "I knew after the divorce that she would never remarry."

From the rubble of her marriage, Nancy managed to re-establish herself and her dignity in the Hollywood community. "There's nothing lower than the abandoned wife of a movie star," claimed Mrs. Van Johnson (Evie Wynn Johnson). "You're dropped from all the party lists, and you don't live in Beverly Hills anymore."

Nancy became a respected figure in Hollywood, enjoying a wide circle of friends, but she always made it clear that her son and her two daughters were her main reason for living. She rarely spoke about Frank's choice of his other three wives, although she did say, "In Ava Gardner, Frank got what he deserved. He found a cheating heart that beat stronger than his own."

She always remained steadfast in her loyalty and, unlike many divorced women, did not try to cut off Frank's relationships with his daughters and son. "He knew that I was always there for him, that I took my role seriously as the mother of his children. Perhaps in his heart he knew that after all his philandering was over, he could always come home again."

In spite of their smiles, there was trouble in paradise. Just before this picture of **Frank with Ava** was taken, Frank had received a mailbag from a former fan club containing the shattered remains of many of his records, deliberately broken into pieces. Nearly all "fan mail" addressed to Ava at MGM began with "Dear Cunt," or more politely, "Dear Bitch."

In spite of Frank's protestations, Ava flew to London en route to Spain to make *Pandora and the Flying Dutchman*. The British press treated her better than their American counterpart, referring to her as "Venus."

On the Spanish coast, where the film was shot, Ava dated the movie star handsome bullfighter, Mario Cabre. Word reached Frank at the Copacabana in New York. The next day he was diagnosed with a submucosal throat hemorrhage and had to cancel his engagement.

Ava took the news not too badly. From her location in Spain, she told her director, "If I can't fuck the man I want, I fuck the man I'm with."

# WHEN "THE VOICE" BECAME "THE GARGLE"

Ava Gardner put through a call to her "gal pal," Lana Turner, in Hollywood. "So how is it to have that love machine all to yourself, at least for the honeymoon?:" Lana asked.

"It's going great," Ava said, "considering that I'm paying for the god damn thing. Frank is terrific in bed. Our fights begin on the way to the bidet."

Whenever she could, Ava showed up for moral support at his concerts, but his engagement at the Paramount in New York City on March 26, 1952, did little business. "Where have all the bobby-soxers gone?" he asked.

At Chez Paree in Chicago, some 150 patrons showed up in a night club that seated a staggering 1,200.

Frank began to resent all the rising new singers like Johnnie Ray. At Ray's opening at the Copa in New York, Frank encountered columnist Earl Wilson. "What do you think of this new guy?" Wilson asked Frank.

"I hear he sucks off guys in men's toilets," Frank shot back.

"It's over for me," he told Ava later that night.

"You'll be big again," she assured him.

But in June of 1952, both Columbia Records and his talent agency, MCA, told him good-bye. Both organizations said the same thing: "No one wants to hear you anymore on records or see you on the screen."

In reference to Frank's performance in a radio show, *Hit Parade*, one critic accurately noted, "Sinatra missed notes, cracked phrases, and attacked melodies with seeming indifference. Gone was the grace of feeling and of phrasing that made him America's dream singer."

Even his friend Earl Wilson said, "Let's face it: You've alienated too many members of the press when you were big. Now that you're down, they love kicking you in the balls."

Although he wouldn't dare say it to Frank's face, his publicist, George Evans, told friends in 1949, "In a year or so, Frank will be all but dead professionally. No more records, no more movies, a footnote in musical history of the 1940s. A lot of stars were big during the war—Betty Grable, Veronica Lake. Look at them now. Has-beens. The public has turned against Frank. Everybody has now learned he's a fucking bastard."

Louis B. Mayer of MGM encountered Frank at a party in Hollywood and asked, provocatively, "How does it feel, Sinatra, to be riding on Ava's coattails?" Frank slugged the mogul in the face.

That was the final straw for the studio chief. He called Frank to his office so he could fire him in person. "Get off the lot!" were Mayer's final words.

For Frank, the lowest point came for him on the evening of May 2, 1952, at the Copa in New York City. Only twenty tables were occupied. As he reached for a high note during his rendition of "Bali Ha'i," the theme song from the hit Broadway musical *South Pacific*, blood poured from his mouth.

At the hospital the next morning, when friends came to visit him. he had to write on a pad and hand it to them. "I can't speak, much less sing."

In December of 1948, *Modern Television & Radio* ran this devastating illustration of Frank.

# Barbara Stanwyck

## NANCY'S FRIEND, FRANK'S RIVAL

They were two of the most famous couples in Hollywood during the 1940s, but their marriages were doomed.

**Frank and Nancy Sinatra** (left photo, above) called it quits when Ava Gardner entered the picture. Nancy never remarried, but developed deep friendships within the Hollywood colony, notably with **Barbara Stanwyck** (*in right photo, above*), whose marriage to MGM heartthrob **Robert Taylor** (*the figure on the far right, above*), also ended on the rocks.

After her marriage to Robert Taylor, Stanwyck never remarried, although she did have an affair with another Robert, young Robert Wagner, whom she met on the set of *Titanic,* where Clifton Webb was also pursuing him.

She was rumored to have had an affair with **George Nader** (*on the right in the left-hand photo, above*), but **Rock Hudson** (*far left*) got to him first.

It's clearly the look of love when **Barbara** (*left figure in right-hand photo, above*) embraces **Joan Crawford** (*far right*), her long-running affair dating from the days they were chorus girl hookers back in New York during the 1920s.

Love was still in bloom when this picture of a married couple, **Frank and Nancy Sinatra**, was snapped in Hollywood. From all reports, she never cheated on him, but he played the field before and during his marriage to his loving and long-faithful wife.

She later recalled that the happiest year of her marriage was in 1939 "when we were together twenty-four hours a day." They drove from one show business gig to another in their new car. "He was doing what he loved," and she was the good wife, often cooking a spaghetti dinner for him on a hotplate in some seedy motel.

Columnist Walter Winchell got it all wrong when he suggested a "romance" between Nancy Sinatra and actor **Tom Drake**. Drake is pictured here playing **Judy Garland**'s "Boy Next Door" in the musical *Meet Me in Saint Louis (1944)*. But instead of Nancy, Drake was in love with Peter Lawford, as was his co-star, Judy herself. "We fought a lot over who was going to get Peter at night," Judy said.

Peter was also romantically involved with two other actors, Robert Walker and Nancy Davis (Reagan) at the time. And as proof of what a small town Hollywood was back in those days, Frank was also carrying on an affair with Judy.

# ROMANTIC RESHUFFLINGS AND INDUSTRY GOSSIP

Long after Frank left her, Nancy Sinatra, Sr. was befriended by Barbara Stanwyck, who had also been dropped by her bisexual husband Robert Taylor. Since Stanwyck herself was a notorious bisexual, there were rumors that she would like to turn her friendship with Nancy into something more intimate. But there is no smoking gun that this ever happened.

Frank himself often spoke contemptuously of Stanwyck, "That dyke is in hot pursuit of Nancy." This was just his opinion based on no facts whatsoever.

Neither Nancy nor Stanwyck ever remarried after their respective divorces. In Hollywood, as their close friendship became known, the pair was known as "the gay divorcees," although the word gay meant something different in those days.

Columnist Walter Winchell promoted *faux* romances, linking Nancy with Tom Drake, who played the role of Judy Garland's "Boy Next Door" in the 1944 musical *Meet Me in St. Louis*. In a very bizarre coupling, Stanwyck was linked with George Nader who logged time in the bed of Rock Hudson. Both Drake and Nader were gay, so Winchell got it all wrong.

One drunken night, Frank drove over to Stanwyck's house, finding her alone. He pounded on her door and demanded to be let in. In the foyer, he shouted at her, "You leave Nancy alone. I forbid you to see her again. She's my wife."

Like she'd confronted men in her *films noirs* of the 1940s, Stanwyck stood her ground. "She was your wife. You're divorced. The last I heard you were married to that Ava Gardner slut. Now get the fuck out of my house and never set foot on this property again. If you don't leave, I'll call the police."

Frank left but not before he slapped Stanwyck so hard she fell down in her foyer. Her hatred of Frank intensified, although she had no intention of generating bad publicity by bringing assault and battery charges against him.

One night in Las Vegas when Frank was too drunk to go on, he did anyway. It wasn't so much of a musical concert, but an attack on all the women he hated, especially those he felt had betrayed him. He delivered rambling attacks on women, everyone from columnist Dorothy Kilgallen to Zsa Zsa Gabor. He also launched into Barbara Stanwyck, shocking the audience by calling her a "card-carrying lesbian. That's why she married that lady, Robert Taylor."

Infuriated, both Taylor and Stanwyck wanted to sue for libel, but were talked out of such action by their attorneys. "Even if you won the suit, the label would stick around for years," Taylor's attorney told the two of them. "Your fans would forever view you as a couple of queers, and Sinatra knows that would happen. That's why he made those reckless charges."

# *The Loves of Barbara Stanwyck*

According to Jerry Asher, a gossipy confidant of **Joan Crawford**: "Joan and 'Missy' (a reference to Stanwyck) had a sexual relationship. Both of them were interested in men and women alike." Crawford and Stanwyck, as well as Bette Davis, were each sharing the sexual favors of **Glenn Ford**.

Stanwyck had a brief fling with **Marlene Dietrich**, but soon after she ended it abruptly. Crawford said that the reason the Stanwyck/Dietrich affair didn't work out was that "each of them wanted to be the man in the relationship."

Stanwyck began a torrid affair with **Gary Cooper** in 1942 when they made *Balls of Fire* together at RKO. A biographer once wrote, "Cooper, known to have affairs with his leading ladies, did not attempt one with Barbara. "

Crawford would have laughed at that. She told her gay pal William Haines, "Barbara told me that Cooper shares a lot in common with those bulls he used to see on the ranch in Montana."

In 1939, Robert Taylor was left to date his boyfriends after Barbara Stanwyck laid eyes on **William Holden** with whom she co-starred in *Golden Boy*. Although the bisexual actors, Tyrone Power and Alan Ladd, had been in line for the role of the young boxer, Stanwyck wanted Holden, a handsome hunk who was at the time only 22 years old. When the director wanted to fire the nervous, inexperienced Holden, Stanwyck wouldn't hear of it. She spent endless hours rehearsing him in her dressing room. "If there's any way I can help you, for God's sake, let me know."

The rather blunt Holden responded, "You can let me fuck you. That will steady my nerves."

Stanwyck welcomed him to go at it. Regrettably, she regularly offered him booze to steady his nerves, a gesture which contributed to a lifelong habit of alcohol abuse that would eventually take his life.

| Marlene Dietrich | Gary Cooper | Stanwyck | Glenn Ford | Stanwyck with Holden |

# Frank Vies With Robert Taylor in Pursuit of Ava

The heterosexual Frank Sinatra and the bisexual Robert Taylor were both pursuing "Hollywood's most beautiful goddess," when Taylor contracted to co-star opposite Ava Gardner in MGM's *The Bribe.*

It was a crime *film noir* that also starred gay actors Charles Laughton and Vincent Price. John Hodiak, married to actress Anne Baxter, was about the only straight member of the cast, and even he was sought after by 1940s gays because of the heavy equipment he carried around in his baggy pants.

In spite of Frank's well-publicized pursuit of Ava, she launched an affair with Robert Taylor, who had told her that his marriage to Barbara Stanwyck was "on the rocks." Since he no longer visited Barbara in her bedroom, she spread the word that he was not only a homosexual, having carried on affairs with the likes of Howard Hughes and Errol Flynn, but that he was impotent as well.

"With other women I'm not impotent," Taylor told Gardner, who had first-hand proof that he was telling the truth. "She's a ball buster. Any man would be impotent with that bitch."

After the beginning of his affair with Ava, Taylor feared that his boss, Louis B. Mayer, would evoke the "morals clause" in his contract. After all, he was still married to Stanwyck. "Ah, that cunt," he told his close friend Andy Devine about Stanwyck one day during a hunting trip. "Barbara always wants to run the fuck, except now there is no fuck to run."

He didn't want to take Ava to a hotel—"too many eyes," he said—so he took her to the safest place he knew, the house of his doting mother, Ruth.

Although she did not approve of the relationship, she wanted to protect her son. One night when she saw her son emerge nude from her guest bedroom, Ruth asked him, "Must you bring Sinatra's whore to my home?"

"Ruth, dear, would you rather I go to a cheap hotel?" Taylor asked his mother. "Get written up in the papers? A scandal? Don't forget, I'm your meal ticket." Ruth conceded the point.

Ava later claimed that her affair with Taylor lasted only about eight weeks. "When we finished *The Bribe,* we were finished with each other. Frank didn't find out about us until the film was in the can. He was seriously pissed off."

When he learned of the illicit affair, Frank told stories about Taylor that were even worse than Stanwyck's. He always referred to him as "the cocksucker. I also heard he takes it up the ass. But most guys who have only four-and-a-half inches have to do that. I can't believe that when she could have what I have to offer, that Ava would settle for Princess Tiny Meat."

Long after Frank had married and divorced Ava, he still listed Robert Taylor among "the top five men on my alltime shit list."

Ava Gardner and Robert Taylor
in *The Bribe* (1949)

When Frank felt that some person had double-crossed him, he never forgot, a trait he shared in common with his mother, Dolly.

The plot thickens: As her luck would have it, Ava had eagerly anticipated an offer for the star role in *East Side, West Side (1949).* However, at the last minute, Barbara Stanwyck became available, having unexpectedly lost a key role in *The Fountainhead.* In lieu of the star role, MGM assigned Ava a smaller part, and even though it was a more dramatic, meatier role, Ava resented the demotion.

The day Stanwyck appeared on the set as the film's headlined star, she approached Ava. "Without saying a word, Stanwyck slapped her face real hard. Ava did not strike back. Obviously, Stanwyck had heard that Ava had seduced her husband. Forever after, Ava topped Stanwyck's "shit list," followed closely by Lana Turner, who had also had an affair with Taylor.

As part of her revenge, Stanwyck—with some degree of accuracy—asserted widely throughout Hollywood that Lana and Ava were lovers, even though Stanwyck had and would continue to have plenty of lesbian affairs of her own.

# The Big Band Sound of

## Frank vs. Tommy Dorsey

**Tommy Dorsey** (*left*) on the trombone and **Frank Sinatra** (*right*) as the boy singer became a familiar combo during the early 1940s. Actually, Frank wanted to be hired by Glenn Miller, but that bandleader rejected him.

"I still get a big kick out of Glenn, and we later became friends. I forgave him his lack of judgment."

At first, Tommy Dorsey didn't want to hire Frank. It took a lot of persuading to get a contract from Dorsey, and later, it took some very serious, almost lethal, persuasion to get Dorsey to release. him. "Long before I recorded 'My Way,' Dorsey forced me 'All the Way.' He was a fucking perfectionist. One time I nearly strangled him to death. Imagine me, losing control of my temper."

Before Sinatra's arrival, Jack Leonard had been Dorsey's "boy singer," and had been quite popular before getting drafted into the army. Joel Herron, who would later compose "I'm a Fool to Want You," joined Leonard "out front at the Paramount to watch this new kid, Sinatra, make an ass of himself. We were practically ready to boo when Sinatra came on to sing 'Who.' When he sang, I sank into my seat and looked at Leonard. I felt humiliated for him. Leonard had just become the oldest kind of news that there was in the world. Go off to the war, die for your country, because Sinatra is holding down the homefront with that dago bastard voice."

# How Frank Made an Offer
## the Bandleader Couldn't Refuse

"**Tommy Dorsey and his trombone** was the greatest," Frank Sinatra said in 1943. "But I hated the bastard most of the time. One night I dreamed I killed the son of a bitch. Yet he had the most influence on me when I was a young singer. I modeled my own style of singing based on Dorsey's seamless trombone playing, if that makes any fucking sense. I called him 'T-Bone Dorsey.'"

"He taught me breath control, phrasing. I became the only singer in the world who ever took voice lessons from a god damn trombone. Later, I found out the secret of his breath control. He took quickie breaths from a pinhole in the side of that trombone. The faker. Under Dorsey, my vocal style became as creamy as the stuff shot into some lucky broad every night. God knows how many babies I must have born in 1943 alone. I didn't like using a rubber."

*"On the road Frank was a young stud. The kid really had it. He could get all the tail he wanted. He had to fight off the broads. All of them wanted to climb into bed with Sinatra, and most of them did. This skinny little guy had an appetite for sex like no one I ever knew."*
—**Fred Tamburro**

*"It is a slightly disturbing spectacle to witness the almost synchronized screams that come from the audience as Sinatra closes his eyes or moves his body slightly sideways."*
—**The New York Herald Tribune**, 1943

*"You can quote Sinatra as saying that he believes it is wrong for anybody to own a piece of him and collect on it when that owner is doing nothing for Sinatra."*
—**Frank Sinatra** talking about Tommy Dorsey

*"Imagine Frank Sinatra making the young gals swoon. He would never have made them swoon in my day."*
—**Franklin D. Roosevelt**

Known as "The Gentleman of Swing," the smooth-toned trombonist, Tommy Dorsey Jr. (1905-56), became one of the key players in the musical life of Frank Sinatra. A temperamental, volatile personality, he was the younger brother of bandleader Jimmy Dorsey. In the mid-1930s, he set out to establish an identity of his own and became one of the key players in the heyday of the Big Band era. His reign lasted from the late 1930s until the early 50s when Big Bands were fading away.

Sexually, he played the field when he was on the road. Dorsey, like Frank, was a married man—"a child molester," as Frank jokingly referred to him. At the age of 17, in 1922, Dorsey had eloped with Mildred Kraft. She was only "sweet sixteen" at the time.

When Frank joined Dorsey's band, he was still married to Mildred, although they would divorce in 1943 in the wake of Dorsey's affair with his former singer, Edythe Wright. Dorsey then wed film actress Pat Dane in 1943, divorcing her in 1947.

Tommy Dorsey is ranked among the top two or three Big Bands of the swing era, having 15 Top Ten hits in 1938, 11 in 1939, and 10 in 1941.

Frank was so excited when he signed with Dorsey that he forgot to ask what his paycheck would be. He soon learned it was $125 a week, a $50 raise from what he'd gotten singing with the Harry James band.

Frank had only four days to spend at home with Nancy before he was changing trains en route to Illinois, where he would be the "boy singer" for the Tommy Dorsey Orchestra.

Meeting up with the Dorsey orchestra, Frank also met their other singers, the most prominent of which included Jo Stafford and The Pied Pipers. When she was introduced to the underweight 23-year-old, Jo eyed him skeptically. She was even insulting. "I can't imagine a bag of bones like you having any vocal power."

"Don't judge me," he told her, "until you see me with my clothes off."

When she did hear him sing, she was impressed. "I knew at once that he was going to become a singing sensation. All the boy singers I knew tried to sound like Bing Crosby. Frank had his own distinctive style. The guy was going places. First stop: my bedroom. I found the bag of bones sexy."

Frank was closely associated with the Dorsey band from 1939 until September of 1942, by which time he'd become famous. His first hit with the band was "Polka Dots and Moonbeams," written by his close friend, Jimmy Van Heusen, and Johnny Burke. He scored a much bigger hit with the dreamy ballad, "I'll Never Smile Again," alongside The Pied Pipers, the vocal group spearheaded by Jo Stafford, and accompanied by the Tommy Dorsey band.

Before he forced Dorsey to rescind his contract, Frank made several recordings, some of which became classics, including "Star Dust" in 1940, "This Love of Mine" in 1941, and "There Are Such Things" in 1942.

Although Frank was becoming the number one rival of Bing Crosby, it was the older singer who suggested that Frank break from Dorsey "before the big bucks start coming in."

The first six months with Dorsey were the roughest. In spite of how

**Jo Stafford** (*third from left*) is seen harmonizing with Frank Sinatra (*fourth from the left*), as **Tommy Dorsey** (*far left, in white suit*) conducts the singing group, **the Pied Pipers**.

With Stafford and the Pipers, Frank would score his first major hit, "I'll Never Smile Again." Recorded months before the attack on Pearl Harbor, it echoed the lonely heart yearnings of Americans already torn apart by WWII.

There was a marvelous harmony among Stafford, the Pipers, and Frank, no individual star outshining the other. "I found Frank kind of thin, but not his voice," Stafford recalled.

For the next four decades, Frank would perform "I'll Never Smile Again" on radio, TV, and in dozens of his concerts, including his so-called retirement concert on June 13, 1971.

well received he was by audiences, Dorsey, a hot-tempered disciplinarian, was rarely, if ever, satisfied. "Why can't you sing like Bing Crosby?" he asked Frank one night.

Many band members resented this cocky intruder from Hoboken and were still loyal to vocalist Jack Leonard, who had been fired by Dorsey.

When one critic first heard Frank sing on radio, he wrote, "he has musk glands where his tonsils ought to be."

When Frank became Dorsey's boy singer, he began to work closely with the musical arranger Axel Stordahl, who would have an enormous influence on Frank's career. Born in Staten Island of Norwegian parents, Stordahl is credited with helping Frank in a metamorphosis of his sound to the quickly evolving technologies of LP records. They formed a working relationship. By January of 1942, Frank's first commercial solo recordings appeared on the RCA sub label of Blue Bird.

In the words of one critic, Stordahl "framed" Frank's voice by "creating a soft, opulent sound with swirling strings, understated rhythms, and woodwinds."

Stordahl also worked with such singers as Eddie Fisher, Dinah Shore, Dean Martin, Doris Day, and even Bing Crosby himself.

[When Stordahl died on August 30, 1963, at the age of fifty, suffering from lung cancer, Frank said, "he helped bring pop arrangements into the modern age."]

In contrast, Frank and Dorsey got off to a bad start and practically ended their relationship in violence, yet Frank benefited from the link. As critics have pointed out, Dorsey's smooth tone, his seamless phrasing, and melodic virtuosity had an enormous impact on Frank, who was on the dawn of his greatest fame.

Although Frank and Dorsey had bitter exchanges, Frank in later life acknowledged his debt to the bandleader in a rather colorful way. "I'm the only singer who ever took vocal lessons from a trombone," Frank said. "Tommy would blow that thing a whole week on one tank of air. I latched on to the secret of breath control from him. If Dorsey had been gay, and with that breath control, he could have given some of the best deep throat blow-jobs in the business."

In May of 1940, Dorsey booked his orchestra and Frank into the prestigious Astor Roof in New York City. He wooed audiences singing "Begin the Beguine." The crowd demanded an encore and another encore and then yet another encore.

As the orchestra finally faded away, and even the piano player, Joe Bushkin, went home, Frank found himself in the early hours singing "Smoke Gets In Your Eyes" *a capella* to the still-delighted crowd.

In July of 1940, "I'll Never Smile Again," sung in perfect harmony with The Pied Pipers, reached the number

**Alex Stordahl** (*background*) is pictured with Frank Sinatra at a rehearsal in 1947. After meeting Frank during the Dorsey years, Stordahl quickly established himself as Frank's musical director. The Stordahl/Sinatra songs of the mid- to late-1940s are considered masterpieces of musical art.

Around 1952, when Frank was failing as a singer, he accused Stordahl of "deserting me when I'm down." When Frank got a call to play at a theater in New York, he phoned Stordahl and announced, "We're leaving tomorrow for New York."

"I can't," Stordahl said. "I'm staging a show for Eddie Fisher. I've got a contract."

"Apparently," Frank said, "you didn't hear me. We're going to be at the Capitol."

"I can't," Stordahl said.

Frank slammed down the phone. A decade would pass before they made up.

one spot on the Hit Parade where it took up residence for several weeks. Music critics have hailed this maudlin ballad as ushering in a new era in American music, when "The Voice" became a bigger draw than "The Big Band."

Frank was on his way to becoming a household word when he sang on NBC's weekly radio program, "Fame and Fortune," between October of 1940 and April of 1941. The program was listened to by millions of Americans. He began to build a fan base.

"I couldn't believe it," Dorsey said. "Women began to show up and swoon at the sound of this skinny kid with the big ears. I never figured out what he did to women, but it was some sexual allure I never possessed. Bing Crosby didn't have it either. No one ever accused 'The Old Groaner' of being a male sex symbol."

For years Crosby had dominated the male singer polls in both *Down Beat* and *Billboard*. But in May of 1941, "The King of Singers" had to move over to make way for new competition "The Voice Out of Hoboken."

"Frank sold himself into bondage when he signed that contract with Dorsey," said Jo Stafford in later years. "It meant until Frank's dying days, Dorsey would own 43 percent of everything he did. He'd even get 43 percent of the $10,000 fee from *From Here to Eternity*. Imagine, 43 percent of 'My Way,' 'Strangers in the Night, 'New York, New York,' the Las Vegas gigs, the Rat Pack movies."

Especially visible was the love-hate relationship between Frank and a Dorsey drummer named Buddy Rich, a Brooklyn-born musician known for his virtuosic technique, speed, power and groove. He was billed as "the world's greatest drummer."

He and Frank liked each other and even roomed together. Sometimes they brought a prostitute back to their double room and took turns with her in the same bed.

But at other times they fought bitterly. "They were birds of a feather," Stafford recalled, "known for their giant egos and explosive tempers. Once Buddy got so mad at Frank, he sat in the orchestra with his arms folded, refusing to accompany Frank as he sang. At the end of his number, Frank stole a pitcher of ice water from a passing waiter and poured it over Buddy's head."

"They were buddies but very jealous of each other," Dorsey recalled. "Buddy wanted billing over Frank. Buddy also wanted me to play more of his kind of music so he could show off his skills as a drummer—not those romantic Sinatra ballads. They were constantly fighting. It got really violent at times. Then they would make up and go out to book a hot prostitute together. Black or white, it didn't matter to those horny bastards."

"Frank was the violent type," Dorsey said. "So was

**"Sinatramania"** was in full swing during one of Frank's gigs at the Paramount Theater in New York City. "I've never been kissed so many times, or been groped so many times, as when the broads surrounded me. All of them were hot to trot. Big Frankie couldn't satisfy all of them, although, god damn it, I tried."

When Frank sang in New York in 1943, "the women swooned, moaned, and gasped." It was reported that some of the more ardent ones "creamed their bloomers."

"The screams grew so loud," said Bob Weitman, the manager of the Paramount, "I thought Frankie's pants had fallen down."

One night he was almost strangled to death, as two girls grabbed at his bow tie simultaneously. Neither was willing to let go of their part of the tie, and Frank's vocal chords were almost crushed.

I. I once hit Buddy over the head with my trombone. Frank could lose it, too. He was heckled one night by a drunk and went off the stage into the room and knocked him down. Fortunately, we settled with that jerk for a hundred dollars."

Backstage one night, Buddy and Frank got into a brawl, evocative of those street fights Frank had had in Hoboken.

Two views of drummer **Buddy Rich**, pictured with **Frank Sinatra** *(on the right in the upper photo)*. "When I roomed with that low-down drummer, Buddy Rich, I found a tough-talking wiseguy from the streets much like myself. He was the real thing—a boozer, a skirt-chaser, and a first-class son-of-a-bitch. I loved the bastard, although I almost killed him on a few occasions."

"Buddy taught me how to live life on the road, a series of one-night stands (both the gigs and the women afterward), those long, boring bus rides, the seedy hotels, the all-night greasy spoons open at two o'clock in the morning. Buddy called himself my best friend, and I guess he was at the time, but he was always jealous of me, both on stage before an audience and after, in our shared bed with the broads."

Stafford witnessed Frank's attack on Buddy and the drummer's retaliation. "I honestly believed they would have killed each other if Tommy hadn't broken up the fight."

With their testosterone soaring, Buddy and Frank, two bantamweights, "went at each other with all their pent-up feelings exploding into curses and swinging fists," in the words of Buddy's biographer, the singer Mel Tormé.

After the fight broke up, Dorsey ordered Frank to go back to his hotel. "I can live without a boy singer tonight, but I need my drummer."

Dorsey told Stafford and others that Frank was striking back at Buddy for trying to sabotage his romantic ballads. However, when Stafford and Frank came together in the late 1940s, Frank perpetuated a very different spin on the events of that violent night. "The incident was so delicious," Stafford said, "that I had to spread it around the music world, especially to friends who knew both Frank and Buddy."

"It seemed that Frank and Buddy used to share the same whore when they roomed together," Stafford claimed. "I mean they took her at the same time in the same bed. One night while Frank was going at it, Buddy must have gotten carried away. In heat, he started to play with Frank's ass. I guess that looked like the only hole available to him at the time. Although Frank seemed to handle it for the moment, brushing Buddy's hand away, Frank's male pride must have been hurt. Secretly he plotted revenge."

According to Stafford, Frank admitted to her that he called two of his mobster friends to catch up with Buddy when he emerged from a late-night restaurant. The drummer was shoved into a back alley and severely beaten. The September 1, 1940 issue of *Down Beat* magazine, claimed that Buddy's face looked "as if it had been smashed in with a shovel."

"Buddy knew that Frank set him up for the attack." Stafford recalled. "But in only a few nights they made up and were back in their shared room screwing the life out of some whore. But I bet Buddy never reached for Frank's ass ever again."

Frank, along with Dorsey's band, didn't just work the

clubs of the East. Hollywood also beckoned to them because of their growing popularity.

Dorsey signed for his band to appear in the 1941 Paramount film, *Las Vegas Nights*, but Frank's name was unbilled and did not appear in the credits. For his appearance, he was paid the sum of fifteen dollars per day. Constance Moore, a popular 1940s singer, was the star, along with Bert Wheeler, playing the husband of Virginia Dale, who is seen dancing with the pigeons.

The Jennings Sisters also appeared in the movie, Frank labeling them "a dime store version of The Andrews Sisters."

Buddy Rich grinned nonstop throughout his drum performances. Dorsey himself, prominently visible in his role as bandleader, displayed all the charm of a wooden Indian.

Singing "I'll Never Smile Again," Frank appeared on the screen for just one minute. His second song, "Dolores," which he recorded on film, ended up on the cutting-room floor.

*Las Vegas Nights* is notable as the venue for which Frank received one of his first ever movie critiques. George Simon, in *Metronome*, claimed, "Sinatra sings prettily in an unphotogenic manner."

The tension between Dorsey and Frank continued gig after gig. Frank wanted out. One night the bandleader, Artie Shaw, came into a club where Frank was singing with the Dorsey band.

"What Tommy was to the trombone, Shaw was to the clarinet," Frank said. "Between numbers, I went over to his table and asked him for a job as his boy singer. The fucker looked me up and down skeptically. 'No job!' he said to me with all the charm of a Tyrannosaurus rex. 'I've got Tony Pastor, and he's better than you,' the creep told me. If the shit hadn't added that last insult, I would have walked away in peace. But he got me riled. 'Well,' I told him. 'I don't want to interfere with your love affair with Pastor. I'm sure he shoves it up your dingleberry-coated ass every night.'"

Ironically, both of these musicians would later marry Ava Gardner.

Years from that night, Shaw was asked about Frank. "If you've heard one dago singer, you've heard them all. One night in a club he insulted me so badly I almost killed him. He didn't know it but I carried a revolver under my coat. I nearly blew the fucker's head off. The world would have been a better place had I done so."

**Frank Sinatra** in the 1942 *Ship Ahoy* got his first good newspaper review in *Variety*. "Dorsey's own tromboning, Ziggy Elman's trumpet, Buddy Rich's drum work, and Frank Sinatra's singing, latter doing 90% of the vocalizing in the film, and doing it well, stands out." Frank was so proud of that critique he carried it around in his wallet for months.

Backed up by the Tommy Dorsey orchestra, Frank sang "The Last Call for Love," and "Poor You." The actual stars of the film were Eleanor Powell and Red Skelton. "Someday," Frank told Skelton, "every movie I appear in will give me star billing," a prophecy, of course, that would eventually come true.

Frank went on to make another movie with the Dorsey band, this one organized and paid for by MGM. In the 1942 *Ship Ahoy*, Dorsey is still the star, with Frank, in a sailor uniform, shunted off to the side. This black-and-white MGM musical starred two big box office draws, comedian Red Skelton and tap-dancing Eleanor Powell.

*Ship Ahoy* was in production when the radio blared the news that the Japanese had attacked Pearl Harbor.

Frank was unbilled. "I was just one of the boys in the band. I would have done better cast as the Jap villain."

He appeared in the film singing "The Last Call for Love." As before, his second song, "Blue Skies," ended up on the cutting-room floor. But Eleanor Powell, playing a character oddly called "Tallulah," steals the show, dancing and doing cartwheels on the diving board over the waters of a swimming pool.

Before its eventual release, the film's title was changed from *I'll Take Manila* to *Ship Ahoy* because the Philippines had already fallen to the Japanese.

"God damn it," Frank said, "if Bing Crosby can be a fucking movie star, so can I." But over at MGM Louis B. Mayer, at least at that point in Frank's career, didn't get him. Mayer called him "a flash in the pan—you know bobby-soxers. In a year or two they'll grow up and forget all about this Sinatra kid with the jug ears."

After *Ship Ahoy* wrapped, Frank wanted to bolt from Dorsey and try to make it on his own as a solo performer. But there was the problem of that iron-clad contract.

After a performance one night, Frank knocked on the door to Dorsey's dressing room and was invited to come in. He was very blunt with his boss. "I want out of my contract."

"When hell freezes over," Dorsey told him. "Forget it. I've got those dago balls of yours in a tight squeeze, and I'm holding on for life."

Frank knew it was not going to be the easy departure that it had been with Harry James. Dorsey demanded that Frank honor his contract—or else.

Frank's press agent, George Evans, even organized pickets by some of Frank's most devoted fans, who staged protests outside theaters demanding that Dorsey release Frank from his "slave" contract. Signs in loud, bold letters proclaimed DORSEY'S UNFAIR TO OUR BOY FRANKIE. The bandleader was enraged, but only stiffened his demands.

The competition, **Bing Crosby**, dominated popular music from the dizzy era of Prohibition through the dark days of the Depression and even into World War II. He practically invented pop singing, and made more studio recordings than any other singer, about 400 more than Frank Sinatra himself.

"Crosby was the biggest thing since baby shit," Frank said. "Every singer wanted to be him. He was my idol, although I'd heard reports that he was a monster. I used to wear a blazer, a sailing cap, and I smoked a pipe, aping him. Of course, I planned one day to kick his fat ass off the throne and be 'The King' myself."

Frank had found a paternalistic Mafia godfather in Willie Moretti (a.k.a. "Willie Moore"), the New Jersey gangster. His relationship with the mobster paralleled the fictional character of Johnny Fontane in Mario Puzo's *The Godfather*.

Moretti had heard Frank singing years before at the Rustic Cabin, and "I loved the kid's music." He owned several gambling casinos—known as "dice barns"—and he hired Frank to sing at them, which gave the Hoboken boy a big push forward in his career.

Until the end of his days, Moretti would remain Frank's greatest fan. Whenever he got into trouble, he knew Moretti was there for him.

One night Frank complained about his contract to his mentor, Moretti. "Don't worry, Frankie boy, I'll take care of it."

"But I don't want you to kill him," Frank protested.

Within the week, Frank was out of his contract. Details are still lacking today, but apparently Moretti and two of his mobsters paid a backstage visit to Dorsey. With a gun down his throat, Dorsey signed the contract releasing Frank for the sum of one dollar.

Other biographers have questioned this, some claiming that Jules Stein, the head of the MCA talent agency, got Dorsey to agree to a $75,000 buy-out, with the promise of some lucrative bookings in his future.

However, shortly before he died, Dorsey himself admitted that Moretti did indeed pay that call on him.

Moretti later bragged to his friends that he had secured Frank's release. Therefore, we are likely to believe Dorsey and Moretti, since they were actually at the scene of the crime.

Years later, one of Frank's closest friends, actor Brad Dexter, who had once saved the singer's life from drowning, admitted that the story of the gangster threat to Dorsey actually happened. "Frank said that it did."

Tommy Dorsey III claimed his father confirmed that it did indeed take place. "Had I kept Frank by the *cojones*, you'd be set up for life," Dorsey told his young son. "Millions would be flowing in over the years."

Frank performed a few more club dates with Dorsey before singing his last song with the band on September 3, 1942. Backstage Dorsey came up to tell him good-bye. Frank turned a smiling face. "No hard feelings, pal?"

Dorsey stared at him. "I hope you fall on that skinny ass of yours, you dago bastard."

Stordahl, with his bald, egg-shaped head and musical genius, also dropped Dorsey and went with Frank "for the ride, although I knew it would be a bumpy haul."

After leaving the Dorsey band in September of 1942, Frank was twenty-seven years old. In just three months, he was on the road to glory. The legend began with his appearance at the Paramount Theater in New York's Times Square area.

An earthquake was about to strike, not in Hollywood, but in New York. The night was December 30, 1942, when Frank opened at the Paramount.

Jack Benny introduced Frank onstage. He later said, "I thought the god-damned theater was going to cave in, that Jap bombers were over New York. In all my years in show business, I never heard such clamor. People ran down to the stage screaming. They were in hysterics. I'd never heard of this Sinatra guy, although I'd met him backstage. I was not impressed. Scream over Johnny Weissmuller in that loincloth—not this skinny little kid from some tenement in Jersey."

During the darkest days of World War II, **Frank Sinatra** was on his way to becoming an American institution when he appeared at the Paramount Theater in New York City in front of adoring masses of bobbysoxers. They "swooned" when he came onto the stage. That word, not much in use since the Civil War, suddenly came back into vogue.

Some critics dismissed his appearances as "wartime degeneracy," but the fans themselves acclaimed his "misty-eyed magic," each young woman thinking he was singing only to her. He literally broke hundreds of young hearts, many of whose sweethearts, or even their dads, had gone to war.

When he became a regular on the Lucky Strike Radio Show, "Your Hit Parade," Frank Sinatra became a household word. He didn't like a lot of the songs he had to sing during that era—"Pistol Packin' Mamma," "Mairzie Doats" and "Praise the Lord and Pass the Ammunition."

He told Jo Stafford, "Let Errol Flynn, John Wayne, and Bogie fight the Japs and Nazis. in the movies. I'm home, engaged in 'the Battle of the Baritones"—a reference to Bing Crosby.

Backstage, bandleader Benny Goodman, the actual star of the show at the Paramount, heard the hysterical roar and couldn't believe his ears. He confronted the manager. "What the fuck is that?"

Unknown to the public at the time, Frank's press agent, George Evans, had planted paid bobby-soxers in the audience to scream. When girls nearby heard them screaming, they joined in the mass hysteria.

Up until a few minutes before it began, the program was envisioned as a star vehicle for Goodman, with Frank billed as "an extra added attraction." But before the gig ended, Frank was the star attraction and Goodman the extra.

Within the week, a dozen mailbags of fan letters had been delivered to the Paramount. Hundreds of bobby-soxers were offering up their virginity to Frank. "Only you, Frankie, can make a woman out of me," one eager fan wrote, hoping to be "deflowered." Ushers hated working at Frank's engagements. They reported to the management that many of the seats were wet. Some of Frank's most ardent fans had lost control of their bladders.

New York's Paramount Theater became known as the "Home of the Swoon," and Frank's gig was extended by more than a month, into February of 1943. The press began referring to Frank as "the Sultan of Swoon." "Swoonnatra" became a word. But the label that stuck to the singer as the decades passed was "The Voice." Peggy Lee jokingly said, "It should be changed to 'The Dick.'"

When Frank Sinatra first arrived at the Paramount Theater in 1943, the marquee was already up, featuring BENNY GOODMAN AND HIS BAND. Down below, alongside billing for the Radio Rogues comedy act, were the words EXTRA FRANK SINATRA. Before the gig ended, Frank Sinatra would be the star of the show, with Goodman's band being relegated to the role of an "extra added attraction."

When theater manager Bob Weitman had first informed Goodman that Frank would be appearing as the singer, the bandleader asked: "Who he?" But by the end of the run, he knew more about Sinatra than he wanted to.

Goodman was not impressed when introduced to Frank, who was sweating and shaking—"like a beautiful blonde broad facing twenty guys who just broke out of jail." He told Weitman. "He looks like he weighs a hundred pounds, twenty of which is hair."

Biographer Tom Santopietro in *Sinatra in Hollywood* tried to explain this show biz phenomenon. "This was the introduction of sex into popular music. Sinatra seduced an audience, both consciously and unconsciously, combining sex and overwhelming feelings of emotion with romance and compassion. He seemed to need the love of the entire world. In the screaming bobby-soxers he nearly found the whole world, because word of the Sinatra hysteria soon spread around the globe. Sinatramania was born."

No one suffered more than Nancy because of Frank's thousands of female fans, many of whom exposed their breasts to him, begging him for an autograph: Frank on one tit. Sinatra on the other. "Some were so small," he later told George Evans, "that I could barely write Frank, much less Sinatra."

"You should have whipped out your dick and had someone write the names of the twelve apostles on it," said Buddy Rich.

In a matter of weeks, Frank was signing fat contracts with Columbia Records and RKO Pictures.

Once Frank left Dorsey, RCA was eager to exploit the hysteria enveloping Frank by launching his career at Columbia. But a musicians' strike made that almost impossible. RCA got around that by issuing Frank's Harry James-era records such as "All Or Nothing At All."

He also did a number of *a capella* recordings, featuring singers who were not in the musicians' union. One of the songs to emerge from this was the wildly popular "I Couldn't Sleep a Wink Last Night."

When the long strike ended, Frank could officially launch his musical career at Columbia with a full backup of band members.

Over the next decade, Frank and Stordahl would cut close to three hundred records for Columbia. Stordahl was the arranger for at least three-fourths of those records, and was also the credited orchestrator for one of Frank's most popular films, *Anchors Aweigh*.

Cutting records wasn't Frank's only ambition. He continued to pursue his dream of movie stardom, even if it meant only a cameo appearance in the 1943 *Reveille with Beverly*, shot at Columbia. For one thousand dollars, Frank appeared on the screen crooning Cole Porter's "Night and Day," backed up by a bevy of beautiful female piano players. The actual star of the film was tap-dancing Ann Miller, who was cast as a switchboard operator who emcees an early morning show for soldiers at a nearby Army camp.

Because of Frank's success singing at the Paramount Theater at Times Square in New York, a lot of fans flocked to hear his one song, earning $3 million for the picture, a huge bonanza back then.

After hawking his talents at several different studios, Frank finally signed a contract with RKO, and was immediately cast in the film version of *Higher and Higher* (1943). It had originated as a Broadway musical in the spring of 1940, starring June Allyson.

For $15,000, RKO had purchased the rights to this film specifically as a vehicle starring Frank, featuring him singing four songs by Jimmy McHugh and Harold Adamson. However, because of pre-existing contracts with Michèle Morgan and Jack Haley that gave these performers the star spots, Frank received third billing.

For some reason, the famous critic James Agee claimed that Frank "has weird fleeting resemblances to Abraham Lincoln." *Variety* was cruel, writing, "At least Frank Sinatra gets in no one's way."

Because of film offers on the horizon from both RKO and MGM, Frank moved to California with his family in the spring of 1944. By that time, Nancy had given birth to both Nancy Jr. and also to Frank

In a movie starring tap-dancing **Ann Miller** (one she would rather forget), Frank Sinatra made an appearance in *Reveille With Beverly* in 1943 for Columbia. Looking rather handsome in a tuxedo, and surrounded by a bevy of beautiful girls (he claimed he seduced three of them), he sang the Cole Porter standard "Night and Day."

For this brief stint, Frank received his first detailed movie critique from John T. McManus, writing for *PM*.

*"And this is Frank Sinatra! Well. I am convinced there has been nothing like him since goldfish-eating. He even out-manias the chain letter rage and the Rudy Vallee crush of 15 years ago. And for the life of me, I can't tell you why. He is a slight young man given to violent sport jackets. He sings, yes—with an almost studied affection of zombie mannerisms. His voice is pleasant enough—a kind of moaning baritone with a few trick inflections that involve going off-key at turning points in the melody.*

*"Reveille With Beverly is his first movie, so it is reportable news that at each moan and trick-turn of the Sinatra voice, in fact each time he so much as turns his dead-pan head or flickers an eye-lid, the adolescent set goes absolutely nuts! They squeal with delight; they rock and moan and make little animal cries. When he is finished, they are emotionally spent."*

Jr., who by now was three months old.

"I plan to learn the difference between New York/New Jersey pussy and Hollywood pussy, and I want to become an expert there after only ten days," Frank told George Evans.

His press agent responded that he should spend some time at home with Nancy and his kids.

In Hollywood, Frank was assigned the lead in RKO's 1944 *Step Lively*, with George Murphy and Adolphe Menjou, formerly big stars now accepting second leads, Gloria DeHaven provided the female interest. The film was based on *Room Service*, a comedy originally released in 1938 that had starred the Marx Brothers.

The role was not particularly demanding of Frank other than he had to sing on cue, which he did best in his number, "As Long As There Is Music."

Had MGM not intervened, Frank could easily have ended up as one of those minor musical stars who emerged briefly during WWII pictures.

But suddenly, MGM mogul Louis B. Mayer opted to buy out Frank's contract with RKO. In August of 1943, Mayer had been moved to tears by Frank's singing rendition of "Ol' Man River" at a charity concert at the Hollywood Bowl. His film salary rose from $25,000 a week to $130,000 per movie at MGM.

Mayer immediately cast him opposite Gene Kelly in *Anchors Aweigh*, a nautical song-and-dance romp. Before filming began, Kelly was called in to "teach Sinatra how to hoof," in Mayer's words.

After only one week of rehearsals, Frank called his press agent, George Evans, "Did you know Kelly is queer and has the hots for me? He got a glimpse of Big Frankie in the shower and is slobbering at the mouth. What to do?"

"You gotta succeed in this movie," Evans advised him. "Let him give you a blow-job—nothing else. Make that clear. Close your eyes and imagine it's Lana Turner down there on her knees."

*Anchors Aweigh* (1945), an American musical comedy directed by George Sidney, was Frank's first big picture. He got star billing over Kathryn Grayson and Gene Kelly. It told of two sailors who go on a four-day shore leave in Hollywood.

Frank played Clarence ("Brooklyn") Doolittle, a screen persona put together in a blatant attempt to pander to his bobby-soxer fans. He played "a romantic type fella," pushing his cuteness for all it was worth.

The war was beginning to turn in favor of the Allies in 1944. **Frank Sinatra** starred with **Gene Kelly** and songbird Kathryn Grayson in his first big movie, *Anchors Aweigh,* set in Hollywood. (Some movie viewers confuse it with *On the Town*, released in 1949, a later Kelly/Sinatra musical that was set in New York. Both vehicles involve sailors on shore leave.)

In *Anchors Aweigh*, Frank played Kelly's gauche buddy, a young man who hadn't had much experience with women. That was an inside joke to his best pals, who estimated that Frank had had at least 1,000 women since he was fourteen years old.

Frank later said, "My dear friend Gene Kelly fondled my body a lot when he was teaching me some dance moves, but a guy has to get his kicks some way, and I've got plenty to fondle."

After the successful completion of his film commitments, in October of 1944, Frank flew back to New York for another appearance at the Paramount Theater. The theater filled with his loyal bobby-soxers, and pandemonium broke out. However, after the first show, they refused to budge from their seats. Thousands of fans waiting outside had bought tickets that day but couldn't get in for the show. A riot, called "The Columbus Day Riot," ensued. New York's finest were called in but it took all day to diffuse the crowds and bring order.

At the time of his appearance at the Paramount, arguably the high point of his decades-long career, his three-week returning gig drew some 30,000 screaming fans, most of them bobby-soxers. They formed frenzied mobs in Times Square, shouting "F-R-A-N-K-I-E! F-R-A-N-K-I-E!"

Except for a homosexual following, Frank wasn't very popular with men, especially those in the service who resented the 4-F status he'd been assigned because of his punctured eardrum at birth.

The author, William Manchester, who gained notoriety for his biography on John F. Kennedy and his literary feud with Jackie, called Frank "the most hated man of World War II," perhaps forgetting Adolf Hitler. At some performances, young men threw rotten vegetables, especially tomatoes, and even eggs at him on the stage.

One such man was almost killed when irate female fans surrounded him and struck blows to his head, kicking him in the groin. "At least we left him impotent for life," said one of the crazed bobby-soxers.

In the immediate aftermath of World War II, in 1945 and 1946, Frank reached the height of his fame and popularity. "Everybody wanted a piece of me," he said. His stamina was amazing. Not only did he keep up a record of seduction that would have challenged Hercules, but he did some 45 shows every week. He estimated that he sang an amazing eighty to a hundred songs in just one day and night.

Frank was often asked to explain his immense popularity on the homefront when other young men were fighting in the European theater, in North Africa, and on islands in the South Pacific.

"It was the war years," Frank said. "There was great loneliness in the land. I was the boy on every street corner who'd gone off to the war. That was all." That was a vast understatement, of course, and for Frank, at least, a relatively modest self-assessment.

\*\*\*

As the 1940s came to an end, Frank's career stalled, both musically and on the screen. He told his boss at Columbia, Emmanuel (Manie) Sachs, "I think I'm all washed up as a singer. I blame no

"Frank Sinatra as a priest—type casting," said director Irving Pichel, sarcastically, when RKO informed him that Frank would be "wearing the collar" in *The Miracle of the Bells (1948)*. "Well, if a bastard like Bing Crosby got away with it in *Going My Way*, why not this little Hoboken gangster?"

In his first non-singing role, Frank appeared opposite top-billed **Fred MacMurray** *(left figure above)*—"from the wooden Indian school of acting," according to Frank.

The movie depicts the rise and death of Olga Treskovna (**Alida Valli**, *center figure above*), who has been brought back to her seedy coal-mining home town for burial. Valli would go on to far greater success in *The Third Man*. Frank claimed, "I made the obligatory (for me) pass at her, but she wasn't intercepting."

In the top photo, **Frank Sinatra** tangles with actress **Betty Garrett** in the 1949 *Take Me Out to the Ball Game.*

In the lower photo, he hoofs up a storm with his partner from *Anchors Aweigh,* gay actor **Gene Kelly**. Garrett is perfectly cast with Frank, as she is a first-rate singer, dancer, and comedienne. Most reviewers thought the pair scored a home run.

Kelly and Frank take on the personas they created in *Anchors Aweigh.* One of the world's most experienced boudoir artists, Frank himself was once again cast as a timid, bashful rube around women. "He was so bashful and timid," Kelly claimed, "that he told Hollywood whores, 'Get naked in the bedroom and work yourself up almost to climax. I've got only ten minutes before I go on camera.'"

*Time* Magazine claimed that *Take Me Out to the Ball Game* "involves Frank Sinatra and Gene Kelly in a whirl of songs and dances that are easy to forget."

one but myself. I did it. I'm my own worst enemy. My singing has gone downhill, and I went downhill with it. It happened because I paid no attention to how I was singing."

His prospects in MGM films didn't look any brighter. His last three films had flopped.

*It Happened in Brooklyn* (1947) reteamed him with Kathryn Grayson, who had starred with him in *Anchors Aweigh.* That film also brought him into contact once again with composers Jule Styne and Sammy Cahn. *It Happened in Brooklyn* revolved around a plot wherein Frank lost Grayson to Peter Lawford, who would soon become his Rat Pack regular.

The only bright spot in the film, which limped along at the box office, is when Frank's scenes coincided with those of Jimmy Durante.

In *The Miracle of Bells* (1948), MGM lent Frank to his former studio, RKO, for his first non-singing role. Perhaps hoping to capitalize on Bing Crosby's priestly role in the Oscar-winning *Going My Way* (1944), Frank was badly cast as a priest who, motivated by kindness and a sense of show-biz razzmatazz, endorses a fake "miracle."

Critics savaged the film, *Monthly Film Bulletin* referring to it as an "offensive exhibition of vulgar insensitivity." He didn't fare much better with the critics at *Time,* who said that his portrayal of a priest was "flea bitten and that he acted like a wooden Indian."

Back at MGM, Frank knew that *The Kissing Bandit* (1948), which once again teamed him with Kathryn Grayson, would be the nadir of his movie career—and he was right. This time around he won Grayson's love in the final reel, but no one seemed to care at that point. When Nancy Jr. presented Frank with his first grandchild in 1974, he told her his dream for the kid—"That she'll never grow up to see *The Kissing Bandit.*"

Frank's next two films for MGM, both released in 1949, teamed him once again with Gene Kelly. Both of them were hits at the box office, but Kelly, not Frank, was cited as the reason for their success.

Frank told Kelly, "The only time one of my films makes money is when you star in it."

"Let's form a partnership," Kelly said. "Get married if we have to. You do the singing, and I'll do the dancing."

Kelly and Frank starred with Esther Williams in *Take Me Out to the Ball Game* (1949), a Technicolor period piece set in 1908. Betty Garrett returned to the screen to work with Frank in this ode to the good-natured nostalgic fun of baseball. Esther was a last-minute choice. Originally, the role had been intended for Judy Garland, who had become undependable because of her drug habit. The part then went to June Allyson, who became pregnant. The film grossed four million dollars, which defined it as a hit in those days. However, most critics claimed that the talented cast was far better than the material.

*On the Town* (1949) featured such famous stars of their day as Betty Garrett, Ann Miller, Vera-Ellen, and Jules Munshin. In an ironic touch, Kelly's character in the film dismisses the beauty of a woman passing by on a New York sidewalk. Munshin asks, "Who are you waiting for, Ava Gardner?"

Frank was having an affair with Ava at the time.

The film's plot involved three sailors on leave in New York, and even today ranks as one of the best MGM musicals. But the rave reviews it generated were for Kelly, not Frank.

In spite of these hits, the patience of Louis B. Mayer, insofar as Frank was concerned, was running out. "He's a pain in the ass," Mayer told his fellow executives.

On April 27, 1950, just four months after the release of *On the Town,* Frank's contract with MGM was terminated.

By then, film studio executives had come to view Frank "as a firecracker ready to explode."

"He's not worth the trouble," Mayer said. "We lose money on him, and he gets the worst press of any star in Hollywood. He's also mixed up with Ava Gardner. I hope he doesn't destroy her career like he's destroying his own."

Although Frank rallied against intolerance, defending Jews and African Americans, among others, against oppression and prejudice, he wasn't always so tolerant in his private life.

His press agent, George Evans, said, "I was in damage control twenty-four hours a day. Frank was unpredictable. He could explode at any minute. He said what he felt. He once told the press that movies stink and so do the people who make them. He was a walking public relations disaster. He became known as a friend of the mob and was widely criticized for his womanizing. He beat up reporters like columnist Lee Mortimer. I mean, on the one hand he could stir a nation's heart with his singing. On the darkest night, he was a first-rate bastard.

Frank Sinatra once stunned one of his concert audiences by falsely claiming, "I never made a movie with **Kathryn Grayson** (*depicted above, with Frank*) called *The Kissing Bandit.* I don't know who you saw up there on the screen, but it wasn't *moi.*"

Of course, as the picture above with Grayson reveals, he did make "the worst movie of my life."

In his outrageous *bandito* costume, he "looks like a male figure skater all set to slide around the rink to Ravel's 'Bolero'" in the words of one critic.

Frank said, "My faggy caballero drag was designed to attract every cocksucker in Hollywood."

Look out if he took a sudden dislike to you."

"By the late Forties, Frank's career had climbed the mountain," Evans said. "There was nowhere to go but down that mountain. Those bobby-soxers of 1944 had married soldiers returning from the war. They had moved to the suburbs and were busy raising a family. These former fans had more on their minds than Frank Sinatra. Also, Frank's cheating heart, his violence, his lack of control, his box-office flops, and his piss-poor records had long ago turned thousands of fans off Frank. He was a has-been. As he faced another decade, new singers were emerging. Frank was yesterday's news."

---

## Frank Sinatra Accused of DRAFT DODGING

Just before Christmas of 1940, about a year before the attack upon Pearl Harbor and America's entry into World War II, Frank Sinatra registered for the draft. Because he was a father, Nancy Sr. having given birth to Nancy Jr., Frank was granted an exemption from serving in the U.S. Armed Forces.

But during the autumn of 1943, with the war raging, and battles going badly for the U.S., draft exemptions were made tougher as the U.S. became engaged on fronts in Africa, Europe, and the Pacific. Many men Frank knew, or would know in the future, had volunteered, including Buddy Rich, Artie Shaw, Gene Kelly, Mickey Rooney, Clark Gable, and Joe DiMaggio. Married fathers were about to lose their exemptions.

Already, young sevicemen were mocking Frank as a "slacker" during his public appearances. "Hey Dago, why in the fuck aren't you in uniform?" was a question often thrown at him.

In October of 1943, Frank was examined by an army physician in Jersey City and classified 1-A. However, two months later, another Army doctor in Newark examined him and declared him 4-F. This doctor, Captain Joseph Weintrob, discovered that Frank suffered from a perforated eardrum, weighed only 119 pounds (four pounds below the accepted minimum for men of his height of five feet, seven inches), and was "emotionally unstable." The latter judgment might more properly have been ruled on by an army psychiatrist instead of by a medical doctor.

When the public learned about Frank's 4-F exemption, it caused a brouhaha. Westbrook Pegler, the columnist, trivialized him as "bugle-deaf Frankie Boy Sinatra," and many of his fans deserted him.

Dr. Weintrob defended his decision by saying, "Mr. Sinatra claimed that he was 'neurotic, afraid of crowds, even afraid to go up in an elevator...He also told me that he suffers from almost constant migraines and becomes extremely nervous and agitated at times, often doing things he regrets. He is rundown, underweight, and appears malnourished."

Frank's publicist, George Evans, tried to put a better face on Frank's patriotism by having him sing at war bond rallies, on American Forces Radio Shows, and on vinyl "V-Disks" sent out to servicemen abroad.

An anonymous tipster, who claimed "my name will be recognizable immediately," penned the following letter on December 30, 1943, addressing it to Walter Winchell at *The New York Mirror.*

> *"The FBI is said to be investigating a report that Frank Sinatra paid $40,000 to the doctors who examined him in Newark recently and classifed him 4-F. The money is supposed to have been paid by his business manager. A former school mate of Sinatra from Highland, NJ, said that Sinatra has no more ear drum trouble than Gen. Douglas MacArthur. Mothers around America who have sons in the service are planning to petition Franklin D. Roosevelt asking for a re-examination of the singer by a neutral board of examiners."*

FBI agent Sam. K. McKee, one of the G-Men whose legend derived from having gunned down Pretty Boy Floyd, investigated. He discovered that Frank had on three occasions denied that he was "emotionally unstable" before asserting in 1943 that he was. On three previous questionnaires, he had denied that he had any physical or mental defects or diseases.

After extensive interviews with Weintrob, the FBI ruled that the doctor had made an honest judgment. At no point was any instance of bribery ever discovered. The FBI marked the case as closed, at least for the moment. In time, however, they would accumulate volumes on Frank based on his association with the Mob.

# Young Frank—Seducing the Songbirds of the Big Band Era

## CONNIE HAINES, JO STAFFORD, AND PEGGY LEE

Frank Sinatra seduced all three songbirds: **Connie Haines** (*top photo*), **Jo Stafford** (*center*), and **Peggy Lee** (*bottom*). Harry James was looking for a girl singer and sat down to listen to Connie, who sang "I Cried for You" and "I Can't Give You Anything But Love." He walked out on her before she could finish the number. "I was furious—what a rude man," she later said. Actually, he had to leave for Penn Station to meet his band en route to Philadelphia. He called her from the station and hired her for forty dollars a week. He also introduced her to his boy singer, Frank Sinatra.

Jo Stafford was already an established singer with The Pied Pipers, backed up by Tommy Dorsey and his orchestra, when Dorsey hired Frank.

She remembered the love/hate relationship Frank maintained with the bandleader. When Dorsey died in 1956, "Frank refused to join in a TV tribute to him. Yet in 1958, he turned an entire episode of his ABC television series into a tribute to Dorsey. He hired me for an entire evening of remembering Tommy," Stafford said.

Frank's flings with Stafford and Connie Haines were little more than passing fancies. But with Peggy Lee, Frank settled into a life-long relationship. "He was a virtual husband to me, though we never actually married," Lee recalled.

# FRANK'S RAPE
## OF "MARIE ANTOINETTE"

On his rise to glory, Frank Sinatra in the late 1930s and early 1940s not only met some of the up-and-coming female singers of his day, he often seduced them, and even raped one of them.

Although there was a certain jealousy in these relationships—"boy singer" vs. "girl singer"—he found a number of the songbirds sexually appealing, or at least convenient to mate with at night when Nancy, his wife, was tucked away in New Jersey. His mother, Dolly, was hovering over the new brood of Sinatras during his absence.

As he had told Harry James, "What do wives expect? I'm on the road away from Nancy. I'm also at my sexual peak. What am I supposed to do for sex? Use my hand? My fingers won't stretch around it."

Connie Haines was still a virgin at seventeen the night she'd first heard Frank sing. Gum-chewing Harry James had stopped his bus in front of the Rustic Cabin in New Jersey. Within a period of twenty-four hours, James had hired Frank as his "boy singer," with Connie filling in as the "girl singer."

Connie was not the most beautiful of the vocalists Frank seduced, but he was mildly tempted by her. When she turned down three attempts to seduce her, he began to view her as a challenge. "Every fucking broad on the planet wants to get in my pants, and you won't let me fuck you," he told her one night backstage.

"It's obvious you save your romance for your songs," she said. "In person, you're a dud when it comes to wooing a gal."

"Connie Haines" was actually named by Harry James when she joined his band. Born in Savannah, her real name (believe it or not) was Yvonne Marie Antoinette JaMais. She'd become famous in Georgia at the age of nine, singing on the radio as "Baby Yvonne Marie, The Little Princess of the Air."

When she won the popular singing competition, "The Major Bowes Contest," she was hired by James, who changed her name. "I didn't get the Marie Antoinette shit at all. You look like a Connie to me."

James had been attracted to the peppy, petite, big voiced but pint-sized singer with her zippy, rhythmic style.

On stage, Connie and Frank had different styles, Connie specializing in rhythmic up-tempo tunes, Frank in ballads and slow fox-trots.

Two views of **Frank Sinatra with Connie Haines.** The girl from the South had a troubled relationship with Frank, "going from hot to cold..mostly cold," she said. "I thought he was a first-rate bastard, and I still think that. But then he could charm the pants off you when he wanted to, and I mean that literally. He could insult me too. Once, we sang a duet together, 'Snooty Little Cutie,' and he told me later that I was so sugary sweet that it left the audience begging for insulin."

Sometimes they were on stage together, Frank ad-libbing to her numbers. In her personalized rendition of "Let's Get Away From It All," she improvised "We'll spend a weekend in Dixie. I'll get a real Southern drawl."

He piped in, "Another one?"

Their days with the financially troubled James band were numbered. At one point, James could no longer pay even their modest salaries.

Both Connie and Frank secured gigs with the far more successful Tommy Dorsey band at higher salaries, and they had to tell Harry they wanted out of their contracts. Ever the gentleman, he let them go. He laughingly said, "If Tommy ever needs a trumpet player, maybe you'll ask him to send for me one day."

Before their departures from him, he amused them with stories of his life. His parents were circus performers, he said. "My mother was known as "The Iron Jaw" because she could dangle from a wire by her teeth with no net below."

James inherited his musical talent from his father, a bandmaster and cornetist. James told Frank and Connie that at the age of five he was known in the circus as "The Human Eel," because he was a contortionist.

"I learned to play the trumpet when I was only eight years old. By the time I was fourteen, I was drinking a quart of booze a day and picking up two or three broads for the night. I got married when I was nineteen. Louise Tobin was only seventeen. On the day I got married to her, I had sex with two other women, a mother-and-a-daughter act."

Frank's ultimate appraisal of James was, "That is one weed-puffing hep cat!" "We both love Harry but we know it's time to hit the road." Connie agreed.

When Connie and Frank appeared on stage together with the Dorsey band, "It was not so much a duet as a fencing match," Dorsey later recalled.

She had a way of singing directly to handsome GIs in the audience, ignoring Frank. "He felt he was hot shit at the time, and I found him too cocky, so I ignored him as best as I could, even though one night he threatened me, 'I'll get you yet, bitch!' Frankly—and I don't mean to play on his name—I just didn't see what all the excitement was about. He was real skinny. I preferred strapping soldiers in uniform, and I had this thing for guys in the Air Force."

In 1945 she married Robert DeHaven, the World War II flying ace.

"When I flirted with the guys, they'd scream and holler," Connie said. "Up until then, he was getting all the hysteria. It really pissed him off. I think he wanted to kill me."

"He was always calling me cornball," she said. "He thought anyone from the Deep South was a redneck. Sometimes to get back at him, I suddenly appeared on stage between choruses doing the lindy or a dirty boogie. That really riled him."

"At one point Frank went to Tommy and demanded he fire me," Connie claimed. "Instead, it was Frank who got fired that night. Tommy replaced him with Milburn Stone who later became a lot more famous on that TV series, *Gunsmoke*, playing the character of Doc Adams. Finally, Frank apologized to Tommy and was hired back."

One night, pretending to be a room service waiter, Frank entered her room. "I ordered him to get out," Connie recalled years later at her Florida home, "but he wouldn't go. He might have looked like a runt but he forced himself on me, pinned me to the bed, and raped me. I tried to fight him off, but he was determined. I'd never had a man before, and he hurt me something awful. I bled. I later learned that most men didn't come in Frank's size. It felt like some huge, blunt instrument that was being inserted inside me. Later when it was over, he became more soothing. He even cried for hurting me. I still ordered him out of my room. At first I was going to tell Tommy, but then one of the boys in the band told me that women who ratted on Sinatra got acid thrown in their face by the mob."

She said she never really forgave him until one night when he saved her life. "It was at Madison Square Garden. There was this idiot smoker who sat in the balcony. He tossed a lit match on to the stage, and it landed on my ruffled tulle dress. I was set on fire. Fortunately, Frank was on the stage with me. He fell on top of me but not for rape this time. He smothered the flames with his coat. After that night, I forgave him for everything. He was welcomed into my room at any time."

In Florida, she got up in her living room and walked about when asked what ultimately happened between Frank and her. "Just as I was getting a big crush on that stringbean, Jo Stafford and Peggy Lee took him away."

"Long after Frank and I had our fling, he would often call me late at night," **Jo Stafford** said. "I was sort of a mother confessor to him. He often talked about his sex life with me, because he knew I was a 'broad-minded broad,' as he liked to call me. A year or so before he married Mia Farrow, he told me he was suffering premature ejaculation. 'That's why I have been going mostly with prostitutes,' he said. 'What's a whore gonna say if you experience premature ejaculation? She'll probably be glad you did so she can take on her next john. With Mia, it's different. I don't have that problem with her. Sex with other gals, present company excepted, didn't mean a damn thing—even with Ava. It was just practice leading up to Mia.' He would then ring off singing 'You Make Me Feel So Young.'"

## FRANK MAKES LOVE TO "G.I. JO"

Born two years after Frank Sinatra, in 1917, Jo Elizabeth Stafford, a native Californian, inherited her singing talent from her parents. Her mother was an accomplished banjo player, and her father would often sing and play various instruments.

Stafford first sang in public at the age of twelve with a sentimental favorite, "Believe Me If All Those Endearing Young Charms." As late as 1941, she was part of the singing trio "The Stafford Sisters," who were heard over radio in the Los Angeles area.

For a while, Stafford worked at the film studios on soundtracks, one of which featured Fred Astaire on the soundtrack for *A Damsel in Distress* (1937). "Astaire had trouble with some of the syncopation," Stafford said. "The man with the syncopated shoes couldn't do the syncopated notes."

Eventually Stafford joined the male singing group, The Pied Pipers, and impressed Tommy Dorsey so much he put them under contract about the same time he signed "boy singer" Frank Sinatra.

In rehearsal with the Dorsey band, Stafford heard Frank sing for the first time. "He had sung only four bars, and I knew at once that he was going to make it. He was *that* good. All male singers at the time sounded like Bing Crosby, but Sinatra didn't sound like Crosby at all. He didn't sound like anybody else I'd ever heard sing. He was his own singer, his own man."

"The song was 'Stardust,'" she said, "and indeed stardust danced in my eyes. I got really turned on by him. He was pretty frail looking with a whole bunch of hair, but there was something about him. I turned to Tommy Dorsey and said, 'Daddy, buy me some of that.'"

Two weeks after meeting Frank, he and Stafford launched an affair. Drummer Buddy Rich said, "On some nights. Frank went from the bed of Connie Haines to the bed of Jo Stafford…or vice versa."

"When I first started working with Tommy Dorsey, The Pied Pipers and I were billed above Frank," Stafford said. "But after his hit recording of 'I'll Never Smile Again,' he was billed over us, and also over Connie Haines. She accepted it with her good nature, but Buddy Rich was furious."

The drummer told Stafford, "The name Buddy Rich will live forever in popular music, when a skinny little prick named Frank Sinatra will end up in the dust bin."

"I wouldn't bet your left ball on that," Stafford told him. "Frank is arrogant and cocksure of himself, but maybe he's got a right to be."

"Fuck that!" he told Stafford. "He's just a lousy singer with jug ears."

The next night Stafford, to her horror, watched as Rich tried to sabotage Frank in his slow, romantic ballads. He speeded up the tempo to throw Frank off his mark.

The first night he did that, Stafford was talking with her fellow Pied Pipers when Frank ran backstage, "I'm gonna kill that fucker!" he shouted. Seeing Rich, he punched him in the nose, bloodying it.

Buddy was holding his cymbal (that High F cymbal a musician plays with his feet). With that instrument, he knocked Frank against the wall, trying to crush the cymbal into his face. It was Dorsey, aided by two band members, who broke up the fight before either or both of them ended up in the hospital. That was but one of several fights between Buddy and Frank that Dorsey would have to break up.

A veteran entertainer like Al Jolson was jealous of Frank's success. He attacked Frank to Stafford, "All that jerk has to do is show up for work

The scene above is of **Al Jolson** in blackface as he appeared in one of the first semi-talking pictures, *The Jazz Singer* (1927). In time, Frank Sinatra would resent the arrival of Elvis Presley and later, The Beatles.

But Frank's presence on the entertainment scene during the war years "pissed off" a lot of established singers whose careers were fading as the taste of the public changed. To Jolson, Frank was the new boy on the block, and the long-established vaudeville entertainer resented all the reports of young girls swooning over this kid from Hoboken.

Jolson was furious when Frank "stole" "The World Is in My Arms" from the trouper's comeback show, *Hold Onto Your Hats*. Frank also "stole" another song from Jolson—at least according to him. It was "Ol' Man River" by Oscar Hammerstein and Jerome Kern. Actually, they had written it for Paul Robeson in 1927. "At least when I sing 'Ol' Man River,'" Frank said, "I don't do what Jolson did and use the word 'niggers.'"

71

and stand before a microphone. The mike seems bigger than he is."

"He may not look like much but, wow, what a voice," she said in defense of Frank.

A dispute between Stafford and her Pied Pipers teamed up against Dorsey led to an argument that could not be healed. The group, including Stafford, walked out on Dorsey.

For two years she had made appearances with the Pipers, but she was gaining too much recognition on her own. Frank urged her to break and go solo, as he himself had done. "You and I are just too good to be part of any group." In 1944, she took his advice, and achieved her greatest fame during in World War II, during which she became one of the USO's most popular entertainers. "Betty Grable had the legs," she once said, "I had the voice." In fact, she was so popular with soldiers that they nicknamed her "G.I. Jo."

Japanese propagandists used her recordings, broadcasting her records on loudspeakers in an attempt to make U.S. troops homesick enough to surrender.

Although Stafford and Frank were friends throughout their lives, he became jealous of her in 1950 when, at Columbia Records, she became the first recording artist to sell 25 million records.

One of Tommy Dorsey's arrangers was Paul Weston. After her "fling with Frankie," as she called it, she began an affair with Weston, which culminated in a marriage on February 26, 1952. Frank couldn't attend but sent flowers.

Once married, Stafford continued a business relationship with Frank. She recorded for his Reprise label, her albums released between 1961 and 1964. They were mostly retrospective in nature. When Frank sold Reprise to Warner Brothers, Stafford bolted.

Five years after Frank escaped from his contract with Dorsey, in August of 1956, she came together again with him for a week-long engagement at the Paramount Theater in New York.

Frank Sinatra took Jo Stafford to see *Johnny Concho*, and later wished he hadn't. "I should not have made the fucking movie," he told her. "I've laid a dinosaur egg."

One night, years later, during a phone call to Stafford, he told her, "I've made five Western films, if you can call *The Kissing Bandit* a film. Not only *Johnny Concho*, but *Sergeants 3*, *Dirty Dingus Magee*, and *4 for Texas*. I've decided to give them up. I'm no Gary Cooper, nor am I John Wayne. This sagebrush shit isn't my style. I belong in a tux, fucking Jackie Kennedy after a presidential inaugural."

Stafford claimed Frank did that only to boost the attendance of his newly released but lackluster film, *Johnny Concho*. It was a minor effort that had Frank starring with B-list stars like Keenan Wynn, whose flamboyant gay off screen expressions bothered Frank, and Phyllis Kirk, whom he spoke about disparagingly. "Who would want to go to bed with her?" Frank asked director Don McGuire.

In *Johnny Concho*, Frank played against type as the movie's villain. Critics panned the movie, one writer claiming "Johnny Concho is Johnny Stinko." Another wrote, "Frank, you are the greatest singer ever, but you don't belong in a movie like this."

Rooster Davis said, "Sinatra just doesn't have the build for a Western bad-guy wannabe. He's just too slight. Maybe he is about the same height as say, Audie Murphy, but Murphy has a pretty solid build. Sinatra comes across as a big-talking little kid who nobody ought to take seriously."

"I sat with Frank in the balcony

watching the screening of the movie with him," Stafford said. "He cringed and sunk down in his seat. I felt real sorry for him. We both knew he was watching one of the worst films he ever made. *High Noon* did it so much better. It was rumored later that Frank actually paid money to have the producers deep six *Johnny Concho*. He was truly ashamed of it. At least the music by Nelson Riddle wasn't all that bad."

Stafford claimed that Frank never spoke to Dorsey backstage. But, like the professional Frank was, he completed the engagement. "There was no love lost between those two," Stafford said. "Both men were very talented and very temperamental. Each was a genius in his own field. I went to bed with both of them. Sleeping with Dorsey was like crawling under the sheets with a rock. He knew how to make love to a trombone better than he did a woman. On the other hand, Frank was a real Romeo. That skinny little kid, like Superman, packed a powerful punch. No wonder the gals were crazy about him."

After the Paramount gig, Dorsey gave an interview in which he called Frank "brittle," which, of course, infuriated him. Dorsey didn't stop there, telling the press, "Sinatra is the most fascinating man in the world, but don't stick your hand in his cage."

"I called Frank when I heard over the radio that Tommy had died. It was just three months after the Paramount gig. Apparently, Tommy had had this really big steak dinner, maybe a lot to drink. Somehow the food backed up on him, and he choked to death in his sleep."

"Frank had already heard the news when I called him," she said. "'Good riddance,' he told me. 'The widow will get no flowers, no card, no acknowledgement from me whatsoever. The music world's a better place without him. He had no talent at all. He couldn't even play the fucking trombone.'"

Even as Dorsey lay rotting in his grave, Frank continued his attack on the bandleader.

Stafford was shocked one night on June 15, 1979 when she attended a concert at the Universal Amphitheater in Los Angeles. Some 6,500 fans purchased tickets that night. On stage Frank gave a tribute to Harry James, introducing him and thanking him for jump-starting his career.

"Then Frank really shocked the audience," Stafford said. "With bitterness on his face, he launched into an attack on Tommy."

"And then there is that dead matter known as Tommy Dorsey," Frank told his stunned audience. "When I wanted to get out of my contract to him, it cost me seven million dollars." That was a blatant lie, of course. He didn't have seven million dollars at the time.

Stafford watched as he stared down at the floor as if he were stomping on the very grave of Dorsey. "You hear me, Tommy?" Frank shouted. "You hear me? I'm talking to you."

"Frank seemed to be having a breakdown on stage," Stafford said. "I couldn't sit through any more. I left before the show was over. I didn't

**Jo Stafford with her husband, Paul Weston**, appears in a pensive mood. She met him when he was a musical arranger for Tommy Dorsey's orchestra.

"I just don't see what broads see in nerdy-looking guys like Weston," Frank said. "It's not his big dick, something he doesn't possess. How do I know? I've flopped out Big Frankie and stood next to him at the urinal. I have finally decided that broads marry guys for reasons other than to get a great fucking every night. That thought had never occurred to me before until I analyzed the Stafford/Weston marriage. I wish them well. But I probably ruined Jo for all other guys, so she had to settle."

have the nerve to go backstage for a reunion with him."

Stafford had drifted into semi-retirement in the mid-1960s when her kind of music was going out of style. She completely retired in 1975, but came back in 1990 to sing at a ceremony honoring Frank.

He called her in 1996 when he heard that her husband, Paul Weston, had died. They talked on the phone for about an hour, recalling with nostalgia the war years.

"I'll make a bet with you, Jo," he said. "I bet you'll outlive me."

"Who are you kidding?" she asked him. "I'll go down in music history as a footnote, a singer who entertained the servicemen who nicknamed me 'G.I. Jo.' With your music, you'll live forever, my sweet, dear loving man." But the songbird did indeed outlive Frank, dying in 2008 a decade after his own death.

When she died, a WWII soldier, Henry Pastor, said, "G.I. Jo got me through many a battle with those Japs. She reminded me what I was fighting to come home too. Jo will live as long as they are singing, 'I Remember You,' 'You Belong to Me,' and 'Walkin' My Baby Back Home.'"

## PEGGY LEE ON FRANK SINATRA: YOU GIVE ME FEVER

"Whenever Frank Sinatra asked me out on a date, I always accepted," said Miss **Peggy Lee.** "I never knew what to expect, but I could be assured it would be fun, followed by a roll in the hay, as we say back in North Dakota.

"I remember the night he took me to Ciro's in Hollywood. It'd been opened to take business from the Cocoanut Grove and Mocambo's. On opening night there was a nude woman—well, almost naked— in a bathtub of champagne. All the guests were told to fill their glasses with champagne and drink it. Then we had three daiquiris before dinner, followed by two glasses of Jack Daniels. Wine with dinner, of course. Then some very old brandy, with a nightcap to follow. That was the ritual...everybody drank like that.

"Outside, the valet brought Frank's car around. We drove off like we were heading down a speedway. About fifteen minutes later, we were pulled over by two members of the California Highway Patrol. They aimed a flashlight into Frank's face. He immediately started warbling 'I'm a Fool to Want You.' One of the patrolmen got behind the wheel of Frank's car, the other following us in the patrol car. They took us to my house. We weren't arrested. Frank fell asleep right away in my bedroom, but redeemed himself at ten o'clock the following morning."

From the cold winds of North Dakota, Peggy Lee, born Norma Deloris Egstrom, the seventh of eight children, emerged to become a legendary singer, actress, and songwriter. She would have a starring role in the life of Frank Sinatra.

Be it poetry, jazz, chamber pop, or art songs, this Scandinavian blonde beauty was a mistress of all these forms of expression.

Beginning as a vocalist on local radio singing with Benny Goodman's big band, she had joined Goodman and his boys in the band in 1941 and sang with him for two years, scoring the first of her Number One hits in 1942. It was called "Somebody Else Is Taking My Place," and it was followed by the even bigger 1943 sensation, "Why Don't You Do Right?", which sold more than a million copies and made her a household word.

That same year, she met and married David Barbour, a guitarist in Goodman's band. Goodman fired Barbour, because he broke the band leader's rule—"no fraternizing with the girl singer."

Today, Peggy is still heard on the radio with her rendition of her signature song, "Fever," released in 1956. Her other big hit, "Is That All There Is?" was released in 1969. By that time, Lee was hailed as one of the most influential jazz vocalists of all time and mentor to such diverse crooners as Frank himself, as well as Bette Midler, Judy Garland, Paul McCartney, and Madonna.

Duke Ellington dubbed her "The Queen," and Albert Einstein adored her. With her platinum cool and inimitable whisper, she sold millions of records and dazzled everyone from Bing Crosby to Frank himself.

In 1942, the worst year of WWII for the United States, audiences needed a distraction, and musical entertainment was a way to forget the ongoing invasions of Europe and Asia by the Germans and Japanese.

Benny Goodman, the "King of Swing," was booked into the Paramount Theater at New York City's Times Square, along with Peggy Lee, his girl singer.

Musician **David Barbour**, pictured with his inevitable guitar, married **Peggy Lee**. "But I understood from the beginning that she might see Frank Sinatra on that odd night. It wasn't written into our marriage contract, but it was understood. I guess she was entitled. After all, he *was* Frank Sinatra, and those two went way back.

"I wanted Peggy the first night I saw her. I was in the band. I stuck out my foot and tripped her. She noticed me all right. She became Mrs. Dave Barbour on March 8, 1943. We both said goodbye to Benny Goodman and his band and struck out on our own. She understood that I had to hit the bottle every night.

"Even though we sold two million copies of our record *Manaña,* I came to love booze more than Peggy."

Although he couldn't read a note of music, a scrawny singer from Hoboken, was also signed for the gig. Frank dazzled the audience singing "For Me and My Gal."

That weekend, "My Gal" was Peggy herself. She would spend the next few years coming and going from his bedside. He later told Benny Goodman, "Peggy and I are the perfect match. She likes to get fucked and I like to fuck—what a combination."

Benny responded, "Frankie my boy, you're gonna grow up to become a dirty old man seducing gals one-third your age."

Peggy was only seventeen at the time Frank took her to bed. She later told Ava Gardner, "I know you and Frank were once in love, and I understand that. Once you've had Frank, he messes it up for you with other men. One of my husbands, Dewey Martin, had the body for love-making but not the drive."

"Frank found Peggy very sexy, and she told me she wanted to marry him," Jo Stafford recalled. "Peggy didn't seem to realize that I too was sleeping with her potential husband. But she claimed that Frank, although finding her alluring as a lover, also considered her too much like himself for marriage."

"We are like the same person," he is alleged to have said to Peggy. "Marrying you would be like me committing incest with myself." Peggy's biographer, Peter Richmond, quoted Will Friedwald as saying, "Sinatra was the first real example of a singer who had the presumption to decide what to sing. And Peggy was the first female singer to follow Sinatra in that regard." Bill Rudman, who helped produce Lee's last great record, "Love Held Lightly," claimed, "What we have here is the Primal Masculine and the Primal Feminine—*yin-yang* to the max. And what deepens it is that Sinatra *also* had a real vulnerability and Peggy *also* had a real toughness—all of which help make their performances so rich. No wonder they were a mutual admiration society. They loved the whole blessed continuum of sexual energy."

To Dean Martin, Frank confided, "Peggy and I got together to fuck between marriages, and sometimes during her marriages. She was my one steady, my one reliable gal. Always dependable, ever ready."

For his TV spectacular, *Star-Spangled Revue*, airing on NBC in 1950, Bob Hope paid "a hell of a lot of money to hire two canaries, Frank Sinatra and Peggy Lee." It would mark Frank's first major appearance on television.

"It takes real courage to get your feet wet in television," Hope told his audience. "I'm really glad this chap decided to take the plunge. I'm thrilled to introduce Mr. Frank Sinatra."

Looking so thin that the wind might blow him away in a mere breeze, Frank sang "Come Rain or Come Shine." He had complete composure, even a cockiness, in this new medium.

Peggy made her appearance and was almost too stunning for the small black-and-white screen. Having just turned thirty the day before, she looked much younger in her chiffon gown and dangling rhinestone earrings. Her rendition of "Bewitched, Bothered, and Bewildered" thrilled audiences across the vast American homeland.

After the show, Peggy and Frank ran off to his hotel suite, where he said he would not let her go until he'd seduced her twelve times in three days.

He was a man of his word.

Peggy knew that Frank had a violent streak in him. But once when he invited her on "The Frank Sinatra Show" on TV, she became sick.

**Frank Sinatra and Peggy Lee** listen to a playback of their own music. "We were our own worst critics," Frank later said.

"To advance ourselves as artists, we have to record a mess from time to time," she claimed. "How else could we grow?"

In 1949 and 1950, both had hit a fallow period in their careers. Frank flew to New York to catch her opening night at the Copacabana. Peggy was worried that she was slipping; Frank knew that he was.

Before her opening, Peggy was a nervous wreck, puffing incessantly on a cigarette. She'd lost her luggage at Idlewild and didn't have the right gown to wear. "I'm as nervous as a cat on a hot tin roof," she said.

Frank held her in his arms, finding her trembling. Backstage after the show, he held her again. "Even Piaf couldn't have sung 'La Vie en Rose' better than you," he told her. "But why are you crying?"

"I've got something like a piece of glass in my eye. I've got to get to the hospital at once."

"I'll always be here to rescue you," he told her. In the back of a taxi, he held her close all the way to the emergency room.

"He was so compassionate, so very caring," she said. "He was like a nurse getting me back to health. When I was shivering, he rushed out to a store and came back with three beautiful wool blankets. He even made tea for me with a little hotplate he brought into my dressing room. He went to a bakery and bought fresh bread to make toast for me with that tea."

Of course, over the years Peggy and Frank had their feuds but they always made up. When asked to evaluate singers, he won some friends but alienated others. Surprisingly he was critical of the vocal techniques of some of his best "gal pals," and praised Tony Bennett as "the best singer in the business, the best exponent of a song."

Amazingly, he denounced his sometimes lover, Judy Garland, as "the worst singer in the business, rivaled only by Ella Fitzgerald for that title. Judy, for example, forgets she's telling a story in a song lyric. Peggy Lee is better with lyrics, but Jo Stafford is even better. She can hold notes for sixteen bars if she has to."

Privately Peggy got her "revenge" on Frank, if it could be called that, when John Lennon weighed in with his opinions on Frank and Peggy. "I can't stand Sinatra's music, not for a moment, but I can listen to Peggy Lee all day. Same praise goes to Ella Fitzgerald. Sinatra's not for me. He just doesn't do it."

Paul McCartney was more charitable to Frank and his music. "Back in the 1950s, I realized that if anyone wanted to go into show business, you were looking at a Sinatra-type person as the most rockin' you were gonna get. When I wrote 'When I'm Sixty-Four,' I was sixteen years old but I thought I was writing a song for Sinatra."

"Frank was much more generous to the Beatles than he had been to Elvis Presley," Peggy recalled. "After all, he did record 'Yesterday' by Lennon and McCartney. He praised them for writing the best love songs in decades. He once made his jet plane available to McCartney, and he even invited George Harrison to Palm Springs as his houseguest. He also recorded Harrison's 'Something.' In time, Frank learned to exist in a rock 'n' roll world and found there was a place for his music to co-exist alongside his. I found that for myself too."

When an interviewer asked Peggy what she thought of Frank, she said, "As a singer, he is refreshingly un-macho. He has a sort of neuter gender feeling that's very appealing. In bed, of course, he is very macho, very in control. Strike that last line. It was strictly off the record."

Frank was always there when Peggy needed him. Her first husband, David Barbour, died on December 12, 1965. She had divorced him in 1951, but told Frank she was getting back with him. Frank paid all of Barbour's final medical expenses.

Ironically, Brad Dexter, Peggy's second husband, whom she married in 1953, saved Frank's life. He had cast Dexter in his 1965 film *None But the Brave*.

On a beach in Hawaii, a riptide carried Frank out to sea. Dexter swam out and rescued him, keeping him afloat until lifeguards could come onto the scene with surfboards.

Frank was so grateful he made Dexter a producer in his film company. "He became my pal, my confidant," Frank said. "After all, I owe my life to him." Peggy had called Dexter "the handsomest man I've ever met." Square jawed like Charlton Heston, he was also broad shouldered. In films, he was labeled "the sweetest meanie to ever slug a hero or tussle with a lady."

When appearing in the film noir, *The Asphalt Jungle* (1950), Dexter had a torrid affair with Marilyn Monroe, something he had in common with Frank himself.

After his failed marriage to Peggy, Dexter told Frank, "I doubt if I'll ever get married again." The bisexual actor would later marry twice, once in 1971 and again in 1994. Between and during marriages, he managed to have affairs with Tyrone Power, Yul Brynner, and Robert Mitchum. A room service waiter once walked in on Mitchum and Dexter in bed with actress Gloria Graham.

Peggy once confided to Frank that she'd chased after Paul Newman but he "turned me down. But when my ex, Brad Dexter himself, called, Paul always came running. I guess Brad had something between his legs that I don't. Hell, what am I saying? I know what the fucker has between his legs. I married him."

"I think the serial seducer is in love with me now," Frank told her. "He's at my beck and call day and night."

"Yeah," said Peggy somewhat skeptically. "He's also on your payroll."

"People wonder how you can survive in show business," she told Frank in later years. "I got my strength from my farm girl training—a hired hand shucking grain and pitching hay. I drove the water wagon for a threshing ring in Jamestown, North Dakota. My school teachers told me I had a good voice, so I put it to work. It beat shucking grain, although I still did some waitressing in between my spots on the radio."

"I was a waiter, too, at the Rustic Cabin in New Jersey," Frank told her, "I always stuck my fingers into the minestrone. That's why I have such clean nails."

As her health became precarious over the years, Frank was "my guardian angel," she later claimed. When she was stricken in New Orleans, he hired a private jet to bring her back to California. When he discovered that her home was not air conditioned, he had workmen arrive the next day. "Long after passion had died, Frank found a true friend in Peggy," said Ava Gardner. "I wasn't even jealous. Friendship like that between a man and a woman is very rare and needs to be treasured. Most men are pursuing the honeypot, not friendship with a woman."

Suffering from poor health, Peggy continued to perform into the 1990s in a wheelchair. She died of complications from diabetes and a heart attack at the age of 81 in 2002. Her body was buried in Westwood Village Memorial Park Cemetery in Los Angeles. Engraved on her tombstone are the words, MUSIC IS MY LIFE'S BREATH.

Her finals words were, "I don't like time. I think of everything as *now*. Is tomorrow all that there is?"

---

## Is That All There Is?

Frank Sinatra died on May 14, 1998. Six months later, on October 27, Peggy Lee suffered a massive stroke at the age of seventy-eight. She came through and survived, but cried that "Frank won't be here to help me face the final curtain."

She'd spent her life communicating in song, but now was unable to express herself, if only to ask for a glass of water. The voice that had thrilled the world was now silent. Even so, she didn't want her doctors to terminate her life, even if it meant putting up with a talking tracheostomy, an artificial respirator, and a feeding tube.

She lived until January of 2002 and died in her own bed at "Peach Palace," so named because she'd painted everything peach. She was cremated, her remains interred in the "Garden of Serenity" within the cemetery at Westwood, Los Angeles. Frank was not around to mourn her.

In announcing her death, one radio broadcaster recalled the first time he met her, in an elevator, decades before. "Are you Peggy Lee?" he asked her.

"Not yet," she said, "but one day I will be."

And so she became.

# Peter Lawford

## THE FORGOTTEN RAT PACKER

Originally, Frank Sinatra was scheduled to introduce **Marilyn Monroe** (above) at the star-studded, fund-raising gala in Madison Square Garden on May 19, 1962, the occasion for President John F. Kennedy's upcoming forty-fifth birthday. But disagreements led to Frank pulling out, and **Peter Lawford** *(depicted in each of the three photos above)* filling in. It seemed appropriate since he was the president's brother-in-law, having married Patricia Kennedy.

Peter later learned that before MM went on, she spent fifteen minutes alone in her dressing room with Bobby Kennedy. Rumor was, she gave him a blow-job. Terrified of going on, she was tipsy when she stood in the wings, listening to Peter's introduction.

"This lovely lady is not only pulchritudinous but punctual. Mr. President: Marilyn Monroe!" But she'd run back in fear to her dressing room. Even after Peter's second introduction, there was still no Marilyn. Finally, after a third introduction, Peter in exasperation said, "Mr. President, the *late* Marilyn Monroe." She came out in white ermine and sang the world's most notorious version of "Happy Birthday, Mr. Pres...i...dent."

The lower photo on the right depicts President John F. Kennedy *(left figure)* with Lawford in the back seat of a limousine. Peter later said, "We were pussy hounds, and I was Jack's guide to the hidden pleasures of Hollywood. He wanted to screw just from the A-list."

# HOLLYWOOD/WASHINGTON BABYLON

In the 1940s, **Peter Lawford** dated both men and women, ranging from Robert Walker to Nancy Davis (Reagan).

Here he is pictured with **June Allyson** as they appeared together in the light comedy, *Good News* in 1947. June was having affairs with both Peter and a young Jack Kennedy when he visited Hollywood.

Frank Sinatra also knew June. When Peter asked him if he'd ever had a fling with her, Frank said, "I'm not dodging the question. I truly don't remember. I may have—in fact, I probably did. But when you had as many broads a night as I did, who had time to count?"

*"I don't know why Peter associates himself with that Rat Pack crowd. That dried-up piece of spaghetti—Sinatra—but I do like his singing. He's the villain of the pack."*

**—Lady Crawford**

*"Peter Lawford could not have an orgasm without getting his nipples delicately cut with a razor blade."*
**—Ripples Darling,** Las Vegas showgirl

*"Unlike Monty Clift, Peter Lawford actually did suck my cock."*

**—Tallulah Bankhead**

*"Frank figured he got JFK elected. He got pissed at the Kennedys for not being thankful enough, not overlooking his mob connections, and he eventually took it out on my old man because he could."*
**—Christopher Kennedy Lawford**

*"Let's show those asshole Hollywood fruitcakes that they can't get away with any shit like nothing's happened. Let's hit Sinatra. Or I could whack out a couple of those other guys. That faggot Peter Lawford, or I could take the nigger Sammy Davis Jr. and put his other eye out."*
**—Johnny Formosa**, henchman to Sam Giancana

*"Jack [Kennedy] loved hearing about Frank's Hollywood broads. He also quizzed me about all the gals I had screwed. He was especially interested in the color of their pussy hair, but sometimes I was too drunk to remember. In those cases, I just said, 'ginger.'"*
**—Peter Lawford**

*"One time at a party in Palm Springs, Frank got so mad at a prostitute that he slammed her through a plate-glass window. Glass and blood everywhere—what a disaster. The girl's arm was nearly severed from her body. Frank paid her off later and the whole thing was hushed up."*

—**Peter Lawford**

*"Frank's a violent guy, and he's good friends with too many guys who'd rather kill you than say hello."*

—**Peter Lawford**

Peter Lawford's parents were Sir Sydney Lawford, called "The General," and Lady May Lawford, who called herself "Mother Bitch." In England they led a privileged life.

Lady Lawford told friends, "The birth of Peter was an awful accident."

Frank Sinatra was born in Hoboken and Peter in England, yet they had something similar in their backgrounds. Initially their mothers dressed them as girls, Dolly abandoning that practice when Frank turned six. Up until he was twelve, Lady Lawford continued to dress Peter as a girl and insisted he sleep between her and her husband, even though he was experiencing "nighttime erections."

His father assisted Benito Mussolini to get his troops into shape before WWII.

Peter was one of the most promiscuous actors ever to set foot in Hollywood, matching Frank's record-breaking scores. But he didn't inherit his libido from Lady May. His mother admitted that she used to slip into the kitchen and rub uncooked meat around her groin. In bed she'd tell her husband, "The General," that she was having her period. Once she admitted to Peter that she never had sex with her husband since Peter was three years old.

She always made Peter feel unwanted, claiming she almost took a revolver and committed suicide rather than endure labor pains. "I can't stand nasty little babies," she once told her son. "They smell like sour milk, or even worse, urine. They run at both ends. Diapers sicken me. There's nothing more horrid than yellowish baby shit."

Peter was the victim of sexual abuse on several occasions when growing up, mostly from his governesses, his first experience occurring at the tender age of ten when he was fellated by a thirty-five-year-old caretaker. He also was molested by several so-called "friends of the family," all male, before he was sixteen.

The book that could not be published — not until after the death of her son Peter Lawford.

**Lady May Lawford**, mother of Peter Lawford, aptly titled her memoir *Bitch!*—and so she was.

The upper photo shows how she preferred to dress Peter as a girl, even after he reached puberty. During Peter's marriage to Patricia Kennedy, and when JFK became president, Lady May referred to her son as "The White House pimp."

She was not impressed with Frank Sinatra, but she claimed, "At least Peter is hanging out with heterosexual men when he's with Frank's cronies—better that than those crowds of homosexuals he usually mates with...Van Johnson and his pack of faggots."

"In England in my circles, I was never fond of Italians," Lady May said. "They were not invited to the really important parties. Guys like Sinatra shouldn't have been fussed over. I would have made him a singing waiter in a trattoria."

Years later, reflecting on his early childhood experiences with predators of both sexes, he said, "Pedophilia is not confined to men. That's the price I paid for being too beautiful as a child."

As a child he severely injured his arm when he plunged it through a door's glass pane. This injury kept him out of military service, and in films he took great pains to conceal that arm so it would not appear lifeless on the screen.

After a life of relative comfort, the Lawfords found themselves broke. They went to America where for a while they accepted invitations from well-meaning friends until they wore out their welcome. After being booted out of a guest cottage in Palm Beach, they moved to West Palm Beach, renting a small, seedy cottage near the railroad tracks.

Peter was able to find a low-paying job as a valet parker at a resort hotel. It was there that he met his future father-in-law, Ambassador Joseph P. Kennedy.

Kennedy cursed one of the parking lot attendants, who was black. "I don't want this damn nigger handling my car," the elder Kennedy said.

"He's the best and most careful driver on the lot," Peter said.

"Confine him to polishing cars," Kennedy advised, "and get out of my way, you silly little British faggot." Kennedy pushed past Peter and went to the manager's office, ordering that Peter be fired.

"We ate rice and beans that week," Peter later recalled.

Arriving in Hollywood with his parents, Peter won a contract with MGM where his first major role was *A Yank at Eton* (1942). He played a snobby bully opposite Mickey Rooney, who had married Ava Gardner, Peter's future lover.

The picture was a smash hit, and Peter went on to appear in such fabled films as *The White Cliffs of Dover* (1944). By 1945, based partly on his appearance in *Son of Lassie*, *Modern Screen* magazine readers voted him most popular actor in Hollywood. MGM was inundated with fan mail from America's bobby-soxers and homosexual young men, some of whom seemed to recognize him as "one of us."

In 1944, MGM mogul Louis B. Mayer threw a party for Henry Ford, inviting Frank and Nancy Sinatra, and also extending an invitation to the studio's newest and, some said, handsomest star, Peter himself.

Almost from the first, Peter bonded with Frank, and within a few weeks he became a regular at Nancy's spaghetti suppers at the Sinatra home. He usually showed up with a different girlfriend every time he was invited.

Frank and Nancy became so fond of Peter that they invited him to their New Year's Eve party to usher in 1947. In a well-tailored tuxedo, Peter looked dashing, but his date stole the show. Wrapped in a white fur stole, a gift from Howard Hughes, and at the peak of her youthful beauty, Ava Gardner made a dazzling impression.

Deserting Nancy, Frank rushed over to her. "How are you tonight, Miss Gardner?" he asked.

She surveyed him up and down, beginning with his

When Peter Lawford first propositioned **Sammy Davis Jr.** *(above)*, Davis turned him down.

But then Sammy (known on Broadway as "Mr. Wonderful") soon got pulled into the swinging, free-wheeling sexuality of the 1960s.

After he'd participated in all-night orgies in his Las Vegas hotel suite with Peter, bringing in prostitutes, it was Sammy who suggested that Peter and he lay off the girls for a night. "I'd like a quickie. I want to see what homo action means."

After their night together, Sammy told Peter, "Let's do it again..and again. You really know how to handle King Kong."

feet. "Looking for love," she said. "Who do you have to fuck around here to get a drink?"

"Frank and I became the odd duo," Peter admitted. "Frank was from the tough streets of Hoboken and could talk with his fists. I was a bit of a sissy, the son of a British Knight of the Realm. In spite of our differences, we liked each other. I found him a cocky low-rent Italian, but very appealing."

"Frank and I ended up seducing some of the same women, namely, Lana Turner, Ava Gardner, Marilyn Maxwell, Dorothy Dandridge, and Marilyn Monroe, plus more prostitutes—black and white—than either of us could count."

Over the years, Frank tried to keep a tally on each of their lovers—female ones, that is. Frank could only speculate as to the identities of Peter's boyfriends.

Some of Peter's other female conquests included June Allyson, Janet Leigh, Lucille Ball, Anne Baxter, Judy Holliday, Gina Lollobrigida, Judy Garland, Grace Kelly, Kim Novak, Lee Remick, Elizabeth Taylor, and even Jacqueline Kennedy Onassis and Nancy Davis Reagan.

Occasionally, but not often, Peter delivered reviews of his sexual trysts in the boudoir. On Rita Hayworth: "She was the worst lay in the world. She was always drunk and she never stopped eating." On Elizabeth Taylor: "I managed to do the deed in spite of her fat thighs and the smell of Chihuahua poop that permeated her bedroom."

His male lovers included Sammy Davis Jr., Merv Griffin, Roddy McDowall, Tony Curtis, Van Johnson, Sam Mineo, Robert Walker, Clifton Webb, George Cukor, Keenan Wynn, Tom Drake, Noël Coward, and lots of male hustlers, young male extras at MGM, studio messenger boys, and young men he met casually in toilets.

Peter teamed with Frank and MGM to make the 1947 *It Happened in Brooklyn*. It co-starred the operatic Kathryn Grayson, boasting the largest bosom of any A-list star in Hollywood. Off the set she developed a powerful crush on Peter.

Released from the Army after four years, the character of Danny Miller (as played by Frank) sang the now standard "Time After Time."

He jokingly mocked Peter's movie role as an aspirant composer, Jamie Shellgrove. "Whether you know it or not, with a name like that, you're actually playing a faggot. Type-casting if you ask me." He had already learned of Peter's secret homosexual liaisons. On the set Peter ignored Grayson, but often disappeared for long lunches with Van

FRANK & PETER WENT AFTER THE SAME WOMEN

Peter...with Marilyn Maxwell

with Ava Gardner

with "La Liz"

with Lana Turner

Johnson, another MGM heartthrob.

Jimmy Durante was cast in the film as its fourth lead, marking the beginning of a long association with Peter. They would later perform in nightclubs together.

After Frank's breakup with Ava, Peter asked her out on a "date" in 1954. It seemed relatively harmless, and apparently did not lead to a renewal of their sexual trysts of the 1940s. But that is not how Frank viewed it.

Peter recalled that he was in bed *alone* when a call came in from Frank who did not identify himself. "Listen, creep, and listen good. You wanna keep your nuts intact? Stay away from Ava. I'm warning you only this one time. Got that, faggot?"

The phone call was followed up by a handwritten note the next day: "Asshole, I will break the legs of any fartface who steps in where he doesn't belong. Frank Sinatra"

Three years would go by before Frank spoke to Peter again.

At a Hollywood party in 1957 at the home of Gary Cooper, Patricia Kennedy Lawford, Peter's wife, had a long talk with Frank. She suggested that if Frank had a reconciliation with her husband, it might lead to "a close relationship with Jack. You know, of course, that Jack is going to win the presidency in 1960, don't you?"

Whether he knew that or not, Frank called Peter the next day. "Hey, Charlie, let's get together for a drink."

Frank "made up" with Peter, although the motives didn't appear to be based on brotherly love. Frank had been impressed when Peter had married Patricia Kennedy. There was talk that

On April 24, 1954, "I became a Kennedy," **Peter Lawford** claimed, after his marriage to **Patricia Kennedy**, sister of the man who, a half-dozen years later, would become President of the United States.

Peter kept both Pat and Joe Kennedy, her father, waiting impatiently at the altar for his arrival at St. Thomas More's Catholic Church in Manhattan. The ushers included Jack, Bobby, and Teddy, along with JFK's gay friend, LeMoyne Billings. Lem had helped Pat pick out her Hattie Carnegie wedding gown in pearl-white satin. "Screaming women and uninhibited bobbysoxers" greeted Peter when he arrived, late, at the church.

The marriage didn't live up to Pat's fantasies of wedding a movie star. On her honeymoon, Pat was shocked at Peter's preference for oral sex. Peter later told Frank Sinatra, "Pat crosses herself every time she goes to bed with me." Months later, he confessed, "I have liberated her sexually, but I wish I hadn't. She's turning into a whore."

her brother, Senator John F. Kennedy of Massachusetts, would evolve into a leader in the race for President of the United States. Frank wanted to ingratiate himself with Peter once again.

"Frank got back together with me, because of Jack Kennedy," Peter later said. "Ol' Blue eyes could see the bandwagon coming."

Peter's son, Christopher Kennedy Lawford, felt that Frank didn't really want to make up with Peter. Both Peter and his son visited Frank in Palm Springs for a reunion. "Sinatra looked old and unhappy," Christopher said. "If he was glad to see my old man, he sure had a funny way of showing it. My father was gracious and open. I could tell he would have liked to rekindle whatever relationship existed before the breakup. But Sinatra was too far down the road. He never really looked at my dad and grunted one-syllable responses. I think Sinatra resented my father—his looks, his style, his command of the language, and his fluency in French. Frank had the power and the voice but my dad had the grace and the style. Those who have been given everything always want more."

"Poor Peter never realized it, but Frank didn't

really want to get back with him," said their mutual girlfriend Marilyn Maxwell. "What Frank wanted more than anything else was an *entrée* into the world of the Kennedys."

In spite of these rather cynical forecasts, Frank gradually allowed Peter back into his life and began to hang out with him. One night he even apologized for misjudging that so-called date with Ava.

After the awkward renewal of their friendship, Frank and Peter became an item. Peter was a closeted homosexual and word spread that he was "servicing" Frank. They appeared together on Dinah Shore's TV Show; they made movies together, and even went into the restaurant business together. They shared suites in London, Rome, and Monaco with hot- and cold-running prostitutes. Peter told the press that Frank "is a fantastic human being, a giant among men."

Peter and his wife, Patricia Kennedy, visited Frank at his Palm Springs villa frequently.

Peter was even invited into what was called "the most exclusive club in Hollywood," the Rat Pack. It was Peter who discovered the script for the film *Ocean's 11* (1960), which endeared him all the more to the Rat Pack. There was one hold-out. Dean Martin never liked Peter but managed to conceal his distaste.

Finally, President Kennedy was elected, and Peter became a highly visible member of America's "Royal Family." It was Peter who introduced Frank to JFK, beginning an extremely close but troubled relationship that would have a short shelf life.

In later life, Peter admitted that it was he, not Frank, who arranged liaisons between President Kennedy and Marilyn Monroe. He brought them together at parties at his house in Santa Monica, which he shared with Pat. Peter also claimed that he was also the man who introduced Bobby Kennedy to Marilyn.

"Frank could turn on you in a minute," Peter said. "One New Year's Eve, Pat and I attended a party at his home in Beverly Hills, along with Robert Wagner and Natalie Wood. We visited so frequently Frank had a room set aside for us, where we kept some clothing. He also reserved a special room for us at his place in Palm Springs. After midnight, Frank wanted all of us to drive with him to Palm Springs. We were exhausted, and Pat told him we'd love to go but it would have to wait until morning. A terrible rainstorm had come up, and driving could be dangerous. Even so, Frank stormed out of the house and told us to go fuck ourselves. We couldn't get him on the phone the next morning. When we went to retrieve our clothing, a servant told us he had thrown all of our stuff into the pool. The message was loud and clear: you did it '*my way*' or else faced the open road."

The first months of the Kennedy administration were all too perfect for Frank, who felt he had a real "in" at the White House and with JFK in spite of his mob connections. When he learned that JFK was planning a short vacation in Palm Springs in 1962, Frank extended an invitation and even expanded his property to include

Clad in a sports shirt and slacks, **President Kennedy** (left) is photographed near the first tee of the Palm Beach Country Club on April 4, 1961. With him on the golf course is actor **Peter Lawford**, his brother-in-law and faithful companion.

After a drunken Peter fell asleep when Jack requested that he read the movie script for the upcoming film, *PT 109*, the president never asked him for advice about film scripts and Hollywood casting ever again. What he depended on Peter for was to supply him with a bevy of beauties on the West Coast.

Peter Dye, of golfing fame, lived next door to Peter in Santa Monica. He revealed that when JFK came to visit, "It was nothing but *La Dolce Vita*, a goddamn whorehouse. Jack Kennedy even hustled my wife and wanted to fly her to Hawaii. It was the most disgusting thing I've ever seen."

extra rooms.

But Bobby Kennedy loathed Frank, and bluntly informed his brother that he could not stay with the singer because of his notorious mob associations. "What great copy it would make for the press—the President of the United States sleeping in the same bed whose sheets were just warmed by Sam Giancana." JFK agreed, and the unwelcome task of informing Frank fell to Peter.

"What a horrible job, telling Frank in person that Jack Kennedy was turning down his invitation," Peter later said. "He might have killed me."

Instead of blaming Bobby Kennedy, the source of the rejection, Frank unfairly accused Peter of sabotaging the invitation. He told his fellow Rat Packers, "The cocksucker is dead meat in my freezer. If one of you wants to hang out with this faggot, feel free, but cut me out." Only Sammy Davis Jr. continued to see Peter in the years ahead.

In future Rat Pack movies such as *Robin and the 7 Hoods* or *4 for Texas*, Peter would be written out of the script.

Milt Ebbins, Peter's manager, claimed, "Peter was destroyed by Frank's rejection. He loved the man, although God knows why, and he relished being a member of the much-envied Rat Pack. Suddenly, he was kicked in the seat of his pants, landing on his ass out the door."

He later blamed Frank for the downward spiral of his career, claiming that it prevented him from getting respectable film roles. "Frank has effectively blacklisted me in Hollywood, and I desperately need to make money acting," Peter said.

Some sources have discounted the story about Frank cutting Peter out of his life forever because of the upset over JFK selecting Bing Crosby's house in Palm Springs over that of Frank's.

In a confessional mood, Ava told director John Huston that the real reason Frank cut Peter off was that the actor told the FBI that they should contact Frank and question him about the death of Marilyn Monroe. Allegedly, according to Ava, Peter told J. Edgar Hoover personally that, "Sinatra knows who ordered the death of Marilyn."

Rat Packers (*left to right*) **Frank Sinatra, Dean Martin, and Peter Lawford** joined Sammy Davis Jr. and Joey Bishop to film the 1962 *Sergeants 3,* essentially a remake of the famous 1939 *Gunga Din,* re-scripted for a setting in the American West.

Frank Sinatra took the Victor McLaglen role, with Martin in the Cary Grant part. Lawford replaced Douglas Fairbanks Jr., and Davis appeared in Sam Jaffe's originally titular supporting part.

After its initial run, *Sergeants 3* was never granted a release on home video. However, on the tenth anniversary of Frank's death, it was finally released on DVD as a single disc, and billed as "The Lost Sinatra Film."

Although Peter was sometimes good at keeping a secret, his loose lips to the FBI earned Frank's eternal animosity. "About the last thing Frank wanted in his life was to become implicated publicly with Marilyn and the mob, although a lot of shit was going on behind the scenes," said Sammy Davis Jr.

Author Michael Munn in his *Sinatra: The Untold Story,* revealed a startling conversation that was said to have occurred in London when he, along with Huston, visited the home of Ava. The year was 1974.

Reportedly, Ava told Huston and the writer that a drunken Peter had visited her in 1969, a year after Bobby Kennedy was assassinated in Los Angeles.

According to Ava, Peter claimed he'd received a mysterious late-night call, warning him that Marilyn Monroe had been the first on the list, then JFK, and finally Bobby. The gangster on the other end allegedly told Peter, "If you open your fucking mouth, you're next."

"Peter was in fear for his life," Ava claimed.

He encountered Frank on several occasions, but Frank would walk on by his former friend, never even giving him a stare with "those cold blue eyes," as Peter called them. Frank told friends such as Dean Martin or Joey Bishop, "Lawford is a God damn limey bum."

Still nostalgic for the good old days, Peter, during his declining years, made several thwarted attempts to see Frank. Once he flew to Las Vegas to catch Frank's opening night at Caesar's Palace. But three waiters removed him from the room. Frank had refused to go on if Peter was in the audience.

Peter had to endure the loss of another friend, the President himself, who was assassinated in Dallas that dreadful November in 1963. Not only that, but Peter's link to the Kennedy family through his wife, Pat, was crumbling.

Tired of his boozing and womanizing, and of constantly being broke, Patricia in 1966 filed for divorce, citing "irreconcilable differences."

"I've just been kicked out of the most famous family in the world," Peter told Sammy Davis Jr. "I expect the phone to stop ringing."

Their son, Christopher, was often around to witness some of the epic battles between Peter and Patricia. "My mother could shrink a man's balls with one glance," Christopher claimed. "She never remarried but settled for gay male friends and dysfunctional drinking buddies."

Haunted by the mysterious death of Marilyn Monroe during his post-Sinatra years, Peter descended into ill health and became a drug addict and alcoholic.

He came to a tragic end. He was rushed to Los Angeles' Cedars-Sinai Medical Center, the hospital of choice for stars, and he was already on the road to death. Both his liver and kidneys were rapidly failing. Since his blood could not clot, surgery was not possible. His doctors put him on life support in a vain attempt to detoxify him.

In December of 1984, he sank into a coma and remained there for four days and nights. But at 8:50am, on the morning of December 24, his body showed some sign of life. He jerked up in bed, as a death rattle escaped from his mouth. Blood spurted from his mouth, ears, and nose. Falling back, he was pronounced dead.

His body was cremated on Christmas Day. After being interred near the tomb of Marilyn Monroe, his ashes were removed in 1988 and scattered at sea since no one had paid the $7,000 owed in funeral expenses to the mortuary.

The *National Enquirer* purchased exclusive rights to cover the removal of Peter's ashes from his tomb and the scattering of them in the ocean, a final indignity after more than two decades of indignities.

When asked for a statement about Peter's death, Frank snapped at a reporter: "No comment."

Today, Peter's claim to fame does not reside in any of the easy-to-forget movies in which he starred, but in the role he filled as an Englishman who married into the Irish "First Family of America," the Kennedys.

Supposedly, he was the last person to speak on the phone to Marilyn Monroe, and he is forever immortalized as the speaker who introduced "the late" Marilyn Monroe to sing "Happy Birthday, Mister President" in 1962..

When he died, Peter was a relic of a bygone era in Hollywood, his glory days a memory from the distant past.

## *Frank Wanted to Know:*
# DID PETER AND JACKIE DO IT?

In the summer of 1966, Peter knew he might be making a mistake when he called Jackie Kennedy and asked her to join him for a vacation in Hawaii. His divorce from Pat had not negatively affected their relationship. Jackie not only accepted his invitation to Hawaii, she even suggested that they fly there together.

Peter asked his best friend and business manager, Milton Ebbins, if the trip would be all right, fearing that it might generate bad publicity. "Why not?" Ebbins asked. "Mrs. Kennedy will be traveling with her children, Caroline and John-John, and you'll be with Christopher and Sydney. Just call it a family affair."

From gossip, Lana Turner, Peter's former lover, heard that he would soon fly to Honolulu with Jackie. Lana took a dim view. "If Lee Radziwill wanted him, Mrs. Kennedy might also want Peter. After all, sisters sometimes go for the same guy. I hear Jackie has a high libido. I can personally vouch for the libido of John Kennedy."

Flying out of New York on June 6, Jackie arrived in San Francisco with her children, where she rendezvoused with Peter, his son Christopher, and his daughter Sydney for the ongoing flight to Hawaii.

A *paparazzo* snapped the arrival of this Kennedy/Lawford party departing from their plane in Honolulu. Pat had given permission for Peter to take their sons to Hawaii, but Ebbins hadn't informed her that Jackie would be along.

When Pat found out, Ebbins claimed she wasn't just boiling mad, she was livid. She'd told friends that she'd long suspected that Peter "had this thing for Jackie."

The so-called Hawaiian honeymoon of Jackie and Peter lasted for seven weeks. To keep up appearances, Jackie technically lived in an oceanfront house near the base of Diamond Head, which she rented for $3,000 a month. Peter's hideaway cottage on the grounds of the Hilton was just down the beach.

In Hawaii, Peter perfected the famous cigarette routine that Bette Davis and Paul Henreid did so well in *Now, Voyager* (1942). Over cocktails in the Hilton bar, he was seen placing two cigarettes in his mouth, lighting each of them, and then handing one to Jackie.

The only time Jackie and Peter were separated was when she took the children, with architect John Carl Warnecke, on an overnight camping trip. John-John fell into the fire and severely burned his buttocks, arms, and hands. A Secret Service agent, John Walsh, rushed him to a local hospital.

Writing for a local paper, reporter Gwen Holson tracked every public move she could of Peter and Jackie. She was hoping to sell a piece to a national magazine. "Throughout their vacation," Holson said, "Peter acted like Jackie's gallant husband. He took her everywhere, and he behaved like a father to her children. Lawford was very familiar with Hawaii, and he became Mrs. Kennedy's tour guide. He introduced her to all his friends, and they were great as a couple, dazzling everyone."

"Lawford even threw this big garden party for Mrs. Kennedy at the Kahala Hilton. *Tout* Honolulu turned out to greet her. Everybody wore their finest clothing, and we expected Mrs. Kennedy to turn up in an Oleg Cassini original. She arrived in a light beach shift with sandals."

"In front of everybody, Lawford hovered over Mrs. Kennedy, even taking her hand to guide her over to the next group of friends to show her off. Unlike that whispery Marilyn Monroe voice she used on camera, Mrs. Kennedy spoke in a normal voice.

"I know that Jackie spent a lot of time at the beachfront house Lawford had rented on Oahu. I paid a servant one hundred dollars for the lowdown. She virtually confirmed on the Bible that Mrs. Kennedy and Lawford slept together. Today, it would be front page tabloid news, but back then no respectable paper wanted to touch it."

"But rumors were flying over Honolulu, and I think many mainland newspapers made veiled references to reports of an affair between Lawford and Mrs. Kennedy. We now know that Jackie slept with Bobby. Why not Lawford? If you sleep with one brother-in-law, why not another?"

Peter, at this point in his life, was deeply troubled, and reportedly Jackie rallied to his side. He was worried now that he was cut off from the Kennedy clan, he would not be offered any more film roles, at least good ones. He admitted to Jackie and to others that he had been too imperial when he was the president's brother-in-law and had made a lot of enemies, including Frank Sinatra. He also feared that he could not provide for his children the way the Kennedys could their brood, and that his kids would lose respect for him.

"I'm going to find a life after the Kennedys, and I'm sure you will too." Jackie said that in front of other guests, as if she wanted other people to believe it. Few did. After the Kennedy connection, it was all downhill for Peter.

In Hawaii, Peter got to know Jackie as never before. Such prolonged intimacy between the two of them would never be repeated. In the future, Jackie would withdraw more and more from Peter upon hearing news of his alcoholism and drug taking.

"Jackie wasn't completely honest about herself," Peter said. "She doctored up her family background. She told social fibs to avoid having to make appearances. She would tell the press practically anything to get them off her back. She obviously had known about Jack's affairs. She told me she knew. She said she once caught him in the act."

When author Truman Capote heard about a possible Peter/Jackie affair, he said, "I'm not at all surprised. Jackie, dear heart that she is, believed in the revenge fuck. She'd always known that Peter supplied Hollywood actresses to Jack. By fucking Peter, she was probably getting even with Jack, even though his bullet-riddled body was in the grave."

**Peter Lawford** and **Jackie Kennedy** disembark from the jet plane that flew them from California to Honolulu for a "family reunion."

89

# Peter Lawford & the Death of Marilyn Monroe

*"Say good-bye to the President."*

—**Marilyn Monroe** to Peter Lawford, August 4, 1962

*"Frank Sinatra believed that the truth about Peter Lawford's role in the death of Marilyn Monroe would never be known. "The drunk seems to come up with a different story every time he recounts that night. I think much that he did was to conceal his own role in her death. I'm not saying he killed her. But I bet he sure as hell knows who did it."*

—**Fred Otash**

Fred Otash, a veteran cop in the L.A. Police Department who later became a private detective, claimed that Peter went to Marilyn's house on the day of her death after her body had been removed. When he entered with a pass key, he found the house deserted. Otash said. "He'd been instructed by Bobby Kennedy to remove all evidence that might link Marilyn with the Kennedys."

Peter's third wife, Deborah Gould, claimed, "Peter told me he was the first one there that morning before the police came. He never admitted that he stole her suicide note, but he didn't deny it either. I still believe to this day that he took it." Of course, many Monroe historians believe there was no suicide note, because Marilyn was actually murdered.

"A massive cover-up began after someone murdered Marilyn, and Peter was the first man on the job to do the dirty work for the Kennedys," Otash said. He asserted in his book that a slightly drunken Peter came to this house after he'd removed papers and a red diary and allowed him to look over the evidence. "You've done good, boy," Otash told him. "The Kennedys will owe you big time for this."

Otash never knew what Peter did with "the stash," including the diary, Otash claimed that he advised Peter to leave town at once to avoid questioning by the police. He claimed that Peter, with the evidence he gathered, hid out at Hyannis Port, where he stayed until the heat was off.

James Spada, in his biography of Lawford, claimed that "Peter, for his part, was never put on tape as saying anything other than that Marilyn's death was a tragic accident that left him deeply remorseful that he hadn't gone to her aid immediately. He insisted until his death that Bobby Kennedy was on the East Coast the night Marilyn died, and that the talk of affairs between Marilyn and the Kennedy brothers was nothing but 'nonsense.'"

When Frank heard these denials, he said, "Has anything connected in any way to Marilyn's death been such a bald-faced lie?"

The last photograph of the once glamorous **Marilyn Monroe**

Throughout the rest of his life, In spite of offers to write his own autobiography and an offer of $100,000 from the *National Enquirer* for serialization rights to the book, Peter refused to talk about Marilyn and the Kennedys. Even when he became desperate for cash, he still refused to do so.

In an enigmatic 1984 interview with *The Los Angeles Times*, Peter backed down somewhat from his original statement. "If the stories about Marilyn, Jack, and Bobby were true, I can't bring myself to reveal anything to the press."

# Frank Sinatra's Mobster Mambo

## HOT TROPICAL NIGHTS WITH THE MAFIA

In the 1940s, after the war, "*La Voz*" (Frank Sinatra) decided that "Havana, not Chicago, is my kind of town." Before Castro's revolution, he discovered a world of tropical nights that had earned for the Cuban capital the title of "Paris of the Americas." High rollers could mambo their way through the casinos, attend sex shows, followed by bordello visits that lasted until dawn. There was a constant stream of beautiful girls, or else beautiful boys, depending on a client's preference.

Frank lived it up in Havana and was even assigned a young boy, "Tito" Perez, whose only job it was to light his Montecristo cigars. Over a series of several of Frank's visits, this same boy grew into a handsome young man. Frank liked him and assigned him to protect Ava Gardner during their fifteen-day honeymoon in Havana.

Unexpectedly, Frank had to interrupt his honeymoon to fly to Las Vegas. With the understanding that Tito's job involved "protecting Ava," the young man later recalled, "Frank had hardly left for the airport when she came on to me. She looked like Miss America. Perfect body. Great tits. Beautiful face. We made love all afternoon. But I was afraid if Frank found out, he would have someone in the Mob cut off my dick. Fortunately, that didn't happen, as a thousand post-Ava women can testify."

"Cuban teenagers today still speak about Sinatra," claimed Bill Lezzi, staff writer for *The Philadelphia Inquirer*. "They listen as their grandparents and parents play his LPs and talk about his music. His photos can be found at the Hotels Nacional and Capri. A nearly life-size cardboard cutout of him greets diners on the rooftop restaurant of the Hotel Seville. Cuban TV occasionally airs his life story. Sinatra is seen by more Habañeros now than when he used to visit."

# HAVANA IN THE OLD DAYS

*"Sinatra told me he'd rather be a Mafia don than president of the United States."*

—**Eddie Fisher**

*"Look, I'm playing with the big boys down here in Havana. Don't ruin it for me. I ain't doing nothing but having fun with plenty of sex. These guys in the mob are great."*

—**Frank Sinatra** to his press agent George Evans

*"I love bums that America selects as its heroes. Take the two draft-dodgers, the left-wing Frank Sinatra and the right-wing John Wayne. Sinatra also brown-noses the Mafia. He's a child molester and has even been arrested for that back in 1938."*

—Columnist **Westbrook Pegler** (speaking off the record) at a private dinner

When JFK was elected president in 1960, Frank Sinatra assumed he'd exert indirect power, and enjoy some degree of protection, thanks to his friendship with the president. From the very first, Frank urged JFK to quietly arrange the assassination of **Fidel Castro,** (*pictured above*), the communist Cuban dictator. For a while, Frank thought JFK would follow his recommendation.

*"Any report I fraternized with goons and racketeers is a vicious lie. I've known some guys who aren't saints, but that's about it."*

—**Frank Sinatra**

Their mutual girlfriend, Judith Campbell Exner, even carried envelopes between Kennedy and her other boyfriend, gangster Sam Giancana, often traveling by train from Washington to Chicago. JFK and especially his brother, Bobby, quickly realized that Frank really wanted to bring the Mob back to Cuba as a means of restoring the lucrative gambling and prostitution of pre-revolutionary Havana.

*"Mrs. Frank Sinatra is the happiest gal in the world."*
—**Ava Gardner,** referring to herself

Ironically, some historians claim that it was Castro who arranged the assassination of JFK in Dallas in November of 1963.

"Oh, Ava. She's just precious. What a charming thing to say as she gives Frank his much-deserved next black eye."
—**Lana Turner**

The war had ended. It was 1947. Frank Sinatra's long-time affair with both the Mafia and with Havana was about to begin. But in Los Angeles, he first had to convince his wife, Nancy, that he'd gotten rid of another love, a blonde goddess by the name of Lana Turner.

Before leaving for Havana, he faced Nancy, telling her that his affair with Lana was over. "It's *kaput*! I don't know what I was thinking. I must have been out of my mind. You're a good woman, a fine wife, and a great mother. I don't know how I could have done this to you. My heart is filled with love but sometimes it doesn't beat in the right places."

"Lana doesn't love me, and I certainly don't love her," he claimed. "She's self-enchanted. The only person Lana loves is herself. She's all glitz and glamour. There's not a real woman lurking there behind all that make-up. Lana is nothing but a starry-eyed extravaganza, nothing real about her. She's completely vain. She took advantage of me and played on my weakness. Deep in my heart I feel a loneliness. I was vulnerable."

"Frank," Nancy told him. "You were always such a bullshitter, even back in Hoboken."

Although she was reluctant at first, he got Nancy to agree to fly to Acapulco to meet him there on Valentine's Day for a second honeymoon. "Just call me the romantic type."

He promised her that there would be no women on his upcoming trip to New York and Miami, where he had professional obligations, such as singing on the radio or giving a benefit concert for needy children. After Miami, he was going to fly to Havana to give a special concert "for the boys."

"In Havana, I'll be a good boy. I'll say my prayers at night and be in bed—alone—by ten o'clock."

A chauffeur arrived to take him to the airport. The driver couldn't help but notice that Nancy turned her face from him when he tried to give her a farewell smooch. He ended up kissing her hair instead of her face.

In Los Angeles on January 31, 1947, Frank had requested a gun permit and was granted one. He was fingerprinted at the time.

Before he left California, he had a German Walther pistol in his holster which was concealed by his jacket. "I felt like a real gangster for the first time," he said.

In New York, Frank had sexual intercourse with four or five prostitutes, including an African-American hooker and a Chinese "Suzie Wong" type beauty.

Sexually satisfied, at least for that afternoon, he flew to Miami where he'd been invited to stay with the Fischetti brothers, three Mafia hoodlums, at their luxurious villa on Allison Island.

The brothers had arranged for three of the most

In spite of the smiles on their faces, there was no love lost between the Cuban dictator, **Fulgencio Batista** (*left figure in photo above*) and the U.S. president of the 1950s, war hero **Dwight D. Eisenhower**. Ike's advisers kept him aware of the corruption in Havana, as brothels flourished, police collected protection money, and the Mob moved in to share the gambling proceeds in the form of kickbacks to Batista.

Ike was furious when Batista announced that he would grant a gaming license to any American who invested at least $200,000 in a nightclub, and at least $1 million in a casino. Based on this, Ike feared a wave of money laundering as a means of avoiding U.S. income tax.

A Republican, Ike was urged by his backers to maintain friendly relationships with the dictator. At the end of Ike's second term, U.S. companies owned some 40 percent of Cuban sugar lands and nearly all its cattle ranches. Not only that, but they owned 90 percent of the mines, 80 percent of the utilities, and nearly all the oil industry. U.S. products counted for two-thirds of all Cuban imports.

desirable and expensive call girls on Miami Beach to share Frank's bedroom at night. "Nothing is too good for our boy Frankie," Joe Fischetti said.

Before greeting Frank in Florida, the brothers had returned from attending their beloved Al Capone's funeral in Chicago.

Charles Fischetti, nicknamed "Prince Charlie," also called himself "Dr. Fisher," claiming to be an art collector. His younger brother, Rocco, claimed he specialized in antiques. An enemy of his said, "Yes, antique coffins."

The third brother, Joe, at least according to an FBI report, was "the least intelligent of the brothers. He's used mainly as an errand boy in their extortion ring." What the report didn't say was that Joe was the best pimp around when it came to rounding up beautiful young women for sex, as Frank was soon to find out.

Frank Sinatra even appealed to the U.S. Supreme Court in an attempt to prevent questioning from the New Jersey State Commission on Investigation. Losing his appeal, he was advised by his attorneys to testify. He agreed to do that but only after midnight in Trenton on February 17, 1970, hoping to avoid reporters.

He was asked about his association with gangster **Meyer Lansky**, pictured above. Frank conceded that "I've met him." When asked to identify the mob boss, Frank said, "I read in the papers that he was an undesirable."

Although Frank had hung out extensively with both Lansky and Lucky Luciano in Havana, he claimed that he was unaware that Luciano was a member of *La Cosa Nostra*. After reviewing Frank's testimony, the senators concluded that they had been stonewalled. "If we are to believe Sinatra, he never even heard of the Mob," said a senator.

Before leaving for Cuba, Frank was driven to Hallandale, north of Miami Beach, where he sang a medley of ten of his favorite songs at the Colonial Inn. This swank gambling casino was owned by gangsters Joe Adonis and Jewish mobster Meyer Lansky. Frank submitted no bill for his performance.

Joe and Frank had known each other since their days on the streets of Hoboken when they'd stolen hubcaps together. On Allison Island, Joe asked Frank, "How would you like to hook up with Lucky Luciano in Havana?"

Frank was thrilled. "I'd love that," he told Joe. "Lucky has been a hero of mine since I was a boy."

No gangster, not even Capone, had ever been as powerful as Charles ("Lucky") Luciano (1897-1962). Although nicknamed Lucky, he didn't always have good luck. In the 1920s, he had run New York's bordello business, taking in illegal profits of a million dollars a year, a vast fortune in those days.

Luciano became known as "The Boss of Bosses" when he eliminated the competition, two rival crime bosses, Joe Masseria and Salvatore Maranzano.

Lucky's luck ran out in 1936 when he was indicted and convicted of ninety counts of extortion and "direction of harlotry."

Released from prison in 1945, he was deported to Italy where he ran the International Crime Syndicate. He directed the shipments of millions of dollars worth of heroin into the United States.

In Miami, Joe revealed to Frank that Luciano had returned from Italy and was trying to establish a base of operations in Cuba, so he would be closer to his business interests in America.

Only a year after the end of World II, *gangsterismo*, a

word coined by U.S. media, ruled the night in Havana, the capital of decadence in the Western Hemisphere.

Mafia kingpins and Hollywood stars, such as Errol Flynn, even Lana Turner, rubbed elbows in the casinos.

The parade of movie stars and entertainers continued into the 1950s, including some who preferred beautiful young boys—Tyrone Power, Marlon Brando, Liberace, and Cesar Romero. Dianne Carroll, Debbie Reynolds, Mamie van Doren arrived, but a really big name who flew in was Elizabeth Taylor herself.

"The sun never rose on an endless party," said expat Ernest Hemingway. "Paris in the 1920s cast only a dim shadow over Havana in the 1950s."

As for big-name entertainers, Havana was Queen of the Night. Appearing or about to appear were such show stoppers as Sarah Vaughan, Xavier Cugat, Abbe Lane, Tony Bennett, Nat King Cole, Maurice Chevalier, and even Edith Piaf. While in Havana, Frank would sign a contract to sing at the Sans Souci.

On the ocean-splashed Malecón, Lansky even hired Ginger Rogers to star at his Copa Room. The Mafia don later said, "She can wiggle her ass, but she can't sing a god damn note."

President Dwight D. Eisenhower referred to Cuba as "The Devil's Playground."

Luciano had ordered a convening of the mob in Havana, a kind of underworld convention, a scene reminiscent of George Raft's appearance in *Some Like It Hot*, with Marilyn Monroe, a picture yet to be made. The last such mobster convention had occurred in 1932 in Chicago.

Every gangster arriving in Havana had big dreams and a hope for some involvement in the money flowing out of Cuba. Of course, Fidel Castro and Che Guevara would turn these mob's aspirations for big money into a revolutionary nightmare.

Luciano was using Frank as a cover, claiming that all these mobsters were gathering in Havana to "honor that skinny little boy from Hoboken." Frank would later provide entertainment for them at the Hotel Nacional, "singing my heart out to all my pals," he told Joe Fischetti.

On the morning of his departure for Havana, Frank breakfasted with the Fischetti brothers, having kicked the hookers out of his bedroom when he'd finished with them.

"Prince Charlie" told Frank that he and his brothers were going to carry attaché cases onto the plane—"a gift to Lucky." To his astonishment Frank learned these cases, one of which he was asked to carry himself, contained $2 million dollars in one-hundred dollar denominations. That would be the equivalent of $16 million in today's currency. Amazingly, Frank did not balk at this assignment. The millions were profits from Luciano's illegal operations within the United States.

With the Fischetti brothers, Frank departed for Havana, board-

In testimony before crime commissions, Frank one time conceded that he (perhaps) had shaken the hand of gangster **Lucky Luciano**. Actually they had a deep and abiding friendship.

Before Senator Estes Kefauver's committee lawyers, Frank said, "When I am introduced to someone, I was brought up to shake their hand without investigating their past."

Later, he told columnist Hedda Hopper, "Even if I'd caught his name when introduced, I probably wouldn't have associated it with the underworld character. In Havana, I sat down at a table with him and other people for about fifteen minutes. Then I got up and went back to my hotel. When such innocent acts are distorted, you can't win."

ing a TWA DC-3 airplane at the Miami International Airport. He asked the brothers, "Does Howard Hughes still own all the stock in TWA? If he finds out I'm on board, he'll order the pilot to nose-dive us into a sea of sharks."

He was photographed wearing a tweed sports jacket in his favorite color of orange which seemed to compete with the brightness of the Cuban sun. He was carrying a heavy suitcase, as were the Fischetti brothers, Rocco, Joe, and "Prince Charlie." All three brothers wore very dark sunglasses, and each had a pinkie ring with a very large diamond that even Elizabeth Taylor would have coveted.

Frank's instruction was to carry his Mafia cash to Luciano's suite. The Fischetti brothers came with him to make sure he carried out his mission. This was the beginning of Frank carrying mob money from the United States to Havana.

Many myths and legends grew out of his trip to Havana. The most reliable source of what really happened was "Johnny" Garcia, whose real name was Juan. He was assigned to take care of Frank during his stay on island. On orders from Meyer Lansky himself, Frank was to be "given anything the fucker wants—*and I mean anything.*"

When interviewed by Darwin Porter, bureau chief of *The Miami Herald* in Key West in 1959, the aging Garcia provided a "blow-by-blow" description of what Frank was up to in Havana.

"He went crazy, just plain crazy. *Loco*, man. In just a few days he wanted to experience all the pleasures Havana had to offer. But I loved the guy, and guided him through all his subsequent trips. He was the world's most generous tipper. But some of his requests, and practically nearly everything he did, was a bit dangerous. He sure loved his *putas*. He was like a man released from jail after ten years of doing nothing but fucking boy ass."

At the Hotel Nacional, two bodyguards escorted Frank up to Luciano's penthouse suite where the gangster was waiting for them and eager to get his $2 million. After dismissing the Fischettis, treating them as no more than delivery boys, Luciano settled in for a long talk with Frank. The two men bonded at once, their blossoming friendship cemented at first because of mutual Sicilian ancestors who came to America from the same little village of Lercara Freddi.

Luciano invited Frank to his seaside mansion in suburban Miramar overlooking the sea. For their spaghetti, the gangster made *salsa di pomidoro* for Frank. "That's the best tomato sauce I've ever had in my life. I thought only my mother, Dolly, knew how to make tomato sauce."

Even though he was not permitted to come back into the United States, Luciano had a dream of remaining the *capo de tutti capi* or the boss of bosses, ruling his empire from Cuba. One by one the delegates to the Mafia convention flew into Havana, including Albert (The Executioner)

Although Frank before senate committes claimed that he did not know that **Willie Moretti** was a member of the Mob, the gangster always said, "I discovered Frankie and gave him his first big break."

Actually, Frank knew Moretti intimately, and Nancy Barbato, Frank's first wife, was a cousin of one of Moretti's senior henchmen.

In the late 1940s and early 50s, Moretti's mental deterioration worsened, resulting from syphilis. The Mob decided to kill him. On October 4, 1951, three of Albert Anastasia's hit men took Moretti to lunch, then shot him repeatedly in the chest. Actually, Dean Martin and Jerry Lewis were originally scheduled to have lunch with Moretti on that fateful day, until Jerry came down with the mumps and cancelled.

Anatasia and Joey (Bananas) Bonanno.

Frank got a kiss on both cheeks from his longtime friend, the gangster Willie Moretti. Moretti, the bookmaker, extortionist, and murderer always claimed, "I discovered Sinatra in a roadhouse in New Jersey."

Meyer Lansky was on hand to greet Luciano, who was in town to purchase a $150,000 interest in the Hotel Nacional casino.

Of all these gangsters, many of them Italian, it was a Jewish member, Lansky, who provided the genius behind the mob.

In just a few years, Lansky had managed to put the corrupt government of the brutal dictator Fulgencio Batista in his pocket.

Luciano had scheduled Frank to entertain the mobsters in a private banqueting hall at the Nacional. When he entered the room, Frank was astonished to find that all these battle-tough veterans of heinous crimes wanted his autograph.

In addition to Frank and Luciano, Ralph Capone, brother of Chicago's notorious Al Capone, was also at the party. Other "honored" guests included a dishonorable gathering of such thugs as Frank Costello, Tommy Lucchese, Vito Genovese, and Joe Adonis.

Frank sang Luciano's favorites, "Almost Like Being in Love" and "Stella by Starlight."

In a strange footnote to his Havana hijinxs, Frank arranged a meeting between Robert ("Chiri") Mendoza, one of a quartet of Cubans who was building the luxurious Havana Hilton. A close friend of Batista himself, "Chiri" came from a family who owned the baseball franchise of the highly successful Almendares Tigers. He wanted Frank to entice Joe DiMaggio to come to Havana to discuss a business proposition.

**Joe DiMaggio** (*left*) and **Frank Sinatra** were devotees of the show-girls of Havana, enjoying their charms on stage and their boudoir skills afterward. But when Frank tried to get DiMaggio hired by the casinos of Havana, the baseball great turned him down. He was much more concerned with his image than Frank and didn;'t want to be linked to the Mob. "I can't know anybody I'm not supposed to." he told Frank.

Lured by the prospect of a bevy of showgirls, as promised by Frank, the baseball great arrived in Cuba. But the offer pitched by Chiri was later rejected. The hotel king wanted the former Yankee centerfielder to be the "greeter" at the new Hilton Casino. "Name your price," Chiri promised.

In spite of the lucrative offer, DiMaggio turned him down. As Chiri later told Frank, "The fool refused to endorse a joint where gambling or liquor was offered. He told me, 'Young boys look up to me as a kind of American hero. I can't do anything to corrupt the youth of America.' What bullshit? While in Havana, he joined the rest of the Yankee whoremongers."

The Mob wanted Joe DiMaggio to patronize their joints—"It's money in the bank," said crime syndicate boss Frank Costello. DiMaggio never saw a tab in any of the Mob-controlled dives he visited, including El Morocco or the Copacabana.

Before the Castro revolution, Frank had planned to become more intimately linked with Havana, as he was listed as a stockholder and possible board member for the projected Hotel Monte Carlo, which was slated to become the most spectacular in the Caribbean.

Frank's plan was to host a television show from the Monte Carlo to be broadcast every week throughout the United States "featuring only the biggest names in entertainment." He also wanted to launch a Cuban movie industry based on profits generated by the TV show. The dream was

The Mob, in fact, set up an account for DiMaggio in 1948 at the Bowery Bank. Every time he appeared at one of the mob-run clubs, a thousand dollars (quite a tidy sum back then) was deposited anonymously into his account.

never to be realized, of course.

One of the manifestos that emerged from that Mafia conference was that a fellow gangster, Benjamin (Bugsy) Siegel, had to go. Lansky personally ordered his death. Bugsy was later shot in the face in California and died instantly by assassins unknown.

The assassination was ordered when it was discovered that a lot of Mafiosi dollars had been siphoned off to Bugsy's private bank account in Zurich.

The gangsters knew they'd be safe from press coverage. "Word got around that what was goin' on at the Nacional was off limits," Luciano revealed to his biographers. "A paper could lose its license to publish if it printed something it wasn't supposed to."

The blackout of news locally did not apply to Robert Ruark, the syndicated American news-paper columnist who was the first to write about Frank's arrival in Havana. In a memo to his executive editor at the *New York World-Telegram*, Ruark claimed that he'd spoken privately with Larry Larrea, the general manager of the Nacional, who informed him that Frank and Luciano were staging orgies in their mutually shared suite. Larrea had advised the columnist not to go upstairs and pound on their door. "There's a lot of women up there right now. I don't think they want company." The manager also warned Ruark not to file his stories at the Havana office of Western Union. "You don't want to wind up with a 'knot' on your head, or something worse."

At the Nacional, a room service waiter told Ruark that he served breakfast to Frank, Luciano, and Lansky in the same hotel suite. "They seemed to be talking very seriously but shut up when I came in."

In one column, entitled "Shame, Sinatra," Ruark wrote that Frank's constant companion in Havana, in public and in private, was Luciano. The public thought he was still in exile in Sicily. The columnist claimed that Frank was surrounded by "Luciano's bodyguards and a rich collec-tion of gamblers and highbinders. The friendship was beautiful. They were seen together at the race track, the gambling casino, and at special parties." What Ruark didn't say was that all those special parties were actually sex orgies.

In a news story that went across the country, Ruark filed this comment:

"If Mr. Sinatra wants to mob up with the likes of Lucky Luciano, the chastened panderer and permanent deportee from the United States, that seems to be a matter for Mr. Sinatra to thrash out with the millions of kids who live by his every bleat. This curious desire to cavort among the scum is possibly permissible among citizens who are not peddling sermons to the nation's youth and may even be allowed to a mealy mouthed celebrity if he is smart enough to confine his social tolerance to a hotel room. But Mr. Sinatra, the self-confessed savior of the country's small fry, by virtue of his lectures on clean living and love-thy-neighbor, his movie shorts on tolerance, and his frequent dabblings into the do-good department of politics, seems to be setting a most peculiar example for his hordes of pimply, shrieking slaves, who are alleged to regard him with the same awe as a practicing Mohammedan for the Prophet."

Ruark went overboard in suggesting that Frank was Luciano's "boyfriend." They did share the same suite and were seen walking around nude together in those quarters. But during Frank's stay with Luciano, they had at least twenty showgirls coming and going.

A servant in Miramar reported seeing Luciano and Frank swimming nude together, but that hardly proved sexual contact.

During Frank's stay with Luciano in the suite at the Nacional, a nun arrived in the lobby with a dozen Girl Scouts, who wanted to present Frank with an award for his music. Through a series of mishaps, a bellhop took them to Frank's suite and even used a passkey to let this group inside. For reasons not known, the bellhop didn't even knock on the door to the suite or call up for permission to enter.

In *Havana Nocturne*, T.J. English wrote: "When the Girl Scouts entered the suite, there were bottles on the floor, lingerie was hanging from lampshades, and the air was filled with the stench of stale perfume. Sinatra entered the front room in a robe and silk scarf as if nothing were wrong. The ruse was exposed when four naked bodies fell giggling into the front room. The nun and her charges quickly left the suite in a state of shock."

Larrea later was almost fired for allowing this innocent, virginal group to enter the suite occupied by whore-mongering Luciano and Frank. Ruark referred to their suite as, "the last stop before Hades."

Sex for Sale might have been the motto of pre-Castro Havana, and Frank enjoyed "every hour there," as he later confessed. Prostitution thrived, especially in the Barrio de Colón. Southern men from such states as Mississippi and Alabama came seeking black prostitutes, a pleasure that was actually illegal in their homeland. One whorehouse advertised, "There is no human sexual desire we can't satisfy."

When he was in Havana, Frank was the best customer at Casa Marina, the most elegant bordello in the Caribbean, which hired only first-rate showgirls, remembered today as "the most beautiful in the business."

Look-alikes Ava Gardner, Betty Grable, and Lana Turner were heavy favorites. It was the most sanitary whorehouse in Havana, with two nurses on 24-hour duty to check the health of each of the prostitutes. These nurses also checked the health of male clients, and performed a genital inspection on each customer before the patrons were allowed into the private rooms with the young women in all colors.

In a report to J. Edgar Hoover in Washington, a Secret FBI agent, working in Havana, wired his chief that shapely call girls had been flown in by the Fischetti brothers from Miami. Why Joe wanted to import hookers from Miami when Havana was thick with them remains an unsolved mystery.

Out by the airport, the Mambo bordello catered to passengers arriving and departing. Many customers wanted a girl the moment they flew in and also another farewell fuck before their departure. Frank was said to have been a good customer. The Mambo specialized in fourteen-year-old virgins, many of whose maidenheads were broken by Frank himself.

For a flat fee of one hundred dollars, a virgin could be deflowered. Somehow the madam here was known for breaking in young girls from the countryside before sending them off to the other bordellos in Havana.

"We had three soundproof rooms for obvious reasons," said the madam. "Frank always preferred a soundproof room. When it

**Dorothy Dandridge,** (*depicted above*) was wildly successful when she completed a one-month run at Lefty Clark's San Souci in Havana. Frank secretly flew into Havana to discuss a similar appearance for himself with the club's owners. He asked the African-American singer and actress if he could visit her in her suite. He not only visited her, but remained there for the remainder of his time in Havana.

His friend, Peter Lawford, had described the delights of Dandridge to him, and Frank wanted to sample her charms. Dating across "the color line" for a prominent entertainer was risky in the 1950s, as Peter learned, but Frank found that in Havana it was no problem at all.

Dandridge confessed to Frank that she taught Peter how to like chitlings—that is, until he found out they were the intestines of a hog. Afrter a long weekend of love-making, the beautiful, coffee-colored star told Frank she had to return to the United States "where I'll be back trying to crack the Jim Crow barrier."

came to women, he had a violent streak in him. If he was like many of my other male clients, he liked to hear a girl squeal during penetration. I think it flatters their male egos. I used to order my young charges to scream even if getting penetrated by a Japanese businessman."

Joe Fischetti took Frank to see the notorious Superman at the Shanghai. The star of the show, El Toro, came on stage boasting a fourteen-inch and very thick penis. He was a tall, slender Cuban of African descent. In addition to his appendage, he made a striking appearance in a scarlet red cape—nothing else.

On Saturday nights he appeared on a trapeze stark nude with an erection swinging high over the heads of the stunned patrons, his monstrous penis flapping in the wind. Three beautiful women lay nude on cots before him. One by one he penetrated each of the women.

In *The Godfather, Part II*, Don Michael Corleone is pictured entering this club and staring at the stage with a group of American mobsters. What they were watching was never identified, but the historical inference was that the infamous El Toro was the centerpiece of their attention.

What the audience didn't know was that the most celebrated heterosexual seducer in all of Cuba was actually gay, preferring to sodomize young boys, many of whom he sent to the hospital with internal bleeding.

In the years to come, Frank saw another sex shows. The year was 1957, and the star of one exhibition was none other than John F. Kennedy, the Senator from Massachusetts.

JFK had been brought to Havana by his close friend, Senator George Smathers of Florida. Kennedy would visit the city whenever he could over a period of the next eighteen months before he sought the presidency.

The purpose of Kennedy's first visit ostensibly was to call on Earl E.T. Smith, the millionaire stockbroker who had been appointed U.S. ambassador to Cuba.

JFK's real purpose was to indulge in orgies. Kennedy also wanted to call on Smith's wife, Florence, a former blond model once known as Florence Pritchard. He and Florence had been having a sometimes affair ever since they began dating at New York's Stork Club in 1944.

Cuban friends of Senator Smathers, including Frank

**Ava Gardner** was called "the world's greatest beauty." But in the golden age of movie-making, the tabloids, which documented her steamy private life, had a lot more to say than that.

Studio packaged, Ava was one of the last of the great Hollywood sex goddesses. But studio chiefs Louis B. Mayer went ballistic trying to keep her personal scandals from destroying her career. "Unless he was a gay blade," said an MGM studio publicist, "every red-blooded male who ever saw an Ava Gardner movie wanted to take her to bed."

Having married Ava, Frank Sinatra was familiar with her charms. Perhaps unknown to him, so was his friend, JFK, who had had a brief fling with her after the war.

Ever since his election as senator from Massachusetts in December of 1957, **John F. Kennedy** had been a devotee of the glories of Havana. Of course, once he became president and Fidel Castro swept into power, the relationship between the U.S. and Cuba grew so tense that the world was almost plunged into war.

Kennedy tried to forget all the happy nights he'd spent in Havana. Frank did, too, expressing his "hatred and disgust with Castro and his government."

When JFK was assassinated in November of 1963 in Dallas, Frank told friends that "Sam Giancana was behind it.. I can't prove it but I know it to be true."

Ragano and Henry and Santo Trafficante, agreed to import Havana's shapeliest showgirls for an orgy at a special suite at Trafficante's Hotel Comodoro, a beachside hotel in Miramar where Luciano lived.

Unknown to Kennedy and Smathers, the suite was outfitted with a two-way secret mirror that allowed anyone willing to pay $500 to watch celebrities in action.

Frank was in town, and he was well known to Trafficante who invited him out to see the future U.S. president in action. Ironically, Frank was scheduled for a private dinner with JFK later that night. He'd met him two years before.

Frank later told Rat Packers, "Jack is not much of a stud. He lies on his back and lets the gal do all the work."

"For God's sake," Sammy Davis Jr. said to Frank, "the guy's got a bad back."

Many movie stars, including on one occasion Joe DiMaggio, were seen having sex by high-rolling voyeurs. Lana Turner and Errol Flynn were also secretly viewed, separately, with partners, in the throes of passion.

"I could kick myself in the ass that I didn't secretly film Kennedy in action," Trafficante later recalled. "Do you know what something like that would be worth?"

By February 14, the day Frank was supposed to fly to Acapulco to meet with Nancy, he was held over in Havana because Luciano had planned a special orgy for him with hookers flown in from Chicago.

Frank sent Nancy a wire: YOU WILL ALWAYS BE MY VALENTINE.

When he finally arrived in Mexico, Nancy greeted him with the news. "I was pregnant, but I aborted our child."

That action inspired a scene in *Godfather II* when Michael Corleone is informed by his wife, Kay, that she did not have a miscarriage. "An abortion, Michael, just like our marriage is an abortion."

Frank was shocked at the extent of coverage his visit to Havana had received in the press. Federal authorities, including the FBI, began to learn of Luciano's plans, which later led to the government of the United States pressuring Cuba to deport the gangland boss.

Columnist Lee Mortimer led the attack on Frank, and was a key figure in forever linking the singer to the mob. Frank's hatred of Mortimer grew day by day, as he plotted ways of silencing him. Johnny Roselli even suggested that Mortimer be "wiped off the map." But Frank knew too many fingers of suspicion would point at him.

Mortimer not only attacked Frank because of his mob links, but became the chief critic of his music and movies.

Two views of **Senator George Smathers**, Florida senator between 1951 and 1969. On left, he's seen relaxing with his close friend **Jack Kennedy** *(right figure in left photo)*.

Smathers, who maintained close ties with pre-Castro Cuba as the staunchly anti-communist senator from Florida, served as JFK's unofficial guide to the nocturnal pleasures of the Cuban capital when they traveled there together.

While Smathers and Kennedy were in town, Santo Trafficante Jr., the most powerful Mafioso in Batista-era Cuba, told his henchman "to give Kennedy and Smathers whatever their little hearts desire."

But the Mob later soured on JFK, and suspicions arose that in some way, Trafficante, along with Sam Giancana, were involved in the President's assassination. However, these allegations, though oft repeated, have not been proven.

After seeing Frank's latest movie, *It Happened in Brooklyn*, Mortimer claimed that the picture "bogs down under the miscast Frank (Lucky) Sinatra, smirking and trying to play a leading man."

"*It Happened in Brooklyn* is a terrible, terrible picture," Mortimer said. "Stay away. Also stay clear of the cheap hoodlums he befriends. As for his fans, they are imbecilic, moronic, screemie-meemie autograph kids."

"If you don't quit knocking me and my fans, I'm gonna knock your brains out," Frank warned the journalist. This was no idle threat.

Frank tried to get his press agent George Evans to get an affidavit from a young man who claimed that Mortimer performed fellatio on him. "I just talked to the guy," Frank shouted at Evans. "They did it last week."

In spite of Frank's shouts, Evans persistently refused to carry out the singer's demand.

Alarmed at what Mortimer had written about his mob connections in Havana, Frank encountered the columnist on April 8, 1947 at Ciro's in Hollywood. He came right up to the reporter's table. "You're a fucking homosexual." He then struck Mortimer in the face. The journalist was grabbed by two of Frank's burly bodyguards who held the columnist down, as Frank pounded him with his Hoboken-trained fists.

"I'll kill you," Frank shouted. "I'll kill you!"

Nat Dallinger, a photographer for King Features Syndicate, tried to come to Mortimer's aid but he could not hold back Frank's assault. Mortimer was being held down until the beating stopped. It was Dallinger who called reporters to cover the incident. He also delivered the badly beaten Mortimer to the West Hollywood Emergency Hospital.

The story of Frank's attack held the American public spellbound. "If President Eisenhower himself had been assassinated, it wouldn't have gotten this kind of coverage," said an outraged Louis B. Mayer, who had been urging Frank to "settle this goddamn mess-and soon—or you'll never work another day at MGM."

Later Frank charged that Mortimer started the fight by calling him a "dago bastard," but eyewitnesses countered that that was a lie.

The police arrested Frank and charged him with assault and battery. His gun permit was revoked.

The columnist sued Frank for $25,000 but settled for $9,000 and an apology.

In addition to the settlement, Frank ran up legal bills totaling $25,000. All in all, in today's dollars that would be worth about $100,000 out of pocket.

When he sued Frank, Mortimer received death threats from the mob.

In her memoirs, Nancy Sinatra Jr., wrote: "Lee Mortimer was the guy who began a fifty-year smear that cost Dad some important jobs and caused the family much heartache. Some applauded my father for teaching Mortimer a lesson he deserved."

In spite of the daughter's defense, the district attorney's office concluded that no slur against Frank had been made and that Mortimer had not provoked the assault. Later Frank was forced to back down, admitting that Mortimer had not made the dago slur at all.

"Frank is his own worst enemy," Evans later said. "He's losing fans every day and may soon become a has-been."

Even after the beating, Mortimer continued to attack Frank, who also spread rumors about the journalist's homosexual life. At one point, Frank claimed he had evidence that "Mortimer is fucking Clyde Tolson, the boyfriend of J. Edgar Hoover. Hoover should hear about this and turn his FBI agents onto that shithead instead of me."

*Variety* claimed, "It looks as if Frankie Boy has taken on the whole Hearst organization."

Even a friendly columnist like Earl Wilson in New York wrote that Frank shouldn't have attacked Mortimer. Wilson claimed, "The Kid has blown his wig. He's acting like a cornball."

The Hearst papers continued to go after him, and Frank finally called Marion Davies, the long-time mistress of William Randolph Hearst. Hearst was eighty-four years old at the time, and his health was failing. Davies, too, hated Lee Mortimer, and she invited Frank for a social call with her once vigorous lover.

The press baron and Frank had tea, and Hearst agreed to "call off my hound dogs—you've suffered enough. Besides, I like your music."

That night, Frank called George Evans, as he'd gone alone to see the mogul. The press agent was eager to learn the verdict. "I smoothed things over with His Majesty. On the way out, I visited Marion in her bedroom and threw her a mercy fuck for helping me."

\*\*\*

Havana continued to be a favorite destination of Frank's. He even took Ava Gardner there on their honeymoon in 1951.

She later told her friends in Hollywood, "I just loved Havana. It's as decadent as the last days of the Roman Empire. There are more dirty deeds going on behind closed doors than anywhere in the West. Even the tradewinds blowing in carry the scent of sex and sin, wicked, wicked sin. My kind of town."

On their first night in Havana, Ava and Frank had one of their biggest fights. She had wanted to go to the Superman show, and he'd denounced her. "You've got Superman right here in the bedroom with you," he claimed. "Why do you want to see some dumb sex show? We're on our honeymoon."

"A honeymoon that I'm paying for," she shouted back at him.

Before marrying Ava, Frank had told her, "Nancy took me to the cleaners in our divorce settlement."

For nearly an hour they fought. Racing to their balconied terrace, she threatened to jump off in a suicide leap.

Finally, by midnight, he calmed her down. "Come to bed, doll," he told her. "I want to fuck you."

She complied and later related to Lana Turner the events of that honeymoon night in Havana. Lana told Peter Lawford who told Sammy Davis Jr. The story made the rounds.

"God, I was crazy," Ava later recalled. "Frank drives me absolutely mad."

\*\*\*

Charges that Frank was a cash courier for the Mafia

Journalist and columnist **Lee Mortimer** at Sinatra's trial for assault and battery.

In court in 1947, Frank admitted having struck Mortimer, but denied he attacked him from behind or that others helped him. Even after a settlement, Mortimer continued to snipe at Frank, calling him "Lucky" Sinatra, suggesting his link to Lucky Luciano.

Three years after Frank's attack on Mortimer at Ciro's, the columnist was beaten unconscious at the Riviera Club in Fort Lee, New Jersey. The dive was owned by mobster Willie Moretti, Frank's close friend.

When Mortimer died in 1963, Frank drove to his gravesite at three o'clock in the morning, unzipped his pants, pulled out "Big Frankie," and urinated on the grave.

kept emerging in the late 40s and early 50s. In fury he responded to the press in 1952:

*"Picture me, skinny Frankie, lifting two millions dollars in small bills. For the record, one thousand dollars in dollar bills weighs three pounds, which makes the load I am supposed to have carried six thousand pounds. Even assuming that the bills were twenties—the bag would still have required a couple of stevedores to carry it. This is probably the most ridiculous charge that has ever been leveled at me. I stepped off the plane in Havana with a small bag in which I carried my oils, sketching material, and personal jewelry, which I never send with my regular luggage."*

In testimony before the Nevada State Gaming Control Board, Frank said, "If you can find me an attaché case that holds two million dollars, I'll give you the two million."

Author Norman Mailer at a bank did just that. In a typical attaché case he discovered that even a larger sum of money could be packed in. When he confronted Frank with this evidence—signed and notarized—Frank refused to give him the two million as publicly promised.

The four attaché cases Frank and the Fischetti brothers carried to Havana in 1947 contained hundred dollar bills, weighing a total of around 60 to 62 pounds. Carried by four different men in four different pieces of hand luggage, and divided between Frank and the brothers, each piece of hand luggage weighed only fifteen pounds.

Jerry Lewis, during his night club appearances, often encountered the *mafiosi*, including the Fischetti brothers. The comedian asserted that Frank carried cash for the mob.

In one incident, Frank was almost arrested by U.S. Customs in New York in the 1950s. He was carrying an attaché case with $3.5 million in high denominations. Customs forced him to open the briefcase. But perhaps the inspector was a fan and let Frank go free without apprehending him as the law required.

Frank visited Luciano every time he went to Italy until his gangster friend died in 1962.

Informants to the FBI learned that Frank carried illegal Mafia money to Luciano at the Hotel Excelsior in Naples, where he met with him when he was on a concert tour.

At Tiffany's in New York, Frank purchased a gold cigarette lighter which he took to Italy to present to Luciano. Frank had the lighter engraved: MY DEAR PAL, CHARLIE, FROM HIS FRIEND, FRANK SINATRA.

Around July of 1958, Frank's valet reported that when he and Frank returned to his suite in Rome, Luciano was waiting for him. "The two men kissed."

Frank later recalled that his reunion with Luciano was "the one joyous moment of my trip to Italy." Frank was deeply saddened when the newspapers carried the news of Luciano's death. "I don't give a fuck what people said about him. He was a loyal friend to me all through my life. In a world filled with shitheads, that means something."

# Frank Sinatra & Dean Martin

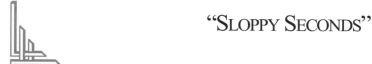

## "Sloppy Seconds"

Brothers-under-the-skin, two hard-drinking entertainers, **Dean Martin** (*left*) has a sip with **Frank Sinatra** (*right*) before launching into their next wisecrack and a duet, leaving their hearts in San Francisco, according to their song.

Frank had met Dean on occasions when he was still teamed with Jerry Lewis, but the two men had not become close. "My star was rising," Dean said, "and I didn't want to hang out with some has-been. Who would have guessed that Frank would make it so big? When I first heard him, I didn't think he was that special."

Dean also had not been impressed with John F. Kennedy, a rising politician from Massachusetts whom he met at Gay Paree in Chicago in 1948. "My partner at the time, Jerry Lewis, liked Kennedy, but he didn't impress me. Later, when he was elected president, I didn't give a damn. Frank invited me to his inauguration, but I was too busy with the booze, broads, and a Hollywood movie. It wasn't like he was Abraham Lincoln or something. He was just another pussy hound like Frank and me."

# "BOOZE AND BROADS—
# NOW, *THAT'S AMORE*"

This was the first nude I ever posed for," **Dean Martin** told Frank Sinatra. "Some chick took it. I figured I'd better get a picture of myself while my Italian sausage was still in its prime. Of course, later on I cut off my better half. No need to give my male friends a case of penis envy."

Jerry Lewis later revealed that his former partner "was very well hung."

By the time Dean had actually passed his prime, his drinking-for-show had evolved into drinking-for-real. He was in pain, having developed ulcers and several liver problems. He'd also become addicted to Percodan, which he had originally taken as a pain-killer for alcohol-induced headaches.

*"The most beautiful broads went crazy for Dean. In truth, I fucked more than he did, but it was always like they wanted to burp me."*

—**Jerry Lewis**

*"Dean screwed some of the same chicks I did, but only after I had discarded them."*

—**Frank Sinatra**

The paths of Dean and Frank crossed at the Copacabana Nightclub in New York in 1948 when Frank was appearing with the comedian Jerry Lewis. "The Dago's lousy," Frank said, "but the little Jew is great." But Frank's friendship would in time develop with Dean, not Jerry.

As writer William Schoell said, "Frank would naturally gravitate to another cool 'wop' like Martin than to a crazy, kvetching difficult Jew like Lewis."

A reporter once asked Dean just how close he was to Frank. "He is my dearest, closest friend," Dean claimed. "We slept together last night, bare ass to bare ass. That's why we're called asshole buddies."

Ironically, Frank's career in 1952 was on the downslide, but Jerry Lewis and Dean were reaching the peak of their popularity.

Dean's second wife, Jeanne Martin, said her husband "had great admiration for Sinatra as a singer, but had no respect for him as a man." Even so, the friendship they'd developed with each other continued and endured in spite of their differences.

Both Dean and Frank felt threatened with the emergence of Elvis Presley in 1956. To their ears, rock 'n' roll was "pure crap," in Frank's words. He told Dean, "We're now appealing just to the parents of those rock 'n' rollers. My bobby-soxer of 1942 is now a middle-aged housewife with a broad ass and three miserable little brats."

The actors started appearing together in 1959 when Frank invited Dean onto the stage at the Sands in Las Vegas. Dean claimed, "It's Frank's world—we're just living in it."

As a team, Dean and Frank didn't always get raves. A reviewer for the *Chicago Sun-Times* claimed, "They performed like a pair of adult delinquents, sharing the same cigarette, leering at girls, breaking up on chatter directed to the Las Vegas fraternity, plugging records, movies, and the places where they eat for free, and swigging drinks at a prop bar."

They were still working gigs together in January of 1964, when the Sands in Vegas billed their act as "Dean Martin & Friend." The joke was that the friend was actually Frank himself.

Las Vegas loved Dean's shows "about booze and broads." At one point he became known as "The King of Las Vegas," outstripping both Elvis Presley and Frank in ticket sales.

When Dean became an integral part of the famous clan, he joked, "Frank is the rat. I am the pack."

Dean and Frank often talked about women, including many of the ones they'd had in common. Frank was especially interested in hearing about Dean's experiences with women Frank had not yet seduced.

If Dean is to be believed, his conquests included such stars as Pier Angeli, Jacqueline Bisset, Dorothy Malone, Lori Nelson, Jill St. John, and even June Allyson, America's "sweetheart" in the mid-1940s.

When it came to men, both Frank and Dean had shared the unwanted sexual advances of gay actor Montgomery Clift, who claimed he fell in love with both men—Frank during the making of *From Here to Eternity* (1953) and Dean during the filming of *The Young Lions* (1958).

Initially Frank had hung out with Monty during the making of *From Here to Eternity* until Monty became too serious about him.

On the set of *The Young Lions,* Dean and Monty became close pals and spent most of their evenings together. Dean nicknamed Monty "Spider," because of the almost spastic nervous gestures he developed because of his abuse of drugs and alcohol.

Author William Schoell in his book *Martini Man*, quotes Dean as describing Monty as "a friend dear to me. Nobody wanted him around, nobody would eat with him. I took him to dinner, or I would have a drink with him, or I would put him to bed 'cause he was always on pills. He was so sad, such a sad, sad man, and he was like a boy, so unhappy and rejected, and so I'd say, 'Come on, Clift, let's go.' I'd bring him with me everywhere."

At first Dean, or so it is believed, was unaware that Monty was a homosexual. "I at first thought he was fucking Elizabeth Taylor," Dean told Frank.

As the days went by during the shoot, Monty very quickly fell in love with Dean and almost became emotionally dependent on him. "I was a bit shaken at first," Dean told Sammy Davis Jr. and Peter Lawford, two entertainers not unfamiliar with some man-on-man action.

"I have been trying to let Monty

**Dean Martin** appears at the Sands in Las Vegas with a bevy of showgirls. He was usually inebriated. "With these broads, it was a question of which one I would pick to get lucky for the night. Women sleep with me for the sex. They sleep with Jerry Lewis just to get even with their philandering hubbies."

Dean became known as a male chauvinistic pig. "In Hollywood, a guy marries a somewhat plain woman who will stand by him on the way up. But when he arrives at the big time, he can go for the sultry siren type. Frank Sinatra is the perfect example of that—from Nancy Barbato to Ava Gardner."

down gently," Dean confessed. "True, he gave me a few blow-jobs. It meant so much to him and was of no importance to me. I got off so I must have enjoyed some part of it. But it's not my thing. I'd rather have a hot blonde down there doing the honors for me. Like Frank, I'm a man for the ladies. Poor Monty. I fear he's doomed."

In return, Monty helped Dean learn his lines and revealed to him some of the secrets of Method acting. "As with Jerry Lewis, Dad was never afraid to show the critics that two men could have a healthy and close relationship regardless of their sexuality," claimed daughter Deana Martin.

When Frank saw Dean bonding with Monty, he told Dean "to watch yourself in a clench. Monty can get so hung up on you he'll threaten suicide—and mean it."

One drunken night, Frank bragged to Dean that both of them were so secure in their masculinity that they could play a joke on the public. Frank reached into his pocket and brought out a jewel box. In it rested matching pinkie rings with an emerald-cut diamond in each of them. "If anybody says anything, I'll just have one of Sam Giancana's boys take them for a ride," Frank said.

Dean wore that pinkie ring for the rest of his life.

Several of their friends noticed the matching rings and inquired about them. In a lisping voice, Dean said, "The Dago and I are lovers. Want to make something of it? The last guy who did that in New York ended up in a barrel of rocks at the bottom of the Hudson River."

When the news came over TV that Monty had died of a heart attack in July of 1966, Dean was devastated. At the time of his death, the tortured, troubled actor was only forty-six years old. Dean told his bisexual friend, Peter Lawford, "Monty is the only man in the world who really loved me. I was so sorry that I couldn't have loved him more in the way he wanted to be loved."

Breaking up is hard to do, at least for the comedy team of **Dean Martin** (*left*) and **Jerry Lewis** (*right*).

Dean began to object to the so-called "nance material" in their movies. "Jerry was always camping it up with faggy mannerisms. Not in real life, but on the screen he seemed to be madly in love with me. I found it embarrassing. We practically tongue kissed each other in *Artists and Models*. We were surely the gayest heterosexuals ever to go before the cameras. At one point I tired of playing straight guy for 'the monkey.'"

In addition to *The Young Lions*, Dean co-starred in another movie that was released in 1958. *Some Came Running* was an adaptation of James Jones' novel about disillusionment in a small Midwestern town in the late 1940s. Frank Sinatra was the star along with his fellow Rat Packers who included not only Dean as a gambler but Shirley MacLaine as a luckless floozie. Vincente Minnelli signed on as director.

*Some Came Running* was filmed In Madison, Indiana.

Dean's daughter, Deana Martin, reported that Shirley developed "an enormous crush" on her father.

Minnelli, who often painted his mouth with lipstick, was a "bit too swishy" for the more macho team of Sinatra and Martin. One beautiful, sunny afternoon, Frank wanted to play golf with Dean. To speed up the fastidious Minnelli, Frank ripped out pages of the script so he could hit the greens that day. "If I didn't do that, Minnelli would still be shooting page one after midnight," Frank said.

At one point during the shoot of *Some Came Running*, Frank got furious at how long Minnelli was taking to set up a camera shot of a Ferris wheel.

"Let's walk out on this one-horse town," Frank told Dean, who agreed to flee from the picture, at least temporarily.

That same night they were seen in Chicago as the chief patrons of Dolores' Place, a whorehouse that flourished briefly in the Windy City before the police shut it down. Obviously, the madam didn't bribe the right people.

"Dolores" (who was later revealed to be a man in drag) claimed that Dean and Frank never put on their clothes "during their entire stay with me. They preferred to share my one suite—painted scarlet red, of course—because they told me they 'didn't want to talk to the hookers, only fuck them.' So between boudoir bouts of sex, they amused each other. At least I assume they did."

"One early morning around three o'clock I entered their room to check out their booze supply and found them sitting buck-assed naked playing poker," Dolores said. "I had wished that both of them had plugged me like they did my gals, but no such luck. I didn't turn them on. I would really have turned them off if they discovered a dick under my gown."

Back in Madison, Dean and Frank returned to the set after a week's absence. They resumed their work with a furious Minnelli, while hanging out with Shirley at night.

She always appears on the list of conquests bedded by both Frank and Dean, but until she releases her sex tapes we can never be sure.

Shirley, Warren Beatty's older sister, was one of the most acclaimed entertainers of her generation. She is outspoken, claiming, "I have only one vice—fucking."

Not everyone in Hollywood endorsed her act. Producer Martin Rackin once said, "Shirley MacLaine is a disaster, a fucking ovary with a propeller who leaves a trail of blood wherever she goes. A half-assed chorus girl, a pseudo-intellectual who thinks she knows politics, thinks she knows everything, wears clothes from the ladies of Good Christ Church Bazaar."

Right after Dean made *Rio Bravo* (1959) with

For the premiere of *Some Came Running*, **Dean Martin** (*left*) and **Frank Sinatra** (*right*) escort co-star **Martha Hyer**, who was nominated for an Oscar as Best Supporting Actress for her part in the movie, where she played Frank's girlfriend. This blonde-haired actress from Fort Worth had worked in *The Delicate Delinquent* (1956), Jerry Lewis' first film without Dean.

In 1966, Martha would marry into the big time, wedding producer Hal B. Wallis.

**HOLLYWOOD TRIVIA**: Hyer came close to winning the role of the doomed Marion Crane in the Alfred Hitchcock thriller, *Psycho*.

**Frank Sinatra** (*left*) boozed it up with **Shirley MacLaine** (*right*) on and off the screen when they shot *Some Came Running* in Indiana. She was cast as the boozy floozie, and he the postwar soldier-cum-tortured-artist who dreams of becoming the new Norman Mailer.

At first, director Vincente Minnelli recommended Judy Garland, his ex-wife, for the role, but Frank nixed the idea. "Life's too short to put up with that," he said.

It was Frank who suggested that Shirley "take the bullet for me at the end of the movie." He accurately predicted she'd win an Oscar nod if she did.

John Wayne, Ricky Nelson, and Frank's girlfriend, Angie Dickinson, Dean called Frank. "In the past few days," Dean said, "I've been solicited for sex eight times. I know that's nothing compared to your record."

I hope none of those came from Angie Dickinson," Frank said. "I've already staked her out."

"No, not from Angie, Dean claimed. "But would you believe from Judy Holliday and Lee Remick? And get this, from Ricky Nelson too."

"Ricky." Frank said. "Be warned that Elvis Presley, so I hear, has already beaten you to him."

In the early 1960s, Dean, Frank, and Sammy reigned as the Kings of Cool, not only in Las Vegas but in Chicago, attracting fans by the thousands.

Frank persuaded Dean to become part owner of the infamous Cal-Neva Lodge on the border between California and Nevada (the casino was carefully positioned in Nevada). Dean purchased seven percent interest in the lodge. He later learned that Frank owned one-quarter of the real estate. Much later, Dean found out that the real owner of most of Frank's share was the notorious Mafia don, Sam Giancana himself.

Dean was not as fond of the mob as Frank was. When Dean learned of the mob's association with Cal-Neva, Dean asked Frank if he could pull out. Frank said he'd make arrangements to have someone else take over Dean's interests.

In the future, whenever Dean entertained at the lodge, he would do so strictly for a salary, as he would no longer perform for free.

Unlike Shirley MacLaine, Peter Lawford, Frank Sinatra, and Sammy Davis Jr., Dean showed the least interest in politics. During the winter of 1959 and 1960 in Las Vegas, while filming *Ocean's 11*, the Rat Pack was the biggest draw in town.

Both Frank and Dean owned a piece of the Copa Room at the Sands and pulled in some $100,000 each per week in salary.

One night Massachussetts Senator John F. Kennedy showed up to see the show. Just weeks before, he had announced his candidacy for President of the United States. Frank introduced JFK to the audience of gamblers and hipsters.

After the show, Dean asked Frank, "What did you say this guy's name was?"

Dean was about to learn more about Jack Kennedy than he ever wanted to know. For a brief time at least, he shared the same girlfriend with the man who was elected President of the United States in 1960. Of course, he also had to share her with Sam Giancana.

She was Judith Campbell (later Exner), whose looks were often  compared to Elizabeth Taylor.

After Frank introduced Dean to Judith in Las Vegas, he was often seen coming and going from her apartment.

When Dean invited her to an out-of-the-way club in the San Fernando Valley, she opened the door wearing a brand new black diamond mink coat. "You look gorgeous," he told her. That night after dinner, Dean seduced her.

"At least until dawn, I belonged just to Dean," Judith later recalled. "Sam, Jack, the others didn't matter. Believe it or not, I didn't know if Dean were married or not. I didn't read the movie magazines. I assume he might be married, but I wasn't sure. I didn't ask. He never said anything, and that's the way we wanted to keep it."

She'd been Frank's girl originally, but eventually, he passed her on to Sam Giancana and JFK.

Over the course of the several cozy evenings Dean and Judith spent together, she revealed various secrets. One of the most surprising was when she told him that Jack had promised her they'd run away together if he lost the election to Richard Nixon. "He said we'd just hang out together for one month on the most deserted island in the South Pacific. He also told me he had a deal with Jackie. He'd grant her a divorce, but only if he lost."

"With Dean there was no commitment." Judith claimed that every time he left her, she didn't know if she'd ever see him again. "Sometimes three weeks would go by without a word, and then he'd call."

Although most of their dates transpired in secret, one night a slightly drunken Dean, seeing how well dressed Judith was, invited her to Romanoff's.

The inevitable happened. That was the night that Frank was also dining there with actress Marilyn Maxwell, his on-again, off-again lover.

Leaving Marilyn at table, Frank approached Dean and Judith addressing them as "Dago" and "Campbell."

"What in hell are you two doing here?" Frank asked.

"Just checking up on you, Frankie," Judith said.

"C'mon join us," Dean said to him. "Ask Marilyn to come on over too."

Later, when Marilyn and Judith excused themselves to go powder their nose, Dean apologized for dating Judith. "I mean, if she's your lady, I'll bow out."

"Oh, hell, get real. I dumped her months ago."

"That's good news to me," Dean said. "I don't want her to come between us."

"Don't worry about me," Frank said, "Worry about Giancana. You just might be singing soprano if Giancana hears about you and Campbell. He's very possessive. Which reminds me. Lucky Luciano has been looking for you."

"Oh, shit!" Dean said.

When Dean finally heard from Lucky Luciano, it turned out not to be a death threat, but an offer.

Another one of Frank's mob associates, Lucky Luciano became interested in having a film made of his life. For some strange reason he wanted Dean—not Frank—to play him on the screen. As far as it is known, no script was ever sent to Dean.

He later revealed that "Frank was furious that Lucky would prefer me to him as the star. Had I ever been asked to appear as Lucky, I would have wired him, 'Roll the dice to someone else.'"

\* \* \*

Introduced to him by Frank, Dean found sex goddess Marilyn Monroe "a bit too exotic for my tastes." But in time he

The two most revered members of the Rat Pack, a term Frank detested, were **Dean Martin** *(left)* and **Frank** himself. They drove the right cars and wore the right clothes.

But more important, according to Dean, "You had to screw the right broads."

The gangster, **Lucky Luciano** (above), fantasized that Dean Martin looked like him, and therefore he wanted Dean to play him in a movie based on his notorious life.

Frank was one of the few people who read a rough treatment of the script that Luciano projected would be "the story of my life."

"Hell," Frank told Martin, "the script is all fucked up. It's not the story of Lucky's life. He's got his life all mixed up with Mother Theresa's."

Lucky once hinted to Frank and Martin that he'd like to join the Rat Pack. "Let's face it: Who's a bigger rat than me?"

entered her web of intrigue and emotional dependency.

He made love to her the first time he visited her apartment with a rewritten script of *My Favorite Wife*, which had starred Cary Grant and Irene Dunne in 1940. Dean hadn't liked the script but he believed that with Marilyn in the movie, it would clean up at the box office.

That night, which was actually the first time he'd ever been alone with her, Marilyn invited him for a sleepover. By morning, he had agreed to star in the picture with her. *My Favorite Wife* had been retitled *Something's Got to Give*. Originally Fox wanted James Garner for the part, but Marilyn held out for Dean.

Dean told Frank, "In the first week of the shoot, Marilyn was a complete mess and told me that she could only face the camera after I made love to her. Not only that, but the director, George Cukor, is also after me. And our co-star, Tom Tryon, told me he'd do anything I wanted in bed—'and I mean *anything*.' Do you think I'm the true sex symbol on this picture and not Marilyn?"

"Dago, you've got a lot of holes to plug," Frank said. "Go easy on them."

Marilyn later told her best friend, Jeanne Carmen, "Dean is not into that mushy stuff. He just gives his performance, and he's good at it, then rolls over and goes to sleep. The next morning a girl is lucky if she gets a pat on her ass. But I like him. He has a thick Italian sausage."

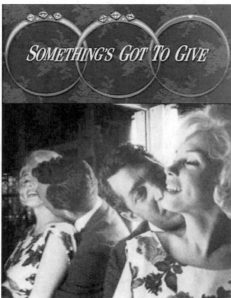

During the course of their ever-so-brief affair, Marilyn engaged in a lot of pillow talk with Dean. She told him she loved being a movie star, "bigger than Lana Turner and Betty Grable ever were," but she hated having to lie on the casting couch to become a star. "Sometimes the price seemed too high. Now that I'm a star, I want roles meant for an actress, not a blonde bombshell."

Marilyn constantly complained about Elizabeth Taylor, "I'm a bigger star than she ever was, and I'm getting $100,000 for a picture, and she's getting a million dollars for *Cleopatra*. It's not fair. I've told my lawyers that I want a million dollars for my next picture, maybe a million and a half. I want to get more than Taylor does. I hear she's a real bitch."

After endless delays on the set, including times when Marilyn didn't even show up, director George Cukor told Dean he wanted to replace Marilyn with Kim Novak, Frank's former girlfriend. Dean held out for Marilyn. "If Marilyn is fired, I walk," he warned Fox executives.

Even though world headlines announced that Marilyn had been fired, she later pleaded with Fox to take her back. She had Dean tell studio chiefs that "Marilyn will be a good girl from now on" [her words].

Fox agreed to take her back, offering a million dollars if she'd complete the film on schedule, and another million dollars if she'd appear in a film musical called *What a Way to Go*.

The movie that never got made with **Marilyn Monroe** and **Dean Martin** was entitled *Something's Got to Give*. Something did...Marilyn's life.

The blonde goddess had every intention of finishing the movie before Fox fired her for holding up production. She even told Martin that she planned to follow their movie with another script called *What a Way to Go*, which would costar Frank Sinatra himself.

Marilyn crossed out entire pages within her copy of the original script, telling director George Cukor, "It's unbelievable. Dean Martin would never be attracted to another woman if he had me," she insisted.

Dean went into a deep depression when he heard of Marilyn's death on August 4, 1962. He tried to attend the funeral with Frank but Joe DiMaggio had left orders for security guards to bar both of them.

The film finally got made under a new title and a new cast. Called *Move Over, Darling*, it was re-shot with Doris Day, James Garner (back in the cast again), Polly Bergen, and Chuck Connors.

"I never went to see the God damn thing," Dean told Frank. "A little bit of Miss Day goes a very long way."

\*\*\*

Lana Turner, Frank's former girlfriend, met Dean when he was performing at Herman Hover's nightclub, Ciro's, in Los Angeles. She came backstage after the show and made herself available. At that time, Dean thought Lana was still Frank's property and avoided her. Actually, he might have been one of the few straight men in the Los Angeles area who wasn't really turned on by her.

But 1962 saw them co-starring together in the film, *Who's Got the Action?*, a strained piece of froth about Lana combating Dean's horse-racing fever by becoming a bookie.

Although in the 1940s, Lana was the blonde goddess of Hollywood in those pre-Marilyn Monroe days, in 1962, at the age of forty-two, she had begun to look matronly.

She did not appeal to Dean at all, yet she "was throwing herself at me," Dean said. He called Frank and asked what he should do.

"Throw her a mercy fuck," Frank advised his friend. "I do that all the time to broads I don't really like but who have a big name."

"The older I get, the younger I like my women," Dean told Frank, "But I'll give it a try. Every other guy in Hollywood has had her."

During the rest of the shoot Lana was seen coming and going from Dean's dressing room. Some of their lunch breaks lasted three hours. He later told Frank, "I did my duty, but now that the filming is over, we're through."

"How was it?" Frank asked. "Vintage stuff."

"She can still get a rise out of me, but the bitch wouldn't even give me a blow-job, and you know I have to have that to get into the mood."

In general, Dean liked working with Frank in his movies. In *4 for Texas* (1963), Frank didn't want Sammy, Joey Bishop, or Peter Lawford, but he asked Dean to join him.

He admired the casting of two beautiful actresses, Ursula Andress and Anita Ekberg. The film's director, Robert Aldrich, was happy to be through with the filming of *What Ever*

Things were "bustin' out all over" when these four stars came together to shoot *4 for Texas*. Left to right are **Dean Martin, Ursula Andress, Frank Sinatra, and Anita Ekberg.**

Ostensibly set in 19th century Texas, the film's values and theme seem to have evolved directly from Las Vegas in 1963. At the film's fade-out, Martin and Frank marry the two well-endowed women whose wedding gowns evoke a Parisian fashion show in the 1960s instead of a scene out of Galveston in 1850.

Frank delivered his performance's epitaph, asserting to *Playboy,* "You can be the most artistically perfect performer in the world, but an audience is like a broad—if you're indifferent, endsville."

*Happened to Baby Jane?* with Joan Crawford and Bette Davis.

"Since I wanted to watch Ursula and Anita in the Battle of the Bosoms, I was only too happy to join the cast," Dean later claimed. "But neither Frank nor Aldrich told me I'd also be working with The Three Stooges."

Dean and Frank may have seduced Ekberg and Andress—at least that was their intention—but they may not have. Crew members reported that a "whole truckload of good-looking hookers" kept arriving from Las Vegas during the shoot.

One drunken night, Frank asked Dean if they could share a double bed when they seduced the prostitutes. "That way," Frank said, "we can study each other's style. Maybe learn a trick or two from each other." Dean was only too willing to watch Frank in action—he'd heard so many stories—so he eagerly volunteered to join in a four-way.

\*\*\*

Early in 1988 in Palm Springs, Sammy and Frank came up with what they thought was a grand idea, a reunion of Dean and the two of them, bringing back the Rat Pack during its Golden Era a quarter of a century before. Dean was reluctant but was finally prevailed upon to sign on for "The Together Again Tour" of nearly thirty cities. Within months the tour of these three legends sold out.

In Chicago, on March 13, 1988, some 16,000 fans turned out to see the Rat Packers. Frank and Sammy performed smoothly, although not quite as good as in their heyday. However, based on his lackluster performance, Dean didn't seem to want to be on the stage anymore.

After the show, Frank confronted him. "Dago, you were off the mark. Get in line for tomorrow night."

In reaction, without even telling Frank, Dean booked a flight to Los Angeles and departed immediately. That was his last tour. Frank and Sammy had to continue without him. They quickly changed the name of the tour and almost overnight hired Liza Minnelli, who did not have an engagement at the time.

It took a long time for Frank to forgive Dean, but one night he called him and invited him out to dinner. "Let's bury the hatchet," Frank said, and Dean agreed.

Dean liked to dine at seven o'clock, but Frank called that "lunch."

Over dinner, Dean, deaf in one ear, discovered that Frank was also partially deaf and needed a hearing aid. Both of them had trouble hearing what people were saying.

After his reunion dinner with Frank, Dean came home depressed.

"I just found out your Uncle Frank suffers from senile dementia," he told his family. "Barbara has to hire a security guard. One night he wandered off by himself and didn't know who he was. Thankfully, the police recognized him and brought him home. As Frank would sing it, 'It's about time both of us old Lotharios faced 'the final curtain.'"

In spite of press reports that Frank and Dean were alienated, they continued to see each other on rare occasions almost until the end of Dean's life.

The curtain descended on Dean in September of 1991, as he performed the last of his live shows in Las Vegas to bad reviews. He did not look well, and at the age of seventy-four was not up to his usual smooth standard. He had to cancel his last appearances and go home.

At Cedars-Sinai Hospital, doctors discovered that his lungs, from which had come so many memorable songs, were riddled with tumors.

His lungs ruined by cigarettes, his kidneys and liver by too much booze, Dean died in 1995 at the age of seventy-eight. Frank did not attend the funeral.

# Frank, Ava, and Lena Horne

## STORMY WEATHER FOR THE BAREFOOT CONTESSA

**Ava Gardner** *(left)*, **Lena Horne** *(center)*, and **Frank Sinatra** might have defined their affairs with each other as "triangular love."

When Lena arrived in Hollywood in the 1940s, she was called "the Negro Hedy Lamarr." She didn't bond with Hedy, but with another sultry brunette, Ava Gardner.

Although Frank and Lena had a brief affair, she ended up siding with Ava in the bitter feuds she had with him. Lena ended up "hating" Frank because of his abuse of Ava, and he suspected "this is much more than mere friendship between Ava and that black bitch."

By the time Lena and Frank came together in the winter of 1960 to tape an appearance on the Timex-sponsored *To the Ladies,* she was referring to him as "my nemesis." Frank told *Life* magazine, "Horne is a beautiful lady but really a mechanical singer. She gimmicks up a song, makes it too pat." He later claimed that in a long Harold Arlen medly which they performed together, she ignored him. "She did all her eyeball-popping shit, playing to the camera, and treated me like I wasn't even there."

In another project, Quincy Jones, the pop jazz arranger and star record producer (Michael Jackson's *Thriller*), conceived pairing Frank and Lena into an "Ultra Deluxe Package," which he predicted would be the recording event of a lifetime.

As Jones had planned it, each artist would sing the other's songs, Frank opening with "Stormy Weather," Lena with "Angel Eyes." "Could you imagine me singing 'My Way'?" Lena asked.

Later, Frank said, "There is no chemistry between Lena and me. I can't imagine my being in the same studio with her, much less singing love duets with the broad."

An African-American woman, singer **Lena Horne** was a star of stage, music, and film, blazing a trail for other black artists in Hollywood and beyond. She was a very independent woman, as noted in the comments she made about herself and delivered to a reporter:

"My identity is very clear to me now. I am a black woman. I'm free. I no longer have to be a 'credit'. I don't have to be a symbol to anybody; I don't have to be a first to anybody. I don't have to be an imitation of a white woman that Hollywood sort of helped me become. I'm me, and I'm like nobody else."

# "LESBIANS! YOU'RE ALL A BUNCH OF LESBIANS!"

### SHOUTS FRANK TO AVA, LANA, AND LENA, DINING TOGETHER IN A CROWDED RESTAURANT

In the early days, before Frank and Lena turned on each other, she used to pour out her career problems to him. Even though she came to despise him, she always said he was accepting of black entertainers in movies—"before it became fashionable to do so, and I don't mean just Sammy Davis."

When filming *Stormy Weather* in 1942, she complained that her leading man, Bill Robinson, her onscreen sweetheart, was talented but still "a Negro character" like Eddie (Rochester) Anderson or Bojangles.

There are a lot of good-looking black men out there—I mean gorgeous men. Harlem is full of them—but I get Robinson!" she complained to Frank "He's practically able to draw a pension, sixty-five if he's a day. I'm only twenty-five. Why not go to Harlem and find an actor who looks like a black Robert Taylor? Maybe even Errol Flynn. Even a beautiful girl-man like Tyrone Power. We have those, too."

Frank very accurately predicted that in years to come, handsome black men would be cast as romantic leads.

"But Frankie, I'm not talking about when I'm old and gray. I want Louis B. Mayer to cast these black dudes now."

One night Frank asked her, "If you want to do scenes with black leading men, why do you date white? Take Orson Welles, for example."

He was referring to pictures that ran in the tabloids of Lena and Orson during the spring of 1943. The actor/producer/director didn't seem to object to being photographed in a night club with a black woman. Other actors such as Frank and Peter Lawford feared that might be suicidal for their careers, although Sammy Davis Jr. defied the conventions of the day.

Frank warned Lena that an interracial scandal might find her in contract violation. "They have moral clauses, you know."

"I know," she said. "But why should it be against the law for a grown woman to date another grown man, in spite of his skin color?"

"I'm on your side, babe," he said. "You're preaching to the choir."

"I don't know why I like white men," she said. "I think it might have something to do with my plantation mentality. For some reason, I view them as protectors. As for black men, I feel they're just as vulnerable as a black woman. Who knows when a hooded posse of white men will arrive on horseback to haul them away to lynch them from some tree?"

Somewhere along the way, Frank's friendship with Lena developed into an affair, but not a very serious one.

They often talked about civil rights. Frank just assumed that she was an admirer of Martin Luther King Jr. and his policy of nonviolent change.

"I don't like him at all," she said. "He's too forgiving; he's too idealistic. For blacks to win equality in this country, they have to take to the streets. Liberty is something that will prevail only if you beat it into the heads of the bigots. King is pussy-footing around the issue. We need someone with bigger balls."

Later, Frank learned that she'd reserved her admiration for Malcom X, the radical Black Muslim minister. "I agree with Malcolm. We have to fight back. Screw Martin Luther King and all that nonviolent shit," she said.

Many black actors wanted to co-star with **Lena Horne** in *Cabin in the Sky,* a screen adaptation of the 1940 all black Broadway musical. It was MGM's first all-black musical since *Hallelujah!*

In 1929, Stephin Fetchit made himself available, and Dooley Wilson, the piano player from *Casablanca,* was considered. But MGM eventually awarded a major role to **Eddie ("Rochester") Anderson**, depicted above. Other stars included Butterfly McQueen of *Gone With the Wind* fame. Also in the cast was Ethel Waters, who detested Lena Horne, viewing her as a threat to her own hard-earned turf.

Waters even accused Lena Horne of sleeping with director Vincente Minnelli. "That's how she got the part," Waters said, apparently unaware that Minnelli was mostly homosexual.

Malcom X didn't share a mutual admiration society with Lena. When he heard she supported him, he said, "How can a Negro woman who sleeps with a white person be on my side?"

George Evans, Frank's publicist, often complained to him about what a difficult client Lena was. "She's trying to bring about integration before its time. I got her into the Copacabana in New York. The first black performer ever to star there. But what does the bitch do? She demands that I get her a suite in a hotel that bars Negroes. The first night, when she heard that black people who came to see her couldn't get in—there were no reservations available for people of color—she threatened to walk out of the gig. She demanded that the Copa open its doors to Negroes as well as whites. I was able to get a few black friends in—Mabel Mercer, for example. I told the doorman that Mabel was the illegitimate daughter of the Duke of Windsor."

Lena rarely spoke of her short-lived fling with Frank, and when she did, she was contemptuous.

"I fucked Frank Sinatra long before he bedded Ava," she boasted. "Later I came to hate the bastard."

\*\*\*

The story of the triumvirate that formed between the mulatto singer, Lena Horne, sultry Ava

Throughout the course of her life, **Lena Horne** would be associated with her most famous song, "Stormy Weather," a song she hated but was forced to sing wherever she went because the audience demanded it.

In 1942, Lena flew to Hollywood to star in another all-black extravaganza, which the studio named after her song. Her co-stars included Cab Calloway and Bill Robinson, with support from Fats Waller and Dooley Wilson. Lena spoiled take after take with renditions of "Stormy Weather" that were completely devoid of emotion, motivated, she admitted, by a fear of the song because it "belonged" to Ethel Waters.

Clarence Robinson, the forrmer Cotton Club dance director from Harlem, sensed the problem and moved in to rescue the "Stormy Weather" segment. He staged it so that it "became the defining image of my screen career." He had her stand on the sound stage as if in her apartment looking out at the rain and thunder. "Sing it like your heart is aching," he told Lena. "That the boy friend, the only man you've ever loved, has left you."

Lena still didn't get it right. "Girl, here's your big chance," Cab Calloway told her. "Don't fuck it up! Put some passion into it. Haven't you ever had a man walk out on you? Think of your career. Think of what MGM is doing to you. A white studio stuck with a sensational *chanteuse* who's the wrong fucking color!"

Suddenly, Lena began to sob. When she sang the next time, there were real tears in her eyes. "There was almost a sob in her voice," Calloway said. "She'd freed herself from the cloud of Ethel Waters hanging over her."

Gardner, and tempestuous Frank Sinatra is the stuff of legend, although largely confined to the closet, especially during the era when this three-star drama took place.

Frank and Lena shared a mutual press agent, a gruff, dynamic, middle-aged man named George Evans. He also represented Duke Ellington and Dean Martin. Frank and Lena were seen on three different occasions at Harlem's Cotton Club.

Ellington learned of the Sinatra/Horne affair, and later asserted, "It wasn't much at all. A shack-up here, a shack-up there, and then they were on their way, only to meet again on stormy seas."

Lena often privately attacked Frank's legendary endowment. "All this talk about Sinatra's equipment bores me," she said. "It's all bullshit. I've known at least a dozen black men with dicks bigger than Sinatra's."

In 1972, Lena told writer R. Couri Hay, "Sinatra and I don't like each other. It started with Ava Gardner."

When Ava was married to musician Artie Shaw, she was introduced to Lena. The two women—one born in Brooklyn, the other in North Carolina—became instant friends. Long before Ava married Frank, she and Lena had long talks.

Night after night, Ava took off her shoes and became a lounge lizard on Lena's black-and-white sofa. She complained about Howard Hughes, as she puffed on a Camel's cigarette and balanced a martini—"easy on the vermouth"—in her other hand.

Lena lived close to Ava's Nichols Canyon house, and they often visited each other. Many a night they sat drinking and watching the sun set over the canyon.

Lena often invited Ava to the bebop clubs of Central Avenue, deep in Los Angeles' black ghetto. Her entrances always were spectacular, recalled a patron. "On some nights Ava was the only white woman in the place."

Actually, Ava confessed to Lena that she was part black. "Poor white trash in the South always have some black blood in them."

It's been suggested that several celebrities were of a mixed race tribe called "Melungeons," an ethnic group made up of Mediterranean bloodlines mixed with African sub-Saharan and Indian.

Throughout her career, Ava was not alone in being charged with being a Melungeon. The same charge was leveled against such stars as Elvis Presley, Dinah Shore, and Joseph Cotten.

In contrast, Lena told Ava that she suspected "I have a lot of white blood in me. I'm sure some dirty old slave master on some plantation in Mississippi raped my poor teenage great-great grandmother."

If both Elvis and Ava were Melungeon, they shared an honorable tradition. It is believed by some historians that President Abraham Lincoln was also a Melungeon. The same revelation has also been made about Tom Hanks, Heather Locklear, and Steve Martin.

The label "Melungeon" was first applied to some residents of Appalachia—that is, people who by appearance were of mixed race, not clearly black or Indian, but not entirely white either.

Lena and Ava often discussed their sexual pasts. Lena told of the night she encountered Tallulah Bankhead at the Cotton Club in Harlem. "First she made a pass at me. I turned her down. That pissed her off. She then told me that she thought my features were too Caucasian. 'I like my black women to be happy and dark, just like they are back in Alabama,' Tallulah told me."

"You'd better stick to Hattie McDaniel," Lena said to Tallulah. Lena had already heard of the bizarre affair between Hattie and Tallulah.

"In wanting you, I think Tallulah showed her good taste before the put-down," Ava allegedly told Lena.

If legend is to be believed, that statement broke the sexual tension between Lena and Ava, each woman revealing "a streak of lesbianism." Their affair was said to have begun in the late 1940s.

During Ava's turbulent marriage to Frank, Lena claimed, "I provided the shoulder for Ava to cry on."

Lena Horne coveted the role of Julie in *Showboat*, which went instead to her friend, **Ava Gardner**, causing tension in their relationship.

But they had another reason to be jealous of each other: Ava married musician Artie Shaw, and Lena had a months-long affair with him. Shaw told Ava, "Lena wanted to marry me, but I warned her it would be the end of both of our careers. Me, marrying a black woman! It was out of the question. Paul Robeson wanted to marry her, but she said she didn't want to go with a black guy."

As her biographer James Gavin pointed out, "Given Horne's raging conflict over whites, her romantic history with them would become one of the great ironies of her life."

Every time Ava had a fight with the man she called "the fucking Guinea," she'd run to the arms of Lena. Ava poured out all her frustrations with Frank, including his inadequacies.

When Frank learned that she was doing that, he exploded. At some point, and it is not clear who told him, Frank learned that the two women—his desired one and his sworn enemy—were making love to each other.

"That was almost more than Frank could handle," said Judy Garland, who also had a strong lesbian streak. "Unlike Ava, I never made it with Lena," Judy once told actor Robert Stack.

As documented in Lee Server's 2006 biography of Ava, *Love Is Nothing*, Frank had long known of Ava's same-sex relationships. Personally, Frank liked to watch lesbians in action, and often hired prostitutes to turn him on by witnessing some girl-on-girl action. But he didn't want those love-making women to be Ava and Lena.

It was not a question of color. Friends such as Sammy Davis Jr. claimed that Frank was "color blind," and he often hired black prostitutes to service him.

The greatest strain in the relationship between Lena and Ava came when Lena did not get the part of the mulatto, Julie, in the hit MGM musical *Show Boat* (1951).

Although it wasn't Ava's fault that she'd been cast in the role that Lena coveted, it did cause a rift between the two friends that took a long time to heal. "There went my chance of a lifetime," Horne told friends. In 1993 she revealed to columnist Liz Smith, "I really didn't mind too much losing *Show Boat* to Ava. I mean, I was a little mad, but only for about fifteen years!"

Miles Kreuger, in his *Show Boat: The Story of a Classical Musical*, denounced the casting of Ava in the role of the mulatto. "The part of the sweetly fragile, highly vulnerable bird who is crushed by circumstances went to (of all people) the voluptuous Ava Gardner, who appears strong enough to take on a cage of wild tigers."

In fairness to MGM, the studio had been warned that if Lena Horne were cast in the role, *Show Boat* would not play in theaters across the South. "The idea of a Nigra gal making love to a white man don't play in Alabama," wired the head of a theater in Mobile, Alabama.

Even as part of her concert appearances, Lena continued to publicly attack Louis B. Mayer, accusing him of "vindictive racism."

Actually, some MGM studio officials said Lena was never even considered for the role of Julie. Samuel Marx, who worked at MGM at the time, said it would have been impossible for Lena to play Julie.

"The most poignant moment of the plot is when Julie's blackness was discovered. With Ava, we could pull that off with what was known as Egyptian makeup. With Lena in the role, there would be no moment of discovery. You'd know she was black from the beginning."

Ava was very sympathetic that Lena was not able to get work in Hollywood during the "Red Scare" of the McCarthy era because of her left-leaning political views. She told Ava, "I'm *black*listed, emphasis on the word black."

One night after Lena and Ava had smoothed out any difficulties because of her lingering bitterness at losing the role, Ava invited Lana Turner and Lena to an elegant dinner in a Beverly Hills restaurant.

Although restaurants were segregated in those days, the maître d' welcomed Lena when she appeared on the arms of the two love goddesses of Hollywood, Ava and Lana.

Someone, perhaps the *maître d'*, tipped Frank off. Within half an hour, an enraged Frank arrived at the establishment, making an entrance so spectacular it became part of the legend of Hollywood.

In front of all the diners he screamed, "Lesbians! You're a bunch of goddamned lesbians!" Then he stormed out of the restaurant as all the patrons watched him go before turning their suspicious attentions on the unholy trio.

All skilled actresses, Lena, Ava, and Lana finished their meal, paid their check, and disappeared into the night together.

Frank, with no evidence whatsoever, later told his cronies that the three of these beautiful women had a three-way. "Once, Ava boasted to me that she was an expert at cunnilingus. She's not a bad cocksucker either. Lana was no good at that. And who knows where Lena Horne has been hanging out?"

# Frank and Judy Garland

## OVER THE RAINBOW

Mostly, **Frank Sinatra** did favors for **Judy Garland**, saving her life on occasion. "The only time I asked her to do a favor for me, she didn't come through," he told Burt Lancaster. "I wanted to play her has-been husband, Norman Maine, in *A Star Is Born,* but she really wanted Cary Grant. He turned her down. Marlon Brando and Laurence Olivier also rejected the role. I found myself competing against Errol Flynn and Humphrey Bogart—yes, Bogie himself—for the role, but I lost to James Mason."

"I didn't speak to Judy for three weeks, until I decided it was not her decision to deny me the part. One night she called me very late and sang *Over the Rainbow* to me. After that, I could forgive her for anything. I did hold out one more request. I asked her to describe in graphic detail what it was like to get penetrated by John F. Kennedy. I figured I should know that in case some chorus gal asked me one night. I wasn't going to find out personally, so I needed a second-hand report from Judy."

"It's funny, Judy and I loved each other when we first met in the 40s *(see photo above),* but we could also become furious with each other. She said she thought of me whenever she sang that song about the man who got away."

To help ratings on *The Judy Garland Show* (1963-64), both **Dean Martin** *(left)* and **Frank Sinatra** *(right)* agreed to appear. Judy was, after all, a fellow Rat Packer.

Both men had made love to her in the past. "Frank was the more romantic of the two," Judy confessed to tap-dancing Ann Miller. "Dean did his duty at night, but all you got from him in the morning was a pat on the ass."

Judy always seemed vulnerable around Frank, telling him, "I need to be needed by a man. So what happened to me? I ended up competing for men with Lana Turner."

As the years went by, Frank often made unflattering remarks and luridly off-color jokes about Judy, yet through it all was a loyal friend as she experienced calamities such as attempted suicide, alcoholism, and drug overdoses. When she was in a hospital, he often flew to her bedside to help pull her through her latest ordeal.

# JAGGED ROCKS,
## NOT YELLOW BRICKS

When Dolly Sinatra went with her son, Frank, to see Judy Garland as Dorothy in *The Wizard of Oz* (1939), he told her after the show, "I'm gonna marry that gal one day."

As life turned out, she would propose marriage to him, not the other way around.

Their romance blossomed in 1949 when both were in New York and secretly headed for a house in the Hamptons which belonged to a mob friend of Frank's.

Judy was on the verge of a nervous breakdown, as her marriage to her gay husband, Vincente Minnelli, was all but over. Their divorce would be finalized in 1951.

In the Hamptons, walking along the beaches, Judy shared many memories of Hollywood in the late 1930s before Frank arrived. She remembered at the age of thirteen when Louis B. Mayer would routinely call her to his office, where he would "grope my adolescent breasts, which were more perky then than full."

According to all reports, Judy and Frank turned out to be very compatible sexually, but he found personality problems he'd never encountered before. She suffered from insomnia and often paced the floor at night, haunted by demons.

She also was in need of constant self-assurance. He liked to be alone to read and to talk to friends on the phone, but she seemed to resent his attention being diverted elsewhere.

"I like Judy a lot, and, except for me, she's the most popular singer in America," he told Ava Gardner. "But she can be suffocating. I don't like it when you bang a chick, and she wakes up the next morning thinking you're going to marry her."

He later told Lawford, "I broke with Judy because neurotic women are not my cuppa."

One night, back in Hollywood, Judy called Joan Blondell at around 10pm. She contacted Joan only when something major was going on in her life. Both actresses identified with each other, having grown up in vaudeville and having had nothing but trouble from the men they loved.

Judy begged her to come over for dinner, and Joan told her she'd already eaten. But after listening to her protests, Joan finally gave in. When she arrived at Judy's home, she found an elegantly set table, still under the glow of candlelight.

Judy confided in her, "Frank was due here for supper. He stood me up."

An hour later she disappeared into her bathroom and emerged looking drugged. Whatever she'd taken seemed to have loosened her tongue. "I'm in love with Frank. He's going to marry me. It's all set. He's definitely going to be my next husband."

"But he stood you up tonight," Joan said, trying to bring reality into the conversation.

"He was just too busy to call," Judy said. Joan feared Judy was heading for major heartbreak. It became four o'clock in the morning, but Judy still wanted her to stay. She insisted that Joan go into Liza's room where the little girl was sleeping.

Judy picked her up tenderly and began to sing *Over the Rainbow* to Liza in a cracked voice. "Tears were running down Judy's face," Joan said. "She crooned the song so gently, so softly, embracing the baby with her eyes, her voice, her arms, seeing perhaps her own youth."

Later Judy collapsed on the floor of her living room, and Joan covered her with a fur rug and quietly left the house.

"I will remember that night forever," Joan said. "And where was Frank? Probably fucking some Las Vegas showgal."

Judy's relationship with Minnelli had reached the screaming stage, and Frank would not accept her phone calls any more, especially the desperate pleas at four o'clock in the morning. She was plagued with migraine headaches and insomnia, and there was more. Her hair had begun to fall out in clumps.

On MGM's set of *Annie Get Your Gun*, she often arrived drugged after a night of heavy boozing. It was a western, and she had a phobia about guns and horses. She was often too drunk or too drugged to perform.

After spending a million dollars (1949 money), there were only six minutes of usable footage. Judy's contract was suspended as of May 10, 1949.

At home, Judy placed an urgent call to Frank, although his career also seemed in a hopeless slump. This time, he took her call, hoping to cheer her up. He didn't want to marry her, but he sure as hell didn't want her to commit suicide. "We'll come back," he told her. "We'll show the bastards. One day in the near future we'll come back bigger than before." His golden voice had a hollow ring.

The next time he heard from Judy was on May 29, 1949. She had checked into the Peter Bent Brigham Hospital in Boston. She was deep into a nervous breakdown, but still had hopes of getting back with Frank. She still fantasized about a possible marriage. Even in her drugged condition, those hopes grew slimmer every day, Frank claiming, "Let's just be friends."

In spite of their occasional rifts, Frank was always there for Judy when she faced her latest crisis. During her stay in the Boston hospital, he did more than send flowers every day. He even flew in a planeload of friends

Although **Frank Sinatra** never agreed to marry **Judy Garland**, he was always protective of her, the way he had been with Marilyn Monroe. He spoke frequently about Judy to his fourth and final wife, Barbara Marx.

One night, he introduced his former love to his new love. "She was so enormous and puffy-faced," Barbara said. "It was sad to see her like that."

Frank was such a loyal friend that he opted to be with Judy the night Liza Minnelli was born.

"I ordered pizzas for the waiting group of Judy loyalists," he said. "When I first heard cries from Lisa's throat, I knew a star had been born."

"Don't marry **Vincente Minnelli**," Frank warned **Judy Garland**. "He's a faggot."

She obviously didn't take his advice, as this wedding picture, taken on June 15, 1945, shows. She was fairly realistic about her new husband, telling Frank, "I know he'd rather be marrying Gene Kelly than me, but you take what you can get in this world."

When Minnelli went to visit Shirley Temple on the MGM set of *Kathleen* (1941), Temple may have been shocked, but even at her young age didn't show it. The rather effeminate director appeared in more makeup that Joan Crawford—heavy mascara and scarlet-red lips that would put a latter-day Michael Jackson to shame.

"I didn't see any false eyelashes, though," Temple reportedly said.

from Hollywood to cheer her up.

When Judy married Sid Luft in 1952, Frank breathed a sigh of relief. "Now I can bed her from time to time, without her asking me if she can become the next Mrs. Frank Sinatra," he told Lawford. "Of course, Luft is one fat prick son-of-a-bitch. Poor Judy. She doesn't know how to pick her men. She went from the bed of that faggot Minnelli into the bed of a whorechaser."

Even throughout her marriage to Luft, Judy's affair with Frank continued on an on-again, off-again basis.

One night over pillow talk, Frank suggested to Judy that he might like to play Norman Maine in *A Star Is Born* (1954). She thought it would be wonderful, but the next day when she presented the idea to Jack Warner, he vetoed it immediately.

Actually both Luft and Judy had already set their hearts on Cary Grant, but he nixed the idea of playing the role of a former matinee idol who had degenerated into a broken, pathetic, alcoholic has-been.

Judy learned the hard way not to cross Frank. In Las Vegas, he had made the Copa Room at the Sands Resort virtually his own room where he was doing it "My Way." He expected his friends to perform at the Sands exclusively. When Judy accepted an engagement at another hotel, he called her and denounced her as a "broken down, drunken old bag, and fat to boot."

"My playing the New Frontier was strictly a showbiz deal," Judy said. "But Frank took it as a personal insult to him. He became really repulsive to me and started making fun of me in his act."

One time on stage he said, "Judy Garland tried to fly Over the Rainbow but was too fat and fell on her ass." The audience didn't laugh.

Yet by December of 1954, Frank had forgiven her for her "disloyalty." He invited her to join him to hear her friend Mel Tormé at the Crescendo on Sunset Boulevard in Hollywood. On the way out, Jim Byron, Tormé's publicist, saw Frank leaving but didn't recognize Judy, who was pregnant. As he was leaving, Frank heard Byron call out to someone, "Who's that broad with Sinatra tonight?"

Byron entered a phone booth to call a newspaper with a late deadline. He wanted to get a plug in a column for his client, Mel Tormé.

Frank rushed back and headed for the phone booth, yelling at Byron, whom he had mistaken for a newspaper reporter. "Take off your glasses, you leech. I'm gonna beat the shit out of you. I'm tired of you fuckers who spend your lives sucking off other people."

Frank slammed his fist into Byron's face, bloodying his nose. Byron struck back but a hotel attendant separated them. As Kitty Kelley quoted in her biography of Frank, the next day he gave his own version. "Byron was trying to make it seem like an illicit date or something. Me, with a star six months pregnant. I told him I resented him calling Judy a broad, and I told him if he didn't know who Judy Garland was, he must have been living under a rock. Suddenly two guys held my arms and Byron tried to knee me. He dented my shin bone and clawed my hand. I broke loose. It ended when I gave him a left hook and dumped him on his ass."

After having previously given birth to two daughters, Judy entered Cedars of Lebanon Hospital where on March 29, 1955 she finally gave birth to a boy, Joseph ("Joey") Wiley Luft.

Humphrey Bogart opted not to go but his wife, Lauren Bacall, went to the hospital with Frank. Later he brought in an array of food, everything from pizza to wine, to feed Judy's loyal friends. The night before, he told Peter Lawford, "Judy may—just may—be giving birth to my child, not Luft's."

After Joey was born, Judy asked her doctor to tie her fallopian tubes.

After separating from Sid Luft, Judy launched "numerous extramarital liaisons, with both men and women," according to her biographer David Shipman. At one point, she was carrying on with both Prince Aly Khan and once again with Frank.

"I am in love for the first time," she told a reporter, not specifying if she meant the Prince or Frank.

Frank told Sammy Davis Jr. and Dean Martin that Judy preferred anal or oral sex. "That's okay with me. I get enough of front door visits with other gals."

One drunken night in Vegas, Judy told Frank the reason she divorced her first husband, the musician David Rose: "He would not perform cunnilingus on me."

"Okay, okay," he said, growing impatient with her. "Every Tom, Dick, and Harry from here to Los Angeles knows it's your favorite thing. So, tell me, which lover was the best at it. Tyrone Power? Peter Lawford? He's very oral. Artie Shaw?"

"None of the above," she quipped. "Ethel Merman."

The Holmby Hills Rat Pack was formed in 1955, with Frank Sinatra as pack master and Judy Garland as first vice-president. Lauren Bacall was den mother, and her husband, Humphrey Bogart, was named rat-in-charge-of-public relations. It was Judy who eventually brought in President John F. Kennedy, making him an honorary Rat Packer.

Vincente Minnelli, who had long since divorced Judy, signed to direct Frank in *Some Came Running* (1958). He suggested that Judy might be ideal for one of the female leads. "There's no way in hell I'm gonna do a picture with her," Frank said. "Life's too short for that." The role eventually went to Frank's pal, Shirley MacLaine.

The other male co-star of the film, Dean Martin, read the script and asked, "Why not Judy? After all, the plot calls for a luckless floozie stuck on Sinatra."

Both Judy and Frank shared violent and suicidal episodes in each other's lives. In the late 1950s, Judy went with him and Peter Lawford to a dinner party at the home of Gary Cooper. Even for the Rat Pack, it was a heavy

**Judy Garland** met **Sid Luft** in 1937 when she was making *Broadway Melody of 1938*, but she didn't marry him until 1952.

Frank and Sid shared one thing in common," said Lana Turner. "Both men were a volcano and might erupt at any minute. Poor Judy. I knew she'd end up with many a black eye from Sid. He was known by a prizefighter name, 'One-Punch Luft.'"

"I was born angry," he told Judy on their honeymoon."

During the course of their marriage, Sid went away on several trips, during which time he shacked up with chorus girls. Back in Hollywood, Judy continued to be attracted to her leading men and others. She told Peter Lawford: "I'm worred about Frank. All he ever wants is a blow job. You gotta fuck once in a while!"

drinking night. The talk grew more raucous as the evening progressed.

Judy seemed to down more liquor than anyone.

In a huddle in the corner with Lawford and Cooper, Judy became quite provocative. She was on drugs that night. "Where I go," she said to Cooper, "my size queens ask me who's got the biggest one—you, Mr. Montana Mule, or Frankie. You should really go into the bathroom with me and put on an exhibition so I can judge for myself. Men are not to be trusted when it comes to giving the exact measurements of their dicks."

"You'll never find out, Judy," Cooper replied. "Ask Marlene Dietrich. She's gone to bed with both Frank and me."

At that point, Cooper jumped up at the sound of breaking glass. Frank had thrown a blonde bimbo through a plate glass window. Blood was everywhere. Judy screamed, and Cooper rushed to the woman's rescue. It was later discovered that the young woman's arm was nearly severed.

Aided by Frank's friend, Jimmy Van Heusen, Cooper called an ambulance to come to his home at once.

Judy had rushed to Frank's aid. His white shirt was covered in blood. Somehow he'd cut himself on the jagged glass. Lawford and Judy helped him into the kitchen where they cleaned him up. His injury was only a flesh wound, and he didn't need to go to the hospital.

Lawford and Judy stumbled out Cooper's front door, where he stood waiting for an ambulance. "No one told Coop what a good time we'd had," said Lawford. "There had been just too much liquor and too many drugs that night. We were a mess. We really put on a horror show for Coop. Frank never told us what that gal said to him that made him react so violently. Another Hollywood night, another Hollywood party. I found out later the girl was paid off, and it never got in the papers."

Many intimates knew how much Judy still wanted to marry Frank, including his valet, George Jacobs, who witnessed the relationship up close and personal.

Aired on February of 1962, Judy had taped a special for CBS, co-starring Frank and Dean Martin. Jack Gould, writing in *The New York Times*, claimed that "Judy Garland held television in the palm of her hand last night. In her first video appearance in six years, the singer carried on the music hall tradition of Al Jolson and other greats.

During the taping, she had been very nervous and uncertain if she could pull off the show. She kept fondling Dean and Frank, as if seeking reassurance. After the taping, and right in front of Martin, she begged Frank to go back to her hotel and "make love to me all night."

He bowed out, pleading other commitments. "I'm free," Martin said, hearing her pleas. Looking at Frank with a mock sneer, Dean said, "The gals tell me I'm better in the sack than Ol' Blue Eyes here." In his good-natured way, Dean turned to Frank. "Can you still get it up, daddy?"

An hour later Dean left the studio with Judy "to do my duty," as he later recalled.

In her final years, when Judy faced venues not worthy of her, she'd say, "Would Frank Sinatra perform in this crapper?"

"No, Judy," a manager would say to her, "but you're not Frank Sinatra, and he's not in hock to Uncle Sam for about half a million."

Judy once told Ava Gardner when they were discussing Frank, "When I sing about the man who got away, I always think of Frank."

The potty-mouthed Ava didn't respond like a jealous former wife. "Whenever a small dick goes in me, I always ask myself, 'Where's Frankie now that I need him?'"

# Shoot 'Em Up, Frank & Ava

## THE SINATRAS GET TRIGGER-HAPPY

Everything's Better In **Indio**

THE FIRST RULE OF A GUNFIGHT IS BRING A GUN

It is said that **Ava Gardner** really taught **Frank Sinatra** how to sing "I've Got You Under My Skin." He was in hot pursuit of her in the late 1940s, although she claimed, "I could take him or leave him." When she learned that he, like herself, was a creature of the night, she became more interested. "I like a man both passionate and restless. I like a man who likes his liquor and is not afraid to keep a cigarette dangling from his lips at all times." In Frank, she'd found her guy.

They went on a drunken spree and shot up the town of Indio, outside Palm Springs, because they were bored. Their arrest was hushed up when they bribed the right people.

Tired of Frank, Ava later deserted him and went back to "shacking up with Robert Mitchum," but she finally left him, too, because he wanted to smoke marijuana all the time, and she, like Frank, preferred booze.

She told Lana Turner, "Bob is a big man, but Frank, except for his dick, is an emaciated crooner who is too macho for too little a man." She changed her mind when he called her one night and threatened suicide. She gave in and decided to go out with him once again. "The rest is history," as she was fond of saying.

As a sultry brunette screen goddess from the tobacco fields of North Carolina, **Ava Gardner** reined during an era otherwise dominated by blonde bombshells like her close friend, Lana Turner.

After two disastrous marriages—to screen star Mickey Rooney and to band leader Artie Shaw—Ava didn't want to settle down and marry Frank Sinatra, even though he begged her.

She was said to have invented the slogan, "Too many men, too little time." This hard-drinking, hard-loving Tarheel was to become *The Naked Maja, The Barefoot Contessa,* Lady Brett, and in spite of herself, Mrs. Frank Sinatra before she deserted him to pursue countless lovers, with Spanish bullfighters her specialty.

# THE MOST BEAUTIFUL WOMAN IN THE WORLD —AND UNTAMED

Indio is a little city, 26 miles east of Palm Springs, that lies in the Coachella Valley of Southern California's Colorado Desert region. Today it's a Latino enclave; an estimated three out of four residents are of Hispanic origin, most of them Mexican dating from the days of the arrival of *Traueros* or railroad laborers who flocked here to get jobs with Southern Pacific beginning in 1910. That was followed by a need for cheap farm labor, which lured penniless immigrants across the Mexican border.

In the 1930s, 40s, and 50s, Indio became a favorite haunt for celebrities on off-the-record weekends.

Before the Indio Airport closed in 1960, celebrities flew in on private planes, either their own or borrowed craft from a friend. Humphrey Bogart was spotted arriving with his long-time mistress Verita Thompson (where was Lauren Bacall?).

Clark Gable flew in with Lana Turner, and was later seen talking to, of all people, Lieutenant-General George Patton, who trained U.S. troops at nearby Camp Young during World War II.

Although celebrities for the most part head today for Palm Springs, Indio still manages to make a headline every now and then. In October 11, 1991 the fire-and-brimstone homophobe preacher, Jimmy Swaggart, was pulled over by the police in the company of a prostitute who claimed that he'd propositioned her for sex.

In 1999, Larry Fortensky, the last "Mr. Elizabeth Taylor," was arrested here for drug possession. In 2000, Robert Downey Jr. attended trial for drug possession.

Today's celebrities are likely to include the notorious Lindsay Lohan (when not in jail) or Salma Hayek. They might be seen at the Indian Palms Country Club, which was founded by one of America's most famous women pilots, Jacqueline Cochran.

But of all the local legends and lore, none tops the night Frank Sinatra and Ava Gardner arrived to shoot up the town. That notorious evening occurred in 1949, at the beginning of their tumultuous love affair.

Frank and Ava were seen attending the premiere of *Gentlemen Prefer Blondes* on Broadway on December 8, 1940. Two weeks later they were spotted in Palm Springs.

While Ava and her sister, Bappie, were enjoying their vacation at a rented villa in Palm Springs, they accepted an invitation to attend a party at the home of producer Darryl F. Zanuck. It was at this party that Ava had what she called "a reunion with Frank."

Frank ignored all the other Hollywood celebrities at the Zanuck party and spent the entire evening coming on to Ava. She seemed to welcome his advances but with a certain reserve. Ever since their shared experiences together in New York, she'd been powerfully attracted to him.

The previous night, Frank had arrived after midnight at the villa that Ava and her sister had rented. Under one of the palm trees, he presented an entire concert of fifteen songs.

Ava opened her windows and stood on the balcony wearing only a bra and panties before retreating inside. "My God," she told Bappie. "I felt like Juliet listening to a singing Romeo. Who wouldn't fall for a guy that romantic? There's also the case of his sexual prowess. He's like Gary Cooper. He can go for hours and hours. He's known for giving us broads multiple orgasms."

The following night at Zanuck's party, the other guests spotted Frank and Ava together in a huddle.

"You know Frank, having an affair with you sounds terrific, but let's not forget. You are married to . . . I don't remember the gal's name."

"Nancy, doll face. But that was a Hoboken romance over and done with long ago. I've gone bigtime since then."

"I'm not exactly opposed to having sex with married men, or beginning a long affair," she bluntly told him. "After all, Robert Taylor was fucking me when he was married to Barbara Stanwyck."

"Faggots don't count," Frank said. "Besides, Babs is Dyke City."

Leaving the party after midnight with Frank, Ava sent Bappie home in a taxi. Before going out the door of Zanuck's home, Frank stole a bottle of Jack Daniels from the bar.

He seated Ava in his convertible, a Cadillac Brougham, and off they went at top speed to enjoy moonlight over the desert and the cool night air.

Once they were beyond the city limits, Frank pressed his foot on the accelerator, and they roared into the cactus-studded flatlands.

A pack of wild coydogs ran across the highway, and he swerved but hit one of them. They didn't stop at the sound of a dying yelp.

Reaching for the Jack Daniels, she drank straight from the bottle before handing it to him at the wheel. He was going 110 miles per hour.

After they arrived in the municipality of Indio, he steered the car to a backstreet where he came to a stop and

At a Palm Springs party hosted by the much-feared, cigar-chomping **Darryl F. Zanuck**, the studio director made a pass at Ava Gardner. He was sensitive about his height, and often compensated with long workouts at a gym. He often bragged that he'd beaten world boxing champion Jack Dempsey at arm wrestling.

Zanuck like to brag about the size of his penis. When he invited Ava into his library, he sat at his desk for a minute or two before standing up to show himself fully erect.

He told her, "You've had nothing, baby, until you've had me. I am the biggest and the best."

Without missing a beat, Ava responded, "I'm sure you are. Now put it back in your pants and zip up."

turned off the headlights. There was no streetlamp on this back street. "It's blacker than a witch's tit," he said.

"Mine are porcelain white with succulent nipples," she told him, inviting him to take out her breasts to suckle on them. For about an hour they groped, fondled, and kissed. At one point she took out his penis and fellated him to a roaring climax.

The reason we know this is that Ava told the story of that night to many of her friends.

Even after all this action, it still didn't seem enough. To amuse her, he opened his glove compartment and removed two .38 caliber Smith & Wessons, for which he had a permit.

He gave her one of the weapons, lowered the windows on both sides, started his Cadillac again, and headed for the main street. The first streetlight he saw, he fired at it, the sounds of its glass canopy crashing against the cement sidewalk.

A member of many a squirrel- or possum-hunting expedition in North Carolina, Ava was also a good shot, taking down the next streetlight. When they ran out of lights, they fired into three glass-fronted store windows. At one point she shot a drunk in the stomach. He fell over on the street.

"Let's get the hell out of here, doll," he yelled at her, heading for the main road leading out of town and back to Palm Springs.

In 1949, **Ava Gardner** and **Robert Mitchum** made *My Forbidden Past* for producer Howard Hughes. He didn't like the picture, and delayed its release for two years.

During filming, Ava came on strong with Mitchum. Knowing that his boss, Hughes, considered Ava private property, Mitchum called him and advised him of the situation. "What am I to do?" Mitchum asked.

"Well, I guess, Bob, you'll have to fuck her," Hughes said. "Otherwise, word will get out that you're a faggot."

Later, Hughes said, "There's not a dame around who won't drop her britches for Bob, including Ava. To make it worse, he doesn't give a damn if they do or not."

Before they reached the main highway, a squad car, its dome lights flashing, pulled them over. To the sound of a roaring siren, and a blinding flashlight, one of the policemen yelled back to the other, "I thought it was a bunch of wetbacks. Hot damn. It's Frank Sinatra and Ava Gardner."

At 3am, Frank placed an urgent call to press agent Jack Keller in Hollywood. He was the West Coast representative of Frank's agent, George Evans in New York. Evans had faithfully represented Frank for more than nine years, getting his client out of "one mess after another," as he put it.

"Ava Gardner and I are in a little hick town called Indio, and we're in deep shit," Frank told Keller. "Ava and I shot up this dump, and we're locked up in jail."

"What?" the sleepy and astonished Keller asked, as if not believing his ears. "Did you guys kill anybody?"

"Nothing like that," Frank snapped. "We were just having a little fun. We took my two .38s and shot out a few streetlights and storefronts. Ava may have nicked this drunk in the stomach a bit, but it was just a flesh wound. The police told me he's some Mexican drunk. I think $5,000 will make him forget all about his wound. He was just a worthless bum."

"Have the reporters in Palm Springs found out about this?" Keller asked.

"No, not a God damn thing," Frank said. "The chief here listens to my records, and thinks I'm a great guy. Maybe a little crazy. We can make a deal. Charter a plane and bring cash. Get as much dough as you can, stuff it in a bag, and wing in like a rescue bird from the sky."

Not knowing how to get that much money, Keller called his good friend, the resident manager of the Hollywood Knickerbocker Hotel.

"How much money have you got in the safe?" Keller asked.

"I know exactly," the manager said. "About fifty thousand dollars. We just hosted a small film convention."

"Frank and Ava Gardner were arrested outside Palm Springs," Keller said. "We've got to pay a few people off. Could you lend me that cash until the banks open in the morning? There's something in it for you."

"Get your ass over here, and the dough will be waiting."

Keller had gotten stars out of trouble before. The moment his plane hit the ground at Indio, he went right to work. He figured it was better to give all the money to the chief and let him spread the wealth around as he saw fit. The arresting officers had to be paid off as well as the Mexican wetback whose stomach had been grazed by a bullet.

Keller warned that in no way was the injured man to be told that Frank or Ava had shot him. "My God, he'll get some crooked lawyer and sue for a million."

The chief told him he'd be discreet. Keller also offered to settle with the city for any damaged streetlights. He asked the names of any store owner whose windows had been shot out. He claimed he'd have more money wired to him at the local bank in Indio and would go to each of the stores, dispensing cash to the injured parties.

Keller obtained the release of Frank and Ava from the jail. By ten o'clock he'd chartered a plane for them, heading to Los Angeles where a black limousine with dark windows awaited them.

Ava was dropped off at her apartment, and Frank was delivered back home to Nancy and his three children.

Ava's sister, Bappie, had been up all night wondering where she was. "What happened?"

"I'm okay," Ava told her. "I spent the night with Frank Sinatra. We had a blast!"

The episode didn't end with Indio. Instead of being grateful to his long-time agent, Evans, and to Keller, Frank later fought with them.

Back in Hollywood, Frank felt Keller had parted with too much of his money, which he could ill afford. "You could have gotten me out of that scrap for ten thousand dollars," he shouted at Keller.

He called Evans in New York and demanded that he fire Keller and find a new representative in Hollywood. Although Frank at the time was his biggest client, Evans refused to fire Keller. "He got your ass out of a jam," Evans told Frank. "I've done nothing but save your ass, dozens of times."

What "seriously pissed me off" [Frank's words] was when he learned that Evans had called Robert Harris, the press agent for Ava. Evans was a blunt-speaking man. He told Harris, "Ava is bad news for Frank. Can you break them up?"

Before Frank started dating Ava Gardner, he would often fly into Indio for weekends with **Lana Turner**, who's pictured above with **Clark Gable**.

Gable and Turner inaugurated an affair during the filming of their 1941 movie *Honky Tonk*. Before Gable realized that Frank was serious about Ava, he told him a story involving Frank's future wife that occurred when Gable was filming *The Hucksters* with Ava in 1947.

"She's a devilish flirt. Between takes, when we sat around waiting to be called, she took off her shoes—the bitch likes to go barefoot—and massaged my crotch with her toes. She's a good Joe, though, very direct about what she wants."

"Like hell I will," Harris said. "She's probably a disaster for a married man like Frank, but the publicity I'll generate for her will be equaled only by the sinking of the *Titanic*. Get one thing straight, Evans, I work for Ava. Sinatra is your fucking problem."

For years, Evans had been on the other end of the phone receiving emergency calls from Frank at two or three o'clock in the morning. Often Nancy called in tears, as she did one night when she desperately wanted to get in touch with Frank and didn't know where he was. Nancy Jr. had become seriously ill, and a very concerned Nancy Sr. feared for her daughter's life.

Evans managed to track down Frank to a flea-bitten hotel outside Trenton, New Jersey. He burst into Frank's motel room but didn't find him until he heard noise coming from the bathroom. In there, Evans pulled the shower curtain to reveal Frank fornicating with a stripper who billed herself as "Lips Luango." Evans ordered Lips out of the room, but she protested. "Frank is gonna marry me and divorce Nancy. He promised me last night."

As Frank slowly dressed, he told Evans, "Handle the broad."

George finally managed to get her out of the room after flashing a hundred dollar bill before her eyes.

At the door, Lips made a final plea to Frank. "You did say you were gonna marry me."

"Fuck off!" he shouted at her. "You seriously think I'm gonna marry a broad named Lips?"

This episode, with variations, was related in J. Randy Taraborrelli's *Sinatra: A Complete Life*.

Although loyal to Frank, Evans was also realistic about him, at one time calling him "a real prick of the worst kind. He not only has to prove you're wrong, but shove it in your face and not let you forget it."

Evans had a long history of criticizing Frank for his philandering. Frank often told him to "mind your own fucking business."

"But you are my business," Evans protested. "I've tried to suppress story after story from your latest whore. You're cheating on your wife. Fans don't like a singer who does that."

"I'm paying you to keep my name out of the paper, not get it linked to some broad," Frank said.

"I'm doing what I can, but give me a break," Evans protested. "Every week I've got to pay off some slut for you. One night in Vegas, I had to pay off three of them. Keep that big thing zipped up in your pants, Frankie."

What finally destroyed the relationship between Frank and Evans was the agent's insistence that he drop Ava.

Evans tried to warn him about Ava. "She's fucked everybody from that Johnny Stompanato to Clark Gable. She's a pouty-mouth broad who goes around in a booze-induced haze most of the time. She doesn't go to bed until dawn. She's another whore like Lana Turner. If a guy's got it hanging between his legs, she's there to service it."

Frank couldn't stand to hear talk like that about Ava. He slammed down the phone.

The next day he cabled Evans that he was fired. Evans had served him well, as he had during this latest disaster in Indio.

But when Frank made up his mind, nothing could change it. Evans was out the door. What wasn't known at the time was that Ava was urging Frank to fire Evans, because Frank had reported to her all the nasty things the agent had said about her.

In despair after his firing, Evans told columnist Earl Wilson, "There's nothing else I can do. If Frank wants to open the door to Hell and plunge down the stairs into the fire, it's his life— or what's left of it."

# Frank & Ava

## BEWITCHED, BOTHERED, AND BEWILDERED

Lonely and isolated from the world, attacked viciously by thousands of their fans, a barefoot **Frank Sinatra and Ava Gardner** walked the empty sands of Miami Beach during their 1951 honeymoon. After a whirlwind courtship, and locked in isolation with each other, they were getting to really know each other for the first time. "Before that, it was a fucking circus," she claimed.

Before flying to Miami, Ava forgot her trousseau suitcase and remembered it only when airborne. "Don't worry about it, baby," Frank assured her. "I plan to keep you naked and in action day and night."

At the Green Heron Hotel on Miami Beach, an outraged receptionist, who looked like a late teenager, said, "Forgive me, Miss Gardner, but I hope you'll fall down one drunken night and break your neck."

"Why don't you mind your own fucking business?" Ava said to the impertinent girl.

"That's telling em', baby doll," Frank said, backing her up.

# FROM TARHEEL POVERTY TO A LIFETIME ROLE AS HOLLYWOOD'S LOVE GODDESS

In Hollywood, a young **Ava** posed for the mandatory cheesecake.

Silas Seadler, a publicist for MGM, studied her pictures. "She took our breath away." he recalled. "There was not a man in the room who didn't want to take her to bed. She was clumsy, and when she talked, she spat cotton. Thank god her first screen test was silent. But what a dame! We sent prints to Mayer's office, with the notation, 'If MGM doesn't sign this broad, they're out of their minds. She'll drive audiences crazy.'"

*"I have seen more sunrises than any other actress in the history of Hollywood."*

**—Ava Gardner**

*"What can Ava Gardner do for Frank in bed I can't do?"*

**—Nancy Sinatra, Sr.**

*"If I hear that Spanish runt [Mario Cabré] has been hanging around you again, I'll kill him <u>and</u> you."*

**—Frank Sinatra** to Ava Gardner

*"Frankie really had hot nuts for Ava Gardner."*

**—Gangster Mickey Cohen**

*"Listen to me, Ava. This Frank Sinatra character has got women all over town. I mean call girls, niggers. I can show you evidence."*

**—Howard Hughes** to Ava Gardner

*"In Ava Gardner, Frank literally met his match. In a woman of spectacularly sensuous beauty, he had found a soul whose turbulence equaled his own. Both had found a true partner in the opera that was his life. Ava was a diva. Like Frank, she was infinitely restless and easily bored. Both had titanic appetites for food, drink, cigarettes, diversion, companionship, and sex. Both were fascinated with prostitution and perversity."*

**—James Kaplan**

*"All my life, being a singer was the most important thing in the world. Now you're all I want."*

**—Frank Sinatra** to Ava Gardner

*"He's a dead man. Even Jesus couldn't get resurrected in this town."*
**—Irving ("Swifty") Lazar** on the stalled career of Frank Sinatra

Ava Gardner was just eighteen years old when she left the tobacco fields of North Carolina and moved to New York to stay with her older sister, Beatrice Gardner (nicknamed Bappie). After getting a few meager jobs as a model, Ava met a talent scout from MGM who arranged a screen test for her.

In Hollywood, MGM mogul Louis B. Mayer saw the screen test. "She can't act. She can't talk. She's terrific. Bring her to Hollywood."

In the summer of 1941, Ava took a train to California. In a coincidence, Hedy Lamarr was on that same train. Both women would eventually vie for the title of "The World's Most Beautiful Animal."

Sometime in 1942, a 130-pound, skinny boy from Hoboken spotted a 36-20-36 daughter of a dirt farmer from North Carolina. The setting was the MGM lot. "I fell head over heels in love with a gal," Frank Sinatra told Gene Kelly. "I'm going to marry her. But first I have to find out her name."

He soon found out who his dream girl was.

During her brief marriage to Mickey Rooney, he introduced her to Frank one night at the Mocambo on Sunset Strip.

Flashing his smile, Frank said, "Hey, why didn't I meet you before Mickey? Then I could have married you myself."

"Well," she said, right in front of Rooney, "I'm sure I'll go through eight or nine husbands in my life—perhaps you'll be one of them, no doubt husband number seven."

Ava was not impressed by Frank, later telling Rooney, "Sinatra struck me as arrogant, conceited, and full of himself."

Over the years she encountered Frank on many occasions, not only on the MGM lot but at Hollywood parties. "That is one stuck-up wop," she told Lana Turner.

"He's really quite sweet when you get to know him," Lana said, "although he dumped me."

"Yeah, sugar with a touch of arsenic," claimed the more cynical Ava.

In spite of Rooney's introduction, it was 1948 before Frank and Ava became serious party animals together.

Frank's marriage to Nancy was a roadblock, but nothing that Frank and Ava's racing car couldn't crash through.

When MGM mogul **Louis B. Mayer** *(right figure, above)* introduced **Ava** to the great actress, **Ethel Barrymore** *(center)* on the set of *The Great Sinner (1949)*, the grande dame of the stage told her. "Miss Gardner, I can act, and you can look beautiful. You'll go much farther in movies than I will. On the stage, however, my dear, that's a different story."

Mayer told Ava, "If you ever learn to talk like someone other than a vaudeville performer on the chitlin' circuit, you'll make it in Hollywood—that is, if you don't do something stupid like marrying Mickey Rooney. That boy gives me cardiac arrest. Right now, he's *schtupping* Irving Thalberg's widow, Norma Shearer."

Rooner later told Ava that Shearer was "hotter than a half-fucked fox in a forest fire."

By 1943, after a year of marriage, Ava had divorced "the midget," Rooney. In 1945, she had married musician Artie Shaw, divorcing him after only a few months. "I guess I'm not the marrying kind," she told MGM songbird Kathryn Grayson. "Besides," Ava added, "marriage gets in the way of your affairs on the side."

After his divorce from Ava, his teenage bride, Rooney later rhapsodized about their sex life. "She has big brown nipples, which, when aroused, stood out like some double-long golden California raisins," he once told Frank on the MGM lot long before he and Ava became romantically involved.

**A SMOOCH HEARD AROUND THE WORLD:** When **Ava Gardner** (*above, left*) married pint-sized **Mickey Rooney**, he was at the very top among box office attractions in America, although his crown was slipping.

Almost overnight, the sultry siren became a household word. During Ava's tour of MGM Studios, she was introduced to Mickey, "the biggest movie star in the world." He was love-struck. She was rather put off by this creature before her, as he was dressed in four-inch wedge shoes and in total drag, with a "fruity" hat for his impersonation on camera of the campy Carmen Miranda.

In 1942, **Ava** took her new husband, **Mickey Rooney** (*center*), back home to meet dear ol' Mammy in the wilds of North Carolina.

To greet her new son-in-law, and to show him some Southern hospitality, **Molly Gardner** offered him a platter of her Southern fried chicken.

"Well, honey, he may have enjoyed the sex, but goodness knows I didn't," Ava said when she heard Rooney's remark. "I'd call our marriage *Love Finds Andy Hardy*."

When she divorced Shaw in October of 1946, she began dating from the A-list. Howard Hughes pursued her for years. Peter Lawford and Howard Duff were among her many lovers, as was gangster Johnny Stompanato, who would later be murdered by Ava's best friend, Lana Turner, who blamed the slaying on her daughter.

Passing through her bedroom over the years were such men as Robert Mitchum, Farley Granger, Porfirio Rubirosa, Clark Gable, Robert Walker, Turhan Bey, Richard Burton, John F. Kennedy, director John Huston, Fernando Lamas, David Niven, and Omar Sharif. George C. Scott lay in her future, as did many other actors, Spanish bullfighters, and an Italian actor named Walter Chiari. Frank Sinatra would become her third and final husband.

In 1949, Louis B. Mayer sent both Frank and Ava to New York to promote their latest pictures, his being *On the Town* and hers being *East Side, West Side*.

During that visit to New York, Ava ran into Frank accidentally on the sidewalk. He was contributing a hundred-dollar bill to the Salvation Army collection pot.

He invited her for a drink, and each star revealed behind-the-scenes tales from the sets of their recent movies. Both lamented being sex symbols and constantly pursued by "half of Hollywood," both male and female.

"I had to bolt the door to my dressing room to keep Gene Kelly out," he boasted. "Gene wanted Big Frankie."

"On *East Side, West Side*, my biggest problem was keeping my panties on around Barbara Stanwyck," she lied. "Fortunately Nancy Davis [later Reagan] stood guard for me at my dressing room door." Actually, Stanwyck detested Ava.

Ava later admitted to Lana that "Frank fucked me that night in New York like I'd never been banged before. Mickey Rooney was a runt, and Artie was interested only in his own orgasm. Howard Duff was pretty good at it, but a lot of the others on a scale of one to ten rated a two."

When Artie Shaw later ran into Sinatra, he told Frank, "You owe me one. I, not Mickey Rooney, broke in Ava for you. She was a sweet, soft-spoken gal when I hitched up with her. Very insecure. After our marriage, she turned into a tough broad, foul-mouthed and hard drinking."

Ava later recalled that she "didn't find Frank so cocksure any more. He still had that cock, but his last four movies had bombed. He was hardly the country's most popular singer, and he was sharing his radio show with Doris Day. In 1949 he didn't have one single record that made the top fifteen. I wasn't doing so hot either. My last three pictures, including *East Side, West Side* (1949), turned out to be box office poison."

In Hollywood that January of 1950, Frank moved out of his Toluca Lake house where he lived with Nancy and his children and into his newly built home in Palm Springs.

He also maintained a bachelor pad at the Sunset Towers in Hollywood, close to where Ava lived, and he invited her to dinner. She accepted, even though she knew he was still married to Nancy, but living apart.

On their first date, Ava admitted they went in for some heavy kissing—and a hell of a lot more. "Why not? That married man had already sampled my honeypot in New York."

To be close to Frank, Ava rented a house with her sister Bappie in Palm Springs. During her first date with him in the desert, she recalled, "We drank, we laughed, we talked, and did I fail to mention it, we fell in love."

Since she was really getting serious about the guy, she asked about Nancy, a subject she'd avoided so far. He admitted that he'd left his wife both physically and emotionally. But as a well-bred and devout Catholic, Nancy was having conflicting feelings about granting him a divorce. More than that, she was absolutely refusing to do so.

His affair with Ava became public early in 1950 when she showed up at the Shamrock Hilton in Houston, Texas, for one of his singing engagements.

He told Ava that Nancy still would not

During the late 1940s, **Artie Shaw** *(right)* was one of the nation's leading swing bandleaders.

After his stint in the Navy during World War II, he returned home an emotional wreck. Even though there was little in his bank account, he still had his charm and, as he admitted, "I've always got to have a woman around."

After his marriage to Lana Turner ended in divorce, Shaw turned to starlet Ava Gardner, and after several spats, married her in 1945.

"I don't really remember being married to him," she said. "He upset me so much I was drunk all the time."

grant him a divorce. Ava responded, "In that case, I'll rub her nose in my affair. I'm so in love with you, I don't care at this point."

Hot-tempered Frank got into a brawl with an invasive photographer when he and Ava were dining as the guest of Houston's mayor, Oscar Holcombe. The scandal at Vincent Sorrento Restaurant not only made the front page of the *Houston Post* but was featured the following day in the *Los Angeles Times*. Nancy was humiliated, and immediately changed the locks on the door to the Sinatra home, barring Frank's entrance.

When Ava's affair with Frank became public knowledge, he lost some of his fan base, especially those 1943 bobbysoxers who had married and settled in the suburbs with husbands who they expected to be faithful to them. As one fan put it, "He's flaunting his affair with the Tarheel bitch. I feel sorry for poor Nancy who's been a good wife to him and a great mother to his children."

"The Aviator," **Howard Hughes,** wanted **Ava Gardner** just for himself, but she somehow always managed to elude his net.

He was immediately attracted to this green-eyed beauty of feline grace and passionate intensity. He told his pimp, Johnny Meyer, "I could live between her breasts, although they aren't in the same league as Jane Russell's."

Hughes especially preferred "wet decks"—his term for a woman who had been recently divorced. He began his hot pursuit of Ava even before her divorce from Mickey Rooney had come through.

"He never really got what he wanted from me," Ava later said.

Some devoted fans sent Frank broken copies of his former hit recordings. Newspaper columnists came down hard on the errant couple, especially Hedda Hopper. "I don't know if I should condemn Sinatra or pity him. Any man who would put a wife of Nancy's caliber in the position of competing with a tramp of Ava's character— or should I say lack of it—is either a low-down skunk or just so insane he should be locked up for his own good."

On Valentine's Day in 1950, Nancy decided to tell the world that she and Frank had separated and that her life with him had become "most unhappy and almost unbearable."

Ava was denounced as a home wrecker and called a "Bitch Jezebel." The Legion of Decency threatened to boycott her films.

Hoping to let the scandal die down, Louis B. Mayer quickly assigned Ava a picture to shoot in Europe, *Pandora and the Flying Dutchman*, co-starring James Mason and set for a 1951 release.

In New York, Frank was booked into the Copacabana for a long engagement, and Ava reserved some time to spend with him before flying to Europe to make the film. Both of them checked into Hampshire House on Central Park South, but, for appearance's sake, booked two different suites, although they adjoined each other with a connecting door.

On Frank's opening night, his diehard fans had never seen him in such a bad condition. Suffering from nervous exhaustion, he was shaking with fever and looked pale and withdrawn. Under the spotlight, he was sweating profusely. Ava was afraid he'd collapse on stage.

When he sang "Nancy with the Laughing Face," there was a rumble in the audience, as all eyes focused on Ava and not on the stage. Even though the song was actually about his daughter, Nancy, Jr., the audience did not make that connection.

He had never before faced such a hostile audience. As he sang, the patrons, whom he later referred to as "stupid, snickering bastards," talked so loud no one could hear him sing.

At one point, he interrupted himself in the middle of a song. "Am I singing too loud for you guys to hear each other?" Finally, he pleaded with the audience, "Please, give me a chance. It's my opening night."

After the third night, he came down with a severe throat infection, but had to continue the gig because he needed the money.

At one of the worst points in his career, he felt threatened with failure and defeated. He took out his frustration on Ava. The manager of the Hampshire House said, "Not since the D-Day landings have there been such carnage. I didn't give their relationship a chance."

Ava had wanted to help Frank, but he made it difficult for her. When his attacks on her became too violent, she fought back. One time she screamed at him, "I won't be dragged down with your failure. My star is on the rise. You're yesterday's crooner."

Although true at the time, it was more than his nerves could take. She was awarded a black eye, Hoboken style.

One night at the Copacabana, shortly before Ava was set to fly away on location, she got "seriously pissed off" at Frank because she'd caught him flirting with a cocktail waitress.

"You fucking guinea bastard!" she shouted at him.

"You Tarheel piece of white trash!" he shot back at her. She fled from the club and rushed to Artie Shaw's apartment for a reunion with her former husband.

During their marriage, Shaw had been her mentor, even assigning her books to read. She presented to him a litany of problems about her relationship with Frank. Since Shaw knew Frank, he was well aware of his temper fits.

But Ava revealed a strange problem. "He doesn't take all that fire to bed with him, and you, of all people, know I like it rough. With Frank, it's impossible. It's like being in bed with a woman. He's so gentle. It's as if he thinks I'll break, as if I'm a piece of Dresden china that he's gonna crack."

After his last show, Frank figured out where Ava had gone—perhaps a doorman tipped him off. He took a cab to Shaw's apartment, arriving spoiling for a fight. When he threatened Ava that he was going to "ruin your fucking face for life," Shaw went to his desk drawer and took out a large caliber pistol. "More trouble from you and that golden throat will run blood red."

Turning his back to them, Frank raced toward the door. "Shits, all of you!" he shouted back at them before slamming the door in their faces.

Back in his suite at Hampshire House, Frank placed an urgent call to Ava, who was still sitting and talking to Shaw in his living room.

"Honey, this is it," Frank told Ava when she came to the phone. "I can't live with you, and I can't live without you. This is the only way out."

All she heard before he dropped the phone were two bullet shots.

Abandoning Shaw, she rushed outside and hailed a taxi to take her to Hampshire House. Meanwhile, David O. Selznick,

The big-mouth columnist, **Hedda Hopper,** led the attacks on Frank Sinatra and Ava Gardner after he broke with Nancy to take up with the screen goddess.

Hopper frequently criticized Frank's relationship with Ava, but he continued to talk to Hopper in spite of her attacks on him. Often, he misled her, telling her that "all the problems between Ava and me have been straightened out."

But then Hopper picked up the paper to read a statement from Howard Strickling at MGM about how Ava and Frank were heading off to the divorce courts. "I'll kill the little dago bastard for lying to me," Hopper shouted at her staff.

who occupied an adjoining suite, had heard the shots. He immediately called the manager. "I think that son-of-a-bitch, Frank Sinatra, in the next suite has just shot himself."

Selznick got the manager of the hotel to use his pass key to enter Frank's suite. When they discovered that he was all right, the manager hastily called his staff and had them exchange the mattress.

When the police arrived, they could find no bullet holes in the suite and reported that Selznick must have been mistaken. That led to a search of other rooms on the floor. No bullet-riddled mattress was found.

When Ava arrived, she found Frank contrite at having performed such a foolish act.

The next morning she called Lana. "It started out like one of my foolish romps. But I think I'm falling in love with the over-the-hill Dago."

"Honey, you're going to Spain," Lana said. "It's full of beautiful men. Shack up with one, maybe two, maybe several. I, too, know about Latin lovers, and I recommend them highly."

One unreported incident associated with that rush of policemen and firemen to the Hampshire House involved a fireman who, having been given the wrong room number, broke into Ava's suite. Once there, he discovered a nude Peter Lawford, Frankie's future Rat Packer, in bed with his longtime lover, Tom Drake, Judy Garland's "boy next door" in *Meet Me in St. Louis* (1944).

Along with Bappie, her sister, Ava flew from New York to London on March 25, 1950. Many letters were arriving at Hampshire House, expressing the wish of her former fans that her BOAC airplane would crash into the Atlantic alongside the *Titanic*.

In Marilyn Monroe's film *Some Like It Hot,* the character she played (Sugar) admitted that she had "this thing" for saxophone players.

In her memoirs, **Ava Gardner** admitted that she had "this thing" for Big Band singers, especially one named **Frank Sinatra.**

"He had a thing in his voice I've only heard in two other people—Judy Garland and Maria Callas. A quality that makes me want to cry for happiness, like a beautiful sunset or a boys' choir singing Christmas carols. I think he was as sexy as hell. Some women fall for writers, some for sailors, some for fighters. I'm hooked on Big Band singers."

*Pandora and the Flying Dutchman* was shot on the Costa Brava in Spain, with its string of little resorts lying north of Barcelona on the road into France. Ava liked the English-born James Mason, who had abandoned the British film industry four years before to work in Hollywood.

She claimed, "I felt I'd come home again when I stepped down on Spanish soil. This place has nothing to do with North Carolina, but it's where I want to live."

Before leaving for Spain, Frank appraised Mason. "I don't have to get too jealous over that limey cocksucker," he told her.

Frank was right. Mason was not the problem.

In Spain, Ava breathed a sigh of relief to be away from Frank. Taking Lana's advice, she selected Mario Cabré, a Spanish bullfighter, as her lover. She later wrote Lana, "He's great sex, but outside the bedroom he leaves me cold. He writes silly love poems to me."

Cabré played Juan Montalvo, Ava's bullfighter-lover in *Pandora and the Flying Dutchman*. The movie's *reel* affair became real. In his case, it was typecasting. He was a real bullfighter and Ava couldn't help but notice how he filled out his "suit of lights."

In her memoirs, she admitted to having gone to bed with him once, but cast and crew claimed that they maintained a torrid ongoing affair throughout the shooting of *Pandora*.

Frank called her daily, begging her to fly back to New York. But she had no intention of abandoning *Pandora*. Finally, he had to cut short his engagement at the Copa after he was hospitalized with a throat hemorrhage.

He had barely recovered when he learned that MGM had fired him. In a face-saving move, the studio announced that Frank had asked to be let out of his contract to pursue other business interests.

As soon as he recovered, he flew to Spain to join Ava on the set of *Pandora*. Fortunately, the matador, Mario Cabré, had an engagement in the Plaza de Toros in Madrid.

Ava was shocked at Frank's appearance, finding him "frail, gawky, and yellow looking." She told him he needed some of her Southern fried chicken with gravy to fatten him up.

The weather on location was horrible, gray and rainy, so she had a few days off from shooting to be with him. Both of them took advantage of it. As frail as he was, Frank made love to her three and at one point four times a day, so strong was his passion for this beautiful woman whom he claimed was "the most beautiful God ever created."

In Spain, cameramen and journalists stood outside Ava's villa trying to taunt Frank. The paparazzi wanted to take a picture of him exploding in anger, which he almost did. One of them shouted, "Frankie, what do you think of Ava's affair with Mario Cabré?"

She wanted marriage and children, but Frank told her, "Nancy will never give me a divorce—she's told me so. I don't want to father a bunch of Dago bastards."

Finally, his time with Ava in Spain came to an end. He flew back to Los Angeles. Cabré returned slightly gored from his latest bout in the Plaza de Toros in Madrid, but still able to make love to Ava "toreador-style" as she called it. She told her friends, "Like Frank, Mario and the bull have something in common."

When he returned to California, Frank drove to the Holmby Hills house where Nancy lived with his three children. He was loaded down with presents for all four family members, many of the gifts paid for by Ava.

When he had spent time with his kids, and they had gone to bed, Frank settled in with a drink to talk over a divorce with Nancy. She suggested that he should be the one to file it.

"I have no grounds," he protested. "You've been the perfect wife, the perfect mother. *You* have grounds for divorce. I don't."

When the press finally cornered him, Frank told reporters that he and Nancy did not plan a reconciliation.

"How does Ava feel about you?" one reporter asked him.

"I forgot to ask her," he snapped back.

No longer in hiding from the press, Ava and Frank let the world know "we're an item, honey child," as she told one reporter who confronted her.

Dumping Cabré in Spain—"except for his dick, he bores me"—Ava flew to London to film the interior sequences for *Pandora* at MGM's studio there.

Frank was delighted as he'd been booked for a singing engagement at the London Palladium. Flying into London, he took a taxi to a flat he'd rented on Berkeley Square near Park Lane where Ava herself had her own apartment. At the time, each of them still found it discreet to maintain separate addresses, even though their affair was public knowledge.

British audiences greeted him with such loud applause, he later told Ava, "I felt it was 1943 and I was at the Paramount in New York singing for all those bobbysoxers."

Ava cheered him on at the Palladium, and also began to nurse him back to health. He'd lost a lot of weight.

Unlike Hollywood, the press in London, more or less, left them alone, figuring their affair was their own business.

On July 12, after his performance at the Palladium, Ava and Frank were invited to the most exclusive parties in town, where *tout* London showed up, even royalty and aristocracy. At one party both Ava and Frank were introduced to Princess Margaret.

The next day Frank received a call from the social secretary to Princess Margaret, inviting him for a private tea at her residence. Ava was not asked to come along.

Without telling her, Frank accepted the royal invitation and disappeared into London for about four hours. It was this occasion that led to rumors that he'd made "love in the afternoon" to Princess Margaret. Frank would not be the only celebrity with whom Margaret Rose had had a fling. She was once even suspected of having a sexual tryst with Marlon Brando.

In public, Frank expressed admiration for the princess as revealed by her authorized biographer, Christopher Warwick, who wrote *Princess Margaret: A Life of Contrasts*.

"Frank Sinatra, who soon became a friend, paid his own compliment to the Princess in the 'hip' jargon of the time when he said, 'Princess Margaret is just as hep wide-awake as any American girl, maybe more so. She is up on all the latest records and movies, and has a lot of wit and charm, too. She is the best Ambassador England ever had.'"

Back on the West Coast, Nancy realized that her refusal to give Frank a divorce was contributing greatly to his nervous breakdown. On April 25, 1951, she filed for a legal separation in the court at Santa Monica.

Although **Ava Gardner**, pictured above with **Richard Burton** on the set of *The Night of the Iguana,* was more than forty years old, she was still a "smouldering siren—not to be trusted," in the words of a jealous Elizabeth Taylor. This Tennessee Williams drama, shot in Mexico, had as its slogan, "One man, three women...one night."

Taylor tried to be around the set as much as possible. Ava later admitted to Lana Turner, "Richard managed to slip around the corner, when Elizabeth was in her toilet, and he knocked off a piece or two when we made the film." When Burton was busy mounting Taylor, Ava amused herself with a string of Mexican beach boys.

She still loved Frank and felt this legal separation would give him some peace of mind. A devout Catholic, she knew that—unlike a full-blown divorce—a legal separation would not break any of the dictates of her church.

Upon their return to New York, both Ava and Frank learned that the press and photographers were still "fanatically interested in us" (Ava's words). He met the press with hostility, but she reminded him, "Sugar, spread a little honey on it, and it might help us with the boys."

Checking back into the Hampshire House in Manhattan, they decided to go to a nightclub with Mr. and Mrs. James Mason. Over drinks, Frank told Ava that, "I'm completely broke. From now on, I'm gonna be your kept boy."

That precipitated a fight which continued after their return to their suite at Hampshire House. As the night wore on and the intake of alcohol for both of them increased, she became violent, striking him in the face. Then, she pulled off her diamond engagement ring and threw it out the window.

Frank called a doorman to go look for it, but some lucky person had already stolen it, not knowing it was Frank Sinatra's engagement ring to Ava Gardner. Had the finder known that, of course, the ring would have been so much more valuable, as they were the most talked about couple in America.

Ava had hoped that Frank would enter into the marriage as an equal partner, and she was bitterly disappointed when she realized that she'd have to be the bread winner.

She found it hard paying Frank's bills as she made only $50,000 a year. After paying everybody else off, including her manager-lawyer, she was left with only $176 a week in expense money. Frank in his heyday used to spend that at a club in less than an hour.

When the tension between them became almost unbearable, Frank suggested, "It's time we went South of the Border, baby, for a little R&R."

Even after Nancy announced that she was divorcing Frank, the press did not let up on coverage of Frank and Ava, "America's *femme fatale.*"

On July 31, during their departure from Los Angeles Airport, an army of reporters and photographers covered the event in spite of a rainstorm. On the way to the plane, Frank struck at least three reporters and two photographers. It was obvious who was going to be voted "most uncooperative" celebrity with the press that year.

After a brief layover in El Paso, where more reporters and photographers waited for them, Ava and Frank finally landed in Mexico City. The press suspected he was going to get a quickie divorce and finally marry Ava.

Reporters would not let them alone even in Mexico. "They want to know everything," Ava protested. "They even want to know if Frank and I get off the can and wipe our asses front to back or from back to front."

A writer for the *Los Angeles Times* reported that "the attempt of Ava Gardner and Frank Sinatra to slip undetected into Mexico turned into the most publicized romantic goings-on since Rita Hayworth and Prince Aly Khan." Another journalist claimed the romantic fling was more publicized than the D-Day landings.

In Acapulco, Frank and Ava vacationed at a resort owned by Ted Stauffer, who was married at the time to the sultry screen goddess, Hedy Lamarr. Stauffer, whom Ava and Frank called "Teddy," was a Swiss-born big band leader whose tireless promotion of the emerging resort had earned him the nickname of "Mr. Acapulco."

Fleeing from the Nazis in the 1940s, and having settled in Mexico, he had once conducted a big band that had introduced American-style Swing music to pre-war Europe. He was also a playboy, night club owner, and a sometimes actor.

As two former rival queens at MGM, Hedy and Ava were a bit chilly with each other. On the first night in Acapulco, Ava joined Hedy for a walk to the powder room. She was brimming with a question for Hedy. "Did you and Frank get it on during your glory days at MGM?"

"We may have," Hedy answered. "There were so many men seducing me at the time—Charles Boyer, Errol Flynn, Clark

Dressed in a velvet bathing suit, **Ava Gardner** appears as Maria Vargas in *The Barefoot Contessa (1954),* which was writen, produced, and directed by Joseph L. Mankiewicz. Ava referred to the bathing suit as "the one with the fringe around my pussy."

In the movie, she co-starred with Humphrey Bogart, a close friend of Frank's. They didn't get along. "I'll never figure you broads out," Bogie told her on the first day of the shoot. "Half the world's female population would throw themselves a Frank's feet, and here you are flouncing around with guys who wear capes and little ballerina slippers."

Gable, John Garfield, Howard Hughes, John F. Kennedy, David Niven, Burgess Meredith, George Montgomery, George Sanders, Jock Whitney, Otto Preminger, Rudy Vallee, Walter Wanger, even Charlie Chaplin.

"Thanks for a *Who's Who* in your bedroom," Ava said. "But I was asking about Frank."

"As I said, I truly don't remember," Hedy claimed.

"If Frank had fucked you, you would have remembered," Ava claimed.

Hedy's response had angered Ava. As she did a final check on her make-up and headed for the door, she turned back to look disdainfully at Hedy. "I noticed you left Adolf Hitler off your list."

Her career fading, Hedy was very jealous of Ava. Even though she was the hostess, Hedy tried to ignore Ava whenever possible. "The sun had set on Hedy's career," Frank later said, "but the sun was rising for Ava—catchy title."

Even today, many of Ava Gardner's most ardent fans consider her role of Julie in *Show Boat* (1951) her greatest. In a part that Lena Horne wanted, Ava played the tragic half-caste. Actually, Judy Garland had been slated to star as Julie, but Louis B. Mayer thought she was too undependable.

Ava co-starred with Kathryn Grayson—"with the big boobs"—and with tall, handsome **Howard Keel**, depicted with **Ava** above.

"Howard and I drank a lot of tequila, which was forbidden on the MGM lot, and we went skinny dipping at night," she said. "He was a very big man all over."

During the filming of *Show Boat,* Ava completed her original, $75-a-week contract, the one she'd signed when she was still a newcomer in Hollywood. Her new seven-year contract paid her $50,000 a year, but demanded "absolute rectitude and teetotalism while working."

Ava had little reason to like Hedy because she'd heard rumors that Frank had visited her dressing room at MGM during the early 40s on more than one occasion.

Hedy claimed, falsely or otherwise, that "Frank had wanted to divorce Nancy and marry me long before Gardner. I remember it well. It was at a party hosted by Elsa Maxwell in Hollywood in August of 1945 to celebrate the liberation of Paris. Arthur Rubenstein played *La Marseillaise*. Charles Boyer, who had starred with me in *Algiers*, sang along with Frank and Judy Garland. That was the week Frank proposed to me. I turned him down. So many men were proposing to me back then."

Later, describing their time as a trio in Acapulco, Hedy wrote, "I showed Frank and Gardner how to enjoy the beaches and the bay."

The way Frank later told it, "Hedy focused all her attention on me and totally ignored Ava." Simultaneous with virtually every encounter with his hosts in Acapulco, Frank constantly hawk-eyed Stauffer, who had once wooed Ava himself.

The press and photographers proved so difficult in Mexico that Frank and Ava decided to return to Hollywood. To afford them more privacy, their millionaire friend in Acapulco, Jorge Pasquel, lent them his private plane, a converted B-26 bomber.

After clearing U.S. Customs in Los Angeles, Frank and Ava faced "a sea of reporters and photographers," who surrounded their car, blinding them with their flashbulbs. Frank bounded out of the car and set a record (for him) of attacking and kicking at least six of them and knocking two cameras onto the pavement. He jumped up and down on the cameras before getting back in the car.

The bravest photographer (or the most foolish), William Eccles, stood directly in front of

Frank's Cadillac, almost daring Frank to hit him. Frank swerved the car, trying to miss him, but crashed into him with his bumper. Eccles was knocked to the ground. "You fucking son of a bitch," Frank had shouted at Eccles. "The next time, I'll kill you, you bastard."

Then Frank and Ava sped away. Of course, a lawsuit followed, as was inevitable. Later the photographer dropped the case. It was rumored that Ava, who had more money than Frank, paid him off.

Years later, Frank was still fuming over that insult in Mexico from Hedy. He vowed to get revenge on her for ignoring Ava. In early November of 1965, Frank at the Cocoanut Grove in Los Angeles stopped by to say hello to Judy Garland's table. She was talking to Hedy and Mickey Rooney.

Frank ignored Mickey, Ava's first husband, and lavishly kissed Judy. At one point, she broke away. "Frank, you remember Hedy?"

He looked long, hard, and critically at Hedy. Then he said, "You look familiar. Didn't you used to be Hedy Lamarr, the movie star?"

***

On September 26, 1951, Ava was rushed to St. John's Hospital in Santa Monica. There were rumors of a botched abortion. Suffering from nervous exhaustion, she had to stay confined to her hospital room for a month to recover from a viral infection. She lost weight. "The great year of 1951 with you has proven far too much for this country gal," she told Frank, who was a daily visitor to the hospital.

"What did the greedy bitch want?" a hospitalized Ava asked Frank when he returned from his divorce lawyers on September 28. He spelled out the horrid details: a third of his annual gross income up to $150,000 and ten percent after that; his Holmby Hills residence, his 1950 Cadillac, and custody of Nancy Jr., Tina, and Frank Jr.

"What's left for you?" Ava asked.

"My '49 Caddy and my old phonograph records."

"My God," she said. "I think I'll stay in this hospital bed for a month."

Frank began to suspect that Nancy was stalling, increasing her demands every day and changing terms orally agreed upon. "No one is getting rich from this but our lawyers," he told Ava.

When he accepted bookings in both Reno and Las Vegas, he also chose to file for divorce himself. Suddenly, Nancy, at long last, swung into action, filing for divorce in California, which had far greater financial advantages for her.

As part of her petition, she sued for $40,000 in back alimony. As if he weren't in enough trouble, Frank's attorney in Los Angeles sued him for $12,250 in legal fees. When the money wasn't forthcoming, he put a lien on Frank's villa in Palm Springs.

Nancy's divorce decree in California was finalized on October 30, 1951, with Frank's Nevada divorce granted on November 1.

By October 19, 1951 Ava was out of the hospital in California and was seen attending a party at Ciro's with the handsome English-born actor, Richard Greene. He'd become a household name in America because of his leading roles in costume quickies which included the bodice-ripper *Forever Amber* (1947). He was in the final throes of his marriage to actress Patricia Medina. Word spread quickly that Ava was having an affair with Greene, and rumors reached New York, precipitating one of Ava's most violent fights with Frank. Ava denied any involvement with the dashing actor, but Frank had witnesses claiming they did have a fling. He

145

demanded that Ava fly into New York, where they had a big fight over the actor. Ava adamantly denied an affair.

Turning the tables, she accused him of having an affair with some anonymous hooker who was seen coming and going from his suite. Their shared commitment to an upcoming marriage hardly survived these accusations.

From the beginning they'd engaged in brawls. "He has a temper that bursts into flames," she said. "I'm the slow burner. But once ignited, call the fire department."

With his divorce papers, Frank flew with Ava to Philadelphia where they had to wait seventy-two hours before they could get married after filing all the documents attesting to their respective divorces.

By scheduling the wedding in Philadelphia, Frank and Ava foolishly hoped to avoid reporters and photographers. They hid out at a private home in Philadelphia that belonged to Lester Sachs, the brother of Emmanuel ("Manie") Sachs, the former head of Frank's label at Columbia.

The night before their wedding, Ava received a letter from "a whore," who claimed she'd been having an affair with Frank. Ava later wrote, "It was filthy, and it gave details that I found convincing." Those details included what was perhaps the most vivid description ever written of Frank's penis and testicles, even a description of the color of his "rosebud," as Ava called it in private revelations to her friends.

The prostitute also described in vivid details Frank's favorite sexual positions, the exact times and places of their trysts.

Ava immediately called off the wedding. It took a night of Frank's pleading before she was convinced to change her mind.

She later learned that Frank's bimbo had been paid $5,000 by Howard Hughes to write the confessional. After reading the letter, Ava told Bappie, "All I could do was vomit."

After Frank's divorce from Nancy came through, it took him only 72 hours before he could legally marry Ava.

Later she told cameraman Robert Surtees, "You know what the son-of-a-bitch did? He sent me the bill for the wedding ring."

In 1941, two of the world's greatest beauties, aspiring starlet Ava Gardner and a star already, **Hedy Lamarr** *(above)* boarded a train, the Twentieth Century Limited, in New York for the long westbound journey to Los Angeles. It would include a change of trains in Chicago for passage across the Great American Plains.

The two 1940s movie queens met in the train's powder room and sized each other up. As Hedy would admit in her autobiography, *Ecstasy,* and as Ava's future biographers would confess, both of these sultry sirens had lesbian tendencies. But apparently, they resisted each other as the train raced across the desert carrying them to stardom and a string of men who would include Frank Sinatra.

Hedy had already lost her virginity at the age of fourteen, when she was raped by a laundryman. Ava, if reports are to be believed, would not lose hers until her wedding night, of January 10, 1942, when Mickey Rooney did the deflowering.

At long last the marriage took place on November 7, 1951. He placed a narrow platinum wedding ring on Ava's finger as she looked camera-ready in a mauve *marquisette* cocktail dress.

They flew to Miami for their honeymoon. Ava's luggage didn't make it, and the honeymooning couple stayed in Miami and delayed their departure to Cuba until her baggage arrived.

"We almost didn't leave that bed in Miami all the time," she later told Bappie. "Did you know that Frank likes to fuck women in the ass? It hurts like hell."

After two days in Cuba, they flew to New York, where Frank did a CBS TV special. They dined with Dolly and Marty Sinatra in Hoboken before returning to Los Angeles, where, after a turbulent flight, they landed on November 15, 1951.

By December 7, they boarded a TWA Constellation jet bound for London. Frank was scheduled to appear at a Royal Command variety performance.

In London, they celebrated his thirty-sixth birthday. They were also invited to a charity benefit sponsored by the Duke of Edinburgh, Prince Philip. Frank became furious when he saw Ava dancing the samba with the prince. "My God," he said to one of the entertainers, "she's pressing her cunt right up against His Highness."

On December 9 their hotel suite was robbed, Ava losing a diamond and emerald necklace, a gift from Frank and one of her preferred pieces of jewelry.

"Don't worry, baby, there's more where that came from," he promised her.

"Only if you rob Tiffany's," she shot back.

Frank told Ava that he did not want her to devote so much time to her career, so she'd be free to travel with him. But she reminded him, "One of us has to work in this family." That remark led to another of their epic brawls.

Because she needed the money and didn't dare risk suspension, Ava agreed to co-star with Clark Gable in a western, *Lone Star* (1952). Frank warned her not to resume her affair with Gable. The warning was not necessary. A has-been at the box office, Gable was hard to photograph. He was overweight and had become jowly, and he was suffering from the first stages of Parkinson's disease.

In a phone call to Frank, she said, "What in hell am I doing playing a newspaper reporter? You know what I think of reporters. I can't even read a newspaper, much less be a journalist."

Suspecting an affair between Gable and Ava, Frank called her three times a day. "Has Gable started fucking you yet?"

"Don't be an ass," she said. "I don't know if Clark can get it up anymore. Besides, what woman in her right mind would want that dick of his? Even Carole Lombard said, 'If Clark had one inch less, he'd be the Queen of Hollywood.'"

Frank flew to the set of *Lone Star* just in time to watch a love scene between Ava and Gable. When he saw that she was very gently trying to conceal his convulsively shaking head from

**Grace Kelly** (*left*) and **Ava Gardner** (*right*) co-starred with Clark Gable in *Mogambo* (1953). Set in Africa, it was a remake of Gable's 1932 film *Red Dust* which had co-starred Jean Harlow and Mary Astor.

Frank traveled to Africa with Ava, but was very sensitive about how he'd be regarded, especially by Clark Gable. "Here I am, a fucking has-been, carrying a shot of booze to my working spouse, the biggest movie star in Hollywood."

In Africa, Frank attacked photographers and spent most of his time in the steamy jungle enraged and lashing out, often at Ava.

The situation on the set didn't get much better when Frank, one drunken night, confronted *Mogambo's* director, John Ford. "Is it true you used to suck off John Wayne back in the good old days? I always wondered how a no talent guy like The Duke broke into show business."

Ford, the most closeted of Hollywood homosexuals, ignored him.

the camera, Frank was no longer jealous of her but applauded her for trying to prevent Gable's embarrassment.

He had to return to the East Coast for singing engagements, and she came back to Hollywood alone. Secretly, even though longing for Frank, she began to date other men. As discreetly as he could, he also saw other women, usually hookers who didn't talk.

At a Hollywood party, Lana Turner and Rosalind Russell found Ava sitting alone smoking a cigarette in a corner. "I have everything," she told these two stars. "Except the things I want the most—Frank, a home, kids. In a sense, these are the same damn things I wanted in North Carolina before I ever knew there was anything else to desire."

***

When Ava was married to Artie Shaw, the couple lived next door on Bedford Drive in Beverly Hills to the reclusive Greta Garbo. Even though Ava often tried to peek through the hedges, she never saw Garbo during her residency there.

While Ava was staying in Frank's Palm Springs house, with her sister, Bappie, she received a call from Frank. He had invited Garbo and a friend for the weekend, and she'd be arriving within minutes.

Ava and Bappie rushed to make her room ready, turning up the air conditioning to fight off the desert heat and filling the bedroom with flowers.

In a taxi, Garbo arrived with her friend, Minna Walls. She wanted to see her room immediately, later sending Minna to tell Ava that Garbo "hated flowers and air conditioning."

That afternoon, as Ava was sunbathing in the nude, Garbo made an appearance. She wasn't nude but topless, attired only a pair of men's baggy khaki shorts.

In her memoirs, Ava wrote: "Other than those shorts, she wore nothing else. Though she must have been in her mid-forties, her breasts and shoulders were glorious. Her face had just a touch of blue eye shadow, her lips a trace of lipstick, and she had that wonderful hair that moved from side to side as she turned her head. She was totally magnificent."

In the original draft of Ava's autobiography, published the year of her death (1990), she devoted almost a chapter to that weekend with Garbo, Frank, and herself in Palm Springs. But someone, perhaps the publisher, decided to censor it because of the lesbian overtones.

Over the years, however, the story has emerged. Frank apparently arrived about an hour and a half after Garbo's arrival. When he changed into a pair of shorts and an orange shirt, he went to join Ava and Garbo around the pool. As he stepped outside, he saw both of them totally nude in the pool, after they'd finished off a bottle of vodka. Garbo was fondling Ava's succulent breasts.

Unlike a future arrival at his Palm Springs villa, when he discovered Ava and Lana Turner, this peep show with Garbo didn't produce any argument at all. He walked over to the pool bar and called out, "When you gals finish your business, come and join me for a drink."

In a few minutes, both Ava and Garbo appeared for another vodka. This time they'd draped beach towels around themselves. When Garbo later excused herself for a siesta, Ava turned to Frank and asked him, "You aren't jealous catching Garbo feeling my breasts?"

"Who wouldn't want to feel your breasts?" he asked. "Besides, it was Greta Garbo. She's entitled."

***

In Palm Springs, Frank's longtime friend Milton Berle—in a serious moment—came to visit Frank. He confessed to "Uncle Miltie," that "I've never felt so alone in my life. I'm desperate for a comeback, but I don't know how."

"Have a hit song or a hit movie," Milton advised him. "You'll be on top again."

"Easier said than done," Frank responded.

He decided to fly back to New York to see what work, if any, was available for him. In the first-class compartment, he sat next to Bob Hope. Knowing of Frank's low ebb in his career, Hope offered him a guest appearance on his TV special.

When CBS signed Frank for a TV series of his own, he felt he was on the comeback trail. Ava had to fly west for wardrobe fittings for MGM's *Show Boat* (1951), in which she played a mulatto. It would become her most famous picture.

As Ava's career in films soared, Frank's return to TV was a bomb. Sponsors for his show dwindled, as did viewers. He began to lash out at Ava again. Her most famous quote at the time was, "The problems were never in bed. We were always great in bed. Our fights began on the way to the bidet."

Ava's fortunes were better. Her *Show Boat* opening that autumn was a financial triumph for MGM and an artistic triumph for her.

Movie roles had more or less dried up for Frank, but he was offered the lead in a film, *Meet Danny Wilson* (1952), in which he would be cast opposite the outspoken and temperamental Shelley Winters.

Frank and Winters had no love for each other. On the set they had a vicious argument as he called her a "bow-legged bitch of a Brooklyn blonde." She retorted, shouting at him, "You're nothing but a skinny, no-talent, stupid Hoboken bastard."

In their final scene, Shelley lay in a hospital bed. Frank was supposed to say to Alex Nicol, his romantic rival, "I'll have a cup of coffee and leave you two love-birds alone." Instead, on camera, he said, "I'll have a cup of Jack Daniel's or I'm going to pull that blonde broad's hair out by its black roots."

Jumping out of bed, Shelley hit Frank over the head with a bedpan and stormed off the set.

It was Nancy Sinatra herself who called Shelley and begged her to return to the set. "If Frank doesn't get that twenty-five thousand for the picture, the bank is going to foreclose on us. My children will be out on the street."

Shelley returned to work.

Unlike Frank, Ava had a more prestigious film assignment.

When she returned with Frank to his Palm Springs villa, a script was waiting. Called *The Snows of*

In *Lone Star*, a quasi-historical tale about the battle for the future of Texas, **Ava Gardner** *(center)* was re-teamed with **Clark Gable** *(pictured in this movie poster on the left)*. Any romance that had flourished between the two of them was already *Gone With the Wind*, as Rhett Butler might have said.

"The end is coming for me at MGM," Gable told her. "A few months ago, I heard that Louis B. Mayer said I had outlived my usefulness. The same could be said for that bastard."

During filming, Ava and **Broderick Crawford** *(right figure in poster above)* often wandered about the set in drunken stupors. Burly, brutish Crawford, with his harsh, barking voice, actually liked sex with handsome young men, but was afraid to approach them, fearing rejection.

One night, Ava spotted a member of the crew, a 25-year-old cowboy from Texas in tight jeans. "Kid, I'll give you a hundred dollar bill if you'll go to Crawford's room tonight and let him suck you off."

"You got yourself a deal, lady," the cowboy said. "But I'd do you for nothing."

"Give me a raincheck," she told him.

*Kilimanjaro*, it was based on a story by Ernest Hemingway. Susan Hayward and Gregory Peck were her co-stars in this film to be directed by Henry King.

Throughout the course of their marriage, Ava and Frank were separated by work. She had turned down several roles to be at his side as he went from one unsuccessful gig to the next. But MGM insisted that she make the prestigious Kilimanjaro picture, and because she was at her peak, Ava felt she had to give more consideration to her own career. Despite Frank's protests, she accepted the part.

The night before she flew away, Frank became more selfish than she'd ever seen him before. Louis B. Mayer had warned her that she'd ruin her career if she didn't take this role. But Frank protested, "Without you, baby, I'll die. I'll just die." He even threatened to kill himself.

She ignored his childish belligerence and left him anyway. A line in the Kilimanjaro movie described her own feelings when she said, "I'm my own lady."

Ava Gardner always thought that Bette Davis was the greatest actress on the screen, but that **Greta Garbo** (*above*) was its greatest beauty.

Garbo could find nothing to admire about Ava's acting, but she thought she was a "sexy siren." and so informed several people at MGM of her opinion. She even told Mickey Rooney, Ava's husband, of how sexy she found Ava.

The pint-sized actor took all that in stride, but Frank Sinatra, Ava's third husband, actually arranged for Garbo and Ava to come together in his Palm Springs villa. "If Garbo has the hots for Ava, I can only applaud her good taste in women," Frank said.

Actually, the eccentric filmmaker, Albert Lewin, had wanted Garbo to return to the screen to star in the 1951 film, *Pandora and the Flying Dutchman*, but happily settled for Ava instead.

She finished the movie and returned to New York in time for Frank's engagement at the Paramount Theater. In many ways, she wished she'd stayed away. Some critics referred to his concert as "a disaster."

Story after story suggested that: SINATRA IS FINISHED! FRANKIE IS ON THE SKIDS! SINATRA IS ALL WASHED UP!

There were stories that he was "a has-been married to the biggest female star in Hollywood."

The first person who calls me Mr. Ava Gardner will get his nuts kicked." Frank threatened.

That night, he told Ava, "Tell all the fuckers writing me off as finished that I'm gonna come back bigger and better than ever."

He seemed more and more dependent on Ava, and was distraught over stories he was hearing from the set of *Kilimanjaro*. So-called friends called him and told him that Ava was having a torrid affair with Gregory Peck, who at the time was considered one of the hottest actors in Hollywood.

To make matters worse, columnist Lee Mortimer published charges that Frank was under the control of the Mafia. That launched a feud between the two that on more than one occasion led to violent confrontations.

While she was in bed with "one of the handsomest male movie stars of all time," as Peck was referred to, Frank was playing seedy dives and losing his once-fabled voice. "I need you with me during this awful time," he pleaded with her over the phone, not knowing her kisses belonged to Peck at night.

*Kilimanjaro* was the film that made an international star of Ava.

On May 24, 1952, back in Hollywood, Ava was

rushed to Cedars of Lebanon Hospital, right after attending one of Frank's performances at the Cocoanut Grove. Depending on which story was spread, she had either a miscarriage or an abortion.

Released from the hospital, she resented the hours Frank spent with the children Nancy had given him.

"They're the only children I have," he shouted at her. "It's not like you've given me any. It seems you've reserved your vagina for other uses."

She threw a vase at him, cutting a gash in his forehead. One of their most bitter fights ensued.

At this point of her feud with Frank, another film offer came in. MGM asked her to shoot *Ride, Vaquero*, a Western co-starring one of her former lovers, Robert Taylor, in the small town of Kanab in southern Utah.

Covered in "Red Dust" (the name of a 1932 movie she'd soon remake with a different title), she experienced 120°F heat at a seedy hotel named Perry's, "the only game in town," she said. "If the termites stop holding hands," she said in a call to Frank, "the God damn place will collapse. You can hear every bed squeaking at night."

"Make sure it's not your bed squeaking," he warned her. "I don't want to hear that you're fucking Taylor again, taking all of his four inches."

By June of 1952, Ava was melting in the heat of Kanab, Utah during her filming of *Ride, Vaquero*. This time Frank heard reports that Ava was spending her nights with the director John Farrow. (Incidentally, Farrow was the father of Mia Farrow, who would become Frank's third wife.)

At first Ava hated John Farrow, the husband of Maureen O'Sullivan. He was cruel to the horses, and he used to import hookers for the weekend, waking up the sleepy town. But by the second week the hookers disappeared.

Farrow was spending his nights at a house Ava had managed to rent. Since Frank had a spy on the set, he soon found out. An epic fight ensued, and he threatened to divorce her.

Hearing reports of her affair, Frank immediately skipped two important singing engagements, even though he needed the money, and flew to her location in Utah. Her affair with Farrow ended almost immediately, but Frank's bitter fights with Ava did not. At one point he denounced her in front of the cast as a "God damn Tarheel whore."

Escaping from Utah, she arrived in Hollywood for a reconciliation with Frank and an offer from MGM to film a remake of *Red Dust*, a 1932 picture that had starred Clark Gable, Jean Harlow, and Mary Astor. The new film, also starring Gable in the same role, had been retitled *Mogambo*.

In New York it was September 5, 1952, and autumn was in the air. She attended the premiere of *The Snows of Kilimanjaro* but without Frank. He was appearing at the Riviera Club in Fort Lee, New Jersey. Ava was able to break away and make Frank's late show in Fort Lee. She arrived but left immediately when she discovered the blonde-haired beauty, Marilyn Maxwell, in the audience. She knew that Marilyn had been Frank's on-again, off-again mistress for years, and she rightly suspected that it was on again.

Then Ava flew back to Hollywood. Once there, she mailed Frank the wedding ring he'd given her. He lost it the first day.

When he returned to Hollywood, he managed to patch things up with Ava.

He joined her during the shooting of *Mogambo* in Africa. But he flew back to Hollywood twice—both for a screen test for the role of Maggio in *From Here to Eternity* and, later, when he actually won the role, beating out Eli Wallach, who had another assignment he preferred.

Tales from the sets of *Mogambo* and *From Here to Eternity* are detailed in other sections of this book.

For a 1953 release from MGM, Pandro S. Berman at MGM cast Ava once again with Robert Taylor in *Knights of the Round Table*, to be shot in England.

In 1953, **Ava**, as Guinivere, starred once again with the aging matinee ideo, **Robert Taylor**, in *Knights of the Round Table* for MGM. Taylor and Gardner had "burnt out on each other" at this point, as Ava so graphically characterized it. She told a reporter, "The fucking picture stinks. I only report to work to collect a paycheck—that's it."

On location for *Knights,* Ava hadn't seen Frank in four months when he showed up on the set. He promised a second honeymoon, but she was suspicious, assuming that he was involved with another woman, perhaps Marilyn Monroe herself.

In May of 1953, Frank got booked on a three-month concert tour of Europe. Ava accompanied him on part of the tour, where he sang to only half-filled theaters. In Copenhagen, a newspaper headline greeted him: MR. SINATRA, GO HOME.

He followed its advice, canceling the tour and flying back to London...and Ava. After a big fight, he flew back to New York alone.

She flew to Spain, where she met the charismatic, handsome, and macho bullfighter, Luis Miguel Dominguin. Ernest Hemingway had told Ava, "He's part Don Juan, part Hamlet."

Ava, shortly after their first tryst, cabled the author back: "Papa, you are right!"

Frank was still away filming the classic *From Here to Eternity*, while Ava was trapped in England shooting this dreary costume drama. MGM's first wide-screen movie shot in England, it was a mini-spectacle re-enactment of King Arthur's Court.

Ava resumed having affairs with other men, and Frank spent drunken nights in bed with a totally inebriated Montgomery Clift, his *Eternity* co-star, who was falling in love with him.

During the filming of *Knights of the Round Table*, Ava risked suspension from MGM for taking time off to join Frank on "his has-been concert tour," as the press called it.

Ava inspired one of his most personal songs, "I'm a Fool to Want You." His arranger, Nelson Riddle, said, "It was Ava who taught him how to sing a torch song."

The tour started in Naples with Ava sitting in the front rows of the audience. In the middle of Frank's first song, the spotlight picked her out of the crowd. The screams of AVA! AVA! AVA! echoed throughout the theater. Frank walked off the stage, and Ava left the theater and went back to their hotel.

It pained her to know that her star was shining so brightly and his had lost its glow. The former idol of all those screaming bobbysoxers played to half-empty halls and jeering former fans throughout the rest of his tour.

At this point, *From Here to Eternity* had not been released. It would in time bring Frank an Oscar for Best Supporting Actor of 1953.

She said, "Our marriage was past saving at this point." Her decision to divorce him came somewhere when he was on that tour.

He called her one night and over the phone informed her, "My big dick, right this moment, is plugged into some bitch. I don't know her name."

Ava put down the phone. She later recalled. "I knew then we had reached the crossroads. Not because we'd fallen out of love, but because our love had so battered and bruised us that we couldn't stand it anymore."

He visited her on the English set of the *Knights of the Round Table*. The weather was gray, dreary, and rainy, just like their love affair. They spent most of their time quarreling.

In a call to Lana Turner, Ava said, "I know you and Frank had something a while back. You're welcome to him again. I'm tired. I want out. His charm is lost on me. He's impossible to live with. This so-called marriage is over. It's been hell. Believe it or not, I still love the Dago bastard. But we get along better on different continents."

The year 1953 was rough on their marriage, as both of them devoted most of their time to their careers. Frank at long last was on the comeback trail, having negotiated a new recording contract with Capitol Records after he'd been dropped from the Columbia label.

The year was also marked by betrayals, adultery on both sides, reunions, and more fights. On one occasion, both Ava and Frank were in New York without realizing the other was there until they read about it in the gossip columns.

Ava's separation from Frank was announced in October of 1953, although the divorce didn't become final until 1957.

"They developed a great friendship," said Kathryn Grayson, who had co-starred with both Frank and Ava in films. "They helped each other. I think they wanted to get together again, but circumstances kept them apart."

Her friend, Arlene Dahl, at the time of Ava's death, said, "She never loved another man as much as she loved Frank."

Their marriage seemed all but over even though they attended the premiere of *From Here to Eternity* in 1953 together. In October of that same year, both of them also showed up arm in arm for the premiere of *Mogambo*. That same month MGM announced for Ava that she was filing for a divorce.

Frank told reporters, "It's not true. We're still very much in love," which in some strange way was the truth.

By Christmas of 1953 his weight had dropped to 118 pounds. Nervous and exhausted, he was on the verge of a total nervous breakdown.

She still remained so enchanted with Spain that she'd moved to Madrid. "There are a lot of bullfighters to audition there," she told Lana.

Although suffering with the flu, Frank flew to Madrid, only to find that Ava had come down with German measles. Their reunion was a disaster.

During their time together in Madrid, she told him she was taking up permanent residency in the Spanish capital. In a bizarre episode, while a resident, she found herself living in an apartment over the exiled Juan Perón, former dictator of Argentina. His ex-wife, Eva (Evita) Perón, had died of cancer, and he kept her body in a crystal coffin in the apartment he shared with his mistress, Isabel.

Idling in Spain, Ava was delighted she didn't have to make a film called *Green Fire* in the steamy jungles of Colombia. Grace Kelly accepted the role instead.

Ava was offered a script called *St. Louis Woman*. She briefly considered it since it would unite her with Frank as her co-star. But the project ultimately fell through. In Frank's absence, Ava renewed her affair with Bunny Allen, the big-game hunter she'd met in Africa on the set of *Mogambo*.

Finally, after months of exasperation, Frank told reporters in Carson City, Nevada, that "Ava and I are washed up."

In Spain, Ava made *The Barefoot Contessa* (1954) and fell briefly in love with Luís Miguel Dominguin, who was handsome, rich, and had been the most famous matador in Spain.

When Ava wanted to divorce Frank, she decided not to "appear like that greedy bitch Nancy Sinatra." However, since he had new contracts, film deals, and money from his recordings again, even a piece of a casino in Las Vegas, she thought it only fair that he repay her some of the money she'd lent him during the years he was broke. He'd always promised to pay her back one day.

To her shock and anger, he absolutely refused. "Why should I pay her one cent?" he asked his lawyers. "She got the best fucking of her life—that's worth something."

When Ava herself became impoverished in later years, he'd be far more generous with her.

Even after their divorce, Ava admitted that Frank ran up "astronomical phone bills" calling her. He wrote to her almost every day, even during his other affairs or marriages. "No matter where in the world I was, I'd get a telegram from Frank saying he loved me and missed me."

Biographer Roy Moseley, a friend of both Ava and Frank, said, "She told me she always wanted to be known as Mrs. Frank Sinatra." She often signed her checks "Ava Sinatra."

Two strokes in 1986 left Ava partially paralyzed and bedridden. After a lifetime of smoking, she suffered from emphysema, in addition to an auto-immune disorder, perhaps lupus.

In 1989, Frank had been warned that Ava might be dying. He called her. "Regardless of what's come down between us, you're still the one," he told her.

"And you're still the one for me, too," she told him.

"I've got a great idea," he said. "Let's get rid of all our excess baggage and get married all over again. If Elizabeth Taylor can marry Burton twice, why can't we?"

"You're on, Little Frankie," she said. "Is Big Frankie still in working order?"

"You'll soon see," he predicted.

Both of them knew that he was not serious in his proposal.

Her last words to her housekeeper, Carmen, were "I'm so tired."

She died in London at the age of 67 of pneumonia. The date was January 25, 1990.

Both **Ava Gardner and Frank Sinatra** *(right)* were introduced to **Prince Philip**, the Duke of Edinburgh *(left)* at a command performance in London in 1951. Later that night, when the handsome royal prince spent most of the evening dancing with a slightly drunken Ava, Frank was both furious and jealous.

Ava later told Robert Taylor, "At one point, Philip and I were dancing so close we felt as one. I really wanted to know if all those rumors are true. I discreetly reached out and very gently groped him. The rumor is true!"

Tina Sinatra found her father slumped in his room crying, unable to speak.

Some reports claimed that Frank attended the funeral in Ava's birth state of North Carolina. It attracted some 500 mourners. A black limousine was parked near the graveyard. Mourners assumed Frank was in the back seat but too grief stricken to get out. Actually, the car had been rented by a Fayetteville hairdresser. "A black limousine was the only appropriate transportation for Ava's funeral," the hairdresser later recalled.

Frank sent a floral arrangement of red and white roses with a simple note that read, "With my love, Francis."

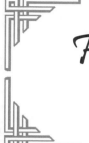

# Frank, Ava, Their Marriage,

## & THE KIDS WHO NEVER WERE

STEPPING OUT!  The love affair and eventual marriage of **Frank Sinatra and Ava Gardner** were doomed from the start. Initially, Ava wasn't impressed with the bag of bones until he took off his clothes, and then she had nothing but praise for "my Frankie boy."  She told Lana Turner, "Only Porfirio Rubirosa is better hung, but then, he's the Ninth Wonder of the World."

She was referring to the diplomat/playboy from the Dominican Republic who went on to marry the world's two richest women--Barbara Hutton and Doris Duke.

In the beginning, Ava was torn between Sinatra and the minor gangster, Johnny Stompanato, a close friend of mob boss Mickey Cohen.  One night she received a call from Stompanato, who told her that even though she'd never received an Oscar, she would get one that night if she invited him over.

"What on earth do you mean, honey chile?" she asked.

"Oscar and I share the same dimensions," he bluntly told her.

"Get over here at once, baby, and let's see how much you exaggerated," she said.

When Frank learned of their affair, he called Cohen and warned him,  "Tell your boy to leave Ava alone or else he might find himself in a ditch somewhere some dark night missing a pair of *cojones.*"

"Oh, Frankie, baby, go back to your wife," Cohen barked at him.  "You belong with Nancy--not Ava."

# A TEMPTRESS
## WHO DROVE FRANK TO THE BRINK OF SUICIDE

**AVA GARDNER**: She was The Naked Maja. The Barefoot Contessa. Lady Brett. The rise of a beautiful North Carolina farm girl—barefoot and with a thick Southern accent—to the pinnacle of Hollywood is the stuff of legend. She became Mrs. Mickey Rooney, Mrs. Artie Shaw, Mrs. Frank Sinatra. She loved booze, bullfighters, and bitches of the night. Her close friends ranged from Ernest Hemingway to Adlai Stevenson.

Her own life, however, was more dramatic than any role she portrayed on the screen.

Ava Gardner was called "the world's greatest beauty." But in the golden age of movie-making, the tabloids, who documented her steamy private life, had a lot more to say than that.

Studio packaged, Ava was one of the last of the great Hollywood sex goddesses. But studio chief Louis B. Mayer went ballistic trying to keep her personal scandals from destroying her career.

"Unless he was a gay blade," said an MGM studio publicist, "every red-blooded male who ever saw an Ava Gardner movie wanted to take her to bed."

*"Straight women, at least at some point in their lives, fantasize about lesbian sex as much as horny men fantasize about lesbian sex. Include Ava Gardner in the first category."*

**Paulette Goddard**

*"She's not a dyke. But Ava likes to pick up ladies of the night and spend the rest of the evening smoking and drinking with them and listening to their low-life tales of lust in the dust. Life on the hustle, the raw edge."*

**Marlon Brando**

*"Howard Hughes pursued Ava Gardner, but all he got from her was a terrific blow-job after that plane crash. Ava told me she never let him screw her. But Mr. Hughes screwed Lana Turner and her boyfriend, Tyrone Power, on a number of occasions. What he really wanted was to go to bed with Lana and Ava, at the same time. Ava said no, but she agreed to make love to Lana and let Mr. Hughes watch one drunken night. He had to settle for that. I think Mr. Hughes told me he masturbated through the entire encounter."*

**Johnny Meyer,** pimp to Howard Hughes

"As much as I would like to believe Ava went for the gals as much as for the cocky bastards like that wop, Frank Sinatra, I just couldn't buy it. In my view, she was too much of a man-eater to like to do it with the girls. At least that was my first impression of her when my son, Peter Lawford, was having an affair with her. But after a thorough interrogation of my son, I now believe Ava was a switch-hitter. Peter supplied names, dates, places, and detailed descriptions of what Ava liked to do with women. I can't stand faggots. Peter was always bringing them around our house in Hollywood. I would retreat upstairs until the perverts were gone. Then I'd order the maid to fumigate the living room. As for lesbians, I'm more like Queen Victoria on that subject. The very thought of woman-on-woman sex makes my blood curdle."

**Lady May Lawford**

"Ava was so drunk half the time she would have gone to bed with a porcupine."

**Mia Farrow**

"Were you once married to the Frank Sinatra?"

—**Young Londoner**'s question to Ava Gardner

"I always knew Frank would end up with a little boy."

**Ava Gardner** learning of Frank's marriage to Mia Farrow

"Ann Sheridan and I were fucking Ava Gardner around the same time, but individually—not as a ménage à trois. I think I would have preferred the latter."

**Peter Lawford**

## They All Had Something to Say About Ava.....

Paulette Goddard

Marlon Brando

Lady May Lawford

Mia Farrow

# AVA GARDNER IN A CATFIGHT
## WITH YVONNE DE CARLO

**Ava Gardner**
The Pride of North Carolina

Most Ava Gardner biographers make no mention of the star's lesbianism. Lee Server, who wrote the definitive biography of the beautiful star, *Love Is Nothing*, at least was aware of it, as were some of the latest Frank Sinatra biographers such as Anthony Summers.

Although unbelievably savvy about what went on when the lights went out in Hollywood, Frank became aware of Ava's fondness for the girls only during the course of their marriage, and that was because the even hipper Rat Packer, Peter Lawford, informed him.

Frank learned even more about Ava's Sapphic streak when Donna Caldwell, a Hollywood madam of the 50s, told him that she had once supplied some of her girls to both Ava and him. "You mean, Ava and I have fucked the same pussies?" he shouted in rage.

Peter Lawford liked lesbians and used to hire them to perform sexual acts together in front of him. Frank, like many straight men, also became excited watching girl-on-girl action.

Ava's rival, both on screen and in the boudoirs of Hollywood, was **Yvonne De Carlo,** who's featured in both of the photos above.

"Howard Hughes told me I was the most beautiful woman in the world," claimed Yvonne. "That bitch, Ava Gardner, is a liar telling people that Howard claimed she, not me, was the most beautiful girl in the world."

Yvonne added a footnote, "Prince Aly Khan begged me to marry him. He only got Rita Hayworth after I turned him down. Another thing: Both Clark Gable and Robert Taylor told me I was far better in the sack than Ava."

*Tout* Hollywood mainly learned of Ava's lesbianism through the mouth of Yvonne De Carlo. Ava and she often dated some of the same men, notably Howard Hughes. They both shared the lovemaking technique of actor Howard Duff, who later became the third "Mr. Ida Lupino." Clark Gable, Burt Lancaster, and Robert Taylor were other men they'd had in common. Ava eventually learned that at one point that De Carlo had sampled the charms of two of her former husbands, Artie Shaw (the musician who had originally been married to Lana Turner) and Frank himself.

De Carlo claimed that one night Ava invited her to her home, and she accepted. "After all, Ava was a big star at the time." De Carlo said that she feared that she might encounter a drunken Ava who'd fly into a jealous rage and attack her for "sleeping with her boyfriends."

"When I got there, Ava could not have been more charming," De Carlo later told friends. "Not once did she bring up the subject of our shared boyfriends, with one exception. She warned me that Howard Hughes might have given me VD, and that I'd better go and get my vagina checked out by a doctor. When I started to leave around two o'clock in the morning, she detained me in the hallway. She invited me to spend the night, fearing I was too drunk to drive. She said she could never stand sleeping alone. I agreed to share her bed. At that point, there was no suggestion of sex."

"In her bedroom, Ava stripped nude—after all, she had a great body—but I modestly retained my lingerie," De Carlo said. We'd been in bed no more than thirty minutes when Ava moved in on me for sex. I was horrified. I have lived and worked with gay people all my life, and I have no problem with their preferences, but anybody who knows me knows I don't go that route. I jumped out of bed and grabbed my clothes, running toward my car. I might have been drunk when I got in bed with Ava but I was sober when I drove away from her place."

The story of De Carlo's night with Ava was just too good to keep to herself. Besides, De Carlo always thought that she—not Ava—deserved the title of "Most Beautiful Woman in the World." At parties and dinners, De Carlo widely repeated the story of her private encounter with Ava, telling some of her lovers such as director Billy Wilder, actor Robert Stack, and even Prince Aly Khan, all of whom knew Ava. Soon the word was all over town.

In his biography of Ava, Lee Server accurately wrote: "She had a continuity curiosity about the sexual demimonde and through the years paid visits to gay bars, red-light zones, and brothels all over the world."

On her most notorious brothel visit, she was accompanied by—of all people—Grace Kelly.

It all began when Grace and Ava signed to co-star in *Mogambo* in 1953, a film to be shot in Africa. The male

When **Clark Gable** arrived in Africa to film *Mogambo* in 1953, he was accompanied by two of the most beautiful women in the world: **Grace Kelly and Ava Gardner.** "I always had trouble deciding whether I liked chocolate or vanilla better," Gable told director John Ford.

He of course was referring to Grace's blonde hair and Ava's dark curls. Mogambo translates from Swahili as "passion," and no other word could better describe the off-screen sex going on during the making of this film.

Ava's all-time favorite movie was *Red Dust* in which a young Gable had starred opposite Jean Harlow as "Honey Bear," a slut in the bush. Now Ava was replacing her idol, Harlow, in Gable's arms.

"As you know," Ava told Grace, "Clark doesn't have all that much to penetrate with, but Frankie's weapon sure knows how to reach virgin territory."

159

star was Clark Gable, who, ironically, had appeared in the first version, called *Red Dust*, released in 1932 and co-starring Jean Harlow and Mary Astor.

On the eve of their first wedding anniversary, Ava announced to Frank that she was heading to Africa to film *Mogambo* directed by John Ford. Frank virtually had no money at this point and was forced to consent to let her go. After another bitter fight, she left California heading for New York, London, and ultimately Nairobi, Kenya.

Since nothing was breaking for him in America, Frank decided to fly to Nairobi with Ava to become a silent member of John Ford's "safari" of 150 whites and 350 natives. An 1,800-yard airstrip had been hacked out of the jungles to receive small planes from Nairobi, carrying food, drink, letters, film equipment, and medical supplies.

When a reporter caught up with Frank as he was departing for his long trip to Africa, he was asked, "Frankie, is John Ford gonna find you a role in *Mogambo*?"

"Yeah," Frank shot back. "I'm gonna go native in black face—maybe with my cock hanging out!"

Ava chimed in, "Frank will be doing his thing in some clubs in Africa, using Tarzan as his opening act."

Celebrating her first anniversary on a plane en route to Nairobi, Ava drank what she called "piss-warm champagne" and accepted a diamond-studded ring from Frank. She would later receive the bill for it.

"I've been married to him for a year," she told the captain. "Marriages to Artie Shaw and that Mickey Rooney runt didn't last that long. I'm the restless type. Show me a man in tight pants, and I'm off to the races." She was drunk before she'd boarded the plane.

In Africa, on the second day of the shoot, Ava discovered that Ford had a gay streak in him. She accidentally walked in on the director when he was deep-throating one of the handsome "white hunters" hired for *Mogambo*.

Frank had nothing to do all day except wait for Ava, who seemed dismissive of him, treating him more like her secretary than her husband. He kept reading and re-reading the novel, *From Here to Eternity*, as his agents worked to get him the tragic role of Maggio in the film.

Ford may have found his white hunter, but Ava also became fascinated by Frank ("Bunny") Allen, another strapping white hunter who arranged movie safaris. But with Frank hanging around, she didn't dare risk chasing after Bunny.

"Our director, John Ford, wanted him, but I got him first," or so proclaimed Ava Gardner during the filming of *Mogambo* in Kenya. She was referring to the great white hunter, **Frank Maurice ("Bunny") Allen**, who's depicted above.

A British-born professional safari guide in Africa, he conducted everybody from Prince Charles to Mick Jagger through some aspects of a shooting expedition in Africa.

Bunny fell bigtime for Ava Gardner during the location filming, and he also came on strong to Grace Kelly. He was also the lover of Isak Dinesen, author of the novel *Out of Africa*.

Before the filming of *Mogambo*, he scouted the Congo River for locations for *The African Queen*, but claimed, "I never had an affair with Katharine Hepburn or Humphrey Bogart, although Robert Morley came on to me."

On days when heavy rains forced her to stay in her tent with Frank, they fought bitterly. Only a week after his arrival in Kenya, word reached him that Columbia had granted him a screen test for the role of Maggio.

Kissing Ava goodbye, and on a ticket she'd paid for, he flew back on the long circuitous route to Hollywood.

In all this jungle heat, Ava discovered she was pregnant.

In Frank's absence, Ava flew to London and aborted their child, although she had previously claimed that her greatest joy in life would involve having Frank's child. When Grace Kelly asked her about this, Ava said, "A lady has the privilege of changing her mind."

In defending her decision to have an abortion, Ava said, "MGM had all sorts of penalty clauses about their stars having babies. Frank and I couldn't even take care of ourselves. How were we going to look after a kid?"

Ava later claimed she'd had a miscarriage. Cameraman Robert Surtees disputed that. "Ava hated Frank so intensely at this point she was horrified at the thought of giving birth to 'Little Frankie Junior,' as she put it. My wife went with her to London. It was a God damn abortion. She told my wife, 'I hated Frankie so much, I wanted the baby to go unborn.'"

Although his Hollywood screen test for the role of Maggio in *From Here to Eternity* had gone well, Frank flew back to Africa, at Ava's expense, uncertain that he'd get the role. He arrived just in time for Christmas, bringing Ava a mink coat and a diamond ring he'd purchased with money from one of his gangster friends, perhaps Lucky Luciano. This would be Frank's last major attempt to win Ava back.

While on location in Kenya, Frank learned of the abortion of his baby and of Ava's affair with Bunny Allen. "All I remember about Christmas of 1953 was Frank denouncing Ava as a whore and a baby killer," Grace said.

Harry Cohn, with a lot of persuasion from Ava, finally agreed to give Frank the role of Maggio, for which he'd be paid only $10,000. Ava told Gable and Grace, "I practically had to agree to fuck Cohn to get Frank that God damn role."

After a brief, troubled Christmas together with Ava, Frank flew back once again on that long trip to Hollywood to accept the role, much of which would be shot on location in Hawaii.

An Oscar for Best Supporting Actor for his role in that film lay in his future. The part would mark a comeback for him.

On the set of *Mogambo*, both Frank and Ava had been witnesses to Gable's affair with Grace.

Ava later said that she wanted Grace to sample Gable as a lover, claiming that she'd already been sexually intimate with him in 1947 during the filming of *The Hucksters*. "I felt it was Grace's turn," Ava was quoted as saying.

When she had first met Ava beside the Kagera River in Central Africa, Grace had been shocked by her heavy drinking, her "potty mouth," and her uninhibited behavior.

But during the long weeks of shooting, Grace gradually warmed to Ava, and in time they became "friends for life."

At the completion of the film, Ava invited Grace to stop over

One of Ava's most famous films, *The Barefoot Contessa*, was actually based on the life of another screen sex goddess, Rita Hayworth. When the film's director, **Joseph Mankiewicz** *(with Ava in photo, above)*, still beaming from his success with *All About Eve*, called Ava in Rome, she invited him up to her suite. He was startled to find her lying naked on the sofa, sipping champagne.

"I can play more than barefoot," she said, wiggling her naked toes at him before raising her legs in the air. "Hop on, big guy."

with her for a few days for a Roman holiday, and Grace accepted. According to the testimony of Guido Volta, a chauffeur in Rome in the 1950s who hauled around everyone from Elizabeth Taylor to Frank Sinatra, Ava took the future princess of Monaco on a tour of the city's brothels. At first Grace declined, but Ava could be persuasive.

With Guido as their guide, the two women set off for visits to establishments that included (according to their English translations), "The World of Earthly Pleasures," "One Hundred and One Desires Fulfilled," "No Pleasure Too Great or Too Small," "Memories Are Made of This," and "The Garden of Delights." At the various Roman bordellos, Ava bought drinks for all the hookers, introducing them to Grace and urging them to tell "only their best stories."

At the final bordello, according to Guido, "Miss Kelly became fascinated by a strikingly handsome young man, Antonio Guarnieri, who at the time was about 23 years old, and who worked as a waiter in the joint. Just before dawn, I drove Ava, Miss Kelly, and Antonio back to the women's suites at the Hotel Excelsior on the Via Veneto. Ava sat up front with me, while Miss Kelly and Antonio got acquainted in back. At the hotel, the future princess of Monaco invited Antonio up to her suite for a nightcap. That must have been one long drink. It lasted for three days and nights and ended only when I came back to drive Miss Kelly to the airport. At the airport, Antonio and Miss Kelly engaged in the world's longest goodbye kiss. When I drove Antonio back to Rome, he cried all the way."

After telling Grace good-bye, Ava flew back to London for more film work. To her horror, she discovered that she was pregnant once again. She didn't want to go to the same hospital for another abortion—"they asked too many God damn questions"—so she checked into a small nursing home near Wimbledon where abortions were quietly performed. She later told friends, "Of course I could have hired Dolly Sinatra. She knows her way around an abortion table."

In her memoirs, Ava wrote, "Clearly someone told Frank about what I was doing, because as long as I live I'll never forget waking up after the operation and seeing him sitting next to the bed with tears in his eyes. But I think I was right. I still think I was right."

After the second abortion, Frank told friends, "I should have beaten her fucking brains out for aborting my kid, but I loved her too much." Later he changed his position, telling Sammy Davis Jr., "I don't think that second kid was mine."

Already in Hollywood, "Frank had found his *cojones* once again," Ava said. "He was no longer as dependent on me as before. His record sales were picking up; he was in a hit movie, and he often preferred nights with his gangland friends instead of me. But I wasn't sitting around the living room knitting at night."

She told Lana, "I've resumed my wild, wild ways—and to hell with Frank."

According to those who knew her well, **Her Most Serene Highness, the Princess of Monaco** in private did not resemble the ice-cold blonde goddess she played on screen.

Gary Cooper, who co-starred with her in *High Noon* (1952), said, "She looked like a cold dish with a man until you got her pants down. Then she'd explode."

A former lover, Don Richardson claimed, "She screwed everybody she came into contact with who was able to do anything good for her. She screwed agents, producers, directors. And there was really no need for it. She was on her way."

Director Henry Hathaway's wife once said, "Grace wore those white gloves, looking all prissy and proper, but she was no saint. Just ask Bing Crosby, Cary Grant, William Holden, Prince Aly Khan, David Niven, Spencer Tracy, Ray Milland, Jimmy Stewart, and countless others."

When she wasn't with one of her male lovers, she cruised Santa Monica Boulevard at night, often picking up as many as three or four prostitutes and bringing them home with her. Sometimes she didn't want sex with them, but just wanted them to talk to her, smoking, drinking, and sharing their experiences with her.

She did have sex with any number of these hookers. According to reports, she paid them well and treated them kindly. Many of Ava's pickups often preferred women to men anyway, and were only too happy to disappear into the night with what the press called "The World's Most Beautiful Animal."

One night, Ava rented herself out as a hooker.

The director, Joseph Mankiewicz, wanted to cast Marlon Brando and Ava Gardner together as romantic leads in *The Barefoot Contessa* after Elizabeth Taylor turned it down. Brando also turned down the role, the part eventually going to Humphrey Bogart. Taking the director into his confidence, Brando revealed that Ava liked to attend bordellos. She became particularly interested in a bordello that specialized in offering "movie stars" to its male clients, and to a few female clients as well.

The madam of the bordello claimed that "if you can't fuck the real thing, we offer you the mock." Clients got a look-alike, and were allowed to spend time with their screen favorite— "Joan Crawford," "Marilyn Monroe," "Elizabeth Taylor," "Jane Russell," "Judy Garland," and even "Margaret O'Brien" for those who liked them really young.

Brando told Mankiewicz that Ava wanted to be taken to the bordello to meet the madam. "That's not all," Brando said. "With the permission of the madam, Ava wanted to exchange places that coming Saturday night with her stand-in."

"That's wild!" Mankiewicz said. "It's incredible. May I be the first customer to hire the real Ava for the night?"

Brando pondered the request for a minute. "If you showed up as Ava's first client, I would just shit my pants. I don't know what Ava would shit."

Brando escorted Ava to the bordello that Saturday night and made the arrangement for Ava with the madam. She was in a bedroom awaiting her first customer when Mankiewicz arrived downstairs to be introduced to the madam. She personally escorted him to Ava's bedroom, while Brando wandered off "to do my duty with 'Betty Grable.'"

The story was spread around Hollywood, and many men queried Mankiewicz about his evening in Ava's whorehouse bedroom, "The lady—and she is a lady—deserves her privacy," Mankiewicz replied.

The next day, Frank learned about what had happened. Instead of phoning Mankiewicz, an angry Frank called Brando. "Listen, creep, and listen good. I know all about you and Ava. Stay away from her! Don't ever come within twenty feet of her even at a party. You got that? First offense, broken legs. Second offense, cracked skull. If you live through all that, cement shoes. One more false step and you've had it."

He slammed down the phone.

One night, Ava agreed to meet Frank for dinner at Chasen's in Beverly Hills. After dinner, he wanted her to come back with him to his apartment, but she refused.

"I have a date," she told him.

"A date at this late hour?" he protested.

"Come on, Frankie, you're the master of the date at two o'clock in the morning."

She ordered a final drink and turned to confront him on the booth where they were sitting.

"I've decided to leave you forever. After that time in the hospital in London, I don't want to have children any more. I told Papa Hemingway only the other day that I wanted to lead a hedonistic life. I don't want to be tied down to you or to any husband—and definitely no children. The dream is over. I'm going to lead the gay life in Madrid.

"I still love you, and I guess I always will," he said. "If you ever change your mind, call me. I'll come running back to you. All you have to do is say the word."

"You're a darling man, Frank," Ava said. "But not for me. You'll find others. All my future lovers will come in quickly through the front door and out the back."

As an afterthought, she added, "Incidentally, unlike you who'll go on to other wives, I'll never marry again."

# *Aging Ava*

Years of sexual dissipation and heavy boozing caused Ava to lose her legendary beauty. Her housekeeper reported that she'd often stare at her face in the mirror and say to her image, "Too many bullfighters, baby. Too many dicks. Too many George C. Scotts. Too many Artie Shaws. Too many Roberts." (No doubt, among others, she was referring to Robert Walker, Robert Mitchum, Robert Taylor, and Robert Evans.)

At night, she'd watch reruns of her old movies, many of which she'd never seen before. After seeing such films as *The Snows of Kilimanjaro,* she'd call one of her former co-stars to reminisce. In that instance, it was Gregory Peck:

"Greg, baby, could it have been true? Was I really the most beautiful woman on the face of the earth, and you its most beautiful man?"

Gallantly, Peck answered: "That's true in your case, Ava, my dear, but I had serious competition back then. After all, Jerry Lewis and Broderick Crawford were two good-looking studs."

Frank Sinatra called January 25, 1990, the "saddest day of my life." He'd just put down the phone after a call from London. His beloved Ava had died of pneumonia at the age of sixty-seven.

Shortly before her death, she told a reporter, "I drank too much, partied too much in the Fifties. It's all caught up with me. I didn't age well, honey child. And all I had to sell was my looks. I was never that great an actress. Now, I'm what is called a faded beauty."

A friend reported on her last comment about Barbara Marx Sinatra. "She may think she's the Queen today. But baby, I sat on that fucking throne when she was just a Las Vegas showgal."

When Frank heard that Ava was sick, he sent her $50,000. Potty-mouthed Ava, in her usual sarcastic way, said, "Is that all there is? I never said that to him when his dick went in me."

Fifty friends showed up at her funeral on a stormy day at the Sunset Memorial Park in North Carolina. The Rev. Francis C. Bradshaw began the oration: "Ava Gardner was no saint...."

Her last phone call had been to her co-star Stewart Granger at three o'clock in the morning. "It's Ava, darling. I was just watching the two of us in *Bhowani Junction*. Weren't we beautiful?"

# *Her Serene Highness, the Princess of Monaco*

## FRANK GETS DOWN AND DIRTY WITH GRACE KELLY

On the set of *High Society,* **Frank Sinatra and Grace Kelly** seemed to be living it up, drinking champagne onscreen, and making love off screen. He told friends that he was completely baffled at her decision to marry Prince Rainier of Monaco. To their co-star, Bing Crosby, Frank said, "I don't think Grace and Rainier will ever reach the altar."

That was good news to Bing. He, too, was in love with the enchanting Grace. "Monaco is too small to contain a gal like Grace," Bing predicted. "Besides, why would she settle for being the princess of a small principality, when she is set to become 'Princess of the World' if she stays in Hollywood and continues her career."

The *Denver Post* grumbled that Rainier was "beneath her station." The Communist *Daily Worker* regretted that Grace had chosen a husband "who can't lay bricks." *The Chicago Tribune* asserted that "Grace Kelly is too well bred a girl to marry the silent partner in a gambling parlor."

Frank himself tried to put a damper on the upcoming marriage. "A hooker in Monaco told me that the prince, unlike *moi,* is lousy in bed," he told Grace.

**Frank Sinatra** made a famous quote about **Grace Kelly**, his co-star in *High Society*. "She is the squarest person I know."

That was his public assessment. In private, he told his cronies, "What I said about Grace was true only before you get her in bed. Once bedded, she's one hot tamale, a crazed nymphomaniac. She'd do it with the pool boy if his bikini was revealing enough. She once felt up the waiter in my presence, perhaps to shock me. But I'm unshockable."

When their co-star in High Society, Bing Crosby, was cast with Grace in *The Country Girl (1954)*, he fell madly in love with her and proposed marriage. In the meantime, Grace was falling for her other co-star in the movie, William Holden.

Rejected by Grace, Bing carried a torch for her for years.

# Steamy Secrets of "The Ice Princess"

*"Grace Kelly was a conniving woman. She almost ruined my best friend Mal's [Mrs. Ray Milland's] marriage. She fucked everything in sight. She was worse than any woman I'd ever known."*
— **Skip Hathaway**, wife of Henry Hathaway, Grace Kelly's director in *Fourteen Hours*.

*"She was a real, white-gloved lady, who only became a whore when the bedroom door was locked."*
—**Alfred Hitchcock**

"What was going on off screen competed with what was going on screen," claimed director John Ford. He'd been assigned to remake *Red Dust* into a new adventure film called *Mogambo* (1953), featuring Clark Gable, Ava Gardner, and Grace Kelly.

Ironically, Gable was cast into the same role [the crusty hero, Vic Marswell], that he'd originally played in the 1932 *Red Dust*. His co-star in that film had been Jean Harlow, cast in a role that was originally intended for Greta Garbo.

Grace was looking forward to going to Africa—"I've read so much about it." She even studied Swahili and was delighted that she'd get to see the wilds of Uganda, Tanganyika, and Kenya during the shoot. She was also interested in having an affair with Clark Gable. She was well aware that her co-star Ava Gardner had already beaten her to Gable.

*Mogambo* had originally been intended to star Stewart Granger (who wrote disparagingly about Gable in his memoirs); Deborah Kerr was envisioned for the role that eventually went to Grace Kelly; and Lana Turner was the inspiration for the part that went to her closest friend, Ava.

Grace had been acquainted with Frank Sinatra before he even arrived in Africa. She claimed she'd met him when she was a teenager, but provided no details of that encounter.

When she wasn't sleeping with Gable, Grace hung out with Ava, who told her that her marriage to Frank was coming to an end. "I don't think we can make it. He's also broke. He's on his way here. I had to pay his plane fare."

Night after night on location in Africa, Grace heard Ava and Frank battling and screaming at each other.

Grace later wrote Cary Grant, "The tent next to mine is co-inhabited by Frank and Ava. After three hours of physical and verbal violence, there is sudden silence. Then their bed starts to creak for the next hour or so."

Sam Zimbalist, who began his career at sixteen as a film cutter, was the producer of *Mogambo*, having produced both *King Solomon's Mines* (1950) and *Quo Vadis* (1951).

While filming 1959's *Ben Hur*, Zimbalist told Gore Vidal, one of the movie's script writers, an anecdote that happened on the set of *Mogambo*.

For location shots, Ford had hired many Watusis, who wore breechclouts. One afternoon in the hot African sun, both Grace and Ava were walking along a row of these elegant men. "Do you think their cocks are as big as people claim?" Ava asked Grace.

"How in the hell do you think I would know that?" Grace said, flabbergasted at Ava's remark.

"I think it's about time we both took a look at some black dick." Impulsively she reached for the breechclout of one of the Watusis and lifted it. A large cock was exposed in the sunshine. The Watusi just smiled at this Western woman as his penis began to harden.

"Let's get out of here," Grace urged Ava.

As she departed, Ava yelled out, "Frank's bigger than that."

Instead of being horrified at Ava's lasciviousness, Grace was attracted to her earthy Tarheel appeal. Ava was profane, outspoken, and outrageous. The more lady like Grace pretended to be horrified but yet was drawn to Ava's sense of ribald humor. Nothing seemed to daunt her, and if she felt like saying something, she did so with absolute freedom.

As the prim, frigid wife in *Mogambo*, Grace delivered a better performance than she did in the 1952 *High Noon*, where she was in love with Gary Cooper both on and off the screen.

Upon the release of *Mogambo*, she received good reviews and was nominated for an Oscar as Best Supporting Actress. She lost the award to Donna Reed, cast as a prostitute on the eve of the attack of Pearl Harbor, in *From Here to Eternity*. Ironically, Frank was nominated for Best Supporting Actor in *Eternity*, and, unlike Grace, he walked home with Oscar.

With Ava gone from his life, Frank was

**Frank Sinatra** *(left)* and **Peter Lawford** *(right)* call on Her Serene Highness, **Princess Grace** of Monaco at her palace. Before arriving at the palace for cocktails, Frank had asked Peter if he had ever bedded Grace. "I like her personally," Peter confessed, "but when it came to sex, she was sort of like an Eskimo pie to me."

"That's because you didn't melt her down," Frank said.

At the palace, Peter and Frank found a confused Grace filled with regret. She missed Hollywood and felt she had made a big mistake, giving up a glorious career. "I was a big fish in a big town, but now I'm a big fish in a small town."

Later that evening, Peter went back to the *Café de Paris* "looking for love" that night, but Frank found it in Grace's bedchamber. Their affair resumed.

despondent after his return to Hollywood. He learned that Grace was also breaking up her relationship with fashion designer Oleg Cassini, who had wanted to marry her. Frank decided to call her for a date, as he'd been wanting to seduce her ever since Africa. He would have were it not for Ava and Clark Gable, who monopolized the off-screen time of both Frank and Grace.

After his breakup with Ava, Frank turned to Grace at a point near the end of her relationship with fashion designer Oleg Cassini. Amazingly, Grace called Cassini in New York and asked him for permission to see Frank. In a jealous rage, Cassini said "no."

"Can't you put it on ice until I get back to Beverly Hills next week?" Cassini asked. "I'll fuck you then."

When Grace put down the phone, she had no intention of obeying Cassini. She called Frank. "I'd love to go out with you. Ava told me you pack a powerful punch." Even though she'd said that, she shocked herself. Perhaps some of Ava's boldness had rubbed off on her.

Frank not only dated Grace but took her back to his hotel suite where he spent the rest of the weekend with her. Ava heard about the off-the-record weekend and called Grace. Ava didn't appear to be jealous at all. "How was it?" Ava asked. "Did I exaggerate?"

"Not at all," Grace said. "It was everything you said and more. What surprised me was how gentle and sensitive he was to a woman's need. I didn't figure that for Frank."

Two of the most memorable moments in *High Society* are depicted above. On the left, Frank Sinatra sings "You're Sensational" to Grace Kelly. On the right, Bing Crosby and Grace record what became a hit song, "True Love," which temporarily convinced Grace she should have been a singer rather than an actress. But that conceit soon vanished when both Bing and Frank convinced her not to pursue a singing career.

Bing later told his close friends that Frank was merely having an affair with Grace. "But I'm seriously in love with her and wanted to marry her. But she chose that prince over me."

Actually, Bing had begun his affair with Grace years before, when she was an unknown, little realizing that one day he'd star in *The Country Girl* and *High Society* with her.

While Bing's wife, Dixie, was at home battling cancer, Bing and Grace used Alan Ladd's residence for their sexual trysts.

"I'm getting tired of going to bed with guys who have had every woman in Hollywood," Ava said. "I've decided I want to break in a virgin male."

In spite of her demure demeanor, Grace had an impish sense of humor. She was fully aware of how provocative Ava had been with Frank, and she devised a scheme that would surpass the best of Ava's outrages. At the end of a very expensive meal at Chasen's, Frank was generously settling the tab.

"I'll pay the tip," she said. To Frank's shock, she unzipped the waiter's black pants and inserted two one-hundred dollar bills into his underwear before zipping him up.

Red faced, the handsome, well-built waiter retreated. Without losing her cool, Grace turned to Frank. "Don't worry, darling, you've got twice as much as he has."

After their inaugural fling, Grace and Frank resumed their secret romance when they were cast together in the 1956 *High Society*, a musical remake of the 1940 film *Philadelphia Story* that had starred Katharine Hepburn and Cary Grant. Along with Celeste Holm, Frank was cast as one of the two reporters from *Spy* magazine sent to cover society nuptials. Grace assumed the role of Tracy Lord.

There was one complication taking place off camera. Frank was pitted against Bing Crosby, starring in the Cary Grant role of C.K. Dexter-Haven. He wanted Grace for himself and didn't welcome competition from Frank. During the making of *High Society*, Frank referred to Grace as "a cross between Aimee Semple McPherson and Queen Elizabeth."

The role called for Grace to make her singing debut in *High Society* in a duet with Crosby called "True Love," a song written by Cole Porter. Unknown to Crosby, Grace rehearsed the number at length with Frank. She told him, "I wish I could duet with you. You sing so much better than Bing."

That was "music" to Frank's jealous ears.

To the surprise of virtually everyone, "True Love" went platinum. Years later in Monaco, the sounds of "True Love" could frequently be heard echoing through the halls of the palace. During one of his visits to Monte Carlo, Frank told Grace, "I taught you well. You went platinum before me."

In September of 1955, a year before Grace and Frank made *High Society*, Grace's eager Monegasque suitor, Prince Rainier, arrived in Los Angeles and installed himself in a luxurious villa in Bel Air. For the next six weeks, Grace discreetly lived with her future husband, sneaking off on occasion to see Frank. "When she wants to play-act being a princess, she's with Rainier," Sinatra told Ava, "But when she wants a good fuck, she comes to the man who knows how to do it."

Frank chose not to attend the April 19, 1956 wedding of Grace to Prince Rainier, an event heralded at the time as the wedding of the century. It wasn't because he was jealous of the prince, but because in London being fitted for his white tie and tails in preparation for the event, he read about the sensational appearance of Ava in Monaco.

He decided that if he arrived in the wake of his bitter divorce from her, it would upstage Grace's wedding. He called her and explained, "I'm not coming, because this is your day." She understood.

After her marriage to Prince Rainier, Grace continued her romantic interest in Frank, even though they saw each other only occasionally. She invited him to Caroline's wedding to playboy Philippe Junot, who was seventeen years her senior.

At that event, Frank sang the grim "My Way," with lyrics expressed by a dying man facing the final curtain. "The song seemed an odd selection for my wedding," Caroline later said. "Couldn't he have sung 'High Hopes' instead?"

In *High Society*, **Grace Kelly** shares a tender moment with **Frank Sinatra**. In her personal life, she shared many tender moments with him. Frank was wise to the changing whims of Grace. "If Grace couldn't be with her *beau du jour*, she loved the man she was with."

"Our affair had hardly ended, and there was Grace seen cozying up to Sinatra at Chasen's," said designer Oleg Cassini.

Between affairs , she didn't let any moss grow on her. Neither did Sinatra. He claimed to be in mourning over his breakup with Ava Gardner. But going in a split second from Ava to Grace wasn't bad. According to Cassini, "In Hollywood, she was the actress on everybody's lips. She was the *numero uno* in Tinseltown. Every producer wanted her for a movie role, and every stud wanted to bed up."

"I once thought she was mine, but I gave up and faced reality," Cassini said. "Grace would have many lovers before and during her reign as princess of Monaco."

In Monaco, Frank resumed his affair with Grace when he sang at the premiere of *Kings Go Forth* (1958), in which he co-starred with Tony Curtis and Natalie Wood (Frank had an affair with her). At some point Frank and Grace managed to slip away to a private villa owned by David Niven, who also had had an affair with Grace. Throughout the remainder of their lives, Frank's sexual link with Grace resumed whenever they came together. On June 9, 1962, Frank showed up in Monaco again, appearing at the Sporting Club. He also made appearances in Grace's boudoir whenever the prince was away.

For one of his many farewell performances, this one at the Los Angeles Music Center on June 13, 1971, Frank gave one of his best shows. In the audience sat Princess Grace herself. The once romantic couple got together for a drink. Reportedly, Frank made a pass at her and asked her, "Can you do it again for old time's sake?" She demurely held him off. "Let's just be dear old friends who cherish a wonderful memory."

He agreed.

During the early 1970s, Frank showed up frequently in Monaco, occupying the most glamorous suite on the eighth floor of the Hotel de Paris. He was seen everywhere from the Monaco Beach Club to the tennis courts of the local Country Club. Business was said to boom in Monaco whenever he was in town.

"If anything, Princess Grace was discreet," said a former assistant manager of the Hotel de Paris. "I assisted Sinatra on numerous occasions. Sometimes he stayed for a month or so with us."

On April 19, 1981 Frank invited Princess Grace and Prince Rainier to celebrate their silver wedding anniversary at his home in Palm Springs. There Grace met a glamorous blonde, ex-showgirl Barbara Marx, who had become Frank's fourth and final wife.

Later in the evening, Grace whispered in his ear. "You married her only because she looks like a dime store version of me."

Grace's friends, Cary Grant and Gregory Peck, joined in the festivities. Privately Grace met Frank and told him the truth. "Where has love gone?" she asked him. "The Prince and I are merely keeping up appearances. We have so many differences these days, and we fight a lot. Both of us have lovers on the side. I miss America so. I miss you. Why didn't you marry me and take me away before I got locked into this Princess role?"

He may have been merely the gallant gentlemen, but he told her, "Not running away and marrying you has been the biggest regret of my life."

In March of 1982 in Philadelphia, Frank saw Grace for the last time. He and Barbara Marx attended "The Tribute to Grace Kelly" at the Annenberg Center. Stewart Granger and James Stewart were also among the honored guests.

As part of her goodbye to Frank, Grace met with him privately. "I'm going to buy a condo very soon in Manhattan, and I want you to become one of my most frequent visitors. If you wish, I'll give you the key. Another place to hang your hat."

"Consider me your number one guest," he promised her.

In a car, on the French Riviera, Grace met her tragic death on September 14, 1982.

Grief stricken, Frank told Cary Grant, "Everyone said Grace lived a fairytale life. A prince. A palace. Her story usually ends by people saying, 'they lived happily ever after.' What has not been written is what comes after they lived happily ever after."

# Howard Hughes, Billionaire

## AND HOW HE ORDERED THE MURDER OF FRANK SINATRA

"The Aviator," **Howard Hughes, pictured above with Ava Gardner,** became intrigued by the sultry brunette when she was still a starlet. He read in the newspaper one morning that she'd filed for divorce from Mickey Rooney. Hughes told his pimp, Johnny Meyer, "that pint-sized midget is not equipped to handle a tomato like that Tarheel bitch. Only I am equipped to do that."

Meyer approached Ava at MGM and found her just as gorgeous as her pictures. He obtained her agreement to go out with Hughes, although she confused him with the director, Howard Hawks. In a touch of irony, Hughes had fired Hawks as director of the controversial film *The Outlaw,* and had recently taken over the job of helming the saga of Billy the Kid himself.

Ava did not find this "rawboned cowboy pushing forty" all that sexually appealing, although their relationship, such as it was, would continue for years. Later, when she dated Frank Sinatra, she told him that Hughes had "an offensive body odor—maybe he can't afford soap." Also, her friend Lana Turner had warned her that Hughes had picked up a veneral disease from his former flame, the actress Billie Dove, and had never gotten over it.

Ava told Frank, "Mink coats, diamonds, and rubies...Howard bestowed it all on me. But his greatest gift of all was a Belgian sheepdog. That dog was better trained than Lassie. The mutt could prepare his own meals."

# HOW AN BILLIONAIRE AVIATOR FROM TEXAS AND A SINGER FROM HOBOKEN BATTLED FOR THE WORLD'S MOST BEAUTIFUL WOMAN

**Lana Turner** *(left)* often referred to **Ava Gardner** *(right)* as "my best gal pal." They often shared the same lovers, such as Frank Sinatra, and on one occasion, the same husband, musician Artie Shaw. Whenever the two screen goddesses came together, their favorite topic involved dishing the dirt on the men they had known.

Lana told Ava that in 1946, Howard Hughes had proposed marriage to her, and that she had accepted, even being fitted for a spectacular wedding gown from the famous MGM designer who billed herself only as "Irene." The secret ceremony had been planned for May 10.

Waiting for Hughes to appear as her groom, Lana looked into the chapel, finding "the world's largest collection of exotic flowers." Even the pianist and minister were waiting, but no Howard.

"I was jilted at the altar," Lana told Ava. "Call him the runaway groom. But I got my revenge. Howard was madly in love with Tyrone Power at the time. I moved in on his boyfriend. Ty said I was much better in bed than Howard."

Two of the screen's greatest beauties, Lana Turner and Ava Gardner, were the best of pals. When they weren't working, each of these glamour queens called each other to report on the seductions (or lack thereof) of the night before.

The first time Ava ever went to bed with Frank Sinatra, she called Lana the next day. Lana had long ago told her that she and Frank had once been "hot and heavy," and had even discussed marriage.

Ava insisted on giving Lana a blow-by-blow description, which was not necessary, as Lana was more familiar at that time with Frank's lovemaking than Ava herself.

"Frank's not very muscular," Ava told Lana. "All his growth has gone into his cock."

Later, Lana jokingly reported the remark to Johnny Meyer, the pimp for Howard Hughes. Meyer sometimes served as Lana's bodyguard. She was well aware that the aviator was in hot pursuit of Ava and would resent Frank moving in on territory he was trying to stake out.

"Bossman became furious," Meyer later said, "when Sinatra's penis got such a high rating. He demanded that my boys investigate to find out the exact measurements of Sinatra's dick. It took us only two weeks to round up more than a dozen prostitutes among the Las Vegas showgals who'd slept with the singer. We vetted them and more or less came up with the same story over and over again. That skinny little runt was hung. A full report was given to Howard, who wanted to find out how he stacked up against Sinatra. I don't recall exactly the final results, but I think Sinatra had bossman beat by an inch—maybe an inch and a half."

"My God, he's got a goddamned hollow chest," Hughes told Meyer. "A stringbean with no lines. His legs are scrawny. He wears padded shoulders on zoot suits from Hoboken. Instead of hair, he's got patent leather. How could his cock be so big? Not only that, he's a has-been with no money. His career is over. And he's no comeback kid."

Hughes even attacked Sinatra's physicality in front of Ava, who reminded him that, "Some gals call you a scarecrow as well, honey chile."

Frank divorced his wife, Nancy, and married Ava on November 7, 1951 in Philadelphia. One hour before the wedding, Hughes called Ava, begging her to jilt Frank at the altar and "marry me." She refused this last-minute proposal, perhaps wondering how serious Hughes really was, as she already knew about Susan Hayward, Jean Peters, and Terry Moore. Defeated, Hughes told Johnny Meyer that he was "giving the marriage only two months."

Howard's hatred of Frank continued, and he even barred him from the RKO lot when Ava was shooting *My Forbidden Past* and having an affair with her co-star Robert Mitchum. For reasons of his own, Hughes kept knowledge of that affair from Frank. However, when Frank was out of town on a singing engagement, Hughes secretly dated Ava, presenting her detailed reports on the women the singer was seducing on the road. After Frank's marriage to Ava, Hughes had ordered that the singer be trailed 24 hours a day.

Raging with jealousy, Frank accurately accused Ava of secretly dating Hughes every time he left town on an engagement.

Hughes had been enraged when he learned that Ava had been cast opposite "his other girlfriend," Kathryn Grayson in MGM's big blockbuster musical of 1951, *Show Boat*. The extravaganza also starred Howard Keel, a dashing, tall, and handsome baritone of the time.

Grayson remembered Ava "shooting daggers at me during the filming." Although Ava had repeatedly turned down proposals of marriage from Hughes, she apparently was jealous of those same offers made to other actresses. She was also furious to learn that Hughes had offered Grayson two million dollars worth of precious gems, whereas he'd once offered her only one million dollars in stones.

One scene in *Show Boat* called for a wedding shot that included Grayson and co-star Howard Keel. She later said that "the other Howard" (Hughes in this case) in a noisy amphibian swept down over the *Show Boat* outdoor set, ruining take after take. He'd become jealous of the younger and more virile Keel.

"Howard Hughes knew every time Frank Sinatra and Ava had a knock-out, drag-out," Meyer later claimed. "There were a lot of slugfests in those days between this stormy pair. Ava arrived in Las Vegas two days before anticipated, and walked in on Sinatra, catching him

**Kathryn Grayson** *(left)*, **Howard Keel** *(center)*, and **Ava Gardner** *(right)* were co-stars in the most popular film for all three of them, MGM's *Showboat*, a spectacular musical released in 1951.

Howard Hughes was embroiled in a torrid love affair with Grayson, while still pursuing Ava. He hired spies to report on the activities of the two stars during the filming, as he didn't trust the handsome leading man, singer Howard Keel. "Never trust a man named Howard," Hughes claimed. "I should know that."

On the first day of the shoot, Ava assured Grayson that there should be no jealousy between the two of them. "You are welcome to Hughes," Ava told her. "I don't want him. Now Frank Sinatra—that's another story."

Knowing that Grayson had previously appeared in films with Frank, Ava bluntly asked her, "Did you guys ever make it?"

Grayson denied any previous sexual involvements with him. "I must be the only one of his leading ladies that he never seduced."

"Perhaps you're telling a lie," Ava told her. "But who gives a fuck at this point? In Hollywood, everybody's fucking everybody else in all known combinations."

in bed with blonde starlet Barbara Payton. That led to Sinatra's biggest brawl with Ava. She was punched in the face and knocked on the floor, where Sinatra repeatedly kicked her."

Fleeing from the Flamingo, she arrived at the Desert Inn where Hughes was staying on the top floor. Allowed entrance to his suite, Ava shocked him with her appearance. He ordered two doctors from the Las Vegas Hospital to come over and treat Ava privately, so as to avoid press coverage.

At about four o'clock in the morning, there was a knock on Meyer's door in the adjoining suite. A sleepy Meyer confronted his bossman in bathrobe and slippers. "I'd never seen Howard this agitated before. He brought me up to date on all that had happened. Inside my suite and in very hushed tones, he told me he wanted two or three of my boys to wipe out Sinatra while he was sleeping at the Flamingo. Somehow, Howard had already arranged for my boys to be admitted into Sinatra's private quarters. I was given a passkey to his suite. Howard said that he didn't want Sinatra shot but beaten to death, the way he'd attacked Ava. I thought bossman had lost it. In fact, he looked like he'd gone completely bonkers. I listened to his intricate orders. He had everything mapped out. I think Howard would have made a brilliant bank robber. He wanted me to offer each of my men fifty thousand dollars to do the dirty deed. I didn't want to tell my bossman but I could have gotten the guys for five hundred dollars each."

Both Howard Hughes and Frank Sinatra had reason to be jealous of the Spanish bullfighter, **Luis Miguel Dominguín**. Iberia's leading matador, Dominguín struck Ava as "very handsome and very sexy." Later, she told Lana Turner, "He didn't speak a word of English. I taught him his first line in English. I had him say, 'I want to go to bed with you.' Once he finally said that, I accepted his invitation."

Dominguín's fans, who numbered in the millions, elevated him to the status of a top-ranking celebrity.

Ava pronounced him "a world class artist in the boudoir. He handled me with the grace he handles a bull in the ring. More than that, he fucks like a man facing death the following afternoon in the bullring. I was a married woman at the time, and at the Hotel Wellington in Madrid I drained Dominguín dry only an hour before Frank's plane landed in Madrid."

Meyer later recalled that he'd listened repeatedly as Hughes told him in minute detail the exact way that Frank was to be bludgeoned to death. "I agreed to carry out his plan. Hughes claimed that Frank was having a raging dispute with some gang members over an alleged $100,000 gambling debt. The singer was refusing to pay because he claimed that the dice were crooked. Hughes believed that Frank's death would be blamed on a fallout with the mob. In those days, Frank was keeping company with some very dangerous characters. 'No one will ever connect us with Sinatra's murder,' my bossman told me. 'No one will even think we're remotely involved. Sinatra has more dangerous enemies than us.'"

Years later, Meyer claimed that he never made the call to his boys to wipe out Frank. Meyer waited in his suite until Hughes summoned him next door around noon of the following day. "I got this distress call from Hughes and rushed over. He looked like hell. He was all alone in his suite. Ava had obviously left some time that morning when Hughes had finally gone to sleep. He had learned that she'd taken the first available flight back to Los Angeles, wearing huge sunglasses to conceal a black eye."

"To my complete surprise, bossman never mentioned his order to kill Sinatra," Meyer claimed. "I was expecting to be fired on the spot. It was the strangest feeling I had, but I honestly believed—and I still do today—that Howard was so demented the night before that he had completely forgotten issuing Sinatra's death warrant. Lucky for me that Howard was that forgetful. It was even luckier for Sinatra."

By the time Ava agreed to appear in *The Barefoot Contessa*, to be directed by Joseph L. Mankiewicz, Frank was admitting to the press that their marriage "was all washed up." There had been published reports that he'd attempted to commit suicide over a marriage gone sour. Privately, Hedda Hopper and Louella Parsons were claiming that his suicide attempt was because of jealousy over Hughes.

*The Barefoot Contessa* was a case of art imitating life. Ava claimed, "I knew I was playing Rita Hayworth and that Humphrey Bogart was playing Howard Hughes."

In Spain, Ava had a scandalous affair with Luís Miguel Domínguín, the country's greatest bullfighter at the time. Back in America, Hughes was the first on the tarmac to greet Ava upon her arrival from Madrid. He found her more evasive than ever. Once again she turned down a marriage proposal from him, even though he promised to "make you the greatest movie star the world has ever known."

She not only refused his offer of marriage, but she turned down an invitation to go to bed with him. Although he pursued her for years, his only memory of any real sex with her came from his hospital bed. He'd survived the crash of his experimental plane, the XF-11, which had crashed into a residential neighborhood of Beverly Hills. Ava had visited him in the hospital. To aid his recovery after the crash, she gave him what she later referred to as "a mercy blow-job."

To Hughes' continuing distress, Domínguín arrived in Los Angeles in hot pursuit of Ava. Hughes still had her house bugged so he could hear every detail of this burgeoning romance.

For the first three days, according to Meyer, Domínguín never left Ava's bed. The trouble began when Ava, with her attention deficient syndrome, threw a party and invited Duke Ellington and his band. Meyer later claimed that the bullfighter caught a drunken Ava going down on the black musician in the bushes of her garden. She ran upstairs and tried to bolt herself inside her bathroom. But Domínguín was too quick for her. He slapped her face repeatedly and dragged her body from the room. Holding a screaming Ava by the hairs of her head, he tossed her down the steps of her house.

She ended up with no broken bones but a severely sprained ankle and lots of bruises. Rushing into the room, her sister, Bappie, screamed when she saw Ava

Frank Sinatra grew to love the music of **Duke Ellington** in the era of the big bands. On the radio, he also listed to Artie Shaw, Benny Goodman, Tommy and Jimmy Dorsey, and Guy Lombardo. But Ellington was a particular favorite.

In 1943, Frank shocked his fans when a picture of him was taken with the black pianist and singer Hazel Scott, when they were together in a night club listening to Duke Ellington.

Frank always defended black musicians. He was horrified when he learned that the Duke's picture could not be depicted on the cover of the album he had recorded with Rosemary Clooney.

Ellington also had high regard for Frank, calling him a "primo non-conformist—nobody tells him what to do or say."

Frank's admiration changed when a "spy" at Ava Gardner's party told him that she had had "some sort of sexual contact with Ellington."

Frank exploded in fury. "I'll kill the son of a bitch!" he threatened. He never did, of course, but Ava got a black eye for her tryst with the musician.

sprawled on the floor. Bappie rushed to call an ambulance to have her taken to the hospital. Even before Ava arrived at the hospital, Hughes with Dr. Verne Mason was waiting in a private room he'd already arranged for her. The next morning, Meyer put Dominguín on a flight back to Madrid.

Hughes was "the most delighted man on the planet" when Ava divorced Frank. Hughes moved her to the Cal-Neva Lodge on Lake Tahoe to establish residency for her divorce. He also ordered his spy brigade to monitor her activities 24 hours a day in case Frank showed up to try to win her back.

---

## *Frankie & Eddie: Onstage Competitors & Boudoir Rivals*

In 1951, *Billboard* listed none of Frank Sinatra's tunes among its top hits. Sponsors were withdrawing from his TV show on CBS because of low ratings. His radio show went off the air in only seven weeks, and advertisers weren't interested. "Fans would rather hear Johnnie Ray or Frankie Laine," his producer told him.

One night in New York, Frank passed a theater where Eddie Fisher, the new sensation, was singing. Lines of fans stretched around the block as they had once done for him. Some fans jeered at him, calling out, "Frankie, you're all washed up!" Another catcalled, "Frankie, boy, time to throw in the dishrag."

Frank returned to the apartment of Manie Sachs, where he was staying. Manie had been a top executive at Columbia Records. Coming home from the theater, Manie opened the door and immediately smelled gas. Rushing to the kitchen, he discovered Frank with his head in the oven and the gas turned on. Pulling him away and cutting off the gas, he called paramedics, who revived him. The next day, he lectured Frank, "Close call, old buddy. You're the comeback kid. You'll be big one day when Fisher is a has-been."

The women who once pursed Frank were now after Eddie. In his memoirs, Eddie said that Zsa Zsa Gabor "wouldn't leave me alone. Hedy Lamarr made a pass at me. Lucille Ball came on to me."

In 1955, Frank starred in a film, *The Tender Trap,* with Debbie Reynolds. When she told him she planned to marry Eddie, he took her to lunch and tried to talk her out of it.

Ignoring all advice, Debbie and Eddie entered into their ill-fated union. After her marriage, Debbie told Eddie that Frank had invited her to go with him to Palm Springs for the weekend.

Frank and Eddie often dated or pursued the same women, yet they maintained some sort of friendship in spite of their rivalries. Each crooner resented the other singer's success, yet it never led to a rift between them.

When Eddie married Elizabeth Taylor after dumping Debbie, he knew she had had an affair with Frank while still married to the English actor, Michael Wilding.

"Elizabeth always spoke about Frank with contempt," Eddie claimed. "I was positive she would never forgive him for forcing her to abort her child. She made it clear that she hated him. She was always cursing him, always criticizing him, always bringing up that abortion."

Eddie met "Frank's girl," Juliet Prowse, at the Cocoanut Grove in Los Angeles and found her body exquisite, especially her long legs. He wanted to have an affair with her. Amazingly, since she was still dating Frank, Eddie called Frank at Claridge's Hotel in London and asked permission to take her out. "Go ahead, have a ball," Frank said. He obviously had decided to dump Prowse, or else he wouldn't have been so generous with her favors.

Walter Winchell in his column wrote "EDDIE/FRANK/JULIET: NEW FILM TRIANGLE."

On their second week of dating, Eddie found out he also had another singer competing for Prowse's affections: His name was Elvis Presley.

# Frank's Sex Triangle With Ava and Lana

## WHAT REALLY HAPPENED THAT NIGHT IN PALM SPRINGS?

**Ava Gardner** *(left)* and **Lana Turner** *(right)* liked to gossip about two of their favorite subjects, musician Artie Shaw, whom both of them married; and Frank Sinatra, whom Ava married but Lana at one time merely planned to wed.

Shaw told Lana that when he enlisted in the Navy a few months after the attack on Pearl Harbor, "Guys would come up to me and say, 'Can I shake the hand that held Lana Turner's tit?'"

Lana told Ava that Louis B. Mayer once called her into his office and lectured her on birth control when she was married to Shaw. Lana warned Ava about Shaw when she started to date her former husband—"the most conceited, unpleasant man I ever met."

Lana also seduced Frank before Ava did and issued warnings about him too. "Frank can turn deadly on a moment's notice. Once, when I angered him, he threatened to have one of his gangster friends scar my face."

"I adored Ava but she was a very strong willed woman," Lana said. "She didn't take my advice about Artie, and she certainly didn't take my advice about Frank. Their marriage was a dreadful fiasco."

# XXX-Rated Soap Opera
## in the Desert

"When Frank was down, he was sweet, but when he got back up, he was hell," **Ava Gardner** told her best girlfriend **Lana Turner**.

"I know that," Lana said. "In fact, I know more about Frank Sinatra than I ever wanted to know."

Ava confided to Lana that she had hoped they would find love and peace in Palm Springs. "Maybe have a kid. But we fought all the time. At first I wanted to redecorate, the place was just too masculine. Dolly Sinatra sent me recipes for Frank's favorite dishes. I was going to learn how to make them like Mama Sinatra did. But things didn't work out. In time, the press came to call us 'The Battling Sinatras.'"

*"Don't worry. Who's gonna believe it?"*
—**Lana Turner** in a retort to Louis B. Mayer, who chastised her for picking up a gas station attendant.

*"Lana was amoral. If she saw a stagehand with tight pants and a muscular build, she'd invite him to her dressing room."*
—**Vincente Minnelli**

*"Ava has been completely victimized by the kind of life she has led and, as a result, has become the slut she is today."*
—Musician **Artie Shaw**, former husband of both Lana Turner and Ava Gardner

*"The difference between Latin and American men is that the Latins give you a little more of everything, more headaches, more heartaches, more temper, more tenderness, and more dick."*
—**Fernando Lamas**

*"I never so much as looked at another gal since Ava. I'm nuts about her and I don't think it's dead. But it certainly is all up in the air now."*
—**Frank Sinatra** to columnist Earl Wilson

*"Hughes's favorite kind of sex was oral, both on the giving and receiving end. Yet he was also the great swordsman, hung down to his knees. Just ask Ava Gardner and Lana Turner. You might also get the lowdown from such lovers as Cary Grant, Gary Cooper, Errol Flynn, Marlene Dietrich, Bette Davis, Jean Harlow, Katharine Hepburn, or Rita Hayworth. If all else fails, ask Marilyn Monroe."*
—**James Bacon**, Hollywood columnist

*"Man, if I could only get her out of my plasma."*

**—Frank Sinatra** on Ava Gardner

*"Ava Gardner is more beautiful than I am. Sinatra told me that one drunken night when he was making love to me."*

**—Elizabeth Taylor**

\*\*\*

# A SCANDALOUS ROMP WITH AN ALL-STAR CAST

It was a week that began with violence and ended in violence.

While Frank Sinatra was on the East Coast, he'd heard that Ava Gardner was slipping around and seeing the aviator mogul, Howard Hughes, once again. In spite of her many rejections, which sometimes led to violence, Hughes had never completely given up hope of snaring Ava into his web.

"In those days Frank had spies all over Hollywood feeding him information on Ava," said columnist James Bacon. "Count me as one of them. I was always hoping for a scoop—nothing wrong with that."

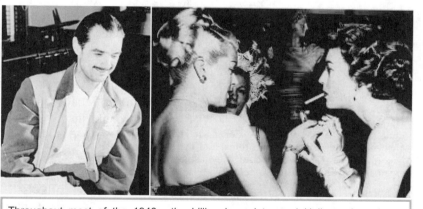

When Frank hit the ground in Los Angeles, he headed immediately to a confrontation with Ava. Barging in the door, he thought he might catch her with Hughes, but instead found her with her shoes off, her feet propped up on her coffee table, listening to his records.

He quickly accused her of two-timing him with Hughes. She fought back, claiming that Hughes had provided her with detailed evidence of his philandering with prostitutes in New York. She also

Throughout most of the 1940s, the billionaire aviator and Hollywood producer, **Howard Hughes** *(above)* hovered over the lives of **Lana Turner** *(left)* and **Ava Gardner** *(right)*, seen lighting up cigarettes at a Hollywood party.

Hughes plied both Ava and Lana with engagement rings and marriage proposals, but how serious was he? Lana found out that when Hughes was "officially" engaged to her, he was also "secretly" engaged to the sultry screen brunette, Linda Darnell.

Ava also learned that when Hughes was "begging to marry me," he was also in hot pursuit of a teenaged Jane Greer.

He told his pimp, Johnny Meyer, "Ava is the most beautiful woman on earth, but if I can't have her, I'll take Lana Turner. She's the second most beautiful woman on earth. If I were a Mormon, I'd marry both of them in a joint wedding."

admitted that it had been Hughes who arranged for one of Frank's mistresses to send her an embarrassing and incriminating letter the day before her wedding.

It was all too much for Frank. He'd been drinking heavily all day, and he wanted revenge. In one of the worst rages of his life, he wrecked her living room but didn't physically attack her at that point.

He grabbed a bottle of Jack Daniels from the bar and with his trusted .38 in his jacket, he set out in a drunken rage to shoot Hughes in the head. "I don't want to wound him. I want to kill him."

Immediately after Frank had departed on his rampage, Ava called Hughes, suggesting that he fly out of town at once. The billionaire thought that was good advice.

Somewhere along the way, Frank picked up two cronies (names unknown), who accompanied him on his rounds. He didn't know where Hughes was, but inquired all over town. Frank even arrived at the Cocoanut Grove night club, but was told that Hughes hadn't been seen there all evening. Frank then went to at least six more places where Hughes might be on any given night. He was nowhere to be seen.

**Lana Turner** and Latin lover **Fernando Lamas** danced together onscreen in a remake of the silent Mae Murray film *The Merry Widow*. They also danced together at private parties *(see above)*.

During filming, Lana had to wear heavy bracelets to cover the scars on her wrists from a recent suicide attempt. She gave her co-star the keys to her home, and he came and went—"mostly came," as Lana told Ava Gardner.

At the peak of their fame, in 1951, Lamas and Lana embodied the ultimate in physical beauty, both male and female. She was particularly attracted to what she saw in his tight pants, and on the first day they met, he invited her to sample his wares—"That is, if you can handle it," he immodestly proclaimed.

Lana was to learn that Lamas was not "the dream prince" he had played in *The Merry Widow*.

Giving up at around 3am, he slept alone that night, since he knew Ava would have bolted her doors and Nancy had already changed her locks.

Three weeks went by before a reconciliation with Ava was even attempted. In October of 1952, he finally reached her on the phone. "I'm crazy for you, honey," he said.

She agreed to have dinner with him, and for two days and nights, as she recalled to her sister Bappie, "we made love in every known position, even inventing a few of our own."

On October 18, they dined at Chasen's. Under the influence of a bottle of Jack Daniels, he brought up the subject of Hughes again. Their fight raged all the way from Chasen's to the Pacific Palisades house where they were staying. Once inside, she didn't speak to him, and he fumed.

She decided to take a bubble bath. She was relaxing and enjoying that until he burst in on her, renewing the charge that she was "nothing but a Tarheel whore."

She ordered him out of the house. Finally, he relented. "Okay, doll, I'll get out. You can find me in Palm Springs. I'll be there *fucking* Lana Turner."

"Fuck Minnie Mouse," Ava said. "See if I care."

The previous week on the MGM lot he'd

encountered his old flame, Lana Turner, who had remained a close friend of Ava's. She'd recently experienced a number of difficulties herself, even violent ones.

After the break-up of her marriage to millionaire Bob Topping, Lana was a free agent once again. She'd considered resuming her affair with Frank, but he was too busy with Ava.

Along came Latin lover Fernando Lamas, who would become known as "the First of the Red Hot Lamas." He would father another actor, Lorenzo Lamas. In the early 1940s, Fernando had become a movie star in his birthplace, Argentina, where he attracted the amorous attention of Evita Perón. He had a torrid affair with "The First Lady of South America."

In 1951, MGM had imported Lamas, known at the time as "Argentina's beefsteak," as a means of giving the already-established Latin lover Ricardo Montalban some serious competition.

Lana was cast opposite Lamas in MGM's 1952 *The Merry Widow*. Throughout the picture, she wore long gloves or a very wide bracelet, even a fur piece on her wrist to conceal the scars from her suicide attempt with a razor blade and sleeping pills.

Before slashing her wrists, she'd called her business manager, Benton Cole, expressing her grave concern over her recent box office flops. Before ringing off, she declared her career "a tissue of fantasies, a hollow success, meaning not a God damn thing."

Late in 1951 and for most of 1952, Lana and Lamas became inseparable, often retreating for long weekends to their favorite desert oasis, Palm Springs. She was careful not to look at another man, because Lamas was ferociously jealous. After the success of *The Merry Widow*, Metro had scheduled the pair to co-star again in the hokey *Latin Lovers*, set for a 1953 release.

As the summer neared its end in 1952, Marion Davies, mistress of William Randolph Hearst, had tossed a huge party for the elite of Hollywood. The party was in honor of her friend, crooner Johnny Ray.

Making a spectacular entrance, Lana and Lamas were seated at table with Ava and Esther Williams. There was a certain irony here. Ava and Lamas had long ago been lovers, and swim queen Esther would eventually become the Argentine's final wife.

Lana became jealous when Lamas began paying too much attention to Esther.

Suddenly, all female eyes turned as Lex Barker entered the room. He was the tenth official Tarzan of the movies and the handsomest. He was smooth-muscled, well educated, and like Lamas himself, known for his "fabulous endowment."

To punish Lamas for his flirtation with Esther, Lana made some comments about Barker's "striking beauty." At the time, Barker was still married to Arlene Dahl (Lamas' future wife), but separated. Hollywood in those days was a very incestuous place. "No wonder he was cast as Tarzan," Lana announced to the table, infuriating Lamas. "I bet he has muscle in all the right places."

"It's not a muscle, darling," a drunken Ava instructed her. "If it was a muscle, it would grow bigger with exercise. If that be the case, Frank's thing would stretch around the block."

As the band struck up another number, Barker broke from the bevy of admiring women at the Davies party and walked toward Lana's table where he asked her to dance, ignoring Lamas.

As Barker graciously escorted Lana to the center of the floor, he held her in a tight embrace, a style quite unlike the courtly dances which Lana and Lamas had executed on the set of *The Merry Widow*.

"Jungle Boy is fucking her right on the dance floor," an angry Lamas announced to Ava and Esther. When he could stand it no more, Lamas jumped up from the table and headed for the dance floor to cut in. He grabbed Lana by the shoulder, spinning her around. He then turned angrily on Barker. Loud enough for the other dancers to hear, he asked, "Why don't you just take her out into the bushes and fuck her?" Lana was furious. Breaking from the arms of Barker, she slapped Lamas' face.

"You fucking cunt!" he yelled back at her, looking as if he were going to strike her. The dancers stopped and turned to take in the floor show.

Lana rushed from the ballroom, heading for the door, as Lamas, later called "a raging bull," trailed her. The ride back to her house on Mapleton Drive was in silence.

Once in the foyer, with the door slammed shut, Lamas slapped her so hard her diamond earring shot across the room. As she tried to kick him in his low-hanging *cojones* with a sequined shoe, he grabbed her right ankle and sent her sprawling onto the marble floor.

With all his fiery temper, he kicked her in her ribs several times before bending over her and pounding his fist into her face twice. Screaming, she tried to protect her face from injury. Before he could inflict more damage, he rose and stormed out of the house, never to return.

When **Lex Barker** asked **Lana Turner** to dance in front of the jealous eyes of Fernando Lamas, it was the beginning of a new love for the blonde goddess. He held her close and whispered into her ear, "I'm unzipped. Reach inside and see if I've got more than Lamas."

Lana must have decided that he did, because Lamas, after a violent confrontation, was kicked out of her house that night.

The next day, the movie Tarzan moved in and remained in her home until Lana discovered that he was forcing sex onto her teenaged daughter.

"For Lana, I was the Jungle Boy stud in the loincloth," he said, referring to the five *Tarzan* movies he made.

*The New York Times* wrote, "Lex Barker is a streamlined apeman with a personable grin and a torso to make any lion cringe."

The following morning, arriving badly bruised at MGM studio, an angry and distraught Lana put through a call to Benjamin Thau, head of MGM casting. "Benny," she said, "forgive me for interrupting your morning blow-job from Nancy Davis, but get to my dressing room at once." Lana was referring to the future Mrs. Ronald Reagan, then a starlet at MGM.

Thau came running, finding Lana "a mess of bruises and scratches." She was set to begin filming *Latin Lovers*, starring Lamas himself.

She burst into tears, sharing all of the horror of her break-up with Lamas. "He said the vilest things to me anyone has ever said. He told me, 'Your pussy's been used so much it's gone limp like a wet dish rag. I practically have to jack-off inside you to get an orgasm. You're a lousy lay. You won't even suck cock!'"

Thau realized at once that Lamas was out of the picture. With the agreement of Louis B. Mayer, Thau replaced him with Ricardo Montalban. There was a certain irony here in that Lamas had been hired by Metro as a possible replacement for Montalban.

Both Mayer and Thau agreed that shooting should be delayed for a week and that Lana should take a vacation in Palm Springs to recover from her bruises.

That afternoon as she was heading to her car, she ran into Frank. "What's up, doll?" he asked her.

"I'm taking a week off in Palm Springs. I'm calling a realtor about a rental."

"Forget it," he said. "My place is yours. It's free this week as I'm tied up with work."

"That's wonderful, dear," she said. "I'll pay you what you think it's worth."

"Come on, Lana," he said. "We're friends from way back. Come to my dressing room. I'll give you the key."

Toward evening, Lana decided she didn't want to be alone. Peter Lawford, her bisexual former lover, had told her about a garage where gas jockeys, some of the best looking and best hung men in Los Angeles, were available.

In 1945, at the end of World War II, a well-built, curly-haired blond former G.I. from southern Illinois moved to Los Angeles. Shortly thereafter, he opened Scott Bowers' Gas Station at the corner of Fairfax and Hollywood Boulevard. Within eight months, it had become the most popular gas station among gays and horny women in Hollywood.

Getting a lube job at Scotty's came to mean something else. He hired as many as a dozen young men to pump gas and to escort certain gentlemen callers into the back rooms. There, the car owners could perform fellatio on these handsome, strapping former servicemen, or else become passive recipients of sodomy. Scotty hired only "tops."

Among the many patrons of the gas station were director George Cukor and the very closeted Spencer Tracy. Robert Taylor often stopped by to get "filled up," and Tyrone Power took some of the young men home with him to perform up close and personal "the down and dirties," in the words of one gas jockey hustler.

"Most of Scotty's men were gorgeous," or so claimed Vivien Leigh, who visited the gas station accompanied by her friend Cukor. Most of Scotty's men were bisexuals and could accommodate either gender. Sometimes one of the gas jockeys was hired for private sessions at the homes of a married couple.

In his investigation, author Paul Young quotes a source who claimed that "Scotty was smarter than some of his competitors. He refused to accept money from his boys or his clients. He'd only accept gifts: gold watches, silver trinkets, stocks, bonds, you name it. Some of his regular clients,

*Associated Press*

**Ava Gardner** (left) and **Lana Turner** (center) both shared the favors of that heartthrob from South America, **Fernando Lamas** (right). Both Lana and Ava also bedded a young JFK before he became president.

Fernando later married the 1950s screen beauty, red-haired Arlene Dahl. Perhaps unknown to him, JFK got to her first. He dated Arlene when he was still a U.S. senator.

Fernando, who was always proud, justifiably so, of his endowment, swore that Ava told him he had "two and a half times as much as JFK."

When he wasn't chasing after Desi Arnaz, the gay actor Cesar Romero pursued Lamas, but to no avail. "Fernando was a beautiful man," Romero claimed. "Very much in love with himself. But instead of with me, he ended up in Esther Williams' swimming pool."

Here Ava, Lana, and Fernando are in a huddle at a lavish party tossed on October 2, 1952 in Beverly Hills by Marion Davies for gay singer Johnny Ray, who later gave Fernando a blow-job in the men's room.

who greatly appreciated his services, even went so far as to give him pieces of property."

Desperate for non-judgmental male companionship, Lana drove her car into the filling station. The first gas jockey who approached her was good looking enough, but she was attracted to another well-built man who looked even handsomer. He sat on a bench in front of the station with his legs apart, revealing his obvious appeal in pants far too tight. She requested that he fill up her tank.

Whatever transaction took place between the two of them can only be assumed, because he showed up after work at her home, arriving with grease on his hands and dirty fingernails. She suggested a joint bubble bath. She would later brag to her confidants, "My God, he's got more than Frank. Seeing is believing."

The twenty-two-year-old man, who was born in Minnesota, was a "Guy Madison look-alike." He'd served in the U.S. Marines during the war. His name was Don Johnson (not the star of *Miami Vice*), and he'd come to Hollywood with some vague aspiration to become an actor, as did thousands of other young men in the post-war era.

Lana invited him to spend a weekend in Palm Springs as her driver. It went without saying that he'd also be her bedmate.

Feeling somewhat uneasy about spending a week with a strange man, she invited her business manager, Benton Cole, who also managed Ava's career for a time.

The plot thickened as the characters moved onto the stage to play out one of the most scandalous dramas in the scandal-rich history of the desert resort.

Before departing from the Los Angeles area, Lana ordered her cook to prepare a large roasting pan of fried chicken.

Johnson, Cole, and Lana arrived early at Frank's villa to enjoy the afternoon by the pool.

Thinking she had the house to herself, Lana was anticipating a period of tranquil recovery from her beating at the hands of Lamas. With a gorgeous, beautifully sculpted, and well-hung lover, plus a faithful business manager, she hoped to recover from her traumas. What she didn't expect was the arrival of two world-famous guests hell bent on destruction and mayhem.

Back in Los Angeles, Ava began to stew over Frank's threat to shack up with Lana for the weekend. On the phone, she called her sister, Bappie, announcing "we're going to Palm Springs, and I'm gonna catch that bastard in the act."

Resisting at first, Bappie eventually gave in to Ava, and they set out across the desert from L.A. In her memoirs, Ava for some reason claimed they

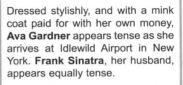

Dressed stylishly, and with a mink coat paid for with her own money, **Ava Gardner** appears tense as she arrives at Idlewild Airport in New York. **Frank Sinatra**, her husband, appears equally tense.

Having flown in from London, Ava and Frank had fought all the way en route. The pilot had to come out of his cockpit and ask them to pipe down.

Chain-smoking **Lana Turner** gets her cigarette lit by a man (**Frank Sinatra**) who has had a lot of experience in doing that. Even though Frank had refused to marry her, Lana had many reasons to be grateful to him.

After she killed her lover, Johnny Stompanato, blaming it on her daughter, Cheryl Crane, Frank talked gangster Mickey Cohen out of his plan to have two of his henchmen permanently damage Lana's bankable face.

arrived after midnight, but in reality they drove up to Frank's villa during the afternoon.

Ava came up with a scheme. Although Bappie warned of the desert land behind Frank's villa—"infested with deadly sidewinders"—Ava persisted. Taking off her shoes, Ava scampered over the six-foot chain link fence, pulling Bappie along with her.

Since the curtains were drawn, Ava and Bappie slipped around the house, trying to peek in some of the windows, hoping to see a little action. It was at that point that Ben came out the back door with a bag of garbage. "Ava, honey, is that you and Bappie? Come on in, honey, and join the party."

Lana was startled to see her since she knew that Frank and Ava were separated. Before kissing Lana on both cheeks, Ava appraised Johnson's body. "Baby," she whispered to Lana, "buy me some of that, momma."

"He's yours for the asking," Lana said, "all bought and paid for, and it's even bigger than Frank's."

"It sounds like a fun weekend," Ava said. "The reason I came is that Frank said he was heading here to 'fuck Lana Turner.'"

"Not at all," Lana said. "Frank told me he's busy in Los Angeles."

No stranger to nudity, Ava began pulling off her clothing. "Let's go skinny dipping like I used to do in North Carolina."

During this prelude to what would evolve into an orgy, Cole wisely removed himself, sitting in Frank's living room reading a book and listening to Sinatra recordings.

What happened next only became known when Johnson tried to hawk the details of that Palm Springs weekend to *Confidential*. The magazine editors did indeed publish an article on that weekend but it was "a vanilla version," since the magazine's lawyers feared a lawsuit not only from Frank himself, but from attorneys for both Lana and Ava.

Johnson claimed to *Confidential* that by 6pm he was in bed with both Lana and Ava. "I was shocked that Ava had a lesbian streak in her. But most of the attention was focused on me and my best asset. They really worked me over. Often at the garage I serviced homosexuals, but I really preferred women. I was afraid that no one back in Los Angeles, certainly not my fellow hustlers, would believe that I serviced both Lana and Ava in the same bed at the same time. I was one lucky guy. Fortunately, I've always been praised for stamina."

"But I had the feeling I didn't completely satisfy these two hot-to-trot mommas, and they'd want more—a lot more—before the night ended."

"We got out of bed about seven that evening, and headed for Sinatra's bar," Johnson said. "All of us had had a little too much to drink, and we were feeling no pain. Cole wasn't part of the action. He stayed more or less to himself. At some point we got really hungry. That's when Lana revealed that her cook had fried a mess of chicken. We headed to the kitchen and had a feast, finishing off about two bottles of wine. I was looking forward to one of the most glorious nights of my life, but things didn't work out that way."

After dinner and more drinking, Johnson, Ava, and Lana retired to the master bedroom. "We were practically involved in a daisy chain when suddenly the door was thrown open. I lost my hard-on at once. There stood Sinatra with murder in his eyes."

"Many stories, mostly denied by Ava and Lana, had been told about that night," Johnson said. "No one got it right. I'm left out of all the accounts."

Actually, Johnson was mistaken about that. Ava in her memoirs has been among the few sources to write about Lana's boyfriend.

Those who dismiss the *ménage à trois* theory haven't checked Ava's autobiography, in which she talks about Lana inviting a boyfriend to Frank's house. Over the years, Lana and Ava exchanged boyfriends if they came across one exceptional "stallion" in bed.

"Get out of my house, you fucking dykes, and take this two-bit hustler with you," Frank shouted at them.

"I'd heard that Sinatra carried a gun, and I jumped out of bed and ran past the crazy fucker," Johnson said. "I managed to escape with just a pair of jockey shorts. Too young to die, I ran out onto the main highway and flagged down the first car coming. Was I in luck."

"A Cadillac stopped," he claimed. "In the front seat sat two queens of the lisping variety. Instead of looking at my face, they eyed my bulge. Without even asking why I was in my jockeys, the men invited me to hop inside. I spent a weekend with them and emerged with two suits of clothes, five hundred dollars in my pocket, and a steady gig with them when I got back to L.A. So the weekend wasn't a total disaster. At least I didn't get shot by that crazed Sinatra creep. By the way, I hate his syrupy music. I was always a Hank Williams kind of guy."

With Johnson removed from the scene, Frank stood over Ava as if he wanted to strike her. Trembling but defiant, Ava blurted, "You said you wanted to fuck Lana Turner. Well, here she is. Go at it."

"Are you kidding?" he asked. "I wouldn't fuck this broken-down broad if she was the last woman on earth."

In tears, Lana ran from the bedroom into the living room where Cole waited with a coat to put over her nude body.

At the sound of violence from the bedroom, they fled from the house. Ben tried to collect their luggage, but Lana told him to run. "Frank's got a gun."

Racing out into the night, they got into her car and drove to a small resort that rented villas by the week. They made arrangements to stay there, planning to return later to see what damage Frank had caused.

Meanwhile, back at Frank's villa, "with red face and blazing eyes," he assaulted Ava, kicking her in the rear as she darted from the bedroom into the adjoining room where she kept some clothing.

"I want you out of this house . . . and now!" he shouted. "You fucking Tarheel dyke-whore!"

In Ketty Kelley's biography of Frank called *His Way*, she accurately quoted Ava as saying to Frank, "I'll get the hell out of the house, but since this is also *my* house, too, I'm gonna take out of it everything that belongs to me. I started taking down pictures from the wall, and Frank exploded. He grabbed everything I said was mine and hurled it outside onto the lawn. It was hysterical."

As the finale to his farewell to Ava, Frank ran upstairs and filled her douche bag with water. Back out on his front yard, he poured the water over her head. "Have a great time fucking either Grace Kelly or Clark Gable in Africa, you whoring dyke bitch."

After checking into her hastily arranged new lodgings, Lana feared for Ava's safety and had Ben drive her back to Frank's villa. When they arrived, they spotted two police cars with dome lights flashing. Spotlights illuminated the house.

The front door was open, and Frank was tossing out both Ava's clothes and Lana's baggage. Lana remained in the car, as Ben identified himself and was able to retrieve her luggage. He asked one policeman, "Can I go into the kitchen and retrieve some fried chicken we left?"

"Get the hell out of here!" the policeman ordered him.

Back at the car, Lana asked Ben to give the policeman the address of the villa where they were staying, inviting Ava to stay with them for the night.

To back up Don Johnson's story of the events that transpired that night, an F.B.I. report, released after Frank's death, mentioned an "unnamed man who claimed that he had sex at the house with both Ava Gardner and Lana Turner."

In her memoirs, *The Lady, the Legend, the Truth*, Lana presented a fantasy version of that night. She completely misrepresented what happened and made it sound like a simple country chicken supper.

When Frank finally retreated and bolted his door, a policeman came to Ava's aid, informing her of Lana's invitation for the night. Not having any other place to go, Ava accepted, and the policeman drove her to Lana's villa. The blonde beauty offered the brunette beauty a stiff drink—and then it was off to bed for both of them.

"Poor Ava," Lana wrote in her memoirs. "She was badly shaken, and after my own grim experience, I could sympathize with her humiliation. I also felt sorry for Frank. It was a bad time for him. His career had slipped badly, and he was losing Ava."

Fernando Lamas, who was still in a jealous rage over Lana in the wake of his beating of her, was also staying in Palm Springs. Somehow he learned that Lana and Ava were both in town and hiding out in a villa.

Perhaps by bribing a policeman, the Latin lover found out where Lana was staying. By then, during the early morning hours, Lana had gone to bed alone, leaving Ava to lick her wounds in the next bedroom.

Ava couldn't sleep and was in the efficiency kitchen when there was a knock on the door. She rushed to the door, thinking it was Frank who had come to apologize. To her astonishment, she saw her former lover, Lamas himself.

"Where's Lana?" he asked. "I know she's here."

Not wanting a second major blow-up, Ava took charge. She kissed Lamas. "Lana's in the bedroom. She's been throwing up all night. Nothing but bile. Why take her when my honeypot is available?"

Lamas seemed to see that that was a reasonable request, and he made off into the night with Ava. Apparently, Lana never found out. Or, if she did find out, she didn't care.

The next morning, the headline in the *Los Angeles Times* claimed SINATRA—AVA BOUDOIR ROW BUZZES. The *Los Angeles Daily Mirror* shouted BOUDOIR FIGHT HEADS FRANKIE AND AVA TO COURTS.

After he cooled down, Frank tried to call Ava but she'd changed her phone number. He didn't even know where she was staying. Apparently, he

"Late in 1949, it was a choice between Frank Sinatra or Robert Mitchum," **Ava Gardner** *(pictured above)* told Lana Turner.

"It was big, burly Bob or this singer from Hoboken with his scrawny limbs, hollow chest...a real stringbean except in one department.

"Believe it or not, I chose Frank because I felt I could mother him, of all things. He was undernourished, frightened, and desperate. The public's changing tastes in music had cut into his record sales. The Sinatra craze was over.

"This gay singer, Johnny Ray, would reign supreme until a fellow named Elvis Presley, like me, rose from a pile of southern white trash."

STEVENSON FOR PRESIDENT

Both Frank Sinatra and Ava Gardner were loyal supporters of Democratic candidate **Adlai Stevenson**, who was making his first run against Dwight D. Eisenhower in a race for the presidency in 1952.

After their biggest fight that night in Palm Springs, Ava and Frank agreed to put aside their differences to support Adlai, who appeared to be losing the battle against the ever-so-popular general who had led the Allied invasion of the Normandy beaches in 1944.

"I did my part for Adlai," Ava confided to Lana Turner. "J. Edgar Hoover had uncovered evidence that he was a homosexual and had even interviewed a male lover of his. Remember this was 1952 and being called a homosexual could kill you in almost any field. Adlai needed to publicly attach himself to some hot tomatoes. There was no one hotter at the time than me. We did it and I spread the rumor that, in spite of his looks, Adlai was a great stud like Frank himself."

never found out that she was warming the bed of Lana's recently discarded lover, Lamas.

Desperate to reach Ava, Frank was a nervous wreck, and he often vomited. In desperation, he called columnist Earl Wilson, begging him to print his pleas for a reconciliation in the wake of the Palm Springs fiasco. Wilson ran the item under the head: FRANKIE READY TO SURRENDER, WANTS AVA BACK, ANY TERMS.

Somehow that won her over, and she called Frank and arranged to get back together with him, an event that occurred in front of hundreds of people.

Ava and Frank had a reunion on Monday, October 27, 1952, at a Hollywood-for-Stevenson rally at the Palladium Ballroom, which attracted four thousand people. The rally was in honor of then-Democratic candidate for president in the upcoming presidential elections scheduled for that November. Adlai Stevenson was running as the presidential candidate against Republican Dwight D. Eisenhower and his Vice-presidental candidate Richard Nixon.

At the rally, Ava's main task involved introducing Frank, who would then sing for the audience. She arrived backstage, but for reasons of her own, decided not to visit Frank in his dressing room.

She stood in the wings until her name was called, and which time she made a spectacular entrance.

Stunning in a black satin strapless gown and a mink stole, she came onstage to face roaring applause. "I can't do anything myself," she told the crowd, "but I can introduce a wonderful, wonderful man. I'm a great fan of him myself. Ladies and gentlemen, my husband, Frank Sinatra."

He came on stage and kissed Ava before singing "The Birth of the Blues" and "The House I Live In."

Ava and Frank's joint appearance at the rally led to their reconciliation, but it did not carry the day for Stevenson, who lost that November to Eisenhower and Nixon.

What Frank didn't know, and what would have ruined everything that night, was the fact that Ava had visited the suite of Stevenson that afternoon and had slept with him.

Republicans had been plotting dirty tricks right before the November election. Privately they'd launched a smear campaign, claiming that Stevenson was a homosexual. There may have been a lot of truth in that accusation.

To counter such smears, Stevenson had systematically initiated a series of affairs with Hollywood stars, pursuing prizes who included both Shelley Winters and Joan Fontaine.

His final seduction, consummated shortly before the November, 1952 election, was Ava Gardner herself.

# Frank's Suicide Attempts

## AND HIS ROCKY COMEBACK TRAIL

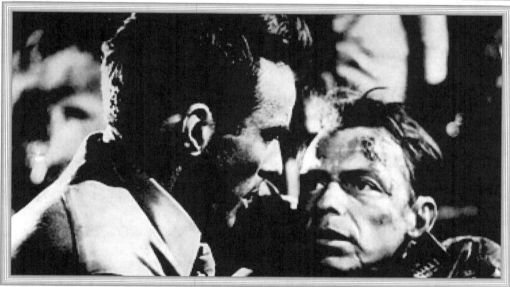

As two doomed soldiers at Pearl Harbor in 1941, **Montgomery Clift** (*left*) and **Frank Sinatra** *(right)* provide tender comfort to each other during the final days of their lives.

"In one long weekend, I read James Jones' first novel, *From Here to Eternity,* and I knew the role of Maggio had my name written on it," Frank Sinatra said. "I got through all 850 pages of it in one weekend." He was referring to the bestseller of 1951, a 430,000-word drama set on the eve of the Japanese attack on Pearl Harbor.

Because of its strong language and "lack of moral character," among its female roles, the book at first was deemed "unfit for the cameras." One of the female leads, played by Donna Reed, is a prostitute, and the other female lead, Deborah Kerr, plays a captain's wife who commits adultery with enlisted men, notably with Burt Lancaster.

Two major studios had rejected the novel, but Harry Cohn of Columbia eventually acquired the rights. The moment Frank read that in *Variety*, he began a long, feverish campaign to convince Cohn that he was right for the role of the scrappy little Italian-American soldier from the tough streets of Brooklyn.

At the time, Frank had come to view himself as a has-been. "No movie deals, no record sales. In Hollywood, you know you're washed up when your so-called friends don't come to the phone. Forget about borrowing money from any of those shitheads. They don't know you. The only collateral I had was my dream that I could make a comeback. But isn't every fallen star in Hollywood dreaming the same god damn dream which often turns into a nightmare?"

## FRANK'S COMEBACK ON THE ROAD TO ETERNITY

Critics pointed out that **Frank Sinatra** *(left figure in upper photo)* was too skinny to be a GI, and that **Montgomery Clift** *(right)* was too reed-thin to be convincing as a boxer.

But in spite of their frail frames, they delivered their most memorable roles in *From Here to Eternity*.

Harry Cohn had wanted Eli Wallach for Frank's role, and the book's author, James Jones, would have preferred Aldo Ray for Monty's part. But these two skinny guys prevailed. When Fred Zinnemann, the director, called Monty with the news that he could play the role of Prewitt, Monty said, "Hooray, now I can play a fuck-up—talk about type casting!"

When Jones met Monty, he apologized for campaigning against him, and he, along with Frank, became drinking buddies.

"They were a motley crew," said the film's press agent. "Jones looked like a bouncer in some sleazy night club. Sinatra was moaning over Ava Gardner, and we kidded him that Clark Gable was giving her a fuck in Africa. Sinatra was suicidal. Only Monty had real class, even when he was taking out his little dick for a drunken piss on the sidewalk."

*"Don't despair. You have to scrape bottom to appreciate life and start living again."*

**—Frank Sinatra**

Merv Griffin, who in time would become one of the biggest names in television, was just a struggling actor when he became roommates and lovers with Montgomery Clift.

When Clift was cast as the soldier boy, Prewitt, in the WWII drama, *From Here to Eternity*, he provided a ticket for Merv to fly to Honolulu to join him during the filming.

The movie would also star Frank Sinatra as Maggio. At a low point in his career, Frank was trying to make a comeback.

When he read James Jones' best-selling novel, *From Here to Eternity*, he became obsessed with playing the role of Angelo Maggio, a tragic figure. "That doomed sad-sack private has the name Frank Sinatra written all over it," he told his buddy, Burt Lancaster. The bisexual actor at the time was pursuing Frank with a gleam in his eye.

When Frank flew to Hawaii, many of his friends had deserted him. Record companies didn't seem to want him. His marriage to Ava Gardner was falling away from him. "My whole world is crashing in on me," he confided to Lancaster.

Harry Cohn, head of Columbia, viewed Frank as a song and dance man. He later admitted, "He was not my first choice for the role."

The rumor that the Mafia forced Cohn to hire Frank is not true. That libel stemmed from the publication of Mario Puzo's novel, *The Godfather* and its 1972 film version. The role of a singer and actor, clearly based on Frank's own life, was disguised under the name of "Johnny Fontaine." In the script, the mob pays a call on a studio chief (actually, Harry Cohn).

In one of the most dramatic scenes in the movie, the mob descends on the studio chief's home, leaving the bloody, severed head of his prize horse on his pillow. The next day the studio chief grants Johnny the role.

Actually Frank's benefactor was none other than Ava herself. She was big box office at the time, and used her clout to intercede with Cohn, asking him to cast Frank in the part.

Even with Ava's intervention, Cohn still objected, telling Frank, "This is a part for an actor, not a hoofer."

Frank even flew to Hollywood to test for the role. He had been in Africa hanging out with Ava when she was shooting *Mogambo* with Clark Gable and his lover, Grace Kelly. Because of a mammoth back tax bill facing Frank, he had to ask Ava to pay his roundtrip fare from Africa to Los Angeles and back to Africa.

Cohn held out for Eli Wallach, who eventually turned it down. Frank won the role by default, getting paid only $10,000.

During the filming of *From Here to Eternity*, Monty had found the ideal drinking partner in Frank. "They didn't just drink," said

During the filming of *From Here to Eternity*, **Merv Griffin** (depicted in the early 50s as the left figure in photo above) flew to Honolulu as the guest of his roommate, Montgomery Clift.

In Hawaii, Merv became intimately involved in the life of Frank Sinatra. "He was a womanizer," Merv said, "but not when I hung out with him. All he could talk about was Ava Gardner, who was in Africa filming *Mogambo* with Clark Gable.

"Frank wasn't interested in other gals. His obsession with Ava consumed his life—that and his role of Maggio. I kept urging him to get over her and get on with his life, but he wouldn't listen. I predicted that Eternity would be big comeback for him, but he was all gloom and doom. He claimed he was finished. He called my talk bullshit."

Merv Griffin, who was vacationing in Hawaii at the time. "They poured it down their throats. It was frightening. Both of them seemed to want to drink themselves into oblivion. Monty was still conflicted over his sexual preference, and Frank drank because his marriage to Ava Gardner was in its death throes."

"Not only that, but Frank was at the nadir of his career," Merv later recalled. "Back taxes, maybe as much as $150,000. His salary for *Eternity* wouldn't cover it. In fact, that paltry fee wouldn't even pay Frank's bar bills. Often, Burt Lancaster and I had to carry both Monty and Frank back to their hotel, where we undressed them and put them to bed like little children. I personally took the responsibility of removing Frank's underwear to judge for myself if the legend was true. It was! Somehow Monty and Frank usually managed to pull themselves together to face the camera the following day, each giving brilliant performances," Merv said. "It was amazing."

When Monty sobered up and Frank sobered up, Monty actually managed to give Frank acting lessons. The singer later thanked Monty and claimed his help was the reason he got the Oscar for Best Supporting Actor that year.

Most evenings, Frank seemed to be trying to place a call to Ava in Nairobi where she was filming *Mogambo*. Word reached Frank that Clark and Ava had resumed their affair, which had been launched when they'd made *The Hucksters* years previously, back in 1947. Frank was misled, as Ava's passion for Gable had long ago cooled. The former "King of the Box Office" was visiting Grace Kelly's tent at night.

After the filming in Hawaii, Fred Zinnemann ordered the cast and crew back to Hollywood, where the final interiors for *Eternity* would be shot at Columbia Studios. Monty booked a suite at the Roosevelt Hotel in Hollywood and invited Merv to stay with him, at least until the end of the picture. "I can't stand to be alone."

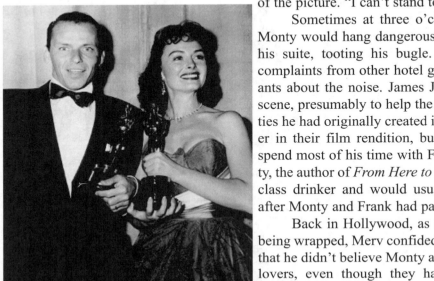

At the Academy Awards, 1954, **Frank Sinatra and Donna Reed**, co-stars of *From Here to Eternity*, walked off with Oscars for Best Supporting Actor and Best Supporting Actress.

On the set in Honolulu, Frank had met Donna and found her very provocative. "As you know I play a prostitute in this film," she told him. "But for you I wouldn't charge."

He turned down her come-on, as he was too obsessed with the woman he'd left in Kenya, Ava Gardner. He told her, "You're Monty's girl in this film—not mine."

She shot back, "You stand a far better chance with Monty than I do."

Later, over a drink, Frank and Donna discussed the *Eternity* script. "Monty and I are the second romance of the film, the big focus being on Burt Lancaster and Deborah Kerr," Frank said. "On the fifth reading, I came to see there was another big romance going on: That of Prewitt and Maggio."

Off screen, all Frank could admit about Monty was, "We had a mutual admiration thing going there."

Sometimes at three o'clock in the morning, Monty would hang dangerously out the window of his suite, tooting his bugle. There were endless complaints from other hotel guests and nearby tenants about the noise. James Jones was still on the scene, presumably to help the pieces and personalities he had originally created in his novel fit together in their film rendition, but Monty preferred to spend most of his time with Frank. Tough and gritty, the author of *From Here to Eternity* was a world-class drinker and would usually still be standing after Monty and Frank had passed out.

Back in Hollywood, as the *Eternity* film was being wrapped, Merv confided to Roddy McDowall that he didn't believe Monty and Frank had become lovers, even though they had occasionally slept drunkenly nude in each other's arms. "I came in many times to wake them up, and saw them huddled together for comfort," Merv confided. "But I think it was more for the moral support they gave each other—not sex. What a contrast. There was Monty's peanut exposed only a foot from Frank's monster Italian salami."

"Frank confessed to me that his vocal cords were hemorrhaged," Merv said. "He'd also received a devastating blow from MCA. His agents informed him that 'no one wants you, Frankie, no more movie deals, no more night club offers.'"

"Every night," Merv said, "Frank threatened to commit suicide. It was Monty, as messed up as he was, who would talk him out of it."

One Saturday morning around 4am, Merv got up to go to the bathroom, which opened onto the hallway. Thinking Monty and Frank were asleep in the next bedroom, he turned the knob and walked into the bathroom. What he saw shocked him. A nude Frank lay sprawled on the tiled floor, an empty bottle of sleeping pills beside him.

Frank appeared to be dead. It seemed pointless to scream for Monty to help, because he was completely wasted. Merv ran into the living room and called the hotel desk, demanding an ambulance and the police.

Covered with sheets, Frank's body was hauled out of the hotel on a stretcher through the back entrance. In the back seat of a squad car, Merv followed the ambulance's flashing dome lights.

At the hospital, while Frank's stomach was being pumped, Merv put through an urgent call to Columbia's chief publicist, strongly advising him to get Harry Cohn involved. "Cohn knows how to keep stuff like this out of the papers," Merv said.

The call paid off. Within an hour, the PR staff at Columbia had launched itself into damage control. Cohn was an expert at keeping scandals about his stars out of the papers, and he managed to cover up Frank's latest attempt at suicide.

Three days later, a sober Frank returned to Monty's suite at the Roosevelt for a reunion with Monty and Merv. He thanked Merv for "saving my rotten life." His weight had dropped to 118 pounds, which Merv thought would make his interpretation of a defeated, burnt-out Maggio all the more convincing in *Eternity*.

He talked openly about why he'd tried to kill himself, claiming that Ava had flown to London where she'd had an abortion. "Her exact words to me," Frank claimed, were 'I killed your son.'" It is not known if Ava ever knew the sex of her unborn child. Perhaps by asserting that it was a boy, she hoped to cause Frank greater grief.

Frank and Monty learned no lessons from the singer's suicide attempt. Within three nights, Frank and Monty had resumed their heavy drinking, referring to their binges as "sloshing good times." Merv joined them on their nightly rounds, having little to drink himself because he knew he had to get both of them back to the Roosevelt intact.

The next day, while Monty and Frank were at Columbia Studios, Merv quietly packed and left the Roosevelt. He'd found an apartment of his own.

One week later, Monty placed a desperate call to Merv, begging him to come over to his suite at the Roosevelt. Once there, Merv found that Monty had been severely beaten. Fortunately, he'd shot his last take at Columbia, because he was far too beat up to face any camera. At first Merv assumed that Monty had picked up some rough trade along Santa Monica Boulevard, who had robbed and beaten him up.

When he wiped the blood off Monty's wounds and put iodine on the cuts, Monty related the details of what had happened. In a drunken rage, Frank had attacked him. Monty refused to tell Merv what had set Frank off.

The house doctor examined Monty, finding no broken bones. Merv called and ordered a male nurse to stay

Hollywood insiders asked the question, "Why would **Harry Cohn** buy a dirty book like *From Here to Eternity?*"

The answer to that was phrased as a joke. "Because Harry thinks everybody talks that way."

To the astonishment of *tout* Hollywood, Cohn paid James Jones $82,000 for the film rights to *Eternity*, with its obscene words and scenes portraying raw sex. Cohn claimed he'd be able to get around the censors, and with the help of screenwriter Daniel Taradash, he succeeded.

The film cost $2,400,000, but brought in $19 million on its first release. The Capitol in New York ran it 24 hours a day to accommodate the lines forming around the block. All five leading players were nominated for Academy Awards, and the film won eight Oscars, tying the record held by *Gone With the Wind*.

in Monty's suite and take care of him. That night he drove to Roddy McDowall's house to tell him what had happened.

Roddy had some ideas about what had caused the uncontrollable rage that had swept over Frank. "I bet Monty confessed to Frank that he'd fallen madly in love with him, and that was more than Frank could take. He sure as hell wasn't going to go from the arms of Ava Gardner into the arms of Monty Clift. No way! Not Frank."

---

## Harry Cohn's One Act of Kindness

The chief mogul at columbia, Harry Cohn, and Frank Sinatra became friends back in his glory as a singer in the 1940s. Frank did Cohn a big favor during his four-week gig at the Capitol in New York. He agreed to allow Cohn to show his lackluster comedy, *Miss Grant Takes Richmond,* starring Lucille Ball and William Holden. Over the objections of Capitol managers, Frank prevailed. Achieving a first-week gross of $122,000, a big figure back then, Cohn made a success of his weak entry.

He didn't forget that favor. When Frank came down with strep throat during the third week of his engagement, Cohn stayed by his side night and day. Frank was in an oxygen tent. No other friends came to call. Cohn read to Frank, shared stories of the golden days in Hollywood, told jokes, and spoon fed Frank. When Frank recovered and Cohn left, his final words were, "You tell anybody about this, you son of a bitch, and I'll kill you."

*From Here to Eternity* lay in their futures.

---

**Frank Sinatra and Ava Gardner** are seen during one of the few happy moments of their turbulent marriage. Within minutes, their smiles could turn into frowns and screaming denunciations.

Three stars in a row: the homosexual **Montgomery Clift** *(left)*, the bisexual **Burt Lancaster** (center), and the heterosexual **Frank Sinatra** *(right)* on the set of *From Here to Eternity* in Honolulu.

Frank may have had a bony physique, but he had hidden endowments that attracted gay interest. Although Burt and Monty pursued Frank, they found him obsessed with Ava Gardner, and completely uninterested.

Frank and Burt remained friends for life, but Frank and Monty broke up one night when a drunken Monty practically unzipped one of Frank's straight friends and wanted action in one of Frank's upper bedrooms.

Ava lobbied to get him the part of Maggio, but privately felt he was heading for disappointment. "How can he pin his hopes on playing one lousy soldier who gets killed?" she asked. "I've starred in big productions that were going to be hotter than baby shit, only to have them flop at the box office."

Traveling from Hawaii, Frank joined Ava in London. She called him "my old man," but later claimed "his batteries were recharged. Six times in one night, not bad. Only Gary Cooper could do that. Frank was full of spunk, and lots of testosterone, enough to take on five whores in one night in a bordello."

# Child Molestation with Frank and
# Natalie Wood

## A HOLLYWOOD STORY

With a patch over his right eye, **Frank Sinatra** helps his lover, **Natalie Wood**, celebrate her twenty-first birthday at Romanoff's in Hollywood on July 20, 1959. At the right is her barely visible other lover, **Robert Wagner**, whom she would marry twice. Frank explained that the eye patch was worn because of a "backfire from a gun" on a movie set.

Frank later confided to Tony Curtis, who had co-starred with Natalie and himself in the 1958 *Kings Go Forth,* "She'd had other guys before me, but they were just boys. Having a young teenage gal like Natalie can really turn on a middle-aged man. I think she'd just had sex in the missionary position, and I could get her to do things that a lot of Vegas whores wouldn't do.

"She desperately wanted to be sophisticated and more or less followed by dictates. It was thrilling for me having a girl that young make love to you and do all sorts of things to you. I always held a special place in my heart for her.

"Okay, already, so I was a dirty old man. So what? Practically any guy in my position would have taken advantage."

# The Girl They Called Natasha
# —Growing Up Too Soon

When **Natalie Wood** made *Kings Go Forth* with Frank Sinatra and Tony Curtis, all the attention focused on her affair with Ol' Blue Eyes.

Several years followed before Tony Curtis made a play for Natalie. It occurred on the set of *The Great Race*, which they starred in together before its release in 1965.

In Tony Curtis' memoirs, *American Prince*, he described their mating:

*"She walked over to the trailer door and locked it. She came back to me and kissed me deeply. It was a kiss that spoke of longing. We both came up for air, and then she leaned forward and kissed me again. That's when I realized that she was naked under her robe. I tore off my jacket and shirt. I don't remember how I got my pants off. The next thing I knew we were making crazy love on the sofa of that trailer. We didn't say anthing before, during, or after. Nor did we need to."*

*"Her dad was a drunk. Her mum ignored her if she failed an audition. So Natalie Wood found happiness in the movies— and men. Frank Sinatra was her longest running affair."*
—**The Guardian**

*"A particularly complex situation arose when Robert Wagner, the star who was the great love of Natalie's life and whom she married twice, was having an affair with Tina, Frank Sinatra's daughter at the very same time Natalie was sleeping with Ol' Blue Eyes himself. On the other hand, she was one of the very few stars to turn down President Kennedy."*

—**The Daily Telegraph**

*"You make better love than Elvis."*
—**Natalie Wood to Frank Sinatra**

Then-*ingénue* Natalie Wood was cast in *The Silver Chalice* (1954), playing Virginia Mayo's character as a young girl. This disaster of a film was Paul Newman's embarrassing debut feature in which he referred to his wardrobe as "a cocktail dress." He later took out an ad in a Los Angeles newspaper apologizing for his role in the film.

One day Maria Stepanovna (*née* Zudilova) was having lunch with her *ingénue* daughter, Natalie, in the studio commissary when she spotted Frank Sinatra dining alone at table. He was on the lot in preparation for his next picture, *Young at Heart* (1954), which co-starred Doris Day.

Maria, the quintessential stage mother who relentlessly coached and pushed her daughter into the public eye, was deeply impressed that Frank had won an Oscar for his role in *From*

*Here to Eternity* (1953) and she was anxious for her daughter to meet him. "Go over to his table and introduce yourself," the pushy Maria urged her daughter. "He's made a comeback and he's really taking off in this town."

When Natalie introduced herself to Frank at table, the dialogue got off to a rough start. "Why do you wear so many silly bracelets?"

"To cover my deformed wrist," she answered bluntly.

For reasons known only to Frank in the deepest cavity of his brain, he found himself powerfully attracted to this blunt-speaking but charming waif.

He even walked her back to her own table to rejoin her mother. Then he invited both Natalie and Maria to his home that weekend for a party.

Later, that evening, Maria decided that it would make Natalie "look too young if I came along as a chaperone. He'll feel like talking to you more intimately if I'm not around."

"But I hear he's still in love with Ava Gardner, and besides he's thirty-eight years old," Natalie protested.

"To hell with that," Maria said. "This is Hollywood. Do you think Sinatra would be the first man here to take an interest in a fifteen-year-old girl? So what if he's pushing forty? He's rich and powerful."

A later boyfriend of Natalie accused Maria of being a "pimp for her daughter. She practically shoved Natalie into Sinatra's crotch."

During her time at Frank's Hollywood party, he devoted most of his attention to Natalie, ignoring his other guests. He also plied her with red wine, and she'd never drunk before. At some point in the evening, she confided two biographical pieces of information: One, that she was no longer a virgin; and, two, that her boyfriend, Bobby Hyatt, called his penis Clyde." This revelation appeared in Suzanne Finstad's *Natasha: The Biography of Natalie Wood.*

Frank seemed to love the word Clyde. A few months later he was singing "Clyde's Song," and even used the word in his act. JFK was also quoted using the Clyde word. Frank never revealed what it meant. When asked, he lied. "It means a guy I don't trust."

When Frank seduced Natalie for the first time, she was no longer a virgin, as some biographers have assumed. When she was fourteen, she'd lost her virginity to Nick Adams, the close and most intimate companion of both James Dean and later Elvis Presley.

"Natalie's mother asked me to teach her daughter the ways of the world," Nick claimed, "and I was only too willing. The mother told me she preferred me to be the one who deflowered her daughter—not one of the sleazy men hanging out with her."

From the bed of Nick Adams, Natalie went on to other boudoirs associated with an impressive A-list group of men, mostly actors. Her main interest always centered on Robert Wagner.

At the time she fell in love with him, he was receiving more fan

A HOLLYWOOD CHILDHOOD ORCHESTRATED BY THE FILM INDUSTRY'S MOST FEROCIOUS STAGE MOTHER

**Natalie Wood**, aged 9, in *The Ghost and Mrs. Muir* (1947)

**Natalie Wood**, aged 11, in *Green Promise* (1949)

**Natalie Wood**, aged 16, in *The Silver Chalice* (1954)

**Natalie Wood**, aged 18, in *The Searchers* (1956)

**Natalie Wood** and **James Dean** (*top photo*) starred in the 1955 classic *Rebel Without a Cause,* directed by Nicholas Ray. All three stars, including **Sal Mineo** (*lower photo*), were destined to end their lives tragically and prematurely. Many reports claim that the concept of "Live Fast, Die Young, and Leave a Good-Looking Corpse" derived from the deaths of these three actors.

During the shoot, both Natalie and Mineo fell in love with James Dean, but he had to tell both of them, "I belong to no one but myself. I can give my heart to no one particular person, but must share it with others."

During the shoot, and in the closeted 1950s, Dean told Mineo "In every scene look at me the way I look at Natalie. We'll fool the censors. All but dummies will know that you are in love with me."

A subtle erotic tension on screen came when the loving threesome spent the night together in a desert mansion which had been scheduled for use as a set in the film the following morning.

"Before we filmed that flirtatious scene," Mineo later recalled, "Natalie, Jimmy, and I spent the night together. Jimmy was Lucky Pierre. All of our love was focused on him."

mail than any other star in America, with the exception of Marilyn Monroe.

While his party was in full swing, Frank escorted Natalie upstairs into one of the bedrooms. Guests were surprised that he didn't emerge until two hours later with her. What happened between the two of them during that time is unknown. But it was obvious to the guests that they had sex.

Without allowing her to say good night to any of his other guests, Frank rushed her out the door and into the back of a limousine. He ordered his chauffeur to take her home.

Maria was waiting up for Natalie. Her mother wanted to know everything that had happened. Far from being horrified that Frank had seduced her underage daughter, Maria seemed delighted. She told friends the next day that Frank one day would co-star with Natalie in a motion picture, perhaps in love scenes.

During the next three months, Frank seduced Natalie as often as the chance arose. On some occasions, Maria drove her daughter to these illegal sexual trysts.

Even when Frank was dating Mia Farrow, another very young woman, he continued to slip away for private sessions with Natalie. Perhaps Mia never found out about these. At least Mia was old enough to marry. Natalie wasn't even old enough to legally have sex according to California's age-of-consent law.

Roddy McDowall, Natalie's close friend, claimed that "Frank really taught Natalie everything about sex and really turned her on. She often described in detail all the things she'd do with him. Before Frank, she thought sex was five minutes of lying on her back enduring a boy on top of her, pounding away. Frank taught her the fine points of sex—rimming, anal intercourse, fellatio, around-the-world, the whole messy thing." He may not have known it, but R.J. really benefitted from all those lessons Frank taught her."

Whether true or not, Roddy said he thought the mother forced Natalie too far in telling her that if Frank wanted unprotected sex, she should give it to him. "I can drive you down to Mexico and get an abortion right away."

Movie star Virginia Mayo met Natalie on the set of *The Silver Chalice* (1954). At her home in Thousand Oaks, California, in 2005, she asserted, "The Natalie I met at a party three years later was a completely different person. She had matured before her time. She was smoking and really drinking a lot."

"I want to be a grown-up actress on the screen," Natalie told Mayo. "All in ermine like Lana Turner. I want to smoke cigarettes through a long holder and drink champagne cocktails—for real—on camera and then be photographed in bed with Paul Newman making love to me."

She told Mayo that she'd seen Vivien Leigh as Blanche DuBois in *A Streetcar Named Desire* thirteen times. "That's who I want to be. Blanche with a notorious past."

"At the rate you're going, you'll create that past before your time," Mayo warned Natalie.

Throughout the 1960s, Natalie was always willing to break a date if Frank called. David Lange, brother of Hope Lange, claimed that in the third week of their affair, Natalie told him she couldn't see him until around midnight because she was going out with Sinatra.

When David arrived at her house, he claimed he "waited in the bushes until four o'clock that morning." Frank had not left the house, so David eventually gave up and went home.

In a touch of irony, Frank in 1972 would date David's sister, Hope Lange, proof that Hollywood can be a small town indeed. And although that night with David didn't work out, sometimes Natalie managed to pull off three dates in one night—Nicky Hilton (after his divorce from Elizabeth Taylor), Dennis Hopper, and perhaps Lance Reventlow, the ill-fated son of the doomed billionairess, Barbara Hutton. Lance told Natalie, "Cary Grant used to be my stepfather. He fell in love with me, and I let him have a good time. After all, he is Cary Grant."

*Variety* referred to Natalie as "boy crazy," and *Movieland* attacked her for dating "Frank Sinatra, a man old enough to be her dad."

Natalie told Pier Angeli—both of them had had affairs with the bisexual actor, James Dean—that Frank was the best lover. "Some of the boys I date are like high schoolers making it in the back seat of a car on senior prom night," Natalie said.

She came and went from the bedrooms of Warren Beatty, Tab Hunter, John Ireland (known for having the largest penis in Hollywood), Steve McQueen,

**Frank Sinatra** (*top photo*) points a gun at the head of his fellow soldier, **Tony Curtis**, in *Kings Go Forth (1958)*.

In the bottom photo, both stars were caught enjoying a leak between takes in this candid snapshot snapped by a member of the crew.

"Pissing with Frank Sinatra could give a guy penis envy," said the underendowed Curtis. He later claimed, "Despite the fact that we were friends, I wasn't sure how well we'd mesh as actors because of his reputation for being difficult.

"If Frank didn't want to work, he just didn't show up. If he wanted to bust the director's chops, he did. People worried that if they pissed Frank off, he might have them bumped off the next day. Everybody tiptoed around him. We were pals. Frank called me 'Boinie,' and I called him 'Francis Albert.'"

Curtis was bisexual. One night after a drinking bout with Frank, he bluntly asked him if he could give him a blow-job. "Check with me later," was Frank's response.

When **Tony Curtis** shot this scene with **Natalie Wood** in *Kings Go Forth*, the character he was playing supposedly did not know that the character she was playing was a mulatto, which would lead to the end of their relationship in the movie.

It wasn't until they had another kissing scene in *The Great Race* that Tony and Natalie really got off on each other. The director yelled "*Cut! CUT! CUT!*" to no avail.

As Tony described it, "Natalie moved up close to me and affectionately toyed with a lock of my hair. I kissed her on the lips. With that, she put her hand behind my head and pulled me down close to her. We just nuzzled each other for a few moments, indifferent to the people around us. I felt a deep, delicate warmth move through me."

He later told the director. "I couldn't get up. I had a raging hard-on that wouldn't go down."

Audie Murphy, Elvis Presley, director Nicholas Ray, and countless others.

On and off throughout the 1960s, her affair with Frank continued. As one biographer put it, "They were friends who occasionally slept together."

One night after sex with Natalie, she told him, "Sometimes when you enter me, you hurt. R.J. always slides in easily. No problem there."

Keeping a long-ago promise, Frank was eager for Natalie to star with him in a WWII drama set in France. Called *Kings Go Forth* (1958), it also starred Tony Curtis. At this point in her young life, Natalie was a much-experienced and worldly wise young actress.

During the shoot, Natalie was in love with Robert Wagner but that didn't prevent her from making frequent visits to Frank's dressing room. Even Tony Curtis claimed that he seduced Natalie during filming. "But that was only because she walked in on Frank with another woman, and was really pissed off at him. I was the beneficiary of Frank being oversexed."

"In some respects, Natalie was the girl who could not say no," claimed Sal Mineo who had appeared with her in *Rebel Without a Cause* (1955). "She even came on to me, but I turned her down. Both of us were also after the star of the picture, James Dean, and both of us got our man . . . again and again."

*Kings Go Forth* was an unusual WWII film for 1958 in that it depicted both Frank and Tony Curtis falling in love with Natalie Wood unaware that the character she plays is half-black. More of a romantic melodrama than a war story, it did not live up to Frank's dream of repeating the success of his Oscar triumph in *From Here to Eternity* in 1953. *Kings Go Forth* might also have been entitled *Race, Love, and War*.

The themes of racism and miscegenation keep the plot turning, but Frank said, "I took the part as an actor, not a lecturer on racial problems." He played Lt. Sam Loggins of the American Seventh Army, who takes an instant dislike to Corporal Britt Harris (Tony Curtis), whom he views as a pretty boy. In the film, Sam claims, "I don't trust him—he was born rich and handsome and I was born poor and not handsome."

Natalie delivers the shocker of the drama—remember this is Eisenhower's 1950's. "My father was a great man," she tells Frank. "He was also a Negro."

What's wrong with this plot? Porcelain-white Natalie Wood is among the last stars who should ever have been cast as half-African American.

In the film, Curtis turns out to be a racial bigot when he discovers that Natalie is a mulatto. He is later killed in battle. Although Frank's character loses an arm, he returns to Natalie's village, presumably to propose marriage, although originally she had preferred Curtis.

When the film flopped, Frank told Natalie, "We laid a great big fat turkey egg."

In November of 1956, before making *Kings Go Forth*, Natalie had skipped out on an appearance at the Hollywood Bowl, standing up 15,000 teenagers. Instead, she flew to

Memphis aboard a plane with Elvis Presley. The trip was a disaster. Elvis' mother, Gladys, detested Natalie.

Back home in California, Natalie said, "Elvis can sing, but he can't do much else."

Secretly, Frank hated Elvis, and Natalie's putdown was music to the aging crooner's ears.

When Natalie realized that no marriage proposal was coming from Frank, she married the handsome young actor Robert Wagner. As a wedding present, Frank sent a hundred-pound sack of sea salt as a house-warming gift. R.J. and Natalie ended up having the only saltwater-filled pool in Beverly Hills.

Natalie's marriage to Wagner occurred on December 28, 1957, before *Kings Go Forth* was actually completed. *Tout* Hollywood showed up for the event. Frank was seen with Lauren Bacall. Louella Parsons covered the event, and even Jane Russell arrived showing no bosom.

Frank later told Natalie, "At one point when we were crowded into a room, Rock Hudson reached over and felt my cock. He told me he wanted to see if those rumors are true."

"They're true," she said flirtatiously. "I should know."

By 1971, Frank's affair with Natalie had begun to wind down after all these years. He was furious that Wagner, Natalie's former husband, was dating Tina, Frank's daughter. "Instead of having intercourse with me, Frank spent most of the evening talking to me about what I could do to break up Tina's affair with R.J.," Natalie told Roddy McDowall.

A very jaded Frank had grown tired of Natalie as a bed partner, although he still liked her very much. But she was no longer the little teenage girl that had sexually attracted him. She often appeared drunk during their trysts together, and he had other, younger women to subdue.

Finally, one night in Palm Springs, he flatly told her, "Kid, it's time we moved on from each other. You and me, we were not meant to be. But we'll still stay in touch and still be the dear friends we always were."

On a Sunday morning, November 29, 1981, Frank was awakened with a call from someone (not known). He'd heard over the radio that Natalie's drowned body had been found off the coast of Catalina where she'd gone for the weekend with R.J. and actor Christopher Walken, her co-star in her last film, *Brainstorm*, which was never completed.

Frank attended the funeral along with Elia Kazan, David Niven, Gregory Peck, and Laurence Olivier. Elizabeth Taylor and Gene Kelly also were among the mourners.

After the funeral, Frank spoke privately to a weeping Roddy McDowall, one of Natalie's closest friends. "Natalie didn't drown accidentally," Frank claimed. "She was murdered. And I think I know who killed her."

He never revealed the name of the murder suspect.

On the town together, a young lover, **Natalie Wood**, and an older lover, **Frank Sinatra**, were an item but not a steady item.

"We were always there for each other," she said. "The day I overdosed on sleeping pills, I called Frank and he made me want to live again. When some asshole director told me my boobs weren't big enough, Frank was there to assure me they were perfectly fine in every way. One night when he couldn't get it up, I consoled him, telling him that I had experienced the same problem with men half his age. I won't name them."

She also shared her fears with him. She was afraid of flying, and of the water. "I know my plane will either fall from the sky or else I'll go down in the murky deep from a boat."

# ROBERT WAGNER ON FRANK SINATRA

"As a man and a musician, Frank Sinatra was a tremendous influence—the dialogue, the Jack Daniels, the manner, everything. Like Brando, he was a combination of overtly tough masculinity on the surface and, just beneath that, total emotional openness. Any kind of dishonesty or bullshit would infuriate him. And people were afraid of him because his explosions were not pretty."

Representative of Hollywood's new generation of star-crossed lovers, **Robert Wagner and Natalie Wood**, married, divorced, and remarried. Initially, their love was the stuff of fairy tales until that dark night off the coast of Catalina when she mysteriously disappeared and was later found drowned.

"She lived fast, died young, and left us with beautiful memories," said Roddy McDowall, her closest friend.

Natalie, the child star of *Miracle on 34th Street,* spotted her "R.J." when he was a dashingly handsome eighteen-year-old heartthrob hanging out with Clark Gable and Gary Cooper.

She told her table companions, "See that guy? He's going to marry me one day." Other marriages, career jealousies, other spouses, lots of love, and ultimate tragedy lay in their future.

One of Natalie's most famous movies was *Bob & Carol & Ted & Alice (1969),* about couples who swing.

Aboard her yacht, *Splendour,* her real life fade-out story could have been entitled *Bob & Natalie & Christopher,* a reference to actor **Christopher Walken**, pictured above.

In November of 1981, Robert Wagner invited his rival, Walken, who at the time was filming *Brainstorm* with Natalie, to sail with them to Catalina Island. It would evolve into an explosive, scandal-soaked voyage.

If this talented actor ever writes a tell-all memoir, maybe he will come clean about what really happened to Natalie that night off the coast of Catalina. Could those rumors about him having an affair with Natalie be true? The most sordid rumors—never proven, but widely published— were that Natalie caught him having an affair with Wagner.

# The Murky Death of a Screen Goddess

*"This is the Splendour. We think we may have someone missing in an eleven-foot rubber dinghy."*

**—Robert Wagner**

The death of the doe-eyed beauty, Natalie Wood, off the coast of California's Catalina Island on November 29, 1981 shocked the world. It was defined as a tragic "accident," but the contradictory statements from the men aboard the yacht, especially those from her husband, Robert Wagner, and her co-star, Christopher Walken, only fueled speculation about one of Hollywood's most enduring mysteries. Not since the death of Marilyn Monroe—suicide or murder?—had Hollywood speculated so wildly about the passing of a movie star.

By drowning on that fateful day, Natalie fulfilled a long-ago prophecy from a Russian gypsy who warned her to "beware of dark water." Over the years, Natalie had been so frightened of water that she even feared having her hair washed because her head would be submerged.

Her drowning followed a jealous, drunken row with her husband, who was feuding with her over her excessive attention to her on-board guest, Walken.

The boat's lonely dinghy was found floating in the waters offshore at Blue Craven Point, with scratch marks on its side, as if the doomed Natalie had desperately tried to climb aboard.

It seemed inconceivable that Natalie, dressed in a flannel nightgown and a red eiderdown jacket, would leave the boat in the middle of the night, especially because of her fear of water.

The "coroner to the stars," Dr. Thomas Noguchi, said, "It was apparent that she had not dressed for a boat ride—and yet the police believed she must have untied the line which held the dinghy to the yacht. But why had she untied it if she didn't intend to go out in the boat?"

One journalist wrote that "the death of Natalie Wood was about as accidental as the shooting of John F. Kennedy in Dallas."

"Every death is a homicide until proven otherwise," Dr. Noguchi said.

In the still unexplained case of Natalie Wood, her death was never proven otherwise.

The ***Splendour,*** however briefly, became the most famous yacht in the world when it sailed from the California Coast in November of 1981. Its passengers were Natalie Wood, Robert Wagner, and actor Christopher Walken.

Only two of those passengers would return alive.

# FRANK SINATRA ON CHARLES MANSON'S HIT LIST

In a communal Death Valley compound, a "dirtbag psycho," Charles Manson and his gang were plotting a mass murder of some of the biggest stars in Hollywood, including Frank Sinatra, Elizabeth Taylor, and Steve McQueen.

Fortunately, the gang was arrested and brought to justice before most of the stars on Manson's death list, including Frank, underwent torture and violent deaths.

The first of the murders of the Manson gang occurred in 1969 at the home of the beautiful, rising actress Sharon Tate, married to the director Roman Polanski who was out of town at the time.

Sharon decided to have a party to which she invited her two close male friends, Steve McQueen and hairdresser Jay Sebring, among others. This party at a French provincial house at 10050 Cielo Drive, in Benedict Canyon, Los Angeles, would become the bloodiest in the history of Hollywood. McQueen never showed up.

Manson hated Frank. For many years, Frank had been his favorite singer. He liked Frank's "style and sense of cool."

But because he couldn't get anywhere near Frank because of the security which surrounded him, Manson decided to stalk him. One night he trailed him in a car to a strip club where Frank had planned to meet three prostitutes.

Manson decided to wait in the parking lot for Frank and two security guards to come out of the club. It was three o'clock in the morning before Frank emerged with two other dark-suited men. A pal of Frank's had agreed to deliver the showgirls back to Frank's hotel suite.

With music in hand, Manson confronted Frank in the parking lot, trying to hand over his compositions to him. Two security guards tackled Manson and reportedly "roughed him up." Actually, it was more than that. One of the guards repeatedly kicked Manson in the testicles until he was bleeding. He became impotent for months.

The guards then got into the car and drove Frank to the hotel with the stripper prostitutes. Perhaps Frank thought no more of the incident because he was often being confronted on some level wherever he went. Manson, however, never got over it.

Frank Sinatra was added to his hit list. He told three of his followers to draw up a plan "for the most hideous death imaginable, and that's what we'll have in store for that arrogant prick. I'll make him regret the day he was born."

Around eight o'clock on the morning of August 9, 1969, the Polanski maid, Winifred Chapman, arrived at the Polanski house.

She discovered the lifeless and grotesquely mutilated bodies of Sebring and Tate, as well as Abigail Folger, the coffee heiress, and her boyfriend, Wojiciech (Voytek) Frykowski.

The body of another victim, Steven Parent, was discovered outside the house. Shortly after his car had pulled into the driveway the previous night, the Manson killers had fatally shot him.

McQueen called Frank who had gone into hiding. "We may be next," McQueen told his friend. Let's face it, we're high-profile people."

"I've beefed up security measures around my place," Frank said.

"I'm not going out the door without a gun."

"As Sam Giancana might tell you, that's always good advice," Frank said.

For Frank Sinatra, the Manson gang had planned a horrible death. After kidnapping him, they would strip him and hang him nude from a rafter where the Manson gang would play an album of his as they skinned him alive. With his skin, they planned to make purses and sell them at high prices at hippie shops "so everyone would have a little piece of Sinatra."

When Frank learned about the fate that had been in store for him, he told Mia Farrow, "So much for you and your hippie friends. The Age of Aquarius has dawned and died."

# *Frank Sinatra Was*
# Too Big for His Pants!

It was once almost unheard of, but all serious biographers tend to comment at some point on **Frank Sinatra**'s legendary endowment. His pre-Nancy Barbato girlfriends in Hoboken first took notice of it and praised his penis long before he put it to Grace Kelly, Ava Gardner, Marilyn Monroe, *et al.*

Before Frank's arrival in Hollywood, the only major star who was frequently cited for his endowment was Gary Cooper. Ava Gardner was one of the few women who got to sample both Cooper and Frank. She confirmed that Cooper was aptly named "The Montana Mule."

Today, the cock size of male celebrities, such as the endowment of Colin Farrell, or the lack of endowment of Brad Pitt, is often presented as news in gossip columns. But in Frank's day, penis size was only whispered about.

The showgirls of Las Vegas were primarily responsible for spreading news of Frank's prowess in the boudoir.

He later complained that he resented so many "broads talking about the size of my dick. Sometimes I don't want to be the greatest lover in the western world. I just want a quick fuck. That's why I turn to prostitutes. They can't complain if I don't deliver the greatest sex of their lives."

# *SINATRA:*

# A LIFE MEASURED IN INCHES

*"Frank had special underpants made, a cross between a panty girdle and a jock strap. The idea was to hold down that big thing of his, so it wouldn't show through his tuxedo pants. He wasn't quite John Dillinger, but he was hung enough to have to take special precautions. This was the Eisenhower era, and 'family values' prevailed."*

**—George Jacobs, Sinatra's valet**

*"Jack [John F. Kennedy] may have ruled the Free World, and Sam [Sam Giancana] may have bossed the Mafia, but Frank was King of the Boudoir."*

**—Judith Campbell Exner**

*"In Las Vegas I found myself standing at the urinals with Frank Sinatra, Burt Lancaster, and Cary Grant. Cary and Burt had their 'shortcomings,' but Frank let it dangle with no hand needed. He lit a cigarette as all three of us took in the long view."*

**—Merv Griffin**

206

*"More would be almost too big."*
**—Dancer and Size Queen Juliet Prowse**

*"It was magnificent, his cock."*

**—Betty Grable**

*"Oh, hell, I got to tell you that has got to be the biggest damn cock I've ever seen in my life."*

**—Natalie Wood**

*"What are you trying to do, break my jaw so your records will outsell mine?"*

**—Judy Garland**

*"Marilyn and I've shared Joe DiMaggio, Frank Sinatra, and John F. Kennedy. Trust me, Sinatra is the prize winner, although Coop [Gary Cooper] was stiff competition."*

**—Marlene Dietrich** to Orson Welles

*"I'd heard all the stories and was very excited when Sinatra took me to bed. When he pulled off his pants, I was expecting something really big. Although he was well endowed, his advance press was a bit exaggerated."*

—Artist, Stripper, and Long-time Hollywood Star-fucker
**Liz Renay**

*"Well, there's only 10 pounds of Frank, but there's 110 pounds of cock."*

**—Ava Gardner**

*"It's like a watermelon on the end of a toothpick."*

**—Jeanne Carmen**,
Marilyn Monroe's best friend

*"We pissed together countless times. I called mine King Kong, and he called his Big Frankie. I told him if Liberace suddenly came into the men's room at that very moment, he'd think he'd found paradise."*
**—Sammy Davis Jr**

*"After a night with Frank, I ended up in the hospital."*
**—Eva Gabor**

*"He threw me on the bed. I said, 'God, no!' But he threw me where my back hit the bed, and just pulled my dress up, pulled down my panties, and did what he wanted to do. I knew I couldn't overpower him. He was forceful and it was over very quickly. I do remember—I found out without wanting to—that he was quite large in that department."*
—Palm Springs Resident **Susan Murphy**
to author Anthony Summers

*"He was a skinny guy, ordinary looking; his Adam's apple protruded. His ears stuck out. But the broads swarmed over him whenever he got off stage. He bragged about the size of his penis."*

**—Joey D'Orazio**,
Frank's boyhood friend from Hoboken

*"Unlike Eva, it was no problem for me. But then I'd been broken in by Porfirio Rubirosa."*

**—Zsa Zsa Gabor**

*"He had sex on the brain. He would make love to anyone who came along. He was hugely endowed. He would swing it around and call it Big Frankie."*

**—Nancy Venturi**, teenage girlfriend in Hoboken

*"Ronald Reagan, so I hear, once bragged to Sinatra that he had eight inches. Our chairman replied, 'I've got that much soft.'"*

**—Peter Lawford**

*"Not bad for a white boy."*

**—Billie Holiday**

*"I'm tired of hearing how big it was. I have Frankie beat."*
                                                    —**Milton Berle**

*"Frank had something in common with Gary Cooper, the Montana Mule."*
                                    —**Grace Kelly** to Ava Gardner

*"Sometimes I let a chorus boy feel it backstage—but that is as far as I go."*
                                    —**Frank Sinatra** to Joey Bishop

*"I fell in love with Frank when I saw his big dick when we slept nude together while making From Here to Eternity."*
                                                    —**Montgomery Clift**

*"It was very, very big, but Joe DiMaggio, who had much less, knew how to use it better."*
— **Marilyn Monroe** to girlfriend Jeanne Carmen

*"By some evidence, Sinatra was proud of his extraordinary endowment; he is even said to have called his penis Big Frankie (unlike the Little Frankie it hung from)."*
— **Biographer James Kaplan**

*"I'm pretty big, but he had me beat by at least two inches."*
— **Dean Martin**

*"Of all my husbands, only Nicky Hilton was up there with Frank Sinatra."*
— **Elizabeth Taylor**

*"From what the broads tell me, no one, not Frank Sinatra, not Milton Berle, ever measured more than yours truly."*
— **Actor John Ireland**

# How Frank Raped the Gabors

## AND ENVIED THE SIZE OF RUBIROSA'S PENIS

Known as "The Last Playboy of the Western World," **Porfirio Rubirosa** is seen with his on-again, off-again mistress, **Zsa Zsa Gabor**. Frank Sinatra *(left)* was often a witness to their affair, and didn't always conceal his jealousy. His fame, of course, has endured, but Rubi and Zsa Zsa were mostly famous for being famous. Rubi often said, "I am a man devoted to the pursuit of pleasure."

Before and during the course of their respective marriages to others, Zsa Zsa and Rubi carried on with their reckless affair. When not doing that, each of them seduced half the planet. Rubi also played polo and Zsa Zsa became celebrated for her provocative TV appearances and an occasional movie.

Zsa Zsa claimed that Frank only moved in on her because he was jealous of Rubi. The Dominican Republic playboy was legendary for his endowment and for affairs that put Frank to shame—Veronica Lake, Gene Tierney, Kim Novak, Susan Hayward, Dolores Del Rio, Eartha Kitt, Patricia Kennedy Lawford, Jayne Mansfield, Marilyn Monroe, and even Frank's own Ava Gardner, plus a thousand more.

As Rubi's biographer claimed, "Women heard about it, wondered about it, whispered about it, had to see it, hold it, have it—and who was he to deny them?"

# SOCIAL GAMES AND SEXUAL COMPETITIONS AMONG THE A-LIST

At a gala, **Zsa Zsa Gabor, with Porfirio Rubirosa** in the background on the left, make a glamorous appearance, the blonde goddess in pink satin, and Rubi with a heavy duty jockstrap.

Author Gerold Frank, who helped Gabor write her autobiography in 1960, describes his impressions of her while the book was being written:

*"Zsa Zsa is unique. She's a woman from the court of Louis XV who has somehow managed to live in the 20th century, undamaged by the PTA ... She says she wants to be all the Pompadours and Du Barrys of history rolled into one, but she also says, 'I always goof. I pay all my own bills ... I want to choose the man. I do not permit men to choose me.'"*

The love affair and eventual marriage of Frank Sinatra with Ava Gardner were doomed from the beginning. Initially, Ava wasn't impressed with the "bag of bones" [her reference to Sinatra] until he took off his clothes. She was awed, having nothing but praise for "my Frankie boy." She told Lana Turner, "Only Porfirio Rubirosa is better hung, but then, he's the Ninth Wonder of the World."

She was referring to the diplomat-playboy from the Dominican Republic who, in time, married, among others, the Woolworth heiress Barbara Hutton and the tobacco heiress Doris Duke, the two richest women in the world.

Duke even went on record about Rubirosa's endowment, claiming, "It was the most magnificent penis that I had ever seen." Society photographer Jerome Zerbe said, "It looks like Yul Brynner in a black turtleneck sweater."

Society's darlings called him "Rubber Hosa," and his fame grew to the point that waiters referred to giant peppermills as "Rubirosas." From possibly hundreds of sightings, his sex organ was described as "eleven inches long and thick as a beer can."

Hearing all these reports made Frank jealous, yet he concealed his green-eyed envy and actually formed a friendship of sorts with his imagined rival in the boudoir.

Frank was made even more sensitive to Rubi's sexual prowess because the two studs often seduced the same women—and the list was long: Joan Crawford, Lana Turner, Zsa Zsa Gabor, Eartha Kitt, Jayne Mansfield, Kim Novak, Marlene Dietrich, Judy Garland, and even Marilyn Monroe.

He knew that all of these beauties had a basis to compare the size of his penis and his boudoir skills, and he didn't like that one bit. He told Sammy Davis Jr., "I'm the great lover of the western world—not Rubirosa."

His friendship with Rubi was severely tested when he read in gossip columns that Rubi was shacked up with Ava before their marriage in 1951.

As Ava was waiting for rewrites on her role as Lady Brett in Ernest Hemingway's *The Sun Also Rises*, she entertained a string of suitors who included Rubirosa as well as bullfighters

Curro Giron and Luís Miguel Dominguin. She also found time to date Peter Viertel, son of Greta Garbo's closest friend, the screenwriter Salka Viertel. While her principal lover, Walter Chiari, was in Rome, Ava had time to work in these various affairs.

And although Frank was none too pleased with any of her flings, the affair that drove Frank ballistic when he learned about it was Ava's affair with Rubi himself. "I guess my dick is not big enough for the bitch," he told Sammy Davis Jr. "She wants a nigger dick instead. Don't tell me Rubi is Latin. I bet he's got more black blood in him than white."

Ava was very attracted to Rubi, as her attraction to Latinos was well documented and even became part of the plot in her film, *The Barefoot Contessa*.

Almost immediately after Ava's divorce from Frank, word leaked out that she was going to wed Rubi, possibly in 1956.

Rubi lied to Louella Parsons when he called her from Paris, telling the gossip maven that, "I hardly know Ava." The call was placed from Ava's suite where he'd just spent the night with the sultry beauty. "She was not bad at deep throating, but she couldn't take my last three inches," Rubi complained to Jimmy Donahue, the outrageously self-indulgent gay cousin of Rubi's former wife, Barbara Hutton. "Try me out," Jimmy said. "I'm a celebrated sword swallower."

Frank was also jealous because Sammy Davis Jr. was deeply impressed with Rubi too. "I really care about my clothes," Sammy said, "but the sartorial sense of Rubi has all of us beat. When I'm next to him, I feel I just fell off a garbage truck."

"Hell, Smoky, I'm practically on all those best-dressed lists," Frank claimed.

"You would be, Frankie, if it weren't for your predilection for the color of orange."

"Better than black," Frank snapped.

Instead of dropping Rubi as a friend because of his involvement with Ava, Frank foolishly set out to make Zsa Zsa Gabor fall in love with him.

At the time of his marriage to Barbara Hutton of the Woolworth millions, Rubi had been engaged in one of Hollywood's most torrid, even violent romances with Zsa Zsa. Frank wanted to seduce Zsa Zsa so effectively that the gossipy star would spread the word that he was better in bed than Rubi. Trouble was, Frank set about his conquest in the wrong way.

Zsa Zsa always said she did not in general prefer Latin men. But Rubi was an exception to her rule. "Maybe this was because, along with his Latin blood, he had a mixture of a lot of other kinds of plasma in him, the way they do in the West Indies,"

**Porfirio Rubirosa** was the world's most expensive gigolo. To maintain his high-living lifestyle, he married, among others, the two richest women of their day, **Doris Duke**, pictured above with Rubi on their wedding day in Paris on September 24, 1947. He also had a short-lived marriage to Woolworth heiress Barbara Hutton but blatantly continued his affair with Zsa Zsa Gabor throughout that marriage anyway.

Duke was enchanted with Rubi's penis, so much so that she purchased a cattle plantation for her new husband in his native Dominican Republic. Among other lavish gifts, she gave him a B-25 bomber fitted out as a private airplane, with a bed for airborne seductions.

The wedding made frontpage headlines around the world—DORIS DUKE WEDS SMOKING LATIN. Rubi smoked throughout the wedding ceremony. The divorce, fourteen months later, was much quieter. Rubi netted a townhouse on the rue de Bellechasse in Paris and an annual alimony of $25,000 (about $200,000 in today's currency).

she said.

"Also he was quite a bit French, since he was brought up and went to school mostly in France. This made for a wonderful combination. I've always said that in animals I prefer pure-breds . . . but not in men! Think of that wonderful Prince Philip, who is Greek and German, and I don't know what else. I seriously considered, for a time, becoming the Royal Mistress of Buckingham Palace. I'm sure Queen Elizabeth would not have minded. But back to Rubi. Talk about mixed bloods. Think of all those American men, the result of a great melting pot. Such men as these mixed breeds are the best of everything. Regrettably, only Italian blood flowed through Sinatra's veins. Italian men, of course, have their charms, but also their flaws . . . many flaws."

In 1955, Zsa Zsa Gabor was thirty-eight years old . . . at least. She'd already survived three divorces—the Turkish diplomat, Burhan Belge; the hotelier Conrad Hilton, and actor George Sanders who later married—briefly—her older sister, Magda.

In Frank's opinion, "Zsa Zsa was ripe for plucking and also . . . rhymes with plucking."

It's true that Frank seduced two of the Gabors, both Eva and Zsa Zsa, but his experiences with each of the glamorous sisters were remarkably different.

He first encountered Zsa Zsa in the late 1950s after she'd divorced actor George Sanders. Over the years she'd seen him at various Hollywood parties, but she had never been alone with him.

When she received an invitation from Mrs. Delmer Davies, the wife of a producer, she was told that Frank wanted to escort her to the party. He arrived on time at Zsa Zsa's house in Bel Air and even met her daughter, Francesca Hilton, the off-spring of her marriage to Conrad Hilton, the hotelier. Francesca seemingly adored Frank and was very impressed that her mother was "dating such a heartthrob."

"I really turn on the eight-year-olds," Frank said jokingly as he drove to the party with Zsa Zsa.

"The girl was a product of a rape by Conrad," Zsa Zsa claimed.

The evening began with dinner at La Rue Restaurant on Sunset Boulevard, where Frank kept his hat on throughout the entire meal. "To hide his bald spot, *dah-ling*," Zsa Zsa later claimed.

At the party later, Zsa Zsa and Frank created a "sensation" with their joint appearance. He then drove her home. "A little kiss with tongue I anticipated," she recalled. "But he pushed by me and forced his way inside."

Once in the hallway, he told her, "When I take a woman out to dinner

"The Fabulous Gabors," three Hungarian sisters—**Zsa Zsa** *(left)*, **Magda** *(center)*, and **Eva** *(right)*—dazzled the world with their beauty and glamour. These *"vonderful vimmen"* brought "guts, glamour, and goulash" to the world, in the word of RuPaul.

Mama Gabor (Jolie) raised her legendary daughters to become great courtesans of the 20th Century. *"But, of course, dahlink."*

Arriving in America from the ruins of Europe after World War II, Jolie Gabor had instructed each of them to "glow in the spotlight. Amass a fortune, break hearts daily, if necessary, and hang out only with kings and millionaires."

Although the sisters didn't always follow Mama's advice, these Budapest bombshells seduced some of the most famous men of their day, everyone from John F. Kennedy to Frank Sinatra.

Frank didn't get around to Magda, but he managed to bed both Eva and Zsa Zsa, even if he had to rape them.

216

and a party, I always make love to her before the evening is over. With you, I have no intention of putting a blot on my record."

"I am not one of your statistics," she shot back at him.

"He just wouldn't move," she recalled. "It was a Mexican standoff. When he pleaded that he had a migraine from hell, I told my maid, Maria, to show him to the guest room."

With Frank out of the way, Zsa Zsa rushed up the stairs and locked herself in her own bedroom. Two hours later he was banging on her door, demanding to be let inside. She adamantly refused and ordered him to go home.

Later she fell asleep. When she didn't hear anymore from him, she assumed that he'd let himself out and that he'd driven himself home in his gold Cadillac.

When she arose the next morning to see Francesca off to school, she found Frank's car was still there.

She knocked on the guestroom door and he told her to come in. He was walking around in the nude. He grabbed her and allegedly told her, "I'm not leaving until you make love to me."

There are various stories about what happened next. Eva once claimed that Zsa Zsa told her that Frank raped her. "I told Zsa Zsa to send word to Frank that he could rape me any night he wanted to," Eva said.

"Since he wouldn't leave, I made love to him," Zsa Zsa wrote in her memoirs, not calling it rape. "I made love to Sinatra so that he would leave, and from then on, I hated him. And Frank knew it."

Initially Zsa Zsa claimed that she didn't want her daughter to leave for school and see Frank's Cadillac still in the driveway. "I didn't want her to think less of her mother."

By 2005, Zsa Zsa wasn't so protective of her daughter's opinion, filing a $2 million lawsuit in which she accused Francesca of larceny and fraud, alleging that she had forged her signature to get a $2 million loan on her mother's Bel Air house.

Zsa Zsa later claimed that Frank wreaked his revenge upon her, especially in Las Vegas. He'd arranged for her to be a guest star on one of his TV series. "He kept me waiting and never showed up," she claimed. On another occasion, she was appearing in a show at the Riviera and Frank in a competing show at the Sands. He asked her to come on with him for ten minutes at the Sands, and he would return the favor and appear with her at the Riviera the following night. "I didn't fear rape that night because Frank was being sexually satisfied by Dinah Shore."

He introduced her at the Sands as "Zsa Zsa Grabber. Oh boy, would I like to grab her."

**Lance Reventlow** *(right)* the son of Woolworth heiress **Barbara Hutton** *(far left)*, looks on mournfully as his mother gets a peck on the cheek from her new husband, **Porfirio Rubirosa**.

The ill-advised wedding took place at three o'clock on the afternoon of December 30, 1953. Hutton looked regal with her upswept hairdo and diamond brooch, wearing a black taffeta dress, a design from Balenciaga.

She told the press that her son was "all in favor of the marriage," but he wasn't. Earlier that day, upon learning that young Lance had homosexual tendencies, Rubi whispered to his stepson-to-be, "Go ahead, feel it. Forget about that small dick of Cary Grant (Lance's former stepfather). I've got one that stretches to the moon."

The next night Frank never showed up at the Riviera, where Zsa Zsa was getting $35,000 a week. "My bosses were furious that I'd appeared at the Sands for free. I was embarrassed and humiliated and knew that this was Frank's revenge on me."

Even though Zsa Zsa made it clear she didn't want to have sex with him again, there was yet another unwanted encounter when he was married to Mia Farrow. She accepted an invitation to a screening of his latest movie at Frank's home on Mulholland Drive. In the middle of the film, Zsa Zsa got up to go to the toilet. She was surprised to find no lock on the door of what she called "the powder room."

Once she was inside, Frank walked in on her without knocking. He bluntly told her, "I want to make love to you again." He grabbed her breasts and began to undo the buttons on her black silk blouse. She pushed him away. "I'm leaving your home—never to return," she told him. "Don't you ever put your hands on me again."

On the way home that night, Zsa Zsa came to realize that Frank wanted to seduce her because of the reputation of Rubi. "Frank's persistent attempts to make love to me had been prompted by his burning desire to prove that he was as great a lover as Rubi."

There was also the battle of the penises: Which of them had the larger organ? Frank wanted to use Zsa Zsa to prove that he—not Rubi—was the better hung.

Zsa Zsa later admitted, "Had Frank not come on to me like a bull in the china shop, I might have been charmed by him—he did have charm. I might have gone to bed with him. We might even have been happy together and embarked on an affair."

***

At the time of Rubi's marriage to Hutton, he'd been involved in a torrid affair with **Zsa Zsa Gabor.** Wearing a black patch to cover a black eye she'd been given by Rubi before his upcoming marriage, Zsa Zsa held up a wedding picture of her estranged lover and the Woolworth heiress. She then publicly mocked the marriage.

Reporters asked Hutton what she thought of Zsa Zsa. "I'm terribly sorry," she said. "I don't know the lady. I read the remarks she made, but I have no comment." Rubi quickly responded, accusing Zsa Zsa of staging a publicity stunt. "Everything she says is fabricated." Actually, Zsa Zsa was telling the truth.

After her breakup with Rubi, Zsa Zsa claimed that she continued to receive unwanted sexual harassment from Frank, even forced sex.

In spite of Frank's jealousy of Rubi, they still saw each other socially, and Frank often extended invitations. Such was the case in May of 1961 when Rubi and his wife, Odile Rodin, were given ringside seats to watch the fight of Floyd Patterson defending his heavyweight boxing title against Ingemar Johansson.

Frank was accompanied by a security guard that night, and Rubi had to take a leak. He asked Frank if he could borrow his guard to go to the men's room. "When I head for the urinals, there's a stampede of gay men who want me to put on a show."

Frank agreed, though he frowned at Rubi's boast. He never liked to hear references to the size of Rubi's penis, especially from the playboy himself.

Milton Berle heard the exchange between Rubi and Frank. After Rubi had left with the guard, Berle said, "I've got both of you boys beat."

Joe DiMaggio, who was sitting next to Frank, chimed in, "With me, it's quality, not quantity."

In the summer of 1961, Frank, along with Peter and Patricia Lawford, Porfirio Rubirosa and his wife, Odile, Mike Romanoff, and Jimmy Van Heusen, rented a luxury yacht to cruise the Côte d'Azur. Joe and Rose Kennedy also joined the party, which was to be highlighted by a stopover in Monte Carlo to attend the International Red Cross Ball hosted by Princess Grace.

In Paris, the party stopped to see Dean Martin, who was heading out for a concert tour in Germany. At one of their reunions, Dean was romancing a beautiful blonde starlet, who was a dead-ringer for Brigitte Bardot. He obviously wanted to spend time with the model, but when he left to take a phone call, Peter Lawford virtually stole the young woman away from Dean. Peter was seen leaving the party with the model.

Fortunately, Rose and Joe weren't there to witness that, but Pat watched her husband leave. When Dean returned and learned what had happened, he made a reference to the Rat Pack. "What happened to one for all and all for one?"

Peter's behavior incensed Frank, who had not really forgiven him by the following night. At a chic Paris bar, Peter spent all his time talking with Pierre Salinger, press secretary to JFK. Thinking they were sharing inside gossip about the Kennedy White House, Frank grew impatient and headed for the bar where he confronted Peter and Salinger. "What secrets are you sharing that I can't hear?" he asked.

"Oh, nothing," Salinger said. "Just making small talk."

Infuriated once again at Peter, Frank stormed out of the bar.

The next morning he called Bob Neal, a Texas oilman and notorious skirt-chaser. Neal was making arrangements for the rental of a yacht to carry Frank, Peter, and their party on a cruise along the French Riviera.

"Count me out," Frank shouted at him over the phone. "I'm going nowhere with that lousy, double-crossing bastard."

"Who's that?" Neal asked.

"Peter Lawford," Frank said. "I'm heading for Germany with Dean."

Frank was to have appeared to sing at Princess Grace's ball. When she heard that he had gone AWOL, she wrote him a note. It was very brief:

FRANK,
I'M SO TERRIBLY DISAPPPOINTED.
GRACE

Frank Sinatra hosted many off-the-record weekends. Perhaps the most bizarre was when he secretly brought together **Porfirio Rubirosa** and his momentary lover, **Patricia Kennedy Lawford** *(top photo)*, and **Cary Grant** *(lower left photo)* and his former stepson, **Lance Reventlow** *(lower right)* for a communal weekend in Rancho Mirage. Until then, Frank didn't know that his friend Cary was an "item" with Lance.

What made the weekend even more bizarre was that both Rubirosa and Cary had been married to Barbara Hutton, the Woolworth heiress, who just happened to be Lance's mother. "The whole thing was very incestuous," Pat Kennedy later said.

Frank wondered if Cary and Rubi would get along together. He need not have worried. The two legends showed more interest in each other than in either Patricia or Lance. According to Frank, Cary was particularly impressed with Rubirosa when he went for a nude swim. "I'm keeping my suit on," Cary told Frank. "I can't compete with that. Who can?"

At one point, Cary apologized for sharing a bed with Lance. "I hope you don't mind. I should have warned you. I didn't mean for it to happen. But it's not that we're actually related by blood."

"Whatever turns you on," Frank said. "Your tastes are certainly versatile. In Spain when we made that awful picture (a reference to *The Pride and the Passion*) you were with Sophia Loren. but I guess cute boy Lance has something that Sophia lacks."

219

The French actress, **Odile Rodin** (*left figure above*), was the fifth and final wife of **Porfirio Rubirosa**. By the time Rubi married her, a woman 28 years his junior, he had settled down at the age of 56.

During his final visit with Frank Sinatra, Rubi had said, "My body, specifically my sex drive, is in low gear."

"Tell me about it," Frank chimed in.

At eight o'clock on the morning of July 5, 1965, Rubi, after a night he spent celebrating a successful polo tournament, crashed his silver Ferrari in the Bois de Boulogne in Paris. It was fatal. One of the 20th Century's most notorious lives came to an inglorious end, wrapped around a tree.

On September 24, 1961, Frank, along with Pat Lawford, flew to Hyannis Port on Kennedy's plane. With them were Rubirosa and his wife, Odile. Teddy Kennedy also went along for the trip. Disembarking from the *Caroline* at New Bedford, Frank emerged from the plane with a champagne glass. He ordered cabbies to drive the party to the Kennedy compound, fifty-three miles away.

When they got there, the presidential flag indicated that JFK was already in residence. At Joe Kennedy's house, Peter Lawford was already waiting, and Rose had ordered that the dinner table be set for twenty-six guests.

The following day the party cruised aboard the *Honey Fitz* where Frank entertained the party, giving details of his recent visit with Pope John XXIII.

"All your friends in Chicago are Italian, too," Peter quipped. His flippant remark was met with an icy stare from Frank.

Jackie was none too happy that Odile had been invited on the yachting trip. Friends had gossiped to her that Odile was having an affair with JFK.

At that point, the White House was trying to distance itself from Frank. Some spin story had to be put out to the press.

Supposedly, Frank was in Hyannis Port to work out an agreement with Joe Kennedy about a souvenir recording of the inaugural gala.

When news of that cruise reached the world, President Kennedy was attacked for "hanging out with such unsavory characters as Frank Sinatra, who never met a Mafia boss he didn't like, and Porfirio Rubirosa, the one-time son-in-law of the notorious dictator Rafael Trujillo of the Dominican Republic." One paper even called Rubi "a notorious international gigolo," referring to his marriages to Doris Duke and Barbara Hutton.

The cruise off Cape Cod lasted only four hours. When it ended, Teddy invited Frank, Peter, and Odile, among others, to go on a tour of the local pubs. Rubi said he didn't feel well, and Patricia claimed she'd gotten too much sun on the cruise, and both of them excused themselves from the pub crawl.

The next day, Frank asked Rubi how he'd spent the day. In whispered tones, the playboy claimed, "I had a pleasant day fucking Ambassador Kennedy's daughter." He was, of course, referring to Patricia Lawford, Peter's wife.

When JFK heard that his sister had been seduced by Rubi, he bluntly asked her, "Is it as big as they say?" His sister refused to answer, but her husband, Peter Lawford, claimed he had the exact measurements. "That guy can balance a chair with a telephone book on the tip of his erection."

In the winter of 1962, the columnist Earl Wilson was startled to see Frank and Ava dining together with Rubi and Odile Rubirosa. "In spite of all the betrayals in love," Wilson said, "they seemed like the dearest of friends. There were rumors going around Broadway that they were engaged in a four-way, but I find that hard to believe."

In September of 1963, Rubi was a guest at Frank's vacation home in Palm Springs. He even tried to teach Rubi, an expert polo player, to play golf but to no avail.

Later Frank invited Rubi for a nude swim. One of his male servants said, "I don't think Frank was gay. But he wanted to see Rubi's cock whenever the occasion arose. It wasn't homosexual desire on the part of Frank, and I'm certain of that. It was a case of penis envy."

# ONE GABOR SISTER DOWN,
## *ANOTHER TO GO*

In 1972 Frank began to pursue Eva Gabor.

Eva, the youngest of the three Gabor sisters—was known as the last great courtesan of the 20th century. At the age of sixteen, Eva was the first member of her colorful family to emigrate from her native Hungary to America. In time, her sisters, Zsa Zsa and Magda, and their mother, Jolie, followed. As they matured, and grew more glib in the ways of America's entertainment industry, Eva and her outspoken sister, Zsa Zsa, were hailed as the world's most beautiful, desirable, and glamorous women.

Before TV talk show host Merv Griffin became more intimately linked with Eva, he often referred to Zsa Zsa and Eva as "my favorite and most amusing guests on TV," the "Gorgeous Gabors" and "The World's Greatest Sister Act."

He later claimed that what especially attracted him to both Zsa Zsa and Eva was their keen ability to deliver one-line zingers. "Take marriage for instance," Merv said. "Zsa Zsa told me, 'I believe in large families—every woman should have at least three husbands.'" On another occasion, Eva instructed Merv that "marriage is too interesting an experiment to be tried only once or twice."

Nine years after the assassination of JFK, in advance of the presidential elections of 1972, Frank was no longer supporting the Democrats, and had switched his allegiance to Richard Nixon and Spiro Agnew. The world learned that Frank was dating Eva when he showed up with her at several Republican Party events at the invitation of Agnew, who had become his close friend.

Because of her unpleasant experiences with Frank in the late 1950s, Zsa Zsa warned Eva about Frank.

"My dah-ling Zsa Zsa, all men are dangerous," Eva came back. "I would think a woman of your age had learned that by now."

Swimming in Frank's pool in Palm Springs, Eva told him an amusing story. Late at night at a hotel in Beverly Hills she decided to swim in the nude, since no one was around. In the middle of her swim, two men came out to use the pool. "Hi, Eva," one of the men called to her. As she jumped out of the pool and ran for a towel, she called back at them, "No, *dahling*, it's Zsa Zsa."

On their fourth date, Frank decided it was time to seduce Eva, and she seemed most willing. But disaster occurred later that evening. Eva had had lovers before, including

Tyrone Power and Glenn Ford, but none with a penis the size of Frank's.

Although known as a gentle lover, he apparently got carried away that night and plunged too deeply into Eva. As she later told her mother, Jolie Gabor, "He split me in two. Something ripped inside me." She had to be rushed to the hospital that night in an ambulance, as she was bleeding.

One would think that was enough to turn her off Frank. But in three weeks they were back together again. But this time they had an agreement. He was not to plunge all the way in.

Instead of being ashamed for harming Eva, he seemed elated. He bragged about it to his fellow Rat Packers. He wanted the story to get back to Rubi. "Zsa Zsa could easily take Rubi, but with another Gabor sister, I sent Eva to the hospital," Frank bragged.

In her memoirs, Eva's long-time companion Camille (also known as Camyl) Sosa Belanger wrote about Eva and Frank in *Eva Gabor: An Amazing Woman,* published in 2005.

Camille claimed that "Eva and Frank were in love, wild about each other, and they were eager to be married." Their hot romance lasted for six months until it cooled down. Eva was between husbands at the time, and Frank was on a rebound after Mia Farrow.

Eva had divorced her fourth husband, stockbroker Richard Brown, and had not yet married her fifth spouse, Frank Jamieson, Vice President of North American Rockwell.

Eva later said that her romance with Frank was "the most passionate I ever had, far more than all my husbands combined. We were both on the rebound, but the right age, and each in the peak of our prime."

"Since we were on the rebound, our only healer was sex," she claimed. "We could not wait to go into the bedroom. We made love on the carpet of my living room, in the shower, on the kitchen table, and everywhere else, even out by the pool."

"One night he was in my kitchen making spaghetti, but couldn't find the oregano," Eva said. "Since he couldn't make the sauce without the oregano, we did the next best thing and ended up making out on the kitchen floor."

"They were very hot for each other," Camille claimed in her memoirs. "Eva was that hot sexy type, and so ardent that she did not hide it and whoever escaped Eva it was their loss."

English, of course, was Camille's second language.

Frank later told Peter, "I had to go slow and break Eva in, but now that she's used to my size, she can't get enough of me. After I finish with her, I will have ruined her for all other men."

"My passion for Frank Sinatra was just too intense," confessed **Eva Gabor** to her longtime companion, Merv Griffin.

"It was just destined to burn itself out. He was at that age when men start looking around for a very young girl—in this case, Mia Farrow. We glamour queens of yesterday had lost some of our glow. He really enjoyed me in the beginning, perhaps too much so. But I watched his roving eye night after night—in restaurants, clubs, and bars. Slowly, ever so slowly, he began to lose interest in me.

"I tried to hold on, but I could see it was a hopeless cause. If he had married me, I would have been very European about his other women. As long as the diamonds and the money kept rolling in, I could forgive an occasional dalliance from a husband."

# Marilyn Monroe & Frank Sinatra
## LOVE ON THE REBOUND

**Frank Sinatra** and **Marilyn Monroe** always wanted to star in a picture together. At least that is what they said. However, when an opportunity arose, such as it did in the projected *Pink Tights*, or in *Some Like It Hot*, either Marilyn or Frank bowed out.

Billy Wilder, in one of his more preposterous moments, tried to convince Frank to play the role of Josephine in *Some Like It Hot,* but Frank turned it down, issuing a violent rejection of the idea of portraying a movie character in drag.

The role went instead to **Tony Curtis** (*see him in drag in the central left photo above*, co-starring with the equally amusing **Jack Lemmon** (*right central figure, above*).

Off screen, Frank and Marilyn starred as clandestine lovers. Jeanne Carmen, a sexy blonde model and occasional B-movie actress, was Marilyn's best girlfriend and lived near to her. As a night person, Carmen stayed up with Marilyn on many a night, talking about sex, drugs, and men. "We were barbiturate buddies," Carmen later recalled.

One night, Carmen confessed to Marilyn that Frank had made her pregnant, and that he had subsequently arranged and paid for an abortion. "If I ever become pregnant with Frank's child," Marilyn said, "I'd go ahead and have it and wouldn't even tell him. Could you imagine the talent a little boy or girl would have with Marilyn Monroe and Frank Sinatra as his mama and papa?"

On another night, Marilyn told Carmen that when she was nineteen years old, she'd given birth to a baby girl. "They took it away from me," she said, without specifying who "they" were, or who the father had been. "I can tell you that will never happen again," she continued." You must never repeat what I told you to Frank. He and that mother of his are known for killing babies. They practically operate an abortion clinic."

## FRANK GAVE HER EMERALDS AND DIAMONDS, BUT HE DIDN'T BRING A WEDDING BAND

Afraid that men do not make passes at girls who wear glasses, **Marilyn Monroe** appeared in the 1953 *How to Marry a Millionaire* with "Man Hunting" co-stars Lauren Bacall and Betty Grable. Over the years, Frank seduced all three women. Marilyn made this film months before she launched a sexual relationship with Frank Sinatra while still married to Joe DiMaggio.

Her psychiatrist, Dr. Ralph Greenson, discouraged her affair with Frank. On call for her day and night, Dr. Greenson said, "I try to keep her from being destructively lonely. During such times, she often retreats to drug use. I told her to avoid destructive people like Sinatra. I viewed their relationship as sado-masochistic, with him acting the role of the sadist. Even though she was seeing me two or three times a week, she would cancel at a moment's notice if Sinatra invited her to his villa in Palm Springs."

Dr. Greenson also claimed that Marilyn confided to him that when she made Frank angry, he was given to violent outbursts. "He could hold his liquor, but he never forgave a woman who couldn't," she said. "I couldn't...at least, not always."

One night, when she was staggering around drunk, he tossed her into his pool. She nearly drowned, as she was too drunk to swim and no one, especially Frank, seemed sober enough to dive in and rescue her.

*"Sometimes I think it would be easier to avoid old age, to die young, but then you'd never complete your life, would you? You'd never wholly know yourself."*
—**Marilyn Monroe**

*"Frank's the best. No man compares to him. I should know."*
—**Marilyn Monroe**

*"Marilyn is nuts about me,"*
—**Frank Sinatra** to Sammy Davis Jr.

Marilyn Monroe first met Frank Sinatra in Los Angeles in 1954 while still married to Joe DiMaggio. Her marriage was heading for a disastrous ending, as was Frank's marriage to Ava Gardner.

Frank, who already knew DiMaggio, had invited him to dinner at Romanoff's, and he requested that Marilyn come along, as he was anxious to get to know her.

During dinner, when DiMaggio got up to go to the men's room, Marilyn slipped Frank her phone number. Imitating Mae West, she said, "Why don't you come up and see me sometime? Joe's visiting relatives in San Francisco next week."

"No red-blooded male turns down an invitation from Marilyn Monroe," he said. "Kid, you're the hottest ticket in America."

According to Marilyn's friend and photographer, Milton Green, the first sexual tryst between Marilyn and Frank occurred on the night of the second day after Joe left Los Angeles for San Francisco.

Over pillow talk, Frank and Marilyn shared a mutual dream of starring together in a movie musical. She told him that she'd been offered the chance to star in a movie called *Pink Tights,* a remake of a film her screen idol, Betty Grable, made during World War II called *Coney Island.* This was the turn-of-the-20th-century story of a saloon entertainer who becomes a famous musical star. Grable herself remade the film seven years later, calling it *Wabash Avenue.*

At first, Frank was reluctant to take on the role originally played by George Montgomery. He told Marilyn that he'd be playing second fiddle to her. But she could be very persuasive, and she finally got his agreement to co-star with her in *Pink Tights.*

What he didn't know was that DiMaggio was dead set against Marilyn starring in the role. His main objection involved the low salary she would be paid. "You're the star of the picture; you're the one who will have them lined up at the box office to see you in those skimpy costumes. But Sinatra will be walking off with the big bucks What you'll get is a bag of peanuts."

Not knowing any of this, Frank showed up on the lot of 20th Century Fox ready for work on the first day of the shoot. When Marilyn hadn't reported to work by noon, he began to curse and steam. He'd already smoked a pack of cigarettes before the lunch break was called. Phone calls to Marilyn's home were not answered. Fox even sent studio emissaries to the DiMaggio residence, but no one seemed to be home.

Back at the studio, Frank, comforted with a bottle of Jack Daniels, waited until closing time. At five o'clock, he stormed out of the studio, telling Fox, "I'm off the picture. Leave a message for that two-bit blonde whore. Tell the cunt never to call me again."

It wasn't until four days later that he learned that Marilyn had flown out of Los Angeles with DiMaggio. They'd landed in San Francisco for a reunion with his Italian family.

News of this reached not only Frank but Fox executives, who suspended their hottest star on January 5, 1954.

Back in Los Angeles, Marilyn made several attempts to reach Frank at his villa in Palm Springs, but he was not taking her calls. He sent her a telegram: "TOO LITTLE, TOO LATE, KID. WE'RE THROUGH!"

When Marilyn Monroe first came to Hollywood, she had one dream and one role model. At 20th Century Fox, she wanted to replace Betty Grable, who had been one of the biggest box office draws of WWII. "The war's over," Marilyn told anyone willing to listen. "It's time Veronica Lake, Lana Turner, and even Betty herself moved over to make room for a new set of gals."

**Grable** (above) is seen in a scene from the movie *Wabash Avenue (1950),* a remake of her earlier film *Coney Island (1943).* Marilyn was offered the lead role in a second remake of *Coney Island,* a film tentatively entitled *Pink Tights.* Its producers had cast Frank Sinatra as the male lead.

"I'd have done it, too," Marilyn later confessed, "had not Mr. Joe DiMaggio put his foot down. He was certain that Frank would be sedcuing me before the first day of the shoot. Joe wasn't always right, but that time he was."

She was not a star who took rejection lightly. On Saturday afternoon, she put on her most alluring dress, with a plunging *décolletage,* and showed up on his doorstep in Palm Springs. Although reluctant to do so, Frank invited her in, especially when he saw how she was attired. As he later told Sammy Davis Jr., "I could say no to working with Marilyn again, but I could hardly say no to a chance to bang the hell out of her. I invited her in, and she delivered...and delivered. By the time she drove back to Hollywood, I was one exhausted dago stud."

In Palm Springs on her first day there, Marilyn and Frank had enjoyed a nude swim in his pool. Later, as they rested on pink *chaises longues* she gave him her version of why she didn't show up that morning at Fox on the set of *Pink Tights.* "I liked the script," she told Frank, "but Joe found it too *risqué.* It was also the money thing, meaning I wasn't getting enough. Joe feels Fox is just exploiting me. There's more. Joe told me that he absolutely wouldn't allow me to make a movie with you. 'I know him too well,' he said. 'Sinatra will spend more time in your dressing room than in front of the camera.'"

"Old Joe was right about that," Frank said. "Now get your sweet ass over here and give daddy a sloppy wet one."

Before she left Palm Springs, she told Frank that she was splitting from DiMaggio. "I'm my own girl again. I control my own life."

Marilyn's trip to Palm Springs came at a time when Frank was at his most despondent from the loss of Ava Gardner. He was virtually in mourning for her. And although Marilyn wasn't Ava, in 1954, she was the most sought after woman in the world.

**Joe DiMaggio** and **Marilyn Monroe** look none too happy in their joint passport photo from 1954.

Only two weeks before, DiMaggio had accused her of slipping around "behind my back and fucking Sinatra." She denied it. As she told her friend, Jeanne Carmen, "I always deny all affairs when I talk to a man. I want each man I'm with to think he's the first one."

"But, Marilyn," Carmen chastised her. "No man will be convinced that he's the first. From the way you tell it, you first got plugged when you were six years old. The guy who did the dirty deed must have had a very small dick."

"When I first met Joe," Marilyn said, "I thought he'd be the loud, sporty type. but he was a real reserved gentleman, in a gray suit, with just a sprinkle of gray in his hair. I was attracted to him. He was smart and alert. but once he married me, he became dull. When I first met him, I'd never been to a baseball game, but after my first night with him, I came to realize he carried around his own bat."

Before leaving Palm Springs, Marilyn made a tempting offer to Frank. She wanted to move in with him as his mistress.

As Dean Martin later advised Frank, "That's an offer no man can refuse. Let's face facts: Ava Gardner is the most beautiful woman in the world, but Marilyn is the sexiest. If you can't have Ava, God has sent the next best thing. No man on the planet can sympathize with you over your loss of Ava if you've replaced her with Marilyn. Hell, man, you'll be the envy of every dude with a hard-on."

In spite of friends such as Martin urging Frank to accept Marilyn's offer, he was still hesitant. She began to call him repeatedly, often late at night. She sounded more and more desperate.

James Whiting, a close friend of Frank's, claimed that Marilyn was becoming dependent on him. "Marilyn always had to have a man in her life. With DiMaggio gone, she had to have an immediate replacement of a male authority figure.

Frank was that lucky man if he could just get over that hangdog, lovesick illness he had about Ava."

Finally, Frank relented and called Marilyn, telling her she could move in.

She was elated, telling Whiting, "If you have any problem in the world, Frankie is the man to turn to. He can solve anthing, even rescuing a damsel in distress like myself."

She sought out her friend, Robert F. Slatzer. He was her long-time confidant who later claimed that he and Marilyn had been married, although only briefly.

After Marilyn's death, he wrote two books about his relationship with her, revealing "the naked truth." One was called *The Marilyn Files,* the other *The Curious Death of Marilyn Monroe.* Both *exposés* claimed that the star had been murdered.

As Marilyn herself later admitted, "Bob was always in love with me, but I could tell him everything about my other love affairs. He was the best listener in the business."

After one week with Frank, she told Slatzer, "Frank Sinatra is the most fascinating man I ever dated. He has always been kind and understanding. When we're together, I feel I don't need pills. He makes me laugh. He makes me feel secure. He makes me happy. He's the man who taught me to love life—not be afraid of it. A real gentleman. Of course, he's still so upset over Ava that he's sometimes impotent, but I'm curing that."

In J. Randy Taraborrelli's *Sinatra: A Complete Life,* he wrote: "Marilyn cured Sinatra of his impotency, at least for a while. She said she didn't care how long it took. She was determined that he was going to perform in bed with her. They were innovative sexually. For instance, they began sharing intimacies outdoors. Sinatra had never done that before Monroe, and it excited him. According to Sinatra's friends, he and Monroe engaged in sexual activity at night on the roof of the Sands Hotel above the Las Vegas strip."

Frank told Whiting that after Ava left to "to fuck every bullfighter in Spain," he became impotent. "But Marilyn is the best cure for that. At home she never puts on clothes, but runs around naked."

With the passage of each day Frank and Marilyn spent together, he thought less and less about Ava, although he was still in love with her, a bond that would last a lifetime.

Those close to Frank claimed that he actually fell in love with Marilyn after his divorce from Ava in 1954.

"He was still in love with Ava," Dean Martin said. "But he also loved Marilyn in a different way. Frank was capable of loving two women at the same time."

During the first two weeks, Frank and Marilyn lived in harmony. But he gradually began to be irritated by her flaws, and she also witnessed firsthand that Frank wasn't always the gentleman that she'd originally thought he was.

Frank's right-man man for many a year, George

In a claim never really proven, **Robert Slatzer** (*pictured above, surrounded with MM memorabilia*) insisted that he had been secretly married to the star when she was a struggling model as part of a ceremony that occurred in Mexico in 1952, before her later marriages to Joe DiMaggio and playwright Arthur Miller. He insisted that Darryl F. Zanuck, head of 20th Century Fox, ordered the marriage dissolved over concerns about Monroe's image, and that the documents were destroyed.

When she was found dead, he launched a private investigation that went on for years and became the subject of two exposé books.

In his books, he charged that the Mafia was involved in MM's death and that Frank Sinatra knew who the culprits were.

"Someone got away with murder on the night of August 4, 1962," he wrote in his explosive book, *The Marilyn Files,* published in 1992. "Marilyn didn't have a chance," Slatzer charged. "Neither did justice."

Jacobs, said that his boss came to regard Marilyn as "a total mess. She was a drunk, and he could put up with that. But he was a very neat man, and he couldn't tolerate Marilyn being a dirty pig. She often didn't bathe. She ate in bed and left foodstuff like pizza under her mattress, sleeping in the filth. Her hair became matted because she didn't wash it. Often she was more than twenty-five pounds overweight, although going on a crash diet right before filming a new movie."

Frank found it "particularly disgusting" that MM didn't use tampons or sanitary napkins and left her sheets with blood on them.

Although Frank was protective of Marilyn when he thought she was being abused by others, he could turn suddenly on her when he was in a foul mood.

Marilyn always liked to walk around naked. "Clothes inhibit me," she told her maid Lena Pepitone.

Arguably, **Marlon Brando** and **Vivien Leigh** appeared in their greatest roles, *A Streetcar Named Desire,* which brought Vivien her second Oscar after *Gone With the Wind.*

Marilyn had a dream of taking the stage play on the road, with the understanding that she would replace Vivien as Blanche DuBois, and that Brando would reprise the role that had made him a legend on Broadway. Of course, that became just another of her fantasies.

In real life, however, Brando became her on-again, off-again lover. He once claimed that he had first met her in a bar in New York, working as a prostitute, when she was Norma Jean Baker.

In England, although Vivien Leigh had already starred in the stage version of *The Prince and the Showgirl,* Marilyn flew to London to replace her in the movie version. Early in the filming, MM seduced Vivien's co-star (Vivien's husband), Lord Laurence Olivier.

Later, she very provocatively announced to Vivien, "Larry didn't really know what to do."

One night Frank called a "Summit" of his fellow Rat Packers—Joey Bishop, Peter Lawford, Sammy Davis Jr., and Dean Martin.

"We were drinking and shooting the shit," Sammy recalled. "In walks Marilyn. Jaybird naked. I think all of us got an erection right away, except Joey. I never saw anything popping up in his pants, but he was true blue to his wife. After that night, and behind Frank's back, all of us 'rats' were determined to fuck Marilyn. One by one we knocked off that piece."

On another night in front of Frank's Rat Packers, a teary-eyed Marilyn was detailing stories of childhood rape, whether true or not. Finally, Frank could tolerate it no more. "Listen, Norma Jean, toughen up or get the hell out. We've all gone through shit. Get over it!" She ran in tears from the room.

One night at Peter Lawford's Santa Monica home, a drunken Marilyn was talking to Sammy, Dean, and Peter about her desire to become a serious stage actress. She claimed that she was considering touring America with Marlon Brando in a repeat of his Broadway and film success of Tennessee Williams' *A Streetcar Named Desire.* "Marlon would get a chance to be Stanley Kowalski again, and I, of course, would play the doomed heroine, Blanche DuBois. I'm sure that darling Tennessee would love the idea."

"Shut up, Norma Jean," Frank shouted at all. "You don't know what in the fuck you're talking about. As Blanche DuBois, you'd be laughed off the stage. Stick to those dumb blonde roles."

She ran in tears from the living room and locked herself into one of Peter's guest bedrooms. Frank stormed out of the house. But in a few weeks he apologized to her, and he and Marilyn started seeing each other again.

Still plagued by impotency, Frank, according to Sammy, flew to Las Vegas for a gig. Once installed in a suite at the Sands, he ordered the most expensive prostitutes, who tried to give him an orgasm. Reportedly, he went through a rainbow of women hailing from Senegal to Thailand, from Canada to Brazil. But no hooker succeeded.

When Frank returned to Los Angeles, he found that Marilyn hadn't quite given up on trying to "get him off." As has been revealed, she took bubble baths with him and went down on him in a giant bathtub. Frank later told Sammy. "Sometimes I get so excited I hold her head down too long. If she's ever found drowned, you'll know who the culprit is."

One morning, unusual for him, Frank awoke early and found Marilyn gone from his bed. In his jockey shorts, he walked into his kitchen. There he discovered a nude Marilyn standing in front of his refrigerator, trying to determine if she wanted orange juice or grapefruit juice.

"I took her right there on the kitchen floor," he later told his friend Whiting. "She cured my impotency. I shot off. Marilyn got her orgasm, rare for her, or so she said. From that morning on, my plumbing was in working order—and to hell with moaning over Ava."

After Marilyn moved out of Frank's house in 1954, he saw her only occasionally and rarely for sex. Sometimes when he was performing in Los Angeles, Marilyn visited him "for that occasional blow-job in his dressing room," according to Peter Lawford.

During the course of their relationship, Frank and Marilyn talked about starring in a film together. The most improbable suggestion came when Billy Wilder offered Frank the role of Joe/Josephine in *Some Like It Hot*, Marilyn's classic comedy. When Frank heard that he'd have to play the role in drag, he immediately turned it down. Tony Curtis took it and gave his most memorable performance.

A more workable idea involved a remake of *Born Yesterday* which brought Judy Holliday her Oscar opposite William Holden and Broderick Crawford. Frank was suggested for the gangster role, but he eventually decided it would be bad for his image.

In 1961, Frank resumed a sexual rela-

In 1955, Marilyn Monroe showed up in the audience at the Broadway premiere of **Tennessee Williams**' *Cat on a Hot Tin Roof. (Tennessee is depicted above.)*

Her hair a shining platinum, she wore skin-tight gold mesh. As she held onto Tennessee's arm, she whispered in his ear. "I know you wrote the role of Maggie the Cat just so I could play it in the movies."

He graciously responded, "Something like that."

As Tennessee wandered off, Marilyn hooked up with columnist Walter Winchell, later inserting herself between the honeymooning Eddie Fisher and Debbie Reynolds, America's so-called "sweethearts."

Although she may have been right—the role might have fitted her like a glove—negotiations didn't work out, and the part of Maggie went instead to Elizabeth Taylor, her rival.

After seeing the movie, Marilyn sent a letter to Tennessee at his base in Key West. "I could have played Maggie so much better. I hate to say this, but Elizabeth just doesn't have the sex appeal the role calls for, and I'm sure you agree."

tionship with Marilyn. Milt Ebbins, the vice president of Peter Lawford's production company, Chrislaw, claimed that Frank actually fell in love with Marilyn all over again, although that is the subject of much dispute.

Press agent Rupert Allan even went so far as to call MM and Frank "star-crossed lovers. In a different time and place, they would have been together," he recalled. "He really loved her. But she was a mess and annoyed him. She became sloppy in her appearance and in her life. One boozy broad. So, she pissed him off. They didn't have a chance to work out their differences."

After her divorce from Arthur Miller, Marilyn was distraught and almost suicidal. To better care for her, Frank moved her temporarily into his home in Coldwater Canyon. Although they resumed their affair, neither party was faithful to each other. Marilyn was seeing John F. Kennedy on the side whenever the chance arose, and Frank was also bedding the dancer Juliet Prowse.

When **Elizabeth Taylor** *(left)* fell in love with **Eddie Fisher** *(right)*, it shocked the world. After all, Eddie was the best friend of her late husband, Mike Todd, who had died in a plane crash. Eddie was also married to Debbie Reynolds, who supposedly was Elizabeth's best friend. The Taylor/Fisher love affair and subsequent marriage became the "scandal of the decade," in the words of one overzealous reporter.

Eddie later claimed that he was not totally surprised one night when Marilyn Monroe called him up and invited him to her apartment.

"I was madly in love with Elizabeth, but what red-blooded male would turn down Marilyn Monroe? I came over and I came once I got there, if you get my drift. Before the rooster crowed, the blonde vixen had me three times.

"Our farewell wasn't all that romantic. 'Thanks, Eddie,' she said. 'I just wanted to experience first hand what turns Taylor on.'"

By February of 1961, the Sinatra/Monroe affair was in full bloom. She referred to it as a "tropical heat wave," evoking one of her old musical numbers.

He presented her with a French poodle, which she named "Maf," short for Mafia. She was always kidding him about his mob associations.

In June of 1961, Marilyn flew to Las Vegas to attend Frank's opening at the Sands. To her surprise, she found herself seated at a front row table with her arch rival, Elizabeth Taylor. Marilyn was not only jealous of Elizabeth's former love affair with Frank, but of her beauty and box office clout. They merely exchanged pleasantries and tried to ignore each other for the rest of the night.

Married to Elizabeth at the time, singer Eddie Fisher watched in horror as a drunken Marilyn made a spectacle of herself. "She was slobbering all over herself," he later claimed. "Normally, she was a beautiful woman. But on this particular night, she looked like a broken-down and washed-up Vegas hooker. But what did I care? I was married to Elizabeth, the most beautiful woman in the world."

At one point when Marilyn was seated between Patricia and Peter Lawford, she fondled his crotch. "For old time's sake," she whispered to him. As Frank sang, she swayed to the music, her ample breasts falling out of her low-cut pink satin dress.

With an entourage of people, Marilyn and Elizabeth went backstage. Marilyn was the first to reach Frank, gushing over his performance and planting wet kisses on his face. Noting her condition, he looked at her with a certain disgust.

"Then the unspeakable occurred," Elizabeth later claimed. "Marilyn was so drunk she threw up on Sinatra." He ordered a security guard to take her back to his suite. A photographer stood nearby and tried to take a picture but Frank knocked the camera to the floor, smashing it with his feet. He then fled to his dressing room to change into fresh clothes.

With Fisher at her side, Elizabeth stood next to the photographer and said, "Monroe is a mess, isn't she? How she holds onto her beauty I'll never know. She drinks far too much and obviously can't hold her liquor. Now, me. I'm a girl who knows how to handle her booze."

Later that night, Frank chastised Marilyn, but she pleaded illness. It was later learned that she was suffering from impacted gallstones. She later had to have surgery.

The first time he visited her in the hospital, he felt sorry for her and forgave her for her outrageous behavior at the Sands.

August of 1961 found Marilyn spending a weekend on Frank's yacht, with Dean Martin and his wife, Jeanne. "Marilyn was into heavy drugs," said Jeanne. Marilyn wandered around the boat nude at three o'clock in the morning, looking for some "reds" to put her to sleep.

That yacht trip proved too much for Frank. Marilyn was so drunk and drugged she couldn't even dress herself, and he had to send Jeanne below deck to assist her.

Later he said, "I can't wait to get her off the boat. The way I feel right now, I could throw her to the sharks. All through this trip, she's been pressuring me to marry her. In a weak moment a few weeks ago, I agreed. But now the marriage is off. I've ordered our return to shore. The trip will continue but without Miss Monroe. It's over between us."

Frank was wrong. It was not over between them. Their most outrageous drama was yet to unfold.

In September of 1961, Frank invited Marilyn to go with him to a Democratic Party fundraiser at the Hilton Hotel. For the occasion, she wore a green-sequined dress that Jean-Louis had designed and crafted for her for $3,000.

Lena Pepitone, Marilyn's tell-all maid, recalled Frank's arrival in the living room to pick up Marilyn. "She flew into his arms like an exotic tropical bird. She electrified the room. They kissed so passionately I was embarrassed to be standing there."

He pulled out of his pocket a gorgeous pair of emerald-and-diamond earrings, clipping them onto Marilyn's delicate ears.

"They're beautiful," she said. "I love them." Actually she never really cared that much for earrings, believing that they distracted from her beauty.

"You oughtta like 'em. They cost me $35,000."

Before the winds of autumn blew in, Marilyn was telling Pepitone, "Frank is going to marry me. He's ready to propose any day now."

Reportedly, Pepitone was living through a web of Marilyn fantasies about possible grooms. Her list included not only Frank, but also John F. Kennedy, even Robert F. Kennedy, depending on what week it was. At one point she claimed that she'd even agreed to remarry Joe DiMaggio.

Regardless of which suitor she picked, Marilyn began to make plans to move into a more suitable residence. She considered renting a home in Beverly Hills "just to show that Liz Taylor a thing or two."

Many biographers have assumed over the years that Frank passed Marilyn on to Jack Kennedy. But JFK had first seduced Marilyn when he arrived in Hollywood after WWII, back when she was still known as Norma Jean Baker.

"The trouble with Marilyn and Frank was the same trouble he'd had with Ava," Dean Martin said. "He wanted to own Marilyn, like he'd tried to own Ava. Considering who those two dames were, they were the unreachable star."

When Frank began to ascertain the complexities of Marilyn's involvement with the Kennedys, and her lingering attachment to DiMaggio, he slowly began to withdraw from her.

If Marilyn clung to the remote possibility that she'd become the third Mrs. Frank Sinatra, her hopes were dashed when she read an item in the newspapers. Frank had proposed marriage to Juliet Prowse, a beautiful, twenty-four-year-old dancer from South Africa.

Marilyn called her friend Jeanne Carmen in desperation. "Frank prefers a younger woman."

By the spring of 1962, Frank was giving up on Marilyn. "She's too emotionally dependent on me," he told Martin. "She's drained me dry. I'll be there for her in the future only when she desperately needs me. But I really want to move on."

Weeks before her death, he seemed to have changed his mind and wanted to marry her after all. "I'm still in love with her," he told Martin. "We may get married one night, but it will be a union blessed by the Devil himself. The ceremony should be performed by a minister from Sammy's Church of Satan."

"Frank kept changing his point of view about Marilyn every day," Martin said. "One day he was going to marry her. Then she'd do something to piss him off, and he would announce that he was 'dumping the broad.'"

To George Jacobs, Frank's valet, Marilyn compared both Frank and JFK as lovers. She claimed that JFK suffered from premature ejaculation, although she turned that around and blamed it on herself for driving him so wild. "He can't hold back." She also said that he was so busy running the country he didn't have time for foreplay. In contrast, she found that Frank took time "for the mushy stuff. He's the best. No man compares to him, and *I* should know."

"Eventually Frank felt more compassion for Marilyn than passion," said Jacobs. "If Marilyn wanted sex, Mr. S would play Sir Galahad and 'rise' to the occasion, so to speak. He called them mercy fucks. On occasion he threw these same mercy fucks to Peggy Lee or Judy Garland."

In the final months of Marilyn's life, her maid, Lena Pepitone, claimed that "the calls she enjoyed the most— and talked the longest on—came from two men who were very, very special to her: Joe DiMaggio and Frank Sinatra."

Many reports claim that Marilyn was washed up in films in the summer of 1962 when she was fired from *Something's Got to Give*, a movie she was making with Dean Martin. But that was not true. Fox would eventually reinstate her.

An Italian company wanted to star her in four big money movies, each a six-figure deal. Frank was talking

**Marilyn Monroe** *(left)* and **Elizabeth Taylor** *(right)* came together in 1961 at the Sands hotel in Las Vegas to attend Frank Sinatra's opening night. Seated with them were Dean Martin and his wife, Jeanne. Eddie Fisher is not visible in this picture, but he's seated to the immediate left of Marilyn.

Before Frank began his act, a drunken Marilyn told Eddie, "I can't tie him down, not Frankie, but I'll always love him."

Far more intriguing than Marilyn's drunken debacle at Frank's opening was what happened the following afternoon, when Marilyn visited Elizabeth's suite to apologize for her outrageous behavior of the previous evening.

As revealed in the April 11, 2011 edition of THE GLOBE, the two women might have had a lesbian tryst.

In her secret diary, Elizabeth wrote that she was entranced by the way Marilyn moved. "She was the sexiest woman I ever met, and her touch was electric."

But back in Beverly Hills two weeks later, Elizabeth was in the bar of the Beverly Hilton when Marilyn entered the room. Elizabeth warned her drinking companion, Roddy McDowall, "Keep that dyke away from me tonight."

with Marilyn and Jule Styne about remaking *A Tree Grows in Brooklyn* as a musical.

On Saturday, August 4, the day before she died, she made an appointment with her long-time friend, the Hollywood columnist Sidney Skolsky, to discuss a script based on the life of the platinum blonde bombshell, Jean Harlow. As a teenage girl, Marilyn had viewed Harlow as an idol and role model.

Gene Kelly wanted to meet with Marilyn to discuss starring with her in *What a Way to Go*. Kelly eventually made the film, which was released in 1964, with Shirley MacLaine, who took the part originally slated for Marilyn.

Frank invited Marilyn to the Cal-Neva Lodge shortly before she died. In Hollywood legend, it became known as "The Lost Weekend," the name taken from the Ray Milland movie about alcoholism for which that star won the Best Actor Oscar in 1945. Frank owned a percentage of Cal-Neva, which was billed as "Heaven in the High Sierras." Its gambling casinos were inside the Nevada state line, its restaurant and hotel accommodations in California. He was appearing in the resort's main showroom that weekend, with backup support by entertainers Buddy Greco and Roberta Linn.

As a stockholder, Frank could invite any guest he wanted to the Cal-Neva Lodge, giving them the best suites. "I felt I had to protect her," he told friends. He never made it clear if that meant protect her from her self-destructive tendencies, or protect her from a person or persons who meant to harm her.

Frank sent his private plane, *Christina*, to Los Angeles to pick up Marilyn, Peter, and Pat Lawford, flying them to Lake Tahoe and Cal-Neva. Peter Lawford was invited, although Frank for various reasons was still "pissed off" at him. Although Pat didn't really want to go, Peter persuaded her. "Turning down Frank would be like ignoring an invitation from the Pope."

Peter, Pat, and Marilyn (with no makeup) flew to Nevada on July 27, 1962. It would be her last weekend out of town.

At Cal-Neva, Frank arranged for Marilyn to be lodged in the luxurious Chalet 52, and he asked to be alone with her there. There is no record of his last detailed conversation with Marilyn, but it is generally assumed they talked about the problems she was having as regards feeling "abandoned" by both RFK and JFK.

Frank later told Peter, "Marilyn is a total mess. She's going over Niagara Falls without a barrel. I'm going to call her psychiatrist, and give him hell." He was referring to Dr. Ralph Greenson. After his second meeting with Marilyn, Frank told Peter, "She should be put in a sanitarium."

He also told Peter, "I can't cut her loose. If it had been any other dame, except Ava, I would have dumped her by now. But Marilyn gives me guilt feelings. I don't know why."

"She was really unkept and often showed up at the night club with no makeup," Buddy Greco claimed. "Most of the guests didn't even know it was *the* Marilyn Monroe. She tried to hide her bad hair with a scarf. She was boozing it real bad that weekend. I heard from Peter she was also taking Nembutal and Seconal."

According to Nevada state law, Sam Giancana, as a convicted criminal, was not supposed to set foot in any gambling casino. In spite of that (or in defiance of that), Frank sent his private plane back to Los Angeles to pick up the mobster. When Patricia Lawford spotted Giancana in the lobby, she told Peter she wanted to fly back home, but he prevailed upon her to stay.

"That's all I need," Pat said, "To have my picture taken with some Mafia boss."

Once word reached the FBI that Giancana was in residence at the Cal-Neva, undercover FBI agents arrived. Peter said, "They were easy to spot. I could spot an FBI agent a mile away."

Giancana found Marilyn "in a dizzy blonde state" [his words]. Nonetheless, he invited her into his suite, and she visited him. Somewhere during the course of that evening, his henchman photographed the star on all fours, with the mobster riding piggyback on her back. She was completely nude, although Giancana wore his shorts. Some sources claim that Frank himself took the pictures, but it is highly doubtful if he would subject Marilyn to such humiliation.

Somebody showed Frank the pictures when they were developed. He looked at them and told an assistant, "They make me want to vomit. Burn them!" So far as it is known, no negative exists of these ghastly pictures. Apparently all of them were destroyed.

Giancana later told Frank, "I fucked Marilyn last night. She's lousy in the hay. I don't know what all the excitement is about."

Back in Hollywood, MM told her friend, "Sam may be a big man in Chicago, but he is nothing in the bedroom. Sometimes when these bigshots get in the saddle they're not such big men after all."

The morning after those pictures were taken, Marilyn tried to commit suicide at the lodge. At the last minute, she placed a call to the Cal-Neva telephone operator who summoned an ambulance. She was rushed to the hospital where her stomach was pumped.

Frank rushed to her bedside and ordered the best medical attention available in that part of Nevada and California. He left her room only when her primary doctor assured him she was out of danger. Privately, he recommended to Frank that she "should be supervised at all times."

One guest said he spotted Marilyn leaving Cal-Neva after Frank had ordered her out. He told Peter, "If she stays here any longer, she's going to die. I don't want her to die on these premises. We have enough problems as it is with Giancana here."

That same guest later told reporters that he followed Peter and Pat as they helped Marilyn onto Frank's private plane to fly back to Los Angeles. Frank would never see her again.

He later regretted his last public comment about Marilyn. A reporter had asked him about his relationship with Marilyn.

Frank delivered a sarcastic reply. "Who? Miss Monroe reminds me of a saintly young girl I went to high school with, who later became a nun. This is a recording."

When Marilyn heard what Frank had said about her, she suggested that he "look me up in *Who's Who*."

Events at the Cal-Neva Lodge went downhill after that infamous weekend. Within a year of its opening, Cal-Neva skidded into trouble with the Nevada Gaming Control Board. The resort's license was revoked on September 11, 1963, partly because Sam Giancana had stayed there.

Frank decided not to defend himself. "No useful purpose would come of it," he told friends. "I'd lose anyway." After his no-show at one of their hearings, the board revoked his license

Without realizing the dire consequences, Marilyn Monroe became involved in dangerous liaisons that starred not only mob boss **Sam Giancana** *(upper photo),* but also **Robert Kennedy** *(lower photo),* the U.S. Attorney General.

A close friend of John F. Kennedy, Senator George Smathers of Florida, claimed, "During Marilyn Monroe's last days, it seemed that everybody wanted to put a bridle on her and silence her big mouth. She was talking too much and threatening too many empires—not only the future of Jack and Bobby, but also the evil empire of that mobster, Sam Giancana, who would sell his own mother down the river for a buck."

Dr. Ralph Greenson, Marilyn's psychiatrist, privately discussed his most famous client with friends. "It's as if she's trying to destroy herself. But in her self-destruction, she plans to take some gentlemen down with her—not Frank Sinatra exactly, but definitely Sam Giancana and those Kennedy brothers. She wants revenge for the real or imagined harm they've caused her."

and ordered him to divest himself of all his holdings in Lake Tahoe and Las Vegas.

Like the rest of the world, Frank learned about Marilyn's death at 12305 Fifth Helena Drive on August 5, 1962.

Frank, for reasons of his own, immediately placed a call to Ava Gardner, who was in Madrid that Sunday morning of August 5, 1962. She had not heard the news.

She told Frank that she had suspected that Marilyn would eventually do herself in.

He astonished her by telling her, "She didn't kill herself. She was murdered."

Ava couldn't believe that. "But who did it?"

"I'm not sure," he said, "but I intend to find out."

Before ringing off, he made a vow. "When I find out the son-of-a-bitch who killed her, I'm going to kill him myself."

She warned him, "Be careful. You might be the one who ends up getting killed."

"Honey, if Frank Sinatra had ever been careful, he would never have ended up leaving Hoboken."

Deeply saddened by the news of Marilyn's death, Frank went into a deep, morbid depression. To pay his respects, he tried to attend her funeral, only to learn that Joe DiMaggio had ordered security guards to block his entrance into the ceremony. Frank even tried to bribe himself into the chapel but failed.

Turned away, Frank stormed out. DiMaggio had committed the unforgivable sin. "No one blocks Frank Sinatra from anything," he said.

One drunken night some time later, Frank placed another alcohol-sodden call to Ava. "I've learned who killed Marilyn. I know who the bastards are."

"Who?" she asked. "Who are you talking about?"

"I can't tell you," he said. "It's dangerous for you to possess such information, and your phone might be tapped. But I promise you this, if it's the last thing I do on this earth, I'm gonna bring the bastards down. One by one. That's how I'll get them. And not a one of the shits will know I was behind their downfall."

---

## *Patricia Kennedy's Final Dialogue with MM*

In 1962, at the Cal-Neva Lodge, on the California/Nevada border, Patricia Kennedy met privately in the bedroom of a somewhat drugged Marilyn Monroe. The rendezvous had been arranged by Patricia's husband, Peter Lawford. Patricia wanted to have a "Come-to-Jesus" meeting with the distraught star, in the wake of Marilyn's disastrous affairs with her two brothers, Jack and Bobby Kennedy.

Here, as Patricia later reported to her husband, are the final words the Kennedy sister said to Marilyn at the Cal-Neva Lodge. When Patricia relayed the substance of their dialogue to Peter, he, in later years, spread the wording of this remarkable exchange. The phraseologies are as Peter remembered them, and may not be exact, but the points Patricia made are reported here as Peter relayed afterward:

\*\*\*

MARILYN: I've been used and abused by your brothers, both Jack and Bobby, and I don't think I could let them get away with it. Each of them at different times promised to leave either Jackie or Ethel and marry me.

PATRICIA: Let's come to our senses. There's no way in hell that Jack or Bobby would leave their wives and destroy their political futures by getting divorced and marrying you. Jack wants to run for the presidency again in 1964. He wants Bobby to run as his vice president. They plan to dump Lyndon Johnson. Bobby then wants to run for president in 1968. Please, be reasonable. They can't give that up, either one of them, to marry you.

MARILYN: Then why did both of them make promises they didn't plan to keep?

PATRICIA: When horny guys are trying to seduce a beautiful blonde goddess, be it Lana Turner or Jayne Mansfield, they'll say anything. Promise anything. Marilyn, let's face it: You've been around the block. You've been in Hollywood long enough to know what the score is.

MARILYN: But I fell in love with them, especially Bobby. He was the best, the most tender. Jack was always in a hurry.

PATRICIA: You'll have to get over it. Bobby and Jack are racing through their lives. They've got big plans, not only for themselves but their country. They have to give priority to their own ambitions and plans. They can't let anything, or anybody, stand in their way.

MARILYN: A promise is a promise.

PATRICIA: What does a promise from a man mean? When I married Peter, he promised me he'd be faithful. That vow lasted for less than twelve hours. Just because a man promises something over pillow talk is valid until he rises from the bed, puts on his pants, zippers up, and heads out the door.

MARILYN: Sam Giancana doesn't like Bobby and doesn't care much for Jack either. Because of his influence in Chicago, Sam claims he won the election for Jack. And now Bobby is pulling a double cross, trying to get him put in jail. He wants revenge on them. Sam said he would privately arrange a press conference if I wanted to expose Jack and Bobby.

PATRICIA: Don't be out of your mind. You're playing with fire. Don't trust Giancana to do anything. He'd use you and then have you knocked off the following day. Don't you see how dangerous it is for you to hang out with Giancana? In fact, I'm leaving Frank's god damn hotel just because he has let Giancana check in. Run from him! You'll regret it if you don't. He could have you killed!

MARILYN: Sam would never do that. He's actually quite sweet and cuddly when he wants to be.

PATRICIA: I'm sure Hitler was, too, with his dog and Eva Braun, in that order. You don't need Giancana, Bobby, or Jack. Peter told me you're having a wonderful fling with this hot Mexican screenwriter, José Balanos. Is that true?

MARILYN: Yes, even in the midst of all my troubles, a girl needs to satisfy her sexual needs, and José is the man to do it. He's incredible.

PATRICIA: Then settle down with him.

MARILYN: But I want more. I wanted to be First Lady like Jackie.

PATRICIA: Now you're dreaming. Don't threaten my brothers and don't get involved with Giancana any more than you already have. I've lived around powerful men such as my father ever since I was born. You are a mere movie star. You don't control empires. You can't pick up a phone and order one of your henchmen to have someone killed.

MARILYN: I bet Bobby sent you here just to scare me.

PATRICIA: Perhaps he did. Someone had to.

MARILYN: GET OUT! I don't trust you.

PATRICIA: I'm leaving, but you were duly warned.

MARILYN: I'm not afraid. I'm Marilyn Monroe. No one would dare harm me because I'm too high profile.

PATRICIA: Being high profile won't save you. Jack is the most famous man in the world, and every day of his life, he's faced with the possibility of assassination.

Patricia Kennedy Lawford could have written one of the 20th century's most scandalous memoirs, but her discretion won out.

# Black, One-Eyed, and Jewish

## SAMMY DAVIS JR.

"We were blood brothers in spite of our different skin colors," **Sammy Davis Jr.** said. "But when I did something to piss Frankie off, and I never knew what that would be, he showed me the highway."

**Frank Sinatra** was uncomfortable about Sammy's lusting after white women, although he was far from being a bigot—in fact, just the reverse. But he realized that in the 1950s and 60s, such a pursuit of blondes not only could damage Sammy's career but perhaps threaten his life.

Once, Frank told fellow Rat Packer Dean Martin, "Sammy has this thing about chasing after my former girlfriends. I know he's gone after Marilyn Monroe. He even sent diamonds to Ava Gardner when he should have used the money to pay his IRS bill. Let's don't even mention the subject of Kim Novak. Smokey seems to feel that if I've had a broad, he's got to go in for sloppy seconds."

Frank was no male beauty himself, but he often kidded Sammy about his looks. Without attributing the quote to columnist Robert Sylvester, Frank, one night during his act in Las Vegas, claimed, "God made Sammy as ugly looking as He could—and then hit him in the face with a shovel."

Even Sammy mocked his own looks: "If God ever took away my talent, I would be a nigger again."

The show must go on for **Sammy Davis Jr.**, with a patch over his left eye which he'd lost in a car accident on November 19, 1954 en route from Las Vegas to Hollywood to record the title song of a new Tony Curtis movie, *Six Bridges to Cross.*

"Here I was, driving a Cadillac, the dream car of every American Negro, and soon both the Caddie and myself were a tangled mess by the side of the road."

At the County Hospital in San Bernardino, Fred Hull, an ear and eye surgeon, delivered the bad news. "Sammy's left eye had been ruptured. Some of the content of the globe of the eye had been lost. I told him I had to remove his eye. Otherwise, in a condition called sympathetic ophthalmia, the damaged eye over a period of time would dilute the power of the good eye.

"He was amazingly calm on hearing the news. He was very brave throughout the ordeal."

# "SAMMY,

## THE GREATEST ENTERTAINER OF ALL"

—Alan King

One afternoon Jack Benny was playing golf with Sammy Davis Jr. "What's your handicap?" Benny asked.

"Talk about handicap," Sammy said. "I'm a one-eyed Negro Jew."

Although he was a world-class entertainer, Sammy Davis Jr. became almost more famous as a member of Frank Sinatra's "Rat Pack."

Frank lived in the age before political correctness. At one point during his onstage introductions of Sammy, he referred to him as "Jungle Bunny." Kinder words were "Smokey the Bear." In front of a Las Vegas audience, Frank said, "You'd better wash up 'cause we can't see you in the dark." In another Vegas appearance, Frank introduced Sammy, "Here's a little black boy who will sing for us."

Frank and Sammy bonded almost from their first meeting in 1941 when he was singing with Tommy Dorsey's band in Detroit. Frank was in his 20s then. He just walked over and stuck out his hand and introduced himself to Sammy.

"That might sound like nothing," Sammy later said, "but it was a big deal in those days. The average top vocalist back then wouldn't give the time of day to a Negro supporting act. Over the next few years, Frank went out of his way to help me along the way. That's the kind of guy he is: a sweet, outgoing, big-hearted soft touch who'd do anything—literally *anything*, to help a friend. But don't ever cross him."

In the Army Sammy had faced strong racial prejudice, which would haunt him for the rest of his life. Although a headliner at The Frontier Casino in Las Vegas, he was not allowed to live there. When he became a star, Sammy refused to work at establishments that practiced racial segregation. In time, he was a key figure in integrating the clubs of Las Vegas and Miami Beach.

Hitting the vaudeville stage at the age of three, Sammy had an uneven career that went from sensational in 1956's *Mr. Wonderful* to slowdown in the late 1960s. In 1954 he lost his left eye in a car accident.

In December of 1967, he appeared on an NBC broadcast entitled *Movin' With Nancy*, in which he co-starred with Nancy Sinatra Jr. They greeted each other with a kiss, one of the first black-white kisses in the history of TV. It shocked the bigots. One newspaper in Mississippi more or less suggested that he should be lynched. "A one-eyed nigger kissing a white woman. How low can television sink?"

For its Christmas issue, *One World*, an African American magazine, wanted to put Sammy—dressed as Santa Claus—on the cover with a celebrity friend. It could have been a male friend such as Frank, but Sammy thought it would attract more attention if it were a beautiful woman.

Both Sammy and Ava should have known in the autumn of 1954 that a white movie star should not pose in the lap of a black entertainer, whispering in his ear what she wanted for Christmas.

Sammy called Ava, and she agreed to be photographed at the Drake Hotel in Manhattan where she was staying. "It was all so innocent," Sammy said. "It was all so public," Sammy later recalled. "Ava's sister was there. Representatives from MGM. Maybe two dozen people in all."

After the shoot, the photographer snapped "private" candid shots of Sammy and Ava—drinks in hand, laughing and talking with each other; one of Ava barefoot resting her foot by Sammy's leg, another of him leaning over her rather possessively. In one he is seen holding Ava's white porcelain hand, in another hovering over her with his arm around her lily-white shoulder.

After that photo shoot, Sammy and Ava sometimes went out together, and were seen at the Apollo Theater in Harlem and at a club called Shalimar.

While both of them were in New York, Sammy was seen coming and going from Ava's suite long after the photo shoot. Even when both of them returned to California, Sammy often was delivered to Ava's home by a chauffeur and picked up the following morning at ten.

Those pictures that Ava and Sammy posed for ended up appearing in the pages of *Confidential* magazine, the leading scandal rag of its day. The exposé magazine clearly suggested that Sammy and Ava were in the throes of a torrid affair.

The article was entitled WHAT MAKES AVA RUN FOR SAMMY DAVIS JR., a play on Budd

Although born in North Carolina, the father of a poor white tenant farmer, **Ava Gardner** had no racial prejudice. When **Sammy Davis Jr.** starred on Broadway in the 1964 *Golden Boy* (upper photo), she went backstage, and in front of cast and crew, gave him a "sloppy wet one."

When Ava and Sammy launched their steamy affair in 1954, she was still married to Sammy's pal, Frank Sinatra, but separated from him. All of America learned of the liaison when *Confidential* exposed the affair. The conservative public of the 1950s was shocked at "a white goddess engaged in a sexual relationship with a black entertainer."

Both Sammy and Ava denied the affair, but pictures taken of the drunken couple at a Harlem nightclub suggested they were lying. When Ava was accused of having "a thing for dark-skinned gents," Frank went ballistic.

The public perception of Sammy changed after the scandal with Ava. As his biographer, Gary Fishgall, put it, "The *Confidential* article depicted Sammy Davis as someone to watch carefully: a cocky, swinging, fun-loving Negro who would stop at nothing to get what he wanted, even when his goal was a glamorous white movie star who had been married to his idol and friend."

Schulberg's novel, *What Makes Sammy Run*. The story also linked Ava with other "colored" entertainers, including Dizzy Gillespie, Cuban mambo king Perez Predo, and Herb Jeffries.

MGM was swamped with letters from former fans, claiming they would never go see an Ava Gardner movie again.

She wanted to sue, but MGM advised her not to. After the dust had settled on that long-ago event, it appears that *Confidential* may have been right. Sammy once boasted to Peter Lawford that he'd been intimate with Ava.

In March of 1955, when the article was published, she was still married to Frank but separated from him.

During an indiscreet radio interview in Chicago, Sammy Davis Jr. claimed that he was a bigger singer than his pal, **Frank Sinatra**. Gossip spread across the continent. Those who didn't actually hear the broadcast got the impression that Sammy, as a black man, was claiming that he was more heavily endowed than Frank.

On all levels, Frank was furious at Sammy. To teach him a lesson, he fired him from his upcoming picture, *Never So Few,* and replaced him with **Steve McQueen**, who had not yet come into his full stardom.

On location, both Steve and Frank (apparently) never got around to seducing the film's leading lady, Gina Lollobrigida, but Frank learned that his fellow Rat Packer, Peter Lawford, had performed fellatio upon Steve.

Steve never actually admitted to the blow-jobs, although he did say, "That Lawford limey is known as the best cocksucker in Hollywood."

Even after Frank had divorced Ava, he went ballistic toward any man who was even seen having a harmless, non-romantic dinner with her. Peter Lawford learned that the hard way. So did Sammy.

"It was all too obvious," Frank said. "All my friends in the Chicago mob interpreted it that Ava wanted black dick for Christmas."

Whether he was lying or not, Sammy went to great lengths to convince a furious Frank that there had been nothing between Ava and himself.

"Frank is not a forgiving person," fellow Rat Packer Joey Bishop claimed. "There was a time he didn't talk to Sammy, didn't talk to Dean."

In a radio interview in Chicago, Sammy was asked who he considered the number one singer in the country.

"I am," Sammy claimed.

"Bigger than Frank?" Jack Eigen, the interviewer asked.

"Yeah," Sammy said.

Frank not only cut off relationships with Sammy, but kicked him off a World War II picture he planned to shoot for MGM, *Never So Few*. The role eventually went to Steve McQueen.

Sammy had had a contract to star in the part for $75,000 but Frank wouldn't budge. Sammy told Peter Lawford that his lawyers had advised him to sue. Peter advised against it. "You don't sue Frank Sinatra if you ever want to work in a night club again." For about a week, Peter later said, Sammy cried night and day.

In the mid-1950s Sammy became romantically involved with "the lavender blonde," Kim Novak. There was still a taboo against miscegenation, even laws against it.

Harry Cohn, head of Columbia Pictures, called gangster Johnny Roselli. "I want you to kidnap the little shit. Scare him half to death."

Roselli's men kidnapped Sammy in Las Vegas and held him for several hours, during which he was threatened. Roselli warned Sammy, "Instead of a one-eyed nigger, we'll turn you into a blind nigger."

Novak at the time was under contract to Cohn. Her romantic link with Sammy provoked widespread condemnation. Cohn was not only in love with Novak, but he was promoting her as Columbia's answer to the love goddess Rita Hayworth, who was aging and had become unreliable.

After his release, Sammy rushed into a marriage to a black dancer, Loray White, in 1958, in an attempt to squelch the controversy. It was an ill-conceived union and soon died.

When his marriage to the African-American woman didn't work out—"She spent too much of my money"— Sammy returned to the pursuit of his first love—hot blonde women. He did this despite the threat of mob violence and the risk of losing his remaining good eye.

Frank had warned him "Don't go there," but Sammy fell under the spell of another blonde actress and succumbed to her charm. She was not just white, but porcelain white, with blonde hair. Born in Sweden, she was the beautiful Mai Britt.

In 1960 he shocked the nation by marrying her.

Mai's most controversial movie was the much-criticized remake of *The Blue Angel* (1959), in which she dared take on the legendary role created by Marlene Dietrich in 1930.

When Sammy married Britt, Frank was his best man. The marriage virtually ended Mai's movie career.

Frank's appearance at the wedding was also attacked. One hatemonger wrote, "Dear Nigger Bastard. I see Frank Sinatra is going to be the best man at your abortion. Well, it's good to know the kind of people supporting Kennedy before it's too late."

When Sammy played at the Lotus Club in Washington, neo-Nazis picketed outside with signs such as "GO BACK TO THE CONGO, YOU KOSHER COON."

Robert Kennedy had asked Sammy not to marry Mai until after the 1960 presidential election, scheduled for November 8, 1960. Consequently, Sammy's marriage took place five days later, on November 13, 1960.

Because of his marriage to Britt, JFK's advisers told Frank to drop Sammy from the list of entertainers scheduled to perform at one or another of the inaugural balls. Sammy never recovered from this snub, and in the early 1970s he switched political camps and supported

Harry Cohn, of Columbia Pictures, was promoting "the lavender blonde," **Kim Novak**, as his new reigning star, hoping to replace Rita Hayworth. He told her, "Remember this, never forget it—you're just a piece of meat in a butcher shop."

What Cohn didn't tell her was that half the men in Hollywood, including Frank Sinatra and Sammy Davis Jr., wanted a piece of that meat.

Her list of alleged lovers is long—Rafael (Ramfis) Trujillo (son of the dictator of the Dominican Republic), Porfirio Rubirosa, Peter Lawford, Prince Aly Khan, John Ireland, Cary Grant, and Sammy Davis Jr. himself.

Sammy became intrigued by Kim when he saw some "racy" photographs that she had posed for when she was a teenager. Somehow he obtained copies of them in 1954 after she had become a star and after Harry Cohn had spent $15,000 to suppress them.

"I don't want a picture, I want the real thing," Sammy said. "And I usually get what I want."

As one of Sammy's biographers, Wil Haygood wrote: "Everything he had, he had to claw for, chase down. But there she was, Kim Novak, pursuing him, wanting to be with him, lying next to him. He did not have to woo. He did not have to send jewelry. She wanted *him*. Not Sidney Poitier, not Frank Sinatra, not Harry Belafonte. Him. The little weasel. The little nigger. Ha. Ha. Ha."

Richard Nixon. In the wake of that change, Nixon, startled, received a tight hug from Sammy on live TV.

Hoping to win support from Black America, Nixon even invited Sammy to sleep over in the White House. Occupying the Queen's Bedroom, Sammy, or so it is believed, was the first African American ever invited there for a sleepover.

"The most controversial wedding of the decade," or so the scandal magazines of the 1950s proclaimed when black **Sammy Davis Jr.** married a blonde Swedish actress, **Mai Britt**.

As Sammy and Frank were known to be supporters of John F. Kennedy in his bid for the presidency, there was fear among political advisers of fallout from this black/white romance. A joke of the day was, "If Kennedy is elected, would he make Sammy Davis Jr. ambassador to Israel or to the Congo?"

Before Mai, Sammy had gone through a sham marriage, two broken engagements, and so many disastrous affairs that he'd lost count. "At last," he told Frank, "I've found someone to love who loves me."

When Sammy left his flu-ridden bride in Los Angeles and flew to San Francisco for a one-man show, the theater manager received eighteen bomb threats and called J. Edgar Hoover of the FBI.

Later, in New York, in anticipation of a show he'd be performing at the Copacabana, Sammy met FBI agents sent by Hoover himself. An agent told him, "We've gotten the word, Mr. Davis, that you're going to be killed tonight."

The greatest amount of hate mail poured in when Sammy starred in *Golden Boy* on Broadway in 1964. He received a Tony nomination for Best Actor. During the run of this play, interracial marriages were forbidden in 31 states, before these laws were ruled unconstitutional.

When Sammy received a threatening letter from a deranged person calling himself *Der Führer*, he read, "You are on my death list." Fearing for his life, Sammy called the FBI.

The Britt/Davis liaison was not destined to last. Eventually neither of them could tolerate the pressure. When Britt found out that Sammy was having an affair with singer Lola Falana, she filed for divorce.

In the late 1960s, as Sammy's career declined, he turned more heavily to drugs. He also entered a bizarre episode of his life, as his behavior and sexual practices became more erratic.

As Frank told Dean Martin, "As the pot, I can hardly call the kettle *black*. I know about the low-lives Sammy hangs with, the extramarital affairs. But when he switched from hash and acid to cocaine and amyl nitrate, that has been too much for me. I've seen too many musicians ruined by heavy drugs."

Jake Austen, in his article, *Sammy Devil Jr.*, writes: "Sammy started his personal relationship with Satan during a 1968 visit to The Factory, a nightclub he partially owned with Peter Lawford, among others."

One night he was invited to a private party at The Factory where he encountered a group of young men and women, each with their pinkie painted in red nail polish, signifying their membership in the Church of Satan.

Founded in 1966 by Anton LaVey, a horror fan with a background in carnival work, ghost-busting, and night clubs, the San Francisco-based ministry combined LaVey's interests in ancient paganism, a media-savvy flair for publicity, and a philosophy of indulgence over abstinence.

Sammy himself described his first meeting at the Church of Satan as "dungeons and dragons and debauchery." All the Satanists were hiding behind hoods or masks. For Sammy, at first it evoked a possible gathering of the KKK.

For the "coven," there was a naked blonde woman chained spread-eagled on a red velvet-covered altar.

He never once believed that the woman was slated for human sacrifice. "That chick was happy," he later claimed in his book. "She wasn't going to get anything sharper than a dildo stuck in her—perhaps a big dick."

During that ceremony in the church, Sammy just enjoyed getting "stoned and serviced." His master fellator at one point took off his hood. Sammy was startled to see that it was Jay Sebring, his allegedly straight hairdresser.

Sebring for a time was the most famous hairdresser in Hollywood, giving that shaggy look to Jim Morrison, for example. Sebring was once engaged to actress Sharon Tate before her marriage to director Roman Polanski. During the Manson family's descent on the Tate/Polanski house for a 1969 massacre, Sebring would be bound to Tate, shot, and then stabbed seven times.

After his first night with the Satanists, Sammy was hooked. "Evil fascinated me. I felt it lying in wait for me. And I wanted to taste it. I was ready to accept the wildness, the rolling in the gutter, and having to get up the next morning and wash myself clean."

Sammy liked the Satanic sex orgies and continued participating for several weeks until he officially joined the Church of Satan. He admitted his links to that organization in his book, *Why Me?*

Although not as much as Sammy, Frank was also a thrill seeker.

One night Sammy invited him to a Satanic gathering. At first Frank refused but finally agreed to attend when he was told he could wear a hood during the entire ceremony.

Somewhere along the way, Frank had learned that Sammy was being fellated by Peter Lawford. Frank ridiculed Sammy without mercy. Accepting this humiliation without a protest, Sammy listened patiently to Frank's harangues, during which time he claimed, "No faggot ever sucked my dick."

When Frank accepted Sammy's invitation for a night of adventure, Sammy saw a chance to get even with the Chairman of the Board.

Through his connections, Sammy rounded up what he called "the three most beautiful transvestites in the world"—one blonde, another brunette, the third a redhead.

In a hidden corner of The Factory, Sammy brought each young "girl" over to Frank and directed each of them to take turns fellating him, instructing the blonde to "ride Frank to the finish line."

After the girls had left and Frank had put back his trousers back on, he told Sammy, "Those chicks gave me the best blow-jobs of my life, and I've known the very best in my day."

At first Sammy had been tempted to tell Frank that he'd been serviced by a trio of men. But, as he later confessed to Peter Lawford, "I didn't dare. I truly think Frank would have had me killed if he'd found out what I did to him that night at The Factory."

Even though Frank never found out the trick Sammy had pulled on him, that night at the Satanic church turned out to be more than Frank wanted to deal with. Slowly he began to withdraw from Sammy, telling Joey Bishop, "Sammy's gone over the edge."

Frank continued to be cordial to Sammy at social or public gatherings, but he ceased to hang out with him privately. "Their bosom buddy days had ended. And this caused Sammy great pain," said Altovise Gore Davis, Sammy's third wife.

The Satanic orgies had been intriguing and in some cases, fun, but he wasn't particularly interested in those devilish games any more. "I got some nail polish remover, and I took off the red fingernail."

243

Then he returned to his adopted Jewish religion.

Removed from his 1980 memoir, *Hollywood in a Suitcase*, Sammy had written, "My interest in the Church of Satan had a short life. But I still have many friends in the church, fellow Satanists. I say this to show that however bizarre the subject, I don't pass judgment until I have found out everything I can about it. People who can put up an interesting case will often find that I'm a willing convert."

After a long illness, Sammy succumbed to cancer on May 16, 1990.

Sammy's last wife was Altovise Gore Davis, an African-American entertainer. The Rev. Jesse Jackson performed their marriage ceremony in 1970.

This would mark Sammy's last marriage, and he would not be faithful to his final wife, often involving her in four-way sexual trysts with others, including porno actress Marilyn Chambers and her husband. Altovise went along with these arrangements because she wanted to hold onto Sammy. As singer Kathy McGee once said, "Sammy had the sexual stamina of a bull. You couldn't be alone in a room with Sammy for five minutes without giving him a blowjob."

Over the decades, Sammy had made millions as an entertainer, but he squandered it all. "But what a hell of a life I had, with everyone from Marilyn Monroe to Ava Gardner crawling under the sheets with me to sample King Kong."

When he died of cancer in 1990, he owed $2,708,901 in unpaid personal income taxes.

Altovise died broke, unable to pay any of Sammy's taxes. Just before her own death, she said, "Everyone thought I was bailed out of my financial troubles by Frank Sinatra, who was said to have given me millions to help me out. Perhaps in his heart, he meant to help me, but I didn't get one red cent from him. Nothing. *Nada.*"

Deserting blondes, at least temporarily, Sammy Davis Jr. decided in London during the 1960s, that black was beautiful. During his appearances in the London stage production of *Golden Boy*, he had three paramours—Lolly Fountain, Lola Falana, and Kim Novak.

Even so, it was Sammy's romps with Mai Britt and Kim Novak that drew the fire of a white neo-Nazi brigade in London. These skinheads picketed Sammy at the Palladium, spewing anti-black epithets at him. He was frequently spat upon when he got into a cab. On two different occasions, sandbags fell suddenly from overhead onto the stage, nearly killing him. During his time in London, a Tory candidate ran for Parliament on the slogan, "If you want a nigger neighbor, vote Labour."

The Palladium had to hire bodyguards to protect Sammy. Through it all, he fell in love with the beautiful, cocoa-colored **Altovise Gore** *(photo above),* He nicknamed her "My Queen Nefertiti."

She became his third wife. In high-heeled boots, she rose to a height of nearly six feet tall, towering over what she fondly referred to as "my beloved midget."

## SAMMY DAVIS PITCHES A SCRIPT TO ELVIS

Backstage, Sammy Davis Jr. and Elvis Presley met during the taping of a TV special on Miami Beach. Unlike Frank, Sammy admired Elvis' music and had great respect for his talent. Knowing that Elvis didn't like Frank, Sammy defended him. "He's the brightest star in show business, but he's got a dark side. Who am I, though, to call someone a darkie?"

Sammy pitched a script he had conceived to Elvis. He wanted to star Elvis along with Butterfly McQueen, who had played Prissy in *Gone With the Wind.*

At first, Elvis thought Sammy was joking. "You'd play a southerner who saves a retarded older black woman, Butterfly, from a mob who tries to burn her house down with her in it because she entertained young white men—and didn't charge."

When Elvis answered, "How many songs do I sing?" Sammy knew he'd come to the wrong actor.

In 1954, it seemed like an "insane" idea, to cast **Frank Sinatra** as a potential assassin of the president in the movie *Suddenly*. But after reading Richard Sale's original screen play, the producer, Robert Bassler, came up with the idea of asking Frank to play the presidential assassin.  Director Lewis Allen tried to nix the idea, claiming "This isn't a damn musical. It's about killing the president."

At the time the movie was shot, **Dwight D. Eisenhower** was sitting in the White House. The script was inspired by his cross-country train trips to Palm Springs to go fishing, although his name is never mentioned in the film. Ike is seen above during his victory speech at the Republican National Convention of 1952, where he'd been nominated as a candidate for president along with his running mate, **Richard Nixon.**

Frank accepted the role, because "I want to show the fuckers that I'm a dramatic actor as well as a singer, and I need a strong, hard drama to follow *From Here to Eternity*."

Frank's sinewy, tightly wound body seemed physically right for the role of the nervous, money-hungry, would-be assassin. "I learned to kill in the war. Only I can do the job because I have no feelings." That is the psycho killer, Mr. Frank Sinatra, talking as he does, most convincingly.

In a touch of irony, a few years later Frank was offered the lead in another movie about a potential presidential assassin. Set for a 1962 release, it was called *The Manchurian Candidate*. In this film, Frank would be on the right side of the law, preventing Laurence Harvey from doing the dirty deed. But since his friend, John F. Kennedy, was in the White House, he met with him privately to see if he had an objections. The president did not.

Actually, JFK had only one question:"What actress is going to play the evil mother? I'd like to suggest Rose. She'd be great in the part."

As a practical joke, Frank sent the script to Rose Kennedy, along with her son's recommendation. She wrote back, "I will not accept the mother role, but I'd like to play the young girl, Rosie, who wants you to date her.  Our love scenes would burn up the screen."

# DID *SUDDENLY* PLANT THE IDEA OF A PRESIDENTIAL ASSASSINATION IN THE MIND OF LEE HARVEY OSWALD?

Gearing up to shoot a president, **Frank Sinatra** shocked his most loyal fans when he played a psychotic monster intent on killing President Eisenhower during his vacation in California. Just as he did in his portrayal of Maggio in *From Here to Eternity*, Frank liked to show the moguls of Hollywood that he could play roles that might, in the 1940s, have otherwise been assigned to John Garfield or Humphrey Bogart.

After John F. Kennedy was assassinated in Dallas in November of 1963, nine years after the release of *Suddenly*, many viewers drew parallels between the film and the real thing.

In his biography, *Sinatra in Hollywood*, writer Tom Santopietro wrote, "Not only are the rifles employed in the shootings similar, but Johnny himself (as played by Frank) is killed, just as Jack Ruby killed Kennedy assassin Lee Harvey Oswald."

In the aftermath of Kennedy's assassination, there were protests demanding that *Suddenly* be withdrawn from circulation.

Four days before the assassination of President John F. Kennedy in November of 1963, the rumored assassin, Lee Harvey Oswald, watched a movie, *Suddenly* (first released in 1954), starring Frank Sinatra in an unlikely role.

This *film noir*, directed by Lewis Allen, also featured Sterling Hayden and James Gleason. Frank played John Barton, a hired assassin who takes over the Benson home as a perfect location to ambush the president when he is scheduled to pass through this small town.

In fairness, it should be noted that some historians claim that Oswald saw another assassination film, *We Were Strangers*, and not *Suddenly*. However, *Suddenly* was known to have played for two months at a movie house in the winter of 1954 and '55 in New Orleans, where a teenage Oswald, a borderline juvenile delinquent, often saw every movie that opened at that certain theater.

For the most part, *Suddenly* received critical praise, the *Hollywood Reporter* claiming, "As an assassin piece, Sinatra superbly refutes the idea that the straight role potentialities in *From Here to Eternity* was one shot stuff. In *Suddenly*, the happy-go-lucky soldier of *Eternity* becomes one of the most repellent killers in American screen history."

After the assassination of JFK, *Suddenly* was withdrawn from circulation. Most critics claimed that Frank was behind such a move, but actually he had no say in the matter. The film was owned by United Artists, over which Frank had no control. However, the copyright on *Suddenly* was not renewed, and it is now in the public domain.

Five years after the release of *Suddenly*, a novel, *The Manchurian Candidate*, was published by Richard Condon, a former Hollywood press agent. It had a remarkably similar ending as *Suddenly*. The book also featured a mentally disturbed former war hero who, at the end, uses a rifle with a scope to shoot at a presidential candidate.

In *The Manchurian Candidate*, released in 1962, the film also starred Frank, but this time his character tried to prevent an assassination being committed by Laurence Harvey.

*The Manchurian Candidate* would not have been made were it not for the friendship that existed between Frank and JFK. At first, United Artists president Arthur Krim refused to put up the money for the film. But director John Frankenheimer worked with Frank to get the movie greenlighted.

When Frank and Frankenheimer moved ahead with the film, Krim issued a threat. "Not only will United Artists not make this film, but I'll call every studio in Hollywood and tell them not to shoot it. The Condon book will never make it to the screen."

Krim feared that such a film might be terribly painful for the president, and might even trigger a potential assassin psychotic who watched it.

Frank still had enough clout back then to call the White House and get through to JFK, who told him he had read the book. "I have no objection to you making a film of it. In fact, I would consider it a favor to me if you guys shot it—forgive the Freudian slip."

Frank urged the president to call Krim and ask him to make the film, although JFK never explained why it would be a "personal favor" to him if UA released such a controversial movie.

Cast as the brainwashed veteran, Harvey pursued Frank throughout the filming. "You're the King of Music," Harvey told him. "Just for one night, let me be the Queen to your King."

Frank consistently turned him down, but one afternoon on the set he came over and tongue-kissed Harvey in front of the crew. Harvey was shocked and so was the crew.

FRANK SINATRA
LAURENCE HARVEY
JANET LEIGH

THE MANCHURIAN CANDIDATE

The controversial film *The Manchurian Candidate* starred Frank Sinatra, Laurence Harvey, and Janet Leigh, but some critics claimed that the real show-stopper of the film was Angela Lansbury, arguably in her greatest role.

In the lower photo, **John F. Kennedy** in an open limousine was photographed by an onlooker only minutes before he was fatally shot in Dallas in November of 1963. Beside him is **Jackie Kennedy**, worried about her hair and her pink pillbox hat.

After JFK's assassination, *The Manchurian Candidate* disappeared from public viewing. Amazingly, Frank's business partners purchased the film's distribution rights in 1972, but someone forgot to tell Frank that he owned them.

It wasn't until 1986 that he learned that he controlled the film, which was then re-released to find a newer and younger audience.

Frank was playing a practical joke. He'd just given an interview claiming that Harvey was a dedicated communist and was addicted to kissing men in public.

Harvey adored the deep throat kiss, but wasn't amused at what Frank said during the interview.

When the film was completed, Frank sent a copy of *The Manchurian Candidate* to the White House where Bobby, Jackie, and JFK viewed it. Jackie found it too gruesome and walked out in the middle of it. She later claimed she had nightmares. The next morning she asked her husband what he thought of the movie.

"A real thriller," he said, "I was on the edge of my seat. Could it happen to me? Anytime any nutbag in America wants to trade his life for mine, he can do so."

Once again, Frank, according to rumor, withdrew the film from circulation following the shooting of the president. *The Manchurian Candidate* was rarely shown after November of 1963, but was previewed on CBS on September 16, 1965, followed by a second showing later that season. NBC picked it up in the spring of 1974 and again in the summer of 1975. Frank acquired distribution rights in the late 1970s, and he later allowed a theatrical re-release.

Although Frank wanted (of all stars) Lucille Ball to play the role of the mother, she turned it down. Angela Lansbury accepted, and in 2007 her character of the incestuous Mrs. Iselin was voted by *Newsweek* as one of the ten greatest villains in cinema history.

In 2004, another version of *The Manchurian Candidate* was released, this one starring Denzel Washington with Meryl Streep taking the villainous role of the mother. Raymond Shaw was cast as "The Manchurian Candidate."

One night in Palm Springs, Frank hit a diner in the face who came up to him with the charge that his playing a presidential assassin "planted" the idea in the brain of Lee Harvey Oswald. When the patron threatened to sue, Frank had his attorneys settle $10,000 on him.

Two killers—one reel, the other real—are depicted above.

On the left, British actor **Laurence Harvey** appears in *The Manchurian Candidate* as a would-be assassin. In the photo on the right, **Lee Harvey Oswald** poses for this mug shot after his arrest in Dallas on suspicion of killing President John F. Kennedy.

The film was made only months before JFK's assassination. Although at the time of his death, JFK had "iced" Frank out of his life, Frank still harbored a love for the slain leader.

After the assassination, Frank's valet, George Jacobs, claimed, "Sinatra wondered aloud (though not too loud) if Mr. Sam Giancana, who knew Jack Ruby from the strip-club circuit in which he had a hand, could have had something to do with it."

# Frank & Elizabeth Taylor

## THEIR ABORTED LOVE CHILD

At **Frank Sinatra**'s villa in Palm Spring, **Elizabeth Taylor** rose from the pool completely naked and reached for a terrycloth robe. As both Frank and her husband, Richard Burton, checked out her not-altogether-fallen breasts, she excused herself "to make myself even more beautiful than I am for dinner."

Both Frank and Richard continued to lie nude in the fast-fading afternoon sun of the desert.

"Sinatra," Richard said, "you've always managed to seduce women by the size of your cock and your baby blues. For my most wicked sexual escapades, I rely on my quick wit. When seductions are particularly difficult, I recite poetry. That gets them every time."

Suddenly, through a drunken haze, Richard confronted Frank. "I really want to know something. What was it like fucking Elizabeth when she was much younger, more beautiful, and her cunt a lot tighter?"

Frank looked stunned. "I don't think I've ever been asked such a graphic question. I hope that's not you at your most poetic speaking. Of course, Elizabeth was more desirable back then. And I'm sure you were a more desirable catch then too, back in 1943 when Laurence Olivier and Noël Coward were sucking your cock."

Burton rose quickly from his chaise longue. "See you guys at dinner."

# Ms. Violet Eyes Meets Ol' Blue Eyes

Of the many movies that starred **Elizabeth Taylor**, Frank Sinatra preferred her screen interpretation of Maggie the Cat (depicted above) in Tennessee Williams' controversial *Cat on a Hot Tin Roof*.

One night in front of Rat Pack members Peter Lawford and Sammy Davis Jr., Frank told them, "Look at me, an aging bag of bones. Yet, believe it or not, the three most desirable women on the planet—Ava Gardner, Elizabeth Taylor, and Marilyn Monroe—fell for me. Each of them wanted to marry me.

"Ava got me, of course, but she regretted it.

"And somehow, I couldn't see myself married to Marilyn. She'd be drunk or drugged most of the time.

"But with Elizabeth, I can only imagine what marriage to her would be like. At the rate her career is going, and at the rate my career is not going, I suspect I'd soon be called Mr. Elizabeth Taylor."

*"Like those crazed bobbysoxers of the 1940s, Elizabeth had this thing for Frank Sinatra. She played his recordings all the time in her dressing room and was wild about him. She once told me, 'I wanted Frank to be the man to take my virginity, but, alas, Peter Lawford beat him to it. It took a little time, but Elizabeth finally got her man, Frankie. Like all our fantasies, it didn't exactly work out the way she dreamed.'*

**—Roddy McDowall**

Nearly all, if not all, Elizabeth Taylor biographies seem unaware of her affair with Frank Sinatra, which occurred in the closing months of her marriage to British actor Michael Wilding, her second husband.

The source for details about the Taylor/Sinatra affair was Peter Lawford, after he was "banished" from Frank. Ironically, Peter was the subject of a biography called *The Man Who Kept the Secrets* by James Spada. Over the years, the "keeper" let a lot of those secrets out of the bag.

Elizabeth had fallen in love with Peter when they made *Julia Misbehaves* in 1948 with Greer Garson and Walter Pidgeon.

A "child woman" at the time, just turned "sweet sixteen," Elizabeth developed a crush on Peter. "He was oh, so very, very handsome, and so very sophisticated.

Peter was the first man she ever knew sexually. It all happened when he invited her to the beach one weekend. There are those who claim Elizabeth lost her virginity to Nicky Hilton on her wedding night, but Peter, although drunk at the time, told friends, "The cherry was mine."

MGM mogul Louis B. Mayer had warned Peter not to "foul" Elizabeth, but he did anyway. "How could I resist?" he later said. "She threw herself at me. I never did have any will power."

That following Monday morning, he became frightened because he learned that Mayer had said that the first actor who took Elizabeth's virginity on the lot would be kicked out of MGM and would never work in Hollywood again.

When Peter heard that, he was very resentful. "That old sod," he said. "Mayer wants to deflower Elizabeth himself." But he finally gave in to pressure, wanting to save his film career at MGM. It was with some reluctance he called Elizabeth to break off their affair before it had really begun. "It cannot be," he said. "Come back in three or four years, and we'll start all over again."

She broke down and cried for three days, according to her mother, Sara Taylor, who wanted Elizabeth to marry Peter in spite of her tender age.

Years later, it was Peter who told Frank that Elizabeth's marriage to Wilding was all but over. "They sleep in different rooms and go for days without speaking to each other. You always claimed you wanted her. Here's your chance to move in."

Frank was ready to take the challenge, because he'd become aware that Elizabeth had had a schoolgirl crush on him.

When he heard that Wilding and his male lover, Stewart Granger, were going away for the weekend, Frank called Elizabeth and invited her to Palm Springs. At first she seemed reluctant to accept, but after a bit of urging gave in. He told her he'd send a limousine to pick her up.

Arriving in Palm Springs, she was greeted by Frank, who wore an orange shirt and white shorts. Her first words to him were, "As you probably know, I adore Monty Clift. You guys were terrific in that *Eternity* picture. But he warned me not to fall in love with you, because he is already in love with you himself."

"Monty's loss will be your gain," he told her, kissing her on the lips.

Peter pressed Frank for details of that torrid weekend. Peter would later learn a lot more, but for the moment Frank said, "I taught her how to drink Jack Daniels."

Later, Peter learned that they had sex "more than once," but a lot of the time was spent listening to her moaning about her loveless marriage to Wilding. In his own sad tale of woe, Frank told her how much in love with Ava he had been—"and still am"—but he added, "She's

In *Julia Misbehaves*, the aging queen of World War II soapy dramas, **Greer Garson** (*top photo, left figure*) confronts the star of tomorrow, **Elizabeth Taylor** (*right figure*). That's **Peter Lawford** standing between them.

"Before she fell for Frank Sinatra," Peter recalled, "She had two crushes—one on me, another on the singer Vic Damone. She virtually stalked Vic. Her busts had fully developed. She practically took over from sweater girl Lana Turner, another one of my passions. Elizabeth's legs were flabby, especially below the knees."

Elizabeth recalled that when she was dating Peter (*right figure in lower photo*), they would go on weekends to Los Angeles' Will Rogers State Beach. As she told Richard Burton and Frank, "He would almost ignore me checking out those hard bodies and bulging crotches. He made a lot of trips to the men's room."

a woman not to be trusted. If you took Ava on a honeymoon, you'd surely catch her at some point in the bushes going down on one of the busboys."

Back in Hollywood, as Elizabeth's marriage to Wilding entered its final death rattle, Frank dated her very secretly and privately. If he feared exposure, he asked Peter to go along with them, serving as a beard.

Peter at the time had his own diversions and didn't really want to do that, but Frank persuaded him. "If you'll do this for Elizabeth and me, I'll let you blow me occasionally when I get horny and there's no broad around."

"You got yourself a deal, big boy," Peter told him.

One night a waiter at a dive in San Fernando Valley must have tipped off a reporter and a photographer from a newspaper. They arrived on the doorstep to the restaurant, hoping to capture Elizabeth and Frank dining together. But the manager alerted Frank, who slipped Elizabeth through the kitchen and out the back entrance. Peter exited from the restaurant's front entrance by himself. "Dining alone tonight," he told the press.

It was not a happy marriage, but **Elizabeth Taylor** agreed to pose for a family portrait with her second husband, **Michael Wilding**. She is holding their first child, Michael Howard Wilding Jr.

Another actor, the doomed John Garfield, had warned Michael that if he married the young goddess of Hollywood, he would become known as "Mr. Elizabeth Taylor." That prophecy came true.

Even Elizabeth later admitted that her second husband was a father figure to her, and, as such, he was doomed to outlive his usefulness after she matured. "I escaped to find peace and tranquility with him," she told Frank Sinatra. "Better that than getting the shit beat out of me every night by Nicky Hilton."

The British actor confessed, "In the beginning, I tried to guide her and influence her, but after a few months, when I opened my mouth, she told me to shut up. In contrast, Marlene Dietrich could listen to me for hours, or at least pretend to."

When Elizabeth tried to get serious about their affair, Frank more or less deflected it, since it was obvious she wanted to marry him after she divorced Wilding.

Both of them were lounging nude by the pool one Sunday afternoon when she asked him, "What is your philosophy of life?"

"You gotta love living. Dying's a pain in the ass."

As the days went by, Elizabeth was growing more and more dependent on Frank, although he was not really in love with her. Without a warning, she arrived on his doorstep one night. Fortunately, he was alone that evening. He secretly had been dating other women during the course of his affair with Elizabeth.

He was alarmed at her physical condition and demanded to know what had happened. Resting on the sofa in his living room, she revealed that she'd told Wilding, "I'm in love with you. I also told him I want a divorce. He's not a violent person, but he slapped my face. I fell back across our coffee table."

"The son of a bitch," Frank said. "I could kill him for that. In the meantime, I'm going to get help for you."

Frank called his doctor who got her slipped into the Cedars of Lebanon Hospital where she lingered for five days without telling Wilding where she was.

When Wilding showed up at Frank's apartment, demanding to know where his wife was, Frank slugged him.

Wilding wasn't the only one to experience Frank's infamous temper. Three weeks after Elizabeth's release from the hospital, he was dining with her at one of his favorite restaurants in Palm Springs. The manager knew to keep fans away from Frank's table, because he was aware of how much the singer hated autograph seekers.

However, that night the manager failed to alert a new waiter. It was the star-struck waiter himself who asked both Elizabeth and Frank for their joint autographs. When Frank refused, Elizabeth graciously agreed. She turned to Frank, saying, "I'll sign for both of us." In large letters, so that he could read it, she wrote ELIZABETH SINATRA.

That was too much for him to take. Right in the middle of the meal, he told her, "We're going back to the house."

"I want to finish my meal," she said.

"Then take a god damn taxi home," he said, barging out of the restaurant.

In a rather drunken state, she arrived about an hour and a half later. A servant let her in. "Where is that Italian bastard?" she shouted.

"He told me to tell you he's driving back to Los Angeles tonight," the servant said. "You can stay on and use the house if you wish to."

She left the following morning. Back in Los Angeles, her calls to Frank went unanswered. When she phoned Peter, he told her Frank had gone to New York.

Elizabeth wanted Frank to abandon all other commitments and romantic entanglements and marry her, but he adamantly refused.

In desperation, she called Peter and told him the sad news. "I'm pregnant. A doctor has just informed me of that lovely tidbit. Maybe Frank will come to his senses. Having a kid out of wedlock doesn't go over big in Hollywood, as you know. I don't want to become another Ingrid Bergman denounced from the floor of the United States Senate."

On hearing the news, Frank bluntly told her, "I'm not going to marry you. We'll have to see that that kid in the oven doesn't become fully baked."

He arranged the abortion. Details are lacking, and Peter

Elizabeth Taylor, among other actresses, looked to the case of **Ingrid Bergman** *(right photo above)* to learn a lesson as to how a movie career could be destroyed. While married to Petter Lindstrom, she'd had an affair with the Italian director, Roberto Rossellini, who had impregnated her.

In the words of her biographer, Donald Spoto, "Joan of Arc was branded a witch and burned at the stake in one quick miscarriage of justice. Ingrid of Hollywood was branded a whore and unjustly burned in the fires of public castigation."

On March 14, 1950, the most vicious attack on a woman ever uttered on the floor of the U.S. Senate, **Edwin C. Johnson** *(left photo)*, Democrat of Colorado, called Ingird a "free love cultist and an apostle of degradation." He wanted her exiled from the United States, claiming that she was "a powerful influence for evil."

He also denounced Rossellini, calling him "a narcotic addict, a Nazi collaborator, and a black market operator." He wanted the Senate to pass a bill to license actresses in motion pictures, allowing only those with "moral decency" to work in films. The bill did not pass.

was not forthcoming with what happened. It is believed that Frank's friend, gangster Mickey Cohen, played a significant role. Somehow Cohen could pull off these things, as he did when he made provisions in Chicago for Judith Campbell Exner to abort the child fathered by John F. Kennedy.

One night at a party when Elizabeth encountered Ava Gardner, these two drunken dames were in a confidential mood. Elizabeth admitted to Ava that Frank had insisted she abort their child, even though she wanted the baby.

"I'm an old hand, darling, at aborting Frank's children," Ava said.

When Simon & Schuster published Kitty Kelley's *Elizabeth Taylor: The Last Star* in 1981, all references to her having an abortion of Frank's child were deleted. However, when Bantam published Kelley's biography of Frank, *My Way*, in 1986, they let the reference of Elizabeth aborting Frank's baby stand.

Even before Kelley's book was published, Frank ridiculously claimed in court that "he and he alone, or someone he appointed, could write his life story, but no one else was allowed to do so." Such a claim would virtually shut down the whole industry of celebrity books. Of course, a saner judge dismissed such a preposterous case.

In the immediate aftermath of her abortion, Elizabeth was very bitter toward Frank and wanted nothing to do with him. But since they were thrown together at several social functions, sometimes involving Ronald and Nancy Reagan, they mutually decided to forget about the mistakes of yesterday. They became friends again, especially when they acquired other lovers like Richard Burton and Mia Farrow.

Sharing a night on the town together, **Frank Sinatra and Eddie Fisher** were fiercely competitive as crooners.

When Elizabeth Taylor dumped Eddie, his promoter, Milton Blackstone, tried to use Frank as a role model for Eddie's hoped-for comeback.

"Look at Sinatra," Blackstone said. "He was down and out after his marriage to Ava broke up. Now he's back on top again. Don't lose your confidence. Sinatra did, but now he's got it back. His fans deserted him, but they're coming back. The same thing will happen to you. And if you play it right, your comeback will be even greater than Sinatra's."

One of the strangest dinners Elizabeth ever attended was in 1957 when she was accompanied by her husband, producer Mike Todd, to a dinner at the Beachcombers along the California coast. Guests included Eddie Fisher, his wife, Debbie Reynolds, Frank Sinatra and his date, Lauren Bacall. Bacall's husband, Humphrey Bogart, had recently died, and Bacall wanted Frank to marry her, although he seemed like a reluctant bridegroom.

What set out to be a peaceful dinner among friends turned violent, as Debbie denounced Eddie for "whore-mongering," and Frank turned violently on Bacall and her hopes for a wedding ring.

Elizabeth also got angry because no one paid her any attention, and she was used to being the main attraction.

The dinner was staged by Jule Styne, the England-born songwriter and composer.

As the evening progressed, it became a total disaster, as tempers flared and the tension became almost unbearable. The first to leave, Todd jumped up and reached for Elizabeth's hand. He turned to his host, Styne, "What a simply fabulous evening. Let's get together and do this again—make a weekly ritual of it."

There was a certain irony to this dinner. Years previously, Elizabeth had been impregnated by Frank and wanted to marry him herself. Within a few short months, Todd would die in a plane crash, and Fisher would divorce Debbie and marry Elizabeth.

Frank and Elizabeth, having not seen each other in months, decided to join forces once again, but not romantically. Both of them agreed to co-star in a film version of Frank Gilroy's Broadway play, *The Only Game in Town*.

When Elizabeth became ill, the film was postponed, and Frank moved on. By the time she recovered, he was no longer available.

Although he'd later regret it, Warren Beatty signed on to fill in for Frank. The lead was the gritty role of Joe Gray, a compulsive gambler. During the filming, director George Stevens drank a lot of martinis and went to bed drunk at night.

Apparently, Beatty and Elizabeth didn't have an affair during the making of the film, though he did occasionally commute to Geneva where Julie Christie, his girlfriend, was shooting *In Search of Gregory*. Back in Paris, where *The Only Game in Town* was being shot, he occupied his nights with French sex kitten Brigitte Bardot and Princess Elizabeth of Yugoslavia, whom he had met through Elizabeth and her then-husband Richard Burton.

Through a connection, Frank asked that a rough cut of the film be sent to him. At his Palm Springs villa, he screened it for visiting friends, including Rosalind Russell. She later said, "Frank sat through only twenty minutes of it before heading for his bedroom. As he was leaving he said, 'Thank God, I didn't film this piece of shit.'"

He agreed with the assessment of Richard Cohen, writing in *Women's Wear Daily*: "Taylor has let herself go to fat. You cannot accept her as a Las Vegas dancer, and you cannot accept her as the girlfriend of a sexpot like Beatty who often looked more like her son than her lover."

In 1970, Frank invited Elizabeth and

**Can this marriage last?**

**Elizabeth Taylor** was supposed to have starred in the dismal *The Only Game in Town* with Frank Sinatra, but that deal fell through. **Warren Beatty** *(left figure in upper photo)* was called in as a substitute to make this box office flop. As critics noted, Elizabeth was horribly miscast—for one thing, she was far too fat to play a Las Vegas showgirl, especially with her stumpy legs.

At this point in their relationship, Frank admitted, "I couldn't care less if Beatty shacks up with Elizabeth—she's not my property." Knowing that the handsome young actor was catnip for women, Richard Burton was jealous, fearing that the two stars would embark upon a torrid affair. "I don't like Elizabeth working without me," he told an interviewer.

Elizabeth was not the only actor who had made a disastrous choice in the role she accepted. At the same time Elizabeth was doing her Vegas showgirl gig, **Richard** *(left figure in lower photo)* was camping it up and playing it gay in one of the worst movies of his career, *Staircase*, opposite **Rex Harrison** *(right figure in lower photo)*.

Darryl Zanuck had high hopes for both pictures. He was bitterly disappointed with *Staircase*, which lost $5.8 million. *The Only Game in Town* racked up losses of $8 million.

Burton to spend time with him at Rancho Mirage, California. Later Burton claimed, "He kept looking at her throughout our little vacation as if he wanted to fuck her. She stared back at him with her best come-hither Elizabeth Taylor *femme fatale* look. Both of them behaved outrageously. I got so pissed at one point that I considered ripping off her pants and yelling, 'Frank, come and get it while it's hot.'"

As Burton later recalled to Ava Gardner, "Frank, Elizabeth, and I spent most of our little holiday lying naked around the pool. I figured it was all right for Elizabeth to appear naked before us. After all, it was nothing Frank hadn't explored intimately. Of course by 1970, things had sagged a little bit since the 50s. But what the hell! Show business people are known for letting it all hang out—no false modesty with us."

Although Elizabeth and Frank continued to see each other mainly at parties over the years, her last known phone call to him was in 1985. She wanted his help in lending his star power to the first major AIDS benefit. Michael Jackson, even Betty Ford, had signed up.

Rather adamantly, he turned down her plea. "Elizabeth, this is one of your lame-duck causes. Back away from it. It's going to hurt you. With the double stigma of homosexuality and AIDS, nobody in this town wants to be a part of it."

She responded in anger, "Without homosexuals there would be no Hollywood, no show business."

Without a good-bye, he hung up the phone on her.

During the 1960s, **Richard Burton and Elizabeth Taylor** *(left photo)* reigned as "the world's most notorious married couple."

In Paris, they spent several evenings with the exiled **Duke and Duchess of Windsor** *(right photo)*, who had held that title during the 1930s. The Duke, during the period he held the British crown as King Edward VIII, abdicated "to marry the woman I love," the American divorcée, Wallis Simpson. "The beating the Windsors took in the press made Richard and me look like chopped liver," Elizabeth later asserted.

Over dinner one night, Elizabeth admired the "Prince of Wales" brooch worn by the Duchess. Inspired by three feathers and a crown, it depicted the symbol of the small country of Wales, birthplace of Richard Burton himself. "It was one of the few royal jewels Lord Mountbatten left me when he came to take back all the gems, upon the Duke's abdication," the Duchess told Elizabeth.

In a touch of irony, Elizabeth would end up owning the brooch, purchasing it after the death of the duchess in 1986. Elizabeth paid $623,000 for it, maintaining a phone connection with Sotheby's when the brooch was sold at auction.

Although Elizabeth loved the royal parties hosted by the Duke and Duchess, Richard found them boring. He compared the couple to "two tiny figures like Toto and Nanette that you keep on the mantelpiece. Chipped around the edges. Something you keep in the front room for Sundays only."

At a *soirée* on November 13, 1968. Richard, tanked up on three bottles of vodka, grabbed the Duchess and swung her around the room. He later compared himself to a "dancing singing dervish."

Afterward, Elizabeth reprimanded him with, "I can't take you anywhere."

## Michael Wilding Beats La Liz

One night, Frank Sinatra invited Elizabeth Taylor and her English husband, Michael Wilding, to dinner on the Sunset Strip. She criticized her husband's sloppy dress, and he said: "Shut your god damn mouth." As she tried to slap him, he seized her wrist and twisted it.

"You broke my wrist!" she screamed.

Wilding walked out, leaving her alone with Frank.

Frank later said, "It was a mistake for any of Elizabeth's husbands to leave me alone with her."

# Sinatra and His Fellow Rats

## HIGH-OCTANE AMERICAN MACHISMO AT ITS MOST CONFIDENT

They called themselves "The Clan." Actually, Frank Sinatra preferred "The Summit." But to the world, they became known as "The Rat Pack," the hippest guys in town—Frank Sinatra, Dean Martin, Sammy Davis Jr., Peter Lawford, and, the most unlikely rat of them all, Joey Bishop, who was mostly a Borscht Belt comedian with a knack for needling one-liners.

These cool cats had talent, power, and money to spend recklessly. Each of them, except home-to-wife-at-night Joey, also had all the beautiful young women they wanted. Bisexual Peter, of course, also had his pick of all the beautiful young boys as well. For as long as it lasted, until tensions, feuds, betrayals, and time drove them apart, The Rat Pack was dedicated to the pursuit of pleasure in New York, Las Vegas, or Hollywood, their main stamping grounds.

The name "Rat Pack" came from Lauren Bacall, who looked at them "the morning after," while they were disheveled and not quite sober. She was the original "Den Mother," when her husband, Humphrey Bogart, was the "Chief Rat." But when he died of cancer, and her subsequent affair with Frank did not lead to the altar, she pronounced the clannish rodents "dead rats."

The obituary was premature. The pack regrouped itself around Frank, designating him as the new Chairman of the Board. Unofficial "mascots" included Shirley MacLaine and Judy Garland, the latter its most unreliable rat.

The scene above from *Ocean's 11* fields a cast almost as gaudy as the free advertising the film gives to Las Vegas. From left to right are **Richard Conte, Buddy Lester, Joey Bishop, Sammy Davis Jr., Frank Sinatra, Dean Martin, Peter Lawford, Akim Tamiroff, Henry Silva, Richard Benedict, Norman Fell,** and **Clem Harvey.**

As *Newsweek* put it, "The major suspense lies in whether Frank, Dean, *et al*, will get their hands out of their pockets long enough to pull the robbery which the movie is all about."

## "The Kings of Cool" Rule Over Bacchanalian Nights

*"The Rat Pack consists of two Dago singers, a kike comic, a limey swell, a hot puta with red pussy hair, and a slightly off-color entertainer."*
—**Sammy Davis Jr.**
[His reference was to Frank Sinatra, Dean Martin, Joey Bishop, Peter Lawford, Shirley MacLaine, and himself.]

Whenever the Rat Pack—(left to right) **Frank Sinatra, Dean Martin, Sammy Davis Jr., Peter Lawford,** and **Joey Bishop**—appeared at The Sands Hotel & Casino in Las Vegas, the box office quickly sold out of tickets. "We never knew what these guys were going to do," said a former manager. "Strip down to their underwear, maybe rape Angie Dickinson on stage, tell the audience that July Garland was a secret dyke."

Whenever he wasn't performing and wanted to see a show, such as the rare appearance of Noël Coward in Vegas, Frank flew the extended members of the Rat Pack in to stay free at the Sands. "Some of us weren't really into the scene," said David Niven, the English actor. "Gamblers and mobsters, all very *déclassé*."

That former Sands manager also made a startling revelation—at least startling for that time. After endless repetitions, including the appearance of his story within *Variety*, it's not so revelatory any more:

"Once, Frank arrived with, of all people, Katharine Hepburn and Spencer Tracy. Privately, he arranged sexual trysts for them—a beautiful showgal for Hepburn ('absolutely no skin blemishes whatsoever,' she demanded) and a virile young male dancer for that dear old closeted faggot, Spencer Tracy."

*"The Rat Pack is the Mount Rushmore of men having fun."*
—**James Wolcott**

*"The Rat Pack depended for its vitality on what Gore Vidal has called the 'great national nap' of the 1950s—at times Frank and the Clan seemed the only people awake after 10pm."*
—**T.H. Adamowski**

*"All this Rat Pack stuff is pure bullshit, but if it pleases my pal Frank, let him have his fun."*
—**Dean Martin**

*"We ain't figured out ourselves what the hell we do up here. But it's fun, baby. It's cool. We're the Kings of Cool."*

—**Sammy Davis Jr.**

*"These boys just didn't want to grow up. It was great to pretend to be adolescent males of fifteen again. They carried on like a bunch of kids with their drinking and their pratfalls. They endlessly ribbed each other with Smokey [Sammy Davis Jr.] carrying the brunt of the insults because of his color. After midnight they retired to their suites for more drinks. That's when they imported whores of all shapes, sizes, and colors for their orgies."*

—**Rosemary Clooney**

*"I went to bed with Sammy Davis Jr., Peter Lawford, and Dean Martin. But Frank was my favorite. He wanted to know if any of the guys were bigger than he was, although I suspected he already knew that. I told him Sammy was the only one who gave him competition, but that he had even Sammy beat by a country mile. He really got excited hearing that. 'So much for fucking racial stereotypes,' he said. 'And Sammy and I are just little guys except in one department.'"*

—**Sadie Hawkins**, stage name for a mulatto showgirl in Las Vegas

*"He was the best lover I ever had. Oh, could the guy kiss. I've kissed several hundred men in my career, and Frank was among the best. Dean Martin wasn't much for kissing. He wanted to plug you and then slip you a hundred while he was showing you to the door. Both men were hung, especially Frank."*

—**Belle Montana**, showgirl in Las Vegas

*"I was a bit disappointed when he (Frank) took me to bed after his last performance at the Sands. He was very drunk, so I guess I didn't get him at his peak. I also got all this black stuff— it was like ink—on my hand when I ran my fingers through his hair. I found out he'd painted his head with some dye to hide his bald spot. Later, of course, he took to wearing wigs. All in all, not my idea of a good night out."*

—**Lola Mercury**, Las Vegas showgirl

*"When Dean Martin hit Vegas, the cocktail waitresses fought to see who would give him a blowjob."*

—Las Vegas casino employee **Ed Walters**

259

"Women were treated like chattels, and Sinatra was probably the first real star to have groupies. Some women threw their room keys onto the stage. But most of the women he fooled around with were professionals—hookers."

—**Count Guido Deiro**, Las Vegas casino dealer

"Success hasn't changed Frank Sinatra. When he was unappreciated and obscure, he was hot-tempered, egotistical, extravagant, and moody. Now that he is rich and famous, with the world on a string and sapphires in his cufflinks, he is still hot-tempered, egotistical, and moody."

—Columnist **Dorothy Kilgallen**

"The Chinless Wonder, Miss Kilgallen, with the chipmunk face has spoken. What an ugly broad!"

—**Frank Sinatra**

"My forty-five-year-old father survived on three or four hours sleep at night. Talk about endless shenanigans day and night."

—**Frank Sinatra Jr.**

"During the heyday of the Rat Pack, of which I was a notorious member, Frank in the wee hours of the morning seemed to be in a marathon race with loneliness chasing on his heels. I know that feeling."

—**Judy Garland**

Overweight—and in what she described as "my ugliest period"—**Judy Garland** receives a sloppy wet one from **Frank Sinatra**. At one point she wanted to marry him, but he turned her down. Over the years, he waxed hot and cold about her, at times viewing her as "a train wreck," which she was.

"She could have starred in some of Hollywood's all-time great musicals, such as *Annie Get Your Gun,* but film by film, she proved unreliable."

Rather unofficially, Judy was the vice president of the Rat Pack. She later told Lana Turner, "The duties of the veep were to sleep with individual members of the Rat Pack when they couldn't find a better shack-up for the night. I gave the boys a lot of blow jobs.

"Both Frank and I fought our way back on the comeback trail together. He came back but I got lost somewhere along the Yellow Brick Road."

"I'm for anything that gets you through the night, be it a whore, tranquilizers, or a bottle of Jack Daniels."

—**Frank Sinatra**

Lauren Bacall chose the name "The Rat Pack" to describe Humphrey Bogart's circle of friends, a motley crew of late-night partiers and heavy drinkers.

The group got its name when Bacall surveyed the "hangover survivors" of an all-night bacchanal in Las Vegas. "You bums look like a god damn rat pack."

The den, or headquarters, for the original Rat Pack was the Holmby Hills home of Bogie and Bacall. Other members who dropped in frequently were Judy Garland, agent Irving (Swifty) Lazar, writer Nathaniel Benchley, composer Jimmy Van Heusen, restaurateur Mike Romanoff, and David and Hjordis Niven.

The informal social club even had officers: Frank Sinatra, pack master; Bacall, den mother; (Swifty), recording secretary and treasurer; Garland, first vice president; and Bogie, rat-in-charge of public relations. Bogie claimed the rats existed "for the relief of boredom and the perpetuation of independence. We admire ourselves and don't care for anyone else."

Kay Thompson, the singer and author of the Eloise books, was also a member of Bogie's pack. She said, "We were all terribly young and terribly witty and terribly rich and old Humpty Bogus was the clan leader, except he didn't wear a white robe."

After Bogie died of cancer in 1957, the original Rat Pack more or less dissolved. Bacall pronounced it "gone forever," although it would experience a resurrection of sorts.

Bogie's widow, Bacall, soon became Frank's lover. It appeared that the two of them were heading for marriage until Frank got cold feet and abandoned her.

Under his chairmanship, a new Rat Pack would be born, with Frank replacing Bogie as the head of the clan. Bacall, of course, was no longer den mother of the ratters' renaissance.

Frank preferred to call his clan "The Summit." Bacall may have lost out on marriage to Frank, but her name for the group stuck and his more affirming label died in some trash can in Las Vegas.

Ohio-born Dean Martin, former prize fighter, card shark, and small-time gangster, was a key member. He warned Frank, "Don't ever let Jerry Lewis become a member—or else I'm out of here."

Harlem's gift to show business, Sammy Davis Jr., worked the vaudeville circuit when it was in violation of child labor laws. When an inspector came around, he stuffed a cigar in his mouth and pretended he was a 45-year-old midget.

He joined the Army in 1942. Later he said, "That's how I ended up with a nose flat against my face. At least four times a week, I was beaten up by redneck soldiers who called me a nigger."

"In Hoboken, Frank was called a wop or a dago, and I was called a coon, so when we got together we really bonded," Sammy later recalled.

Peter Lawford, brother-in-law of Senator John F. Kennedy of Massachusetts, rounded out the membership, along with comedian Joey Bishop, who was called "The Mouse of

**Lauren Bacall and Frank Sinatra** did have some happy moments together before their relationship turned sour.

Her first husband, Humphrey Bogart, always called Frank "a Don Quixote chasing imaginary windmills across the plains of La Mancha, always ready for a fight at the slightest provocation. Even when he hit it big, he was still that angry little boy from Hoboken with a chip on his shoulder. If the spaghetti wasn't just right, meaning the way his mother cooked it, he didn't send it back to the kitchen. It was likely to land in the waiter's face."

At the end of his life, weakened by cancer in his Holmby Hills house, Bogie began to suspect that his wife's affair with Frank had already begun. He confided his concern to his close friends, Spencer Tracy and Katharine Hepburn. Kate told him, "The heart wants what the heart wants."

the Rat Pack."

Peter and Frank not only drove matching Dual-Ghias *[Editor's note: a rare, short-lived automobile, produced in the United States and modified in Italy between 1956 and 1958. Only 117 of them were ever manufactured]*, they often shared the same woman in the same bed. "I'm sure Peter seized the chance whenever he got it to go down on Big Frankie when Frank didn't have it occupied elsewhere in some puta," claimed Sammy.

Frank admired Joey Bishop's talent as an ad-libber, but was not impressed with his credentials as a stud. "Okay, so he doesn't want to cheat on his wife. So he's not a babe magnet like Deano and me. Every clan needs a court jester."

The birthplace of the Sinatra Rat Pack was Madison, Indiana, a small town used as a setting for the movie, *Some Came Running* (1958), based on a then-new James Jones novel published in 1957. Filming began in August of 1958, the movie co-starring Frank, Dean Martin, and "Rat Pack cuckoo mascot," Shirley MacLaine.

She later claimed that both Frank and Dean came knocking at separate times on her bedroom door. "They were just going through the motions. Neither of them ever put the make on me." Her virginal claims have been widely disputed in certain biographies.

Unlike Bogie's Rat Pack, which was purely social, Sinatra's Rat Pack often performed together, either on stage or in the movies.

Frank set the rules for the club. The drink of choice was a bottle of Jack Daniels. The dress code was crisp white shirts, shiny sharkskin suits, and thin dark ties. Penises were "birds," and women were broads, and you called everybody Charley.

Of them all, Dean was the best example of *menefreghista*, which MacLaine defined as an Italian word "meaning one who does not give a fuck."

The setting for most Rat Pack "conventions" were the gambling casinos and bordellos of Las Vegas. When the Rats were in Hollywood, they had to go home to their long-suffering families.

Las Vegas was more "my kind of town" than Chicago ever was for Frank, "The Knight of the Night."

For a brief time, Tony Curtis was a member of the Rat Pack, but he dropped out. He later told friends, "Both Sammy Davis Jr. and Peter Lawford were after me. Sammy wanted to fuck me, and Peter wanted to blow me. I came between them. At the time I was the hottest kid in town. Everybody—men, women, even chickens—wanted my golden body."

"The Summit," as Frank still preferred to call the clan, launched one of the most popular revues in the history of Las Vegas at the Sands.

Tickets were priced at $3, but often were scalped for $100, an astounding figure for a show in the early 1960s. At one point the 800-seat Copa Room at the Sands had to turn down 18,000 requests for tickets.

"With Sammy," Frank said, "we get our token black and our token Jew, all rolled into one little tap-dancing fool. For the steam room, all of us guys wore white robes. But I ordered one made for Sammy in midnight black."

Of all the Rat Packers performing on stage, Peter was viewed as the least talented—"a *louchemeister* of limited gifts who was there only because he was married to JFK's sister," in the words of one critic.

Unknown to many biographers, Marilyn Monroe became a temporary but rather unstable member of the Rat Pack. She had sexual trysts with Frank, Sammy, Peter, and Dean, and most definitely with another honorary member, John F. Kennedy.

"The Summit" on February 7, 1960, got a surprise visitor. He was presidential candidate,

Senator John F. Kennedy, who showed up one night at the Sands in Las Vegas to see the Rat Pack perform. He had a motive. Like no president before him, he wanted to use celebrities to promote his candidacy, namely, the high-profile Frank Sinatra.

"I'm all behind this guy for president," said Dean Martin jokingly. "What was his name again?"

For his fellow Rat Packers, Sammy lined up the most dazzling array of showgirls in Vegas, most of whom were eager to jump into bed with the Rat packers.

Columnist Dorothy Kilgallen, an enemy of Frank's, wrote that he dated some of the great beauties and stars of their day, including Lana Turner. "Others," she claimed, "were fluffy little struggling dolls of show business and some were gals for hire."

While performing at the Sands at night, the Rat Packers decided to make the first of several movies together. It was called *Ocean's 11* (1960).

Frank starred as Danny Ocean, Martin as Sam Harmon, Davis as Josh Howard, Peter as Jimmy Foster, and Bishop as Mushy O'Connor.

"We didn't want Sammy to get too uppity, so we cast him as a garbage collector," Frank said.

Peter had acquired the rights for *Ocean's 11* for only $10,000, using Patricia Kennedy's money. "She can afford it," he told Frank.

Peter's original investment earned him $500,000, although he'd wanted a lot more, but Frank said "no way, my way."

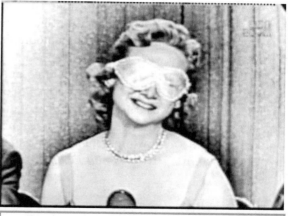

Frank Sinatra detested the newspaper columnist **Dorothy Kilgallen**, referring to her as "the chinless wonder," and satirizing her appearances as a contestant on the TV game show *What's My Line (photo above)*.

Originally, she'd been one of his main supporters in the press, but in 1956 she made him "boiling mad" by writing unfavorable articles about him, calling him "a Jekyll and Hyde dressed in sharpie clothes."

In retaliation, he mocked her in public, even ridiculing her as part of his stage act, which ultimately embarrassed many of his fans.

At his home in Rancho Mirage, Frank installed a dartboard with what he called "the ugliest pictures ever taken of the female face." He attached photos of three columnists: Kilgallen in the center, with Louella Parsons on her left and Hedda Hopper on her right. For amusement, he hurled darts at the board, almost always hitting Kilgallen between the eyes.

When he heard that she'd died, he said, "Guess I'll have to change my nightclub routines." He didn't. For two more years, he continued to attack her, even bringing up the charge that "she'd once lusted for a homosexual."

That was a reference to Frank's rival, the gay singer, Johnnie Ray, whom the police once arrested in a men's room on a morals charge.

One of the most startling lines in *Ocean's 11* is when Peter says, "I think I'll buy me some votes and go into politics." Audiences assumed that was an obvious reference to his brother-in-law John F. Kennedy.

Directed by Lewis Milestone, who had helmed *All Quiet on the Western Front, Ocean's 11* dealt with eleven friends who had known each other during WWII. Pooling knowledge learned in the military, they set out to rob five of the biggest casinos in Las Vegas—all in the same night.

Gay actor Cesar Romero played a slick mobster engaged to Jimmy (Peter Lawford) Foster's mother. Frank sarcastically told Sammy Davis Jr., "At least our bill for prostitutes is being cut down a bit now that Peter is getting all those blow-jobs from Romero."

The female star of the picture, Angie Dickinson, had had a brief affair with Frank. She also had an affair with President Kennedy. "She's a real gentleman and doesn't talk about it," Frank said. According to rumor, she had an autographed photo of JFK. It was inscribed: "Angie, to the only woman I've ever loved."

Sammy was forced to stay at a "colored only" hotel during filming.

He was the first Rat Packer to discover "Hot Box." No one knew where she came from or what her real name was. But for three years before she disappeared from the radar screen, Hot Box was one of the most sought-after and one of the most beautiful hookers in Las Vegas. Unlike most of her fellow prostitutes, she was a real blonde. She may have taken her name from the "Hot Box Girls" in *Guys and Dolls* (1955) that had co-starred Marlon Brando and Frank himself.

Although Shirley MacLaine denied it, she was said to have "fallen hard" for Frank Sinatra when they made *Can-Can* together in 1960. As one biographer noted, "Frank had his fling with her, put her in the movies with him more than once, but that was that."

Frank went from Shirley into the arms of leggy Juliet Prowse. Shirley appeared in a cameo as "Tips Girl" in *Ocean's 11*, but Frank seemed more enchanted at the time with Angie Dickinson, the female lead. He told Dean Martin, "I'll have to share her with the newly elected president of the United States," a reference to John F. Kennedy.

When Frank cast Sammy Davis Jr. in a role of the garbage collector in *Ocean's 11*, he asked him, "Do you mind doing the role in black face?"

During the filming, Frank complained to Sammy and to Dean Martin, "That fucking faggot, Lawford, isn't carrying his weight in our stage shows. He can't sing or dance or do impressions. He's definitely the odd man out, the fifth wheel."

Dean protested, perhaps jokingly, "But Frankie, baby, we need to keep him around to give us blow-jobs in our dressing room."

After Sammy informed fellow Rat Packers that, "I've just had the hottest sex of my life," each of his fellow rodents was eager to sample the charms of Hot Box herself—all except Joey Bishop who was busy at night writing their "ad-libs" for the following evening's performance at the Sands.

As the chairman, Frank got first dibs on Hot Box. He called Sammy the next day. "You're right on the money, Smokey. The broad does—and did—everything. My libido is satisfied for a week, maybe a month. The big toes, the armpits, the rosebud, Hot Box leaves no part of a man's body untouched. She milks you so dry. I've nicknamed her 'The Milk Maiden.'"

After Frank's rave review, Dean Martin and Peter Lawford lined up to sample Hot Box's special charms. In some ways, Sammy seemed the most sexually sophisticated of the crew. One night when he was performing an act of cunnilingus on Hot Box, he rose up, smacking his lips. "You weren't born a woman, were you?"

She broke down in tears and confessed that she'd been born a boy—"But I always looked like a girl." Far from turning Sammy off, he became all the more intrigued and found her even more sexually exciting. "I like a change of pace," he told her. "It's a hell of a lot more fun to have sex with gals who used to be boys. If you're an example, such gals try harder to please a man. They go that extra mile."

As a private joke, Sammy never told Frank, Dean, and Peter that Hot Box was transgendered. He continued to listen to their rave reviews of her sexual gymnastics, only smiling smugly. "I looked like the cat who swallowed the canary," he told Joey Bishop, who also didn't dare tell his fellow rats she was "fucking transgendered."

***

Married to Elizabeth Taylor at the time, singer Eddie Fisher claimed that he was present at the "beginning of the end of the Rat Pack."

While Elizabeth was still filming *Cleopatra*, and while she was shacked up with her co-star Richard Burton, Fisher returned to the Desert Inn in Las Vegas in 1961. That was followed by an engagement at the Cocoanut Grove in Los Angeles. *Le tout* Hollywood showed up for his opening, including Frank and his fellow Rat Packers that he was still calling "The Summit."

Their partying had begun long before Fisher's opening. The singer viewed this as a sort of comeback after eighteen months out of work except for that Vegas gig. As he started to sing, Frank, Sammy, and Peter started heckling him. On wobbly legs, this trio of Rat Packers climbed onto the stage to take over Fisher's performance.

Hopelessly giving up, Fisher took a seat while Frank and his cronies went into a drunken routine, which had once been so popular only a few months before in Vegas. The audience shouted down the Rat Packers, including Frank. The boos became so strong that management sent two burly waiters to remove the drunks from the stage.

With them out of the way, Fisher mounted the stage again and asked his fans, "Join me in singing 'God Bless America' to show President Kennedy we're behind him." That brought loud clapping.

Fisher was a bit too hasty in predicting the demise of the Rat Pack, but the peak of their popularity had certainly faded that night at the Cocoanut Grove.

Frank went on to develop another movie, *Sergeants 3* (1962), with his Rat Pack buddies, Dean Martin, Sammy Davis Jr., Joey Bishop, and Peter Lawford. It was an updating of *Gunga Din*, based on the Rudyard Kipling poem that had first been made at RKO in 1939. From India, the setting moved to the American West of the early 1870s, where three hard-drinking, lusty calvary officers (each played by a Rat Packer) play anti-heroic jokes on each other while rescuing the U.S. Army from an Indian ambush.

It was less successful than *Ocean's 11*, *Variety* calling it "warmed over *Gunga Din*, with American-style Indians and Vegas-style soldiers of fortune."

"Of course, these are not great movies," Frank said. "But you know what's great about them? They make money, and isn't that the name of the game?"

In *4 for Texas* (1963)—each Rat Pack movie had a number in its title—Bette Davis knew what she was doing when she declined a role in the film. Director Robert Aldrich took an instant dislike to Frank's "non-professional attitude," and, almost unbelievably, tried to get the producers at Warner Brothers to fire him.

The only Rat Packer in the cast of this American western comedy was Dean Martin. About the only real comedy in the picture was provided by The Three Stooges.

Female leads were Anita Ekberg and Ursula Andress. Frank himself personally supervised nude screen tests—the first in Hollywood for major stars—but censors removed all nudity from the finished film. "Instead of the breasts, I guess I'll have to flash my dick instead," Frank said. "In that case, we'll need a wide screen."

Peter Lawford was supposed to be cast in *4 for Texas*. Frank had an argument with him and expelled him from the cast and the Rat Pack. Likewise, Peter's proposed role in *Robin and the 7 Hoods* also disappeared.

**Frank Sinatra** is captured in a rare photograph with then-Senator **John F. Kennedy** at the Democratic National Convention in 1960. Columnist Dorothy Kilgallen mocked the friendship, quoting JFK as saying, "Sinatra is no friend of mine. He's a friend of Pat and Peter Lawford."

Frank shot back, "Like hell, the cunt says. I have a white telephone in my house in Palm Springs with a direct line to the White House."

*Time* magazine did not doubt the friendship, but questioned the propriety of it. "Some of JFK's biggest headaches may well come from an ardently pro-Kennedy clique that is known variously as the Rat Pack or the Clan."

Frank told Dean Martin, "I will have access to the White House any time I want it. I can pick up the phone and get Jack on the line any time of the day or night. I'm an unofficial member of the cabinet."

In *4 For Texas*, some critics wondered whether the real plot centered on which of the two women, Andress or Ekberg, would show more cleavage. "Oh, to bury my face between those four suckling breasts," Frank told Dean.

*Time* magazine led the attacks, calling the film a Hollywood Clanbake. "Sinatra and Martin seem bored with the outside world. Sometimes, perish the thought, they even are obviously bored with each other."

The final Rat Pack film, *Robin and the 7 Hoods*, was released in 1964 starring Frank as Robbo, Dean Martin as Little John, and

Sammy as Will. Bing Crosby took the role originally intended for Peter, with Peter Falk filling in for Joey Bishop. Edward G. Robinson, a major star of yesterday, also found himself cast in the film.

A bizarre event happened during filming. There was a funeral scene for Edward G. Robinson's character, and it was shot in an actual cemetery. Frank discovered a gravestone marked John F. Kennedy (1800-1878).

The cast joked about it all morning and even at lunch. But someone turned on a car radio, as news from Dallas claimed that the 20th century John F. Kennedy had been assassinated.

All joking ended, of course, and the cast seemed to go into mourning, especially Frank who locked himself away in his dressing room and wouldn't come out.

Ironically, a kidnapping scene in *7 Hoods* was filmed on the same day that Frank Jr. was kidnapped. It was later cut from *Robin and the 7 Hoods*.

The film introduced one of Frank's standards "My Kind of Town," written by his pal Jimmy Van Heusen with lyrics by Sammy Cahn.

In 2001 a remake of *Ocean's 11* starred George Clooney, Brad Pitt, and Matt Damon, followed by a pair of sequels—*Ocean's 12* in 2004 and *Ocean's 13* in 2007.

It's a debatable point, but the Rat Pack lasted for four years—or maybe six years in the view of some critics. Each of its members had fame, gorgeous women, and a fabulous playground where they ruled the night. Crime lords backed them and, for a while at least, a President of the United States.

But the fire in their bellies eventually burned out, as the clan broke up to go their separate ways. When asked about the Rat Pack before his death on Christmas Day in 1995, Martin said, "I don't remember any such group."

Peter Lawford retained bitter memories about getting expelled from the group up until his death on December 24, 1984.

Sammy Davis Jr. died in 1990. "I guess I knew it was all over when I sang 'Bang! Bang!' in *Robin and the 7 Hoods*. Bang! Bang! It was all over. When we shone, we sparkled—talent, money, any broad we wanted, even power. We had it all to burn, and we had a hell of a time as we set about destroying ourselves."

From left to right, **Frank Sinatra, Dean Martin, and Peter Lawford** were each in uniform for their appearances in *Sergeants 3*, released in 1962. The not-very-bright idea involved a remake of the original *Gunga Din*, based on the Rudyard Kipling poem.

Sammy Davis Jr. was also in the cast. Before his marriage to the blonde-haired Swedish actress, Mai Britt, Frank threw a bachelor party, really a celebrity roast, for Sammy.

Milton Berle appeared in full drag, with high heels, a blonde wig, and black hosiery, impersonating Mai in *The Blue Angel*. Tony Curtis and Peter Lawford embarrassed themselves with a silly duet. After the ribbing, Frank told Sammy he was lowering his advance money, but giving him seven percent of the profits, which he estimated would come to about $250,000.

"You'll need the extra cash to hire bodyguards to protect you from KKK members who will try to shoot you down for marrying a blonde."

"I know you and Mai will want to have kids," Frank said. "The first one will look like Little Black Sambo, but the second one will pop out of the womb looking like Heidi."

## FRANK TANGLES WITH GOD

"When he gets to heaven, Frank's gonna give God a hard time for making him bald."
—**Marlon Brando**

# IN MEMORIUM R.I.P.

# THE RAT PACK

"Listen, you little dago bastard," Frank Sinatra said one drunken night to **Dean Martin**. "You learned to sing by listening to Bing Crosby."

There was always a slightly jealous edge to their relationship, each trying to outdo the other in front of a microphone and in a bedroom with the same women.

"King Rat" **Frank Sinatra** set the agenda for his fellow rodents. Before the Rat Pack, Frank liked to hang out with a group of lackeys, who were after "the booze, the bucks, and the broads."

"A guy could make out like a bandit picking up Frankie's cast-offs," said Jerry Hiller, one of Sinatra's pals. "Of course, some of the guys were petty criminals."

**Shirley MacLaine,** Warren Beatty's sister, was often called "the Lady Rat Packer."

She had a certain jealousy with Angie Dickinson, perhaps feeling the chief rodent preferred her. Although Shirley found Frank mesmerizing, she could also be realistic about him, referring to him as "a perpetual performing child who wants to please the mother audience."

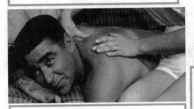

**Peter Lawford** never really fitted into the Rat Pack.

"He's the president's brother-in-law," Frank said to Dean Martin, "but he speaks like an upper-crust British pretty boy, and he's only a degenerate B-movie actor. He brags about his record of cocksmanship—Lana Turner and the like—but those homosexual rumors won't go away."

One day Peter shared with Frank his impressions of bedding Elizabeth Taylor and Marilyn Monroe. "With Marilyn, I stepped in chihuahau poop all over her bedroom, and with Elizabeth Taylor, those fire hydrant thighs reminded me of Nancy Davis" (later, Reagan).

Sometimes jokingly, because he was anything but a bigot, Frank claimed that **Sammy Davis Jr.** was "the Rat Pack's token nigger." When asked if he were a member of "the Clan" (another name for the Rat Pack) Sammy denied it.

"Do I look like I'd belong to an organization called THE CLAN? We're just a group of ordinary guys like Frank Sinatra. Speaking of him, how ordinary can you get? We have an annual meeting to plot world domination—that's all."

Once, stuck in "Fuck All, Utah" (Sammy's term for his movie location at the time) Peter Lawford asked him where he was going.

"I'm gonna catch a lounge act in Vegas. I hear that onstage, Eddie Fisher is going to bottom for Vic Damone."

**Joey Bishop**, the self-styled "mouse" of the Rat Pack, was once asked about his membership in "The Clan."

"Clan, Clan, Clan," he said. "I'm sick and tired of hearing about The Clan. Just because a few of us guys get together once a week with sheets over our heads..."

Frank called Joey "The Hub of the Big Wheel," because he anchored the group onstage and off. Frank was a major influence in launching Joey into the Big Time. In the years ahead, he was known as "Sinatra's comic." Frank dubbed him "the Frown Prince," because of the comedian's perpetual hangdog face.

# How Frank Struck Out With

## "Joltin' Joe" DiMaggio

**Joe DiMaggio** (left) and **Frank Sinatra** were casual buddies, but became more intimately involved when they married the most sought-after women in the world—Marilyn Monroe and Ava Gardner. The four of them were seen drinking and dining together, more drinking than dining.

Ava was rather skeptical of Marilyn, and very acccurately felt that her MM persona was just for show. Once the editor of *Confidential* was asked, "What was the hottest story you ever suppressed?" He immediately answered. "We had it on good authority that Marilyn, Joe, Frank, and Ava once engaged in a four-way."

The chief waiter for room service at the Beverly Hills Hotel delivered two bottles of Jack Daniels to a suite that Frank had rented in his name. He caught all four of them in bed together. Frank slipped him a hundred dollar bill. "There's more where that came from, kid," Frank allegedly said to the waiter.

"Ava and Marilyn seemed to be cuddling and giggling in the middle of the bed," the waiter claimed. "I'm not sure, but I think DiMaggio and Sinatra had wanted to watch them engage in some girl-on-girl action."

# "Where Have You Gone, Joe DiMaggio?"

**Marilyn Monroe and Joe DiMaggio** pucker up on their wedding day, January 14, 1954. The hero athlete and the blonde sex goddess launched a storybook romance that didn't end happily ever after. To their public, it was a match made in heaven. But their close friend Frank Sinatra knew differently. "It was nine months of hell," he said.

From the day of that kiss, seen above, they launched into their own searing drama of powerfully clashing egos. On her wedding night, he told her what it felt like to hear the roar of the crowd when he was "the Emperor of Yankee Stadium."

She told him that she understood the intricacies of baseball, although she'd never actually attended a game. "I learned all about it when I played softball in the orphanage," she claimed.

She told him, "I heard this song about Joltin' Joe DiMaggio. The lyrics went, 'He'll live in baseball's Hall of Fame. He's got there blow-by-blow.' I understand that. That's exactly how I climbed the ladder in Hollywood."

Joseph Paul ("Joe") DiMaggio, nicknamed "Joltin' Joe" or "The Yankee Clipper," spent his entire thirteen-year baseball career playing for the New York Yankees and was elected into the Baseball Hall of Fame in 1955. He was a disappointment to his father, Giuseppe, who wanted all his five sons to grow up to become fishermen.

"But the smell of dead fish makes me puke," DiMaggio told his father who denounced him as a "good for nothing."

In the Depression-stricken 1930s, DiMaggio became America's icon as the immigrant boy who made it big. He became a national hero partly because of an astonishing string of home runs, (a 56 game "hitting streak") he executed between May 15 and July 16, 1941. Despite his acclaim at the time, he styled himself as "the loneliest hero who ever lived."

Except for his baseball fame, DiMaggio is known today for his marriage to the blonde bombshell Marilyn Monroe. The press dubbed them "Mr. and Mrs. America."

Their searing drama, the clash of two powerful egos, was played out in public, although many secrets were not known. Nevertheless, the Monroe/DiMaggio love affair and their subsequent doomed marriage became one of the 20th century's most dazzling pairings. But shadows loomed on their path—her need for endless love, her affairs, his temper, his jealousy. In time the hawk-faced baseball hero and the screen goddess ended their marriage because, as he claimed, "I was tired of sharing my wife—*naked* at that—with the world."

Hovering in the background was Frank Sinatra, the player who would loom large in their drama.

Contrary to many reports, DiMaggio and Frank were not intimate friends. They had a casual relationship. A year older than Frank, DiMaggio also had a Sicilian background. They attended boxing bouts together and occasionally hung out but usually in the company of other cronies, so there were few head-to-head intimate talks.

DiMaggio once called Frank a "blowhard," and the athlete claimed that when he went to a place, he liked to be discreet and keep it a secret. "I would sleep with Marlene Dietrich on the side," DiMaggio once confessed. "But when Sinatra slept with her, he practically took out an ad in the newspapers."

Frank, Marilyn, and DiMaggio were often a "threesome," but it was at a restaurant or club, never in the boudoir, so far as it is known. Of course, one can never be certain of these things among the rich and famous, who are likely to do anything at any time it suits them.

At 20th Century Fox, executives wanted to co-star Marilyn and Frank in *Pink Tights*, a remake of Betty Grable's 1943 *Coney Island*. At first, Marilyn was open to the idea of co-starring with Frank in a film in which her character evolves from a prim schoolteacher to a torch-singing cabaret *artiste*.

From the beginning, DiMaggio had reservations about it, fearing first off that Marilyn and Frank would have an affair.

"It's another dumb blonde part where Darryl F. Zanuck will strip you half-naked and parade you out," DiMaggio said. "I've got money. Marry me. Then you could tell Zanuck to shove those pink tights where the sun don't shine."

He also reminded her that Frank was getting $5,000 a week as opposed to her $1,250. "You'd be the star attraction at the box office, not Sinatra. You're the biggest star at Fox, and they treat you like shit, someone to fuck and discard."

Although DiMaggio socialized with Frank, he never completely trusted him, especially around Marilyn. That caused a rift in the trio. Marilyn didn't always take DiMaggio's advice. Secretly she wanted to do the picture, but one night she decided that she preferred Gene Kelly, not Frank, as her co-star. The role would suit Kelly better.

Finally, DiMaggio prevailed. Without notifying Frank, Marilyn flew to San Francisco where she married her baseball star. No one told Frank. He'd flown in from Rome and showed up at Fox, as agreed, to begin shooting on January 4, 1954. But no Marilyn.

"I've never seen a star so pissed off," said Zanuck. "I was pissed off, too, and I had a temper as big as Frank's. I suspended Monroe."

The rift between Frank and Marilyn took some time to heal. He began to see Marilyn and DiMaggio again, and Frank had a front row seat to watch "the marriage of the century" disinte-

During their honeymoon, **Joe DiMaggio and Marilyn Monroe** discussed his own mortality, or so she claimed to Frank Sinatra and her best girlfriend, Jeanne Carmen.

Joe said, according to Marilyn, "When I reached my thirty-seventh birthday, both my shoulders ached and my knee throbbed. My reflexes were slow. The Yankees wanted to keep me on, but I knew it was time to make my exit. There's nothing for a retired baseball player past his prime to do but marry the world's most desirable woman."

Then Joe, also according to Marilyn, told her what she didn't want to hear. "You won't be able to carry on this blonde bombshell bit after the age of thirty-five. You don't want to appear on the screen naked when you've reached middle age."

Before her marriage, Marilyn paid a call on gossip maven Louella Parsons and talked about her love for Joe and her plans for marriage. "I think he's the right man for you," Parsons told her. "I'm never wrong about these things. Forget that Sinatra. He'd leave you alone in your honeymoon bed while he's out pursuing some showgals in Vegas."

Joe DiMaggio suspected he might catch his wife, **Marilyn Monroe**, in bed with her drama coach, Natasha Lytess, during his spectacularly botched "Wrong Door Raid." He'd heard lesbian rumors.

It wasn't Lytess, but a handsome young man MM was bedding that night. He was **Hal Schaefer** (depicted in both photos, above), a brilliant composer and pianist who had once been a protégé of Duke Ellington. Marilyn had launched an affair with him when they'd met on the set of Gentlemen Prefer Blondes.

Hal admitted years later, "I wasn't the world's greatest lover. I wasn't Tyrone Power. But I did give what she needed most—help. I didn't use her. I was supportive, and I cared about her."

He also insisted that he was not the reason for her breakup with DiMaggio. Hal admitted that sex was not the real reason for his relationship with MM. "She felt she was supposed to have sex with a man because that was something she had to give in return for my help. But I felt it wasn't very fulfilling for her."

Marilyn helped Hal recover from the suicide he had attempted on the night of July 27, 1954, when he drank typewriter cleaning fluid (carbon tetrachloride), a quart of brandy, and swallowed a hundred sleeping pills. It was a long, slow recovery, but he survived.

grate. "I read in the press that it was a coupling made in heaven," Frank told Sammy Davis Jr. "From what I saw, it was nine months made in hell and scripted by the Devil."

Unknown to DiMaggio, Marilyn met privately with Frank and told him she planned to go ahead and divorce DiMaggio in a court in Santa Monica. "He's cruel to me, goes for days without speaking, and holds my film roles in contempt. One time he went ten entire days and spoke not a word to me. I begged him to tell me what I'd done wrong. Finally, when he did speak, he said, 'I'm tired of your God damn nagging.' Then he stormed out the door and was gone for an entire month."

Before leaving Frank's villa at Palm Springs that hot afternoon, she made an astonishing request. "If I divorce Joe, will you promise to marry me when we're both free of entanglements? Knowing you'll eventually marry me will give me the courage to go through with the divorce."

"You're on, kid," he told her, although it is highly doubtful if he meant it.

Privately, he told Dean Martin and others, "I wish Marilyn would divorce Joe. He's not right for her. She even offered to give up her career for the sucker, and even that didn't help the relationship. For Marilyn to give up her career—now that's making the big sacrifice."

Marilyn called Frank when Judge Orlando H. Rhodes granted her interlocutory decree, with her divorce scheduled to become final in one year. "I've just counted the days on my calendar. I was married to Joe for 286 days."

Frank was playing a dangerous game, being Marilyn's confidant and protector on the one hand, and DiMaggio's good pal on the other. He seemed torn in his loyalties.

DiMaggio didn't want the divorce and developed a plan to sabotage it. Frank agreed to meet him for dinner at one of their favorite Italian restaurants in Hollywood, Villa Capri. Previously, Frank had lent DiMaggio the services of his private detective, Barney Ruditsky. As a favor to DiMaggio, Frank agreed that Ruditsky could "get hot on Marilyn's trail and learn the dirt, especially who she's fucking."

When Ruditsky arrived at the Villa Capri, he

told both DiMaggio and Frank that Marilyn was "shacked up with some woman" at an apartment at Waring Avenue and Kilkea Drive.

This came as no surprise to either DiMaggio or Frank, both of whom had heard of some previous lesbian involvements of Marilyn's, with such stellar lights as Shelley Winters, Joan Crawford, and Barbara Stanwyck.

DiMaggio told Frank that he wanted him to accompany him to the apartment house and break in on Marilyn. That way, he might stall the divorce, or make Marilyn forget all about it, if he had a detective photograph her in a compromising situation with another woman. "Marilyn might have survived that nude calendar scandal, but none of her fans would stand for it if she's caught in some lesbian affair," DiMaggio said.

"After all these years in Hollywood, I'm never surprised at what men will do with other men when they're alone or women with women," Frank said. "Surely you've had a few blow-jobs in your day in some lonely shower room."

"Forget that shit," DiMaggio said. "I want you to go with me. I need you to back me up."

"Okay, God damn it," a drunken Frank said. "I think it's a stupid stunt, but you seem determined to go through with it."

That night of November 5, 1954 would live in infamy in the annals of Hollywood scandal. In separate vehicles, Frank and DiMaggio, and four "private dicks," arrived at the apartment house where they hoped to entrap Marilyn.

Frank later maintained that he waited in his automobile outside, but witnesses asserted otherwise. The corps of private detectives consisted of Ruditsky himself, along with his cohorts, John Seminola, Philip Irwin, and Patsy D'Amore.

One of the detectives had brought an ax to cut through the door; another carried a camera to capture the sexual tryst in a photograph.

After the apartment's door was smashed in, DiMaggio led the "posse" into the room as one of the detectives shined a flashlight on the lone occupant in the bed who had gone to sleep.

It was not Marilyn and a girlfriend, but the fifty-year-old Florence Kotz, who had retired for the night. Thinking it was a "band of burglars," as she later claimed, she screamed at the top of her lungs.

She later told friends, "I thought they were going to rape me."

When Frank turned on the light, she recalled, "I couldn't believe my eyes. Along with these other guys, I recognized Frank Sinatra and Joe DiMaggio, two of the most famous men in America. I suspected those two Lotharios wouldn't have needed to break down any woman's door for rape."

DiMaggio had ordered the break-in at the

The house at 8120 Waring Road in West Hollywood became one of the most notorious in America. It was here that a "posse" led by Joe DiMaggio and Frank Sinatra, broke into the wrong apartment. Instead of catching Marilyn in bed with her *beau du jour* (or even a lesbian lover), they found a hysterical middle aged woman, Florence Kotz, who feared rape and robbery.

When columnist Hedda Hopper heard the news, she privately told friends, "If DiMaggio and Sinatra broke in on me, I'd invite them to strip down and show me what they could do."

The building contained two other apartments, one of which was occupied by Marilyn and her male lover. Hearing the commotion, MM and her beau fled through the back door. DiMaggio and Frank hadn't thought of stationing a guard in back of the house.

wrong door. Marilyn, along with her lover, Hal Schaefer, were in the upstairs apartment, which belonged to a girlfriend of hers, Sheila Stewart, who had graciously lent it to Marilyn for the night. Grabbing Shaefer's arm, Marilyn fled with him out the back door and hailed a taxi, leaving her own car parked in front of the building.

Schaefer remains one of Marilyn's least publicized lovers. His career spanned seventy years, and he was one of the leading vocal coaches of Hollywood. He'd worked with Marilyn on *Gentlemen Prefer Blondes*, orchestrating her biggest hit, "Diamonds Are a Girl's Best Friend."

It wasn't until September of 1955 that *Confidential*, the reigning scandal magazine of its day, broke the story of the "Wrong Door Raid" by Joe DiMaggio and Frank Sinatra in November of 1954.

Thinking that Marilyn Monroe was inside, DiMaggio and his goons broke in on Florence Kotz, a middle aged secretary. "I was terrified," she told the press. "The place was full of men. They were making a lot of noise and lights flashed on. I saw one of them holding something up towards me, and I thought it was a weapon." It was actually a camera.

Instead of catching the sexy blonde actress in the naked throes of passion with her paramour, the paparazzo caught poor old Flo in her nightgown and curlers. "We've got the wrong place!" DiMaggio shouted.

Later, after she learned the details, Kotz said, "In all my life, I could never even remotely dream that I would be caught up in a tabloid scandal with the three most famous people on earth—Frank Sinatra, Marilyn Monroe, and Joe DiMaggio."

Schaefer was also a pianist, conductor, arranger, composer, and accompanist. As long as it lasted, he had a romance with Marilyn.

The police were called, but by then the "burglars" were back at the Villa Capri, ordering fresh pasta. In the police report, the raid on Florence Kotz's apartment was reported as an attempted burglary.

There was an ironic end to that night that was not reported. Yet another private detective had been assigned to stake out Marilyn's official residence. After the raid, the blonde bombshell drove up alone and entered her house. About an hour later, DiMaggio by himself also drove up.

The detective saw Marilyn answer the door in her panties, wearing no bra. She let DiMaggio into the house. The detective remained at his post until five o'clock that morning. DiMaggio had not left the house all night.

As Frank had anticipated, Kotz filed a $200,000 lawsuit, but Frank's attorney was able to get her to settle for $7,500. When word about the raid leaked to a reporter, Frank angrily shouted, "Case closed."

Frank paid the final settlement himself. "Tightwad Joe didn't cough up a penny. And it was the fucker's idea, not mine."

The story might have died, but *Confidential* magazine published the details in its September, 1955 issue. The break-in on Kotz became known as "The Wrong Door Raid."

In the wake of the exposé in *Confidential*, one of the detectives linked to the Wrong Door Raid, twenty-four-year-old Philip Irwin "spilled the beans" to police investigators and later to a California State Senate investigative committee.

The scandal ripened and spread. The California State Senate Investigating Committee, although not specifically investigating the Wrong Door Raid itself, was probing how stories of the "ilk" that the magazine published were leaked to the tabloids. Committee members were concerned that laws were being broken by private detectives as a means of gathering data which could then be sold to *Confidential* and other magazines for a handsome profit.

Shortly thereafter, at 4am on February 16, 1957, three policemen, using a pass-key, entered the star's residence in Palm Springs.

All of the cops entered Frank's bedroom at the same moment, and one of them shined a flashlight directly in his face, as his bed partner for the evening rolled over, the face concealed. Frank started cursing the policemen, and his fury, even for him, went beyond the boiling point. He was served with a subpoena, summoning him to testify before the Senate committee.

He later said, "I'm the fucking sap who got raided. These cops were lucky I was asleep when they broke in. Had I been awake, I would have gotten my gun and started shooting up the place." He later threatened to sue the force but dropped the case for one very embarrassing reason.

DiMaggio was also called to testify but cabled his regrets, remaining in New York out of the range of the California State Senate and its subpoenas.

One of the most gossiped about stories in Hollywood concerned Frank's bed partner during the pre-dawn hours of the morning of that raid in Palm Springs. Most gossips assumed it was a woman, later learning that Frank had been caught nude and in bed with Burt Lancaster, who'd been his co-star in *From Here to Eternity*. Burt had become powerfully attracted to Frank in Hawaii during the making of that film, and a friendship was cemented between the two of them that lasted a lifetime.

When columnist James Bacon heard that it was Burt in bed with Frank, he privately claimed, "If Montgomery Clift fell in love with Frank during the shooting of *Eternity*, why not Burt? Monty is as queer as a three-dollar bill, and Burt is one of the most notorious bisexuals in Hollywood. If the public only knew."

After their return to Hollywood, Burt and Frank were often seen together, dining alone at secluded restaurants or going to nightclubs together without female dates. Like Yul Brynner, another bisexual actor with a crush on Frank, Burt spent many weekends with Frank in Palm Springs with no women invited.

Their being caught in bed together

Frank Sinatra himself was caught in a "Right Door Raid" in February of 1957, when policemen broke into his villa in Palm Springs. Instead of knocking on the door during daylight hours, the policemen, for reasons of their own, broke into his home in the pre-dawn hours. "It took me ten years to cool down my temper," Frank later said.

He, of course, wanted to sue, but his attorneys talked him out of it.

It was widely assumed that he was caught, drunk and in bed, with Marilyn Monroe. At least that was the gossip of the day. Hedda Hopper speculated, in print, that Ava Gardner had returned to the villa. Her rival, Louella Parsons, wrote that it was Lana Turner, who, she said, had made up with Frank.

Who would have suspected that the person caught in bed with Frank at the time of that pre-dawn police raid was the macho he-man of dozens of films, muscle-bound **Burt Lancaster** (*photo above*), Frank's co-star in the 1953 *From Here to Eternity*?

was probably more innocent than it sounded. Perhaps both of them had had too much to drink that night, as was often the case, and tumbled into bed together. Or it could have been something else.

Since no video camera was there to record their sleepover, and since neither man ever discussed it, it must remain their private business.

At the very least, their sleepover demonstrated what a strong and abiding friendship, and a very intimate one, that both men had for each other. If on a dark, drunken night Burt pressed his sexual demands upon Frank, that must remain their affair.

The discovery of Burt in Frank's bed certainly explained why Frank's attorneys advised him to drop his lawsuit against the police. If word got out that Frank and Burt were in bed together, and "jaybird naked," the unwanted publicity would have dwarfed the "Wrong Door Raid" in search of Marilyn.

Before the grand jury, Frank swore that he did not participate in the raid but remained outside in his Cadillac. The landlady, Virginia Blasgen, refuted that testimony and claimed she was in the hallway when she spotted Frank fleeing from the Kotz apartment.

Phillip Irwin, one of the detectives, also claimed that Frank participated in the raid. He stated that "almost all of Mr. Sinatra's statements made today are false."

The detective also confessed that shortly after the story in *Confidential* came out, he was severely beaten by some thugs. "Mr. Sinatra may have sent his thugs after me and may have believed I was the source of the *Confidential* story, but I was not."

State investigator James J. Callahan testified, "Irwin had a black eye. I don't think his nose was broken, but it was badly bruised. He had severe welts from his shoulders to his belt line. His arms and legs had been kicked. He was pretty thoroughly worked over."

When Frank was called back to the stand, he asked the jury, "Who are you going to believe, me or a guy who makes his living kicking down bedroom doors?"

The headline the following morning in the *Los Angeles Mirror-News* shouted at its readers: WITNESS SAYS SINATRA LIED."

Frank narrowly escaped indictment, and perjury was ruled out by the district attorney, who nevertheless noted the "bald conflict" in Frank's testimony.

The entrance to Westwood Memorial Cemetery is at 1218 Glendon Avenue, just off busy Wilshire Boulevard.

On August 8, 1962, the fallen sex goddess of her era, Marilyn Monroe, was placed in a wall crypt here in the "Corridor of Memories."

For every year in the wake of MM's death, Joe DiMaggio journeyed to Westwood on the anniversary of his wedding day to Marilyn. He placed red roses on her grave and whispered something to her in her crypt. For every other week of the year, he ordered fresh red roses sent to her grave site.

On the 20th anniversary of her death, during August of 1982, that order to the florist was abruptly canceled.

After this scandal, the friendship between DiMaggio and Frank ended. DiMaggio, in fact, came to hate Frank when he learned that he was secretly dating Marilyn and later "passing her around to his friends," such as the gangster Sam Giancana and both President Kennedy and his brother, Attorney General Bobby

Kennedy. DiMaggio called the Kennedys "brothers in crime. As for that faggot pimp, Peter Lawford, I'd like to take him three miles off the coast and drop him off somewhere. But he'd probably be too pickled for even the sharks to eat."

Frank allegedly told his friend Jilly Rizzo that he wanted to keep information about his sexual involvement with Marilyn private from DiMaggio. "I don't need the aggravation. Joe would get seriously pissed off at me. Of course, if Marilyn and I get really serious about this thing, Joe is gonna find out. If she becomes the next Mrs. Frank Sinatra, the whole fucking world will know. Joe already suspects us. He's not as dumb as he looks."

From what DiMaggio learned, Marilyn was serious about marrying Frank, and DiMaggio found this out.

Marilyn's secretary and confidante, Lena Pepitone, who wrote a book entitled *Marilyn Monroe—Confidential* in 1979, claimed that she asked Marilyn why she would consider marrying Frank if she were still in love with DiMaggio.

"Joe will never marry me again," Marilyn said. "Never. He loves me, but he's insisting I give up my career. I'll never do that."

Ironically, Frank, if he'd agreed to marry her, would have insisted that Marilyn give up her career, too.

During the last vacation weekend of her life, Frank invited Marilyn to the Cal-Neva Lodge, whose location famously straddled the border between California and Nevada. When DiMaggio heard of this, he too headed here.

He'd told friends, "If Sinatra doesn't want her, why doesn't he let her alone? He's only fucking up her mind. And those are gangsters he's got her mixed up with!" He was no doubt referring to mob boss Sam Giancana who was a guest at the Lodge that weekend.

After Monroe died, Giancana boasted, "I was the last man on earth to fuck Marilyn Monroe."

The resort's bell captain, Ray Langford, had been instructed to tell DiMaggio that there was no more room at the inn. Langford did help him book a room at the nearby Silver Crest Motor Lodge. Langford also pretended that he didn't know Marilyn's room number and the desk could not put through a call to her, even though DiMaggio insisted that it was an emergency.

On that following foggy Sunday morning, DiMaggio from his motel grounds could look down at the pool of the Cal-Neva. Marilyn stood at the edge of the pool, dropping her robe to reveal that she was totally nude.

She looked up at the foothill above the rustic lodge. In *The Assassination of Marilyn Monroe*, Donald H. Wolfe wrote, "Standing there in the mist staring back was Joe DiMaggio. It was the last time he would see her alive."

Wolfe also quotes Harry Hall, a close friend of DiMaggio, "He was furious with Sinatra, and he was furious with the Kennedys. He was very upset. Marilyn went up there; they gave her pills, they had sex parties. I don't think DiMaggio ever talked to Sinatra again."

DiMaggio was devastated when he heard the news of Marilyn's death. "Suicide, hell. She had our future life together. We were going to remarry. It was the fucking Kennedys, that Bobby in particular. I hate him. And that fucking bastard Sinatra. I'm through with him. He was part of the plot to murder Marilyn."

DiMaggio would never forgive the Kennedys or Frank. At Marilyn's funeral on August 8, 1962 in the Mortuary Chapel on the grounds of L.A.'s Westwood Memorial Cemetery, Frank showed up with Sammy Davis Jr., and they tried to bully their way into the chapel to say their farewells to Marilyn. But DiMaggio had hired security guards to keep them out.

Furious, yet fighting back tears, Frank stood with Sammy on a grassy lawn outside, as the sounds of *Over the Rainbow* came from an organ inside.

Inside the chapel, DiMaggio waited for all the guests to file past Marilyn's open coffin. When they had departed and right before the casket was closed for eternity, he bent over and placed a gentle kiss on her cold lips.

He also placed three beautiful roses in her hands. As the casket came down, he sobbed, "I love you! I love you! I love you!"

When a cynical Frank heard about DiMaggio's theatrics at Marilyn's casket, he said, "Joltin' Joe always said he and I would be friends until the end. This is the end."

---

## HOW BILLY WILDER EVALUATED FRANK SINATRA
## DURING THE FILMING OF *HIGH SOCIETY*

*High Society* (1956) was a pleasant but mild musical remake of a classic film, *The Philadelphia Story* that had rescued Katharine Hepburn's career in 1940. Her co-stars included Cary Grant and James Stewart.

This time around the star parts went to Bing Crosby, Grace Kelly, and Frank himself. Grace was said to have broken the hearts of both Frank and Bing during filming when they learned of her engagement to Prince Rainier of Monaco. She wore her actual engagement ring for her character's engagement ring in the film.

She, of course, took the Hepburn role of Tracy Lord, but did so less effectively. This was Grace's last feature film before retiring from acting.

Bing takes Cary Grant's husband role of C.K. Dexter-Haven, who had been married to Grace, and Frank is the nosey reporter for *Spy Magazine*, Mike Connor, as originally played by James Stewart.

Although Grace ends up remarrying Bing in the film, the on-screen chemistry is actually generated between Frank and Grace, especially when he sings "You're Sensational."

Director Billy Wilder dropped onto the set and found that Frank was brilliant in the scene he witnessed. "He makes other actors look like faggots," Wilder proclaimed. "I wouldn't work with him, though. He'd run after the first take, chasing some broad, in this case a future princess, Miss Grace Kelly herself. I hear he has a perpetual erection when he's around his leading ladies, and has to keep it taped to his belly so it won't show in his trousers. Some men have all the luck with the chicks."

Because Frank was a nervous bundle of energy during filming, the crew named him "Dexedrine" after the stimulant. Bing was cool and very relaxed, and he was called "Nembutal" after the sleeping pill.

The Cole Porter song, "Well, Did You Evah?", was added from a previous musical by Porter when the director realized at the last minute that it didn't have a song for Bing and Frank to sing together.

Another Porter song, "True Love," was a million seller for both Grace and Bing. This is the only platinum-designated record ever associated with sitting royalty. Grace had become Princess Grace prior to the award ceremony.

For months afterward, the sounds of "True Love" echoed through the palace in Monaco.

Celeste Holm claimed that "Frank was terribly in love with Grace during the shoot, and followed her around like a lovesick puppy. There was never a girl Frank couldn't get, including one engaged to be married to a prince."

# Eva Bartok:

## "My Love Child with Frank"

Born in Hungary, the actress **Eva Bartok** *(left photo)* competed with Zsa Zsa Gabor as "The Budapest Bombshell," and was frequently cited in the British press as "The Hungarian Rhapsody."

But whereas Zsa Zsa maintained that Frank Sinatra raped her, Eva was only too willing to submit to the singer.

The story of her own life was far more intriguing than any of the films in which she appeared.

Since her father was a Jew, she was sentenced to a concentration camp at the age of fifteen. A sadistic Nazi officer became intrigued by her beauty and forced her to marry him. Eva later characterized the marriage as a series of ruthless rapes of a teenager.

Famously married to the German/Austrian actor Curt Jürgens, Eva finally made it to Hollywood and into the arms of two of Frank's closest friends, Burt Lancaster and Dean Martin.

"I was pretty used goods by the time I got around to that charming man, Frank Sinatra. But he didn't seem to mind. I desperately wanted to be the mother of his baby, and so it came to be, although it didn't work out like I wanted it to. What I really wanted was for him to marry me and be the father of our daughter. Alas, it was the stuff of dreams, at least where Frank was concerned."

## WAS SHE A GABOR, OR MERELY THE MOCK?

*"Deana, the daughter I had with Frank, is like me. We do it our way. She will make her own decisions. But I have my memories of Frankie, and I see him in her eyes whenever I look at her."*

—**Eva Bartok**

Eva Bartok became familiar to American audiences when she co-starred with **Burt Lancaster** in *The Crimson Pirate,* which was widely distributed in France as *Le Corsaire Rouge.* Burt *(left figure in the lower photo)* shows off his muscled torso as he battles Spaniards.

Eva later admitted that she learned that Burt was bisexual—"and although he was a skilled lover of women, too, he perhaps wanted Frank for himself. He oozed masculinity. He never liked having sex in a bed. He preferred it on the floor with his naked partner lying on a mink coat. That was some erotic vision from his past that he was always trying to relive."

Jackie Bone, Burt's longtime companion, more or less echoed Eva's impression, and she also claimed that "Burt loved to go to bed with his leading ladies," and with some who were not.

Burt told Eva that his two biggest conquests had been Marlene Dietrich and Ava Gardner. "Frankie got them too, of course, especially Ava when she wasn't getting plugged by some other stud."

It's Sunday afternoon and you're bored. You turn on Turner Classics just as *The Crimson Pirate* (1952) comes on, starring Burt Lancaster.

Having seen her film, *A Tale of Five Cities,* Burt Lancaster was impressed and asked her to play his love interest in *The Crimson Pirate,* to be shot off the coast of Naples on the island of Ischia. She accepted.

The perfectly muscled and buffed Lancaster looked gorgeous, but so did his female co-star, Eva Bartok. Her career was on the rise. Not only was Lancaster seducing her in her dressing room, but she was publicized in the 1950s as "Britain's answer to Sophia Loren," even though she was Hungarian.

Some movie viewers mistakenly identified her with the fabulous Gabor sisters—Eva, Zsa Zsa, and Magda, but they detested her, viewing her as competition.

Cast as Consuelo, Eva played the daughter of a revolutionary on a Caribbean island who persuaded Lancaster to join her father's rebellion against a Spanish tyrant.

\*\*\*

Born on June 18, 1927 in Budapest, Eva, then known as **Eva Ivanova Szöke,** was the daughter of a Hungarian Catholic mother and a Jewish father, a political writer for local newspapers.

Eva was imprisoned in a concentration camp during World War II when she was just 15 years old. But a Nazi officer, Giza Kovas, spotted her, rescued her, and forced her to marry him or face the gas chamber. She chose marriage to this child molester. She later recalled her "honeymoon" as "a series of ruthless rapes."

Her Nazi husband, really her abductor, disappeared when the Soviets took over Hungary. She was able to get the courts to annul her forced marriage on the grounds of "coercion of a minor."

After the war and Hungary's subsequent Communist takeover, Eva married Alex Paal, a man she hardly knew. The Hungarian film producer promised to take her out of her native country to live in Britain.

Paal cast her in one of his films, *A Tale of Five Cities*, in 1948 although the movie would not be completed and released until 1951 because it ran into financial difficulties. This marriage of convenience didn't last long, and Paal divorced her. But in England, another more famous Hungarian, Alexander Korda, hired Eva and signed her to a movie contract for 80 pounds a month.

Eva met and married British publicist William Wordsworth in 1951. Her third husband was a descendant of the famous English poet. Having little money, she designed her own wardrobe and even her hats from "scraps of this and that." Soon she became known throughout London as "the girl with the crazy hats."

She particularly became famous for her "Bartok bucket hat," whose design was copied and adopted by women across Europe and America.

As Eva pursued her agendas, she had less and less interest in her marriage to Wordsworth.

In Germany while filming *Rummelplatz Der Liebe* in 1953, opposite the formidable German/Austrian actor Curt Jürgens, the couple fell in love. They were married in 1955 when her divorce from Wordsworth finally came through. Their first movie was a success, and it was followed by a string of other pictures.

Jürgens, who kept a glowering, almost militaristic air about him in most of his films, never understood her spiritual side and lavished furs and jewelry upon her. There was also violence, particularly one night in Rome at the Hotel Hassler, where he beat her so severely she ended up in the hospital. The paparazzi loved them.

They lived together in an elegant château in the Swiss Alps. For a little girl who had endured life in a concentration camp, it was like a fairytale which, however, turned into a nightmare. Because of work commitments, the couple spent little time together. Often their nights were spent in the arms of others.

In 1953, when **Eva Bartok** (right) made the German film, *Rummelplatz Der Liebe,* she fell in love with her handsome leading man, **Curt Jürgens** *(left),* one of the most successful European film actors of the 20th century. Of Franco-German parentage, he was born during the closing days of World War I, in Hohenzollern Imperial Germany.

Even as a young man, he was a liberal and made disparaging remarks about the Nazi Party. For that, in 1944, he was labeled "a political unreliable" and thrown into a concentration camp,

He once told Eva that because he was a beautiful young blond-haired man, he was often taken at night to the quarters of the officers in charge. "There, they tied me to a bed and used me like a woman," he said. His worst night, he claimed, was when he was sodomized by more than a dozen men. "I lost count and was left bleeding."

Although he'd been born in Munich and was not Jewish, like Eva, Jürgens had also been a prisoner during WWII in a concentration camp. Josef Goebbels had viewed him as a "political unreliable."

For a brief reign, Eva and Jürgens were the toast of Europe, especially among the paparazzi. Her former press agent called her "at one time one of the most photographed women around and one of the most beautiful women in the world."

Eva begged Jürgens to father a child, and she tried desperately to achieve that dream. Although she always had unprotected sex with him, no pregnancy resulted. Finally, he admitted he was infertile, the result of a car accident in 1933 when he had to submit to a surgery that removed his spermatic cords.

Eva joined the jet set of the 1950s and was seen everywhere with the playboy millionaire David Michael Mountbatten, Marquess of Milford Haven, who had been best man at the wedding of Prince Philip to Princess Elizabeth in November of 1947. The Marquis and Eva were photographed at every posh watering hole from Monte Carlo to Capri. The Marquess of Milford was the cousin of Prince Philip.

When the Marchioness of Milford Haven named Eva in her divorce suit, the scandal only made Eva more famous or rather, more notorious. The Royal Family disapproved of the union, and she and Mountbatten eventually drifted apart.

She could often be seen on the streets of London driving a chocolate-colored Rolls Royce. Later, she referred to this period as "the most wasted time in my life."

Movie offers were pouring in because of her infamy as a frivolous party girl, although she abhorred this reputation, having a sensitive side that was especially interested in meditation and a quest for understanding and meaning in life.

She was better known for her private life than for her string of mediocre films. Even so, Hollywood beckoned.

When she accepted the role in *Ten Thousand Bedrooms* opposite Dean Martin, her life changed drastically. His closest friend was Frank Sinatra. Like his buddy, Dean often seduced his leading ladies whenever possible, and Eva was no exception.

In Hollywood, he told her that he had "commitments," but that "my pal Frankie is breaking up with Ava Gardner and needs some company at night."

She later believed that Dean Martin, with whom she'd had a recent affair, had given her a glowing report on what a delight she was in the boudoir.

Eva claimed that she met Frank at a

Here, the **Third Marquess of Milford Haven, David Mountbatten** (a cousin of Prince Philip, the Duke of Edinburgh) is seen on his wedding day, November 17, 1960.

He really wanted to marry Eva Bartok, but Buckingham Palace did not approve of the Hungarian-born actress with "the notorious past." David was one of Philip's closest friends, and had been best man at the wedding of the prince to Princess Elizabeth in 1947.

He married **Janet Bryce**, the Bermuda socialite and ex-fashion model, when she was 23. He was marrying for the second time; she for the first. Prince Philip did not attend, because the Queen, as head of the Church of England, was prevented from attending the wedding of a divorced person.

During the time it lasted, David's affair with Eva was the tabloid scandal of Europe, intriguing readers with lurid headlines from London to Paris, from Monte Carlo to Capri.

party at the home of Charles Feldman, the producer. That night she was accompanied by Rex Harrison, Kay Kendall, and David Niven.

"Frank never took his eyes off me all evening," she said. "When he came on to me, I rather arrogantly told him, 'I'm not one of your adoring female fans.' Amazingly, that didn't turn him off. It only seemed to pique his interest. Before the evening ended, I had fallen victim to his charm. I ended up giving him my phone number."

"Just as I was getting ready for bed, he called me and told me he was very lonely and needed me," Eva said. "Like a fool, I said I'd come over." She claimed they talked until dawn, and she found him well read. "He was one movie star who read something other than film scripts. By the dawn's early light, he took my hand and said, 'Come with me.' That invitation led right to his boudoir where I could not even count the number of women who must have gone there before me."

The relationship lasted three months. She saw no one else, but she suspected he had women on the side when he was not with her.

After the first night, she was seen about town with him—at recording sessions, on a studio lot leaving his dressing room, at night clubs along Sunset Strip, at casinos in Las Vegas, and most definitely for long weekends in Palm Springs.

Then tragedy struck.

In Los Angeles she learned that she had developed a cancerous ovarian tumor, which required immediate surgery. "Oh, yes," her doctor said, "you are also pregnant."

She was told that she had to submit to surgery at once to save her own life, but there was no hope for the baby. The news was devastating to her. She knew that the father was Frank Sinatra, and she desperately wanted to have not just his child but any baby. She longed to be a mother to "fulfill myself."

She preferred to go back to London for the operation. She chose not to tell Frank. "An attractive woman doesn't complain to her lover about her poor health. I think a man would lose his erection if he felt he was plunging into a woman with a cancerous tumor."

An obstetrician told her, "If you have your baby, you might bleed to death, and it is highly unlikely the baby would live anyway." Needing help and guidance, Eva, through a friend, was put in touch with Pak Subuh, a guru from Indonesia and the leader of an international spiritual movement, "*Subud*," a meditative introspective affirmation of life used by an estimated 10,000 devotees worldwide to achieve a deeper understanding of their personal religious beliefs. The movement came to the consciousness of the western world through Indonesia in the late 1920s, and through England in the 1940s.

Two dancing couples, *(left to right)* **Dean Martin and Anna Marie Alberghetti** and **Eva Bartok** and **Dewey Martin** (the ex-Mr. Peggy Lee) hit the dance floor in *Ten Thousand Bedrooms*, a lackluster comedy graced only by Dean's masculine charm.

"Dean's relationship with Jerry Lewis had gone *kaput*, and there was threat of legal action," Eva said. "I caught him when he was insecure about his future as a solo act. He was also in hock to the government.

"I never had a child with Dean, but with Frank. But Dean was practically a walking sperm factory, having another *bambino* every nine months. He turned to me for comfort.

"At times, he couldn't go home and face all those children and all those problems. I was cut out to be a mistress more than a wife."

Eva had been told that her birth canal had become blocked and that the cyst could rupture at any time, causing her to bleed to death.

"I had to have the cyst removed," she said. "By doing that, I would also abort my child with Frank, and I desperately wanted his baby.

Meeting with Pak Subuh, he told her, "No abortion."

A follower of Mohammed, Subuh claimed that the "sole presence of their leader could lead to wondrous results." Those results included the healing of both body and soul. Eva postponed her surgery.

She had never believed in faith healers or even in self-suggestion hypnosis. In the midst of her chanting and introspection, Pak Subuh came and told her that if she believed that God could heal her, He would. The day before her scheduled surgery, her pains reached an almost unbearable point.

But then the guru announced to her that the surgery was no longer needed, and she believed him, postponing it indefinitely.

When Eva's mother arrived and sent her back to her doctors, "no trace of the tumor could be found," Eva claimed. "I was out of danger."

Of course, there is no way of verifying this seemingly preposterous claim.

Later Eva claimed that her cancerous tumor disappeared because of her spiritual conversion to *Subud*. Based on these experiences, she became a follower of Pak Subuh and his movement, *Subud*. She would remain a follower, and eventually, a teacher, for the rest of her life.

A premature baby girl was born to her on October 7, 1957. Eva chose not to notify Frank.

Eva named her Deana "Grazia," the latter name in Italian for "grace." The father's name was not written on birth certificate.

At the Coombe Springs (England) Subud Convention in 1957, **Eva Bartok** *(left)* asserted that she had been miraculously healed from a cancerous tumor. She had turned to **Pak Subuh** *(right photo, also snapped in 1957)* an Indonesian mystic, for a miracle, and, she widely asserted, it happened. Or so it was said.

"She spoke to me about a serious operation for cancer and how she needed to prepare herself for death," the guru claimed. He also said that as she was speaking, "a clear indication came to me that she was destined to be cured through Subud."

The spiritual leader visited her bedroom, where she lay dying, for only forty minutes, but assured her that the pain would subside and that she would not need an operation. He told her she could give birth to what she claimed was Frank Sinatra's baby, without complications.

Later, obstetric surgeons told her there were no more cancerous tumors and a strong healthy baby was eventually delivered.

Because Deana had been born prematurely, Eva could not see her for three days. She weighed only five pounds. "My eyes filled with tears when the nurse brought Deana in. The little baby turned her head slowly and opened her eyes. There was no more to be seen of them than a line of blue. That pair of eyes seemed to look into the core of my being. Frank looked at me with eyes that color of blue whenever he made love to me. I knew I had given

284

birth to his daughter."

She informed Jürgens that Frank was the father of her baby. Without Eva's permission, he cabled Frank, informing him that Eva had given birth to his baby daughter. "I wish she were mine, but she's not," Jürgens wrote. "She's yours. I felt I had to tell you."

Frank cabled back. "Thank you." That was that.

Very gallantly, to avoid a scandal, Jürgens offered to give Deana his last name. She turned him down, and news of her "single motherhood" became tabloid fodder in Europe and America.

Many reporters raised the question: "Who was the father of her child?" Two papers speculated that it was Sinatra but didn't pursue it beyond that point.

A friend of both Eva and Frank, Cary Grant, visited her in London. When he saw Deana, he said, "I know this is Frank's daughter. Her face looks just like his."

Eva told Deana that Frank was her father when she was three years old. But it wasn't until she was fourteen that Deana began pressuring her mother to contact Frank. Eva adamantly refused.

Although it told virtually nothing, Eva wrote her autobiography, *Worth Living For,* in 1959. In spite of its lack of candor—it didn't even mention Frank—it sold very well.

At the time her daughter was eighteen, and at her extreme urging, Eva broke down and wrote that long-delayed letter:

> *Dear Frank,*
>
> *This is a difficult letter to write, so please bear with me. This is about my daughter Deana. I have sometimes wondered during the past eighteen years whether you ever suspected that she is also your daughter. Deana has known this truth since she was three years old. Rightly or wrongly, I have always dissuaded her from contacting you. But now she is virtually a woman, with a mind of her own, and her emotional needs are too strong to be denied any longer. Very simply, she needs that you should know and understand. After all this time, Frank, I don't have to tell you that we have no material needs from you whatsoever. I can only tell you that it is an emotional crisis in her life and quite honestly I can no longer deny her. I cannot let her continue to be hurt in this way. It would have been so much better to have been able to discuss it with you in person, but you are not the easiest man to meet up with.*
> *Love,*
> *Eva*
>
> *P.S. I'm enclosing a recent picture of Deana. She really is very beautiful.*

The only child of Eva Bartok, **Deana Sinatra** never got to meet the singer from Hoboken, the man she believes is her father.

The daughter bears a strong resemblance to Ol' Blue Eyes, both in her own blue eyes and in the shape of her face. She told the press that she never sought to legally share in the Sinatra estate. "I only wanted recognition from him when he was dying that I was, indeed, his daughter. Is that too much to ask?"

She said that to satisfy some inner need within herself, and "to acknowledge that other half of me, I legally changed my name to Sinatra."

Frank's three legally recognized children—Nancy Jr., Frank Jr., and Tina—have never issued a comment on claims made by Deana.

Legend has it that as a toddler, Deana rifled through Eva's stacks of LPs and picked out a Sinatra album. "Daddy," she is alleged to have said to a dumbstruck Eva.

Frank responded to her plea with a message delivered

through his lawyer. "At the moment, please understand and forgive him. He told me he is in no state to deal with an emotional teenager."

***

During the 50s and 60s, Eva made 38 films in five languages, but her career faded.

By 1968 she'd given up her career and was living with Frank's daughter in Jakarta, Indonesia, in a Subuh compound. Later she became a sort of guru herself, teaching Subud philosophy when she moved to California and later to Hawaii.

In London, reporter Danae Brook was given a rare interview with Eva the year she died. It was published in *The Mail on Sunday*. Brook found Eva living in a seedy Paddington hotel in a cell-like room. Outside her window, teenage prostitutes and drug dealers prowled the night.

All of Eva's final possessions in life had been stolen when a gunman invaded her hotel room and robbed her of anything valuable.

Ironically, when this interview took place, Eva was near death herself, as was Frank, who was fading in Palm Springs at the age of 82.

"I could and should have made a claim on him for the sake of Deana, my daughter," Eva said with regret. "I never asked him for money, and I don't want to do so now that he is desperately ill. His memory is too precious to me."

She also said that she knew "the moment we first made love that I had conceived a child."

When Deana was thirty-six, she wrote Frank herself: "My sense of loss at not ever having known you, except at a distance, is breaking my heart. I would like us to meet before it is too late. Your loving daughter, Deana."

He might not have received the letter. If he did, he never answered.

Deana, now living outside Sydney, Australia, was contacted by a local newspaper and asked if she were the daughter of Frank Sinatra.

Deana was married and was the mother of two sons, Oliver and Damon. Frank would be their grandfather. She admitted to the Sydney reporter that she was indeed "a love child," the daughter of Eva Bartok and Sinatra.

"I am so deeply saddened," she told a reporter. "How could it have hurt him at the end to be a gentleman? It is theoretically possible that he will acknowledge my existence in his will. I really don't want money—just the words that I am his daughter. His cowardice makes me feel endlessly angry."

There was no mention of Deana when Frank's will was read. Her appeals have gone unanswered by the Sinatra family. Neither Eva nor Deana ever filed a formal paternity suit against Frank.

"As in the case of another unacknowledged daughter of Frank's, Julie Sinatra, the siblings seem very reluctant to admit another member to the family," wrote reporter Philip Lazlo. "No need to share the pot of gold if not forced to by a court."

Reporter Brook noted that Eva in her final months of life went around London incognito, wearing a wig and dark glasses because she didn't want her former fans to recognize her. "Apart from her classic bone structure," Brook wrote, "it is difficult to believe anyone would now see in her tiny frame any remnants of the glorious Hollywood star she once was. Would Sinatra recognize her? Even that is doubtful."

Alone and forgotten, Eva was found dead in London on August 1, 1998.

# Frank and "Bogie's Baby"

## LAUREN BACALL: JILTED AT THE ALTAR

According to the press, **Frank Sinatra and Lauren Bacall** were heading for the altar, but he stumbled on the way there. As Frank told Dean Martin and others, "Bogie's shoes were too big for me to fill." Of course, that was just a lame excuse. He actually didn't want to get married.

Frank had been a member of the original Rat Pack when Humphrey Bogart was the chief rat. Frank's relationship with Bogie's widow, Lauren Bacall, heated up when the screen legend died of cancer in 1957.

Years before that, Frank found nights at Bogie's Holmby Hills house the most entertaining in Los Angeles. "What an array of talent," he recalled. On any night, he might encounter Spencer Tracy, Katharine Hepburn, agent Swifty Lazar, Mike Romanoff, Billy Wilder, David Niven, John Huston, and even Adlai Stevenson.

Once, Bogie invited Frank to join Lauren and him for a sail to Catalina aboard his yacht, *Santana*. Frank said, "No way. My way of doing a sail to Catalina is to rent a power yacht, hire a dance band, stock the best booze that Mike Romanoff has, and hire the best broads in Tinseltown."

After he left his first wife (Nancy) Frank moved to Holmby Hills, just blocks from Bacall and Bogie. "He was always there," Bogie said. "I think we're parent substitutes for him, or something."

Later, Bogie changed his mind, fearing that Lauren herself had become the attraction for Frank.

## A Dying Bogie Competes with Sinatra for the "Den Mother" of the Rat Pack

In *To Have and Have Not* (1944), a very young **Lauren Bacall** (also known as Betty Bacall), lights up a cigarette for **Humphrey Bogart**, but she did more than that, rekindling a passion in this balding, middle-aged man.

Years later, Frank Sinatra told agent Swifty Lazar what an impact that movie had had on him. "The presence of that dynamic duo on the screen sparked an ambition in me. When I first started dating Ava Gardner, I proposed to her that we become on the screen of the 1950s what Bogie and Bacall were in the 1940s. I wanted to make one film after another—tough, gritty roles, not musicals, that would make us evoke the screen legend that Bogie and Betty became."

"I always regretted that too many clouds got in our way, and my dream was only to be dreamed," Frank said. "Like most dreams, mine didn't come true."

*"Sinatra behaved like a complete shit!"*

—**Lauren Bacall**

*"He's a hell of a guy. He tries to live his own life. I like his style."*

—**Humphrey Bogart**

At the end of World War II, Bogie confronted Frank with the provocative and perhaps drunken comment, "They tell me you have a voice that makes girls faint. *Make me faint.*" From such an unlikely beginning, a deep friendship emerged.

Beginning with *The Maltese Falcon* in 1941, Frank had admired Bogie's screen presence. In fact, he wanted to work with the star. An opportunity arose when the bisexual director Nicholas Ray cast Bogie as an impassioned lawyer in the 1949 *Knock on Any Door*. Frank wanted to appear opposite his screen hero as the tough street kid.

Meeting with Ray, Frank allegedly promised him, "I'll let you suck on my big dick every day during the shoot if you'll give me the part."

He exploded two weeks later when he read in *Variety* that the role had gone to John Derek. "That pretty boy is more Ray's type," Frank charged. "When he's not chasing after eleven-year-old girls, Derek is a card-carrying faggot. He was a male hustler. He's fucked half the queens in Hollywood. That son-of-a-bitch preferred Derek over me. Derek no doubt agreed to let Ray pound his rosebud. He wouldn't have gotten that from me."

Frank desperately wanted Bogie's approval but never got it. Frank arrived on his doorstep, having won the Best Supporting Actor Academy Award for playing Maggio in *From Here to Eternity* (1953). He asked Bogie, "What did you think of me in the role?"

"Not much," Bogie said. "Maybe Eli Wallach could have pulled it off."

Bogie almost never made any public comment about Frank. Once when he did, it became a famous quote. "Sinatra's idea of paradise is a place where there are plenty of women and no newspapermen. He doesn't know it, but he'd be better off if it were the other way around."

In virtual mourning over the loss of Ava Gardner, Frank called Lauren Bacall (born Betty

Perksy) and asked her to deliver Ava's favorite dessert, a coconut orange cake, to his estranged spouse in Rome. Bacall was flying there to join Humphrey Bogart, who was filming *The Barefoot Contessa* (1954) opposite Ava.

Bacall agreed, carrying the cake across the Atlantic on her lap. She stopped off in London and continued on to Rome "with that damn cake."

In Rome, Bacall, with Bogie, checked into the Excelsior Hotel along the Via Veneto. She called Ava, and "that coconut cake sat there rotting for two days."

Finally, Bacall decided to deliver it to Ava's dressing room at the studio. "I felt like an idiot standing before Ava with that bloody box. Frank sent this coconut cake to you from New York. He said it was your favorite."

"Put it on the table," Ava said. She didn't say thank you, although Bacall had carried it on her lap all the way so it wouldn't get crushed.

Bacall later told friends, "I knew then it was all over between Frank and Ava. She had moved on to her next conquest."

Far from mourning Frank, Ava was making love to the handsome, dashing Luís Miguel Dominguin, Spain's leading matador. He was more than that; aficionados called him "the greatest bullfighter in the world." Ava had another billing: "A bull in the ring, a bull in the boudoir."

Bogie, still loyal to Frank, chided Ava on her new passion. "Half the broads in the world are trying to get Frank in their bed. And you turn him down, preferring a guy who shows off the size of his dick in toreador pants and flounces about in little ballerina slippers."

Frank, in one of the low points of his career, more or less joined up with Bogart's Rat Pack in 1953. He was deeply depressed about the failure of his love affair with Ava.

Bacall named the original Rat Pack. A gang of Bogie's friends, including Frank himself, David Niven, Judy Garland, Angie Dickinson, Irving (Swifty) Lazar, Jimmy Van Heusen, and Mike Romanoff had flown in a chartered plane to Las Vegas, ostensibly to catch Noël Coward's opening at the Desert Inn. After a week of partying, Bacall walked in late one morning and surveyed the disheveled, debauched crew. "You look like a goddamn rat pack," she charged.

Even though Bogie was CEO of the Rat Pack, he named Frank its president.

Back in California after his breakup with Ava, Frank practically crash landed at the Bogart's. In the beginning, Bogie virtually adopted Sinatra, and he became a regular at their

"I had my heart set on playing opposite Bogie in *Knock on Any Door* (1949)," Frank recalled one night in Palm Springs. Even after the passage of many years, a bitter disappointment still reflected on his face.

In the film, **Humphrey Bogart** was cast as a lawyer, Andrew Morton, defending the rights of Nick Romano, a troubled young man from the slums, as played by a young **John Derek**.

"Who knows troubled young men from the slums better than I do?" Frank asked. "Bogie had set up his own production company, Santana, and he had the power to give me the role. But he didn't."

"Amazingly, he gave the part to a former hustler, John Derek, who was the prettiest face in Hollywood at the time. The kid couldn't act, but he was sure eye candy.

"If I thought Bogie had been gay, I would have understood. But he wasn't. A boy who looked like Derek wouldn't have lasted in the slums one day. A rich queen would have picked him up and moved him immediately into a penthouse apartment in Manhattan."

home. He joined in their dinners and their parties.

But when Frank started showing up every night, Bogie decided "enough was enough." He pulled back, wanting to make the get-togethers with Frank less frequent.

"I know he's lonely," Bogie said. "But he chose to live this way. *Alone.* It's too bad if he's lonely. That his choice. I don't feel sorry for him. He can walk into any party in Hollywood and leave with the most beautiful gal in the room." He told Bacall, "We can't live Frank's life. We have our own road to travel."

One night in L.A., Dean Martin and some showgirl walked into Romanoff's and spotted Bogie, Bacall, and Frank at table. "I couldn't believe it," Dean claimed. "Betty was sitting right on Frank's lap. It couldn't have been more obvious. I knew Betty and Frank later had an affair. But had the affair begun already? Right in front of Bogie? Maybe Bogie and Bacall had made an agreement, since he was in such poor health. He looked like he couldn't take care of a woman any more. Of course, I don't know that for a fact. I'm only speculating."

As Bogie was dying, Frank visited him frequently. Bacall recalled, "He cheered Bogie up, made him laugh. He kept the ring-a-ding act in high gear for him."

**Gene Kelly** is making a phone call in the 1945 movie, *Anchors Aweigh,* as a very young **Frank Sinatra** eavesdrops.

When Humphrey Bogart's longtime mistress, Verita Thompson, came to see him for a final visit, she found him lying in bed— "all skin and bones"—in the final throes of cancer. She was surprised to see him watching what she called "such fluff," *Anchors Aweigh.*

Bogie explained it to Verita, whom he had continued to seduce throughout the course of his marriage to Bacall: "Frank is moving in on my turf, and my body's not even cold yet. I wanted to see this movie to study Frank very closely. I never got his appeal, but apparently, the gals are crazy about this little dago runt. I'm almost certain he'll propose to Betty while I'm being embalmed. For all I know, I'm looking at this silly little guy who can't even fill out a sailor's suit and thinking, 'Oh, my God, there's the future stepfather to my son and daughter.'"

If Kitty Kelley's quote in her biography of Frank is to be believed, Bacall later said, "Bogie was somewhat jealous of Frank. Partly because he knew I loved being with him, partly because he thought Frank was in love with me, and partly because our physical life together, which had always ranked high, had less than flourished with his illness."

Kelley also quoted playwright Ketti Frings, who paid several "death bed" visits to Bogie. "All of Bogie's friends knew what was going on in those last days. Everybody knew about Betty and Frank. We just hoped Bogie wouldn't find out. That would have been more killing than the cancer."

When Verita Peterson Thompson, Bogie's longtime mistress, came to visit him on his death bed, he told her, "I think Betty has fallen in love with Frank Sinatra. If she's not in love with him, then he's in love with my wife."

The last movie Bogie ever watched on his television set was Frank's *Anchors Aweigh* from 1945.

Bogie died on Monday, January 14, 1957, of throat cancer, right after his fifty-seventh birthday. Frank was so shaken by the news that he was too emotionally unstable to attend the funeral.

Throughout the remainder of 1957, Lauren was seen on Frank's arm as he escorted her to galas and dinner parties. She became a regular visitor to his home in Palm Springs, the hostess of small dinner parties, and she showed up at the premieres of his pictures, both *The Joker Is Wild* and *Pal Joey* (1957).

But reportedly, Frank felt he was being smothered. He

called Dean Martin, "How can I get out of this? I feel like I'm trapped. I want to be a free man."

Even though Bacall and Frank were "an item," he saw less of her than he did when Bogie was alive.

"He just couldn't devote himself to one woman," said director John Huston. "Betty was a one-man woman. He just couldn't commit himself. He wanted to lead the life of a swinging bachelor. He wanted to hang out with his pals. And there were all those gals to lay in Hollywood, Vegas, and New York."

On the night of March 11, 1958, Frank perhaps surprised even himself and proposed marriage to Bacall. She was thirty-three years old. The proposal came about a year and a half after his divorce from Ava.

Sinatra biographer, Michael Freedland, claimed, "Bacall even went so far as to sell her house—because she thought Bogie's ghost would be too much for Frank to handle."

She had her clivia plants dug up at the Bogie manse on Mapleton Drive and transferred to her new rented home. The clivia plants were in Frank's favorite color, orange.

One of Frank's many anonymous dates slept over with him in his Palm Springs house. She remembered Frank taking a call from someone he called "Boss." When he finally put down the receiver, he identified the caller as Lauren Bacall. "That is one pushy woman," Frank told his shack-up. "It's Betty Bacall. I don't know how Bogie put up with that."

In their book *The Rat Pack: Neon Nights with the King of Cool*, co-authors Lawrence J. Quirk and William Schoell tried to analyze the reasons that the marriage never took place: "Like a little girl, she clung to him, she smothered him. He ran out of patience and asked her to leave his house when she began acting too much like a girl-bride. Bad enough she came on like a wife, a potential ball and chain."

Judy Garland was also a member of the Rat Pack, and for a while she was hoping that Frank might marry her. Reportedly she tried to explain him to Bacall one night. "His behavior toward me is pretty repulsive, but I have to take Frank for what he is—that is, a first-class bastard who also has a sensitive, caring side on that odd Monday morning. You invite him to a party. He might not show up. If he shows up, he might be three hours late and he's with a dame he's just fucked."

Just as Bacall was falling for Frank, some so-called friend called her and warned her that the reason Frank wasn't seeing her every night was that he was dating Kim Novak, the lavender blonde goddess and his co-star in *The Man With the Golden Arm* (1955) and *Pal Joey* (1957).

The collapse of the Sinatra/Bacall engagement, according to reports, came about in the most trivial way. The day after

At the end of the war, Frank Sinatra saw this publicity still of **Lauren Bacall** from the film *To Have and Have Not*. He told Gene Kelly that she was next "on my list of gals to seduce."

But before he could get around to that, he'd heard that she'd fallen in love with Bogie.

In Bacall's 1978 autobiography, *By Myself,* she recalled: "I can't remember how it all began—there must have been a special feeling between Frank and me from earlier days. Certainly he was then at his vocal peak, and was wildly attractive, electrifying. And Frank had always carried with him not only an aura of excitement, but the feeling that behind that swinging façade lies a lonely, restless man, one who wants a wife and home but simultaneously wants freedom and a string of 'broads.'"

proposing, Frank flew to Miami.

Back in Hollywood, Bacall attended a party that Zsa Zsa Gabor was giving for Noël Coward.

Bacall was escorted by the agent Irving ("Swifty") Lazar. Gossipy Louella Parsons, with too many drinks in her, accosted Bacall at the party. "Is it true that you and Frank are going to get married?"

What happened next is the subject of some dispute. One account has Bacall dashing off to the powder room so she wouldn't have to answer the big question. Parsons could be very persistent. Perhaps while Bacall was gone, Lazar confirmed the engagement to Parsons. In her column the next morning, Parsons falsely reported that Bacall had confirmed her upcoming marriage to Frank.

LOS ANGELES EVENING

# MIRROR NEWS

It was a four-way drama, starring **Frank Sinatra and Lauren Bacall** (upper photos) and agent **Swifty Lazar** and gossip maven **Louella Parsons** (lower photos).

After Bogie died, Frank became Lauren's "best chance for a future romance." He called her frequently and even invited her to rest and recuperate in his home. They did not want to be seen together in public in the immediate aftermath of Bogie's death, but their romance flourished. There was talk of marriage.

But Frank admitted one night to Judy Garland, "As you know, I adore my broads. I don't think Betty will be able to handle my need for other broads." Even so, Lauren told Swifty about their plans to marry, and somehow Swifty indiscreetly leaked word to Parsons.

The next day she broke the headline news "SINATRA TO MARRY BACALL."

Frank was furious and called off the engagement.

The news that broke in the *Los Angeles Mirror* proved disastrous for the Bacall/Sinatra engagement. The story claimed, "Frank Sinatra and glamorous Lauren Bacall will be married in the near future, climaxing a fast and furious romance which has been Hollywood's number one gossip topic for several months, the actress revealed today." The *Mirror* even suggested that March 26 might be the wedding day. "Why else had both stars cancelled plans to be at the Oscar ceremonies that night?"

Instinctively Bacall knew that a premature announcement "would seriously piss off Frank." She called him in Miami. Some woman picked up the phone in his suite, and Bacall asked her to tell Frank to call her. As the hours drifted by, Bacall began to realize that Frank might never return her urgent call.

It was evening before she finally reached him. His angry voice came over the phone. "Why in hell did you make that announcement without consulting me?"

She explained that it was Lazar with the loose lips, not her.

In Miami Beach, the announcement had set off pandemonium, and Frank was besieged with reporters and photographers. There was a lot of unattractive gossip going about, including the charge that Frank and Bacall had launched an affair when Bogie was upstairs suffering and ultimately dying from throat cancer.

Frank's final words to Bacall was, "We'll have to lay low for a while. Not see each other."

Unknown to Bacall, Frank's mother, Dolly, had placed a call to Frank in Miami Beach, warning him to drop her and call off the marriage. "She's a ball buster. The marriage will be a disaster. You're still whining over Ava, and Bacall hasn't really gotten over Bogie yet. She'll try to run your life. If anybody's gonna run your life, it's your mother."

Frank celebrated the breakup of his love affair with Bacall by calling his pimp at the Fontainebleau. "Send over the two most beautiful broads in Miami—one blonde like Marilyn, another *café au lait*."

When a reporter finally caught up with Frank on Miami Beach and asked him about the upcoming marriage, he responded in anger, "What for? Just so I'd have to come home early every night? Nuts!"

George Jacobs, Frank's valet for years, later remembered that he complained to him about "Bacall's unwillingness to perform oral sex."

Swifty Lazar was "an ugly little creep with a truckload of pure shit and *chutzpah*," in the words of David Niven. The agent may have pushed Frank away from Bacall. He took no responsibility for breaking the news to Parsons, more or less blaming Bacall.

When Frank returned to Hollywood, Lazar warned him, "Don't marry Betty. You married Nancy who found out you were fucking other gals before you married her. She took you to the cleaners and could never accept your need to fuck other bitches. Ava, now take Ava. She cuckolded you on numerous occasions. As if your dick wasn't big enough, she wanted every slab of Spanish sausage she saw in toreador pants. Betty doesn't want you. She wants another Bogie. He made her a star. With him gone, she's history unless she can ride on your coattails to another decade of stardom. Otherwise, she's washed up in this town—and you know it. Don't become her meal ticket! She'll just use you. Dump her."

That was the last Bacall ever heard from him until he ran into her six years later.

Originally she'd been planning to attend Frank's opening at the Sands in Las Vegas. Instead she attended Dean Martin's opening at the Cocoanut Grove in Los Angeles. When confronted by a nosey reporter, she said, "Do me a favor. Never mention me again in the same breath with Frank Sinatra."

It soon became clear that Bacall had simply been dumped outright by Frank, without any explanation and for the most ridiculous of excuses. She'd stood by him and comforted him through the throes of his divorce from Ava, and this was how she was repaid. "Frankie humiliated Betty in front of the world," Martin recalled. "He shouldn't have done that. He just dropped out of her life after proposing to her. He's done that to dames before, and I'm sure he will do it again."

When Frank read what Bacall wrote about him in her autobiography, *By Myself*, he said, "There's another side to it, but I'm not going to give it. Let it rest."

After years had gone by, Swifty Lazar threw a party, inviting both Bacall and Frank, although neither of them knew that. A devious sort, the agent wanted to see some fireworks when the legendary couple came together again.

Although Bacall and Frank tried to avoid each other at the party, at one point they accidentally came face to face. He looked into her eyes, but his face was a total blank, as if he didn't recognize her. Of course, that was an act. She had one of the most famous faces in America. He walked right past her without a word.

Loud enough for her to hear, he said to one of his pals, "Who was the broad? She looked familiar."

Even though Bacall had named the original Rat Pack, she was more contemptuous of the "second coming" of the Rat Pack, which by then consisted of Frank, Peter Lawford, Dean

Martin, Joey Bishop, and Sammy Davis Jr.

Biographer Freedland reported that, as far as Bacall was concerned, "The Rat Pack was dissolved at the time of Bogie's death."

"I don't recognize the present group at all," she allegedly said. She was also reported to have called them "small minded—any color they might have escapes me because I think it's pretty manufactured stuff."

In a contrasting opinion, Frank weighed in, telling Joey Bishop, "The old Rat Pack, including Betty Bacall, died years ago. Today I have my own Rat Pack. I'm too old to play second fiddle to Bogie any more. Today I'm Chairman of the Board."

Frank's final word on the subject, uttered to Dean Martin and Sammy Davis Jr. in Las Vegas ten years after the breakup with Bacall, was this: "I woke up late one morning after Bogie's ghost paid me a visit. He told me not to become the new Bogart in Betty's life."

---

# THE DEATH OF DOLLY SINATRA

In August of 1976, Dolly had begun to complain and perhaps to prophesize to her friends and to Frank, "I don't have much longer to live."

"You're gonna live to be a hundred and ten," Frank assured her. "You're too tough to die."

In the last months of her life, she complained to Nancy, Sr., with whom she retained a dialogue, about Frank marrying that "horrible, horrible woman. What a little bastard of a son I have, to pull a trick like that on his mother, who has sacrificed so much for him." She was referring, of course to Barbara Marx, whom she frequently denounced in the vilest of terms.

Frank invited Dolly to his opening at Caesars Palace in Las Vegas, a glitzy event scheduled for January 6, 1977. Dolly loved to gamble with Frank's money. From New Jersey, she flew first to Palm Springs with a friend, Anna Carbone.

The women stayed at Frank's villa in Rancho Mirage. On the day of his appearance, he rented a Lear Jet to fly them from the Palm Springs airport into Las Vegas, the proposed flight to take only twenty minutes.

At the Palm Springs airport, the pilot was advised not to take off because of a violent storm raging in the Coachella Valley. Dolly cursed him and insisted that the flight depart anyway. Once airborne, the pilot found that visibility was zero, and he'd have to navigate the plane by radar. After two minutes aloft, ground control in Palm Springs lost communication with the Lear Jet.

Frank received a call in Las Vegas. It was feared that Dolly's plane had crashed into the San Gorgonio Mountains. He went ballistic. Yet amazingly, within three hours, he went on stage and delivered a performance that met with thunderous applause. As he sang, a search was still on for the missing aircraft.

At the end of the show, he flew immediately to Palm Springs, as weather conditions had improved. Anxiety-ridden, sleepless hours dragged on. Three days after the disappearance of the aircraft, Frank received the phone call he dreaded.

The wreckage of the Lear Jet had been found. And although the bodies of the passengers had disintegrated, Dolly's muu-muu dress was found hanging from the limb of a tree, blowing in the wind. Ironically, this was the same mountain that would, a decade later, claim the life of Dino Martin, (i.e., "Dino" of the 60s rock group *Dino, Desi, and Billy* and the son of his best friend, Dean Martin) when his F-4 Phantom II jet fighter crashed during a test flight with the California Air National Guard.

On January 12, 1977, the Associated Press reported that Frank's eyes "were unswerving from the casket covered with white lilies and pink roses."

# THE KIDNAPPING OF FRANK SINATRA JR.

Ever since President John F. Kennedy was assassinated in Dallas in November of 1963, that news and the subsequent fall-out had dominated the frontpage of every newspaper in the United States.

But on December 8 of that same year, an event happened that knocked even the post-assassination coverage of a president off the frontpages. It prompted news bulletins throughout America and Europe.

Frank Sinatra, Jr., had been kidnapped at 9:30pm, thirty minutes before he was scheduled to go on stage at Harrah's Club at Lake Tahoe. Trying to follow in his father's footsteps, Frank Jr. was struggling to make it as a singer.

In his underwear, the nineteen-year-old boy was sitting in his dressing room talking to John Foss, a twenty-six-year-old trumpet player with the Tommy Dorsey band. "I was just killing time before putting on my tuxedo," he later recalled.

Three kidnappers had descended on the resort. The leader of the pack was Barry Keenan, who at the age of twenty-one was the youngest member of the Pacific Stock Exchange in Los Angeles. Joe Amsler was a semi-pro boxer, but mainly a drifter, and John Irwin was a former underwater demolition team expert. He'd also been a decorated hero during World War II.

Pretending to be a room service waiter, Keenan burst into the room with a long-barreled blue steel .38 revolver. As the other two kidnappers entered the room, Foss was tied up and gagged. Blindfolded and tied, the scantily dressed Frank Jr. was led across the blizzard-swept parking lot and into a getaway car.

Within twenty minutes, Frank Sr. was contacted at his villa in Rancho Mirage and informed that his son had been kidnapped. "I'll pay anything to get him back," Frank promised. "A million dollars, whatever."

Within the hour, he was flying to Reno, Nevada, to meet with agents of the FBI. Once there, he received sympathetic, helpful calls from two of his enemies, both FBI director J. Edgar Hoover and U.S. Attorney General Bobby Kennedy.

By this time, the kidnappers, with Frank Jr. under threat of death, had slipped beyond police roadblocks and were hiding with their prisoner in a house in the San Fernando Valley.

It was Frank Sr. himself who took a call from one of the kidnappers, who demanded $240,000 in used currency. The distraught father quickly agreed and was given instructions where the pickup of the money would occur. As a means of evading police, the kidnappers demanded that Frank communicate with them through a series of public phone booths. As instructed, Frank arranged for a "drop." The courier made off with the money in a black valise.

Four hours later, Frank Sr. was instructed to pick up his teenaged son at the Mulholland exit of Los Angeles' San Diego Freeway. Frank drove there, but saw no sign of his son. Morbidly despondent, he drove home, cursing that he had been double-crossed. He even considered calling Sam Giancana at this point, with a request to bring the Mob in on the case.

Ironically, Frank Jr., had indeed been dropped at the designated dropoff point at the designated time. But fearing that his kidnappers would return, he fled from the site and walked to a random spot two miles away. It was at that point, a street corner in Bel-Air, where an FBI agent spotted him and picked him up. To avoid members of the press gathered at the Sinatra home, the agent put Frank Jr. in the trunk of his car.

Frank Sr. and Nancy Sr. couldn't stop hugging their son when he was freed after being held captive for fifty-four hours. Unknown to either of the parents at the time, there were many charges and much speculation in the press that the kidnapping had been a hoax, staged as a publicity stunt. Both Franks vehemently denied this, and even successfully sued in London, winning judgments against both the ITN and the BBC.

At the trial in late February of 1964 in the U.S. District Court in Los Angeles, attorneys for the kidnappers claimed that Frank Jr. had staged the kidnapping "as an advertising scheme," but the judge dismissed such charges.

The perpetrators, Joe Amsler and Barry Keenan, drew a sentence of life imprisonment, John Irwin getting off with sixteen years because he had befriended Frank Jr. during the ordeal. The sentences were later reduced, and the men became eligible for parole. Keenan spent four and a half years behind bars, and his other two partners served three and a half years each.

When Frank Jr. resumed his singing career, audiences for the next three months heckled him at his gigs, believing those false speculations that the kidnapping had been "staged."

It was later revealed that Keenan had known Nancy Jr., and had often visited the Sinatra household. On occasions, he'd even talked to Frank Sr., finding him "a pretty hard-boiled character who would be at home hanging out with gangsters."

**Frank Sr.** hugs **Frank Jr.** in the most affectionate embrace of these two ever captured on film.

"I knew Dad loved me when we came together after the kidnapping," Frank Jr. said. "His face seemed to have aged ten years."

Keenan had gone to University High School in West Los Angeles with Nancy Jr. Amazingly, he had met Frank Jr. on several occasions. "Because of the four-year difference in our ages, we didn't hang out together, although he might have been my best friend," Keenan claimed. "I really liked the guy, and felt that his father idolized his daughter, Nancy, not his son. I could tell that Frank Sr. wasn't close to his son, but I would bet that he would pay a pretty penny if Frank Jr. were kidnapped."

In an amazing interview with author J. Randy Taraborrelli, Keenan claimed that he felt a "good kidnapping would only bring the father and son together."

Keenan also revealed that the original plan involved kidnapping Frank Jr. at the Ambassador Hotel in Los Angeles during November of 1963, but because of the assassination of John F. Kennedy in Dallas, the kidnapping was postponed.

After Keenan was released from prison, he said that he often ran into Frank Jr. at social gatherings in Beverly Hills. "I once extended my hand to him, but he didn't shake it. He just looked at me, turned his back to me, and walked away. Can you blame the guy?"

# Frank, Lana Turner, Adultery, & Murder

## WHO KILLED JOHNNY STOMPANATO?

When they were very young and still getting started in Hollywood, **Frank Sinatra** feeds **Lana Turner** a popsicle. "That's not all I'd like to feed her," he told Gene Kelly. "Someday I'm going to divorce Nancy and marry Lana. Call it destiny. We were made for each other."

Peter Lawford, one of Lana's lovers, laughed at the remark. "Both Lana and Frank were made for a thousand lovers. Their charms were to be shared. Before each of them retired from heavy schedules in the boudoir, everybody got a crack at them, including myself."

With the possible exception of Ava Gardner, Frank never met another star like Lana, who'd gone from a discovery in a Sunset Boulevard malt shop to become one of the biggest blonde bombshells in Hollywood history, topped only by Marilyn Monroe. "I saw her through it all," Frank once said. "All seven husbands and a telephone book of love affairs that included Lex Barker, Fernando Lamas, Howard Hughes, and Tyrone Power. Her greatest role involved impersonating Lana Turner herself. No one did it better."

Columnist Hedda Hopper nailed it: "To Lana Turner, men are like new dresses, to be donned and doffed at her pleasure. Seeing a fellow that attracts her, she's like a child looking at a new doll."

# BUT WHY DID FRANK GET SO DEEPLY INVOLVED?

A deadly trio meet at the airport: a suntanned **Lana Turner, Johnny Stompanato**, and **Cheryl Crane**, daughter of Lana's second husband, Stephen Crane. Lana and Stompanato had just returned from time together at their favorite resort, Acapulco.

Lana was hardly truthful when she told reporters, "Marriage—forget it. I'll never marry again." She even denied reports that she was having a torrid affair with Stompanato, one of Mickey Cohen's gangster boys and an acknowledged Hollywood hustler to size queens of both sexes.

Later in their relationship, when Lana complained of physical violence from Stompanato, Janet Leigh, who was the first Hollywood star that Stompanato had seduced, had a different reaction:

"He was a perfect gentleman with me. Maybe he shouted once or twice when I forgot which cleaners I put his most expensive suit in—and lost the ticket. But that was that. He never raised a hand to me. He raised something else...and frequently. Too frequently, if you ask me."

*"I killed the son-of-a-bitch and I'd do it again."*
—**Lana Turner**
to Eric Root, her escort, occasional lover, confidant, and "spiritual brother" for two decades.

*"I wonder if the screwing I'm getting is worth the screwing I'm getting."*
—**Lana Turner**

*"When it comes to men, Lana and I are the world's lousiest pickers."*
—**Ava Gardner**

*"You'll never get rid of me."*
—**Johnny Stompanato, 1958**

In his first recording of "Nancy," a song about his infant daughter, Frank warbled, "Keep Betty Grable, Lamour, and Turner." He did not follow his own advice.

Frank and Lana launched one of the most tempestuous affairs in Hollywood. When she published her autobiography in 1992, she called it *Lana: The Lady, The Legend, The Truth*. It was advertised as "the naked, intimate truth—finally, she tells it all!" She certainly didn't tell the truth. Nor did she tell it all. In fact, truth had little to do with her memoirs—call it selective memory.

In her original version, she'd written a blow-by-blow account of her love life with Frank. But at the last minute, she changed her mind and killed three chapters devoted to their on-again, off-again tempestuous relationship that stretched over the years. In her so-called "tell all," she claimed, "The closest thing to dates Frank and I enjoyed were a few box lunches at MGM." This was a complete lie, of course.

Ava Gardner was Lana's closest friend. She contradicted Lana's "memory" of her affair with Frank. "We met one night in the ladies room during a Hollywood party, and she told me the whole story. She'd been deeply in love with Frank. She thought he was in love with her too. He broke her heart. But she later told me she denied the affair in her memoirs because she didn't want to give him the satisfaction of reading about himself."

By Hollywood standards, their romance got off to a slow start. If Lana met a man she wanted to seduce, it rarely took her more than a day or night. With Frank, a world war had to be fought and won.

Lana first met Frank in 1940 at a night club in the San Fernando Valley. He sang that night with the Tommy Dorsey band. He asked for her telephone number, and she willingly gave it to him, but he didn't call.

Six long years would go by before he actually asked her out on a date. In the meantime, she'd encountered him on several occasions, even appearing together with him on radio. Perhaps Lana had been reluctant to get involved with him because she'd become a close friend of his wife, Nancy.

As far as it is known, Frank and Lana did not become romantically involved until 1946. It happened on the MGM lot. Staffers and co-stars noted that Frank had become a frequent visitor to Lana's dressing room, sometimes staying there for three hours when they weren't due on the set. When Lana went to New York to promote *The Postman Always Rings Twice*, she stayed in Frank's hotel suite. He was in Manhattan for location shooting and radio shows.

Their affair heated up. There was talk that Frank was going to divorce Nancy and marry Lana. After sleeping with Lana for four months and rarely showing up to stay with Nancy, word leaked out. Frank's press agent, George Evans, was the first to announce that Frank and Nancy had separated. When confronted by a reporter, she said that she preferred a separation to a divorce.

At a Hollywood party, Louis B. Mayer noted that Frank

On the streets of Jersey City *(top photo)* a very young and skinny **Frank Sinatra** dated **Nancy Barbato**. "We were going steady," he said, "and there was talk of marriage. He later told his chums, "You known me. I can go steady with twenty broads at a time."

Frank and two of his Jersey pals went to see a crime drama, *They Won't Forget* (1937), starring Claude Rains. The picture opens with Lana Turner walking along the streets in a sweater, her breasts bouncing in the wind. "Wow, look at those knockers!" one of Frank's friends shouted in the dark theater. The whole world seemingly was captivated by Lana's breasts—she became known as "The Sweater Girl."

Before Frank headed to California, he told his male friends in New Jersey, "My first mission will be to fuck Lana Turner." As the lower photo clearly indicates, he was soon on his way to fulfilling his dreams.

and Lana danced throughout the night cheek to cheek and appeared very much in love. The studio chief, of course, opposed the relationship, warning both Lana and Frank that they ran the risk of seriously damaging their careers.

Frank spent weekends at Lana's villa in Palm Springs. At the celebrity-haunted Chi Chi Club, they made no effort to conceal their affair.

To some journalists, Lana insisted that she and Frank were just good friends. "I have never in my life broken up a home. I can't take all these accusations."

In less than three weeks, following a public scolding in the press from columnist Hedda Hopper, Frank was back home with Nancy. At Slapsie Maxie's night club on Beverly Boulevard, he sang, "Goin' Home" directly to Nancy, who sat at a table by herself. They left the club together arm in arm. When the press converged on him, he told them to get lost. "I'm going home and let's forget it."

He called Lana the next morning, telling her, "It's all off."

During the late 1940s, the public came to see a different Frank Sinatra. He began a vicious cycle of fighting with reporters and photographers. He often threatened them and, on occasion, beat them up. As early as 1946, he'd been named "least cooperative star of the year" by the Women's Press Club.

A few weeks later, Frank was in New York for his opening at the Waldorf Astoria. He'd invited Nancy to accompany him. Lana was also in town, and Frank called her to resume their affair. "I've missed you, babe," he told her. "Can't live without you." During his stay in Manhattan, he maneuvered between Lana's bed and Nancy's.

"I began to make wedding plans," Lana confessed to Ava Gardner. "He proposed marriage to me, and I accepted. He told me that he was definitely going to leave Nancy this time. His exact words were, 'There can be no turning back. As far as Nancy is concerned, the spark is gone.'"

But back in Los Angeles, he changed his mind once again. He spent a long weekend with

After his arrival in Hollywood, Frank Sinatra decided he wanted to live in two separate worlds. By day, he could be a family man, as the family portrait of (left to right) **Frank Jr., Nancy Sr., Frank himself, and Nancy Jr.** indicates.

At night, however, he preferred to date from the pool of what he called "the goddesses," one of whom was **Lana Turner** (right photo). "I like brunettes," he'd later say. "Ava Gardner proved that. But when a blonde like Lana, Marilyn Maxwell, or Marilyn Monroe came along, I was as erect as the Empire State Building."

He was always mad at Peter Lawford for dating Lana. "The guy was screwing her, but telling me she was all boobs and no brains. I didn't like the cocksucker putting Lana down like that. Lana was A-okay in my book."

Nancy. The details of what was said are not known, but he emerged Monday morning with an uneasy alliance with his estranged wife. Their marriage would stagger through another four years, and in the meantime he would date other women.

On occasion he even bedded Lana. But by now she realized that a marriage to Frank was not to be.

She launched another torrid affair, this time with Tyrone Power, even though she'd been warned that he frequently indulged in homosexual relationships with young men. Frank and Lana would remain "best pals" in the years to come.

He made a promise to her, which years later, she would ask him to keep. He'd told her, "If you need me, babe, I'll be there."

It was almost like the refrain from a song.

***

Johnny Stompanato, the trusted henchman and pimp for Mickey Cohen, read in the papers that Hollywood's blonde goddess, Lana Turner, was recently divorced from Lex Barker, who played Tarzan in the movies.

A handsome man, Stompanato stood five-feet eleven, weighed 180 pounds, and had flashing brown eyes and black wavy hair.

He'd obviously learned how to dress from movie gangster George Raft, and was most often described as "cunning and cocksure," with an emphasis on *cock*.

After Cohen had to do time on a Federal tax rap, Stompanato became a high-priced gigolo, servicing some of the fading beauties of Hollywood who had kept their money long after their careers had faded.

Word of his endowment became legendary. "He was the John C. Holmes of his day," said columnist James Bacon, a reference to the famous porn star.

In his memoirs, *In My Own Words*, Cohen had written, "Johnny Stompanato was the most handsome man that I've ever known that was all man. He was an athlete and a real man, without any queerness about him." The gangster left out the fact that Johnny hustled not only rich women but "rich queers," as he put it.

Stompanato obtained Lana's private phone number and began placing calls to her, which she refused to accept. Since she wouldn't speak to him, he started sending her "the most exquisite flowers in all the world" [her words]. Later she would find out that they came from a florist shop owned by Cohen. Stompanato even began to send her jewelry, which she did accept because there was no forwarding address. Finally, she decided to take one of his persistent calls.

**Lana Turner** denied that her gangster boyfriend **Johnny Stompanato** was great sex, but her love letters to him revealed otherwise.

"She was hot for the bastard," Frank Sinatra said. "I hated the shithead. He was selling his dick to the highest bidder."

After his friend, Stompanato, was murdered, his gangster friend, Mickey Cohen, came into possession of Lana's "hot, hot" letters to her lover. To embarrass her, Cohen released the letters to newspapers all over the world. A horrified Lana assumed that her career "was all but over."

She was mistaken. As an aging actress about to disappear from the radar screen, she found that the scandal had put her back on top again at the box office. She was in demand and her earnings per film, such as *By Love Possessed*, were higher than ever.

Stompanato had presumably saved the love letters Lana had sent him to use as blackmail against her if she ever planned to ditch him and move on to another stud.

He introduced himself as "John Steele," a Los Angeles businessman. On the other end of the phone, she heard a smooth talker with a strong, masculine voice. "Ava Gardner, as you know, is in London now, but she gave me your phone number. She told me to call you. She said that you and she often share the same tastes in men."

"I trust Ava wasn't referring to Mickey Rooney," Lana said in a teasing voice.

He immediately picked up on that innuendo. "That's not me at all. In fact, I have something in common with Oscar."

"What might that be?" she asked, knowing full well what he was implying.

"We're both a foot long," Stompanato claimed. A date was arranged, and one of the most notorious affairs in the history of Hollywood was launched.

He was thirty-two years old, Lana thirty-seven, a dangerous age for an actress in Hollywood in the 1950s.

From the very beginning, and from all reports, Johnny Stompanato at first was the perfect lover, both in bed—he had not exaggerated his endowment—and as an escort. But gradually he began to try to take over management of Lana's life and money. She resisted these intrusions.

That led to months of physical abuse, violent arguments, and repeated reconciliations. The question is often asked, "Why did Lana put up with such abusive behavior? Why didn't she dismiss him when he first attacked her, giving her a black eye which she concealed with large sunglasses?'

Stompanato bragged to his cronies that "Lana can't get enough of it. She told me I went deeper than any of her former lovers, including Frank Sinatra."

Frank had detested Stompanato ever since he'd learned of his affair with Ava. At Mickey Cohen's house, Frank pleaded with the mob boss to intervene and forbid him from seeing Ava. The mobster refused.

Cohen told Frank, "I don't mix in with no guys and their broads. Why don't you go on home to Nancy where you belong?"

Lana began to date Stompanato in the spring of 1957, shortly after ending her marriage to Lex Barker. Her daughter, Cheryl Crane, whose father was Stephen Crane, Lana's second husband, had claimed that Barker had repeatedly molested and raped her.

Lana went to England in 1958 to film

In happier days, **Lana Turner** had been deeply in love with her second husband, **Stephen Crane**. After she'd divorced musician Artie Shaw, Lana claimed that this new attempt at marriage, on July 17, 1942, was for "forever and ever." In December of 1942, she announced that a baby was on the way. It would be Cheryl Crane, a child marked for tragedy.

She had known her new husband only nine days before she married him. He was twenty-seven years old and a junior executive in a firm that sold hot dogs at baseball parks. When Stephen married her, he forgot to tell her that he was in the midst of finalizing a divorce from another wife, Carol Kurtz of Indianapolis.

To Lana's heartbreak, she learned that her groom of two months would not be officially divorced until January 19, 1943, which meant that her marrriage to him was invalid, and that both she and Stephen were bigamists. She sought an annulment and had to remarry him.

Cheryl Crane was born on July 25, 1943. Six months later, on January 21, 1944, Lana divorced Stephen. In court, Lana told the judge that her marriage to Stephen caused her "to catch colds."

*Another Time, Another Place* with a very young Sean Connery. When word reached Stompanato that she was having an affair with the future James Bond, he flew to England, where he confronted Connery at the studio, brandishing a gun. Connery was too quick for him, disarming him and chasing him off the set.

Lana was just beginning to realize the extent of Stompanato's temper and potential for violence.

Because of the incident with the gun and the fight with Connery, Scotland Yard deported Johnny from England.

Weeks before his murder, Lana and Johnny had quarreled endlessly. As she related in her unreliable memoirs, *Lana: The Lady, The Legend, The Truth*, "He threatened me constantly. He'd kill me or cripple me. He'd disfigure my face, carve it up with a knife, so that no man would ever want me again. I'd never act again or be able to earn a living."

On Good Friday, April 4, 1958, the world was about to learn that Johnny Stompanato had been murdered at Lana Turner's house at 730 North Bedford Drive in Beverly Hills.

\*\*\*

As told to the police, Stompanato threatened Lana only minutes before his murder. She'd ordered him to leave her house, telling him their affair was over.

Her fourteen-year-old daughter, Cheryl, was waiting outside the door eavesdropping, or so the story went. "I'll cut you up and I'll get your mother and daughter too," Cheryl claimed she heard him say. "That's my business," he went on, "killing people."

According to highly disputed accounts, Cheryl ran to the kitchen and grabbed the first weapon she found, a nine-inch butcher knife. Racing back up the steps, she rushed into the room and stabbed Stompanato in the stomach. Or so this particular scenario goes.

At the trial before a jury, Lana gave what many consider her all-time best performance, worthy of an Oscar. She testified about the violent argument she and Stompanato had right before his slaughter.

"And I said, 'Don't—don't ever touch me again. I am absolutely finished. This is

After Lana Turner learned that her husband, Lex Barker, the devastatingly handsome movie Tarzan, was seducing her daughter, Cheryl, she divorced him. She began to drink heavily and felt lonely and despondent. "She was ripe for plucking," Mickey Cohen told his former bodyguard, **Johnny Stompanato,** who's pictured with **Lana** above.

Famous among Hollywood patrons of hustlers, he was olive skinned and ruggedly handsome. He had thick, wavy black hair and an endowment that was widely hailed as "unbelievable." With the collapse of Cohen's underworld empire, Stompananto was looking for a new "gig," and Lana was it.

Frank Sinatra warned her about him, but she didn't listen.

"I'm passionately in love with Johnny," she told her former lover. Frank's final warning was, "You'll live to regret it. It's not fair to Cheryl either to move some lowlife like Stompanato into your home."

the end. And I want you to get out.'

"And after I said that, I was walking toward the bedroom door, and he was right behind me, and I opened it, and my daughter came in.

"I swear it was so fast, I—I truthfully thought she had hit him in the stomach. The best I can remember, they came together and they parted. I still never saw a blade.

"Mr. Stompanato grabbed his abdomen. He started to move forward, and he made almost a half a turn, and then dropped on his back, and when he dropped, his arms went out, so that I still did not see that there was blood or a wound until I ran over to him, and I saw his sweater was cut, and I lifted the sweater up and I saw his wound.

"I remember only barely hearing my daughter sobbing and I ran into my bathroom which is very close, and I grabbed a towel. I didn't know what to do.

A chicly groomed **Lana Turner** poses in 1957 with her new heartthrob, an unbelieveably young **Sean Connery**. The future James Bond was just breaking into movies when he co-starred in England with Lana in *Another Time, Another Place*. From a photograph, Lana had personally selected Sean as her leading man, with seduction looming in the background.

Leaving Johnny Stompanato behind in Los Angeles, she flew to London and into the arms of her dashing new leading man.

Hearing of the affair, Stompanato also flew to London. Before leaving, he had threatened Lana, promising to "carve up your face with a knife if I find you're sleeping with this creep."

Showing up on her movie set with a gun, Stompanato confronted Sean, who wrestled the gun from him and laid him out cold with a right hook.

Lana arranged for Stompanato to be quietly kicked out of Britain by Scotland Yard. He promised her, "I'll be waiting for you in Hollywood, bitch."

"And then I put the towel there, and Mr. Stompanato was making very dreadful sounds in his throat of gasping, terrible sounds and I went to the telephone and I called my mother because I had been out of the country for so long, and I could not remember my doctor's number.

"And I said, "Mother, quick, call the doctor, Dr. Macdonald.""

She told her mother, Mildred Turner, "He's been stabbed to death." She did not identify who had been stabbed or who had actually murdered Johnny. Mildred dressed hurriedly and drove to her daughter's house, arriving about the same time Stephen Crane was pulling into the driveway.

Without Lana's knowledge, Cheryl had rushed to the phone to telephone her father, Stephen Crane.

Crane would later admit only to his most intimate friends, "I'll never forgive Lana for making our daughter take the blame for her murder. What was she thinking in the first place? Having a notorious gangster in the house."

After Lana determined that Stompanato was dead, she was back on the phone, placing a call to the attorney, Jerry Geisler.

Short and plump, with a high nasal voice, Geisler had defended Charles Chaplin and Errol Flynn on statutory rape charges, even gangsters Mickey Cohen and Bugsy Siegel.

The word had always been, "If

304

you've murdered someone, get Geisler."

A world-famous voice came over the wire. "This is Lana Turner. Something terrible has happened. Could you please come to my house?"

When Geisler arrived, he found the bloodied corpse of Johnny Stompanato (alias Johnny Valentine) lying on the floor.

Lana also placed a call to Frank Sinatra. His role in that infamous night is often overlooked. But Lana in desperation had phoned him, thinking he would know how to handle a murder.

Geisler summoned Fred Otash, Hollywood's most celebrated private eye, to the scene. Otash was called because he'd been working for months spying on Stompanato and Cheryl. He had been employed by Stephen Crane.

"Crane hired me to find out how deeply involved Cheryl was with Lana's two-bit gangster boyfriend."

Otash stabled some horses in San Fernando Valley where Stompanato was teaching Cheryl to ride. "But the only ride that interested Johnny was fucking Cheryl," Otash claimed. "I saw them together many times. He was all over her like skin."

Lana trusted Frank more than Otash and Geisler. She may have known that Otash was working for Crane.

To Frank, she revealed the complete story. "You've got to tell Otash and Geisler. I can't bear to do it. I arrived home early and walked in on Cheryl and Johnny in my bed. I took that butcher knife I keep by my bedside in my nightstand. I don't know what happened to me. I went berserk. I grabbed the knife. Johnny was on his back, resting up after having done his dirty deed. I plunged the knife into his stomach. I was aiming to castrate him. Cheryl saw me and screamed."

Otash later admitted that he was the one who changed the bloody sheets on the bed and moved Stompanato's body to the floor.

According to Otash, Lana was running around screaming, "My career. What's going to happen to my career?" Otash later claimed that he was also the one who wiped Lana's fingerprints from the knife.

Frank pointed out that Cheryl as a juvenile "Won't get more than a slap on the wrist." He

The war was over, and **Frank Sinatra** *(left)* and **Peter Lawford** *(visible in the background)* were not only enjoying the popcorn and drinks but **Lana Turner** as well.

Almost daily, widely read columnists wrote that Lana was "the most sought out actress in Hollywood." Chief among her seekers was Frank himself. While he was making *Anchors Aweigh* on the MGM lot, Lana was filming *Weekend at the Waldorf*, also on the MGM lot. *"I lost fifteen pounds,"* he claimed, "running between my set and her dressing room."

Because of their crotch-to-crotch dancing at a party hosted by Sonja Henie, reporters got wind of the romance. Since Frank was married, he began to slip about and arrange for a rendezvous with Lana in discreet places such as Palm Springs.

The beginning of the end of their romance was when he escorted Lana one night to the Chi Chi Club in Hollywood. Howard Hughes showed up with his date, Ava Gardner. Hughes liked to switch partners during many of his outings. He asked Frank, "Do you mind if I dance with Lana tonight, and you dance with Ava Gardner here?"

Frank lost Lana that night to "The Aviator." Within weeks, Lana was making plans to marry him.

"My consolation prize was Ava," Frank said. "What a change. Blonde to brunette."

**Fred Otash** *(photo above)* became the most famous private detective in Hollywood, most of his early duties involving the setup of abortions for the mistresses of movie stars. "I've had enough kids aborted to populate a small country," he said.

He was also the chief investigator for the tabloid scandal rag *Confidential.*

Although he was called in on the Lana Turner/Johnny Stompanato murder case, he was employed by the mob specifically to report on the affairs Kennedy was having on the West Coast. Today, he's best remembered for his private work investigating Marilyn Monroe and the Kennedy brothers. In the wake of Marilyn's death, his files were confiscated by the FBI and never returned.

Otash told James Ellroy, the novelist, that he sometimes spied on JFK in action. Otash claimed that from what he'd seen spying on JFK, that he was "a two-minute man" and "hung like a cashew." In Ellroy's novel, *American Tabloid* (1995), the president was called "Badback Jack," because he used his bad back as an excuse for his lack of virility.

Frank Sinatra paid Otash to find out what really happened that night between Stompanato and Lana. Otash gave him a full report, beginning with the words, "Lana did it."

preyed on Lana's worst fear—that her career would be ruined and she'd be sent off to face all the lesbians in prison.

Geisler later agreed to go along with Frank's plot and urged Lana to "go for it, too."

After kissing Lana good-bye, Frank said he had to leave, as he didn't want to be caught in the house when the police arrived.

As he was leaving, Cheryl came into the room. Geisler and Lana had to rehearse her on what to say, and both of them had to repeat the exact same story to police. Geisler warned them that the police would question them separately, looking for inconsistencies in their testimony.

Clinton Anderson, the Beverly Hills chief of police, suspected that Otash had been involved in some sort of cover-up. He was brought in for questioning. Eric Root, in his memoir, asserted that "Fred had some damaging political information on Anderson, so he was never charged."

Swimming star Esther Williams, who knew both Lana and Frank, said, "There have always been cover-ups here because Hollywood protects its own."

Lana's former lover, Howard Hughes, was telephoned in his bungalow at the Beverly Hills Hotel. The call was from his pimp and right-hand man, Johnny Meyer, who was blunt, "Lana has stabbed Johnny Stompanato in the gut. He's dead. They're setting up her teenage daughter to take the rap."

Rising from his bed, Hughes swung into action. He knew that Mickey Cohen would want revenge, and indeed, death threats from the mob came in within twenty-four hours of Stompanato's murder.

Through Meyer, Hughes ordered a 24-hour security guard. He'd heard from Meyer who quoted a source that Cohen didn't plan to kill Lana, but to have one of his goons throw sulfuric acid in her face.

For eight months, Hughes had Lana under 24-hour protection until fear of mob reprisal had died down.

Stompanato had been Cohen's best and most trusted friend, and he wanted revenge on the murderer, whom he believed was Lana herself. The police called him and asked him to come to the morgue to identify the body. Cohen refused claiming the reason why: "I won't do it on the grounds that I may be accused of this murder."

Cohen went into a rage when he determined that Lana "was getting away with murder." Before the police arrived, he ordered two of his henchmen to search Stompanato's former living quarters at the Del Capri Motel in Westwood and remove anything that was incriminating, or anything that would link him to Cohen.

He also wanted all the blackmail evidence that Stompanato had accumulated on those fading stars and "rich queers" he'd seduced for profit. Among the cache, and to Cohen's surprise, were some very personal love letters Lana had written him. Cohen decided to release them to the newspapers to cause her more embarrassment than what she was already suffering.

All the readers of the *Herald Examiner* and later the *Herald-Express* got to read Lana's love notes. "I miss you, want you, and ache for you. I'm your woman and I need MY MAN!" The letters directly contradicted Lana's testimony to the police, in which she stated she had "little interest in Mr. Stompanato."

Cohen later came up with a completely different story from the version recited by witnesses on the scene. He didn't believe that Cheryl had stabbed Stompanato. "There's no way that a clever fox like Johnny would let a fourteen-year-old girl stab him. He would have blocked her move and disarmed her. Somebody else, and I know who, rubbed Johnny out but only when he was asleep in the bed."

Cohen was right about one point: Stompanato had been stabbed in bed with his eyes closed.

Carmine Stompanato, Johnny's brother, was furious at what he viewed as an inept police investigation. "Lana called her mother, her ex-husband, and her press agent before calling the doctor, and she never called the police. And Johnny lay there dying all this time."

The police in Beverly Hills reported that there was a lapse of at least two hours between the time of the slaughter and their arrival on Lana's doorstep. Others familiar with the murder scene claim there was a lapse of five hours.

The case was not without its irony. Cheryl's father, Stephen Crane, had been a close pal of gangster Bugsy Siegel. Siegel was Mickey Cohen's mentor, and Cohen had been Stompanato's boss.

At the inquest, an anonymous man leaped up. He violently objected to the testimony. "This is all a pack of lies. Johnny Stompanato was my friend. The daughter was in love with him, and he was killed because of jealousy between mother and daughter." He was immediately ushered from the courtroom.

At the actual trial, and after hearing Lana's sobs and testimony, the jury took only twenty minutes to render a verdict of justifiable homicide.

\*\*\*

Far from destroying Lana at the box office, the Stompanato murder marked her return to films with some of her biggest hits, notably *Imitation of Life* (1959).

Her long-time companion, Eric Root, revealed that

The two most beautiful women in Hollywood, **Ava Gardner** *(left)* greets **Lana Turner** *(right)* at a party. Ava and Lana liked to talk about men they'd shared, specifically Artie Shaw, the musician, to whom both woman had at one time or another been married.

Sometimes, they talked about Artie's sexual performance, as opposed to that of Frank, with Frank winning on every score.

Long before Ava had started to sleep with Frank, Lana had bragged about his priapic endowment. When Frank actually bedded Ava, she called Lana, "You did not exaggerate." Frank's pal, Jackie Gleason, said that "Frank, naked, looked like a tuning fork."

When Lana learned that Ava was falling for Frank, she warned her, "The bastard will hurt you, make any promise, and even claim he's leaving Nancy. But he won't—believe me on that."

"He'll leave her," Ava said. "Frank and I are too far gone on each other. This time it's for keeps."

Lana was still getting huge royalty checks for *Imitation of Life* (1954) from her profit participation plan up until her death.

In his memoir, *The Private Diary of My Life with Lana*, published in 1996, Root revealed a story that, if true, would require a lot of rewriting of Hollywood biographies.

Lana told Root, "I've done so many things wrong in my life I've had to live with, but darling, if I die before my daughter, you should tell the truth so I can rest in peace. Don't let my baby take the rap all her life for my mistake."

She confessed that Cheryl did not go down to the kitchen to get that butcher knife. "I kept that knife in the nightstand. The one by my bed." She feared that Stompanato might attack her one night, as he had so often threatened, and she wanted to defend herself.

In his memoirs of Lana, Root writes, "The last remaining link to the truth behind this sordid affair lies buried within the private memories of Cheryl Crane. All her life she has not changed her version of the story in any substantial manner, but she may have come close. In [Cheryl's 1988 memoirs] *Detour*, she recounts an incident wherein she tried to explain the murder to her lover, Josh. Although she later glosses over the conversation as though it were merely an attempt at wishful thinking, the words ring true."

Cheryl wrote, "I didn't do it. I love you so much more than anyone else in my life, Josh, that I don't want you to think I could do a terrible thing like that."

Shortly before his death in 1973, Lex Barker was intimately involved with actress Karen Kondazian. He made a startling revelation to her. "It was Lana who stabbed Johnny Stompanato to death. She called me five days after she'd murdered him and told me that she'd followed Frank Sinatra's advice to let Cheryl take the blame. But she added a tantalizing note without ever revealing actually what she meant. She said, 'Cheryl is not entirely without blame in this whole mess.'"

To this day, Cheryl consistently denies all these reports about any sexual involvement with Stompanato, although sticking to her story that Lex Barker repeatedly raped her.

Lana's daughter also still claims that she, and she alone, fatally stabbed Stompanato. But witnesses and those close to the scene believed Lana was the murderer.

Diagnosed in 1992 with throat cancer, Lana died in 1995 at the age of 74. All her life she'd been a heavy smoker. Cheryl, her only child, survived her and was living with her long-time partner and lover, Joyce ("Josh") LeRoy. Lana had referred to Josh as "my second daughter."

Lana left her fur coats to Cheryl and the balance of her estate ($50,000) to Carmen Lopez Cruz, her long-time maid and companion.

Lana was a great believer in reincarnation, and was absolutely convinced that in a previous life she had been the Queen of Egypt, Cleopatra herself.

To escape the post-murder trauma after Stompanato's murder, she often envisioned herself at court in Egypt and told friends how much in love she had been with Marc Antony. Again, retreating into fantasy to avoid reality, she also told friends that Tyrone Power was the reincarnation of Marc Antony.

When she conveyed this belief to Frank during one of his last phone calls to her, he asked: "And what role do I play in this drama? Julius Caesar no doubt."

# *How Frank Pimped S& M Pinup Queen Bettie Page*

## TO THEN-SENATOR FROM MASSACHUSETTS, JOHN KENNEDY

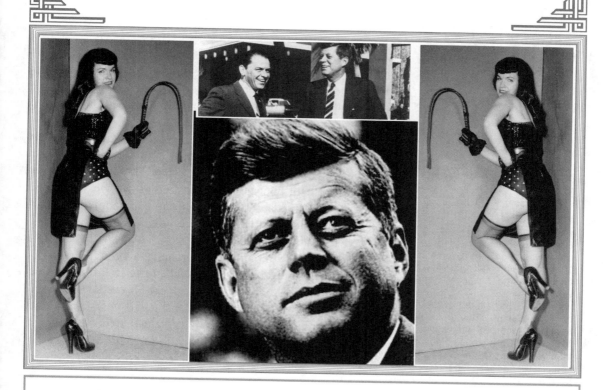

"Who would believe that I would grow up to seduce such famous men as John F. Kennedy, Frank Sinatra, and Howard Hughes?," said pinup **Bettie Page**, depicted above. "I could only dream about such things when I was born to redneck white trash in Nashville, Tennessee. Most of us gals in those days never escaped our hillbilly backgrounds."

"When I did move away and started posing for cheesecake, my career really took off. One of my bestsellers was a series I posed for called 'Battling Babes.' I learned how to use a whip. Men get turned on watching one scantily clad woman spank another woman. Sometimes I was on the receiving end. My ass was red a lot in those days."

"But I got into trouble. The coonskin-wearing senator from Tennessee, Estes Kefauver, was a moral crusader. He targeted me, calling my pictures indecent. He made so many threats against me he drove me into hiding. He told his aides, 'Bettie Page is a pervert—no doubt, a lesbian. Only a card-carrying lesbian would pose for some of those sordid pictures. I vomited looking at them.'

"Twice, Kefauver sought the Democratic Party's nomination for president. I hated him. But I really liked another man who sought and won the nomination for president. He was John F. Kennedy. I'd vote for him over Kefauver any day. Frank Sinatra wasn't bad either."

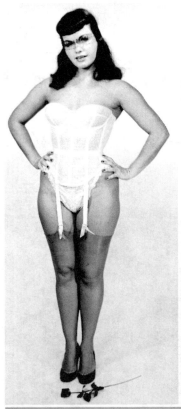

# Frank Introduces the "Empress of Kink" to JFK

Bettie Page, Queen of the Pinups in the 1950s, died after a turbulent life at the age of 85 on December 11, 2008. She was one of the earliest "Playmates of the Month" for *Playboy* magazine. After aging in seclusion, no one would recognize Bettie Page in later life as the former "Empress of Kink."

She enjoyed a renaissance during the 1980s and 90s that continues to this day. "I'm more famous now than I was fifty years ago," she said in 1993. Her bust was 36", her waist 23", and those measurements became known around the world. Her jet black hair—all bangs and bob 'do—became an iconic trademark during the rockabilly subculture of the Eisenhower years.

**Bettie Page** was exploited by photographers who had taken pictures of her in the 1950s and were making a living by hawking those long-ago images. In the last few years of her life, when she was living in near poverty, she hired a law firm to help her recoup some of the profits being made from her likeness. It seems that everybody has profited from Bettie Page except the model herself. There are tribute songs, countless web sites, and more than a thousand products for sale on e-Bay. At first her videos were sold under the counter or mailed in plain brown wrappers. Yet decades later she was elevated to the status of pulp goddess. The "Bondage Babe" had gone mainstream.

According to her business agent and long time friend, Mark Roesler, Bettie was hospitalized in critical condition on December 6, 2008. She had suffered a heart attack, which led to her falling into a coma. When her funeral was conducted at California's Westwood Village Cemetery, there was a large blowup of Bettie in all her cheesecake glory resting among the tribute flowers.

Displaying soft core porn at a funeral may have been a first.

"She was a remarkable woman, an iconic figure in pop culture who influenced sexuality, taste in fashion, someone who had a tremendous impact on our society," said *Playboy*'s founder Hugh Hefner, who years previously had provided Bettie with her greatest "exposure."

In 1995, Bettie was referred to as "Miss Pinup Girl of the World," "The Dark Angel," and "The Queen of Curves."

Bettie Page images have spawned picture books, biographies, fan clubs, dozens of websites, comics, beach towels, and even lunch boxes.

Look-alike contests in the 1980s and 90s brought out "kitten-with-a-whip Betties," all in leather and lace.

Celebrities took note. Uma Thurman in bangs reincarnated Bettie's image in Quentin Tarantino's *Pulp Fiction*. Madonna ordered that her own bondage photographs, some of them inspired by Bettie, be widely distributed.

When someone showed Bettie a copy of Madonna's *Sex* book, the former pinup beauty wasn't impressed.

"She's not much of a looker," Bettie said. "If I was Madonna, I'd keep my clothes on."

At a lonely, desperate time in Bettie's life, a call came in from Johnny Meyer, who identified himself as the publicist for Howard Hughes. Throughout the entertainment industry, Meyer was known as Hughes' pimp.

Hughes regularly, even systematically, flipped through girlie magazines and selected the model of his choice whom he then lured to Hollywood with the promise of an RKO contract. He had taken over the studio, and was using it as a vast casting couch. Hughes was a notorious bisexual, seducing as many good-looking young actors as he did young actresses.

Thrilled at the prospect of a movie contract, Bettie accepted the offer. The next day a thousand dollars in spending money, plus an airline ticket on TWA, arrived at her hotel.

Wanting to leave the pinup world behind her, and fearing that time was running out for her, she was eager to make it as a legitimate actress. Upon her arrival in Los Angeles, she was not met by Meyer, but by one of Hughes' chauffeurs. He drove her to a fairly luxurious house in Beverly Hills, where she was installed.

The next day, Meyer called and warned her not to leave the house. "Mr. Hughes' schedule is never certain because the boss man is very busy," Meyer told her. "But he wants you there in case he drops in unexpectedly. Try to have yourself camera ready day and night because he keeps some strange hours."

Bettie later recalled that she was a virtual prisoner in that house until one night Hughes arrived on her doorstep.

"He was a man of few words and had a hearing problem," she said. "He must have found me appealing. We retired to the bedroom where he pulled off his jacket but none of his other clothes. He performed oral sex on me and then left. I tried to ask him about the screen test, but he told me that Meyer would make those arrangements."

Meyer called the next day and said "the boss man has talked to Frank Sinatra in Las Vegas. Frankie is very interested in using you in his next picture. I'm arranging for you to be picked

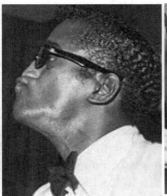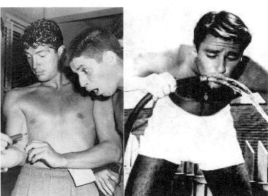

When Frank Sinatra invited **Bettie Page** (*left photo*) to Las Vegas, she thought he meant to spend a week with her in an expensive hotel suite at the Sands. He had failed to inform her of a major point: She was to be the "party favorite" for his fellow Rat Packers, including (*left to right*), **Sammy Davis Jr**, bare-chested **Dean Martin** (pictured here with "the geek," Jerry Lewis), and **Peter Lawford**, shown on the far right taking a drink (water, for a change).

Those wild nights in Vegas happened before Bettie "found Jesus." But instead of granting her peace of mind, religion seemed to bring out "the slasher" in her.

During her later years, this former pinup girl became a psychotic, raging against the world. In one murderous knife attack, she stabbed an elderly woman, but not fatally, before she was subdued. Arrested by the police, she pulled her panties down in the back seat of the van where she was being held in custody and began masturbating.

up in a limo and driven to Las Vegas to attend Frankie's opening night at The Sands."

"It all sounded so glamorous at the time," Bettie recalled. "I was thrilled. All the way across the desert to Vegas, I dreamed that stardom for me was just around the corner."

She not only attended Frank's star-studded opening night but accepted an invitation to dinner in his suite.

"It was the most thrilling night of my life. I adored Frankie. He was romantic and sensitive to my feelings. By morning I think I wanted to marry him."

"He made arrangements for me to stay at another suite at The Sands for a whole week, with all expenses paid," Bettie said. "But the next morning I realized that Frankie had other plans and other gals. I'm afraid he treated me like a whore."

"During that week, my suite was visited by Dean Martin, Peter Lawford, and, much to my horror, Sammy Davis Jr.," Bettie said. "All three of them treated me well. Although I was initially afraid of Sammy, he turned out to be the nicest of them all. I kept waiting for a call from the fifth member of the Rat Pack, Joey Bishop, but he never showed up."

"I had all of them," Bettie later confessed. "All of them had big dicks, all except Lawford. In Las Vegas they were cool cats but had a dark reputation. Pity their shamefully neglected wives and children. They discarded women like a used razor blade. They had talent; they brought joy to millions; and they were great in bed, except for Peter."

At the end of my stay, a bellhop delivered a note from Frankie," she said. "It contained two thousand dollars. He wrote, 'You showed me and my boys a great time. Let's do it again sometime.'"

"Except for Frankie, I never heard from the other Rat Packers again," Bettie said. "If I did, I guess I would have come running. After all, they were stars, weren't they?"

Bettie Page was aptly named. She formed only a "page" in the life of billionaire **Howard Hughes**, one of the 20th century's greatest Lotharios. He seduced an all-star cast of lovers—male and female—and even managed, for a while at least, to become an American hero.

"He was an equal opportunity seducer," said Johnny Meyer, his pimp. "The gender of the victim didn't matter. He had just one requirement. Beauty."

"There was a screen test at RKO and some still pictures, but nothing came of it. Hughes never showed up at the studio while I was there. Personally, I think he decided I was too old for him."

A month later, Frank called her again. She mistakenly thought that he was arranging another date or a trip to Las Vegas for her. He told her that he had a friend—"a very important friend"—who wanted to meet her, as he was one of her biggest fans. "He refused to divulge the name of his friend, however, but told me he was charming, rich, and handsome. Trusting Frankie's judgment, I agreed to meet this mysterious stranger."

The rendezvous was to be not in Las Vegas, but at a place Frank either owned or rented in Palm Springs. "I don't know which," Bettie said. "At the last minute, Frankie called again. The plans had been switched. Instead of having a limousine take me to Palm Springs, a chauffeur would drive me to a mansion in Beverly Hills. I still didn't know the name of this man, but I was mighty intrigued."

The date was set for four o'clock the following afternoon, Bettie claimed. "I must have changed clothes two or three times before deciding on the right outfit. I figured this was a man of culture who had taste, so I decided to go for the demure, girl-next-door look instead of arriving with whips and chains. I figured that if this guy was into S&M, Frankie would have warned me."

A manservant ushered Bettie through the living room and out toward the pool area where she saw a young man swimming. He called out to her. "Bettie, why not take off your clothes and jump in? It's a hot day."

"I told him I didn't have a bathing suit with me."

"You of all women aren't ashamed to show the human body, are you?"

"Not at all," I said. "Right before him, I pulled off all my clothes and jumped completely jaybird naked into the pool with him. I swam to him. He didn't swim to me. When I got close to him, he pulled me to him and gave me a long, lingering kiss. 'I've waited a long time for this,' he said, hugging me close. 'I collect your pictures.' It was all too obvious that he was naked and aroused. Our kissing continued until he wanted it consummated under a cabana."

When pressed for details, she hesitated. "It was nothing out of the ordinary. He lay on his back. He wanted me on top. After he finished with me, he showered by the pool but didn't invite me to join him. He didn't kiss me goodbye but thanked me."

"By the way," he said, "I'm Jack Kennedy."

"I know it seems unbelievable, now that he became the most famous man on earth in the 1960s," Bettie said. "But you have to believe me. I only knew Ike in the White House. I had never heard of the Kennedy family. Millions of Americans in the 1950s didn't know who the Kennedys were, even though Jack had once sought the nomination for Vice President on the Democratic ticket. He didn't get it. I didn't even know that about him at the time. I never listened to those nominating conventions."

Bettie said that when she dressed and headed for the door and the waiting limousine, she expected to be handed a thousand dollar bill. "The man at the door offered me nothing," Bettie said. "I was a bit pissed off. Frankie had told me he was rich. However, the very next day, Frankie sent over ten one-hundred dollar bills and two dozen red roses. He also enclosed a note: 'JACK LIKED YOU A LOT AND WANTS TO SEE YOU AGAIN THE NEXT TIME HE'S IN LOS ANGELES.'"

"He never called me again," Bettie said. "I would have gone to meet him in the White House when Jackie wasn't around. I regretted not seeing him again, although the sex was hardly special. But he was the president. I heard stories that he was seeing Marilyn Monroe, but I didn't know if they were true or not. I was real sad that day he was shot in Dallas. He was far too young to die."

"One night months later I was watching television, and I heard that **Jack Kennedy** had been nominated to run against **Richard Nixon**," Bettie said. "That night on the TV news I saw his beaming face."

"I couldn't believe it. It was the man who seduced me. He was running for president of the United States. Personally, I didn't think he would beat Nixon. Everybody knew who Nixon was. But who was this Jack Kennedy with the funny accent?"

"They would make fun of an accent like that in Tennessee where I grew up."

---

### BETTIE PAGE MEETS RICHARD BURTON

At one point in her career, Bettie accepted a job in Port-au-Prince, Haiti, where she fell in love with a well-built mulatto whom she called "My Mandingo." He turned out to be a sex performer known as "Superman."

One night, roaming the grounds of the Hotel Olaffson, she met Richard Burton, in town with Elizabeth Taylor during the filming of *The Comedians.*

"I bet you can guess what he wanted from me," Bettie said.

# *For Frank, Between Marriages, There Was* PEGGY CONNELLY

An aspiring singer from Shreveport, Louisiana, young and virginal Peggy Connelly first came to Hollywood early in 1955. She was safely ensconced at the Hollywood Studio for Girls, its residents, all of them aspiring actresses, protected from the wolf pack. Frank Sinatra meant nothing to her. She was strictly a Perry Como fan.

Dining with a girl friend in Los Angeles at the Villa Capri, she spotted Frank Sinatra enjoying pasta with Jackie Gleason and three other unknown men. Her girlfriend had been one of Frank's fanatically loyal bobbysoxers during the war and she was dying to meet him.

Peggy noticed that Frank kept looking at her table, but eying her, not her dining companion. At the end of his meal, he got up and walked toward her. "I don't like a broad who wears orange."

That was an unlikely way to launch an affair. But his charm and baby blues warmed her heart.

They began an affair that lasted through 1957, when his divorce from Ava Gardner was granted. Frank was thirty-nine at the time, Peggy only twenty-four.

"The first time he took me to Palm Springs, I discovered he didn't really hate the color of orange—only on women Actually, orange was his favorite color. His sweaters were orange, and many of his shirts were orange. Even a Jeep he had for rides through the desert was orange. Halloween orange accents were all over the house. We even ate off orange-colored ceramic dishes. His blazers and handkerchiefs were orange. His private plane was orange inside and out. But he hated orange ties. He even had orange underwear dyed especially for him.

"I once asked him, 'Why orange?'" she said.

"His answer was enigmatic. He said it was from a poem about the color orange called 'The Gay Deceiver' He quoted from that poem, 'My shade is correct and stylish, but never will it pierce my skin to affect my soul.' Then he turned to me, 'You know, red can destroy a human soul.'"

Peggy admitted that during their months-long relationship, she came to realize that he both "loved and hated Judy Garland, finding her a mess most of the time. He was working with Marlon Brando at the time on *Guys and Dolls* and often considered having him wiped out."

"He was definitely connected to the mob, and I met many of them. He always warned me, though, never to ask their names. When he wasn't with me, I knew he was with one of his many prostitutes. Twice, he proposed marriage to me, but I didn't think I could tolerate his whores."

Frank eventually flew with Peggy to Madrid, where he'd signed to appear with Cary Grant and Sophia Loren in *The Pride and the Passion* (1957). Ava Gardner lived in Madrid. One night he got a call from her. She told him, "You fucker, you're in Madrid, and I had to read about it in the newspapers."

The next day, Frank hired a chauffeur to drive Peggy to Toledo for an overnight visit. When she returned to Madrid at noon the following day, she entered their suite only to discover Ava Gardner in bed with Frank. She didn't speak to Peggy.

"I ran from the suite," Peggy said. "The next day, I found that a maid had packed my bags. Frank was sitting shirtless and drunk in the living room smoking a cigarette. He told me he'd booked me on a plane leaving that night for New York. He also said he'd arranged for me to be given five-thousand dollars in American Express traveler's checks."

"His final words to me were 'Ava and I are back together. We're gonna live in New York. It was swell, kid, while it lasted.'"

"And that was that," Peggy said.

314

# How Frank Pimped His Gun Moll

## TO THE PRESIDENT OF THE UNITED STATES

After the election of **John F. Kennedy** as U.S. president, **Frank Sinatra** was on his way to assuming the unofficial postion of "First Friend" at the White House. Frank promised that he'd deliver many "treats" to the president, notably **Judith Campbell Exner** (*right photo*), a beautiful, high-class prostitute who fell in love with JFK, something the president hadn't anticipated.

She also became pregnant with his child. As JFK told Frank and others, "Having a baby with a hooker while being commander-in -chief with a beautiful, faithful wife is strictly a no-no. Just ask any politician. My friend, George Smathers, the senator from Florida, told me 'There are two things you can't do as a politician. One is to be caught in bed with a young boy; the other is to be caught in bed with a dead girl. Getting a hooker pregnant seems to be the third thing not recommended."

Frank had invited JFK as his guest to his compound in Rancho Mirage, near Palm Springs. Before the president arrived, Frank asked him if he had any "special requests."

JFK had been blunt. "I want to fuck every woman in Hollywood. But to begin with, I want to have a Naked Lunch," a term he had borrowed from the hip heroin novel by William Burroughs.

"Sure, we can do that," Frank said, thinking he meant dining in the buff around a swimming pool. When JFK saw that Frank didn't get it, he explained more fully—"Shaved pussy sprinkled with cocaine."

Frank looked startled for a minute. "Sure, I can arrange that."

# Frank Sinatra, the U.S. President, and a Prominent Mobster Each Sample Judith Exner's Charms

*"I was Frank Sinatra's pimp, and Frank was Jack Kennedy's pimp. It sounds terrible now, but then it was really a lot of fun."*

**—Peter Lawford**

Almost everyone who ever met **Judith Campbell Exner** *(top photo)*, the high-toned hooker, claimed that she was an **Elizabeth Taylor** *(lower photo)* look-alike.

Peter Lawford, who'd slept with both Elizabeth and Judith, didn't quite get the comparison, but her other dates did. "As time went by, Judy began to make her face up to look more like Elizabeth," Peter said.

Frank noted that when Judith started visiting the White House, she adopted Jackie Kennedy as her role model, not Elizabeth.

"Of course, when Judy came to call, Jackie was riding some horse in Virginia."

*"The Kennedys treat Frank Sinatra like a whore. You fuck them, you pay them, and they're through."*

**—Johnny Roselli**

*"Judith Campbell Exner was a user, a manipulator— common as dirt!"*

**—Jackie Kennedy**

Judith Campbell (later Exner) had met Frank three times before at parties. But no real contact was made until she was seen dining at Puccini's in Beverly Hills, a restaurant he co-owned with Peter Lawford. It was November of 1959.

Frank said to Peter, "That dame looks gorgeous. I think I'll invite her as my date when you, Pat [Patricia Kennedy], and I fly down to Honolulu. She looks a bit like your old gal pal, Elizabeth Taylor, but a nicer version."

He called his factotum, Nick Sevano, and ordered him to approach the woman. Nick already knew her. "That's Judith Campbell," he told Frank and Peter.

"Judy," Nick said to her. She was sitting alone at table, perhaps looking for a pickup for the evening. "Sinatra wants to date you."

She looked up and smiled. "Tell him he's on." She quickly retreated to the ladies' room for some emergency repairs to her makeup. When she came out, she looked even more gorgeous as she sat down at table with Frank and Peter.

The rest, so the saying goes, is for the history books.

In Honolulu, Judith found herself sharing a suite with Pat and Peter at the Surfrider Hotel. She later admitted in her highly unreliable memoirs that she was physically attracted to Frank and was looking forward "to a good time."

On a mammoth patio that afternoon, "we had drinks and got stewed," as she remembered. She also recalled a lot of "ring-a-ding-ding" talk between Peter and Frank. "They were speaking a language all their own." Before the afternoon ended, Judith determined that Peter "was a steer, not a bull. Pat was the strong one."

With enough drinks in him, Peter suggested that all four of them pull off their bathing suits and go skinny dipping in the pool. Frank didn't need any encouragement. His orange-colored swimsuit came off almost immediately, revealing his large endowment. Peter was next, jumping into the water with Frank. Pat and Judith were the last to remove their suits.

After about thirty minutes in the water, Judith reported that, "Peter began deep kissing Pat before moving on to me."

"Pat seemed to have no objection to that," Judith said. "I could see that Peter and Frank were becoming aroused."

It was Peter who suggested that they engage in "wipe swapping."

"You're married to Pat, but here in Honolulu what wife of mine are you talking about?" Frank asked.

"Judy," Peter said. "I'd like to bang her. And Pat has long had the hots for you—she told me so."

"You've got to be kidding," Frank said. "You want me to get it on with Pat here?"

"Let's all four retire to

If the tabloids had only known at the time, the Hawaiian vacation of **Frank Sinatra** *(left)* and **Peter Lawford** *(right)* would have made headlines around the world. The women who accompanied these two Rat Packers to Honolulu were **Judith Campbell Exner** *(top photo)* and **Patricia Kennedy Lawford** *(bottom photo)*, the sister of President John F. Kennedy.

Frank later claimed that of all the Kennedy women, "Pat was the wild one. When it came to sex, she tried to match the exploits of her brothers—Jack, Bobby, and Teddy."

In Palm Springs, Peter and Pat spent so many weekends with Frank that they had a room assigned to them which was more or less permanently stocked with their clothes so they wouldn't have to pack before their visits.

Frank's valet, George Jacobs, was the first to notice that Frank was planning to seduce Pat. That was made relatively easy for him, since she'd harbored a crush on him for years. In Honolulu, Pat finally found the answer to a question that had intrigued her for months:

What was Frank Sinatra like in bed?

317

your king-size bed, and let the party begin."

"Let's go for it," Frank said.

There's no one to record what happened that night, but Judith in later life claimed that Frank seduced her in bed with Peter and Pat, and that Peter then mounted her while Frank "plugged Pat."

"The next day," Judith said, "Pat told me she'd always wanted to get it on with Frank and welcomed the chance to have him. Apparently Peter wasn't the jealous or possessive type."

**Marlene Dietrich** *(photo above)* and Judith Exner came from such different worlds that it seemed unlikely that they would ever meet.

The man who introduced them was Frank Sinatra, who knew both of them as David knew Bathsheba. In time he would invite both of them to share his bed at the same time.

Marlene and Frank went way back to 1942. When the blonde goddess first showed up in public with Frank, it was at ringside to watch a title fight at Madison Square Garden. Her other date that night was Joe DiMaggio. Rumors still persist that they had a three-way that night.

Frank found Marlene versatile. He could bring another man to her bed—in this case DiMaggio—or a woman, in one case Judith Exner. Marlene considered Frank and Joltin' Joe as trophies to add to her collection of seductions. They had already included Joseph P. Kennedy Sr., his son, Jack, John Wayne, and the French singer, Edith Piaf.

The day after, no one acted as if anything unusual had happened. Frank drank a lot of Jack Daniels the second day and made love to Judith alone that night. "He was very gentle, romantic, expressive, and sensual," she later wrote. "He just kept his arms around me all night long. We made love again during the night."

As one lazy afternoon drifted into another, Judith reported that two beautiful Japanese girls appeared in the suite, and Frank and Peter disappeared with them into a bedroom for "massages." "It was blatantly obvious," Judith said. "Pat knew what was going on. She was furious."

Frank had been kind and sweet, but one night he seemed to turn on everybody, especially Judith, but also Peter and Pat. "Frank gets considerably shorter when he takes his shoes off," Judith said. "In his mind, he feels he's a big man, that he has power, and the way he proves it is to push people around."

"He was Dr. Jekyll and Mr. Hyde. You didn't know which one you were going to get. Frank's Dr. Jekyll was a charmer, but his Mr. Hyde was frightening, truly frightening."

The following night, Frank turned on Peter. Judith later admitted that she didn't "have an ounce of respect for Peter. I think he's an ass. He makes the best flunky in the world because it's important to him to be with VIPs. He'll sacrifice himself, take a tremendous amount of punishment, just to be there with Frank."

After several miserable nights in Honolulu, Judith said, "You would think I'd had my fill of Frank Sinatra." But in spite of her reservations, she made herself available to him time after time in the months ahead.

"I kept coming back to Frank because there is something compellingly attractive about him that draws you to him like a magnet," Judith said. "I think that's why so many gals and cronies stick to him even when he grinds his heel into their soul." There would be more evenings together, including one particular evening at Frank's Palm Springs house where another four-way orgy took place, again with Peter and Pat.

Back in Beverly Hills, Frank tried to lure Judith to his home for a *ménage à trois* with a tall black woman. She turned him down, but would later consider such a proposition. "If a big name was involved—movie star, politician, Mafia don—Judith would do almost anything, even do it with a woman if it were a big star and Frank ordered it," Peter claimed.

In her memoirs, Judith falsely stated that she quit having sex with Frank because he "was too kinky for me." Her refusal to have sex with the black prostitute may have been based on shyness, moral qualms, or on something to do with the color of the woman's skin. Later, in other circumstances, she did, in fact, agree to sex with other women in the same bed with Frank.

When Judith wrote her tell-all, *My Story*, in 1977, it was considered shocking to some. In later years she admitted, "I told only part of the story." She never quite revealed that she was a high-class prostitute, but made herself appear somewhat like a wayward Catholic schoolgirl who got mixed up with a U.S. president, a singer from Hoboken, and big-time Mafia bosses.

She also confessed, "I left out a lot of the good stuff from my memoirs, especially all that lesbian shit Frank wanted me to indulge in. He was such a voyeur. But then many men like to see girl-on-girl action. It turns the bastards on for some reason that I don't get."

One time in Las Vegas, Frank brought two white prostitutes into their suite for an orgy. In fairness, she may not have desired that form of sexual involvement, but Frank reminded her, "You want a paycheck, don't you? So don't give me any lip unless you put those smackers to good use. Ever hear of a deep throat blow-job?"

In her confessional she claimed, "Perhaps if I had been in love with Frank, I would have tried harder to please him. I was infatuated with him. He knew how to make you feel like a complete woman—that is, until he became Mr. Hyde."

Nearly all biographers have found Judith Campbell Exner's "confessions" rather selective. There was certain decadence to her story that she omitted. She later claimed she was afraid to tell her full story—"somebody might kill me."

She denied knowing gangster Johnny Roselli before she met JFK. "I was seeing the gangsters because of meetings arranged by Jack Kennedy," she said. "I wouldn't have been seeing them otherwise."

That was a lie. Long before she met JFK, Judith was dating Roselli. Years later he bragged about his link with JFK. "Me and him like to fuck the same broads, Marilyn Monroe and Judith Campbell."

In spite of her denials, FBI agents spotted Roselli and Judith leaving Romanoff's Restaurant in Beverly Hills in January of 1962, a month before meeting JFK. They were seen going into his hotel suite.

Judith knew Roselli even before she met Frank. But it was Frank who would later introduce her to Chicago mobster Giancana, who also became her lover.

Mob boss **Sam Giancana** is pictured handcuffed to a chair during one of his many arrests in Chicago. The son of Sicilian immigrants went to work in the 1920s for the ultimate *Mafioso*, Al Capone. Giancana rose to the pinnacle of the Chicago mob, implicated in beatings, kidnappings, and murder.

During World War II, the Selective Service rejected him, finding him a "constitutional psychopath showing strong eremitic [*editor's note: not concerned with the temporal world or swayed by mundane considerations*] trends."

Frank Sinatra became a crony of his. This led to a connection with Joseph P. Kennedy. Giancana later claimed he helped run a vote-stealing fraud in Chicago's Cook County, a district that helped push JFK to victory during the presidential elections of 1960.

During his tenure as president, JFK shared the same girlfriend with both Frank and Giancana—Judith Campbell Exner.

The gangster told her he was a businessman named "Sam Flood," and that he was a widower. She was wearing costume jewelry. "A woman like you should be wearing real jewels," he told her.

She began to suspect he was a mobster, especially when she met his pals who sported names like "Crackers," "Teets," "Horse," "Turk," and "Dutch."

Frank also arranged Judith's introduction to a rapidly rising politician, launching an affair that would live in political infamy.

On February 7, 1960, when Frank introduced "girl-about-town" Judith Campbell to JFK at the Sands Hotel in Las Vegas, she had never heard of him. She didn't know that JFK was the U.S. Senator from Massachusetts, and she had no idea that he was running for President.

Teddy Kennedy also met Judith that same night and came on strong to her, but she turned him down.

"I didn't even know Jack was married," she later said. "All I knew was that he was gorgeous. After one night of lovemaking, I fell for him, little knowing it would ruin the rest of my life."

"Jack was the world's greatest listener," she recalled. "I was a nobody and the first day we spent together, we talked for three hours before bed, and he seemed fascinated with everything I said."

"Something wonderful was happening to me," she claimed. "I was almost giddy. It was a feeling that I had when I was young and had a crush on someone—that first meeting when you realize that he's someone special. It's all anticipation, hoping and wondering and feeling good. Then doubt creeps in: I wonder if I'll ever see him again. There was not much doubt after that first time I met him. I slept well and woke up feeling like Scarlett O'Hara the morning after Rhett Butler had carried her up the stairs."

After JFK returned to Washington, Frank called Judith, wanting a play-by-play description of what had gone on. He told her that he was to be informed every time she met with JFK. "I want to know everything going on. I want to be in the loop. There's a reward in it for you."

Since she was getting paid, she told Frank the truth, something she didn't tell her memoir writer.

Ironically, Judith's meeting with JFK did not represent her first link with the Kennedy clan. Frank Sinatra's valet, George Jacobs, wrote a memoir (*Mr. S: My Life with Frank Sinatra*) chronicling his years working

JUDITH EXNER

"I knew them when the dream of Camelot was real—Jack Kennedy, Frank Sinatra, Sam Giancana, and John Roselli."

MY STORY

as told to Ovid Demaris

Judith Campbell Exner, hooker and frequent lover of President John F. Kennedy, Frank Sinatra, and gangster Sam Giancana, later claimed that "the publication of my autobiography extinguished the candle of Camelot."

It may not have done that, but its revelations led to an array of other books and tabloid exposés that extended her story to include the likes of Marilyn Monroe, Jackie's affairs, Teddy's philandering, and Bobby's sexual trysts. (He wasn't that choir boy after all.)

Even though her confessional appeared to be an unvarnished account of her involvements with powerful men, Judith later admitted that "it was a virtual whitewash compared to how I was really involved with these guys."

For years, harrassed by the FBI, Judith had kept a tight lid on her secret love affair with JFK in the upper bedrooms of The White House.

But then, in 1975, fifteen years after her involvements with the president, she was hauled before a Senate investigating committee, where she told her story. It immediately hit the front pages of newspapers across the country.

close-up and personal within the singer's entourage. He claimed that Joseph Kennedy, Sr., JFK's father, had visited Frank during the late 1950s in Palm Springs, where he expected his host to pick up the tab for sexual services arranged with local prostitutes. In Palm Springs, according to Jacobs, Frank introduced Joe Sr. to the sexual services of Judith.

As described by Jacobs in his memoir, Judith Campbell "was the perfect Eisenhower era pinup of the girl next door. That she charged for her wholesomeness was beside the point. Judy would go on to infamy as the fourth corner of a quadrangle that included Sinatra, Sam Giancana, and JFK. But before his son took a bite off the poison apple, the father was there first. Talk about chips off the old block!"

***

Judith was born in New York City into a wealthy family in 1934. When she was a child, her father, a German-born architect, moved his family to a 24-room Mediterranean-style villa in Pacific Palisades, a suburb of Los Angeles. Their home was later bought by movie star Joseph Cotten of *Citizen Kane* fame.

As a child, she remembered her family associating with Hollywood celebrities, including Jack Warner, Cary Grant, and Robert Stack.

Shortly before Judith's death in 1999, she confessed that as a teenager, she lost her virginity to Bob Hope, who, while posing as a family friend, forced sex onto her at a beach cottage. "Hope hurt me, and I bled, but I didn't tell my father," Judith claimed. "I was brought up a strict Catholic. I feared that he'd kick me out of the house, even though it wasn't my fault. Bob Hope made me do it."

Based on her belief that she had been "ruined" by the comedian, she claimed "I had to get married." She met actor William Campbell, marrying him in 1952 over her parents' objections.

"I divorced him in 1958 when I became intimately involved with Sinatra," Judith said.

In later life, she claimed that Sinatra "used me like a prostitute for the Rat Pack. It all began one night in Las Vegas when he demanded in his hotel suite that I 'deep throat' Sammy Davis Jr., Dean Martin, and Peter Lawford. Sinatra was such a voyeur. He wanted to see me blow his friends. First I objected, but then I gave in. I actually ended up enjoying it and liking the guys, especially Dean Martin. He was my favorite. I had affairs with all of them."

**Judith**, age six, holds her pet on Sunday, December 7, 1941, a day that would "live in infamy," when the Japanese attacked Pearl Harbor, plunging the United States into World War II. She was too young to understand the war, but she grew up quickly. When she was an early teenager, **Bob Hope** *(inset photo)* was a frequent visitor to her parents and their home.

Once, he dropped in and gave her a large pink teddy bear. When he found out her parents were away, he invited her out to the pool. In the beach cottage, he stripped down and urged her to take her clothes off too. She'd never seen a naked man before. Afraid, she tried to run back to the house, but he held her down and raped her. She kept that "dirty secret" until later in her life when she became more confessional.

Not at first, but in later revelations she claimed that Frank liked three-ways with two women in the bed. Originally, she had said, "When he brought another woman to join us in bed, I absolutely froze. I went rigid. No one could have moved my arms or legs."

But as the years passed, she altered her story, ultimately asserting that she did join Frank in three-ways with other women, most memorably in Las Vegas with the legendary Marlene Dietrich. For years, Frank had conducted an on-again, off-again affair with Marlene. Judith felt they had "some sexual arrangement between them."

Al Capone sent gangster **Johnny Roselli** (pictured above at four different periods of his life) to Hollywood in the 1930s to rule as its Mafia lord. He moved between Capone's Chicago, Harry Cohn's Hollywood, Howard Hughes' Las Vegas and ultimately within John F. Kennedy's Washington.

A ladies' man with surface charm, he seduced everyone from Judith Campbell Exner to Marilyn Monroe. Frank Sinatra became a close friend of his and was often seen coming and going from his address at 1333 South Beverly Glen in Los Angeles.

Johnny ended up knowing too much about too many major American figures and suffered a grisly murder in Florida.

The public would not learn of the JFK/Judith link until twelve years after the President was assassinated, and she was called before the Senate's Church Committee, investigating the CIA's involvement with organized crime in its effort to have Fidel Castro assassinated.

"Frank wanted to watch Marlene make love to me," Judith claimed in one of her later interviews. "She was an oral artist with both men and women. Fortunately, I didn't have to do anything but lie there. She brought me to a climax which so excited Sinatra he immediately penetrated me. He was real kinky at times."

After her inaugural meeting with Sam Giancana in the spring of 1960, she became more intimate with him during the months following JFK's conquest of the presidency.

A short, dour, and rather ugly Sicilian, Giancana, or so it is estimated, had directly organized, arranged, or been personally responsible for some 200 murders up to 1960, when Kennedy became president. He was a leading member of *La Cosa Nostra*, the international crime syndicate.

As Chicago's Mafia boss, he was the successor to the notorious Al Capone. Amazingly, he'd been arrested 70 times, including three times on charges of murder. His close friend and associate in crime was John (Johnny) Roselli, who represented the Chicago mob on the West Coast.

As part of an ironic coincidence, the Mafia boss and the President of the United States ended up sharing the same girlfriend—Judith Campbell Exner, with Frank on the sidelines.

"What tangled lives we lead," JFK later told Bobby Kennedy as their ties with Giancana became more linked. Giancana was enlisted to help win the 1960 presidential election for Kennedy against his Republican opponent, Richard M. Nixon. Giancana provided both union support and money for the campaign.

It was Frank who had originally arranged the link between the mob (as represented by Giancana) and the Kennedys. It was perceived as vital by JFK's advisers that he carry the "swing state" of Illinois. The plurality was narrow, but JFK was pronounced the ultimate winner, though even today there is a claim that the 1960 presidential election, thanks partly to the collusion of then-mayor of Chicago, Richard J. Daley, was stolen from Nixon.

"I wouldn't have gotten involved with Sam if Jack didn't tell me to," Judith later claimed. "After all, I was being ordered to by the President of the United States. I did what he wanted me to do."

She claimed to Frank that she had personally organized a meeting between Giancana and JFK at the Fontainebleau Hotel on Miami Beach. Although she did not attend the meeting, she said that the President (then a Senator) later came to her suite and gave her $2,000 in cash after making love to her.

Frank didn't bother to conceal his eagerness in hearing every detail. Apparently, the gangster and JFK had discussed the upcoming West Virginia primary, where JFK's Catholicism had emerged as something of a problem—a definite factor to consider.

Frank was kept well aware of what contacts were being made between JFK and Giancana, both friends of his. "I have a vested interest in learning everything, because it affects me," he told Judith.

JFK later reported to Frank that Giancana was going to use his influence to help him win the hard-fought West Virginia primary.

Giancana, as JFK told Frank, came through for him. The gangster convinced his associate, Paul ("Skinny") D'Amato, to urge sheriffs to get out the vote for Kennedy. Various bundles of cash were exchanged. JFK trounced Hubert Humphrey in the primary.

The mobster firmly believed that JFK was going to become president. He told Judith, "I want him to owe me one. As president, Jack will go easy on the mob. Frank has given me his word that Jack will give me a pass."

Judith told Frank she was amazed when JFK sent her a plane ticket and money to fly to Washington. She had thought he'd meet her in some out-of-the-way hotel, but he invited her to dinner on April 6, 1960 at his home in Georgetown. "I learned Jackie was away. We did it that night in the same bed where he slept with her."

"He told me that Jackie was no good at the oral stuff, and that he had to turn elsewhere for that," Judith claimed. "He wanted to know all the details about how I'd become such an accomplished deep throat artist. I told him I was broken in by Sinatra and The Rat Pack. He told me his greatest sexual fantasy would be to go to bed with both Shirley MacLaine and me at the same time. That never happened."

On July 11, 1960, the opening day of the Democratic National Convention in Los Angeles, JFK summoned Judith to his hotel suite. "He told me he was highly nervous about the convention and needed to relax. On our previous encounter when we'd kissed passionately, and with his lips on me, he'd asked me, 'Do you think you could love me?'"

"'Yes, yes, yes,' I said into his open mouth. 'I love you.' When I said that, he plunged his tongue into my mouth and ordered me to drink all his saliva until his mouth was completely dry. At that point, I was under his spell."

After such passion and such a declaration of love, Judith later said she was shocked when he told her there was another woman who would be arriving soon. "I just couldn't believe it," she said. "I thought he was satisfied with me, but he seemed insatiable."

"We were sitting in robes in the living room when this other woman was ushered in. To my surprise, it was Marilyn Monroe. I'd heard stories that Jack was having an affair with her. I knew that another three-way was in the offing. I'm about the last woman on earth who could be called a lesbian, but I found Marilyn attractive. She kissed each of my cheeks before turning her attention to JFK."

323

As time went by and JFK's sexual tastes became more decadent, he began to prefer three-ways. For the most part he had no trouble luring two women into the same bed with him.

His fantasy, as he revealed to Florida Senator George Smathers, involved bringing together **Judith Campbell Exner** *(top photo)* **and Marilyn Monroe**, an event his aides arranged on the eve of his nomination for president at the Democratic Convention at Los Angeles in 1960.

Before Marilyn's meeting with Exner, JFK's makeup man had made Exner look as much like Elizabeth Taylor as possible. "Marilyn detests Elizabeth Taylor, so I know I'll never get those two into bed at the same time," Jack told Smathers. "Marilyn will be real, of course, but instead of Elizabeth I'll have to settle merely for the mock."

"She pointed a finger at Jack like he was a naughty boy," Judith said. "'You brought along this lovely girl,' MM told Jack. 'She looks like Elizabeth Taylor. What fantasy are we having tonight, Mr. President?'"

"He wasn't president yet, but she had already started calling him that," Judith said. "Right in front of me, she went over to the sofa where Jack was sitting. She unzipped his trousers, took out his penis, and began to give him a blow-job. She took her mouth off him and looked back at me. 'This is just to get the party going,' she said. 'Come over here and give it a try so I can rest my mouth for a minute.'"

"Nothing could have surprised me more when Jack was elected president," Judith said.

Frank, too, had his doubts about JFK's chances. "Too much scandal, too much sexual baggage," he told Judith. "Imagine what they'd dig up on me if I ever ran for office."

"I know you voted for him," Judith said to Frank, "but I voted for Nixon. I did that to protect myself. I feared that if Jack became president, I would be exposed and featured in all the tabloids. Talk about a fear coming true."

She felt that "once Jack became president, he'd clean up his act. He was being watched by too many people, and he had a lot of political enemies who were working to destroy him. But he was completely reckless. Once in the Oval Office, he had power. With that power, he became more reckless than ever. It was like he felt he was above being harmed by a scandal, especially a sexual scandal."

Frank was intrigued to hear that, like himself, JFK often preferred three-ways. "He invites whores to the White House for nude swims," Judith said. "He invited me to the White House one night when Jackie was in Virginia. I found him in the pool with another woman. I would have preferred to keep him to myself, but at that point I was giving in to all his wishes."

"After we swam," Judith said, "we went to his suite in White House bathrobes. He wanted to watch this whore go down on me. He became so excited that when I climaxed he penetrated me at once. He was so worked up at that point that it took him only twenty seconds to reach his own climax."

Although JFK seduced dozens of women during his tenure in the White House, Judith was the first in public to admit to having had an affair with the sitting president. "I realized that it was a blow to his image. It virtually destroyed the public image of Camelot, and it led to scandalous stories to come, including his sexual trysts with Marilyn Monroe. I came to realize that Jack's affair with me exposed him to blackmail from the mob."

In her most startling claim, Judith said that when he became president, JFK often used her as a courier between the White House and Giancana. Her role as an intermediary became even more important after the bungled Bay of Pigs invasion of Cuba in April of 1961.

She remembered bringing JFK and Giancana together on April 28, 1961 in a suite at Chicago's Ambassador East Hotel.

JFK was scheduled that night to address a Democratic Party dinner, but not before he talked over a possible assassination of Fidel Castro with the Mafia don. Judith was not privy to the details of that plot.

During a period of eighteen months between 1960 and 1961, Judith was the president's link to the mob. In that capacity, she crisscrossed the nation, carrying messages from Washington to Florida, Chicago, and Los Angeles.

In her later recollections to Frank, Judith went on to assert that she had arranged a total of ten meetings between JFK and Giancana, two of which were within the White House. Kenneth O'Donnell, JFK's aide, had Giancana slipped in *incognito*, of course.

Judith said that she was once asked by JFK to carry $250,000 from Washington to Giancana. On this trip, Kenneth O'Donnell, part of JFK's Irish Mafia, shadowed her, sitting on the train in the same compartment with Judith, even though she was unaware of his role as a watchdog and spy. In Chicago he watched her get off the train and hand a satchel to Giancana, who was waiting for her. Before heading back to Washington, O'Donnell watched Judith and the Mafia boss leave the railway station together in a black limousine.

With Frank's hand looming in the background, she also delivered "gobs of money" from California businessmen to the Kennedys, to help finance JFK's re-election campaign of 1964. Later, after JFK's death, charges were leveled that some of this money went to the president's personal use, including bills to madams who imported working girls into the White House for orgies when Jackie was away.

Judith also revealed to Frank that she carried pay-

Historians are still debating the role that gangsters Sam Giancana and Johnny Roselli played in plotting the unsuccessful assassination of Cuban dictator **Fidel Castro**.

Working with the CIA in Miami, Giancana came up with a rather inventive plot that involved reaching Castro's mistress and settling a few million dollars on her to "drop a poison pill in Castro's food or drink." Even before JFK became president, the CIA Office of Medical Services in Miami had been given a box of Castro's favorite cigars with orders to treat them with a lethal dose of poison.

The mob hated Castro because when he had taken over Cuba, he had ruined their profitable gambling and prostitution businesses.

Through Bobby, President Kennedy was alleged to have sent word to the mob that "assassination of a foreign leader is a dirty word. Don't use that word on paper."

offs, in cash, into the White House from California defense contractors wanting government business.

One night during dinner at the White House—Jackie was away, of course—JFK introduced Judith to Bobby. As she told columnist Liz Smith, "He squeezed my shoulder solicitously and asked me if I was OK carrying these messages from Jack and him to Chicago. 'Do you feel comfortable doing it?' Bobby asked me. I told him I did."

As she told Frank, her most memorable moments in the White House came that night after dinner when she retired with the president to his suite. "Jack stripped down and got into bed, while I went to the bathroom to freshen up a bit. When I came back into the room, all the lights were turned off. I crawled into bed with Jack. To my surprise and shock I found it was Bobby in the bed with me. He was completely naked."

"I always thought Bobby was the cuter Kennedy, and I was only too glad to have sex with him too," she said. "As we were going at it, Jack, also nude, crawled into bed with us. After Bobby shifted my body to accommodate Jack, the president entered me from the rear. I became the meat in a Kennedy sandwich."

***

The death of Marilyn Monroe on August 5, 1962, had a profound effect on both Judith and Frank. She urgently came to him, finding him despondent. She later admitted that she felt he knew a lot more about the death of Marilyn than he was letting on.

"Marilyn was gone and no one could save her now except, perhaps, God," Judith recalled. "I told Frank I wanted out of the whole mess. I feared for my life."

This was not just paranoia. It's been rumored, but never proven, that Judith was indeed on some hit lists, perhaps not from mob boss Sam Giancana, but from his henchman, Johnny Roselli.

During that frantic meeting with Frank, she informed him of her last visit to see JFK at the White House.

"When the president called me to come to the White House for another roll in the hay, I didn't let him know that I was leaving him," she said. "I arrived at the White House in the usual way. I don't think Jack suspected a thing."

"When we came together, I told him, 'I can't see you anymore—it's too painful, too dangerous.' Even when I told him that, he still wanted to be intimate with me for one final time. I was still in love with him, as much as that was possible, and it broke my heart to tell him goodbye. I never saw him again after that cold day in Washington."

After that final sexual encounter with JFK, she discovered she'd become pregnant. "Since I knew it was Jack's child, I called him at the White House, not knowing if he'd speak to me. He came to the phone right away."

This news stunned Frank because he knew that if Judith wanted to, she could blackmail the President.

"When I told Jack I was pregnant and wanted to have his child, he went ballistic," she said. "First he claimed our kid might belong to you—'Let Ol' Blue Eyes pay for it.' He also claimed that the child might belong to either Sam or Roselli. But the timing wasn't right. I knew he was the father. During sex together, he refused to wear a condom, claiming it deadened the sensation for him."

"I pleaded with him to let me have the child, but he insisted that I have an abortion," she said. "Both of us were devout Catholics, but he demanded I abort our baby. As I always did, I gave in to him."

Finally JFK said, "Do you think Sam would help us?"

"I realized then I wasn't going to get help from him, and I called Sam. Unlike the president, he was very loving and caring and arranged for me to have the abortion at Chicago's Grant Hospital on January 28, 1963, even though such an operation was illegal at the time. The president's kid was not to be."

She stayed in Chicago and, when she recovered, had sex with Giancana one final time. "In spite of his awful reputation, he was rather gentle in bed. I much preferred him over Johnny Roselli, his friend. Johnny treated women brutally and wanted to cause them pain. He once told me he wasn't satisfied until he made a woman scream in agony."

"I think if you and I want to live a long and healthy life, we'd better keep some of these sordid details under our hat," Frank told Judith. "Let it be our little secret—or big secret in this case."

None of the Exner/JFK/Sinatra/Giancana shady dealings escaped the eagle eye of J. Edgar Hoover, head honcho at the FBI. When he'd gathered enough evidence to impeach a sitting president, he called his "boss," Attorney General Bobby Kennedy. At a tense meeting between these two men who hated each other, he displayed his evidence to Bobby.

"Associating with Sinatra and his mob ties is child's play compared to a link with Sam Giancana," Hoover warned. "If the public finds out about your brother's involvement with the Mafia, it could bring down his presidency."

Knowing that Hoover had accumulated blackmail evidence on JFK, Bobby promised him that he personally would see to it that the affair was ended abruptly.

"Hoover had done his homework," Bobby told his brother that night.

\*\*\*

In the wake of JFK's assassination, Frank received alarming reports that Judith was on the point of a complete nervous breakdown. He feared she might somehow involve him in nasty headlines, making revelations about his own links between the president and the mob.

FBI Director **J. Edgar Hoover** *(center)* captures the attention of two listeners during his revelation of the scandalous information he had unearthed about **President John F. Kennedy** *(left)* and his brother, U.S. Attorney General **Bobby Kennedy** *(right)*. Bobby loathed Hoover, but was actually his boss. Neither of the brothers wanted to hear the results of Hoover's investigations into their private lives, and didn't even want to look him in the eye.

Hoover's spies had uncovered compromising details about every meeting between the Chicago mob boss and JFK. They also knew that Judith had frequently functioned as the courier between the White House and Giancana.

Hoover also delivered a devastating report about Frank Sinatra's links to mob figures and urged the president to break off his relationship not only with Judith but with Frank.

"There's no way you can accept another invitation to stay at Sinatra's villa in Palm Springs," Hoover said.

Hoover's warnings against Frank were dire: When the FBI Director left the Oval Office, JFK told Bobby, "I've not only got to end it with Frank, but I have to throw our singer friend under the bus."

He learned that she was occupying a suite at the Beverly Crest Hotel in Los Angeles. The manager knew Frank because the singer had booked the hotel for sexual trysts in the past.

Using a pass key, Frank was allowed into her suite, where he found Judith lying nude on the bed in an alcoholic stupor. A normally beautiful woman, she looked gaunt and disheveled.

She told him that FBI agents were tailing her and that she had once been brought in for questioning.

"Your name came up several times," she warned him.

"Tell the bastards nothing," he told her. "Loose lips will bring our house of cards down on all of us."

Roselli arrived at her suite a day later and almost forced her to go for some rest and recuperation with him in Palm Springs, where she gradually pulled herself together.

After a week, Roselli and Judith returned to the Los Angeles area. He invited her to dinner at Romanoff's where, in a touch of irony, they encountered Frank dining with actress Marilyn Maxwell.

On the way to the men's room, Frank walked past their table but did not acknowledge either of them.

"The story's over," Judith told Roselli.

"Like hell it is," he said. "Some fucker one day will probably make a movie about all of us."

***

As she became less and less afraid as the years went by, Judith added to her story and changed details significantly.

She was interviewed, for example, by columnist Liz Smith for an article in *Vanity Fair*, and also by Seymour Hersh for his book, *The Dark Side of Camelot*. It soon became apparent that she had delivered what Nixon called "a limited hangout" in her earlier testimonies.

As her shadows deepened and as cancer continued to eat away at her body, Judith in her final years provided more and more details to what few friends she still had. To the percolating brew, she added increasing numbers of florid tidbits about her sexual intimacies with JFK, Sinatra, and The Rat Pack. Of course, she preferred to be paid for these interviews, so embellishments were to be expected.

Weeks before her death, she was deeply wounded by her critics, many of whom still denied her role in JFK's life. She particularly resented being portrayed as a vapid party girl, the mistress of both a president and a Mafia don.

"I was not a tramp! I was not a slut!" she said. "I was never anybody's kept woman."

Each night for the final ten years of her life, she'd fallen asleep with a gun under her pillow, a gift from Giancana, who warned that the Kennedys "might have you wiped out one night. And don't trust Frank Sinatra either."

Suffering from breast cancer, Judith Exner died at the age of 65 on September 24, 1999.

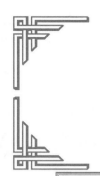

# Juliet Prowse
## FRANK'S ENGAGEMENT TO
## "THE SEXIEST DANCER I'VE EVER SEEN."

**Frank Sinatra** has **Juliet Prowse** eating out of his hand at a celebrity costume gala where he came dressed as an Indian." I've played cowboys in my life—never an Indian. If I joined the Navajo tribe, I bet they'd call me 'Sitting Bull.'"

Dancer Juliet came into Frank's life as he was entering his third decade as an American phenomenon. He was not just a singer and actor, but a businessman, launching Frank Sinatra Enterprises.

When Frank appeared on the set of *Can-Can*, his latest film, he met Juliet of South Africa, a newcomer to Hollywood. The day before, he'd been driving along the street and stopped his car and asked her if he could drive her to where she wanted to go. She told him, "I don't get into cars with strange, dirty old men."

But on a sceond meeting, she was more receptive when she recognized the star of the picture, Frank himself. For the first time since Ava Gardner, he found a woman truly fascinating. During the filming of *Can-Can*, he fell in love with her and proposed marriage, although his offer was not immediately accepted.

Breaking up with Arthur Miller, Marilyn Monroe was "on the string," and she too wanted to marry Frank after her divorce. "Torn Between Two Lovers," as the song goes, Frank settled on Juliet. "She has better hygiene," he told Eddie Fisher.

Frank wanted "Love and Marriage," as his song went, and Juliet wanted "Career and Marriage." She ended up with something of a career, but no Frank.

# JULIET PROWSE—FRANK SINATRA'S HIGHEST "KICK"

In a dance role where she interpreted a serpent, wearing a sexy version of simulated snakeskin, **Juliet Prowse**'s dance performances were some of the highlights of *Can-Can*. This was in spite of the fact that the Soviet dictator Nikita Khrushchev, on a visit to the movie set, defined her dancing as "immoral."

"Nikita, such a big teddy bear, was my greatest press agent," she recalled. "Before him, I was unknown. After his visit, I became a household word like Frank Sinatra himself. My career took off thanks to this 'Red Menace.'"

For the film, Frank was paid $200,000, plus a percentage of the gross, and she made $300 a week. "Through a translator, Nikita spoke to me about this," Juliet said. "He claimed that in Soviet Russia I would be paid the same as Frank."

As the 1950s came to an end, Frank still owed a debt to 20th Century Fox for having walked off the set of *Carousel* in 1954. In the aftermath of that eruption, his part was assigned to Gordon MacCrae. Frank wasn't that excited to star in a frothy, French-inspired musical, *Can-Can* (1959), but he eventually agreed to make it for terms which were sweet—$200,000 up front with a quarter of the gross. No more $10,000 paychecks for playing Maggio in *From Here to Eternity*.

*Can-Can* would be Frank's first musical in three years. With a score by Cole Porter, *Can-Can* was based on a long-running Broadway hit with the same name.

But after the first week of filming, it was obvious that Frank had been miscast. Stacked up against the ultimate Frenchman, Maurice Chevalier, Frank did not evoke a Parisian in any way—and he made no attempt to do so.

Likewise, his Rat Pack co-star, Shirley MacLaine, made no attempt to project even the slightest French inflection. So although they'd been cast as Parisians interacting with issues of decorum and censorship during the late 19th-century's *Belle-Époque*, both Frank and MacLaine came off as pure mid-20th-century Americanese. At one point Frank even inserts, "*Ring a ding ding ding*" into a Cole Porter lyric.

Partly as a means of countering the Americanizations of Sinatra and MacLaine, the devastatingly handsome *je ne sais quoi* quotient of Louis Jourdan and the French-to-the-core Maurice Chevalier were also cast in *Can-Can*, based on their success in the mega-hit, *Gigi*, with Leslie Caron, which had won nine Academy Awards after its release in 1958.

The actual female star of *Can-Can* was Frank's long-time girlfriend, Shirley MacLaine. But as tensions on the set mounted, Barrie Chase, the dancing partner of Fred Astaire in three landmark TV specials, walked out on *Can-Can*. This seriously pissed off Frank.

He said, "How dare any broad walk out on one of my pictures? Who in hell does she think she is? I'm gonna replace her, and I assure you I'm gonna make her replacement famous."

That replacement was Juliet Prowse, and Frank lived up to his word. She did indeed become famous.

Frank was 44 when he first met Juliet, age 23, on the set of *Can-Can*. He was immediately attracted to her striking beauty, sultry smile, and eyes as blue as his. He spent more time looking at her legs than he did her face. He later told Dean Martin, "What man wouldn't want legs like that locking him into a death grip?"

He immediately set out to learn as much about her as he could. She'd been born in what was then Bombay, India, but was reared in South Africa.

He'd also told Martin, "I wonder if her pussy is the same color as her flaming red hair. She's like a trim Brigitte Bardot—talk about sex kittens. She's got the highest kick of any showgal in Vegas."

On camera they emoted well together. His most memorable song to her was "It's All Right With Me."

MacLaine recalled, "He was singing a love song to her. You know the tune—'*It's not her face, but such a charming face that it's all right with me.*' He fell in love with the person to whom he was singing. She fell in love with his voice and the fact that it was *the* Frank Sinatra. Do you call that love? I don't."

Far more impressive than anything that happened in the movie itself was the arrival on September 19, 1959 of Soviet dictator Nikita Khrushchev. He was accompanied by his dowdy wife, Nina, a dour and unphotogenic matriarch who looked like a Soviet bag lady. The setting was Fox Studios Sound Stage 8 in Los Angeles, outfitted in the desert heat to resemble Montmartre in 1896.

The idea of staging a performance of the Can-Can dance in front of Khrushchev originated with Frank.

As Frank stood looking helpless, the irrepressible MacLaine rushed over to the Soviet boss. "How the hell are you, Khrush? I'm goddamn glad you're here. Welcome to our country; and welcome to 20th Century Fox. I hope you enjoy seeing how Hollywood makes a musical. I'm going to shoot the Can-Can number without pants just to honor you."

But it was Juliet Prowse, or so it seemed, who captured the attention of the world that day. It was she who was at the center of the international spotlight when she danced the "Can-Can" in front of Khrushchev.

The old perv was secretly thrilled at the racy dance, especially the ending when the Can-Can dancers turned their backs to the stage to reveal

Although the antecedents for *Can-Can* were authentically lodged in the *Belle Époque* of Marcel Proust, Frank's interpretation of his own role, and Shirley MacLaine's interpretation of hers, were pure Americanese, without a shred of continental suave.

Whereas Europeans were appalled, American audiences of the late 50s loved it.

On the set of *Can-Can*, Nikita Khrushchev greeted the stars of the picture, Louis Jourdan, Shirley MacLaine, and Frank Sinatra. The Soviet boss was blunt in assessing the appearances of the stars. He told Jourdan, a Frenchman, "I was briefed this morning on who you are. I was told you were voted the handsomest man in the world. We have far better-looking soldiers in the Soviet Army."

He suggested to Shirley that she shouldn't wear her gowns cut so low. "My wife believes that a respectable woman should not show so much."

As for Frank, Nikita told him, "Even in the Soviet Union we've heard of Frank Sinatra. But your Chicago gangsters would not be allowed in Russia. There is no crime in my country."

In the ironic saga of Juliet Prowse, she turned for sexual trysts to two of Frank Sinatra's musical competitors, Elvis Presley and **Eddie Fisher** (depicted above). Perhaps she was getting even with Frank for the collapse of their engagement.

As Eddie related it, "She came to me at the Cocoanut Grove in Los Angeles. I was attracted to her immediately, but I knew she had been going with Frank Sinatra, and I thought it wise to check with him first. No one wanted to anger him. I called him in London, where he was appearing after a tour of performances that had taken him around the world. He gave me his gracious permission to date Juliet and then invited me to come to London when my engagement at the Cocoanut Grove was over. A lot of his buddies were there and he was forming some new kind of Rat Pack."

In his 1999 biography, Eddie admitted that he and Juliet were so attracted to each other upon first meeting that "We did it in my dressing room—what wild sex!"

their butts. Ideologically, at least, he had to pretend to be shocked by this open sexuality of decadent capitalism on display. After the show, he said, "The face of mankind is prettier than its backside. We do not want that sort of thing for the Russians. The dance is lascivious, disgusting, and immoral."

When Juliet heard of Khrushchev's put-down of her, she said, "Well, it isn't exactly *Swan Lake*."

After that, *Can-Can* became such an international scandal that filming continued. So did Frank's affair with Juliet.

Frank fell in love with her, or so it was rumored, during the filming of one particular scene in the movie. With a twinkle in her eye, she whips a formidable hip in his direction. "Don't point," he gasps, obviously turned on. "It's rude."

She was sensational in her solo as "The Snake" in an Adam and Eve Ballet in *Can-Can*. She slid sensually down branches of the Tree of Life dressed in blue-green snakeskin. Of course, she had a big red apple in her hand, Temptation itself.

Temptation it was for Frank. Contrary to many reports that suggested otherwise, he later told his Rat Packers that he was bedding her the first week.

In a surprise move, one of the hit songs of the musical, "I Love Paris," was sung by the chorus in the opening credits, although it would have seemed an obvious choice to have Frank actually sing it in the film. However, the movie soundtrack album did feature Frank singing "I Love Paris."

In his shower, he rewrote the words, singing "I Love Juliet."

At first, some people couldn't believe that Frank had fallen for Juliet. He met her in the late summer of 1959 and dated her for about ten months, until their relationship came to a shattering conclusion.

Some Hollywood insiders speculated that Frank was just helping launch her career, and that his intense dating of her was a mere publicity stunt for this newcomer.

Before the announcement of his engagement to Juliet, Frank called Marilyn Monroe, who was holding on to some vague idea that he was going to marry her. "I like what we have between us," Frank told the disappointed blonde star. "Let's don't spoil it with marriage." He'd later change his mind.

Marilyn was said to have been devastated by the news. "I can't believe Frank would betray me in this way," she told Jeanne Carmen, her best friend. "He told me he loved me and wanted to spend the rest of his life with me."

"Oh, Marilyn," the more realistic Jeanne said. "How many men have told you that?"

Sammy Davis Jr. speculated that Frank had launched an affair with Juliet "just to get Marilyn out of his hair."

It was said that Frank proposed marriage to Juliet five times before she accepted. He even flew to South Africa to meet her parents. When they came to Los Angeles in 1960, during JFK's run for the presidency, Frank hosted them.

He dated Juliet seriously, and even gave her a pearl necklace priced at $12,000.

Before they really understood what was happening, Frank's friends were attending an engagement party hosted by Michael Romanoff, at his restaurant. In front of everyone, Frank presented Juliet with a five-carat diamond.

The announcement of Frank's engagement to Juliet was a crushing blow to Nancy Sinatra, Sr. She told the press, "Frank and I are a closed chapter. He wants a new life."

Sergio Fadini had toured Italy with Juliet as a dance partner. He'd also been her lover.

Fadini, now her former boyfriend, was very dismissive of Frank. "Juliet is a sweet, shy, reserved girl. I don't see what she sees in a man like Frank Sinatra."

When Sammy Davis Jr. heard Fadini's putdown of Frank he said, "I know what Juliet sees in Frankie. A big dick with money."

"Gossip about Frank Sinatra and me doesn't bother me," she told the press. "I'm an open person. I've mixed around in this business long enough not to be embarrassed by anything pertaining to sex."

To her friends, Juliet pretended to be almost virginal. "She was anything but," claimed Dean Martin. "From reports getting back to me, she'd fuck any guy with a dick big enough."

It is not known how many tricks Juliet turned, but during her so-called engagement to Frank, the names of two of those so-called tricks have surfaced—Elvis Presley and a notorious male prostitute named William Parker, nicknamed "Big Willie."

Unknown to Frank at the time, Juliet met "Big Willie," who was a strapping six-foot, three-inch "walking streak of sex," known for his legendary endowment. He'd bedded some of the top stars in Hollywood, but he charged for his services, at least two hundred dollars a night, which was considered an outrageous price back then. "I'm worth it," he told his women clients, and seemingly most of them agreed.

It is not known how Juliet hooked up with him, but "Big Willie" called on her several times when Frank was otherwise engaged. She paid him for his services, as she was known to like men with "heavy equipment."

She admitted to MacLaine, "That's what I like about Frank. He will never ask the way to the little boy's room."

Their engagement was long over before Frank discovered that she'd made use of a male prostitute. He exploded. In the future, whenever anyone dared bring up her name, he referred to her as "a slut" or "a whore."

Simultaneous with her off-the-record life, her on-record engagement with Frank continued, and soon she was a guest on his television show, where he brought on such stars as Hermione Gingold, Ella Fitzgerald, Peter Lawford, and Nelson Riddle and his Orchestra. On occasion, he would be filmed singing adoringly to

With her red hair, pouting lips, and long legs, **Juliet Prowse** had the highest kick in films during her all-too-brief career. When her movie career faded, she became a sensational night club performer. Hanging out with Frank Sinatra and Nikita Khrushchev had made her notorious. If the Soviet dictator had learned about what eventually happened to Juliet in the 1970s, he would have doubled up on his denunciations—"lascivious and disgusting" would at least in Khrushchev's opinion be too tame.

Always interested in the size of a man's appendage, she finally hired John C. Holmes, the legendary "King of Porn," to entertain her on certain nights. As millions of his fans know, John was known for his legendary 13.5 inches. Juliet apparently found this country boy from Ohio very penetrating.

Juliet. It was no act. He was falling for her big time, or at least he'd convinced himself of that.

Their official engagement lasted only forty-three days. Their breakup was met with ridicule in some quarters. On *The Tonight Show*, Johnny Carson said, "Talk about short engagements. Frank has had longer engagements in Las Vegas."

Juliet later asserted that Frank wanted her to give up her career, which she refused to do. "After working this long and this hard for a career, I'd hate to give it up—and I won't!"

That's what Juliet told the world, concealing what really happened behind the scenes.

On the set of *Can-Can*, Frank had noted that **Nina Khrushchev** appeared to be making a comment about him, in English, no less. Later, he asked a Fox Studios' security guard what she'd said.

She had said, "In the Soviet Union, we'd regard this little man, this Sinatra, as a shrimp, not a big star." Frank wanted revenge.

When he heard that **Jackie Kennedy** was going to pose with Mrs. Khruschev at an upcoming Summit in Vienna, he wrote the First Lady at the White House:

"Jackie, show that fat Soviet Lady Bear what chic is all about. I know you'll pose for pictures with her. She looks like a butcher in a slaughterhouse. Show her what American style, fashion, charm, and beauty are all about."

Jackie did just that when she posed with Nina. She really didn't need the advice from Frank.

In Jackie's navy blue suit and matching beret, in her pearls and ruby diamond pin, America's First Lady was a billboard for the capitalism of the West.

When she received word of the breakup, Nancy Sinatra didn't hold out much hope for a reconciliation, especially when Frank told reporters, "I love Nancy, but I'm not in love with her."

Juliet would later recall, "He was incredibly possessive of me. He was seeing his hookers on the side, and I felt it was okay for me to turn a trick or two. But when Frank found out about that, he went ballistic."

Straight from *Can-Can*, Juliet segued almost immediately into *G.I. Blues* starring Elvis Presley in a reworking of the 1942 film *The Fleet's In*.

Frank may not have found out about Juliet hiring a male prostitute until months after their engagement was off, but he did uncover her affair with Elvis [see following feature].

Although Juliet would prolong her career for years to come, her prestige and her fan base faltered after her breakup with Frank. She performed in many TV shows and often appeared in night clubs, sometimes as a headliner at the Desert Inn in Las Vegas, where she did a charming and very funny impersonation of Elvis.

In 1994, she was diagnosed with pancreatic cancer. But a year later it went into remission, and she toured with Mickey Rooney in *Sugar Babies*. Regrettably, she succumbed to the disease on September 14, 1996, two weeks before her sixtieth birthday.

Before she died, she told friends, "Maybe if Frank hadn't found out so much about me, maybe I should have married him when he proposed. But I insisted at the time on doing it *my way*. Trouble was, I didn't do it *his way*."

---

### FRANK ATTACKS ELVIS' MANHOOD

"The only good news I ever heard about Elvis Presley was when I learned that Juliet Prowse turned down making a second film with him after *G.I. Blues*." Frank said.

"Elvis didn't make it in the sack. Natalie Wood told me he was all foreplay, no action."

# The Rat Pack Becomes

## THE JACK PACK

The stories that revolved around the Rat Pack and **John F. Kennedy** in the 1970s took the place of folk mythology, especially when Marilyn Monroe was involved. (Incidentally, that is not MM in the far right corner, as some captions have it.) Performing in Las Vegas are Rat Packers (*left to right*) **Peter Lawford, Frank Sinatra, Dean Martin, Sammy Davis Jr., and Joey Bishop.**

In honor of his friendship with JFK, Frank suggested to Judy Garland and others that the Rat Pack—a name he loathed, incidentally—should be renamed "The Jack Pack."

When Judy, in one of her phone calls to the president, informed him of this, he exploded. Perhaps jokingly, he said, "It won't do my image any good to be the leader of a pack of whoremongers and drunkards like those guys. I hear Sammy Davis Jr. is a member of the Church of Satan. My brother-in-law's a queer, and Frank and his mother run an abortion clinic."

"You've got a point, Mr. President," Judy said.

# JFK JOINS THE RAT RACE—
# BUT NOT FOR FOREVER

*"All the girls from the hotels were vying for an invitation to the Sands when word got out that the handsome young senator from Massachusetts, Kennedy, was there. Jack Kennedy was so gorgeous, all the gals wanted to meet him."*

—**Dawn Lindner Lewis,** former showgirl at the Stardust Hotel in Las Vegas

Before he switched to right wing politics, Frank Sinatra had supported Democratic candidate Adlai Stevenson for president in 1952 and 1956. Later, he became a pal of both **Teddy Kennedy** (*center*) and **JFK** (*right*), but developed a strong antipathy for **Bobby Kennedy** (*left*), U.S. Attorney General

.

When a young Teddy came to Hollywood, Marilyn Monroe and Frank used to throw "sex parties" for him. Frank would also ask JFK "What do you want on the menu tonight?" Frank then delivered the goods, the most beautiful hookers imported from points between Las Vegas and Palm Springs.

An advocate of civil rights for African Americans, Frank discussed the subject with the new president. "I'm more interested in the broads you can get for me instead of helping the plight of the disenfranchised," JFK said. "See my brother Bobby about that. He's much more of a social activist than I am. You've done your part. By including Sammy Davis Jr., you've integrated the Rat Pack."

*"JFK enjoyed hanging out with Frank and his Hollywood crowd, which was so different from the somber mood in Washington. After the Cuban Missile Crisis in December of 1962, he said he needed 'the distraction' of Palm Springs."*

—**Gerald Blaine,** Secret Service Agent

Nancy Sinatra Jr. asked the right question: "My father was the most charismatic entertainer of the 20th Century. Why shouldn't he be best friends with the world's most charismatic politician at the time?"

Frank was first introduced to JFK by Peter Lawford in 1955 at a Democratic Party rally. At the Democratic National Convention in Chicago, in 1956, Frank supported Adlai Stevenson and was disappointed when JFK lost his bid to run as Stevenson's vice president.

JFK was temporarily defeated, but he told Frank, "I'll skip this VP shit job and seek the presidency itself in 1960."

"I'm right behind you, Prez," Frank promised him and kept his word when the time came. "I'll be your chief supporter."

Dean Martin later accused Frank of "brown-nosing—the best rimmer in the business."

A friendship quickly developed between the two men because each had something the other wanted. JFK had political power, and Frank, in the Senator's own words, "had access to Hollywood movie stars, the most fuckable."

Frank was rather cocky, arrogant and a bit autocratic about his association with the Kennedys, which was kept alive mainly through JFK's brother-in-law, Peter Lawford.

"Unknown to a lot of people, Jack loved Hollywood gossip, and Sinatra knew every scandal that had not yet made *Confidential*," said Kennedy aide David Powers.

When they had first talked about Hollywood stars, JFK wanted to know "Is Shirley MacLaine's pussy red? Or are her legs as good as those of Cyd Charisse?"

In 1959, Jack stayed at Frank's compound in Palm Springs. Hollywood columnist James Bacon, a former lover of Marilyn Monroe, claimed it was always New Year's Eve when JFK was in Palm Springs.

Richard Burton, a friend of Frank's, wrote in his Journal: "I know that when Jack Kennedy was plotting his run for the presidency in 1960, and stayed with Sinatra in Palm Springs, the place was like a whorehouse. Kennedy was the chief customer."

As guests at Frank's villa in Palm Springs, Peter and Senator Kennedy were openly spotted by the household staff snorting lines of cocaine. The senator said it relieved his back pain. Peter made no such pretense, claiming, "I did it for the hell of it."

Although Frank indulged his guests, he did not partake of cocaine, since he frowned on drugs—"all except for those in the bottle," as he was fond of saying.

The FBI learned that Frank and Peter had thrown a sex party at Frank's home in Palm Springs, where the future president was an overnight guest.

Frank later put a plaque over the bed, JOHN F. KENNEDY SLEPT HERE. Peter later cracked, "Jack did more than sleep in that damn bed."

Details are lacking, but the FBI learned that two mulatto prostitutes imported from Las Vegas were used to entertain the three men. Neither of this unholy trio had any trouble crossing the color line, and all three of them had on occasion specified that they wanted women of color, yet all three had also slept with blondes like Marilyn Monroe and Lana Turner. "We are equal opportunity fuckers," Frank said of himself, Peter and JFK.

Frank found JFK a far smoother operator than his father, Joe Kennedy, Sr., had been when he was a house guest of Frank's in Palm Springs. "Joe called

Frank Sinatra once hired **Mort Sahl** (*left*), a Canada-born comedian and actor, as the Democratic Party's weapon against Bob Hope, who was writing jokes for Richard Nixon and the Republicans.

Sahl occasionally wrote both jokes and speeches delivered by JFK. *Time* magazine, putting him on the cover, called him "the patriarch of a new school of comedians." But when his quips came "too close to home," he angered **Joseph P. Kennedy** (*right*), who didn't want him at any more Democratic fund raisers.

Although Sahl was no longer welcome at Hyannis Port, he was deeply wounded by JFK's assassination and became obsessed with it. A lifelong Democrat, Sahl turned his witticisms and his wrath onto Ronald Reagan and Nixon: "Washington couldn't tell a lie; Nixon couldn't tell the truth, and Reagan couldn't tell the difference."

In the aftermath of that, Nancy Reagan invited Sahl to the White House where President Reagan roasted him at a White House tribute. "The Reagans are very, very forgiving," Sahl said. "But not old Joe Kennedy."

337

my help 'niggers' and burned one of the whores I'd rounded up for him with a cigar," Frank confided to Sammy Davis Jr.

If Peter Lawford was Frank's pimp, Frank became JFK's pimp. He both introduced the Senator (and later president) to movie stars, or in many cases, prostitutes. FBI agents filed reports with J. Edgar Hoover about orgies in Palm Springs, New York, Beverly Hills, and Las Vegas, that revolved around Peter, Frank, and JFK. Frank called them sex parties.

To show JFK's increasing closeness to Frank, he frequently invited him to his sexual hideaway at Washington's Mayflower Hotel. "There's where Jack staged orgies," Judy Garland later claimed. "I should know."

JFK watched "The Summit" (alias the Rat Pack) perform on the eve of the 1960 New Hampshire primary.

Without Frank's ever knowing it (possibly), he shared two women with JFK. They were Angie Dickinson and Juliet Prowse. One night Juliet was told to wait in Frank's suite at the Sands until he finished his late show. She'd been to the early show, as had JFK.

To her surprise, she found JFK in the suite, also waiting for Frank. Apparently, Frank had arranged for some other entertainment for the presidential candidate.

"He may have had Angie earlier in the evening," Julie later claimed, "but he had me that night while Frank was singing on stage. I felt I couldn't say no. After all, he was soon to become President of the United States. And as our supreme commander, he could have ordered me to go to bed with him. Angie was right. JFK didn't take long to get off."

To get elected president, JFK depended on Frank's mob ties and his fund-raising concerts.

Joe Kennedy asked Frank to use his influence to secure 120,000 votes in the West Virginia primary. Frank then appealed to mob boss Sam Giancana to deliver the votes, doing "whatever is necessary" to get them. Frank emerged as a politically useful combination that included being an entertainment-industry heavyweight with the ability to enlist the help of organized crime.

Giancana, of course, was eager to win favor with the new administration. Basically, Giancana cooperated because he wanted the government to let

Actress **Angie Dickinson** *(left)* and dancer **Juliet Prowse** *(right)* shared intimate times with both Frank Sinatra and John F. Kennedy. JFK became more intimate with Angie, Frank with Juliet. "Changing partners" could have been the president's theme song with Frank.

Dean Martin may have been the first rat who "dallied" with the sexy Angie while filming *Rio Bravo*. But by the time the Rat Pack was filming *Ocean's 11*, Angie seemed to have moved on to Frank himself. At one point, Frank announced, "I want Angie to be the leading lady in all the Clan's movies."

Juliet Prowse was seduced by JFK, but Frank's fellow Rat Packers stayed away from her because she was considered "Frank's girl," at least during their engagement. When she made *Can-Can* with Shirley MacLaine and Frank, he seemed to pay little attention to Shirley. "I've drifted on," he told his co-star Maurice Chevalier.

"The story of my life," the French entertainer replied.

him alone. Evidence indicated that he didn't expect a lot of favors. As he told Frank, "Both of us didn't take into account that Kennedy would make his brother Bobby the god damn attorney general," Giancana said. "He has all the charm of a cobra and he's after our asses."

FBI records have revealed that large donations from the mob were being collected by Frank to pay off officials in West Virginia. Key people were faced with a challenge—get out the vote even if it cost money. "If they're voting for Hubert Humphrey, pay them to vote for Jack," Joe Kennedy ordered.

Right wing Bob Hope was practically a joke factory for his candidate Richard Nixon. To counterattack, Frank turned to comedian Mort Sahl to write jokes attacking Nixon and the Republicans. At one Kennedy fundraiser, Sahl said to Joe Kennedy, "You're not losing a son, you're gaining a country." The ambassador considered that "impertinent," and let Frank know that. Sahl was shown the open road.

JFK, at least for a while, defined Frank as an ideal friend. He could not only raise money from the mob, but "he knows where all the best pussies are stored," JFK told his close buddy, Senator George Smathers of Florida.

Brother-in-law Peter Lawford claimed, "Let's just say that the Kennedys are interested in the lively arts, and Sinatra is the liveliest art of all."

Justice Department files claimed, "It is known fact that the Sands Hotel in Las Vegas is owned by hoodlums and that while the Senator, Sinatra, and Lawford were there, showgirls from all over the town were running in and out of the Senator's suite." All of these show girls were supplied by Peter and Frank.

Frank campaigned avidly for JFK during the campaign of 1960, working closely with Joe Kennedy. "I've practically assigned New Jersey to Sinatra," Joe claimed. "Dolly Sinatra, when she's not aborting babies, still has a lot of political pull there."

Sammy Kahn reworked the lyrics for Frank to sing "High Hopes":

*K-E-double-N-E-D-Y,*
*Jack's the nation's favorite guy.*
*Everyone wants to back Jack*
*Jack is on the right track.*
*And he's got HIGH HOPES*
*High apple-pie-in-the-sky HOPES.*

**Bob Hope** *(right photo, inset)*, a lifelong Republican who wrote jokes for **Richard Nixon** *(left)*, was startled when a longtime Democrat, Frank Sinatra, switched sides and agreed to support Nixon. Throughout the 1950s, Frank had always said, "I hate Nixon's guts." Obviously, later in his life, he wanted revenge on the Kennedys for dumping him.

A fellow Rat Packer, Sammy Davis Jr., also threw his tiny weight behind Nixon. "Ever since Jack froze me out of his inauguration ceremonies, I know the word Liberal doesn't mean a God damn thing," Sammy told Frank. "Even though he's to the right of Goebbels, I actually think Tricky Dickie will do more for us black folks than any Democrat."

Despite massive demonstrations for Adlai Stevenson, the Democratic Convention of 1960 finally nominated JFK as their presidential candidate. Frank pounded Peter on the back. "Charley, we'll soon be sleeping in the Lincoln Bedroom, but I've got to find a better bedmate than you," Frank said, "Maybe

Jackie herself. Jack doesn't seem to get around to her very much."

Before and after the election of 1960, Frank had been devoted to the Kennedys, especially Jack. Bobby always seemed to hold Frank in a bit of contempt, primarily because of his mob associations.

Frank admired JFK's politics and power, and the president admired Frank's "way with women, his personal charisma, and his talent as a singer—the best popular singer in America," as JFK once called him.

FBI men, in a report published in the *Washington Post* in 2011, said that "Sinatra was wooing JFK through Peter Lawford so that Joe Fischetti and other notorious hoodlums could have an entrée to the Senator, especially after he became president."

Somehow Frank acquired a copy of a private investigator's report. It revealed that Richard Nixon, the Republican nominee, had made several visits to Dr. Arnold Hutschnecker, a New York psychiatrist. With a certain glee, Frank turned this over to Bobby Kennedy, JFK's campaign manager. Even though Frank knew that the report could be very damaging if revealed, Bobby locked it in his safe and never used it against Nixon.

Frank was furious because he felt he'd delivered a killing blow, and Bobby wasn't taking advantage of it.

As a sign of trouble to come between Frank and the Kennedys, he almost derailed his participation in the campaign when he hired Albert Maltz, one of the notorious "Hollywood Ten," to write a screenplay of *The Execution of Private Slovik*, about the only American soldier executed by the U.S. Army, after approval by Dwight D. Eisenhower, for desertion since the Civil War.

Frank wanted to direct the picture himself. Maltz had been famously imprisoned and blacklisted for his refusal to provide answers put to him by the members of the House Un-American Activities Committee during Joseph McCarthy's "Red Scare" of the late 1940s. After that, in 1951, he'd fled to Mexico. Like many others in Hollywood, Frank wanted to end this notorious blacklist of some of the most talented artists in Hollywood.

Once Frank made the announcement in March of 1960 that he'd hired blacklisted Maltz, he faced accusations across the country. *The New York Mirror* denounced him for hiring "a hard Communist revolutionary." But Frank also received support from such papers as *The New York Post*, who

Every now and then, Frank Sinatra developed an obsession, and one of them involved bringing to the screen the tragic story of **Eddie Slovik**, seen in the photos above both alive and dead.

The unfortunate young man, who was charged with desertion during World War II, was the only American soldier executed by the U.S. Army since the Civil War. When arrested and tried, he thought his sentence would involve a simple court martial, but he was shocked to discover that he'd been sentenced to death.

On the firing squad, one of his executioners said, "I don't feel sorry for the son of a bitch. He deserted under fire while the rest of us got hell shot out of us."

The execution was carried out in France on January 31, 1945. Slovik's final words were, "They're not shooting me for deserting, as thousands of guys have done that. They just need to make an example out of somebody because I'm an ex-con. They're shooting me for the bread and chewing gum I stole when I was twelve years old."

As a chaplain blessed him, Slovik faced the firing squad as eleven bullets slammed into his chest.

awarded him an "Oscar" for his attempt to defy the secret blacklist that had sent terror racing through Hollywood studios.

John Wayne attacked Frank, calling him a "crony of the Leftist Kennedy," and wondered how the new president might feel about using communists in the film industry.

To counterattack Wayne, Frank purchased full-page ads in the trade papers in Hollywood. He claimed, "I did not ask the advice of Senator Kennedy on whom I should hire."

A loyal American like Frank was also attacked "for following the communist line."

Many Americans vowed to never see another Frank Sinatra movie, claiming, "We'll never buy another record." One former fan wrote, "If I hear his voice on radio, I'll turn it off." Yet another fan club in Georgia deserted him, its former president claiming, "Sinatra takes his marching orders directly from the Kremlin."

The pressure, particularly from Roman Catholics, became so severe that Ambassador Kennedy called Frank. "That pro-Communist shit is more than our campaign can take. Jack being Catholic is enough to derail us. Now this. Make up your mind. It's either Maltz or the road."

After that threat, Frank caved in and removed Maltz, although in some quarters that brought condemnation too. "Chalk up another victory for the lynch-law mentality," screamed *Publishers Weekly*.

In a very generous move, Frank settled $75,000 on Maltz, which is what he'd have received if he had finished the script. Then Frank abandoned the entire project.

*The Execution of Private Slovik* finally made it to the screen as a made-for-TV movie in 1974 starring Martin Sheen.

About five nights later after the Maltz firing, Frank encountered his arch enemy at a celebrity dinner at the Moulin Rouge. Still "boiling mad" over his treatment in the right wing press, Frank spotted John Wayne at the bar. Rising drunkenly from the table, he headed for Wayne. At six feet, four inches, Wayne towered over Frank.

"I got a bone to pick with you," Frank said to Wayne.

"Let's talk about it in another place, another time," Wayne said, heading for the door to prevent a public spectacle.

To his back, Frank yelled, "Dietrich told me you've got the smallest dick in Hollywood."

Wayne didn't turn back but hurriedly left the room. Later he told friends, "I could have cleaned up the floor with the dirty little Mafia wop."

In the words of Frank Sinatra, "**Albert Maltz** *(above)* is the best goddamn writer around." That's why Frank hired him to write the screenplay for a film based on the Army-executed soldier, Eddie Slovik, during the closing months of World War II.

This was the writer's first screen assignment since he'd been convicted of contempt of Congress in June of 1950. He declined to answer queries from the House Un-American Activities Committee regarding membership in the Communist party. Maltz was fined $1,000 and sentenced to a year in prison for contempt. Disgraced, he was released in 1951 and became known as one of the infamous "Hollywood Ten."

Frank's hiring of the blacklisted writer sent shock waves through the Kennedy campaign, creating an enormous backlash. "If Sinatra loves his country, he won't do this," wrote columnist Hedda Hopper, a fervent right winger.

Under the most intense political pressure he'd ever endured, Frank was forced to come to a settlement and take Maltz off the picture. On hearing the news, the *Los Angeles Examiner* published, in red ink, a massive headline: "SINATRA OUSTS MALTZ AS WRITER."

At the Democratic National Convention in Los Angeles on July 11, 1960, Frank, among others, opened the ceremonies singing "The Star-Spangled Banner." The Rat Pack was there, and delegates from Mississippi booed Sammy Davis Jr.

Sammy left the stage in tears, even though Frank pleaded with him. "You lose if they see they've made you cry, Charley."

The obscenely prejudiced condemnation was expressed not just because Sammy was black but because he had announced his plans to marry Swedish actress, blonde-haired Mai Britt. Frank got Sammy to postpone his marriage until after the election.

Like much of the nation, Frank stayed up on the night of November 8, 1960 to listen to the election results. By midnight NBC had gone on the air predicting a victory for Nixon, but an hour later, the race became too close to call. Frank watched at 3:10am, when Nixon appeared on television at the Ambassador Hotel in Los Angeles. He refused to concede.

Frank went ballistic and called the hotel. "This is Frank Sinatra," he shouted at the operator. "Put me through to Nixon's suite." Nixon refused to take his call. Frank was going to demand that the GOP candidate concede.

In the final tally, rigged or not, JFK carried Illinois by 8,858 votes. Mafia honcho Skinny D'Amato said, "Sinatra won the election for Kennedy by mobilizing mob support—and all that money."

Dozens of political observers claimed that Frank made JFK a media star months before he was seated as president. Frank's most dazzling achievement was on January 20, 1961, the day before JFK was inaugurated, when he organized the presidential gala. He invited A-list stars, including quite a lot of black performers such as Harry Belafonte, Ella Fitzgerald, and Nat King Cole. Leonard Bernstein, a personal favorite of Jackie's, was there, along with Tony Curtis, Janet Leigh, Laurence Olivier, Gene Kelly, and, of course, Angie Dickinson.

However, he had the unpleasant task of calling Sammy and telling him that he was not invited to the inauguration. "Jack told me to tell you, and he hopes you will understand," Frank said.

Frank himself did not understand. Only hours before the night of the inauguration, he threatened "to pull the plug" and fly out of Washington. Peter practically had to beg him to stay on and see it through.

As a tribute to African-Americans, Frank sang at a benefit for Martin Luther King Jr. in the days that followed, even though he was "overloaded" with Jack Daniels when he went on stage.

In spite of all his work at the inauguration, Frank was snubbed on that bitterly cold day when JFK took the oath of office. He showed up thinking he was among the 600 guests invited to the section set aside for the president's friends.

He arrived drunk at the ceremony. When he asked to be shown to his seat, the security guard told him, "You're not on the list."

"I guess you don't understand, Charley," he said. "I'm Frank Sinatra."

"I don't give a fuck who you are," the guard told him. "You could be the Pope for all I care. You're not on the fucking list."

Frank struck the security guard and was escorted out of the area by two men from the Secret Service.

Frank had dared dream the impossible dream. "He actually thought Kennedy would appoint him ambassador to Italy for all the work he did on his campaign," Ava Gardner said. "Could you imagine the questions that would have been put to Frank at the Senate confirmation hearings?"

During the first weeks of his presidency, JFK made several calls to Frank for informal chats. He always picked up the phone saying, "Hi ya, Prez." Mostly JFK wanted to hear the latest gossip, and was especially eager to know which stars were sleeping with which other stars.

One night, JFK told Peter that he wanted to do something special for Frank for all his help in the campaign. An invitation to the White House was suggested. The president said it would have to be extended when Jackie was in Middleburg. "She hates Sinatra," JFK said.

Of course, after JFK's assassination, Jackie would change her mind about Frank, especially when she launched an affair with him in the mid-1970s.

Peter later claimed that as prelude to his invitation to visit JFK in the White House, Frank was slipped in through the southwest gate to avoid reporters and photographers. "Jackie must not find out," JFK warned.

Peter later said that Frank always wanted to fly on Air Force One, but never got an invitation. "He also wasn't invited to state dinners or to spend a weekend at Camp David. Jack did take him on a personal tour of the White House, and they enjoyed Bloody Marys on the Truman Balcony."

Over dinner, Frank told JFK about his recent visit to the Vatican and delivered "a very special message" from the Pope to the president. The secret in that message has never been revealed, but it may have had something to do with abortion.

For a while, JFK and Frank were sharing Marilyn Monroe and Judith Campbell Exner as lovers. Sam Giancana also seduced both women.

Frank was just a pawn for J. Edgar Hoover to use in his battle with the Kennedys, especially Bobby, who, as attorney general, was technically Hoover's boss. Hoover was afraid he was losing his grip on the FBI, and his agents fanned out to link both Frank and the Kennedys to the mob. The FBI chief knew that information such as that could bring down a president, or else be used as blackmail to hold onto his job.

An FBI wiretap revealed that gangster Johnny Roselli was far more skeptical of Frank's ties to the White House than his boss Giancana was. "You know Pierre Salinger [a reference to JFK's press secretary] and those guys, they don't want Frankie," Roselli claimed. "They treat him like they treat a whore."

Immediately after Bobby launched his war on organized crime, several mob mem-

When child star **Shirley Temple** came to inspect FBI headquarters in Washington, **J. Edgar Hoover**, its director, personally showed her the latest crime-detecting equipment. At the end of the tour, Shirley asked him, "Are you married?" He answered that he was not. "Then I will give you a kiss," she said. Hoover got a big smack on the lips from the little box office champion, who had always been a favorite of his.

On January 20, 1949, Hoover invited Shirley, then a mature, 21-year-old actres whose screen popularity was fading, to be his guest at the inauguration parade of newly elected U.S. President Harry S Truman. "He (Hoover) gave me his best Santa Claus smile and a present, a tear gas gun disguised as a fountain pen," Shirley said.

Hoover's homosexuality would not be a problem with Truman, who told author Merle Miller, "They brought me a lot of stuff about his personal life, and I told them I didn't give a damn about it. It wasn't my business."

The "dreaded" Kennedys lay in the FBI director's future.

In the Oval Office of the White House, President John F. Kennedy told Bobby and two of his aides, "If I accept Sinatra's invitation to stay with him in Palm Springs, I might encounter **Sam Giancana** (depicted above) over the breakfast table. We've got to cut our ties to Sinatra. That cocksucker, J. Edgar Hoover, is making a huge stink about it."

Frank was bitterly disappointed when the president rejected his invitation to stay with him.

"Look at all the broads I've supplied to that little prick. The booze. The babes. And the Mafia dough!" Frank said. "Now the door to the White House has been closed to me forever. As for you, Lawford, you're dead meat."

He ended their long-standing friendship. He also called producer friends. "I know he's the president's brother-in-law, but don't offer this limey shit any more film roles."

bers went to Giancana with requests to kill Frank in revenge. "The son of a bitch tricked us," Roselli claimed. "He needs to die. But first we'll cut off his overused *cojones*."

Giancana rejected all assassination attempts on Frank. However, Giancana wanted "something to settle the debt."

He called Frank in November of 1962. Giancana was secretly operating the casino Villa Venice outside Chicago. When he got Frank on the phone, Giancana was blunt. "For what we did for your Kennedy fuck-up, I want you, the nigger, and Dean to show up and perform for us. There will be no paycheck coming your way, of course."

In London Ava Gardner once told a reporter that Giancana "would have killed Frank in an instant but, perhaps held back, figuring he had some use for him in the future."

A 1962 visit to Palm Springs marked the beginning of JFK trying to distance himself from Frank, at least at public events. Columnist Dorothy Kilgallen quoted JFK: "Sinatra is no friend of mine. He's a friend of my sister, Pat, and her husband, Peter Lawford."

Even though Jackie Kennedy was escorted into the pre-inauguration ceremonies on the arm of Frank, she later told Peter, "He disgusts me. I don't want him in the White House. Besides, I know for a fact that he arranges whores to seduce my husband." Ironically, in her dialogue with Peter, she was addressing a pimp who also arranged sexual trysts for JFK.

Bobby intervened and warned his brother that he had to break with Frank, because "a noose is tightening around our neck. If we're not careful, that Judith Campbell and Sam Giancana will end your presidency." [See separate article.]

Jack took Bobby's advice, and soon an invitation was forthcoming from Bing Crosby, a Republican who also had a vacation home in Palm Springs.

In his memoir, *Palimpsest*, Gore Vidal found it ironic that Frank was exiled from "The Holy Family," meaning the Kennedys, for hanging out with mobsters that Joe had done business with all his life. He also claimed that Peter was "Jack's Plenipotentiary to the girls of Hollywood." But Vidal could also have cited Frank as a major pimp as well.

When JFK announced that he was going to stop over in Palm Springs, Frank immediately extended an invitation through Peter. Without hearing differently, Frank assumed the president would stay with him. He added extra bedrooms, tightened the security system, and installed a helipad. He even went so far as to arrange the installation of a direct phone link to the White House.

Peter had assured Frank that the president would be his house guest. It came as a shock when Peter learned that the Secret Service had opted for Crosby's house instead. Agent Floyd

Boring claimed that "Sinatra's house is too exposed."

Frank had to be notified, and Boring agreed to go with Peter to Frank's villa to relay the bad news. Another agent, Gerald Blaine, also accompanied Peter to Frank's house.

It was Blaine who informed Frank that JFK would be staying with Crosby. Frank looked shocked. "I'm sorry, Frank," Peter protested. "I was overruled. I just found out myself . . . just an hour ago."

"It's purely for security reasons," Boring told Sinatra. "No other reason."

Concealing Bobby's role in the decision, Peter blamed the shift in plans on the Secret Service. Whereas Frank's house opened onto the Tamarish Country Club with much open space around it, Crosby's house backed up against a mountain and was entered only by a solitary road.

The moment the Secret Service agents left the house, Frank turned on Peter. In front of the U.S. government agents, he had remained relatively calm. Alone with Peter, he smashed a glass-framed photograph in his living room that had been autographed by the president himself.

"I've seen Frank mad before, and I've seen him violent," Peter later said. "But he became a madman that afternoon. He lunged toward me and began choking me. I was strangling to death. I tried to fight him off, but his anger seemed to give him a strength he never had before. He was killing me. All I remember was that someone intervened. It was a servant no doubt. I passed out."

Peter later recalled he woke up alone in the desert outside Palm Springs. "I didn't know where I was. My throat was aching and parched. I stumbled toward the highway and flagged down a car filled with fraternity boys from Los Angeles."

"Aren't you the president's brother-in-law?" the driver asked. "What in hell are you doing out here?"

"I tried to think of a reason," Peter recollected afterward. "I told them that I'd gotten fresh with Ava Gardner, and that she kicked me out of her car. The frat boys understood that. On the way into town, they related various stories about girls who had reacted violently to their come-ons."

The next day Frank sent word to Peter that he was *persona non grata* in Rat Pack circles. To prove his point, he fired him from two upcoming movies. "If I meet the faggot again, I'll give him a punch in the nose."

"Forget the Kennedys," Frank told his remaining Rat Packers. "Fuck them. I think I'm gonna become a Republican like Bing Crosby. In fact, I will give Bing

A distant relative of Jackie Kennedy's, gay author **Gore Vidal** *(depicted above)* for a time was welcomed at the White House until Bobby Kennedy had him bodily removed for getting too personal with the First Lady. Like Frank Sinatra himself, Vidal became *persona non grata* at the White House.

In his memoirs, *Palimpsest*, Vidal wrote: "Since Joe Kennedy had exiled the singer Frank Sinatra from the Holy Family (Sinatra was alleged to have met those underworld figures that Joe had done business with all his life), Peter Lawford became Jack's plenipotentiary to the girls of Hollywood. But then, all Jack's Hollywood connections were put to use. Jack would ask me endless questions about the 'availability' of this or that star. Since my own approach to sex was not unlike Jack's I have never been as shocked as people still appear to be by his promiscuity."

a role in our next Rat Pack feature. After the experience I went through, even Nixon is beginning to look good to me."

Although JFK didn't see Frank during that particular trip to Palm Springs, he ran into Barbara Marx at her Racquet Club where she was playing tennis. She would later become Frank's fourth wife. He didn't remember propositioning her on the *Queen of Bermuda*'s sail from New York to The Bahamas, and, according to her memoirs, he started to flirt with her all over again.

Ultimately, even after JFK rejected Frank's invitation, the singer still tried to improve their relationship. In May of 1962, for the president's birthday, Frank sent JFK a large rocking chair made of flowers. Kenneth O'Donnell, a Kennedy aide, said, "The god damn thing was so gaudy that it was embarrassing. I decided not to show it to the president to avoid embarrassment and sent it out the back door along with John-John's diapers."

During the final weeks of the Kennedy administration, Frank told Dean Martin and Sammy Davis Jr. that, "I've been exiled to Siberia." Even so, he spoke with respect about JFK, but was painfully hurt by the Kennedys casting him out.

News of JFK's assassination in Dallas in November of 1963 caused Frank acute agony.

Immediately after the assassination, Frank called the White House and spoke to Patricia. He did not ask to speak to Peter. He was hoping that she would invite him to the funeral, but she didn't.

"I did so much for them, and now I'm not good enough to come and pay my respects," Frank told Dean Martin. "With friends like the Kennedys, you don't need enemies."

Emerging from seclusion, Frank issued a statement about the president's assassination. "I'm just one of the hundreds of millions of people who carry in our hearts a profound affection, respect, and lasting sense of loss for John Fitzgerald Kennedy. I dearly wish I could find more ways to live those words of his: 'Ask not what your country can do for you . . . .'"

In the month following JFK's assassination in Dallas, Frank suddenly had another major disaster on his hands—the kidnapping of his son, Frank Sinatra Jr.

 ## FRANK AND ELVIS REACT TO THE MURDER OF MARILYN

Marilyn Monroe died on August 5, 1962, and both Elvis Presley and Frank Sinatra mourned her passing. Both of these singers had been her lover, Elvis fleetingly so, Frank of a more enduring nature. Both men, in their very different ways, did not buy the suicide theory. Friends claimed that both Elvis and Frank uttered the same accusation: "Marilyn was murdered."

"It was Robert Kennedy," Elvis claimed. "That son of a bitch had Marilyn murdered. She knew too much. She was threatening to destroy the Kennedys, and she could have if she'd wanted to."

Frank had a very different take on Marilyn's murder. Although he knew Bobby Kennedy was implicated, he did not believe for a second that RFK would actually murder MM himself. Frank viewed Marilyn's death as being orchestrated by the Mob, and he began his own investigation, beginning with his highly unreliable "friend," Chicago mobster Sam Giancana.

346

# Frank, Elvis Presley, & Juliet Prowse

## SIZE DOES MATTER

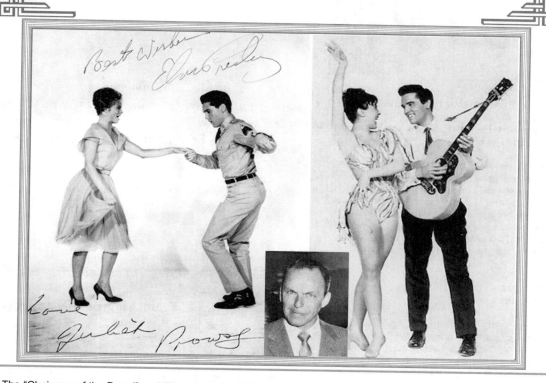

The "Chairman of the Board" and "The King" didn't like each other, at least not at first.

That is an understatement. **Frank Sinatra** may have wanted the Mob to either wipe out **Elvis Presley** or at least "teach the fucker a lesson." Usually there was some gangster around, perhaps Johnny Roselli, to do Frank's bidding, even if it was expressed as a drunken whim.

Elvis and Frank certainly tangled over **Juliet Prowse**, the actress-dancer seen above dancing with Elvis in *G.I. Blues.* Frank was particularly bitter when he read, "Juliet Prowse has dumped Frank Sinatra to take up with Elvis. Maybe it was because of his Pelvis."

Elvis idolized Dean Martin, not Frank, but there were similarities between Elvis and Frank. Both recorded modern versions of "Old MacDonald," Elvis besting Frank. Frank got an Oscar for a movie, and Elvis, in contrast, always won the Golden Turkey as worst actor in Hollywood. Both men maintained genuine friendships with Sammy Davis Jr, and separate affairs with Juliet.

Eventually, Frank softened toward Elvis, and even lent the singer his jet when he flew to Las Vegas in 1967 to marry Priscilla. Shortly before Elvis died, Frank called him and pleaded with him to "get your act together."

In 1977, midway through one of his concerts, when Frank was informed that Elvis had died, he switched the lineup of his songs and ordered his band to start playing some of Elvis' most famous numbers. He sang them, including "Love Me Tender," before informing the stunned audience "We have lost a dear friend tonight. If I know Elvis, the kid's rockin' in heaven tonight."

# "The Chairman of the Board" Versus "The King"

**Juliet Prowse** never became the third Mrs. **Frank Sinatra**, although she came close. They were seen everywhere together, even at White House galas.

In the movie *(Can-Can)* which they made together, Juliet pranced onto the Fox sound stage with shrill cries, kicking those long legs of hers and whirling her skirts. When she ended her act, a routine which was later presented to a visiting Nikita Khrushchev, Frank said, "*C'est magnifique.*" To Louis Jourdan, his co-star, he said, "I'm gotta get into that ass."

"Why not go through the front door as well?" Jourdan replied.

As Frank moved toward marriage, Juliet prematurely started to boss him around when he presented Nancy Jr. with a mink coat when she turned "sweet sixteen." He had plans to order her the first pink Thunderbird in the United States for her birthday the following year.

"He was ignoring Frank Jr., and spoiling his oldest child, and I told him that," Juliet said. "That was the last advice I gave him. He turned around and slapped hell out of me and told me to 'mind my own god damn fucking business.' And so I did after that."

"If I'd been his wife, I would have tried to get him to cut back on the Jack Daniels, but as his girlfriend, I didn't dare. He worked booze into his act, both talking and singing about it. That was one man who could really hold his booze, unlike Dean Martin. He'd drink a quart and then order another one. But when he got a gig, he could go cold turkey—I mean completely off it. After a few days, the timbre of his voice would return. But once the gig was finished, it was a case of 'Where in the fuck did you stash the Jack Daniels?'"

*"She's gonna be real disappointed going from Big Frankie to Little Elvis. The thing with Elvis won't last. Juliet is a size queen."*
— **Frank Sinatra** to Sammy Davis Jr.

*"Frank cannot stand to be in the same room with you."*
— **Mia Farrow** to Elvis Presley

*"Elvis Presley is a degenerate redneck, his music a rancid-smelling aphrodisiac. An abomination, like the man who sings it."*
— **Frank Sinatra** to Ava Gardner

*"That truck driver from Tupelo, Mississippi, can put his brogans under my bed any damn night. That swivel-hipped action could get any gal off."*
— **Ava Gardner** to Frank Sinatra, who slapped her

*"Elvis was very different from Frank. He wasn't that hot for penetration, preferring the oral route. Mostly he liked to cuddle and fondle. When he did engage in intercourse, his tight foreskin would tear. On several occasions, this caused bleeding."*
— **Juliet Prowse** to actor Nick Adams

*"Been there, done that."*
— **Nick Adams** responding to Juliet Prowse

Frank Sinatra detested not only Elvis Presley as a person, but his music as well. Later Frank's hatred of "the competition" would indirectly lead to violence.

Nonetheless, he agreed to tape a TV show for ABC called "Frank Sinatra's Welcome Home Party for Elvis Presley." When Dean Martin asked him why he was doing that, Frank said, "It's show business, *dah-ling*," doing a bad imitation of Tallulah Bankhead.

Full of barbiturates to stave off his fear of flying, Elvis landed at McGuire Air Force Base near Fort Dix, New Jersey, at 7:42am, on March 2, 1960.

Devilishly handsome, and trim after two years of military training, he was "lean and mean," all 170 pounds of him. He was even welcomed back by Nancy Sinatra Jr., who presented the King of Rock 'n' Roll with two formal, lace-fronted dress shirts, a gift from Frank himself, who really didn't want Elvis to come home, but had decided to take advantage of his homecoming in his upcoming TV special.

At the peak of his fame, during the spring of 1958, Elvis had been inducted into the U.S. Army. The event created a frenzied carnival of reporters and photographers at the induction center at Memphis. The singer's privacy was outrageously invaded. The photographer even snapped a picture of a nearly naked Elvis in his jockey shorts, with the outline of his penis clearly revealed. The picture was flashed around the world.

What was never photographed was when Elvis had to take down those jockey shorts and let a doctor, his hand sheathed in a rubber glove, shove his finger up Elvis' ass. A rumor spread that when this happened, Elvis got an instant erection, but there appears to be no truth in that charge.

Elvis passed the Army's physical and was assigned an Army Identification number: US53310761. Of course, his mythic sideburns as well as most of his hair ended up on the floor of a barbershop. The locks were scooped up and sold to his most ardent fans. Facing photographers, Elvis said, "Hair today, gone tomorrow."

While in Germany, Elvis had fallen for Priscilla Beaulieu, then a student in the ninth grade, who Elvis promised to send for and whom he'd eventually welcome at Graceland. TV cameras watched as the most famous GI in the world fell madly in love with this fourteen-year-old, whom he defined as "just a baby."

Although frequently drunk and drugged during the evenings of his military service, Elvis would eventually complete his required tenure and be discharged during the spring of 1960.

After his induction in Memphis and a transit across the Atlantic aboard the *USS General Randall,* Elvis docked at Bremerhavn in West Germany on October 1, 1958. Waiting to greet him were some 1,500 screaming fans caught up in Presleymania.

During most of his time in the Army, Elvis was stationed in the historic West German spa town of Bad

At a press conference, reporters read to G.I. **Elvis** *(depicted above)* Frank Sinatra's vicious attack on rock 'n' roll. Without naming Elvis in his assault, it was really a biting critique of Elvis's music. The rock 'n' roll star was asked for a rebuttal.

"I admire the man," Elvis said. "He has a right to say what he wants to say. He is a great success and a fine actor. But I think he shouldn't have said it. He's mistaken about this. Rock 'n roll is a trend, just like what Sinatra faced when he started out years ago to challenge Bing Crosby. I consider rock 'n' roll the greatest music. Namely because it's the only thing I know how to do."

Nauheim, where he rented a private home for $800 a month.

Approximately two years later, when he returned to the U.S., during a hastily convened press conference at Fort Dix, Elvis faced two hundred reporters and photographers.

Frank Sinatra's nineteen-year-old daughter, Nancy, perhaps a bit old at that stage for Elvis, was obviously enamored of the glamorous rock 'n' roller. Although he'd later regret it, Frank had sent his daughter to officially welcome Elvis back to America. Frank was also seeking publicity for the upcoming TV spectacular where they'd be on a concert stage together. At the time, Nancy, Jr. had no way of knowing that Elvis had "promised my heart" to an underaged teenager back in Germany.

Of course, Frank had no intention of allowing his oldest daughter to get involved with Elvis.

Not only that, but Nancy at the time was engaged to marry singer Tommy Sands, a knot they would tie together during September of 1960.

Four years before the TV show, Frank had fallen into a deep depression when Elvis's "Hound Dog," "Don't Be Cruel," and "Heartbreak Hotel" changed pop music history, knocking Frank off the charts.

Reacting to the widespread perception that the music industry was being destroyed by Rock 'n' Roll, Frank had written an article for *Western World* in which he said:

*"My only deep sorrow is the unrelenting insistence of recording and motion picture companies upon purveying the most brutal, ugly, degenerate, vicious form of expression it has been my displeasure to hear and naturally I'm referring to the bulk of rock 'n' roll. It fosters almost negative and destructive reactions in young people. It smells phony and false. It is sung, played, and written for the most part by cretinous goons and by means of its almost imbecilic reiterations and sly, lewd, and plain—dirty lyrics, it manages to be the martial music of every sideburned delinquent on the face of the earth."*

Although this opinion was actually a lambast against Elvis, Frank, at least on the surface, pretended to welcome the singer back from the Army. He and his producers, along with the sponsor, Timex, agreed that Elvis and Frank would attract half the TV viewers in America with the release of this special, "Welcome Home, Elvis."

For his appearance, Col. Tom Parker, Elvis' manager, had demanded the then unheard of fee of $125,000 for a single show.

Taping would take place on March 26, 1960, at the Fontainebleau Hotel on Miami Beach.

Prior to showtime, Elvis told Nancy Jr., who was also booked as a performer in the special, "I have butterflies eating away at my stomach." She helped him with the arrangement of his massive bow tie. In the mirror, he adjusted his luxuriant pompadour to ensure that it was lacquered into place.

Frank had agreed to round up three hundred teenage girls to give Elvis a hysterical welcome, evocative of those which Frank had himself generated during the war years among the bobby-soxers.

Even though he despised "Elvis the Pelvis," Frank welcomed him warmly on his TV special.

Bouncing onto the stage, Elvis appeared in a glittery but ill-fitting tuxedo that had obviously not been tailored for him. He sang "Fame and Fortune" and "Stuck on You," and looked fabulous. Although his sideburns had not grown back, his post-Army pompadour had. He practically towered over Frank, and was in better voice than either Frank or Sammy Davis Jr., one of the show's guest stars, who appeared along with Nancy Sinatra Jr.

Frank also sang Elvis's "Love Me Tender," and Elvis stole Frank's "Witchcraft." The two singers harmonized on the former for the presentation's climax. At the end, Frank said, "Gee, that's pretty."

On Frank's TV special, it was a new and different Elvis who faced the cameras. As stated by his biographer, Albert Goldman, Elvis appeared "very delicate and vulnerable, as if he were recovering from major surgery. He wrings his hands as he talks. He has become extremely wary. With his preposterous Little Richard conk, his limp wrist, girlish grin, and wobbly knees, which now turn out instead of in, he looks outrageously gay. When he confronts the much smaller but more masculine Sinatra, Elvis's body language flashes, 'I surrender, dear.'"

Frank's bet on Elvis paid off, but it was a bittersweet victory. The Sinatra special drew a staggering 41.5% of prime-time TV viewers, the highest of any TV show in the previous five years.

A TV reviewer wrote: "Talk about a lack of chemistry. Have you ever tried to mix oil and water? The meeting between the King of Music of Yesterday and the King of Music Today lacked any spark. Sinatra seemed reluctant to give up his new throne to the newly crowned King back from the wars."

Elvis, not Frank, was the singer of the hour, as world attention focused on him, the *New York Journal-American* claiming he'd turned "from a hillbilly hoot 'n holler huckster to a crooning Croesus."

Nancy almost stole the show from both Elvis and her father. Columnist Dorothy Kilgallen, no friend of Frank, wrote that she was a "charming talented doll and the best thing on the TV special." Critic Jack O'Brien saved all of his attacks for Elvis himself, comparing his hair to Mr. Vesuvius and asserting that his songs were "as deplorable as ever," and his voice "as tortured as ever."

In spite of any personal animosity, Frank was too much of a pro to let any personal antagonism be detected during the broadcast. Before and after the show, Frank treated Elvis, in the words of one observer, "like a long-lost son."

But Elvis was not taken in so easily. The next day, he told Col. Parker, "Sinatra hates my guts. The feeling is mutual. In a fight, I would mop up the floor with this

Concealing the uneasy truce between them, **Frank Sinatra** and **Elvis Presley**, a fresh arrival from Army duty in Germany, staged a "Welcome Home" TV special in 1960, and the ratings shot skyward.

A pal of Elvis, Marty Lacker, watched the TV show from backstage. "Those Sinatra people treated our boy like he was King Elvis. Sinatra may have thought Elvis was sexually dangerous, but he really wasn't until he came home from the army, and then he became a sexual predator."

This former truck driver from Tupelo, Mississippi, made Frank uncomfortable "He wiggles and shimmies as he sings this rockabilly shit," Frank said. "But he drives the hot bitches in the audience wild. I recognize the sexual moans coming from those gals. I had my bobby-soxers, all wanting to get laid. But I was the class act. Elvis is a degenerate redneck."

351

dago perv."

Nancy, Jr. and Elvis would not become the romantic target that Frank had initially feared. A very different type of woman would soon come between Elvis and Frank.

In a touch of irony, "Frank's gal," Juliet Prowse, was cast opposite Elvis Presley in *G.I. Blues* (1960), his first motion picture after his return to the entertainment business.

Probably because she was still involved with Frank after her inaugural meeting with Elvis, Juliet at first snubbed him, trying to ignore his sexual advances. "Boy oh boy," Elvis told his Memphis cronies, "that is one cold chick." He also confided to his boys, "That Sinatra needs to be taken down a peg or two. Snaring his girl might do the trick for the arrogant prick."

Eventually, Elvis won Juliet over with his charm and physical appeal. Soon the director of *G.I. Blues,* Norman Taurog, was having to cry, "Cut! Cut! God dammit. Get a room."

Elvis used his free hand to shoo Taurog away. "Get away from us, fucker!"

He later told his henchman, Sonny West, "The Ice Queen has melted. The bitch can't get enough of my meat." As the crew later noticed, Elvis's portable dressing room was soon rock 'n' rolling.

His affair with Juliet marked the beginning of many torrid trysts with his leading ladies.

Frank Sinatra was particularly nervous when **Elvis** teamed with his older daughter, **Nancy Sinatra Jr.**, (*right figure above*) to make a film called *Speedway* in 1968.

Despite Elvis' well-publicized marriage to Priscilla, Elvis "is not to be trusted around my baby doll," Frank said.

Nancy Jr. was a virtual icon of the 1960s, a decade that belonged in part to her. But Elvis admitted that "I feel more at home in the 50s. Today, everyone is going wild, taking drugs and having orgies. At these orgies, or so I hear, it doesn't matter who you screw—male or female. It makes no difference to these weirdos. I'm not gonna be sucked into this crap."

"I'm twenty years younger than Sinatra, and I've got red pepper on my dick," Elvis claimed.

"Juliet's got the most gorgeous belly button in the business and can go *ooh-la-la* with a guy. I've seen some red-haired pussy in my day—it's common in The South—but hers is foxy, almost like it's got a life all its own. As for the rest of her body, it would make an archbishop stamp his booted foot through a stained-glass window."

Elvis soon became "Chickie Baby" to her, although he didn't think Chickie was an appropriate name for a he-man.

Juliet told the press, "Elvis would make a damn fine dancer—the guy's got fabulous rhythm."

When Frank heard that, he asked, "What kind of fucking rhythm is the broad talking about?"

An Elvis crony, Red West and his cousin, Sonny West, often teased Elvis by knocking on his dressing room door, shouting "Frank's coming!"

In attack mode, Elvis would throw open the door. "Christ, almighty, where's the fucker?" The West boys would then run off laughing. Finally, one day, it became no laughing matter. Frank did show up on the set, but the West boys had cried wolf too often, and Elvis thought they were joking.

It took a little persuasion, but Sonny finally convinced Elvis that Frank was indeed on the set of *G.I. Blues.* With only minutes to spare, Juliet and Elvis put their clothes back on.

When Elvis opened the door, Frank found the

rock 'n' roller and Juliet studying their scripts.

"Hi, baby," Juliet said, getting up and rushing into Frank's arms.

"How about lunch, doll," Frank asked.

"You're on," Juliet said, looking back at Elvis. "Want to join us?"

"No," Frank said. "Three's a crowd."

Frank may or may not been fooled by the charade that early afternoon. He was smart and intuitive about who was sleeping with whom. Unknown to Elvis, he hired a spy to report activities on the set between Juliet and Elvis.

Within days, he learned that his girlfriend was "shacking up" with Elvis. Elvis was partially to blame for that. He told several people that "Juliet was great in the sack. It takes a dancer like her to spread her legs that wide—in fact, she spreads them so wide you almost fall in. She locks those dynamite gams around you, and doesn't let a dude up until he's completely satisfied her. And she doesn't satisfy easily. I don't know how a grandfather like Sinatra keeps up with her."

Word soon leaked to the press of the affair. One reporter called Elvis and Juliet "a torrid twosome," much to Frank's annoyance. He despised being replaced by a younger man, either in the music field or in the boudoir.

The scandal magazine, *Top Secret*, was blunt: "Right from under Sinatra's nose, the *gee-tar*-twanging kid from Memphis moved in and moseyed off with Frankie's girl."

The night that Frank uncovered the truth about the affair of Juliet and Elvis, he threw a drunken party in his hotel suite. The gangster, Johnny Roselli, showed up and Frank invited him and some of his boys up for a drink.

Frank always had a "soft spot" in his heart for Roselli. Although it was later denied by almost anyone involved, Roselli was the go-between with Harry Cohn at Columbia, who got Frank the coveted role as Maggio in *From Here to Eternity*.

Ever since that day, Roselli had told Frank, "If you need me, you usually know where to find me. You don't need to get dirt under your fingernails—you're too big a name—but I can see that your business is carried out for you. And you won't know a God damn thing."

That night at the party Frank was in one of his worst moods. "I didn't just have to lose Juliet, I had to lose her to that faggot Elvis Presley." Frank had learned about a few of Elvis's male-on-male affairs, including his longtime tryst with actor Nick Adams,

**Juliet Prowse**, Frank Sinatra's "former girl friend," cuddles up to guitar-picking **Elvis** when they made *G.I. Blues* together.

"Everybody said Juliet ditched me for Elvis," Frank claimed. "That's a fucking lie. I was the one who told the whoring bitch to go.

"I thought she was a sweet gal when I met her, perhaps not virginal. Then stories started to reach me. I found out she was the whore who never charged. If I had brought Sammy Davis into our bedroom, or Dean Martin, especially Dean, the broad would have shouted out, 'the more the merrier!'

"I didn't want that kind of dame. She was not to be trusted when she saw something wearing pants.

"She put Lana Turner and Ava Gardner to shame, that one."

and Frank always referred to Elvis as "the faggot" in private.

Reportedly, Roselli told Frank, "Prowse is a dancer, ain't she? A crippled dancer can't do the high kick."

"No, I don't want to see her hurt," Frank cautioned Roselli. "It's that Presley hillbilly I'm after."

"Say no more," Roselli said.

At this point, the stage lights dim on the plot. After denouncing Elvis to Roselli, Frank may have not thought any more of it. But three nights later, a drunken Elvis was lured away from his boys from Memphis and into a chauffeured car that was to take him to the house where Juliet was staying.

He never got there. Somewhere along the way, Elvis was drugged and carried into a house where he was forcibly raped by three of Roselli's mugs. He was tied to the bed, and it is not known if he were conscious during this ordeal.

But incriminating pictures were taken, which were later sent to both Frank and Elvis. The rapists were masked, so neither Frank nor Elvis knew who the men were. Elvis told the colonel what had happened. "Man, I've got the sorest ass in the history of sodomy," he confessed.

"Word of this must never get out," Parker warned. "It would destroy your career. You'd become a laughing stock."

Frank told members of the Rat Pack, and even showed them the pictures of Elvis's rape. Peter Lawford, Sammy Davis Jr., and Dean Martin saw the photographs. Judy Garland also claimed that she'd seen the pictures.

Show-biz history may never accurately record what **Johnny Roselli**'s boys did "that night" in Vegas to humiliate the King of Rock 'n' Roll.

The stories that were spread at the time may have been more or less true, but over the years, the scenario has turned almost into a mythology. All that Roselli *(photo, above)* said on the subject of Elvis was a bit vague:

"He pissed off Frankie—not a good thing to do. I've settled scores for Frankie in the past, and I plan to do so in the future, especially if Marilyn Monroe gets out of hand."

Elvis had been brutally humiliated. Frank apparently never asked Roselli if he were behind this kidnapping and sexual assault on Elvis. Perhaps Frank already knew and didn't want it confirmed.

But he did tell his fellow Rat Packers, "If Presley were conscious at the time, I bet he loved taking it up the ass. He probably liked it so much that when he returns to Memphis, he'll demand that his boys line up every night to plug him."

Frank disappeared from Juliet's life for a week. Finally, he agreed to accept one of her frantic calls.

"Frank, darling, what is the matter?" she asked him. "I've missed you terribly. Is something wrong?"

"Why don't you go fuck a Hound Dog?" he asked, before slamming down the phone.

By making love to Elvis on the set of *G.I. Blues*, Juliet had humiliated Frank. But she was due for her own humiliation, and payback was on the way.

She wasn't due on the set one day, and she decided to pay a surprise visit to Elvis's dressing room, having had her cook prepare his favorite dishes which she'd carefully packed into a picnic basket.

Unknown to her, Elvis had already ordered Sonny West to go out and get him a take-out lunch of juicy hamburgers, not only for himself, but for his surprise visitor.

When there was a knock on his dressing room door, Elvis obviously assumed it was Sonny. "Jaybird naked," as he later recalled, he threw open the door to discover not Sonny, but Juliet herself.

Dropping the basket of goodies, she ran in tears from the set but not before she recognized the nude blonde woman standing behind him. It was Miss Marilyn Monroe herself.

Elvis's last words to Juliet were, "My God, it's you."

Marilyn and Elvis, the two most legendary sex symbols of the 1950s, had met only two days before in front of a sound stage at 20th Century Fox. The chemistry between them had been explosive. For fickle Elvis, Juliet was out and Marilyn was in.

An hour later, Red West, Sonny's older cousin, escorted Marilyn off the set. On the way out, he said, "The gals really go for Elvis. Just how was it with him?"

"I found him very penetrating," the sex goddess said demurely, the same remark she'd made about John F. Kennedy.

***

In the months that lay ahead, the Elvis/Marilyn affair continued. Neither star expected the other to be faithful, as they continued to make love to other people. Unknown to their fans at the time, Elvis had an occasional fling with a man, and Marilyn was not entirely opposed to a little girl-on-girl action on the side.

When they were together, they often talked about co-starring in a movie together. But Col. Parker had the biggest idea of all. In spite of Frank's difficulties with Elvis, the colonel had maintained a friendship with Frank. In fact, he came up with what might have been the greatest act in show business during the entire 20th century—the teaming of Elvis, Marilyn, and Frank for a spectacular act in Las Vegas.

Backers for the show claimed that "the ticket line would form in Los Angeles and stretch all the way across the Nevada desert to Las Vegas."

After Marilyn's death, Frank lamented, "Alas, it was not meant to be. If we had appeared together, and it would have been put on film, it would be a show that viewers would be watching two hundred years from now." Rather arrogantly, he also said, "During rehearsals, I would have fucked Marilyn every day and let Elvis blow Big Frankie. That's what they both really want."

***

Frank and Elvis would eventually tangle once again over a young woman—not a girlfriend this time, but Frank's own daughter, Nancy Jr. Frank suspected she was having an affair with Elvis when she made *Speedway* with him, released in 1968.

In his calls to his wife Priscilla, Elvis told her not to believe the tabloids. "I hardly know Frank's daughter. I met her once or twice at a party—that's all. Honey, if you're gonna be with Elvis, you can't believe a word these farts write about me. You know I belong only to you, and you belong only to me."

In her book, *Baby, Let's Play House*, Alanna Nash wrote that Nancy offered to throw a baby shower for Priscilla on the set of *Speedway* when Elvis announced that she was pregnant.

Actually, according to Nash, Nancy Jr. was "busy fighting off Elvis's advances on the set. She had fantasized about him for years, even before she met him on the day he returned from Germany in 1960. Now that she was divorced from Tommy Sands, it was easier to think about being involved with him. But she refused to have sex with a married man, even as she indulged in his adolescent games."

In her biography, Nash wrote: "At lunchtime, they'd go back to her dressing room trailer. Elvis would mess up her hair and her clothes, teasing her, and when he got especially frisky, he'd pin her to the floor and dry hump her. They'd laugh and giggle and toss back and forth in the mock throes of ecstasy. 'Did you come yet?' he'd ask, a big smile on his face. But there was no mistaking that Elvis was truly turned on. 'Do you feel Little Elvis?' he'd whisper in her ear. And of course, she did."

Priscilla saw pictures of her young husband with Nancy in the fan magazines. She called him: "I thought you had forgotten me and that you have fallen in love with Nancy Sinatra like the papers say."

"It's not true, *wittie nungen*" [his pet name for her], Elvis told her on the phone. "I love only you."

When Elvis made *Speedway* with Nancy, the blonde, brassy, go-go-booted queen of the late 1960s was at the peak of her star power, having recently topped the charts with "These Boots Are Made for Walkin'" as well as "Somethin' Stupid," her duet with Frank.

On the set of *Speedway*, Elvis camped out in Nancy's dressing room. Once, he hid in her wardrobe and jumped out to catch her half-dressed.

She recalled, "He just held me and then he lifted up my face and he kissed me and I started to melt."

But before things got more serious, Elvis withdrew and apologized. He gave her "a warm, sincere, I-love-you kiss," and then left her trailer. At least where Nancy was concerned, Elvis maintained his marital fidelity with Priscilla, whom he had recently nicknamed "Belly," because of her pregnancy.

Nonetheless, Frank lived in horror that his daughter "was fucking Elvis," and he suspected that she was in spite of denials from her. One drunken night, he told Sammy Davis Jr. and Dean Martin, "If I find out that Elvis has been fucking my daughter, I'll cut off his dick—that is, if I can find the little worm."

Colonel Tom Parker, Elvis's manager, maintained a strict policy of rejecting the insertion of duets (Elvis performing with girl singers, regardless of who the singer was) on any of Elvis's albums. He was particularly incensed at Ann-Margret, accusing her of "riding on Elvis's back without a saddle." But The Colonel made an exception with Nancy, who had recorded "Your Groovy Self," from *Speedway*, singing a solo rendition with the understanding that in the movie, Elvis would be very much a part of the visuals. But that was because of the Colonel's continuing friendship with Frank.

In later years, Frank said, "One of my favorite people, Elizabeth Taylor, went to fat. One of my least favorite people, Elvis Presley, also has gone to pot. How disgusting how he comes out on stage in that white jump suit. What a paunchy rock 'n' roller, with those humongous side-burns."

On August 16, 1977, Frank heard the news about Elvis's premature death in Memphis. He immediately placed several calls, even to Col. Tom Parker, wanting as many details as he could learn.

Later he told Dean Martin, "So Elvis Presley is dead. One should speak only good of the dead. *Good!*"

Over a drink with Martin, he told him, "From the colonel, I learned what Elvis's last words to Ginger [a reference to his girlfriend Ginger Alden] were: 'Honey, I'm gonna go take a shit.'"

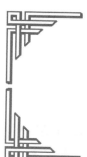

# Frank and Mia

## THE SWINGER & THE TEENY-BOPPER

When a teenaged **Mia Farrow** arrived at the Rancho Mirage villa of **Frank Sinatra** to begin their affair, she was mildly perturbed that the house was filled with photogaphs of Ava Gardner looking her loveliest. Although Frank and Ava had long ago divorced, he seemed to be living in the past. The place was a bit like a memorial to her.

On their second night together, he talked about his singing, claiming he learned a lot about phrasing and the technique of "sneaking breaths from Tommy."

Who's Tommy?" she asked her startled middle-aged boyfriend. He patiently revealed that Tommy was actually Tommy Dorsey, one of the great band leaders of America in the late 1930s and early 40s. "I was his boy singer."

"I never knew you sang with a band," she said.

"I also made movies in the 1940s," he told her.

"You did?" she said. "I'm amazed. I thought *From Here to Eternity* was your first picture."

"Kid, you've got a lot to learn." He lit a cigarette and headed out to the pool, perhaps wondering what a fifty-year-old man had in common with a nineteen-year-old.

"The sex is good," he later told Dean Martin. "I guess that's reason enough to keep her around. She's a very sweet girl, a little mixed up, perhaps. She's up on Elvis and the Beatles, but she's never heard Bing Crosby sing or seen one of his movies."

When **Mia Farrow**, pictured above with heartthrob **Ryan O'Neal**, arrived on the lot of the once fabulous 20th Century Fox, she found the studio soundstages silent. Elizabeth Taylor's *Cleopatra* had virtually bankrupted one of the world's greatest movie producers. Those dressing rooms where Tyrone Power put on his makeup, where Betty Grable checked out her legs, or where Shirley Temple sucked a lollipop were empty.

Mia was set to film the pilot for what became a successful TV series, *Peyton Place*. At first she begged to be released from her commitment to the series, but she was forced to carry on.

On the set, for the TV series which aired in half-hour episodes between 1964 and 1969, she met the very handsome Ryan.

"Teenagers across the country fell for Ryan, and I was no exception. But there was a problem: He was married, not that that ever stopped him from scoring."

# "BEWARE OF YOUNG GIRLS"— A SONG BY DORY PREVIN, WHOSE WORDS WERE INSPIRED BY MIA FARROW

*"I always knew that Frankie would end up in bed with a boy."*
**—Ava Gardner**

*"I've got Scotch older than Mia Farrow."*
**—Dean Martin**

*"Frank Sinatra should be marrying me— not my daughter."*
**—Maureen O'Sullivan**

Frank Sinatra met Mia Farrow when she was only eleven years old. She was the daughter of writer/director John Farrow and the beautiful actress Maureen O'Sullivan ("Me Tarzan, You Jane"). Frank was dining at Romanoff's with Farrow, discussing a possible film deal. "You've got one pretty gal for a daughter," Frank told Farrow.

"Talk about robbing the cradle," Farrow said. "You stay away from my daughter."

Frank took that as a command. After all, there are laws against child molestation.

John Farrow and Maureen O'Sullivan had been living in separate bedrooms since Mia was eight years old. Around that time, O'Sullivan learned that her husband was having an affair with Ava Gardner. Mia was the quintessential Hollywood child, having gossip maven Louella Parsons as her godmother, and gay director George Cukor as her godfather.

Unlike Ava, Mia had measurements of 20-20-20.

Eight years would go by before he saw her again. She appeared on the set of *Von Ryan's Express* (1965), a CinemaScope production where Frank was cast as a POW colonel who leads a daring escape by highjacking a freight train transporting prisoners.

He looked at her on the set but didn't approach her. She found his face beautiful "but full of pain." Perhaps he stayed away from her because her long hair was in braids. "I'm sure I still looked eleven years old."

Being shot simultaneously on the same 20th Century Fox lot was the TV series *Peyton Place*, in which Mia played Allison Mackenzie.

The next day, her teenage heart lured her back to the set. This time Frank took the bait, but he sent a grip over to ask her how old she was. "I'm nineteen," she said.

The grip repeated that to Frank. "Good," he said, "I don't want to pick up jail bait." She was invited to approach Frank, and she did, awkwardly spilling the contents of her straw bag all over the floor, including bubble gum and tampons which landed at his feet.

In spite of that introduction, he invited her to a screening of his first directorial attempt, *None But the Brave* (1965), a taut war drama focusing on the crew of a cracked-up plane and a Japanese army patrol who make peace on a remote island during WWII.

After the screening, he invited her to Palm Springs that night. Terrified, she turned him down. She wanted to go but bowed out, claiming she had a deaf cat at home that ate only baby food. "No pajamas. No toothbrush."

He told her he'd send a private plane for her the following day. "Oh, yeah, bring that advertisement for Gerber's Baby Food."

The next morning Mia flew to Palm Springs with her cat. Waiting for her at the airport was Frank in a Halloween orange shirt. She was quickly learning that his favorite color was orange. "He looked handsome," she recalled. Could all those rumors about his sexual prowess really be true? What about his legendary endowment?

He invited her to sleep in a bed where John F. Kennedy had slept, or so a brass plaque claimed. Out by the pool, a beautiful red-haired woman was crying, and Yul Brynner was drying her tears. Mia later learned that she was supposed to have been Frank's date for the weekend. When Mia showed up, Frank had turned her over to Yul.

That night Mia slept with Frank in the master bedroom, not in the room where JFK had snoozed and seduced. "The cat slept alone that night," she later recalled.

The only star who knew about Frank's relationship with Mia was Yul Brynner, who often spent weekends with them. Frank called him "The Chinaman," and Yul referred to Frank as "Charlie." It was later rumored that the bisexual actor had fallen in love with Frank. Even though Yul may have wanted to be in Frank's

In 1965, looking like a Texan more than a boy from Hoboken, **Frank Sinatra** escorted **Mia Farrow** to "The Share Party," which was the first time they were seen in public as a couple.

Dressing up in western garb, Frank and Mia went with Sammy Davis Jr. and Shirley MacLaine to this annual charity show. It was a star-studded event where the entertainers themselves performed on television. Mia was playing a shy sixteen-year-old girl, and here she was with that famous late middle aged saloon singer, barroom brawler, and womanizer. From the stage, Dean Martin announced, "Thank God there are no laws in California prohibiting child molestation."

After that inaugural night, Mia was sucked into a glittering social whirl that extended from Beverly Hills to Palm Springs and on to New York and London. Frank was definitely on the A-list.

bedroom at night, and envied Mia, he still befriended her. "I even called him Dad."

Frank told his valet, George Jacobs, that Mia's father, John Farrow, had had an affair with Ava Gardner when they filmed *Ride, Vaquero* in 1953. "Sinatra had his score to settle, even if it had to be done over John Farrow's dead body," said Jacobs.

Jacobs, who had opportunities to observe Yul up close for years, called him not only the "king of the tightwads, but a closet AC/DC himself." Yul, at least, certainly didn't accuse Frank of child molestation with Mia, because Yul had seduced a very young Sal Mineo when they'd appeared together on Broadway in *The King and I*.

Mia later said, "Life with Frank was about as normal as living on the third ring of Jupiter."

On her second night in Palm Springs, Mia admitted to Frank that she had never heard him sing a song—"I like The Beatles." Nor had she seen a movie of his except one that he'd screened for her.

He set about to remedy that oversight, screening 1940s films of himself and playing all his popular albums day and night.

Another world was opening for her. The hippie revolution was in full swing. Wearing a long, white dress, Mia had once accompanied Salvador Dalí to watch a Greenwich Village orgy. Rumored affairs lay ahead with Eddie Fisher, Peter Sellers, even Roman Polanski and singer John Phillips of "The Mamas and the Papas" when he wasn't seducing his daughter, Mackenzie Phillips. But at the time she met Frank, she was almost virginal.

Frank was conscious of their age difference, and for weeks he kept his passionate relationship a secret, even from the Rat Pack. He was finishing *Von Ryan's Express*, and she was working too. Weekends were reserved for private time together at Palm Springs.

In his kitchen, he made a spaghetti sauce whose recipe had been taught to him by his mother, Dolly. To the sound of his favorite composer, Ralph Vaughan Williams, he made love to her.

When he learned that two strange men were following her one night in a car, he purchased a small pearl-handled gun for her and taught her how to shoot. "He was a great shot himself," she said.

She was called the poster child for hippiedom, wearing flowers in her hair, collecting Beatle records and rock stars, chasing after Eastern religion gurus.

She liked to announce that she was going to meditate just when Frank was so hot and horny for her that he'd often rip off her "flower child" dress.

Mia's first "outing" came when Frank took her to a charity event, *The Share Show*, which was attended by *tout* Hollywood. Here she was officially introduced to such friends as Dean Martin (who made a pass at her); Sammy Davis Jr. (who also made a pass at her), and Shirley MacLaine, who wanted to know what sign she was born under.

The paparazzi went wild, snapping pictures of this fifty-year-old singer and his teenage mistress.

"The secret months" were over, and they would never come again. Once their pictures appeared in the press, she was thrown into an elite social world, centering around Las Vegas, Beverly Hills, and Manhattan—not just the Rat Pack, but Claudette Colbert, Rosalind Russell, Jack Benny, and Edie and Bill Goetz became part of Mia's life.

Edie was the daughter of Louis B. Mayer. Sometimes Frank's friends would be invited to Palm Springs and would bring their children with them. Some of these kids had gone to school with Mia. But whereas they were seated at the kid's table, Mia sat with the grown-ups.

He finally introduced her to Nancy Jr. and Tina who "soon became like sisters to me."

Mia's bosses on the TV series, *Peyton Place*, had the script writers put the character she played into a coma so she could sail along the East Coast on a yacht with Claudette Colbert and Rosalind Russell.

All the paparazzi in the world descended. Frank tried to ignore them. He stopped at Hyannis Port, where Mia and Frank visited Rose Kennedy, Teddy, and the stricken family patriarch Joe, who was bound to a wheelchair and could not speak. Eunice and Jean came for food and drink aboard Frank's yacht. Patricia also made an appearance, and from the distance the press mistook her for Jackie. The cruise ended abruptly when a member of the crew fell overboard and drowned.

*Time* magazine called the pleasure trip "probably the most closely watched since Cleopatra floated down the Nile to meet Marc Antony."

The marriage took place in Las Vegas without her parents being informed. Before they left for London, Spencer Tracy, Katharine Hepburn, Edward G. Robinson, and Dean Martin turned up to wish them well. Mia remembered talking to Red Skelton, "who," she said, "had just shot

Roman Polanski, the film director, cast a hot Hollywood property, **Mia Farrow**, to star in his 1968 *Rosemary's Baby,* along with Ruth Gordon and John Cassavetes. Mia played an unsuspecting young wife whose husband becomes involved with Satanists and their diabolical plans. Word soon reached Frank that Mia was having an affair with Roman, whether it was true or not.

Also being filmed in New York was Frank's latest picture, *The Detective*, in which he had a role for Mia. But the shooting schedule for *Rosemary's Baby* was extended, preventing Mia from appearing in Frank's film with him. Frank urged her to abandon *Rosemary's Baby* before its conclusion, which would certainly have led to the end of her career, but she refused to obey him.

"Have it your way, babe," he told her. "We're finished." Then he slammed down the phone.

Before Mia Farrow married Frank Sinatra, **Eddie Fisher** (*depicted above*) almost had the pleasure. "Frank and I often screwed the same women," Eddie said, "Elizabeth Taylor being the most classic example."

Eddie started out with a crush on Mia's mother, actress Maureen O'Sullivan, but eventually shifted his focus onto her daughter, Mia.

Before her marriage to Frank, during periods when she may have been feuding with him, Mia often dated Eddie, joining him for dinner one night at George Hamilton's house where Hamilton was shacked up with LBJ's daughter, Lynda Bird Johnson.

When Eddie invited Mia for an off-the-record weekend in Mexico, she proposed to him as they crossed the border. But before she'd ultimately commit herself to Eddie, she wanted to call Roddy McDowall in Hollywood to ask his permission. "That pissed me off big time," Eddie recalled. "After all, Roddy was Elizabeth Taylor's best friend, the cocksucker who had advised Elizabeth to dump me."

When Mia couldn't reach Roddy, Eddie asked her, "Does that mean you won't marry me?"

"I guess not," she told him. "Guess I'll have to marry Frank Sinatra, but only if Roddy gives his okay."

"Well, when you break up with Frank, which is inevitable, you can propose to me again."

"Okay," she said, but her response was a bit too noncommittal for him. He returned to Hollywood to find a call waiting for him from Marlene Dietrich, who wanted to seduce him.

"Marlene was old enough to be my grandmother, but she always liked to take Elizabeth's discards," Eddie claimed.

his wife."

[Actually Mia misstated the case in her memoirs. Georgia Skelton had wounded herself in an "accidental" shooting. That was in 1966. Ten years later Red's then ex-wife would indeed commit suicide by gunshot on the anniversary of her son's death.]

Eventually it happened. Frank introduced Mia to the woman said to be the love of his life, Ava Gardner. She treated Mia warmly and came to like her very much, at one point in their relationship calling her "the child Frank and I never had." She told Mia, "Frank is so wild, so full of love and energy, that he is like three men rolled into one. Behind the booze and the womanizing, he is highly sensitive and intelligent, and he has a heart of gold."

Privately, Ava told friends that "Frankie has married a fag with a pussy."

Ava constantly hounded Frank that he was a latent homosexual in having an affair with the boyish-looking Mia. "I look like a real woman; she looks like a catamite's fancy."

When Mia cut her hair and looked like an effeminate boy, Frank told Ava, "Now I really will look like a fag."

With such two different temperaments, the marriage went up and down. When Mia was away shooting *A Dandy in Aspic* with the gay actor, Laurence Harvey, Frank dated showgirls.

Mia's big chance came when Paramount offered her her first feature film, *Rosemary's Baby*, to be directed by Roman Polanski. The worst part of the film for Mia was when the director forced her to eat raw liver on camera, even though she was a vegetarian.

Shooting on *Rosemary's Baby* dragged beyond its schedule, and Frank became furious. At one point he issued Mia an ultimatum. "Leave the picture or our marriage is over." She knew she couldn't just walk out on the picture, as she was needed in virtually every scene.

Frank wanted her to star with him in *The Detective* (1968), but Mia's role went to Jacqueline Bisset. Lee Remick was also in the film, and Frank turned to her for an affair.

Lee told her dear friend, Merv Griffin, about her bizarre relationship with Frank. "When my husband, Bill Colleran, had a car accident, I flew to Los Angeles and stayed at the Beverly Hills Hotel for a week. Bill had directed Sinatra in a TV special, but I didn't know him. That's why I was shocked when he paid my hotel bill."

"Mia could not finish *Rosemary's Baby* in time to star in *The Detective*. With no Mia, I thought Frank and I were just going to have a mere fling on location, but he fell for me big time. He said he was going to divorce Mia to marry me, but I didn't want that. I was scared to turn him down. After I left the set, I wrote him a 'good-bye Frank' note and pasted it on his dressing room door. He exploded. I didn't take his calls, but he left a dozen phone messages for me, calling me every vulgar name you could ever call a woman— 'whore' being the kindest word."

The real reason Lee turned Frank down was that she was madly in love with Bobby Kennedy. The actress had told another of her lovers, Peter Lawford, that "Bobby was the best sex I've ever had, and as you know, I've had your pal, Sinatra."

Lee could barely tolerate mention of Ethel Kennedy, and she threw temper fits whenever she heard rumors about RFK with other women. She became furious when she learned that her suitor had developed a crush on Claudine Longet, who had at one time been married to singer Andy Williams. Columnist Hedda Hopper got wind of the Peter Lawford/Lee Remick affair and ran a blind item in her syndicated column. "The big news in Hollywood is a romance that can't be out in print. I guarantee that if this one hits the papers it will curl hair from Washington to Santa Monica."

Imagine what Hedda would have written if she'd known Bobby himself was having an affair with Lee?

Tipped off by Peter Lawford, Frank learned about Lee's affair with Bobby Kennedy. He'd never liked the man and he now had another reason for "despising" him. Peter also told Frank that Lee had had an affair with Jack Kennedy when he was president.

She later said, "I fucked Bobby for love; I fucked Jack because he was President of the United States."

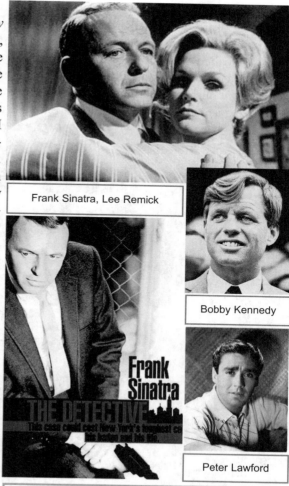

Frank Sinatra, Lee Remick

Bobby Kennedy

Peter Lawford

**Frank Sinatra,** appearing with **Lee Remick** (*top photo*), starred in *The Detective* (1968), among the last few movies he ever made.

He often referred to it as "my gay film." Actually, he didn't play gay, but in his role of Detective Joe Leland he arrives at the scene of a brutal mutilation murder of a homosexual. As part of his investigation, he makes the rounds of gay hangouts.

During the making of the picture, he dumped his wife Mia Farrow and developed a crush on Lee Remick. But Remick rejected him, as she much preferred Bobby Kennedy, "the true love of my life."

Of course, RFK just happened to be one of Frank's most despised people, an ironic coincidence.

Peter Lawford also fell in love with Lee Remick, although both of them were married to other people at the time. Hedda Hopper, in her column, warned Peter, without naming him, that he stood a chance of losing "his million dollar baby," a reference, of course, to his wife, Patricia Kennedy Lawford.

When Lee became too aggressive in her attraction to Bobby, he backed away from her, fearing exposure. Most of RFK's lovers found him more sensitive to a woman's needs than Jack, who did not linger for pillow talk. Once the deed was done, "he (JFK) put back on his shorts and called the Kremlin," in the words of Lee.

Frank's dislike of Bobby only grew stronger when he learned that Mia was supporting him for president during his anticipated bid for the presidential election of 1968, a bid that was cut short by his assassination. Frank didn't really like Hubert Humphrey, but threw his support to him because he was Lyndon B. Johnson's pick, and because of his contempt for Bobby. These political differences spilled over into many an argument, driving Frank farther and farther away from his young wife.

When Bobby heard that Mia was supporting him, he called her when he was in Los Angeles. Fortunately, Frank was out of town. At that point, Frank positively hated Bobby Kennedy, viewing him as the anti-Christ.

Mia was young and eager to go dancing, and so was Bobby. He invited her to go with him to a Democratic fund-raising event at The Factory, a popular disco on Santa Monica Boulevard.

Mia accepted. Frank's spies were immediately on her trail, later reporting that she was seen dancing cheek-to-cheek with Bobby Kennedy.

Whether falsely charged or not, these same spies told Frank that Mia was seen leaving the disco with Bobby later that night, presumably heading for his hotel. Frank had the lobby staked out. His spy asserted that Mia left Bobby's suite at 10am the following morning, although this could have been a total lie.

Frank was confronted with this news in New York, and he exploded. The affair between Bobby and Mia may never have happened. What is important is

In the top photo, **Ava Gardner** smiles at her former lover, actor **Robert Taylor** *(center)* and at her present lover, director **John Farrow** *(left)*. Farrow just happened to be the father of Mia Farrow, who married Frank after Ava's exit from her marriage with him.

Ava had just signed a new seven-year contract with MGM, which had offered her from $90,000 to $130,000 per picture. In her new contract, she demanded that the studio add a formal agreement to produce a picture starring Frank and herself.

They wanted to make *St. Louis Woman*, based on a then-popular Broadway musical. Instead of that, however, she was assigned *Ride, Vaquero* (1953). It was scheduled for shooting in Kenab, Utah, a locale which co-star Howard Keel defined as "the asshole of creation."

that Frank believed that it had taken place. He immediately called his press agent, announcing that he and Mia were going to have a trial separation.

Later, Mia's love for going out dancing got her into even more trouble when Frank heard that his butler, Jacobs, had been seen dancing with Mia at the Candy Store. That was it for him. In Jacobs' own words, Frank viewed that innocent dance as a betrayal—his "young movie star wife having a thing with his black valet." Jacobs, after long years of service, was fired.

In spite of some "fuck you money," Jacobs was told "never to darken Sinatra's door again." In his memoirs, Jacobs likened it to a "Nigger, Go Home," order.

Mia didn't believe that Frank would abandon her in spite of his threat to do so. When she returned to work, she heard rumors about Frank's affair with Lee Remick.

Frank's lawyer, Mickey Rudin, arrived on the set of *Rosemary's Baby* with an official application for a divorce from Frank.

Mia agreed to the divorce. While waiting for it to go through, she began to spend her weekends with Polanski and his beautiful wife, actress Sharon Tate, little knowing how short Sharon's life would be. When Mia heard of the gruesome murder of Sharon and her friends at the hands of the Charles Manson goons, she said, "But for the grace of God, I might have been at that party."

Unknown to nearly everybody in the press at the time was the real reason for Frank's break with Mia. Although he felt it was permissible for him to have a girlfriend here or there, he did not want his young wife taking on a lover. He just hadn't trusted her during her excursions with either Bobby or Jacobs.

Even Bobby's assassination by Sirhan Sirhan brought Frank "no satisfaction," as he himself proclaimed.

*Rosemary's Baby* was a hit, and new film offers poured in. Mia wrote, "At twenty-one I had lost my husband, my anonymity, and my equilibrium, and it was peace I yearned for."

She was still in love with Frank, even though he had discarded her and moved on to others. Heavily medicated and perhaps suicidal, she stayed at his London apartment on Grosvenor Square before her doctor heavily medicated her and sent her to a clinic.

Confused and bewildered, Mia was befriended by one of Frank's former lovers, Elizabeth Taylor, who was in London at the time with her husband, Richard Burton, making *Where Eagles Dare*.

Mia was cast in *Secret Ceremony* (1968) with Elizabeth and Robert Mitchum.

Her divorce from Frank was finalized in August of 1968. On the way to Mexico, she compared the experience of being married to him to a backstreet abortion.

Two years after her divorce from Frank, Mia married the German-born pianist, conductor, and composer André Previn. He became the adoptive father of Soon-Yi Previn, the future girlfriend and later wife of filmmaker Woody Allen.

Following her divorce from Previn in 1979, she had adopted eight-year-old Soon-Yi.

In 1980 Mia and Woody Allen became lovers, adopting two additional children, Misha Farrow and Dylan Farrow. When Mia discovered that Woody and her adopted daughter, Soon-Yi, were having sex, she broke off with him. During a custody battle over their adopted children, Mia also gave birth to Satchel O'Sullivan Farrow. Mia charged that Allen had molested Dylan, then seven years old. Allen adamantly denied the charge, but Mia ultimately won custody.

At the 1992 Republican nominating convention, Mia and Woody Allen would be cited as "representative of the family values for the Democratic party."

Mia's story with Frank, which had begun when she was a teenager, hardly had come to an end.

During her confrontation with Woody, Frank rallied to Mia's side, even offering to break Woody's legs, as she related in her tragic memoir.

In 1997, Soon-Yi married Woody, and Mia broke off her relationship with her adopted daughter. The young Korean woman charged that "Farrow is no Mother Teresa."

Not discouraged that Soon-Yi didn't work out as a daughter, Mia, since her break with Soon-Yi, eventually adopted six more children. "Lark Song," a Vietnamese orphan she had adopted with Previn in 1973, died of AIDS in 2008.

Frank had remained grateful at the way Mia handled their divorce. When Rudin asked Mia what she wanted as a settlement, she said, "Just your respect and friendship."

That she got. She and Frank remained friends for life. "I came to Frank as an impossibly immature teenager. I loved him truly. But this is also true. It was a little bit like an adoption that I had somehow messed up, and it was awful when I returned to the void."

On the eve of his marriage, Frank told Dean Martin, "I don't know, maybe we'll have two years together. She's so young. But we have to try."

Even thirty years after the divorce, Frank still spoke to Mia almost every day, and each of them shared their mutual problems.

In Palm Springs he called her right before his death. "We should have stayed married to each other. In many ways, I was just as young and foolish as you were."

At Frank's death, Mia cried for two days and was invited to the funeral by Nancy Jr.

After **Frank Sinatra** (far right) gave Eddie Fisher permission to date Juliet Prowse, he invited "the junior singer" to join him in London. There was some vague idea that Frank was going to reorganize the Rat Pack, having tired of or feuded with its former members. Eddie wanted to be a charter member of the new club.

In London, he discovered **Yul Brynner** (left photo) hanging out with Frank, breakfasting with him, lunching with him, and dining with him. "There were rumors that the bald-headed star of The King and I had the hots for Frank, and I believed he did," Eddie claimed.

Another possible candidate for a revamped Rat Pack was another bisexual actor, Laurence Harvey, who had already made The Manchurian Candidate with Frank.

In London, "the women who came and went changed every night," Eddie said, "but Princess Margaret was a frequent visitor, and she would often excuse herself and disappear for an hour or two into the bedroom with Frank."

"One morning, I arrived for breakfast and thought **Princess Margaret** (left figure in right-hand photo, above) had slept over," Eddie said, "but this time it was her highness, Princess Alexandra. I expected Queen Elizabeth to show up the following night, but she never did. That item about Frank and Alexandra was leaked to the London tabloids, and Frank blamed me. I was innocent, but he didn't think so."

*"Now I know why I was born."*
--**Mia Farrow** at a party where Frank officially announced their engagement

*"I'll get you down from that drug if I have to pull you down by your pubic hairs."*
--**Peter Sellers** to **Mia Farrow** after he discovered that she had experimented with mescaline

# "Deep Throat" Gets Personal

## PORN STAR LINDA LOVELACE MEETS THE RAT PACK

*Deep Throat*, the largest-grossing porno film of all time, inspired both Frank Sinatra and Sammy Davis Jr. to seduce its female star, **Linda Lovelace**. Here she is, seen with a "doctor," **Harry Reems**, who discovers that she has a misplaced clitoris. It is not tucked behind the lips of her vagina, but lodged several inches down her throat.

Shortly after its release, Sammy Davis Jr. did more than any other celebrity to popularize this XXX-rated flick in California, even renting a theater for a private screening for his friends. They included Frank Sinatra and Spiro Agnew, the disgraced vice president under Richard Nixon. "If he'd been in town, I would have invited Nixon, too," Sammy said. "He has to get off too."

In 1972, *Deep Throat* opened on the same day in about three hundred theaters across America. Many liberal newspapers ran reviews of it, never having promoted a porno flick before. *Deep Throat,* a 59-minute film with graphic scenes of oral copulation, got millions of dollars worth of free advertising. Chuck Traynor, Linda's husband, began getting calls from movie stars who wanted to sleep with Linda. Sammy Davis Jr. was the first big star to call.

GERARD DAMIANO'S

# DEEP THROAT

HOW FAR DOES A GIRL HAVE TO GO
TO UNTANGLE HER TINGLE?

EASTMANCOLOR Ⓧ ADULTS ONLY

*Deep Throat* brought **Linda Lovelace** fame but not fortune. In her suit to divorce Chuck Traynor, she claimed that he forced her into porno at gunpoint, pointing an M-16 rifle at her head. She wrote in her autobiography that her marriage had been plagued by violence, rape, forced prostitution, and private porn sessions with paying customers.

Her co-star, Harry Reems, described the experience of working with Linda. "I knew the anal scene was coming up and I asked her, 'Would you like some K-Y jelly or something?'"

"'No, no,'" she panted. "'Just let me give you some more head.' Giving more head, she became frantic—her tongue and lips were everywhere. Then I felt the muscles in the back of her throat opening up. Her head lowered over me. Suddenly I could feel my cock go right into her throat. I couldn't believe she ate the whole thing! My cock and balls and half of my pubic bush were all engulfed in that cavernous deep throat."

## STRANGERS IN THE NIGHT

*"Frank Sinatra was almost handsome and wore neatly tailored clothes that he'd take off for the right woman. What he lacked in muscles he made up in staying power. He was also well hung. Frank should have been the star of Deep Throat instead of Harry Reems. He found I had many talents, and he was anxious to try them all. When he plunged in, he didn't want to pull out again. Of course, he also sampled my deep throat. Not only that, he ended the night by a blast up my rear. He was some kind of man."*

—**Linda Lovelace,** the era's most famous porn star, on **Frank Sinatra**

Sammy Davis Jr. not only flirted with Satanism, he was also a devotee of XXX-rated porn flicks, especially those depicting acts of sadomasochism. Of all the Hollywood stars, he was said to have amassed the largest collection of what he called "blue movies," and that was in a day when they were not openly sold in stores or exhibited on cable TV.

In the days before videos, Sammy spent a huge part of his budget for his bootleg film collections, many of which were stolen from private collections. His favorite was a secret tape of Errol Flynn seducing a fourteen-year-old boy and a fifteen-year-old girl at the same time.

Sammy not only collected porn, he often appeared in it. He purchased some of the best video equipment of his day and had a cameraman film orgies of both men and women fornicating at his home. In addition to straight sex, he encouraged some of his friends to indulge in woman-on-woman action or male-on-male lovemaking.

When *Deep Throat* starring Linda Lovelace opened at the sleazy Pussycat Cinema in Los Angeles, Sammy attended the midnight showing and sat through four screenings.

It had caused a scandal when it had first opened in New York in June of 1972 at the same time the Watergate burglars had broken into the offices of the Democratic National Committee. In fact, the informant who provided the secrets to bring down the Richard Nixon administration during the Watergate scandal was called "Deep Throat" by reporters Carl Bernstein and Bob Woodward.

Culture vultures later claimed that the release of *Deep Throat* changed America's sexual attitudes more than anything since the Kinsey Report in 1948.

It also gave the Mafia its most lucrative business since Prohibition, and altered the nation's laws on obscenity forever. The film continues to make money to this day. So far, during its decades-long run, it has grossed more than $600 million, perhaps a lot more, making it the most financially successful porno film of all time. Men and women across America who had never attended a porno showing before went to see *Deep Throat* for reasons never fully explained.

Sammy had read that Ed McMahon, the sidekick of Johnny Carson on *The Tonight Show*, had attended the showing of *Deep Throat* at the World Theater in New York and had invited his celebrity friends.

After attending the Los Angeles showing, Sammy got an idea. In fact, he later credited himself with inventing "porn chic." He decided to rent the entire Pussycat Cinema for an evening and invite some of the biggest names in Hollywood.

For his screening, Sammy, of course, invited Frank and recommended that he bring "a hard-to-get-chick. After watching Linda in action, she'll get so hot you'll have her before the night is over."

Sammy later claimed he was absolutely shocked when Frank turned up with his "date" for the evening. It turned out to be Spiro Agnew, the former Vice President of the United States, who had been forced to resign in disgrace for accepting a bribe.

In the audience that night were Milton and Ruth Berle, Warren Beatty, Mr. and Mrs. Dick Martin, even Lucille Ball and Gary Morton, her husband. Among other A-list guests were Truman Capote, Rat Packer Shirley MacLaine, and Nora Ephron.

At the end of the showing of *Deep Throat*, Sammy had made a special point of inserting a porn "loop" called *The Masked Bandit: He Steals Pussy*. In it, two beautiful girls were completely naked and exposed to the camera, but the lone male star, who looked very young and skinny, had his face covered by a mask throughout the entire loop. Although he had a small frame, the boy in the film, who looked under twenty years old, boasted a prodigious endowment. Unknown to the audience, the actor was a very young Frank Sinatra.

Since his friends weren't likely to recognize Frank's younger self, especially through the mask, Sammy wanted to have the projectionist run the clip as a prank on Frank. They were always pulling practical jokes on each other.

Previously, at the Sands in Las Vegas, Frank heard that an elderly man had died from a heart attack within one of the bedrooms. Frank asked the manager to have the corpse delivered secretly and very late at night to Sammy's suite when he was asleep.

The next morning around 10am, Sammy walked into the living room of his suite to discover a nude dead man sitting upright on his sofa. "I shit bananas," Sammy later told Frank. "Wait till I get even with you."

Sammy's revenge included a screening of *The Masked Bandit* at the Pussycat Cinema in front of dozens of Frank's friends.

"After the showing, Agnew and Frank filed out of the Pussycat. All of the guests thanked Sammy for his hospitality—except one and that was Frank himself.

Later that night Sammy told his wife, Altovise, "Ol' Blue Eyes looked at me. No polar night ever had such a chill. I think I've really fucked up big time. Obviously, Frankie didn't appreciate my little joke on him."

"It wasn't so little," Altovise told her husband.

*Editor's Note: For more on this, please refer to FRANKIE'S LOST YEARS, a feature appearing at the end of this chapter.*

"Let's face it," **Richard Nixon** told Henry Kissinger. "We can't rely on Sinatra's support. He's really a Democrat. He's only hanging in with Spiro Agnew and me because he hates the Kennedys for kicking him out of the White House. I saw a poll. Black Americans hate me, but I know how to solve that. I'm going to invite **Sammy Davis** to visit me in the Oval Office. I hear he's wildly popular with the Negroid vote. I'm appointing him to the National Advisory Council on Economic Opportunity."

When Sammy arrived at the White House on July 1, 1971, Nixon was waiting with a photographer. They made small talk for a few minutes. Within the hour, a White House photo of Sammy with Nixon was going out over the wires.

Later, Sammy said, "Now I'm bigger at the White House than Frank. Tell him I'm now summoned by presidents for my advice."

Later, Nixon said to Kissinger, "I'm going to mention that Davis boy at a press conference. Is it appropriate to call him—what is it they say?—a soul brother?"

In Sammy Davis' discussions with Peter Lawford during his organizing the rental of the Pussycat Cinema, he admitted that he'd watched the Lovelace/Reems scenes from *Deep Throat* "a hundred times—and that is no exaggeration."

But Sammy wasn't satisfied by just watching scenes from *Deep Throat*. He personally wanted to sample the special oral talents of Linda Lovelace. Through an agent, Sammy arranged an off-the-record weekend with Linda and her porn-industry husband, Chuck Traynor, at Frank's villa in Palm Springs. Frank was not given any details about who would be on the guest list when he turned his property over to Sammy.

At first, Sammy had the agent ask a crucial question: "Do Chuck and Linda fuck with niggers?" When he learned that they had no racial prejudices, he asked the next question. "Do they believe in wife swapping?" He was told that Traynor and Linda frequently performed with multiple partners and were willing to play at orgies. For a price, of course.

First, Sammy had to get the approval of his wife, an African American entertainer, Altovise Davis, whom he'd married in 1970. Reared in Brooklyn, she was both an actress and a chorus-line dancer. The Rev. Jesse Jackson had officiated at their marriage ceremony.

Far more conservative than Sammy, Altovise did not want to join in wife swapping or any other sexual games. But as a means of holding on to Sammy, she became an unwilling participant. "But my heart was never in it," she once confided to Peter Lawford and Frank.

At Frank's villa in Palm Springs, Traynor arrived with Linda. Like Sammy, Traynor wore beads and Linda was provocatively attired in hot pants. Traynor, a well-built ex-Marine, had brought along some short porno "loops" in which he, not Linda, was the featured star. As the night unfolded, Traynor showed the loops to Sammy, who was impressed, and Altovise, who was not. Even so, Sammy's wife ended up as Traynor's sexual partner for the night, and Sammy retreated to the master bedroom to experience firsthand Linda's famous and widely publicized talents.

Over pillow talk, Linda confessed to Sammy that

Traynor had kept the $1,200 she'd made for performing in *Deep Throat*. She also claimed that he beat her and at gunpoint made her endure rape from various men he brought to their apartment. Since Sammy was fascinated by S&M, he seemed turned on listening to Linda's trauma.

Later, in Las Vegas, Sammy relayed details of his encounters with Traynor and Linda to Frank. Frank himself wanted to try out Linda, and asked Sammy to have her flown into Las Vegas and delivered to his suite. Frank gave his permission for Traynor to accompany her to Vegas, but he didn't want him in his suite. "I want Linda to arrive by herself. I generally don't like to seduce women in front of their husbands." There was a smirk on his face that followed, when he looked at his friend. "Unlike you, Sammy boy."

Linda never described her encounters with Frank in any of her biographies and provided only a "vanilla account" of her experiences with Sammy himself, since both Frank and Sammy were still alive when she was wrote autobiographies which included both *Meet Linda Lovelace* and *Ordeal*.

In fact, Linda was discreet in not offering Sammy a particularly detailed overview when Sammy called her a week after her encounter in Frank's suite in Las Vegas.

Like a voyeur, Sammy wanted a blow-by-blow description of what went on between Frank and herself. "Unlike you, Sammy, he seems to prefer normal sex—you know, with the man on top, regular fucking preceded by a deep-throat blow job. I did my duty and was paid for it—and that's that."

In the months to come, Linda broke from Traynor and inaugurated plans which eventually culminated in their divorce.

She made several attempts to get in touch with Frank, wanting to become his mistress, but he never returned her calls. She scribbled a message for him and asked the receptionist at the Sands in Las Vegas to deliver it to his suite.

"I'm still waiting by the phone, Frankie," she wrote. "Just give me a call at any time, day or night, and I'll come running."

The message, if it were ever delivered, was never answered

More pimp than husband, **Chuck Traynor** *(center)* was called "the luckiest man in America." He was married at various times to two of the most visible porno queens in the world—**Linda Lovelace** *(left)* and **Marilyn Chambers** *(right)*.

"I don't think Linda was a prostitute before I met her, and she really wasn't one after I met her either, " he claimed. "But she was not the little inexperienced farm girl from northern New York like she'd have you believe. She was a kind of hot-to-trot, sleep-around kid."

While in Las Vegas, Linda attended a performance of Elvis Presley. "He was fat. It wasn't the guy that was hanging on my wall when I was a kid. I felt sorry for him. I went backstage, and he invited me up to his hotel suite. Once I got there, he showed me karate moves, not much else. I don't think he could get it up anymore."

When Marilyn Chambers met Traynor, she told him she wanted to do only one or two erotic films, then move on. "I really wanted to go on stage in Vegas. I wanted to be the next Ann-Margret."

# Frank Gets "Soapy"
## with the Ivory Snow Model

In 1972, Sammy Davis Jr. invited Frank Sinatra to attend the twentieth birthday celebration of Marilyn Chambers, the blonde beauty from Providence, Rhose Island. At the time, she was the talk of the country, thanks to the recent release of her XXX-rated flick, *Behind the Green Door.*

Frank was intrigued when he learned that Marilyn was available for a private rendezvous, even though she had a boy friend, Chuck Traynor (whom she later married), who didn't mind pimping her out if the price was right. Sammy told Frank that he'd had already had three-ways on several previous occasions with Chuck and Marilyn.

Frank asked Sammy to arrange a one-on-one meeting with Marilyn, alone in his hotel suites. She arrived on the scene with Traynor, who described to Frank and Sammy his plans for Marilyn's upcoming 21st birthday party. "I'm going to arrange for 21 guys to fuck her, one for every day of her life on this earth."

Frank thought this was ridiculous, saying so at the time. "Hell, man, that's almost one an hour. No woman could hold up under that."

As it turned out, Frank was wrong. Chuck kept his word, having no trouble rounding up 21 studs in Las Vegas. Sammy later described the scene to Frank. "Chuck and I just sat in two arm-chairs nearby, directing the action." Sammy claimed.

In 1974, Sammy functioned as best man at Chuck and Marilyn's wedding, to which Frank was invited, but declined.

Frank continued to see Marilyn on and off for a number of years, especially when she starred in Vegas for a year in her play, *The Mind with the Dirty Man* at the Union Plaza Hotel.

One night, their talk turned to Sammy, the "agent" who had brought them together for the first time. "He's going to be the host of *The Tonight Show,* filling in for Johnny Carson." she said. "He's promised to have me on as a guest."

"Don't get your hopes up," he warned her.

Indeed, he was right. NBC rejected an appearance by Marilyn. She was very disappointed. "No one will take me seriously as an actress. I'm viewed as nothing but a slut, a wild bitch who has lesbian, straight, and interracial sex on demand."

"Don't worry about it," he told her. "If you're going to be a slut, then be the best slut there is."

At one point, a nosey Sammy asked Frank what he

thought of Marilyn in the boudoir.

"She shows a guy a great time, but hasn't mastered that special skill that Linda Lovelace has acquired."

Be*hind the Green Door* was not the high-grossing phenomenon that Linda Lovelace's *Deep Throat* had been, but it made a porno star of Marilyn Chambers.

She was hired by the producers because of her resemblance to Cybill Shepherd. But soon, the tabloids discovered that she had been "The Ivory Snow Girl," posing, as part of a national advertising campaign, with a baby on every box of the soap.

The producers of *Behind the Green Door* promoted her as the "99 and 44/100% pure girl." She pleaded with Procter & Gamble not to fire her for being an XXX-rated actress, claiming that her newfound notoriety would help sell more soap for them, but they were not convinced.

Her film shocked viewers with its (rare for the time) group sex scenes with women. Causing even more shock were the blonde beauty's scenes with the African American boxer, Johnny Keyes. Those orgasms in the film were real, not faked.

Despite the notoriety she'd generated through her roles as a porn star, Chambers still hoped for a mainstream career as an actress. In 1977, she won a starring role in the low-budget Canadian movie *Rabid*, directed by David Cronenberg, and three years later, her fans saw her in *Insatiable,* a top-selling adult video.

Five years before she died, she warned aspirant actresses, "Don't work in XXX-rated film if you want to become a serious actress. It's heartbreaking. It leaves you kind of empty. Stick to your day job."

In her final years, she occasionally appeared in films that not many people saw, including *Bikini Bistro, Angel of Heat,* and her final role in *Solitaire.* She attempted a singing career with the release of a disco single, "Benihana" in 1976.

In a surprise move, she ran twice for vice president of the United States on the Personal Choice Party ticket alongside running mate Charles Jay. They got 946 votes. They tried again, unsuccessfully, in 2008. Chambers was an alternate write-in candidate for vice president, running in states which included Oklahoma, South Dakota, Hawaii, and Utah.

On April 12, 2009, at the age of 56, Chambers was found dead in Santa Clarita, California. The coroner's autopsy revealed that she had died of a cerebral hemorrhage and an aneurysm related to heart disease.

MARILYN CHAMBERS:  "I may have been the Ivory Snow Girl, but my snow-bank started to drift when I turned to porn. I was a topless model and a bottom-less dancer as well. When I was in high school, I was the biggest prick-teaser there was. Young boys are always so horny and so unfulfilled. My first affair was with this crazy football player and his brother in the same room. A young boy is part kid and part man, just shedding his skin and coming out of the cocoon as a male, a real man. I think his cock leads him."

# FRANKIE'S LOST YEARS

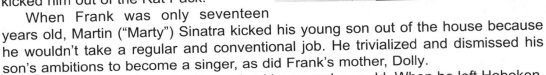

Somewhere beginning in the summer of 1933 and lasting until September of 1935, details about Frank Sinatra's life are almost nonexistent.

But over the years, Frank shared fragments of his life with friends, relating how he supported himself during the months that he was forced to live away from his childhood home because of a feud with his father. One such incident was relayed by Peter Lawford after Frank kicked him out of the Rat Pack.

When Frank was only seventeen years old, Martin ("Marty") Sinatra kicked his young son out of the house because he wouldn't take a regular and conventional job. He trivialized and dismissed his son's ambitions to become a singer, as did Frank's mother, Dolly.

For eighteen months, Frank survived however he could. When he left Hoboken, he had only ten dollars in his pocket. When that ran out, he slept in an all-night theater in Manhattan's then-sleazy Times Square area. The following morning, he was scheduled for a temporary job delivering pizzas.

But before that happened, he had to sleep. He chose a remote corner of the upper balcony of the theater. When he had to descend the steps to the men's room in the basement, he was followed by a man in an overcoat.

The man stood next to Frank at the urinal. When Frank saw the man gazing down at his large penis, he said, "Back off, pal, or I'll charge admission."

"Hey, kid, I'm not one of the faggots who hangs out here," the stranger said. "I've got a job offer for you. For two hours' work, a hundred bucks."

"No way, José," Frank said.

"All you have to do is fuck two beautiful teenage gals on camera," the man promised.

After Frank buttoned up, he trailed the man into the lobby of the theater to work out the details. The stranger was a cameraman who shot blue movies up in the Bronx.

"But I can't appear in that shit," Frank told him. "I might be famous one day. It could ruin my career."

"Don't worry about it," the stranger said. "You'll be wearing a mask throughout the movie. The flick is called *The Masked Bandit: He Steals Pussy*. No one can identify you. All you need to show is your big cock plugging these gals, a blonde  and a redhead."

"You're on, pal," Frank said. "I've never held a hundred dollar bill in my hand before."

In the 1950s, the staff at *Confidential* was tipped off by an anonymous caller, who sent the magazine a copy of Frank's porno debut. Two staff members traced the female star of the movie, who billed herself as "Dawn Day," to Betty Joe Calahan, a well-known stripper on Miami Beach who used a boa constrictor in her act. Once reached by a reporter, she admitted that she had been the sex partner of Frank Sinatra in the movie.

She claimed, "Of course, he was a nobody then. I didn't know who he was until a boyfriend of mine at the time took me to see *Anchors Aweigh.* I almost stood up in the theater and shouted, 'That's him!' Of course, if I had a copy of that film today, I wouldn't be working this seedy joint. If you guys ever see Frank in Hollywood, tell him that Dawn Day says hi and that he was a good boy with me. No rough stuff."

The story was never run in *Confidential.* Frank got wind of it and threatened a massive lawsuit.

For a month after the screening of his porn at the Pussycat, Frank didn't speak to Sammy. Then Frank became worried. If he continued to alienate Sammy, his friend, or former friend, might show that blue movie to even more of Frank's friends as well as to members of the press, and identify to them who the Masked Bandit really was.

He decided to call Sammy and make up. "Hey, Smokey," Frank said when Sammy came to the phone. "How's it hanging?"

Sammy and Frank bonded that night, and Sammy agreed to destroy his copy of *The Masked Bandit.*

Years later, a segment of *The Masked Bandit* was considered for insertion within a feature film about stars such as Joan Crawford who had appeared in porno before they became famous. When Frank heard about this, he called his friends in the mob. The bandit loop never resurfaced.

Sammy may have heard about this and bought the loop, or a copy of the loop, that was cut from the final version of the *Hollywood Blue*, which opened in 1970 as a feature film in New York's Times Square area.It is believed that screenings of *The Masked Bandit* were shown at "smokers" for years. Of course, patrons at these private screenings never knew they were watching *the* Frank Sinatra in full-steam sexual heat.

If somebody out there still has a copy of it, it might eventually end up on the internet, something for the viewing titillations of millions, as Paris Hilton, in the decades to come, would one day discover.

# LINDA LOVELACE AND HER SPINOFF INDUSTRIES

Since Linda Lovelace didn't make any money off *Deep Throat*—her husband, Chuck Traynor, confiscated the $1,200 she was paid—she became a virtual publishing cottage industry, turning out book after book relating her experiences.

The first and most successful was *Meet Linda Lovelace*. It begins with the claim, "Somebody told me that the two best-known names of 1973 were Henry Kissinger and Linda Lovelace." In the book, she shared the secrets of her deep throat techniques, claiming that after months of practice on many different men of all shapes and sizes, she became "one of the supreme cocksuckers of all time."

"Everyone wants to be the best in some field of endeavor, and since I'm not exactly material for a Nobel Prize in literature, I do what I can with what I have," Linda said. She invited her readers to get inside her throat. Some hookers used to have trouble deep-throating Frank Sinatra, but Linda, with all her experience, claimed that once Frank's penis passed her throat muscles, "length became no problem."

# What Ever Happened to
# *Linda Lovelace?*

Linda Lovelace recalled that her initiation into prostitution was a gang rape by five men arranged by her husband, Chuck Traynor.

"He threatened to shoot me with a pistol if I didn't go through with it. I had never experienced anal sex before, and it ripped me apart. They treated me like an inflatable plastic doll."

After divorcing Traynor, she married Larry Marchiano, with whom she had two children. Later, she claimed he drank to excess and indulged in violence against both her and her children. She divorced him in 1996.

In her later years, she joined the feminist anti-pornography movement, backed by such supporters as Gloria Steinem.

In 1987, she had to undergo a dangerous liver transplant, which greatly extended her life. But on April 3, 2001, she suffered massive trauma and internal injuries in an automobile accident. At the age of 53, on April 22, 2001, she was taken off life support and died in a hospital in Denver.

# Frank & "The Showgirl From Hell"

## BARBARA MARX

**Barbara Marx**, former showgirl, and **Frank Sinatra** get affectionate on their wedding day in 1976. He had two pronouncements to make: "Barbara is no ordinary gal," he told his honored guest, Ronald Reagan, four years before he became president of the United States.

"Barbara will be the last Mrs. Frank Sinatra," he also told Reagan. "It's time for me to settle down, but on my terms only. Of course, even a man of my advanced age will stray from time to time."

Frank told another of his honored guests, the disgraced ex-Vice President Spiro Agnew, something more shocking. "My mother, Dolly, does not approve of the marriage. I sent my attorney to tell her the bad news. I was too afraid. I also made one final call to Ava Gardner begging her to take me back. She told me, 'I'm not the marrying kind.'"

In London, Ava complained to her longtime companion, Reenie Jordan, "Frankie finally tied the knot with his gal. But that god damn wedding fucked up my plans to have a vacation in Palm Springs. I need one...real bad. I've got this hangover from hell that won't go away."

377

# Barbara:
## "The Girl with the Betty Grable Legs"

In her memoirs, **Barbara Marx Sinatra** wrote, "For a long time I had to pinch myself almost daily to believe that I, Barbara Ann Blakeley, the gangly kid in pigtails from the whistle stop of Bosworth, Missouri, had somehow become the wife of Francis Albert Sinatra. A big part of Frank's thrill was the sense of danger he exuded, an underlying ever-present tension."

When Barbara was a beautiful model, depicted above, she was wooed by John F. Kennedy. She resisted his advances, as she did an early come-on from Frank Sinatra. However, Bobby Kennedy may have fared better than his brother, and, of course, Frank finally won her over, even though she was still married to Zeppo Marx.

Changing her early tomboy image, Barbara dyed her hair "Rita (Hayworth) Red, lost my twang, and acquired a cashmere hubba-bubba sweater."

At the age of fifteen, she heard her first Sinatra record, "I'll Walk Alone."

"I shivered to the toes of my bobby sox," she said.

*"I don't want no whore coming into this family."*
**—Dolly Sinatra**

*"Barbara Blakeley was one of the most striking women I'd ever seen. Take it from me, she's come a long way from my humble showroom to the lavish Palm Springs compound she enjoys today. Barbara, like her husband, Frank Sinatra, did it 'her way.'"*
**—Mr. Blackwell**

Some people still remember her as Barbara Blakely; others call her Barbara Marx or Barbara Sinatra. The fourth and last of Frank's wives is far lesser known than Nancy Barbato Sinatra, Ava Gardner, and Mia Farrow, wives No. 1, No. 2, and No. 3 (Frank's "trophy bird")

The paths of the world famous crooner, Frank Sinatra, and Barbara Blakeley seemed unlikely to cross. The daughter of a struggling butcher, she was born in 1926 in Bosworth, Missouri (pop. 500). Even as a little girl, she had a dream, not to marry Prince Charming, but to wed a rich man who would provide a life of luxury for her.

Not able to make it financially in Missouri, Barbara's father moved his family to Long Beach, California, hoping for a better life.

Her first big break came when she was named

"Miss Scarlet Queen" in a Long Beach Beauty pageant.

In later years, Barbara would marry both Zeppo Marx and Frank Sinatra. But before that there was an early marriage to a wannabee singer, Robert Harrison Oliver, an executive with the Miss Universe pageant. The date of the actual marriage is the subject of some dispute. She is known to have married him in the 1940s following the end of World War II. The marriage ended in divorce some time in the 1950s and produced her only child, Robert (Bobby) Oliver.

She later became a model, working for Richard Blackwell, who became famous as "Mr. Blackwell." He was notorious for compiling a "Worst Dressed List" that roasted the fashion felonies of everybody from Madonna to Elizabeth Taylor. The acid-tongue gay designer referred to Madonna as, "helpless, hopeless, and horrendous." Of Elizabeth Taylor, he said, "In tight sweaters and skirts she looks like a chain link of sausage."

While modeling clothes for Mr. Blackwell, Barbara learned all the right maneuvers according to him, meaning how "to coo, to seduce—and still remain aloof."

"Little did I realize that hidden beneath her soft smile and honeyed voice lurked a mind as cunning as Bette Davis in *All About Eve*. I was merely a pawn in her elaborate and ambitious game of chess."

He called Barbara's taste, "Vegas toned." Before taking her to New York's Savoy, he borrowed furs, jewelry, elaborate hats, and silk shoes for her. "No one knew better than Barbara the power of illusion in catching and keeping a man."

Although she had not been a beautiful girl, by the 1950s Barbara had blossomed into a blonde beauty. She set out for Las Vegas to make it as a showgirl. "Mr. Blackwell" claimed she was "a regular at the hotel casino bars in order to come into contact with the high rollers."

In one of the casino bars, Barbara met "Zeppo" Marx, who was immediately attracted to her. Herbert Manfred Marx, born in 1901, is the least known of the Marx brothers. Although he appeared in the first five Marx Brothers films, he left the act to start a second career as a theatrical agent. He is still seen on the screen in such films as *Monkey Business*

After **Dolly Sinatra**'s death, **Frank Sinatra** decided he wanted to get married in a Catholic church— "Dolly *(right figure, above, photographed shortly before her death in 1976)* would have wanted that for me," he told Barbara Marx.

But there was a problem. Frank had been married three times before. In the eyes of the Church, his marriage to Ava Gardner and Mia Farrow didn't count, only his marriage to Nancy Barbato. However, if he got an official annulment of that marriage, he could remarry Barbara in a Catholic church with full pomp and circumstance.

Amazingly, after much maneuvering, Frank procured such an annulment, even though Nancy, Sr., and his three legally recognized children were horrified.

Barbara asserted, "From the day we were married, Frank had always referred to me as his 'bride,' and I suddenly felt like one again, in another lovely gown with tropical flowers threaded through my hair."

(1931) and *Duck Soup* (1933). He had been married before (1927-1954) to a Marion Benda.

Barbara was thirty-two years old when she married the fifty-eight-year-old Marx brother. He was married to Barbara from 1959 until 1972.

In its review of *Cocoanuts* in 1929, *The New York Times* referred to Zeppo as "the handsome but dogged straight man with the charisma of an enamel washstand." Noted filmmaker Rainer Werner Fassbinder made the surreal assertion that Zeppo was one of "the ten greatest film actors of all time," a ridiculous exaggeration, of course.

Groucho once told Paramount executives, "We brothers are twice as funny without Zeppo." Others, such as critic James Agee, disagreed with this assessment, calling Zeppo "a peerlessly cheesy improvement on the traditional straight man."

Barbara and Zeppo were often a guest of Frank in Palm Springs. Parties included Ronald and Nancy Reagan, Rosalind Russell and her husband Freddie Brisson, and Spiro and Judy Agnew.

One morning at Frank's house, Judy Agnew rose early. As she was going down for coffee, she saw Barbara slipping out of Frank's bedroom. At that point, Judy became aware that Barbara had spent the night with Frank.

Frank later told Judy that he had let Barbara sleep over because it was late. "I couldn't let her go home alone. She might be attacked by a coyote."

At a gala in 1979, the glamorously dressed **Mrs. Frank Sinatra and her husband** dazzled onlookers. On the left is her longtime friend, **Cary Grant**. At the mike is **Dean Martin**, wearing glasses "because I am technically blind."

Frank used to tell Barbara, "I spill more than Dean drinks." His relationship with his fellow Rat Packer had its rough spots, but upon Dean's death in 1995, Frank said, "You like people and then they die on you."

Barbara may not have gotten along with Frank's children, but she "adored" Cary Grant. He was one of Frank's most devoted fans, and often shed tears at some of his more moving songs.

Barbara was always protective of her son Bobby, and wanted to do everything in her power to see that he had a good life. She prevailed upon Zeppo to adopt her son. Zeppo agreed but never did the legal work. Nonetheless, Bobby started using Marx as his last name.

Even though still married to Zeppo, she had begun her pursuit of Frank, but was willing to take a detour with Bobby Kennedy, who had signaled his interest in her right from the beginning.

Zeppo seemed little interested in sex at that point in his life. He liked to play poker with his cronies. On the night Barbara met

Bobby, Zeppo was sailing on a yacht he owned in Acapulco.

Stopping over in Las Vegas in 1966, Bobby went to see "The Summit" perform—Frank Sinatra, Sammy Davis Jr., and Dean Martin. Joey Bishop and the estranged Peter Lawford were not in the act. Bobby spent more time watching Barbara at a nearby table than he did the floor show.

The socialite Mary Harrington was an eyewitness to Bobby's attraction to Barbara. Jacqueline Susann (*Valley of the Dolls*) had nicknamed Mary "Magnolia" and featured her as a character in her novel.

"I had gone to see Frank perform the night Barbara met Bobby Kennedy," Mary claimed in an interview in Palm Beach. She was to die in 1987, and at that stage of her life she didn't mind spilling a few secrets. "We saw Sammy Davis Jr. and Martin who also appeared on stage with Frank. I was shocked to see Bobby Kennedy in the audience. I'd always heard he didn't like Frank. I knew all the Kennedys from our years in Palm Beach. I hadn't seen Bobby for a long time when he suddenly showed up."

"Let me add that on this particular night, Barbara had never looked more gorgeous," Mary said. "She was known for having the best showgirl legs in Vegas. Bobby was only three tables from us.

Throughout Frank's singing, he'd never taken his eyes off Barbara. After the show ended, the band played music for dancing."

"As I expected, Bobby rose from his table and headed for ours," Mary said. "I introduced him to Barbara, and he asked her to dance with him. I sat alone at the table and envied Barbara, as she just glided smoothly into Bobby's body. I guess I would have liked to be the one dancing with Bobby myself."

Within the hour Barbara and Bobby had disappeared from the club. "I didn't see Barbara until the following night," Mary said.

"I just assumed that she'd spent the night with Bobby." Mary had known the Kennedys for years,

**Frank Sinatra** admitted that "I may not have been the best father in the world," but he loved his children. **Nancy Sinatra Jr.** *(top photo)* was snapped with him during a 1966 CBS TV special. She was his particular favorite.

In the center photograph, Frank wraps an affectionate arm around his son, **Frank Jr.**—"If only critics wouldn't compare him to me."

In the lower photo, snapped in the early 1970s, Frank is seen attending a gala with **Tina Sinatra,** his youngest child.

His daughters had a hard time adjusting to his marriage to Barbara Marx. Nancy Jr. expressed her feelings and the feelings of her fellow siblings. "We felt we were losing him. He had begun a new life and a new family. I felt almost uneasy and almost unwelcome in his home."

and without really wanting to she became the "beard" for Barbara and Bobby, or so she claimed. This trio was seen in public over the months to come—Mary, Bobby, and Barbara. "Those who saw us thought we were just old friends getting together to catch up on each other's activities and gossip."

Although details are lacking, biographer Michael Munn in his book, *Sinatra: The Untold Story*, estimates that Bobby's alleged affair with Barbara lasted for the better part of a year, but was conducted in utmost secrecy, evocative of his affair with Marilyn Monroe. In his book, *RFK*, author C. David Heymann gives a more detailed account of the Bobby/Barbara liaison.

During the mid-1960s, while still married to Zeppo, Barbara, according to Frank's friends, including Martin and Davis, began to date Bobby "seriously."

Details associated with **Bobby Kennedy** have remained an enigma in the life of Barbara Marx. An affair with him has been described by others, but she doesn't speak of such a thing in her memoirs. Frank Sinatra told Sammy Davis Jr. and Peter Lawford that he suspected that Bobby and Barbara did have an affair.

Although Frank invited John F. Kennedy to his Rancho Mirage compound, Bobby was *persona non grata*.

"He is a complete shit," Frank said about Bobby. "He fucked up Marilyn Monroe's mind, and god knows what he did with my Barbara. He pretends to be holier than thou, but he's really an alleycat chasing poontang, At least he keeps Ethel barefooted and pregnant while he runs around doing whatever in the fuck he wants to do. When poor Jack was assassinated, Bobby put the moves on Jackie."

In New York, Mary alleged that Bobby and Barbara used her apartment at the Hotel Carlyle, former stamping ground of JFK, as their love nest. "I always went to another apartment when they wanted to use it," Mary said.

She later made yet another astonishing claim. During one of her sojourns in Jamaica at the Half Moon Club, she encountered Bobby there. "He came on to me. When Bobby comes on to you, it's not subtle. On the dance floor that night, he pressed his body against mine. He was clearly aroused. So was I. I prefer not to reveal what happened later that night."

Mary admitted guilt for "violating my friendship with Barbara. And, let's face it, Bobby was a married man. It was against my principals."

All this talk about an affair between Barbara and Bobby could have been mere rumor, even though the gossip was widespread. Many turned to Barbara's memoirs, *Lady Blue Eyes*, published in 2011, for the final word. In it, Barbara mentioned Bobby on only one page, revealing that she was invited to play tennis, joining Bobby on his side of the net to defeat their opponents. And that's all we get.

Was all this gossip about Bobby and Barbara a mere invention, a fantasy romance, one that never existed? Perhaps. But perhaps not. Chances are, we'll never know for sure.

RFK's biographer C. David Heymann quoted Mary, "Bobby had animalistic vibrations about him. When he talked to a woman, he would not only look directly at her, he would also speak in a soft, low tone.

He was far better with ladies than Jack."

When unconfirmed rumors of the affair reached Frank, he was furious. Although he was a decade away from marrying Barbara, he had already staked her out for himself, in spite of Zeppo.

Complicating matters was the fact that privately, Frank and Bobby had entered into a secret agreement. Although Frank pretended to be a friend of Sam Giancana, he no longer was. He had "a million and one reasons" to hate Giancana, including the fact that Frank blamed him for the deaths of both Marilyn and JFK.

The deal was that Frank would secretly provide incriminating evidence against Giancana, in return for total immunity from his prosecution, regardless of what the Justice Department might discover. He also held out for total anonymity. Bobby agreed to the deal—in essence, forming a secret pact with Frank.

In December of 1972, Barbara filed for divorce from Zeppo and moved into a condo within walking distance of Frank's Palm Springs home.

To this day, Barbara denies having a torrid affair, or any affair, with Bobby Kennedy. As late as December 8, 1997, in *The New York Post*, she claimed, "I was never that lucky. But I got even luckier than that when I married Frank Sinatra in 1976."

Journalist Douglas Thompson referred to Barbara as "a Barbie with honey hair and a Carnation complexion. She's also regarded as the Showgirl from Hell. The girl from the chorus who married the Chairman of the Board and is now the woman who runs the board."

Frank had been slow to fall for Barbara's charm, although he always had thought she was beautiful, especially her shapely legs. Originally, she had appeared to have popped up coincidentally in Palm Springs wherever he went. It later appeared that she

Many Democrats hoped that **Frank Sinatra** would "come home again," returning to the more liberal party and the causes he had supported for so long. But that wasn't going to happen, as this picture, taken at the 1988 GOP convention in New Orleans, clearly indicates.

Frank supported George H.W. Bush for the presidency, even though he did not expect to have as cozy a relationship with him as he'd had with Ronald and Nancy Reagan. Basking in the glow of Republican sunshine are **Barbara Marx Sinatra** and diplomat **Henry Kissinger**, who had been U.S. Secretary of State under Richard Nixon.

Despite his links to the Republicans, Frank remained dedicated to his pet causes, including a woman's right to an abortion and handgun reform.

Shirley MacLaine, a liberal Democrat, once claimed that Frank had become a Republican because of pressure from the mob, whose Dons seemed to think they'd fare better under Bush than under any of his Democratic competitors.

Memories of (Democrat) Attorney General Bobby Kennedy lingered on.

was stalking him. He once asked George Jacobs, his valet, "Who invited her?"

During her marriage to Zeppo, she often passed Frank in their golf carts, showing off her long-stemmed Betty Grable legs.

By 1974, Frank was being seen everywhere with Barbara. She was also spotted leaving his house in the early hours of the morning. He was not dating her exclusively, and she was well aware that he was seeing other women. By March of 1976, Frank had become even more serious about Barbara, and asked her to marry him.

Nancy Jr. and Tina were not aware that Barbara was about to become "Frank's bride-to-be." But when she showed up at a gathering of the clan wearing "a diamond the size of a quail's egg," the Sinatra kids got the message.

At first Nancy Jr. couldn't believe that her father would marry Barbara. "She wasn't Daddy's type," Nancy Jr. claimed. When her father married Barbara on July 11, 1976, Nancy Jr. said she cried for a week before the wedding. "No chance now for him and my mother to get together and grow old together, spend the rest of their lives together. It was finally and forever over, and my mother would have to come to grips with it."

The marriage was performed at Sunnylands, the Rancho Mirage estate of Walter H. Annenberg, publisher of *TV Guide* and the former Ambassador to the Court of St. James's.

When the judge asked Barbara if she took Frank for richer or poorer, he answered for her: "Richer, richer."

There was a problem that led to a serious disagreement. Right before the wedding, Frank had insisted that Barbara sign a prenuptial agreement. She balked at having to sign it, but he was very insistent, almost forcing her to give in under threat of calling off the wedding. He did agree, however, to give her a generous monthly allowance.

Right before his wedding, Frank and Nancy Barbato Sinatra ("Nancy, Sr.") reportedly had a romantic weekend together, which led the children to believe that they might remarry.

What he didn't tell his children was that he was also clinging to the romantic fantasy that he might remarry Ava. The morning before he married Barbara, he called Ava, who was in her apartment in London, and proposed re-marriage to her. She turned him down, later telling her assistant, Reenie Jordan, "I'm not a good nurse for geriatric patients."

Ronald and Nancy Reagan, too, took time out of his presidential campaign to attend the wedding. Gregory Peck and Kirk Douglas were among the honored guests, even Spiro Agnew.

When they married, Frank was a ripened sixty and Barbara was already forty-six but hardly "over the hill."

"Barbara is one woman that Frank never called a broad," said fellow Rat Packer Joey Bishop. "She always wanted to be more than Arm Candy on the arm of a Vegas deity."

When potty-mouthed Ava first heard of Frank's marriage to Barbara, Ava revealed her streak of lesbianism. "She's a good looking bitch. I'd like to fuck her myself."

But as the months went by, Ava grew more disenchanted with Frank's final marriage. His calls and notes became fewer as time drifted by.

"I can't prove this," Dean Martin said, "but I think Barbara let it be known to Frank that he should only have one wife at a time. Like a popular refrain from a song, she allegedly told Frank that 'yesterday is dead and gone.'"

For some two decades, the marble statue of Ava that had been created for *The Barefoot Contessa* had been a graceful monument within Frank's garden. One afternoon in 1976, when Frank was away on a concert tour, movers arrived and hauled the statute away. It was never seen again. It may have been destroyed.

Barbara had a far greater influence on Frank's career than was realized by most of his friends. She talked him out of playing the Mafia Don in *Godfather 3*.

Dean Martin later claimed that Barbara was the only person in the world who could prevent Frank from drinking the last Jack Daniels.

Barbara, according to her friends, is a woman with a mind of her own—determined, opinionated, dedicated to protecting the image of Sinatra. She was the force that drove him from "The Compound" (his home within the desert resort of Rancho Mirage) back to Beverly Hills, which was filled with the glitter of galas and the popping of flashbulbs.

During the course of her marriage, when Barbara felt she was in a strong position with her Frank, she prevailed upon him to adopt her son Bobby. Frank had become very fond of his stepson and included him on some of his tours. He trusted Bobby and warned him not to be a spy, reporting his nocturnal activities back to his mother.

Tina asked the pertinent question: "Who adopts a twenty-five-year old man?" To outsiders it seemed like Barbara wanted Bobby cut in for a share of Frank's estate.
Tina asked another question, "Does Bobby get a new name every time Barbara snares a husband?"

By the time Nancy Jr. and Tina had matured to the point where they became too preoccupied in their private lives, Bobby filled in as a surrogate son for Frank, spending long weeks on tour with him.

Bobby, or so it appeared, eventually assumed a role that might, at first glance, have been more suited to Frank's biological son, Frank Jr. As Tina put it, her biological brother, Frank, Jr. "found himself saddled with this gregarious stepbrother (Bobby) for whom Dad had all the time in the world."

All of Frank's women—Nancy Sr., Nancy Jr., and Tina—rallied against Frank, urging him not to adopt Barbara's son. Frank hated confrontations and finally gave in to the demands of his blood family. He called Frank Jr., and with a large dose of cynicism, said: "Tell your sisters to relax. The adoption is off. Their money is safe."

Tensions between Barbara and Frank's brood reached a boiling point when the children urged Frank to divorce Barbara and remarry Nancy, their mother. Nancy Jr. once asserted, "I will always wish that my parents had remarried. It was more than a child's wild fantasy. At one point it became a probability because they were spending a great deal of time together."

When a journalist asked Barbara how she felt about her three stepkids, she said, "Just because we're in the same family doesn't mean we have to like each other."

It's amazing the marriage lasted. Frank and Barbara had bitter fights. She threatened to leave him, and he'd volunteer to pack her baggage. She often went for days without speaking to him, sleeping in separate bedrooms. At dinner parties, Barbara would be the perfect hostess, but then sometimes gave Frank her silent treatment after the guests left.

Their first decade of marriage was the toughest for both of them. To get her to speak to him again, he often purchased expensive jewelry from Tiffany's

Tina compared his marriage to Barbara "like a long, wasting disease."

In the summer of 1996, to honor twenty years of a turbulent marriage, Frank and Barbara went to the Catholic Our Lady of Malibu Church, in Malibu, California, to renew their marriage vows. Frank's children did not attend. The "bad blood" between Barbara and Frank's stepchildren had not been drained.

After years of marriage, during which he considered divorce time and time again, an unhappy Frank eventually came home to Barbara. "This is it," he told Dean Martin. "I can't stand the pain and humiliation of another divorce. I've had it with women. In my time, I've had my share."

"More than your share," Martin corrected him.

"Barbara and I will hang in for the duration," Frank said. "But the fires of September will burn on a very low flame."

---

## THE DEATH OF MARTY SINATRA
### *"Frank, Your Papa's Dead"*

Suffering from emphysema, Marty Sinatra, Frank's father, had died in 1969 at the age of seventy-four. In a last ditch effort to save him, Frank had flown him to Texas to have his heart operated on by a specialist, but the effort was in vain. At the funeral, Marty's wife (i.e., Frank's mother), Dolly, had tried to throw herself into his grave.

Although she claimed "I hate California," Dolly moved there after her husband's death. She hovered over Frank, and she and her son had constant fights. He loved his mother, but sometimes tried to avoid her. "She drives me batshit," he told his wife, Barbara. "If everything is going peacefully, she'll pick a fight."

Yet, following her death in 1976 in a plane crash, "my life fell apart," he claimed.

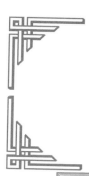

# Frank and Jackie

## ROMANCING THE FIRST LADY

One night in Manhattan, Fiat czar **Gianni Agnelli** *(inset photo, above)*, the richest man in Italy, had arranged to have dinner with **Frank Sinatra**. "We Italians must stick together,"

"The Rake of the Riviera," as Agnelli was called, had what he termed "a monkey curiosity about gossip." Pamela Harriman had once kept him amused about what was going on in London and Paris, but Frank was the best source for the peccadilloes of Hollywood scandal. Over the course of their dinner, Agnelli revealed a scandal of his own: While **Jackie Kennedy** had been married to the president, he had asked her to seek a divorce and marry him.

Jackie had met Agnelli when she went on a holiday to Ravello, Italy, to visit her sister, Lee Radziwill. The two-week holiday stretched on for a month. The paparazzi took pictures of Jackie and Agnelli swimming together off the Fiat heir's 82-foot yacht. JFK cabled his wife: "A LITTLE MORE CAROLINE AND LESS AGNELLI." As an answer to her husband, Jackie was photographed the next day going scuba diving with Agnelli.

Wild stories began in Washington and spread to Los Angeles. One report claimed that the CIA had received word to retrieve Jackie's diaphragm from the White House and have it sent by plane to Ravello.

Agnelli told Frank, "I was in love with Jackie. But we decided to view our relationship as a summer romance."

"You've got me excited," Frank said. "Up to now, Jackie has disliked me very much because she knew I pimped for her husband. But now, you've convinced me that this babe can be had."

In 1975, **Frank Sinatra** escorted **Jackie Onassis** into the 21 Club in Manhattan, following a concert he had delivered at the Uris Theater. He was in a playful mood and over dinner joked with her.

"After Jack died, you were quoted as saying you'd have the respect of the American people, just so long as you didn't run off to marry Eddie Fisher. Why didn't you say Frank Sinatra instead of Eddie?"

"I figured he needed the publicity and you didn't," Jackie shot back.

Before their final brandy of the evening, she made a proposition to him—no, not that kind. "Frank, you must write your memoirs. I'll volunteer to be your editor."

"There are just too many things I've done in my life that I'm not proud of," he told her.

"Perhaps we can skip over the really horrible ones and tell a tantalizing story at the same time," she responded.

"Perhaps. Let's you and I sleep on it."

"Is that an offer?"

In separate limousines, they left 21 Club for the Hotel Carlyle for a sexual tryst. Ironically, this was the same hotel where her husband had had several sexual encounters with Marilyn Monroe.

# JACKIE O, "CHICKY BOY," AND "LOLLIPOPS"

*"Even in the pre-JFK years, Jackie had more men per square inch than any woman I've ever known."*
**Letitia Baldrige**, longtime friend and social secretary

During his 1960 campaign for president, JFK, in Jackie's opinion, was seeing too much of Frank Sinatra. She voiced her suspicion to Peter Lawford that "Sinatra seems like an endless wagon train hauling young women to Jack,"

Whenever possible, Jack took time off from the campaign to party with Frank either in Las Vegas or Palm Springs. Party time meant available women, and Jackie knew that.

She was particularly furious about his dangerous liaison with Judith Campbell Exner, who had been introduced to JFK by Frank. Jackie was enraged when she learned that Exner had slept over at their Georgetown house when Jackie was out of town.

Behind JFK's back, Frank called him "Chicky Boy." Somehow Jackie found out about that nickname and used it to taunt her husband when she discovered yet another of his infidelities, many of which were arranged by Frank himself. She referred to the young women that Frank set up for a JFK seduction as "lollipops."

JFK asked Frank to organize the entertainment for his 1961 inauguration. Frank gladly accepted and later claimed that the gig was the highlight of his life.

During the frenzied weeks he spent arranging the events, Frank was on the phone day and night, getting commitments from an impressive array of leading stars who promised to appear for the president's inauguration. Ella Fitzgerald was willing to fly in from Australia, and Shirley MacLaine agreed to wing in from Tokyo. Frank located Gene Kelly in Switzerland, where he was shacked up with a ski instructor. Sidney Poitier flew back from Paris. Ethel Merman got permission to leave her Broadway show, *Gypsy,* for one evening performance so that she could fly to Washington to entertain. Frank even got Eleanor Roosevelt to agree to show up, although she really would rather have seen Adlai Stevenson as president instead.

Joey Bishop signed on as master of ceremonies, and Leonard Bernstein agreed to conduct a rendition of "Stars and Stripes Forever."

Frank brought his girlfriend, Juliet Prowse, although he planned to devote most of the evening to Jackie herself. Because of their interracial marriage, Sammy Davis and Mai Britt were not on the guest list, but Kennedy loyalists Janet Leigh (one of JFK's mistresses) and Tony Curtis (who wanted to be JFK's mistress) were invited, as were Bette Davis, Jimmy Durante, Mahalia Jackson, Harry Belafonte, Milton Berle, and Nat King Cole.

Dean Martin called Frank, "I'm too busy on this shit movie in Hollywood to come. By the way, who won? I was drunk that night."

Finally, the inauguration got underway in spite of Washington's worst snow storm. John F. Kennedy was the epitome of youth, and surely no First Lady had ever looked as glamorous as Jackie that night—not Martha Washington, Mary Todd Lincoln, and certainly not Mrs. Calvin Coolidge or Bess Truman.

Arriving at the National Guard Armory, Jack and Jackie were treated like the newly crowned King and Queen of the World, despite the snowdrifts blowing across Washington.

Frank opened that gala with his hit song, "That Old Black Magic." Except for this night the lyrics were changed to "That old *Jack* magic."

"It wasn't Black Magic, it wasn't Jack magic, it was Jackie magic," Frank said. "I

The pre-inaugural gala of January, 1961 was "the biggest night of my life," **Jackie Kennedy** said. She was about to become the First Lady of the land. Elegantly attired and coiffed, she is escorted up the steps of the National Guard Armory in Washington, D.C.

As host of the proceedings, a tuxedo-clad **Frank Sinatra** is her escort. At the *Washington Post* an editor saw this picture and asked, "Where is JFK?" A reporter replied, "He's probably in a broom closet somewhere fucking Angie Dickenson."

At the time this picture was taken, Jackie held Frank and his Rat Pack, including Peter Lawford, in disdain, claiming that the Kennedy family was merely star struck. "The Rat Pack is the wrong image for you, Jack," she told her husband. She was credited with eliminating the presence of the Rat Pack during JFK's quest for the presidency.

Even though he had escorted her into the ballroom, she kept Frank "at arm's length." Later, she changed her mind about him. "Once you melted his protective façade, he was one of the most sensitive men I ever met, so unlike Jack."

literally came under her spell, and before my life ends, I'll be god damn if I'm not going to get her."

Back in Hollywood, Frank, over drinks, discussed the inauguration with Lawford. "I was speechless when Jackie emerged from that limousine with that bouffant hairdo. I wanted her just for myself and to hell with Jack. She wore a long white gown—the women reporters called it "organza"—along with sparkling jewels. She literally left me speechless. I got a hard-on. Fortunately, I was able to conceal it as I escorted her up the steps to the armory, thanks to my heavy duty jockstrap."

One evening during the early weeks of his presidency, based on JFK having told Jackie that he wanted to dine alone with her, she was expecting a romantic evening. But when she came in for dinner, she discovered Frank with Jack, discussing women. The moment she entered the room, they abruptly changed the subject.

It turned out that JFK had created what he called "a dynamite idea for a film," and he wanted Frank to star in it, playing himself as president. The plot involved a Texas-based *coup d'état* and a plot to remove him from the presidency.

Ironically, after JFK's own assassination in 1963, that half-formulated idea became a central point in many of those claims about how Lyndon B. Johnson had engineered the assassination of JFK so he would become president.

In later years, Jackie and Frank discussed JFK's premonitions about how he was going to die in Dallas.

In April of 1961, some malicious person, no doubt a Republican within the F.B.I., sent Jackie an anonymous letter which asserted that the Bureau had learned that *Confidential* magazine had affidavits from two mulatto prostitutes in New York stating that Jack and Frank, from within a suite at the Hotel Carlyle, had had sex with both of them. The anonymous letter went on to assert that the magazine would soon after release the story.

Without alerting her husband, Jackie placed a call to Frank himself for verification. At first he denied it but then he relented, admitting the story's validi-

When then-First Lady Jackie Kennedy was conducting her month-long affair with Gianni Agnelli off the Amalfi Coast in Italy, Vice President **Lyndon B. Johnson** *(photo above)* was working behind the scenes to discredit both Jackie and JFK, hoping to bring their extramarital affairs into the light of public scrutiny. He'd learned that JFK planned to dump him in favor of his brother, Bobby Kennedy, as vice-presidential candidate during the upcoming elections of 1964.

Johnson wanted to use any of dozens of percolating Kennedy scandals to chase them from the Oval Office.

J. Edgar Hoover kept Johnson informed about the romantic and sexual conduct of Jackie with Agnelii. Secretly, the vice president was instrumental in getting a conservative public advocacy group, Concerned Citizens of America, to threaten to picket the White House.

Although they didn't actually protest *en masse*, the group's president wrote an open letter to Jackie, urging her to return immediately to U.S. shores: "Would you not better serve the nation and the President by remaining here at home by his side? We have honored you greatly with the position of First Lady of our land. We ask only that you not violate the dignity of that title."

ty after he learned that the report was about to be printed.

"You created this mess. Now get rid of it!" Jackie reportedly admonished Frank. Then she slammed down the phone. It is believed that Frank then called Joe Kennedy, who had gotten him involved in the campaign in the first place, and persuaded Joe to buy off the magazine for $50,000. The story was never run.

Jackie later told Peter Lawford, "My call to Sinatra may have saved Jack's presidency in its early stage."

This same unknown informant within the F.B.I. also sent Jackie a detailed report from Belden Katelman, who was identified only as a Las Vegas investor. In the report, Jackie read that Frank and JFK had shared a suite at the Sands during the campaign and that Peter Lawford had also arrived for a visit. "Showgirls from all over were seen running in and out of the Senator's suite all hours of the day and night," the report alleged.

After he was elected president, JFK often called Frank just to talk to him. The president was especially interested in hearing about the latest young movie stars, especially those Frank had seduced.

One night over an after-dinner drink, Jack told his brother-in-law, Peter Lawford, "I should really invite Frank to the White House. Throw something special as a means of thanking him for all he did for me in the campaign."

"That's impossible," Peter said. "Jackie hates Frank."

"The next time Jackie goes horseback riding in Middleburg, ask Frank to come and see us," JFK said.

Peter called Frank that very night and found him elated by the invitation. Two weeks later he flew to Washington where a limousine was waiting to drive him to the less-frequently used southwest gate of the White House as a means of avoiding photographers.

From left to right, **Peter Lawford, Sammy Davis Jr.**, and **Frank Sinatra** are engaged in one of their most embarrassing confrontations. The brother-in-law of John F. Kennedy and Bobby Kennedy has informed Frank, organizer of the president's inauguration entertainment, that Bobby didn't want Sammy to perform with the other stars.

"Bobby feels he's too controversial," Peter explained." He turned to Sammy. "This planning to marry a blonde Swedish actress is a bit much even for the liberal Democrats to take," Peter said. "Bobby is afraid we'll lose our Democratic base becase of Sammy. They might even vote Republican next time."

At first, Frank balked, threatening to walk out the door, but Sammy urged him to stay on. "It's not the first time that a darkie was shown the back exit," Sammy said.

Peter Lawford later whispered to JFK, "I think Frank wanted us to send Air Force One to fly him here from California."

"People don't get what they want in life," JFK said, "except for me."

Jack himself escorted Frank on a personalized tour of the private rooms of the White House, which ended with Bloody Marys on the Truman Balcony.

The next day Teddy Kennedy and both Patricia and Peter Lawford accompanied Frank on a private Kennedy plane to Hyannis Port where they went boating on a yacht.

Back in Washington, Frank hooked up with the president for a sail on the Potomac, this time aboard the Kennedy yacht, the *Honey Fitz*.

Before they had a falling out, JFK would lavishly entertain Frank, in league with other celebrities who included both Judy Garland and Audrey Hepburn, at Washington's Mayflower Hotel, where he maintained a suite. Jackie was never invited, but she was made aware that Frank often arranged the presentation of beautiful starlets for the president to sample.

These three men shared the privilege of seducing Jackie Kennedy Onassis. From left to right, **Frank Sinatra, Peter Lawford,** and **Bobby Kennedy** meet under the hot sun of Los Angeles during July of 1961.

Bobby didn't like either of the other men in this photo, including his brother-in-law Peter. He especially despised Frank. His brother's relationship with Frank and the Mob had made this meeting especially painful for Bobby, who knew that at some point the White House would be forced to drop Frank from its guest lists.

With Jackie, Peter and Frank would sustain mere flings. But with Bobby, her post-assassination love affair would be the real thing.

In a touch of irony, all three men would also become the lover of Jackie's chief rival, Marilyn Monroe.

Although MM came to view Peter as "my sister," she fantasized about marrying either Bobby and/or Frank.

As a senator, Jack had used the Mayflower, in the words of one observer who worked in the White House, as "his personal Playboy mansion."

In his 1987 book, *Capitol Hill in Black and White*, Robert Parker detailed the challenges associated with catering JFK's private parties at the Mayflower. At the time, Parker worked for Harvey's, a first-class restaurant adjoining the Mayflower. Food was delivered to room 812. Frank often supplied the women for these parties, which turned into orgies.

In 1962 Marilyn Monroe called Jackie at the White House, and, surprisingly, the First Lady took the call. The two women would meet months later within Truman Capote's New York apartment. On their initial call, Marilyn urged Jackie to step aside and divorce her husband so she could marry him.

She later told Lawford, "Marilyn really must have been on something. Welcome to reality, something she obviously doesn't know anything about."

Jackie was furious that Marilyn would have the audacity to actually call her. "The woman has no shame," she told her secretary. "I know she calls Jack at the White House. But phoning me is unforgivable. I blame Frank Sinatra for all of this."

Through Peter Lawford, Jackie sent word to Frank that "you are no longer welcome at the White House."

Years would go by before they made up. The flare-up with Frank occurred at the same time that Bobby

Kennedy began to go after some of Frank's mob associates, including Sam Giancana, Johnny Roselli, and Mickey Cohen. Ultimately, it was Bobby who warned Jackie to steer clear of Frank.

On March 16, 1974, Peter Duchin, the pianist and band leader, brought Jackie and Frank together again after a long alienation.

In an interview with Duchin, Sarah Bradford, author of *America's Queen*, claimed that as a friend of both Jackie and Frank, Duchin managed to convince them to bury their hatchets.

In the wake of their reconciliation, Frank invited her to attend his concert in Providence, Rhode Island. Claiming "that sounds like fun," she accepted. He sent his plane to pick her up.

Accompanied by Peter and Cheray Duchin, Jackie flew to Rhode Island, where she hooked up with Frank after the show. They then flew on his private plane back to New York where a limo waited to whisk them into Manhattan for a late dinner.

Reportedly, at the end of the meal, Jackie told Duchin, "I don't think Frank is my type."

"Nothing happened," Duchin told Bradford. "I think either she would have told me or Frank would have told me."

Perhaps Duchin's impression is right. Nothing happened on that particular night. Their brief fling would occur later.

In 1974, Frank called Jackie and asked her to the Uris Theatre in New York. She accepted the invitation. To the awe of the audience, he sat in the center of the theater with Jackie, listening to his opening act of Ella Fitzgerald and Count Basie. At intermission he excused himself and left to perform. His seat was taken by a member of the Secret Service.

After his performance, the romantic pair had a late night dinner and then departed in separate limousines. She was taken to the Hotel Carlyle, where she had time to change into something more comfortable. He discreetly arrived thirty minutes later and was escorted in through a secret entrance.

Jackie must have been impressed with Frank's performance, because he was invited back for "a second show." This was not to be the beginning of a long-running affair. They would not be alone together until almost another year had passed.

As *People* magazine so blatantly and accurately maintained, **Maurice Tempelsman** (above) was **Jackie Kennedy's** last love. What he didn't have in looks, he made up for in financial savvy.

"After having me, Jack and Bobby Kennedy, Peter Lawford, William Holden, Gianni Agnelli, and even that thing, Marlon Brando, Jackie is settling for this?"

Frank Sinatra was talking about Jackie's final romantic involvement, this time with a married man, Maurice Tempelsman. A friend of Jackie's for years, and later her financial adviser, Tempelsman had become her constant beau and companion during her later years.

She said, "I truly hope my notoriety doesn't force him out of my life." It didn't. This Orthodox Jew who had fled Belgium to escape the Nazi onslaught was with Jackie to the end, tending to her needs on her final day.

Frank finally declared that he understood the relationship. "I just heard that Tempelsman has turned Jackie's $20 million into $200 million."

Many Jackie watchers felt that that time at the Carlyle marked the end of the Jackie/Sinatra affair.

Not so. In J. Randy Taraborrelli's *Sinatra: Behind the Legend*, he reports another sexual tryst between Jackie and Frank, this one occurring at the singer's suite within New York City's Waldorf Towers in 1975.

Several sources, including Sammy Davis Jr., confirmed that afterward, Frank bragged about his conquest. One source, an employee of Frank's, told Taraborrelli that he dropped Jackie off at the Waldorf and picked her up there the following morning.

According to the book, Ethel Kennedy may have been instrumental in convincing Jackie not to take any more of Frank's calls.

When Truman Capote asked Jackie about the Sinatra rumors, Jackie jokingly said, "I should have stuck with Eddie Fisher."

Capote told Jackie, "I don't know how you could let Frank get away. He let me feel it one night, and I'm a good judge of cocks, having seen enough of them in my day. If I were you, I would still be swinging on it. Of course, it wasn't as big as that of Porfirio Rubirosa, who seduced your sister-in-law, Pat Kennedy."

Frank met Jackie one final time in New York. It was in 1994 at 21 Club when Jackie was an editor for Doubleday. Spotting her, he asked the *maître d'* to invite her to his table. She accepted.

Without mentioning their shared past with each other, she urged him once again to write his memoirs.

"As I've said before, I can never do that," he told her. "Too many secrets. But for you, I'll think about it one more time."

She had long ago forgiven him for sharing Judith Campbell Exner with President Kennedy, or the role he played in bringing Marilyn Monroe back into JFK's life. At the end of the dinner, as she got up to leave, he kissed her goodbye on the lips.

The next morning he sent her a bouquet of exquisite flowers and a bottle "of the most expensive perfume in New York." He wrote: "You are America's Queen. I can't write those memoirs. God bless you, always. Love, Frank."

He knew her days on this Earth had grown short, and when he heard of her death he wept bitter tears. "I could have loved her. She could have loved me. The saddest words are always what might have been."

At Jackie's funeral, on May 24, 1994, Frank sent two dozen red roses but didn't show up.

---

*"The Kennedy media image that shielded Jack's peccadilloes also protected Jackie, and neither one could divorce the other while in the White House. 'We are like two icebergs,' Jackie said, 'the public life above the water, the private life submerged.'"*

**—Dr. David Eisenbach**, political historian

# Frank and the G.O.P

## VERY STRANGE BEDFELLOWS

**Frank Sinatra**, pictured above with **Richard Nixon**, was in Palm Springs listening to his own music when a late night call came in from Jackie Kennedy, who had not recovered from the assassination of Bobby Kennedy in 1968. Now it was 1972, and time for another presidental election. She had read in the papers that Frank was throwing his support to Nixon who, as a Republican, was running against George McGovern on the Democratic ticket. "How could you, Frank," Jackie asked. "You've been such a great Democrat all your life. I read in the paper that even your own daughter, Tina, is supporting McGovern. Nixon is a crook, and I know you know that."

"Nixon's okay," he told her. "I didn't use to like him, but we've made up. He's all right in my book, and Spiro Agnew and I are friends."

Months before the November election, Frank was seen dining with Richard and Patricia Nixon in New York. When they left the restaurant, a sixteen-year-old boy, Juan Garcia, snapped a picture of Frank with the Nixons. Frank flew into a rage and knocked the camera out of the boy's hand, crushing it with his feet. Martin Venker, a Secret Service agent, witnessd the scene.

Frank warned Venker, "Get that God damn kid out of here or I'll take him out."

"Just get in the car and cool it," Venker said. Frank shut up and got into the car.

After dropping Frank off at his hotel, Nixon settled back into his seat. "That dago is one hot-headed bastard from hell, but I need all the support I can get, even if it comes from spaghetti eaters."

## THE SECRET SERVICE'S CODE NAME FOR FRANK WAS:

# "NAPOLEON"

Plagued by millions of protesters opposing the Vietnam war, Lyndon B. Johnson had bowed out of the 1968 presidential race. **Frank Sinatra** *(left)* was delighted. "It's about time for Johnson to return to Texas where he can spend his final days kicking horse shit."

Frank announced he would support **Hubert Humphrey,** *(right)* the vice president who was in a close race on the Democratic ticket against his Republican challenger Richard Nixon, who had twice been vice president under Dwight D. Eisenhower in the 1950s.

Despite the gag picture *(above)* of Frank with Humphrey, Frank had very little enthusiasm for the candidate, but was nonetheless putting up a brave front.

In spite of what the picture above implies, Humphrey didn't exactly welcome Frank's support. When Frank flew to Washington in May of 1968 to have dinner with Humphrey, the candidate slipped him in through the back door of the White House. In the summer of 1968, Nicholas Gage of the *Wall Street Journal* published a scathing *exposé* about Frank and the Mafia. Humphrey aides urged him to drop Frank. "You don't need the support of the underworld," advised Washington attorney Joseph L. Nellis.

Humphrey refused eight phone calls from Frank, but finally accepted one. "You fucking prick!" Frank screamed at him as he came onto the phone. "How dare you treat me like this after those concerts I did for you. "You're an ungrateful shit."

Humphrey had channeled the call through a speaker phone, and five aides heard Frank's lambast. Humphrey slammed down the phone.

Amazingly, Frank kept stumping for him, even though Humphrey had made it clear that he didn't welcome the support.

When Humphrey lost the election, comedian Mort Sahl said, "Once Sinatra backs you, it's the Mafia kiss of death."

*"Frank was changing his political mind with alarming speed. He hated Nixon with deep vitriol but then before long would campaign for him. It was almost the same thing with Reagan."*

**—Shirley MacLaine**

*"Both Nixon and Sinatra had deep ties to the Mafia. It was only natural that after President John Kennedy dumped Sinatra that Ol' Blue Eyes hooked up with the biggest politician in the Mob's pocket. Sinatra hung around with Nixon and Vice President Agnew so much he even acquired a Secret Service code name, 'Napoleon.'"*

**—Don Fulsom** in *Crime Magazine*

Author Gore Vidal called Frank "a neutered creature of the American Right, an Italo-American Faust." Political consultant Joseph Cerrell claimed "Sinatra likes attention. He's still that little kid from Hoboken who likes to be stroked by presidents."

These pundits and others were weighing in on Frank's sudden shift from Democratic Party to the Richard Nixon camp. In the 1950s and 1960s Frank had had only contempt for Eisenhower's vice president.

When Lyndon Johnson, no friend of Frank's, announced in 1968 that he was stepping down in favor of his vice president, Hubert Humphrey, Frank backed Humphrey, but without any real enthusiasm. He certainly didn't want Bobby Kennedy to get the Democratic nomination for president. Of course, an assassin's bullet in Los Angeles ended Bobby's chance. "I'd do anything to defeat that bum Nixon," Frank said in public. As late as the summer of 1970, Frank was telling *The Los Angeles Times* that Nixon would "run the country into the ground. The Democrats have got to get together and beat him."

In spite of Frank's attacks on him, Nixon felt there was a real possibility that the singer could be wooed to his side. The president wanted Frank's support because of his connection to Hollywood celebrities and other public figures, and because of his proven ability as a great fund raiser.

When John F. Kennedy had dumped Frank because of his mob ties, Nixon was gleeful to see Frank banished from the Court of Camelot. Bobby Kennedy had begun to crack down on organized crime, and some of his targets focused on Frank's best friends, including Sam Giancana of Chicago. Bobby told JFK, "Sinatra is in the mob's pocket, and I can't fight crime if you're hanging out with the bastard or using him as your pimp."

Nixon's political strategist, Charles Colson, suggested to Nixon and Agnew that they should try to win Frank over to their side in the 1972 election campaign. Agnew was selected as the emissary from the White House, and he began at once to ingratiate himself with Frank.

Nixon told Agnew, "We've got to start courting Sinatra like he was the jilted bride left at the altar by his Democrat bridegroom."

Agnew secretly arranged a "chance meeting" at the Palm Springs Country Club, and the Agnew/Sinatra "romance" was on. Soon Agnew was a regular houseguest at Frank's villa in Rancho Mirage. They were so intimate that Frank was soon showing him porn, especially *Deep Throat*.

In early 1971, Agnew told Nixon that "we can welcome Sinatra aboard."

Frank and Agnew were labeled "the odd couple" when they came together and bonded as close friends. The Vice President was treated like royalty at Frank's compound in Rancho Mirge. He named his guest cottage the "Agnew House," and ordered monogrammed sheets.

Awakening early one morning, Judy Agnew, the VP's wife, saw Barbara Marx slipping out of Frank's bedroom. She later told her husband, "Silly me, I always thought Zeppo Marx was a

Sammy Davis Jr. claimed that he never understood the instant chemistry between **Spiro Agnew** *(left)*, Nixon's vice president, and **Frank**. "The Chairman of the Board was a *ring-a-ding-ding* kind of hipster, and Agnew was a conservative square attacking 'those god damn hippies.' Frank had married one of those hippies, Mia Farrow."

But Agnew and Frank formed a tight bond, and the vice president became a frequent visitor of Frank's in Rancho Mirage. "Frank treated him like he was King of America," Davis said, "even naming the guest house he'd built for JFK 'the Agnew House.'"

Frank revealed to Agnew how shabbily the Democrats had treated him. "Humphrey introduced me to Johnson at the White House. He gave me a souvenir booklet and a tube of lipstick bearing the White House seal. Then the Texas longhorn told me, 'It'll made a big man of you with your women.'"

great friend of Frank's. I wonder if he knows that Frank is sleeping with his wife."

"Don't worry about it," Agnew told her. "We're in California now. Things like that are the norm out here."

Frank supported the Nixon/Agnew ticket in 1972. He even rented a house on Embassy Row in Washington with Peter Malatesta, Agnew's aide, so as to be near the seat of the Republican Party's political action. His boss, the Vice President, was a frequent visitor.

After Frank's so-called "retirement" in the spring of 1971, the Agnews spent more and more time with the singer, including Easter, Thanksgiving, and New Year's.

Frank became so close to Agnew that soon the two men were flying on official trips together aboard Air Force Two. Frank had wanted to travel with JFK on Air Force One but no invitation had ever been offered.

Agnew was attacked in the press for his friendship with Frank, but he did not turn his back on him as JFK had done.

**Spiro Agnew** (center) introduces **Frank Sinatra** to **Tricia Nixon Cox**, the daughter of Richard Nixon. Once she left the room, Frank whispered to Agnew, "I'd like to bang that chick. Can't you set that up for me?"

The Veep jokingly responded, "To have you backing the Republican ticket, I'll not only set that up, but arrange trysts with Patricia and my Judy." He was referring, of course, to Patricia Nixon and his wife, Judy Agnew. The two men often indulged in that kind of vulgar talk.

Agnew also told Frank that he had rushed away from Tricia's wedding in Washington to attend Frank's "retirement concert" in California.

Agnew certainly turned Frank's political head around. As late as July of 1970, Frank was telling *The Los Angeles Times* "Nixon is running the country into the ground. The Democrats have got to get together and defeat Agnew and Nixon in the '72 campaign."

A year later, actress Rosalind Russell, a close friend of Frank's, arrived for a weekend at his villa. "I couldn't believe my eyes," she said. "Agnew was at the piano hitting the keys as Frank sang 'Night and Day.'"

Two years into their friendship, both Frank and Agnew learned about Nixon's plan to knock Agnew off the ticket in 1972. The vice president was to be replaced by Texas governor John Connolly, the same man who rode with Jack and Jackie Kennedy on that November day in 1963 when JFK was assassinated.

In Palm Springs, Frank and Agnew conspired to prevent Nixon from dumping him. First off, Frank orchestrated a massive write-in campaign, urging Nixon to keep Agnew on the ticket.

Frank knew he had little influence with Nixon, but he felt he could exert a powerful control over Agnew if he ran and won the presidency in 1976. To do that, however, Agnew had to remain on the 1972 ticket as the vice presidential candidate.

Also as a means of countering Nixon's plan to dump Agnew, Frank launched a mammoth fundraiser in Baltimore at the Lyric Theater. He even lined up Bob Hope as the master of ceremonies, and attracted an array of stars to perform. Emerging from retirement, Frank sang "The Gentleman Is a Champ," evoking his famous "The Lady Is a Tramp." Following that outpouring of support, Nixon was more of less forced to keep Agnew on the ticket.

After this highly visible event in Baltimore, within the heart of Agnew's home state of Maryland, Frank was subpoenaed—but later "invited"—as a hostile witness before the House Select Committee on Crime. The board was investigating organized crime in horse racing and sports. Frank was questioned about his investment in the Berkshire Downs Racetrack in Massachusetts.

He turned the occasion into an attack on the committee, claiming he was called "only because my name ends in a vowel. Anyone who has Sicilian ancestry is automatically called a crook," he charged.

Eventually, after his sparring with the committee, Frank, with all his swagger and counter charges, won the day. "You're still the Chairman of the Board," said Representative Charles Rangel, Democrat of New York.

Later Frank sent the committee a bill for $18,750 to reimburse personal expenses it had forced him to incur as a result of his appearance in Washington. The bill went unpaid.

Frank told the press that the members of the committee wanted publicity during an election year, and they did so by dragging him in for questioning.

President Nixon called Frank and personally congratulated him on his performance before the committee. Frank was so flattered by the call that he agreed to support the president in his reelection bid in 1972, posting $55,000 of his own money.

Frank turned down the offer to stage the inaugural gala of 1972 after Nixon and Agnew were reelected. "I'm a president maker, not a performer," he bragged to friends.

He did fly to Washington to his Embassy Row mansion, where he staged a series of pre-inaugural parties, inviting everybody from Henry Kissinger to Senator Barry Goldwater.

Nixon invited Frank to the inauguration celebration in January of 1973, and Frank said that he would attend but would not perform. Previously he had sung at a dinner Nixon held for the prime minister of Italy, Giulio Andreotti. Frank sang "The House I Live In."

Afterward, the president said, "Once in a while there is a moment where there is magic in the room. A great singer and entertainer is able to capture it and move us all. Frank Sinatra has done that tonight."

Frank showed up at Nixon's second inaugural with a beautiful blonde girlfriend on his arm. She was Barbara Marx, a former showgirl in Las Vegas and the wife of Zeppo Marx.

*(Left to right)*, **Judy Agnew, Frank Sinatra, and Spiro Agnew** appear at a banquet.

"Unlike the Democrats, I'm not ashamed to be photographed with Frank, but welcome his support," Spiro said. Allegedly, Judy was a bit put off by Frank's "loose morals," but she went along with her husband and was always gracious to Frank when she was his house guest, a venue that occurred a total of at least eighteen times.

Frank showed his loyalty to Nixon and Agnew through his performances at the White House, even though the administration was already enmeshed in the Watergate affair. "What the hell!" Frank said. "I've known a few guys in my day that break into places." When Tina Sinatra confronted her father with news about the extent of the charges, he told her, "Nobody's perfect."

Frank did waver a bit at one point. Three months after Nixon was forced to resign from his presidency because of Watergate, Frank made a surprise appearance at a fund-raiser for New York Democrats. He never warmed to the presidency of Jimmy Carter, however, referring to him as "that redneck, Born Again peanut farmer from Georgia."

As he was opening a car door for Barbara, Maxime Cheshire, a columnist for the *Washington Post*, rudely approached Frank. "Mr. Sinatra, do you think that your alleged association with the Mafia will prove to be the same embarrassment to Vice President Agnew that it was to the Kennedy administration?"

Remembering a similar question asked in front of the California governor, Ronald Reagan, Frank was furious. He called Cheshire a "cunt. Get away from me you scum. Go home and take a bath."

He shoved two one-dollar bills at the woman. "You know what that means, don't you? You've been laying down for two dollars all your life."

Later Henry Kissinger told Frank, "You overpaid."

After she got back from the Nixon inaugural, Barbara sued Zeppo Marx for a divorce and was awarded $1,500 a month in alimony for the next decade.

Through White House channels, Agnew recommended that Nixon name Frank as director of the American Revolution Bicentennial. John Ehrlichman, one of Nixon's head honchos, promised to pass the suggestion on to the president. But Ehrlichman later said, "I'd seen Sinatra's thick FBI package, full of innuendos about connections with organized crime. I can't imagine trying to get him through a Senate confirmation."

When Ehrlichman presented Agnew's suggestion to Nixon, the president laughed. "I have long ago concluded that Agnew is lazy, incompetent, and dumb."

The bicentennial job went to future U.S. Republican Sen. John Warner of Virginia, who became better known as one of the husbands of Frank's former lover, Elizabeth Taylor.

Frank ultimately headed "Entertainers for Nixon," a post that did not require Senate confirmation.

Nixon always wanted to back off whenever a staff member presented him with evidence of Frank's ties to the Mob. During his first race for Congress in 1946, Nixon had the secret financial support of gangster Mickey Cohen.

He also had links to another gangster, Meyer Lansky. Once, in Havana, when Nixon lost $50,000 at one of Lansky's gambling casinos, Lansky did not insist on payment. Also, as a guest at Lansky's Hotel Nacional, Nixon was not presented with a bill for his stay in the presidential suite.

Nixon's almost constant companion, Bebe Rebozo, had been involved with Lansky in illegal gambling rackets in South Florida.

In October of 1973, Frank was in Rancho Mirage when he received a phone call from his lawyer, Milton Rudin. The Associated Press had just carried a story that Agnew might be heading to jail. He'd been charged with systematically taking bribes since he'd held political office in Maryland back in 1967. At one point he bagged $100,000 in cash, according to reports.

When he read the charges, Frank concluded that his friend was "dead-ass guilty, but I want him to walk."

When Agnew flew in to visit Frank, he asked Rudin, his attorney, if he knew a way to get the vice president off. "The only way I can get him off is jerking it," Rudin allegedly said. "Otherwise, he's going up unless he receives a presidential pardon."

To help with Agnew's mounting legal costs, Frank gave him $30,000. More money was on the way.

At another private confab at Frank's villa in Rancho Mirage, Agnew delivered the bad news. "Nixon wants me to resign." "Fuck that!" Frank told him. "Shit! Hell! Damn! If you resign, you'd be admitting guilt. Fight the bastards."

Frank wanted to line up at a cartel of the best five or six lawyers in America to defend

Agnew.

With Frank's coaching, Agnew faced the press, claiming, "I am innocent."

Much to Nixon's horror, Agnew took Frank's ill-conceived advice. Before a meeting of the National Federation of Republican Women, Agnew defiantly shouted, "I will not resign if indicted."

Within an hour, Nixon was on the phone to his veep. "Don't you ever make a speech like that. If you don't resign, you'll face jail. Politically, I can't afford to give you a presidential pardon. It would ruin my political future." As events moved into October of 1973, Agnew faced no choice but to resign. The evidence against him was overwhelming. To avoid criminal prosecution, he resigned his office as vice president.

Frank was bitterly disappointed when Agnew resigned. "There goes Frank's dreams of taking over the Lincoln bedroom in 1976," said Dean Martin, and he wasn't joking.

When queried by the press about Agnew's disgrace, Frank said, "I don't believe in deserting a friend when he's in trouble."

Agnew faced mounting debts, and Frank lent him $200,000 to pay back taxes. He'd lost his salary of $62,500 as vice president, and also his government pension.

Frank even tried to get a publisher to put up half a million dollars for Agnew's memoirs, but no one was interested.

The post office virtually had to put out extra staff to process the hate mail pouring into Frank's letterbox because of his support of Agnew.

A few months later, in astonishment, Frank watched as Nixon became entrapped in his own lies and deceit which culminated in the Watergate scandal. The president was forced to resign unless he wanted to face impeachment. Shortly after Gerald Ford took over the Oval Office in April of 1974, he granted Nixon a presidential pardon.

When Frank was asked about Nixon's roll in the Watergate scandal, he said, "Nobody's perfect." In private he told friends, "I always knew Nixon was a crook."

Once Nixon was out of office, he had no more use for Frank and dropped all contact with him after the summer of 1974. "I never listened to his music anyway," he told Ford. "I'd advise you to stay away from him. His influence is vastly overrated."

In contrast, Agnew remained a loyal friend. "As time went by and my business improved through my numerous trips abroad, I earned an adequate income and paid back the last of the Sinatra loans in 1978."

Visitors to Agnew's mansion in Rancho Mirage were greeted by the bust of Frank resting on Agnew's piano.

After two years of involvement with Republican office seekers, Frank gave in to Agnew's urgent pleas that he come out of retirement. In 1973, he mounted a TV special which he called "my comeback."

"How many times did Judy Garland retire?" Burt Lancaster asked. "Frank is a great artist, and great musicians like Frank can't sit in the desert painting pictures until the end. He'll be back—bigger than ever."

Frank began work on a new album, "Ol' Blue Eyes Is Back." Up until that time, he had never been known as Ol' Blue Eyes. The nickname came from an art director at Reprise Records, and the tag stuck. He would forever after be identified by the name of that album.

On his TV special in 1973 Frank, nearing the age of sixty, faced the world again with a "rug" on his head, jowls on his face, and, in the words of one critic, "movements that were once panther-tense, but now are self-conscious hoodlum bustle."

Nevertheless, he was wildly cheered when he sang:

*I know I said that I was leaving*
*But I just couldn't say good-bye*
*It was only self-deceiving*
*. . . Let me try again.*

Cecil Smith, writing in *The Los Angeles Times*, noted that Frank was "puffier, rounder in the jaw, and had a paunch."

*Variety* claimed, "Not much of that voice remains." But *The New York Times* claimed that Sinatra's "new material seems almost calculated to capture the new mellowness, the effective element of a bittersweet maturity."

For the most part, the reviews were devastating, the ratings poor. As for the album, *Ol' Blue Eyes Is Back*, only serious aficionados bought it.

As Frank hit the comeback trail, he found that he still had old fans in the press, notably Kay Gardella of *The New York Times*. She wrote: "In a way, it's like a champ returning to defend his title. When Sinatra came out of retirement, he came out swinging. For a man who wanted a quiet place in the sun in Palm Springs in place of glaring spotlights, his turnabout rocked a musical world inundated with rock, young groups and new faces, but one that was not entirely ready to place Ol' Blue Eyes in the musical archives."

## *Politics and the Mob: Blowing Sinatra's Horn*

Hubert Humphrey had reason to worry about Frank's ties to the mob. It was during the filming of one of his worst films, *Come Blow Your Horn* (1963) that its director, Bud Yorkin, is reported to have said jokingly: "This Paramount film is the one that Frank made with Sam Giancana." It was shot during the most intense period of Frank's relationship with the Chicago Mobster. *Come Blow Your Horn* was based on a Neil Simon Broadway play. Frank's supporting cast included Lee J. Cobb, Molly Picon, Barbara Rush, and Jill St. John.

Prior to its filming, Frank and Giancana were seen playing golf on the courses together outside Las Vegas. The gangster was a frequent visitor to Frank's villa in Palm Springs, attracting FBI attention.

Frank took Giancana to Hoboken for one of Dolly's big Italian banquets that took her three days to prepare. With the party was Phyllis McGuire, Giancana's girlfriend. While at Dolly's dinner, Frank offered her the role of Mrs. Eckman, a buyer for Neiman-Marcus in *Come Blow Your Horn*. She accepted the part only after Giancana approved.

Giancana showed up every day Phyllis had a scene to shoot. "He hovered about," Lee J. Cobb said. "He didn't kill anybody—just sat there watching. I think he wanted to make sure we treated his gal right."

Phyllis was a singer with the McGuire Sisters, and their road manager, Victor LaCroix Collins, also visited the set. "From what I saw, Frank was brown-nosing Sam. He practically ran errands for him. Usually everybody catered to Frank, but when Sam was around, Frank was the Go-Fer. He even presented Sam with a star sapphire, some sort of a Mafia 'love ring.'"

The film got some good reviews, but mostly it was attacked by the critics, Bosley Crowther of *The New York Times* citing "vapid boredom." He also wrote that Frank is "so indifferent that he moves and talks in the manner of a well-greased mechanical man."

In spite of the pans, Frank still managed to win a Golden Globe Award nomination as Best Actor in a Comedy or Musical.

# Frank Sinatra and The Reagans

## A LOVE TRIANGLE

This photograph, taken on July 5, 1981 at the White House on the occasion of Nancy Reagan's sixtieth birthday party, shocked the nation. It was published on the frontpages of newspapers throughout the United States, even abroad.

**Nancy** was dancing in the arms of "the man of my dreams," **Frank** himself, although he's wearing one of his worst *toupées*. She obviously regrets the intrusion of her husband, **Ronald Reagan**, who always suspected that "something was always going on between those two."

Frank was well aware of Nancy's "scarlet past," as some reporters in Hollywood of the 1940s defined it. Long before she even dreamed of becoming First Lady of America, Nancy Davis was an attractive and ambitious starlet known otherwise as "The Fellatio Queen of Hollywood," as described by Kitty Kelley in her unauthorized biography.

As an aspiring actress in the late 1940s and early 50s, she had dalliances with Clark Gable, Peter Lawford, Spencer Tracy, Milton Berle, Alfred Drake, and Yul Brynner. Reagan himself was a handsome man about town. His conquests didn't match those of Frank's, but included such A-list names as Lana Turner, Betty Grable, Doris Day, Ruth Roman, Ann Sothern, and even a very young Marilyn Monroe.

**Ronald Reagan and Nancy Davis** are seen as a happy couple on their wedding day on March 4, 1952. She'd finally won her long-sought-after prize, a future president of the United States, although she could hardly have imagined that at the time. Reagan's best friend, actor/dancer George Murphy (later a U.S. senator from California) urged his pal not to marry Nancy—"too mousy and no personality," but Reagan went ahead anyway.

Unlike Reagan's first wife, Jane Wyman, Nancy pretended to be vitally interested in Reagan's political views, listening to him talk for hours. She used every feminine wile to attract his attention, later telling Spencer Tracy, "I am wholeheartedly in love."

But Reagan wasn't ready to commit. He was still vaguely considering proposing to Doris Day. But fear of an "early" pregnancy drove him to the altar with Nancy.

In 1957, the studio thought it might be inspired casting to put the husband-and-wife team together in *Hellcats of the Navy*. It wasn't.

FRANK ON RONALD REAGAN:
"A STUPID BORE WHO CAN'T
GET A JOB IN PICTURES"

FRANK ON NANCY REAGAN:
"A DUMB BROAD WITH FAT ANKLES
WHO CAN'T ACT"

Starlet Nancy Davis was first attracted to Frank in the late 40s, when she was introduced to him in the MGM commissary where he was seated at table with Judy Garland, Elizabeth Taylor, Lana Turner, and Esther Williams, all of whom at some point already had or would co-star with him either in his movies or his bed.

When these glamorous women left, Nancy had remained behind to speak to Frank privately. "Talk about insecurity," she said. "What if you had to go into makeup every morning, and you found yourself seated between Ava Gardner and Elizabeth Taylor."

"They're just dames," he told her. "You look great. When Liz or Ava wake up in my bed, they look like hell before they apply that God damn grease paint."

Katharine Hepburn, a friend of Frank's, was very outspoken on the subject of Frank and Nancy. She shared her opinion with director George Cukor, who spread the rumors around. "Personally, I think Nancy wanted Sinatra more than she wanted Reagan," Kate claimed. "I know she went for him in a big way around 1948 and 1949. I'm sure Nancy wanted to take him away from his other Nancy. But Frank told me Miss Nancy Davis, girl starlet, wasn't his type at all."

Marilyn Maxwell recalled that she attended a party in the mid- 1960s with Frank. "Reagan and his squaw, Nancy, arrived and were welcomed by the host. Frank grabbed my arm. 'Come on, babe, we're out of here. I can't stand the fucker. Wind up a Reagan doll, and he starts spouting politics.' Jane Wyman told me he should always be standing on a soap box. He's a golly shucks kind of guy, a real gee whiz right-wing dope."

On September 19, 1959, Frank was asked to host a luncheon at 20th Century Fox in honor of Nikita Khrushchev. Such stars as Cary Grant, Elizabeth Taylor, and Marilyn Monroe were only too eager to meet the Soviet leader. But when Frank called to invite Reagan, he was told, "I wouldn't even be in the same room with this bloody dictator."

"I'll take that as a no," Frank said sarcastically.

His longtime valet, George Jacobs, wrote a memoir, *My Life with Frank Sinatra*. In it, he exposed Frank's opinion of the Reagans in the 1960s.

"Mr. S. was apoplectic that a bozo, or Bonzo, like Reagan would have the audacity to run for any office higher than dogcatcher. If anyone in Hollywood should be governor, it was Mr. S. Besides, at the time, Sinatra was still a liberal."

Jacobs claimed that Frank saw the candidate running for governor as a "right wing John Bircher, a Pacific Palisades Klansman."

Over the years, Frank had made fun of Nancy, and he claimed that she had attempted to seduce him when she was a starlet at MGM during the late 1940s. "If you liked gals, you could have her," he told Gene Kelly.

Frank loved beautiful legs, the type he'd known on Betty Grable, Marilyn Monroe, Ava Gardner, and Lana Turner, among countless others. "Nancy Davis has fire hydrant legs," he was fond of saying.

Frank was slow to warm to the Reagans. "He despised Reagan as much as he did Nixon," said Peter Lawford. "He didn't like Nancy either. He knew that she and I had been lovers."

When California Gov. Edmund (Pat) Brown, a Democrat, sought his third term as governor in 1966, Frank supported him against his challenger, Reagan himself. Frank staged benefits for Brown in both San Francisco and Los Angeles.

In his benefits for Brown, Frank lined up an armada of stars, including Ella Fitzgerald, Joey Bishop, Connie Francis, Dan Rowan, Dick Martin, the Smothers Brothers, and Dean Martin, with Nelson Riddle's orchestra providing the music.

Reagan's arsenal of stars include Irene Dunne, Roy Rogers, John Wayne, and Pat Boone. Frank called Boone's singing "syrupy—Mr. Goodie Two-Shoes, a real jerk. John Wayne is an asshole, and the 'King of the Cowboys' is to the right of Josef Goebbels."

When Reagan defeated Brown, Frank said, "Son of a bitch. Can you believe that this asshole is going to be governor? I'm leaving California. Selling my house. I've told Mia [Farrow] to start packing our bags."

As the newly installed First Lady of California, Nancy Reagan called Frank and asked him to partici-

Actress **Barbara Rush** is seen here seated between **Ronald Reagan** (left) and **Frank Sinatra** at Puccini's Restaurant in Beverly Hills. A former Democrat, Reagan was moving to the right. Frank would follow in his footsteps a decade later.

A Denver-born beauty, twelve years younger than Frank, Barbara doesn't get mentioned in most Sinatra biographies. But for a time, he was immensely attracted to her and considered "putting the moves on her." But nothing much ever came of that.

Frank worked with her in the 1963 movie *Come Blow Your Horn,* in which their lips certainly came together. Their screen smooch was used in publicity stills.

In the movie, Alan (Frank) proposes to Connie (Barbara), marries her, patches up a marital split between his parents, and bequeaths his bachelor pad to his younger brother.

Frank liked Barbara so much that he also cast her in *Robin and the 7 Hoods* (1964), co-starring Dean Martin and Sammy Davis Jr. In that movie, Barbara was cast as the daughter of a bigtime gangster evocative of Sam Giancana.

In the film, she offers Robbo (Frank) $50,000 to kill the men who murdered her father.

pate in an upcoming concert. He slammed down the phone on her.

Throughout the 1960s, Frank made disparaging remarks about Nancy, the most notorious of which was when he called her "a dumb broad with fat ankles who can't act."

In his Las Vegas acts, he changed the words to his hit. "The Lady Is a Tramp." The song states, "She hates California where it's cold and it's damp." He changed the lyrics to "She hates California, it's Reagan and damp."

Gradually, while Reagan sat in the governor's seat, Nancy won Frank over to their side. She was reported to have had many long face-to-face conversations with him. He later told his friends that "Nancy is misunderstood. She's picked on by the press same as I am. She's not some cold, heartless cunt but a very sensitive woman who has warm feelings for her friends and a love of her country."

Even though he remained a registered Democrat, Frank shocked his friends on July 9, 1970 when he announced that he was supporting Ronald Reagan in the Republican's bid for a second term as governor of California. Frank was a liberal and Reagan to him had been "a stuffy uptight shit with no imagination."

So, why was he supporting him? There may have been a hidden motive. Running against Reagan was Jesse Unruh, former speaker of the California Assembly. He had been a *protégé* and early supporter of Bobby Kennedy, and Frank's hatred of Bobby had not diminished over the years since his assassination. He told Sammy Davis Jr., "I'll get even with the Kennedys if it's the last thing I ever do."

When Lyndon B. Johnson, another Democrat, took over the U.S. Presidency after JFK's assassination, he loudly proclaimed, "I am not a Sinatra fan. I can't stand that guy's singing. I like Western singers. Now, take Gene Autry. That's a real singer, not this Sinatra mobster. Also, I heard the fucker said I wasn't elegant like those Camelot Kennedys 'cause I conduct some of my business with men while I sit on the toilet. Hell, Louis XIV did the same thing."

Steve Allen sent Frank an open letter reminding him of some of Reagan's statements. In 1962, the future American president had made a comment about African Americans: "In their own country they're eating each other for lunch."

Frank claimed he supported the GOP platform—"except for abortion." Considering all the abortions he had arranged over the years,

A lineup of mixed political persuasions showed up in Sacramento on January 5, 1971 for the Inaugural Gala of Ronald Reagan, newly elected governor of California. From left to right are **Frank Sinatra, Governor Reagan, Vicki Carr, Nancy Reagan, Dean Martin, John Wayne, and Jack Benny.**

Later, Dean asked Frank, "What in hell am I doing here? I don't hate niggers, Jews, or faggots."

The gala marked the night that John Wayne told Frank, "Let's bury the hatchet now that we're playing on the same team."

"It's okay, Duke," Frank responded. "Over the years we've had things in common. Like you, I went to extraordinary lengths to get out of active duty. At least you got to fight World War II on the screen."

At that point, Dean Martin walked over to join Frank and Wayne. "Now take Dean here," Frank said. "He told me he got the first real fright of his life when he received his draft notice. Thank God he was saved by claiming a double hernia."

he could hardly go along with the so-called "pro-lifers." Had he done so, it might also have been disrespectful of his mother, Dolly Sinatra, who had performed countless abortions in Hoboken.

After spending most of his professional life mocking Reagan behind his back, he was now referring to him as "Ronnie."

Dean Martin claimed that "Frank liked to stay close to the center of power regardless of party affiliation. In his heart, he was always a Democrat just pretending to be a right-winger."

At Governor Reagan's inaugural gala in Sacramento in 1971, Frank flew in, giving Nancy a big kiss and Reagan a bear hug.

Although Frank did not spend many private evenings with the Reagans, he was always encountering them at galas. Nancy may have been jealous, but she, along with Reagan, showed up in Rancho Mirage when Frank married showgirl Barbara Marx, who long ago had dumped Zeppo.

The ceremony was held on July 11, 1976, at the estate of media baron Walter Annenberg, a close friend of the Reagans. Spiro Agnew also showed up, as did Frank's close friends, Kirk Douglas and Gregory Peck.

After the completion of his second term as governor in 1975, Reagan and Nancy kept Frank in their camp during his long run for the presidency. In 1980 he ran against sitting President Jimmy Carter, whom Frank called "that redneck peanut farmer from Georgia." In the aftermath of that election, Reagan, as we know, unseated an unpopular sitting president (Carter) who went down to a bitter defeat.

In January of 1981, Frank once again hosted a presidential gala, raising some $5 million for the event, making it the most expensive inaugural in American history.

As Frank had conceived it, the first Reagan inaugural gala was a three-hour show staged in front of 20,000 GOP supporters. In his $3,000 form-fitting tuxedo, Frank escorted the president-elect and Nancy to throne-like chairs covered in blue velvet. He later said, "The two of them looked like they were about to be crowned King and Queen of America. It was more of a coronation than anything else."

The gala was held at a giant sports arena, the Capital Center, in Landover, Maryland. Frank had lined up a series of performers who included everybody from Ethel Merman to Bob Hope, with Johnny Carson functioning as master of ceremonies.

Carson ran the show, with his usual quips, ridiculing how exclusive the $500 to $2,000 tickets were. "I went to the men's room and found it was by invitation only."

Merman, the "gal pal" of J. Edgar Hoover and his lover, Clyde Tolson, sang "Everything's Comin' Up Roses." She altered the lyrics: "I had a dream, a dream about you Ronnie baby."

The Reagans' old friend, Jimmy Stewart, repeated the tired old line that Jack Warner, Reagan's former boss, had said when he heard the actor was seeking the presidency. "No, Jimmy Stewart for president," he quoted Warner, "Reagan as his best friend."

In an outrageous example of political incorrectness, Ben Vereen appeared in blackface. Several critics noted they'd never seen such a portrayal of black stereotypes since Stepin Fetchit left the screen.

Frank took the mike. "I should like to do something special for our new First Lady. This is one of my favorite songs, and we've had just a little change in the lyrics. And I hope you'll like this, Nancy."

He sang "Nancy with the Laughing Face," which had originally been an homage to his first-born, Nancy Jr.

*"I'm so proud that you're First Lady, Nancy.*
*Also so pleased that I'm sort of a chum.*
*The next eight years will be fancy as fancy as they come.*
*Nancy, Nancy, Nancy, with the smiling face."*

When Frank sang that Nancy song to the First Lady, the crowd at the inaugural noticed that she seemed to be gazing at him with glazed eyes. That night the rumors started flying that she was actually in love with him.

"Nancy was very flirtatious with Frank," claimed Ethel Merman. "He told me that she had long had a crush on him. Later that night Nancy herself told me that Frank was the most attractive and the sexiest man she'd ever met. She was one gone gal. And she had even shacked up with Clark Gable, among countless others. That didn't say much for Gable, now did it?"

Frank had set out to impress, but he was appalled by the press reviews the next day. The acerbic movie critic, Rex Reed, called it "a cross between *Dial-a-Joke* and *Hee Haw*." Tom Shales in *The Washington Post* dismissed it as a "Kiwanis Club talent contest."

Barbara Marx Sinatra accompanied Frank to the inauguration ceremonies in front of the U.S. Capitol. Evocative of the Kennedy inauguration, Frank was furious to discover he'd been excluded from the "chosen few," the one hundred people given special passes for viewing. "To hell with this," he told a security guard, barging right by him and taking a choice spot, even without an invitation. No one dared evict him from the stand.

This photograph snapped in Sacramento in 1970 shows **Frank Sinatra** *(left)*, **Nancy Reagan,** and **Ronald Reagan**. Usually, when Nancy was around Frank, she gazed wistfully into his blue eyes. But in this picture, she gazes adoringly at her husband, who had made her First Lady of California.

Frank used to tell his friends that he thought Ronald Reagan was stupid. But when Reagan ran for reelection as governor of California in 1970, Frank backed him. The news hit Los Angeles like the explosion of a political time bomb. In a statement to the press, Frank claimed he'd known Reagan for two decades and that both of them wanted what was best for the people of California.

As an afterthought, Frank added, "I don't agree with everything Ronnie does, and I am the first to tell him so."

Reactions from the very liberal disbanded Rat Pack were swift, Joey Bishop referring to it as "shocking."

"It figures," Peter Lawford said enigmatically, not explaining what he meant."

Frank told some Republican stalwart standing next to him, "Without me, Reagan would never have been elected."

In the White House, Nancy played Frank's music over the public address systems day and night, especially her favorite, "Strangers in the Night." Reagan was said to be annoyed by Nancy's "schoolgirl crush" on Frank. "We grow out of these things. In the 1940s I fell in love with my leading ladies, but I got over it soon enough. Usually after the picture was finished."

During Nancy's first year as First Lady in Washington, Frank defended her to Larry King in a radio interview. Nancy was being attacked for her *haute couture* wardrobe, her immaculate grooming, and even the new and expensive china she'd selected for the White House. On the show Frank revealed that Nancy did not spend $200,000 of taxpayers' dollars on the china, but accepted it as a gift to the White House from some anonymous donor.

Unlike the rejections he'd endured

during the days of Camelot, Frank was invited to numerous White House functions and fund-raising events. Reagan told his staff, "We raise more money at these things when Frank shows up."

When Kennedy was elected president, Frank had every hope that he would become a White House insider. That didn't happen, but his dream came true with the Reagans. He was even invited to their most intimate birthday celebrations.

Sometimes he was asked embarrassing questions. When it was discovered that Ron Reagan Jr. was a ballet dancer, there was press speculation that he might be gay. In New York, Frank was asked about this, because it was assumed that Nancy had discussed her son with him. Frank delivered an answer he knew no paper would print. "I don't know if Ron Jr. is gay or not. He hasn't sucked my dick."

Ron Jr. had an answer to Frank. He told friends that "I am ashamed of my parents for maintaining that friendship with Sinatra."

Frank was invited to celebrate Reagan's seventieth birthday party on February 6, 1981. A picture snapped that night became notorious. Frank and Nancy were dancing, bodies pressed close together. The president cut in, much to Nancy's annoyance. She looked as if she were practically swooning in Frank's arms, resenting the intrusion of her husband.

Nearly every paper in the country ran that revealing photograph. Reagan aide Michael Deaver stormed into the office of the chief White House photographer. "You dumb shit," he shouted at him. "What a stupid idiot. The whole world will now know that Nancy is in love with Sinatra."

A White House aide said that Nancy carried around that picture of Frank and herself dancing for years, but she cut Reagan out of the photograph.

Frank, jokingly or otherwise, later told Sammy Davis Jr., "Here I was pressing my big hard-on against Nancy to give her a thrill. Then Reagan cuts in, leaving me without my shield. I'm standing in the middle of the dance floor with this huge erection and no place to hide it."

In March of 1981, Frank was performing at Caesars Palace in Las Vegas when he heard that Reagan had been shot in Washington. Although he was scheduled to give a final performance, he cancelled it to fly to Washington to comfort Nancy.

**Frank Sinatra** *(left)* campaigned with his newly acquired friend, **Ronald Reagan**, when he sought reelection as governor of California in 1970. The comedian **Pat Henry** stands behind the two men.

"Before we could work together, we had to bury a bloody hatchet," Frank confided to Dean Martin and the very liberal Shirley MacLaine.

When Reagan functioned in the 1940s as president of the Screen Actors Guild, he had suspected Frank of being a communist, and played a role in how close Frank came to being blacklisted by the House Un-American Activities Committee. Frank later learned that Reagan had supplied damaging information to the committee.

Frank had recorded a song, "*The House I Live In (That's America to Me),*" written by Earl Robinson and Lewis Allen. The song appeared as part of a ten-minute short film of the same name written by accused communist Albert Maltz, who was blacklisted from all aspects of Hollywood production, and was eventually included in the public eye as a member of the infamous "Hollywood Ten."

Produced by Mervyn LeRoy, the film, which was shown in theaters across America, was really about anti-Semitism and racial prejudice. The film received an honorary Oscar.

But during the witch hunt for Reds during the late 1940s and early 50s, Frank was labeled "a commie" by Reagan and others because of his association with people in the film industry like Maltz.

Referring to the White House, she told him, "It's a big house when you're here all alone."

Elizabeth Taylor was in Washington starring in the play, *The Little Foxes*. She called Frank and told him to tell Nancy that she was canceling her show in remembrance of Reagan and with hope for his speedy recovery. Frank delivered the message, but with a stinging bite. "Liz has gotten real fat. That gal has really let herself go."

In Tina Sinatra's memoir, *My Father's Daughter*, she revealed that Nancy Reagan, right after the attempted assassination of her husband, was calling Frank every night for long talks. She had learned that Barbara and Frank had separated.

Seen in social triumphs at the White House, **Frank Sinatra** was frequently photographed with **Nancy Reagan**, who adored him, and **Ronald Reagan**, who smiled and put on a brave front, although he privately resented Frank, suspecting (rightly or wrongly) that his wife was in love with the crooner.

In the upper photo, Frank is congratulated by Nancy and the president for being a recipient of the Kennedy Center's Honor for Lifetime Achievement. On the same night, James Stewart, Elia Kazan, and dancer Katherine Dunham were also honored. Gene Kelly told the audience, "There is not the remotest possibility that Frank will have a successor."

The lower photo was taken on January 19, 1985, after Frank had performed at the Presidential Inaugural Gala, singing "We, the People."

The night before, he'd performed at Vice President George Bush's inaugural program. When Frank was cornered by the press, Bush snapped, *"Leave him alone! Just leave him alone!"*

When Nancy reached Frank on the phone, he told her that he wanted to talk things over with his estranged wife, but had to wait for her to finish her massage.

"You have to wait for her *massage* before you can see her?" Nancy said. "Francis, this woman is not for you. She's not going to make you happy. You've got one foot out the door—keep going."

Frank didn't listen to Nancy's advice and came back together again with his wife.

Another White House secretary claimed that Nancy became hysterical when preparing herself to go and hear Frank at a May 7, 1981 luncheon in her honor at the Congressional Club in Washington. "She changed her outfit six times just to impress him. "If Francis Albert," as she called him, "is coming to town just to see me, I'm going to look my best for him."

Frank also showed up on July 5, 1981 in Washington for Nancy's sixtieth birthday party. There was always some confusion about her age. She was born on July 6, 1921 but had given the year of her birth as 1923 on many an occasion.

"At least she shaved only two years off," Frank was quoted as saying. "Marlene Dietrich shaved a decade off."

The "dancing with Frank" photograph may have done damage enough, but then along came Kitty Kelley's biography of Nancy, published in 1991. In it, she insinuated that whenever Frank visited Nancy at the White House for a private luncheon, only when Reagan was gone, these visits turned into sexual trysts.

There have been many denials of an affair between Nancy and Frank, but according to Kelley, one White House staff member, who refused to be named, later claimed he walked in on Frank while he was lying on top of Nancy deep kissing her. He did report, however, they were fully clothed. "They were so into each other that I quickly got my ass out of there. I don't know what happened next, but I can imagine."

A California friend of Nancy's, who also refused to be

named, said, "I knew that Frank and Nancy were having sex. It did her good. She wasn't getting a lot from Ronnie by then. Frank could still get it up, and Nancy was the horny broad she always was. I'm glad she got some pleasure out of her life, although privately Nancy was calling herself 'the old crone.'"

In her unauthorized biography, Kelley was the first major author to "out" the affair of Frank and Nancy. The biographer quoted a White House staffer: "Nancy usually would arrange those 'lunches' with Sinatra when the president was out of town, and they'd last from 12:30 to 3:30 or 4:30pm. All calls were put on hold. We were told not to disturb. No matter what. When the First Lady was with Frank Sinatra, she was not to be disturbed. For anything. And that included a call from the president himself."

After the worldwide release of the Kelley book, Frank threatened to sue her for suggesting that he'd had an affair with the First Lady in the White House. His lawyers talked him out of it. "It would be a media circus," Frank was warned by one of his attorneys. "And Nancy would be dragged into it. The defense would bring up all that shit about her being the former Fellatio Queen of Hollywood. Both of you would go down in disgrace."

In 1981, Frank applied for a Nevada gaming license, in spite of his links to the mob. He had to prove that he was a person of good character, and he brought such heavy duty witnesses as Gregory Peck and Kirk Douglas to testify on his behalf. Although Ronald and Nancy Reagan did not appear as character witnesses, their names were on the list of personal references submitted to the Nevada board.

President Reagan wrote the board a letter of recommendation, claiming that Frank was "an honorable person, completely loyal and honest."

With that letter from Reagan, I got my sweet revenge for Jack Kennedy considering me too controversial to be my house guest in Palm Springs."

Frank even brought the sheriff of Los Angeles to a meeting of the Nevada board, who testified, "If Mr. Sinatra is a member of the Mafia, then I'm the Godfather."

The Nevada board voted four-to-one to grant Frank a "key employee license."

"I am not suggesting that Frank Sinatra is a saint, by any means, but in the areas we have investigated, we have not found any substantive reason why he shouldn't have a gaming license." So said Richard Bunker, the head of the Nevada Gaming Control Board.

Having been cleared by the board, Frank could go

**Frank Sinatra** tried to avoid **Ronald Reagan** whenever he could. But in the picture above, taken in the 1950s, they accidentally ran into each other in a line-up for coffee at a public event.

Long before Reagan entered politics, they sometimes talked about women. Reagan had learned that Frank was "shacked up" with Marilyn Monroe. Reagan admitted that he'd had an off-the-record weekend with Monroe when he took her on a trip to Miami Beach in the late 1940s.

"She fell madly in love with me, but I had to tell her it couldn't be between us. A gal like Marilyn just doesn't fit into my plans."

To her friend Shelley Winters, Marilyn claimed that Reagan was "the only man I know who took a shower before and after sex. He was not terribly passionate, though. He felt my breasts but didn't go in for armpit licking and toe sucking, like some guys."

on to earn $8,000 a week in his role as a "consultant" at Caesars Palace in Las Vegas. After the hearings, he proclaimed, "I am completely cleared of all Mafia links." That was, of course, a vast overstatement of the facts.

When Nancy heard that he had been approved for a gaming license from the Nevada board, she was the first to call him to congratulate him. That night, she told Reagan, "Isn't this the greatest news you've ever heard?"

"Not really," he said. "For me the greatest news was the end of WWII with the good guys winning."

Usually Nancy was pleased with Frank's sponsorship of major events. But all went wrong during the visit of Queen Elizabeth to the United States in March of 1983. Nancy designated Frank as producer of her state dinner for the queen.

But when he learned that he had not been invited for a dinner the following night aboard the Queen's yacht, H.M.S. *Britannia*, he threatened to withdraw as sponsor of her dinner. Through various appeals and manipulations, the queen reluctantly, and only under pressure, agreed to invite Frank.

At Nancy's welcoming dinner for the queen, Frank "blew it," as he later admitted, forgetting his lines and stumbling awkwardly. He blew kisses to Nancy but ignored the queen, forgetting to welcome her.

"Frank was at his worst," Bette Davis said. "He thought he was performing at some drunken Rat Pack show in Vegas. He didn't even introduce me to the queen. Fred Astaire and Jimmy Stewart were also ignored."

To top things off, Frank left the dinner before the queen did, a violation of royal protocol. Most of the British press, in Washington covering the event, denounced Frank and the event as "filled with mistakes, outrageously bad, and a tedious bore."

With the Reagans in the White House, **Frank Sinatra** had finally achieved what he'd failed to do during the Kennedy years. He was a frequent guest at state dinners. He is seen here enjoying amusing conversation with **the First Lady** and **the President of Sri Lanka** on June 18, 1984.

Frank had been called upon to stage the January, 1981, Inaugural Gala when Reagan was elected to his first term.

For the program, Frank lined up an impressive array of talent, everyone from Jimmy Stewart to Bob Hope, to those less talented as entertainers, notably General Omar N. Bradley. He'd also asked Charlton Heston, but warned him, "Don't bring a rifle. This is not an NRA convention."

What he didn't tell the president was that twenty performers he'd called had rejected the invitation, protesting how much they detested "Reagan and his right-wing friends.'

Although Frank had made it a point never to bring his wife, Barbara, to the White House lunches he shared with Nancy Reagan, he did bring her to White House state dinners, where Nancy demanded that Frank occupy the seat directly next to her own. At such events, she "sent Mrs. Sinatra to Siberia for her seat and placed her between the two most boring people at the dinner," claimed a White House secretary.

As he lavished attention on Nancy when she was First Lady, Barbara fumed, especially when she heard that Frank had offered to buy Nancy the Bulgari jewelry she'd borrowed to wear to the London wedding of Prince Charles to Lady Diana.

When Reagan sought reelection in 1984, he once again called on Frank for fund raising. Flying to seven cities for appearances and cocktail parties, Frank raised half a million dollars for Reagan's successful campaign.

During Reagan's 1984 reelection campaign, Frank returned to Hoboken, showing up on the president's arm. The last time Frank had been in Hoboken, a lot of guys threw rotten tomatoes at him when he came out on stage. Maybe they were jealous of a hometown boy who had made good.

But when he showed up with this "old, old man," Reagan, the crowds cheered him. Hoboken itself had changed. The city seemed to have decided that it loved Frank after all. They even had opened a shrine to him at the public library.

Hoboken was a blue collar town that normally voted Democratic, but Reagan hoped that by appearing with the city's most famous hometown boy, he could sway voters. Both of them attended the Festival of St. Ann during that July of 1984. The festival honored the mother of the Virgin Mary, the patron saint of women.

Embarrassing Frank, Reagan delivered an attack on the practice of abortion, all this in front of Frank whose mother was still remembered as "Hat Pin Dolly."

Not able to stand the scrutiny, particularly because he'd authorized so many abortions on his girlfriends, including Elizabeth Taylor, Frank skipped out of town early. He told the president he had to appear at a concert in Hartford, Connecticut.

Once he returned to Manhattan, Frank had few kind words for his hometown. "Ronnie and I were there for about half an hour. Everything's changed, everything's different. I don't know anyone there any more, so I don't plan to go back."

He was even more emphatic to reporters. "I have no plans to ever set foot in New Jersey. As for me, America consists of just forty-nine states."

Frank's anger at New Jersey grew especially heated when he faced charges from the New Jersey Casino Control Commission. It was alleged that he had intimidated four workers at the Golden Nugget Casino in Atlantic City, getting them to "break blackjack rules." The Golden Nugget was fined $25,000 for this infraction.

Frank was appearing as a performer at the hotel with Dean Martin. At the end of their gig, he told Martin, "I'm out of here. My last visit. I've got no more friends in Jersey. The bastards have turned on me."

Actually Frank did go back to his home state. Ten months after his visit to Hoboken with Reagan, the Stevens Institute of Technology awarded him an honorary doctorate. Even that honor brought protests from some students. "We worked for our degrees," said one irate student. "What did Sinatra do? I heard he never finished the sixth grade before dropping out."

When Reagan once again put Frank in charge of an inaugural gala—this time Reagan's second, in the wake of his re-election in 1976, an editorial in the *New York Daily News* shouted: FIND ANOTHER SINGER.

When he was presented with a newspaper editorial by Joseph Kraft claiming that Reagan's

**Frank Sinatra** is seen on the campaign trail in 1984 with **Ronald and Nancy Reagan**, when he was seeking reelection as president of the United States.

Barbara Marx, Frank's final and fourth wife, came to resent Nancy's calling her husband all the time—"and not just because she flirts outrageously with him."

Barbara complained that Nancy constantly took up Frank's time, seeking his help in causes she espoused. "I felt that she took a little too much advantage of Frank's huge heart. She invited him frequently to perform at fund-raisers and dinners, often at the White House. I think he became her therapist more than her friend."

friendship with Frank was "sleazy," the president refused to read it.

On the eve of the inaugural, *The Washington Post* ran a very unfavorable article, "The Rat Pack is Back—Sinatra and his Sidekicks."

Captured on a TV camera, Barbara Howar, working for *Entertainment Tonight*, confronted Sinatra and grilled him about the article.

In front of the world—it was later played on TV—he turned in fury to attack her. "You read the *Post* this afternoon? You're all dead, every one of you. You're all dead!"

Frank's outburst on camera caused agitation at the White House, which was also under fire for Nancy's inaugural wardrobe, which was estimated to have cost more than $50,000.

Reagan ignored the protests, and Frank went to the White House to receive, on May 23, 1985, a presidential award, the Medal of Freedom, America's highest civilian honor.

Also sharing the Presidential Medal of Freedom honor with Frank was Mother Teresa, who flew to Washington to receive it.

In front of cameras, Reagan placed the medal around Frank's neck. He told the audience, "His love of country, his generosity for those less fortunate, his distinctive art, and his winning and compassionate persona make him one of the most remarkable and distinguished Americans, and one who truly did it his way."

In the White House, Reagan also appointed Frank to the president's Committee on the Arts and Humanities. When he did so, the press grilled him about Frank's alleged ties to the Mob. "We've heard those things about Frank for years," Reagan said weakly. "We just hope none of them are true."

Frank was insulted by the president's weak response. "Was that the best the great communicator could do?" he asked.

On Mother's Day, 1988, Don Regan, the former Chief of Staff to Ronald Reagan, released his memoirs of his days in the Reagan White House, about seven months before the end of Reagan's presidency. Nancy had always disliked Regan. In his remembrances, he got back at her, disclosing how she used astrology to force her husband to make decisions affecting the nation. In doing so, she was following in the footsteps of everybody from Mary Todd Lincoln to Adolf Hitler.

Without naming Don Regan specifically, Frank attacked the "pimps and whores" who write such confessions. "Suddenly they are out making a buck because they got a pigeon," Frank charged.

Although Reagan and his Nancy returned to California after he'd served two terms as president, Frank saw less and less of them. His own health was failing, yet he stayed in touch.

Long before the world knew that Reagan in his retirement was showing distinct signs of Alzheimer's disease, Nancy had alerted Frank "of this oncoming night."

His response was warm and sympathetic. "This is the saddest day of my life. I'll want to see him while he still knows who I am."

"I'm afraid there will come a time when he won't know even me," she said.

Frank predicted, "His last sight on earth will be of Nancy with her smiling face. Look deeply into his eyes. He'll know it's you."

On June 5, 2004, she did just that.

"Oh, Frank," she said quietly, perhaps to her own memories of Frank. "You were right. He knew. Ronnie *knew*."

Frank could not hear her, as he had already departed from this world six years prior to that, on May 14, 1998.

# Death and Eternity

## FACING THE FINAL CURTAIN

At a costume party in California, **Frank Sinatra** (*right*) was seeing longtime friends and companions, many for the last time. He gathered with **Milton Berle** (*left*) and **Burt Lancaster** (*center*), each of them dressed in Western garb, for a few laughs and remembrances of yesterday. Both men had met Frank in 1940 and had bonded for life.

Milton remembered appearing on a bill with Frank when he was with the Harry James band. When a man in the audience threw popcorn onto the stage, Frank jumped into the audience to punch him in the face. "The trouble with hanging out with Frank is that I always seemed to end up in fights," Milton said.

The bisexual actor, Burt Lancaster, who had a crush on Frank since their first meeting, once shared the embraces of Ava Gardner, but not at the same time, although Burt would have been willing. "You are one crazy mother fucker," Frank told Burt as they were saying goodbye for a final time. "I don't know why I've kept you around all these years."

"Because you love me, Frankie," Burt said. "You always did. We were brothers under the skin. Sooner than later, I'm going to be taking the night train to Heaven."

Burt was right, as he was the first to go, passing on on October 20, 1994. Four years later, Frank would die on May 14, 1998. Uncle Milton would outlast his friends, going on his way on March 27, 2002.

# "LAST NIGHT, WHEN WE WERE YOUNG"

As **Frank Sinatra** neared the end of his life, he loved going over albums of pictures from when he was young.

He told friends, "I was sorta cute. I could understand why the gals went wild for me. I didn't look like Tyrone Power, Robert Taylor, or Errol Flynn, the reigning matinee idols of my day, but they were faggots and I wasn't.

"I could really show a gal a good time. If I remember it, I showed quite a few of them a good time. On more than one occasion, I've run into some old broken down hag, married to some stuffed shirt, at a party. Many of them tell me, 'Don't you remember, Frankie? We did it in a seedy Times Square hotel back in 1943.' How can I be expected to remember after all these years? Besides, people change.

"If they're famous, I usually remember it. But lately, my memory grows dim. Did I—or did I not—screw Joan Crawford?"

*"Regrets, I've had a few."*
—**Frank Sinatra** on his dying bed.

By 1997, Frank Sinatra had reached the "deep December" of his years, at times hardly remembering the "fires of September" that had not made him mellow, but bitter.

The love of his life, Ava Gardner, had died in 1990.

His other loves of yesterday—Lana Turner, Marilyn Monroe—lived only on late night television.

The Rat Pack had long ago been exterminated. He hardly remembered Peter Lawford, dead in 1984, citing some "betrayal," although no one was sure what that was. Sammy Davis Jr. had died of cancer in 1990.

Shirley MacLaine failed in her attempts to speak to him. Frank Jr. had called three times in one week, but Frank Sr. wasn't available. He wasn't angry at his son, just withdrawn.

At one point he said, "Everybody still left is old and dying." He had memories of Claudette Colbert and Rosalind Russell, close friends. Russell had died in 1976, Colbert in 1996.

"It seems like yesterday they were here with me, and we were going sailing," Frank said.

A Merry Christmas was not celebrated in the home of Dean Martin. On that day in 1995, he had died at the age of seventy-eight. His liver and kidneys had been destroyed by alcohol, his lungs by thousands of cigarettes.

Frank did not attend Martin's funeral. But he suffered greatly at the "loss of my brother." Frank went into a weeks-long and very morbid depression. He told Barbara, "I'm next."

Frank felt deep guilt over Martin's death because he had never really made up with him after Martin had deserted their reunion tour in 1988. Martin had sent Frank an urgent message during the summer of 1995: "If we don't meet now, it's going to be too late."

Frank's reply was, "I'll think about it."

He never spoke about the death of his friends, only claiming that "they have gone to the mountain."

Long since divorced from Frank, Nancy Sr. would on occasion have a limousine deliver him her classic eggplant parmigiana which he savored, as he did jars of her spaghetti sauce that she sent over. "Now that Dolly is gone—she was the best—Nancy is a close runner-up when it comes to home cooking the way I like it."

Much to the annoyance of Frank's children, Barbara began to sell at auction some of Frank's once-valued possessions, including his 1976 Jaguar XJS which went for $79,500 and even his black lacquered grand piano which fetched $51,750. "No more songs for me," Frank said.

He and his wife, whom some people still referred to as "Barbara Marx," had already realized that the party was over and had sold their luxurious Rancho Mirage desert estate in 1995 for nearly $5 million. He had been the proud owner of it since 1954, when Eisenhower was president. They still retained their $5.2 million mansion in Beverly Hills and their $6 million beachfront home in Malibu.

He lived in Gatsby like opulence in Beverly Hills behind high security gates.

On May 1, 1993 Frank had drawn up the most recent version of his Last Will and Testament, dividing his multimillion-dollar estate among his fourth wife, Barbara, and his three children—Nancy Jr., Frank Jr., and Tina.

Knowing how much his offspring resented Barbara, Frank instructed his lawyers to put a "zinger" into the will—and they did. The document stated that if any of his heirs contested the will, he or she would automatically be disinherited.

On his eighty-first birthday on December 12, 1996, Nancy Jr. watched as he weakly blew out the candles on his banana shortcake. "What's your wish, dad?" she asked.

"Another birthday," he said.

Frank feared that this might be his last birthday on earth. After the sale of his home in Rancho Mirage, he had begun to miss it dearly. At one point, he looked around the vast ground floor of his Beverly Hills mansion and felt he'd checked into a hotel that was doing no business.

It was hard for him to do it, but Barbara urged him to begin auctioning off mementos of his life. When he finally agreed, he said, "There go the memories."

His paintings by every artist from Andrew Wyeth

At the dawn of the 1990s, **Frank Sinatra** said, "What a depressing decade. At long last, the time has come for all of us to die. I don't think any of us will make it to the millennium."

In spite of failing eyesight and hearing, he decided to die on stage.

He didn't have to. Financially, of course, he was a multimillionaire but he performed live, until—onstage—he eventually collapsed. "If I stop working, I know Death will come knocking on the door."

His first major heart attack hit him in November of 1996. Doctors discovered at the time that he had suffered a number of minor strokes prior to that. He also learned that he'd developed ureter cancer. "It won't be long now."

He finally came to view himself as "an American hero of sorts." But he'd quickly add, "But a very flawed one. When all the bad stuff is long forgotten, future generations will judge me only for my music."

to Grandma Moses went first. Many items put up for sale had been gifts from friends—a gold-and-silver cigarette case from composers Sammy Kahn and Jule Styne; a diamond-studded watch from Sammy Davis Jr.; two 1930s vintage radios over which Frank's singing voice was first heard; and a mounted bust of John F. Kennedy, his former house guest from friendlier days. Even his Bösendorfer grand piano was sold. "My life is disappearing out the door," he lamented.

A lot of collectors wanted a "piece of Sinatra" and an auction at Christie's brought $2 million. News of this auction alerted the press, who sent out investigative reporters to determine the state of his physical condition.

Above, an aging trio of Rat Packers performs on their final legs. Left to right, **Dean Martin, Frank Sinatra**, and **Sammy Davis Jr.** sing before an appreciative audience. Frank and Sammy wanted to go on a final tour which they thought would be called "The Together Again Tour," although their public quickly dubbed it "The Rat Pack Tour."

Dean was seventy years old, Frank two years younger, and Sammy ten years younger. Dean felt old and tired, but finally gave in to their wishes. When Sammy saw only three black musicians in the band, he demanded that Frank fire nine of the white musicans to make room for "more folks like me."

The tour began in Oakland, California, and the press came down hard on them, tagging them as "senior citizens."

Frank and Dean feuded because, according to Frank, Dean "didn't give a damn. He was drunk most of the time."

One night Frank got so exasperated with Dean, he picked up a plate of spaghetti and emptied it over Dean's head. That night, Dean checked out of the hotel and dropped out of the tour.

Later in his life, Frank seemed to regret his harsh treatment of Dean and stated, "Dean Martin was my brother. Not through blood but through choice. Our friendship traveled down many roads over the years, and there will always be a special place in my heart and soul for Dean."

The extent of his deterioration was first revealed in April of 1996 in the *National Enquirer*. The report, although attacked at the time, was accurate. The tabloid claimed that he was suffering from microangiopathy of the brain. This disease actually causes the brain to shrink in a patient, as the network of tiny blood vessels leading to the brain begin to wither.

There was a perception that, like his long-time friend Ronald Reagan, Frank was suffering from Alzheimer's disease. On a radio show, Nancy Jr. was asked about this. She claimed she didn't know for sure.

At times during the past few months, Frank didn't know where he was. When old friends came to call, he often didn't recognize them. He stunned long-time acquaintances by asking "Who are you?"

On certain days he would wake up and seem fairly coherent. Even so, he required 24-hour care from nurses.

In November of 1996, he made his last public appearance, singing at the Carousel Ball Benefit in Los Angeles. That same month he suffered a major heart attack and was rushed to Cedars-Sinai Hospital. He had also come down with pneumonia. Undergoing extensive tests, he was told by his doctors that cancer had been discovered in his ureter. Additionally, Barbara was informed, privately, of what she might have already known: Frank's brain scans revealed a diagnosis of dementia.

In his hospital bed, perhaps thinking he was dying, Frank summoned each of his three children to his side. He held each of their hands and looked deeply into their eyes. "Kids, I'm facing the final curtain."

Throughout America, newspapers were

preparing his obituaries. But Frank fooled them. His lungs cleared up, and he checked himself out, heading for Beverly Hills where he sat down in his living room and lit a Camel cigarette and asked a servant to bring him his favorite drink, a glass of Jack Daniels. "I came through," he told Barbara. "I showed the fuckers."

Sometimes Frank slept eighteen hours a day. He often watched his old movies. The last known movie he saw was *Guys and Dolls*. "Brando still can't sing," he said.

At times, Frank would slip into dementia as when he demanded that his mother, Dolly, be removed from his room. Barbara tried to comfort him. "Dolly is gone . . . gone forever."

The world was remembering him during the summer of 1997. Pushed through by Senator Alfonse D'Amato, a Republican from New York, Frank was awarded a Congressional Gold Medal. Previous honorees had included Frank's friends Bob Hope and John Wayne. (Frank and the Duke had agreed to put aside their differences).

An interview that Frank gave to Walter Cronkite in 1965 became almost an epitaph for Frank. "I think I would like to be remembered as a man who brought an innovation to popular singing, a peculiar, unique fashion that I wish one of these days somebody would learn to do so it doesn't die where it is. I would like to be remembered as a man who had a wonderful time living his life and who had good friends, a fine family, and I don't think I could ask for anything more than that, actually. I think that would do it."

Nancy Reagan called him shortly before his death. She seemed to sense that he was failing. He bluntly told her, "Dying is a pain in the ass."

And then it happened. Barbara was out of the house dining with friends when she received an urgent call to go to the Cedars-Sinai Hospital.

Leaving her dinner engagement, Barbara rushed to the hospital to find three doctors working on Frank. She took his bony hand and told him, "You have to fight, Frank."

He opened his blue eyes for one final time. In a voice that had once thrilled the world, he said, "I can't."

He closed those dazzling blue eyes for a final time, shutting out the world.

In the words of one radio announcer, Frank Sinatra "had a gig with eternity" on May 14, 1998. At 10:50pm, in the Emergency Room of the Cedars-Sinai Medical Center in Los Angeles, he suffered a fatal heart attack. Barbara had rushed to his side, without alerting her husband's children.

Tina Sinatra said, "My father did not die. He escaped."

For his burial, Frank's body was returned to the beloved desert at Palm Springs where he was placed in the ground beside Dolly and Marty.

At the top of his simple grave marker were the words THE BEST IS YET TO COME.

Lost in grief and standing at his grave side, Barbara, in a soft, barely audible voice, said, "The best has come and gone."

Frank Sinatra may have been a rascal in private moments of his life, and he often displayed violent outbursts in public, but he performed at more charity benefits than almost any performer of his era.

In the picture above, taken with **Dean Martin** (*left*) and **Jerry Lewis** (*right*), he surprised Dean by unexpectedly bringing out Jerry Lewis at a charity benefit for muscular dystrophy. The famous comedy team hadn't spoken in years.

# FRANCIS ALBERT SINATRA

## 1915-1998

*"May you live to be one hundred and the last voice you hear be mine."*

—**Frank Sinatra**

# About the Authors

## Darwin Porter

One of the world's leading celebrity biographers, **Darwin Porter**, as an intense and precocious nine-year-old, began meeting movie stars, TV personalities, politicians, and singers through his vivacious and attractive mother, Hazel, a somewhat eccentric Southern girl who had lost her husband in World War II. Migrating from the depression-ravaged valleys of western North Carolina to Miami Beach during its most ebullient heyday, Hazel became a stylist, wardrobe mistress, and personal assistant to the vaudeville comedienne Sophie Tucker, the bawdy and irrepressible "Last of the Red Hot Mamas."

Virtually every show-biz celebrity who visited Miami Beach paid a call on "Miss Sophie," and Darwin as a pre-teen loosely and indulgently supervised by his mother, was regularly dazzled by the likes of Judy Garland, Dinah Shore, Veronica Lake, Linda Darnell, Martha Raye, and Ronald Reagan, who arrived to pay his respects to Miss Sophie with a young blonde starlet on the rise—Marilyn Monroe.

Hazel's work for Sophie Tucker did not preclude an active dating life: Her *beaux* included Richard Widmark, Victor Mature, Frank Sinatra (who "tipped" teenaged Darwin the then-astronomical sum of ten dollars for getting out of the way), and that alltime "second lead," Wendell Corey, when he wasn't emoting with Barbara Stanwyck and Joan Crawford.

As a late teenager, Darwin edited *The Miami Hurricane* at the University of Miami, where he interviewed Eleanor Roosevelt, Tab Hunter, Lucille Ball, and Adlai Stevenson. He also worked for Florida's then-Senator George Smathers, one of John F. Kennedy's best friends, establishing an ongoing pattern of picking up "Jack and Jackie" lore while still a student.

After graduation, as a journalist, he was commissioned with the opening of a bureau of *The Miami Herald* in Key West (Florida), where he took frequent morning walks with retired U.S. president Harry S Truman during his vacations in what had functioned as his "Winter White House." He also got to know, sometimes very well, various celebrities "slumming" their way through off-the-record holidays in the orbit of then-resident Tennessee Williams. Celebrities hanging out in the permissive arts environment of Key West during those days included Tallulah Bankhead, Cary Grant, Tony Curtis, the stepfather of Richard Burton, a gaggle of show-biz and publishing moguls, and the once-notorious stripper, Bettie Page.

For about a decade in New York, Darwin worked in television journalism and advertising with his long-time partner, the journalist, art director, and distinguished arts-industry socialite Stanley Mills Haggart. Jointly, they produced TV commercials starring such high-powered stars as Joan Crawford (then feverishly promoting Pepsi-Cola), Ronald Reagan (General Electric), and Debbie Reynolds (selling Singer Sewing Machines), along with such other entertainers as Louis Armstrong, Lena Horne, Arlene Dahl, and countless other show-biz personalities hawking commercial products.

During his youth, Stanley had flourished as an insider in early Hollywood as a "leg man" and source of information for Hedda Hopper, the fabled gossip columnist. When Stanley wasn't dishing newsy revelations with Hedda, he had worked as a Powers model; a romantic lead opposite Silent-era film star Mae Murray; the intimate companion of superstar Randolph Scott before Scott became emotionally involved with Cary Grant; and a man-about-town who archived gossip from everybody who mattered back when the movie colony was small, accessible, and confident that details about their tribal rites would absolutely never be reported in the press. Over the years, Stanley's vast cornucopia of inside Hollywood information was passed on to Darwin, who amplified it with copious interviews and research of his own.

After Stanley's death in 1980, Darwin inherited a treasure trove of memoirs, notes, and interviews detailing Stanley's early adventures in Hollywood, including in-depth recitations of scandals that even Hedda Hopper during her heyday was afraid to publish. Most legal and journalistic standards back then interpreted those oral histories as "unprintable." Times, of course, changed.

Beginning in the early 1960s, Darwin joined forces with the then-fledgling Arthur Frommer organization, playing a key role in researching and writing more than 50 titles and defining the style and values that later emerged as the world's leading travel accessories, THE FROMMER GUIDES, with particular emphasis on Europe, California, and the Caribbean. Between the creation and updating of hundreds of editions of detailed travel guides to England, France, Italy, Spain, Portugal, Austria, Germany, California, and Switzerland, he continued to interview and discuss the triumphs, feuds, and frustrations of celebrities, many by then reclusive, whom he either sought out or encountered randomly as part of his extensive travels. Ava Gardner and Lana Turner were particularly insightful about Frank Sinatra.

Darwin has also written several novels, including the best-selling cult classic *Butterflies in Heat* (which was later made into a film, *Tropic of Desire,* starring Eartha Kitt), *Venus* (inspired by the life of the fabled eroticist and diarist, Anaïs N in), and *Midnight in Savannah,* a satirical overview of the sexual eccentricities of the Deep South inspired by Savannah's most notorious celebrity murder. He also transformed into literary format the details which he and Stanley Haggart had compiled about the relatively underpublicized scandals of the Silent Screen, releasing them in 2001 as *Hollywood's Silent Closet,* "an uncensored, underground history of Pre-Code Hollywood, loaded with facts and rumors from generations past." A few years later, he did the same for the country-western music industry when he issued *Rhinestone Country.*

Since then, Darwin has penned more than a dozen uncensored Hollywood biographies, many of them award-winners, on subjects who have included Marlon Brando, Merv Griffin, Katharine Hepburn, Howard Hughes, Humphrey Bogart, Michael Jackson, Paul Newman, and Steve McQueen. He's also co-authored, in league with Danforth Prince, four *Hollywood Babylon* anthologies, plus four separate volumes of film critiques, reviews, and commentary.

In 2011, Darwin, along with co-author Roy Moseley, won a total of four literary awards for *Damn You, Scarlett O'Hara—The Private Lives of Vivien Leigh and Laurence Olivier*. They included either First Prizes or Honorable Mentions from the San Francisco, Paris, and New York Book Festivals, and the coveted Grand Prize from the Beach Book Festival, which defined that title as "The Best Summer Reading of 2011," and as "the most forthright and honest biography of the Romeo and Juliet of the 20th century ever published."

Darwin is presently at work on a book about celebrity, voyeurism, poltical repression and blackmail within high-level circles of the U.S. government, *J. Edgar Hoover & Clyde Tolson: Investigating the Sexual Secrets of Amerca's Most Famous Men and Women*.

Darwin can be heard at regular interviews as a radio commentator discussing celebrity events, pop culture, and politics. He's also a Hollywood columnist, pouring out bi-weekly and monthly newsletters which include *Blood Moon's Dirty Laundry*, which anyone can receive without charge by registering an email address at **www.BloodMoonProductions.com**. Additionally, through South Florida's *Boomer Times Magazine*, he crafts a monthly column, *Hollywood Remembered,* about the complicated and competitive lives of players, past and present, in politics and the entertainment industry.

# Danforth Prince

**Danforth Prince**, president and founder of Blood Moon Productions and co-author of this book, is the hottest producer and publisher of celebrity exposés in America. In 2011, a respected consortium of literary critics and book marketers, The J.M. Northern Media Group, organizers of a string of literary award ceremonies across North America, defined him as "Publisher of the Year."

Publishing in collaboration with the National Book Network, he has documented some of the controversies associated with his work in more than 30 videotaped documentaries and book trailers, all of which can be watched, without charge, either on his company's website, **www.BloodMoonProductions.com,** or by performing a search for his name on YouTube or Vimeo.com.

During his early 20s, Prince was a resident of France, studying religion at the Catholic Institute and supporting himself as a building contractor, translator, and salesman in Paris' garment district. Prince launched his journalistic career in 1976 in the Paris bureau of *The New York Times*. Since his original encounter with Darwin Porter in 1982, he has also functioned as the co-author and director of research for as many as 50 of THE FROMMER GUIDES, describing and reviewing the hotels, restaurants, nightclubs, and cultural monuments of France, England, Italy, Germany, Switzerland, Austria, Portugal, Spain, Hungary, Morocco, the Caribbean, and America's Deep South.

A graduate of Hamilton College, and proud of his Moravian roots in Bethlehem, Pennsylvania, and distant ancestral roots to Harriet Beecher Stowe, he is a resident of New York City.

# Frank Sinatra
## Index

433

435

Salvaging the unrecorded
histories of the Entertainment Industry's
"off the record" past

And its affiliate, the Georgia Literary Assn

THE GEORGIA LITERARY ASSOCIATION
ENTERTAINMENT YOU WOULDN'T NECESSARILY EXPECT FROM THE DEEP SOUTH

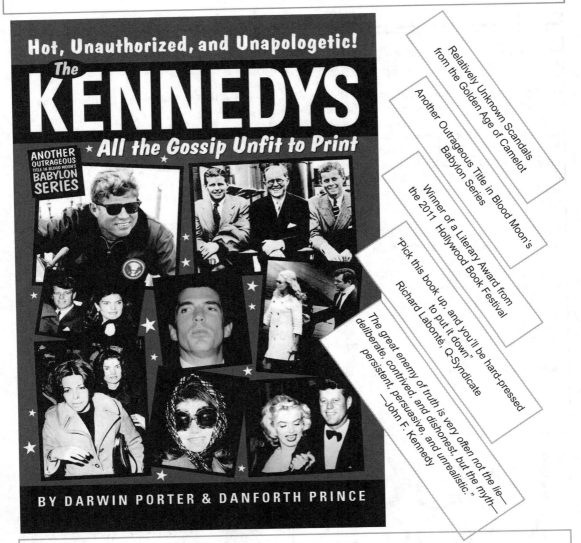

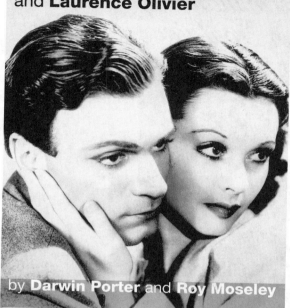

# Damn You,
## Scarlett O'Hara
### The Private Lives of **Vivien Leigh** and **Laurence Olivier**

by **Darwin Porter** and **Roy Moseley**

Here, for the first time, is a biography that raises the curtain on the secret lives of **Lord Laurence Olivier,** often cited as the finest actor in the history of England, and **Vivien Leigh,** who immortalized herself with her Oscar-winning portrayals of Scarlett O'Hara in *Gone With the Wind,* and as Blanche DuBois in Tennessee Williams' *A Streetcar Named Desire.*

The spotlight shone on this famous pair throughout most of their tabloid-fueled careers, but much of what went on behind the velvet curtain remained hidden until the publication of this ground-breaking biography.

Dashing and "impossibly handsome," Laurence Olivier was pursued by the most dazzling luminaries, male and female, of the movie and theater worlds. The influential theatrical producer David Lewis asserted, "He would have slept with anyone." That included Richard Burton, who fell madly in love with him, as did Noël Coward.

Lord Olivier's promiscuous, emotionally disturbed wife (Viv to her lovers) led a tumultuous off-the-record life whose paramours ranged from the A-list to men she picked up off the street. But none of the brilliant roles depicted by Lord and Lady Olivier, on stage or on screen, ever matched the power and drama of personal dramas which wavered between Wagnerian opera and Greek tragedy. *Damn You, Scarlett O'Hara* is the definitive and most revelatory portrait ever published of the most talented and tormented actor and actress of the 20th century.

**Darwin Porter** is the principal author of this seminal work. Winner of numerous awards for his headline-generating biographies, he has shed new light on Marlon Brando, Steve McQueen, Paul Newman, Katharine Hepburn, Humphrey Bogart, Merv Griffin, Michael Jackson, and Howard Hughes.

**Roy Moseley,** this book's co-author, was an intimate friend of both Lord and Lady Olivier, maintaining a decades-long association with the famous couple, nurturing them through triumphs, emotional breakdowns, and streams of suppressed scandal. A resident of California who spent most of his life in England, Moseley has authored or co-authored biographies of Queen Elizabeth and Prince Philip, Rex Harrison, Cary Grant, Merle Oberon, Roger Moore, and Moseley's long-time companion during the final years of her life, Miss Bette Davis.

## DAMN YOU, SCARLETT O'HARA
### THE PRIVATE LIFES OF LAURENCE OLIVIER AND VIVIEN LEIGH
by Darwin Porter and Roy Moseley

ISBN 978-1-936003-15-0     Hardcover, 708 pages, with hundreds of photos.   $27.95
Also available for E-Readers

# What Pair of Famous Hollywood Sisters Refused to Forgive the Insults of their Lifelong Feud?

Of the hundreds of movie stars who flourished during the 1940s, the constantly feuding sisters, Olivia de Havilland and Joan Fontaine, outlived their contemporaries and jointly survived as the last remaining superstars of Hollywood's Golden Age. Their war with each other smoldered and flamed for more than ninety years, as they clawed at and sabotaged each other for the same maternal affection, the same roles, the same Oscar awards, and the same men. Jointly, they nurtured the movie colony's most ferocious case of sibling rivalry.

This new collaborative effort by two of the publishing industry's most respected celebrity biographers involves more than just the untold story of a primal and particularly bitter intra-sibling feud. It's a bittersweet ode to a sweeping but vanished era, with keen and startling new insights into the sisters' top-drawer colleagues and competitors, with a flooding sense of wisdom about the enduring legacy of bloodlines, no matter how blurred and complicated.

## OLIVIA DE HAVILLAND AND JOAN FONTAINE
### TWISTED SISTERS: TO EACH HER OWN

As relayed by **Darwin Porter** and Olivia's former business manager, **Roy Moseley**

A Comprehensive Hardcover, with 450 pages, hundreds of photos, and More Scandalous Gossip than either Melanie (from *Gone With the Wind*) or the second Mrs. De Winter (from *Rebecca*) would ever have tolerated.

ISBN 978-1-936003-27-3    $27.95    AVAILABLE EVERYWHERE, INCLUDING ON E-READERS, EARLY IN 2012

## CRIMINAL ACTIVITIES AND VOYEURISTIC MANIA
## FROM AMERICA'S CHIEF LAW-ENFORCEMENT OFFICER

It was 1928. Into FBI Director J. Edgar Hoover's Office walked a job applicant. Clyde Tolson, fresh from America's Corn Belt. He was handsome, macho, well-built, and soft-spoken. Later, he'd be called "the Gary Cooper of the FBI."

Hoover sat up and took immediate notice of Tolson's commanding presence, especially his piercing black eyes. After an hour of chatting with Tolson, Hoover proclaimed, "Our bureau needs more men like you."

When Hoover invited Tolson to his home for dinner that night, the meal would mark the beginning of thousands served over the next forty years. Before the rooster crowed, Hoover had been nicknamed "Speed," and Tolson was called "Junior." In public, of course, Tolson referred to Hoover as "The Boss."

But as Tolson, one drunken night, told their "fag hag," Ethel Merman: "When we go home and shut the door, I'm the boss."

For their sexual amusement, but often for blackmail purposes, Junior and Speed viewed the obscene files of the FBI. Illegal wiretaps and hidden microphones were used to destroy their enemies.

"Hoover ruled as the head of America's Gestapo," claimed an angry Harry S Truman. Through nine different presidents, Hoover kept his job, even blackmailing Dwight D. Eisenhower. The files he accumulated on "my worst enemy," Eleanor Roosevelt, silenced her opposition to him.

As time went by, Hoover and Tolson opened a celebrity version of Pandora's box, learning the darkest secrets of Errol Flynn (was he a Nazi?), Frank Sinatra, Jane Fonda, the Kennedys, Marlon Brando, Rock Hudson, and especially Martin Luther King, Jr., among countless others.

"For decades, America has been in the grip of two homosexual lovers," Lyndon B. Johnson told his pal, Florida Senator George Smathers. "And there's not a God damn thing I can do about it. He's got us by the cojones, and he'll never let go."

For nearly half a century, this peculiarly private man, who carefully guarded his own dark secrets, held virtually unchecked public power. He manipulated every president from FDR (*"Sometime, J. Edgar, we'll catch you with your pants down"*) to Richard Nixon. He used illegal wiretaps and hidden microphones to destroy anyone who opposed him. And just for fun, he and bedmate Clyde Tolson investigated America's greatest entertainers, including Marilyn Monroe and Elvis Presley; its greatest scientists (including Albert Einstein), and its greated civil rights leaders.

Darwin Porter's saga of power and corruption has a revelation on every page—cross dressing, gay parties, sexual indiscretions, hustlers for sale, alliances with the Mafia, and criminal activity by the nation's chief law enforcer.

It's all here, with chilling details about the abuse of power on the dark side of the American saga.

But mostly it's the decades-long love story of America's two most powerful men who could tell presidents "how to skip rope." (Hoover's words.)

*Darwin Porter* has been fascinated by the American concept of fame since he worked as an entertainment columnist for The Miami Herald early in his career. Since then, he's evolved into one of the most acclaimed celebrity biographers in the world.

**WHAT does a man really have to do to make it in Show Biz? Finally--A COOL Biography that was too HOT to be published during the lifetime of its subject. TALES OF A LURID LIFE!**

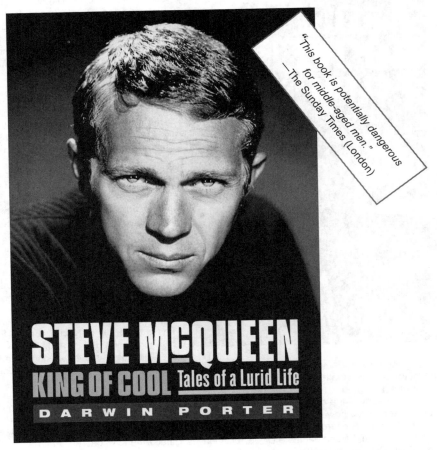

"This book is potentially dangerous for middle-aged men."
—The Sunday Times (London)

The drama of Steve McQueen's personal life far exceeded any role he ever played on screen. Born to a prostitute, he was brutally molested by some of his mother's "johns," and endured gang rape in reform school. His drift into prostitution began when he was hired as a towel boy in the most notorious bordello in the Dominican Republic, where he starred in a string of cheap porno films. Returning to New York before migrating to Hollywood, he hustled men on Times Square and, as a "gentleman escort" in a borrowed tux, rich older women.

And then, sudden stardom as he became the world's top box office attraction. The abused became the abuser. "I live for myself, and I answer to nobody," he proclaimed. "The last thing I want to do is fall in love with a broad."

Thus began a string of seductions that included hundreds of overnight pickups--both male and female. Topping his A-list conquests were James Dean, Paul Newman, Marilyn Monroe, and Barbra Streisand. Finally, this pioneering biography explores the mysterious death of Steve McQueen. Were those salacious rumors really true?

### *Steve McQueen    King of Cool    Tales of a Lurid Life*
**Darwin Porter**

ISBN 978-1-936003-05-1    A carefully researched, 466-page hardcover with dozens of photos    $26.95
Also Available for E-Readers

# PAUL NEWMAN
## THE MAN BEHIND THE BABY BLUES, HIS SECRET LIFE EXPOSED

### Darwin Porter

**THE MOST COMPELLING BIOGRAPHY OF THE ICONIC ACTOR EVER PUBLISHED**

Drawn from firsthand interviews with insiders who knew Paul Newman intimately, and compiled over a period of nearly a half-century, this is the world's most honest and most revelatory biography about Hollywood's pre-eminent male sex symbol, with dozens of potentially shocking revelations.

Whereas the situations it exposes were widely known within Hollywood's inner circles, they've never before been revealed to the general public.

If you're a fan of Newman (and who do you know who isn't) you really should look at this book. It's a respectful but candid cornucopia of information about the sexual and emotional adventures of a young man on Broadway and in Hollywood.

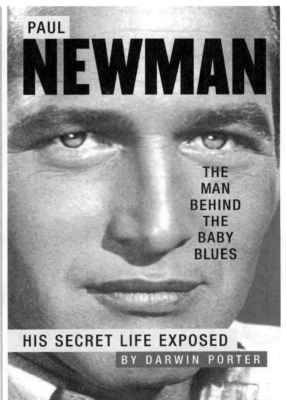

**PAUL NEWMAN WAS A FAMOUS, FULL-TIME RESIDENT OF CONNECTICUT. SHORTLY AFTER HIS DEATH IN 2009, THIS TITLE WON AN HONORABLE MENTION FROM HIS NEIGHBORS AT THE NEW ENGLAND BOOK FESTIVAL**

This is a pioneering and posthumous biography of a charismatic American icon. His rule over the hearts of American moviegoers lasted for more than half a century. Paul Newman was a potent, desirable, and ambiguous sex symbol, a former sailor from Shaker Heights, Ohio, who parlayed his ambisexual charm and extraordinary good looks into one of the most successful careers in Hollywood.

It's all here, as recorded by celebrity chronicler Darwin Porter--the giddy heights and agonizing lows of a great American star, with revelations never before published in any other biography.

## Paul Newman, The Man Behind the Baby Blues
## His Secret Life Exposed
### Darwin Porter
Hardcover, 520 pages, with dozens of photos. Also available for E-readers
**ISBN 978-0-9786465-1-6   $26.95**

THE DEFINITIVE PAUL NEWMAN:

"One wonders how he ever managed to avoid public scrutiny for so long."

# MERV GRIFFIN
## A Life in the Closet

Darwin Porter

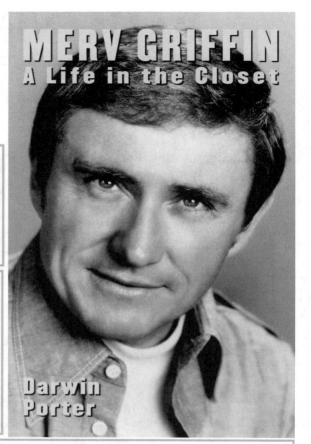

## *Merv Griffin, A Life in the Closet*

Merv Griffin began his career as a Big Band singer, moved on to a failed career as a romantic hero in the movies, and eventually rewrote the rules of everything associated with the broadcasting industry. Along the way, he met and befriended virtually everyone who mattered, made billions operating casinos and developing jingles, contests, and word games. All of this while maintaining a male harem and a secret life as America's most famously closeted homosexual.

In this comprehensive biography——the first published since Merv's death in 2007—celebrity biographer Darwin Porter reveals the amazing details behind the richest, most successful, and in some ways, the most notorious mogul in the history of America's entertainment industry.

Most of his viewers (they numbered 20 million per day) thought that **Merv Griffin**'s life was an ongoing series of chatty segués—amiable, seamless, uncontroversial. But things were far more complicated than viewers at the time ever thought. Here, from the writer who unzipped **Marlon Brando**, is the first post-mortem, unauthorized overview of the mysterious life of **the richest and most notorious man in television**

### HOT, CONTROVERSIAL, & RIGOROUSLY RESEARCHED

## HERE'S MERV!

Hardcover, with photos.  Also available for E-Readers.

ISBN 978-0-9786465-0-9    $26.95

449

# BRANDO UNZIPPED

### An Uncensored Exposé of America's Most Visible Method Actor and Sexual Outlaw
### by Darwin Porter

**BRANDO EXPOSED!!** This "entertainingly outrageous" (*Frontiers Magazine*) biography provides a definitive, blow-by-blow description of the "hot, provocative, and barely under control drama" that was the life of America's most famous Postwar actor.

"Lurid, raunchy, perceptive, and certainly worth reading...One of the ten best show-biz biographies of 2006." **The Sunday Times (London)**

"**Yummy**. An irresistably flamboyant romp of a read." **Books to Watch Out For**

"Astonishing. An extraordinarily detailed portrait of Brando that's as blunt, uncompromising, and X-rated as the man himself." **Women's Weekly**

"This shocking new book is sparking a major reassessment of Brando's legacy as one of Hollywood's most macho lotharios." **Daily Express (London)**

"As author Darwin Porter finds, it wasn't just the acting world Marlon Brando conquered. It was the actors, too." **Gay Times (London)**

"*Brando Unzipped* is the definitive gossip guide to the late, great actor's life." **The New York Daily News**

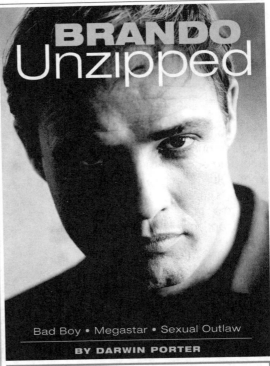

Bad Boy • Megastar • Sexual Outlaw

**BY DARWIN PORTER**

This is one of our most visible and most frequently reviewed titles. A best-seller, and recipient of several prestigious literary awards, it's now in its fifth printing, with French, Portuguese, and Dutch editions available in Europe.

Shortly after its release, this title was extensively serialized by THE SUNDAY TIMES in the UK, and in other major Sunday supplements in mainland Europe and Australia.

A definitive and artfully lurid hardcover with 625 indexed pages and hundreds of photos
Also available for E-readers

**ISBN 978-0-9748118-2-6**. $26.95

# Jacko
# HIS RISE AND FALL

## The Social and Sexual History of Michael Jackson

Darwin Porter.

He rewrote the rules of America's entertainment industry, and he led a life of notoriety.

Even his death was the occasion for more scandal, which continues to this day.

Read this biography for the real story of the circumstances and players who created the icon which the world will forever remember as "the gloved one," Michael Jackson.

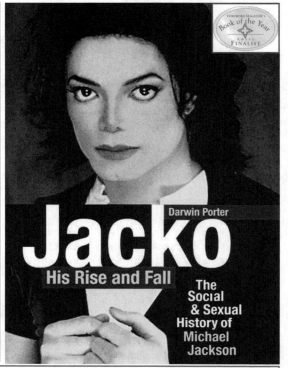

Darwin Porter

Jacko

His Rise and Fall

The Social & Sexual History of Michael Jackson

# HOLLYWOOD BABYLON STRIKES AGAIN!

## THE PROFOUNDLY OUTRAGEOUS VOLUME TWO OF BLOOD MOON'S BABYLON SERIES

Volume Two of Blood Moon's overview of exhibitionism, sexuality, and sin as filtered through 85 years of Hollywood indiscretion.

"Monumentally exhaustive...The Ultimate Guilty Pleasure"
Shelf Awareness

Winner of the Los Angeles Book Festival's Best Nonfiction Title of 2010, and the New England Book Festival's Best Anthology for 2010.

"If you love smutty celebrity dirt as much as I do, then have I got a book for you!"
The Hollywood Offender

*"These books will set the graves of Hollywood's cemeteries spinning"*   **Daily Express**

## *Hollywood Babylon Strikes Again!*

Darwin Porter and Danforth Prince
Hardcover, 380 outrageous pages, with hundreds of photos

**ISBN 978-1-936003-12-9**   **$25.95**

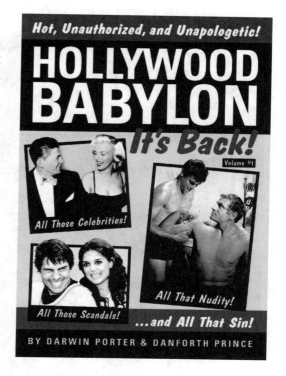

# HOMOSEXUALITY IN THE MOVIES

*For Private Homes and Libraries, This Is a Book of Record, Reference Source, and Gossip Guide to 50 Years of Queer Cinema*

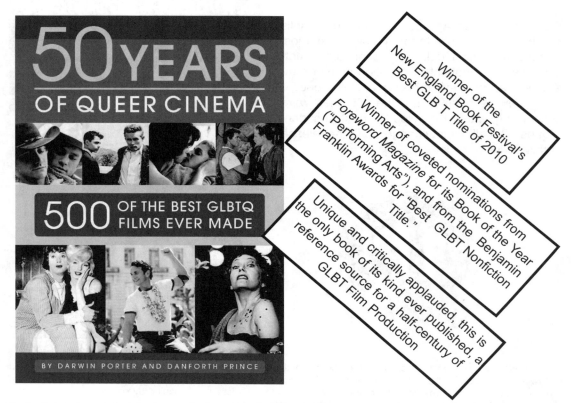

"In the Internet age, where every movie, queer or otherwise, is blogged about somewhere, a hefty print compendium of film facts and pointed opinion might seem anachronistic. But flipping through well-reasoned pages of commentary is so satisfying. Add to that physical thrill the charm of analysis that is sometimes sassy and always smart, and this filtered survey of short reviews is a must for queer-film fans.

"In part one, Porter and Prince provide a succinct "A to Z romp" through 500 films, with quick plot summaries and on-point critical assessments, each film summed up with a pithy headline: *Yossi & Jagger* is "Macho Israeli Soldiers Make Love, Not War.

"The films surveyed in part two are quirkier fare, 160 "less publicized" efforts, including—no lie—*Karl Rove, I Love You*, in which gay actor Dan Butler falls for 'George W. Bush's Turd Blossom.'

"Essays on Derek Jarman, Tennessee Williams, Andy Warhol, Jack Wrangler, Joe Gage and others—and on how *The Front Runner* never got made—round out this indispensable survey of gay-interest cinema."

RICHARD LABONTÉ
BOOK MARKS/QSYNDICATE

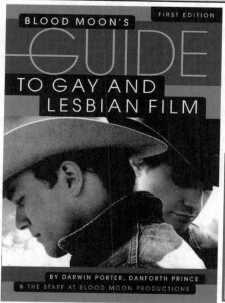

457

# Midnight in Savannah

### A Horrifying, Bittersweet Parody of Sexual Eccentricities in the Deep South

## Darwin Porter

**Midnight In Savannah**

First there was THE BOOK, the one that exposed the sexual priorities of Georgia's steamiest city.

Now there's Midnight in Savannah, a decadent novel that tells a whole lot more.

This is the Savannah of today: Gay, straight, and transgendered, presented with affection and verve by the Georgia Literary Assn and Blood Moon Productions.

Scandal is no stranger in Georgia!

After its publication in 2000, Darwin Porter's *Midnight in Savannah* quickly established itself as one of the best-selling gay novels in the history of the Deep South.

Eugene Raymond, a filmmaker in Nashville, writes, "Porter disturbs by showing the world as a *film noir* cul-de-sac. Corruption has no respect for gender or much of anything else.

"In MIDNIGHT, both Lavender Morgan (at 72, the world's oldest courtesan) and Tipper Zelda (an obese, fading chanteuse taunted as 'the black widow) purchase lust from sexually conflicted young men with drop-dead faces, chiseled bodies, and genetically gifted crotches. These women once relied on their physicality to steal the hearts and fortunes of the world's richest and most powerful men. Now, as they slide closer every day to joining the corpses of their former husbands, these once-beautiful women must depend, in a perverse twist of fate, on sexual outlaws for *le petit mort*. And to survive, the hustlers must idle their personal dreams while struggling to cajole what they need from a sexual liaison they detest. Mendacity reigns. Physical beauty as living hell. CAT ON A HOT TIN ROOF's Big Daddy must be spinning in his grave right now."

*"If you're not already a Darwin Porter fan, this novel will make you one! We've come a long way, baby, since Gore Vidal's The City and the Pillar."*

**Time Out for Books**

*"An artfully brutal saga of corruption, greed, sexual tension, and murder, highlighted by the eccentricities of the Deep South. Compulsive Reading."*

**The Georgia Literary Assn.**

A wildly popular, supremely entertaining parody of a famous murder that will haunt you long after your return from Georgia. From Blood Moon and the Georgia Literary Assn.

Softcover, 498 pages **$16.95** **ISBN 978-0-9668030-1-3**

A supremely informativie "info-novel" about orgiastic highlights of pre-code Hollywood

# Hollywood's Silent Closet by Darwin Porter

An anthology of star-studded scandal from Tinseltown's very gay and very lavender past, it focuses on Hollywood's secrets from the 1920s, including the controversial backgrounds of the great lovers of the Silent Screen.

Valentino, Ramon Novarro, Charlie Chaplin, Fatty Arbuckle, Pola Negri, Mary Pickford, and many others figure into eyewitness accounts of the debauched excesses that went on behind closed doors. It also documents the often tragic endings of America's first screen idols, some of whom admitted to being more famous than the monarchs of England and Jesus Christ combined.

The first book of its kind, it's the most intimate and most realistic novel about sex, murder, blackmail, and degradation in early Hollywood ever written.

A banquet of information about the pansexual intrigues of Hollywood between 1919 and 1926 compiled from eyewitness interviews with men and women, all of them insiders, who flourished in its midst. Not for the timid, it names names and doesn't spare the guilty. If you believe, like Truman Capote, that the literary treatment of gossip will become the literature of the 21st century, then you will love *Hollywood's Silent Closet.*

"The *Myra Breckinridge* of the Silent-Screen era. Lush, luscious, and langorously decadent. A brilliant primer of **Who Was Who** in early Hollywood."

***Gay Times, London***

A compelling, show stopping paperback, 7" x 10", with 746 pages and at least 60 vintage photos

**ISBN 978-0-9668030-2-0**     $24.95

Millions of fans lusted after **Gary Cooper** (background) and **Rudolph Valentino** (foreground) but until the release of this book, **The Public Never Knew.**

# BLOOD MOON

**An Artfully Brutal Tale of Psychosis, Sexual Obsession, Money, Power, Religion, and Love.**

by Darwin Porter

In 2008, this title was designated as one of the ten best horror novels ever published
in a survey conducted by the British literary club *Boiz Who Read*

**Blood Moon** exposes the murky labyrinths of fanatical Christianity in America today, all within a spunky context of male eroticism. If you never thought that sex, psychosis, right-wing religion, and violence aren't linked, think again.

*"In the gay genre, Blood Moon does for the novel what Danielle Steele and John Grisham have been publishing in the straight world for years."*

**Frank Fenton**

Rose Phillips, Blood Moon's charismatic and deviant evangelist, and her shocking but beautiful gay son, Shelley, were surely written in hell. Together, they're a brilliant—and jarring—depiction of a fiercely aggressive Oedipal couple competing for the same male prizes.

*"**Blood Moon** reads like an IMAX spectacle about the power of male beauty, with red-hot icons, a breathless climax, and erotica that's akin to Anaïs Nin on Viagra with a bump of meth."*

**Eugene Raymond**

A controversial, compelling, and artfully potboiling paperback that describes what really happens when The Moon Turns to Blood.　　**ISBN 978-0-9668030-4-4**　　$10.99

# Rhinestone Country

An Erotic Thriller about Love, Sex, Applause, and the Music Industry     Darwin Porter

### All that glitter, all that publicity, all that talent, all that pain...

The *True Grit* of show-biz novels, *Rhinestone Country* is a provocative, realistic, and tender portrayal of the Country-Western music industry, closeted lives south of the Mason-Dixon line, and three of the singers who clawed their way to stardom.

*Rhinestone Country reads like a scalding gulp of rotgut whiskey on a snowy night in a bow-jacks honky-tonk.*
  **-Mississippi Pearl**

DARWIN PORTER

Author of
Butterflies in Heat,
Blood Moon and
Hollywood's
Silent Closet

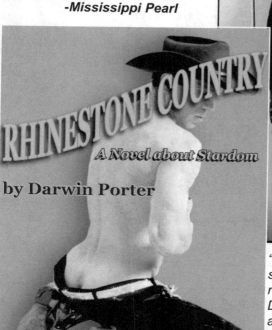

*A Novel about Stardom*

**by Darwin Porter**

"Beautifully crafted, *Rhinestone Country* sweeps with power and tenderness across the racial, social, and sexual landscapes of the Deep South. This is a daring and dazzling work about trauma, deception, and pain, all of it with a Southern accent." **Peter Tompkins**

*"A gay and erotic treatment of the Country-Western music industry? Nashville has come out of the closet at last!"*

**The Georgia Literary Assn**

Softcover, with a Southern accent, some memorable men and women, and a whole lot of pathos

569 pages     **ISBN  978-0-9668030-3-7**     $15.99

# BUTTERFLIES IN HEAT

## Darwin Porter

### A compellingly retro softcover expressing some eternal truths about LOVE, HATE, GREED, MONEY, AND SEX

**Tennessee Williams,** who understood a thing or two about loss, love, and drama, had this to say about **Butterflies in Heat:**

"I'd walk the waterfront for Numie any day."

*"The most SCORCHING novel of the BIZ-ZARE, the FLAMBOYANT, the CORRUPT since Midnight Cowboy. The strikingly beautiful blond hustler, Numie, has come to the end of the line. Here, in the SEARING HEAT of a tropical cay, he arouses PASSIONS that explode under the BLOOD-RED SUN."*
**Manor Reviews**

*"A well-established cult classic. How does Darwin Porter's garden grow? Only in the moonlight, and only at midnight, when man-eating vegetation in any color but green bursts into full bloom to devour the latest offerings."*

**James Leo Herlihy, author of**
**_MIDNIGHT COWBOY_**

This title, a cult classic now in its **16th printing**, has sold steadily to a coterie of Darwin Porter fans since its inauguration in 1976, when it was the thing EVERYBODY in Key West was talking about, and the inspiration for the movie (The Last Resort/ Tropic of Desire) that EVERYBODY wanted to be in.

ISBN
978-0-9668030-9-9
$14.95

*"Darwin Porter writes with an incredible understanding of the milieu--hot enough to singe the wings off any butterfly."*
**James Kirkwood, co-author of _A CHORUS LINE_**

*"We know from the beginning that we're getting into a hotbed that has morbid fascination for potential readers. The novel evolves, in fact, into one massive melée of malevolence, vendetta, and e-v-i-l, stunningly absorbing alone for its sheer and unrelenting exploration of the lower depths."*
**BESTSELLERS**

Blood Moon maintains its ongoing commitment to a FREE monthly newsletter
wherein **Darwin Porter,**
America's most literate and outrageous muckraker, analyzes recent celebrity gossip.

This is Blood Moon's response to the 21st century tabloids.
Blood Moon: Putting the *oooomph* back into editorial coverage of
current events and celebrity scandal,

### SALACIOUS CELEBRITY DISH
### LIKE YOU'VE NEVER SEEN IT BEFORE. WHY?

## BECAUSE DIRTY LAUNDRY MAKES WASHDAY FUN!

The water's hot, and the soap is free, but you won't get really clean
unless you sign up for it first, **FREE AND WITHOUT CHARGE,**
from the home page of

# WWW.BLOODMOONPRODUCTIONS.COM

In May of 2010, Blood Moon rented a booth at **Book Expo, 2010,** the world's largest literary marketplace, and made a 75-minute movie about what happened during the maniacal goings-on that followed.

In June of 2011, we filmed a 60-minute updated version, reflecting the previous year's evolution of the thousands of events affecting the book trades.

We offer these films, plus dozens of other videotaped book trailers, to anyone who dreams about maneuvering his or her way through the shark-infested waters of the book trades. Watch these films, download or share them, without charge, from the home page of

## www.BloodMoonProductions.com

**BLOOD MOON PRODUCTIONS ANNOUNCES** THE AVAILABILITY OF A PAIR OF DOCUMENTARIES AND INFO-MERCIALS it filmed at two separate instances of the world's largest literary trade fair, *Book Expo America.*

**BLOOD MOON'S VIEW FROM THE FLOOR**, Versions 1 and 2, represent history's first attempts to capture—close, in-your-face, uncensored, and personalized—the interactions, alliances, scandals, and dramas that explode for a small book publisher during a bookselling mega-event devoted to the marketing, pricing, and sale of its literary products.

Conceived as a means of increasing public awareness of Blood Moon's literary products, these films were developed as publicity and promotion pieces by the company's founder and president, Danforth Prince. "Book publishers operate in a state of barely controlled hysteria, especially in this economic climate," he said. "Within these films, we've captured some of the drama of how books are promoted and hawked at highly competitive events where everyone from Barbra Streisand to the Duchess of York will enthusiastically shake his or her bon-bon to sell something."

"At BEA, enemies, competitors, and authors evoke Oscar night in Hollywood before the awards are announced," Prince continued. "These films are the first attempt to depict, without charge, on video, how a small press swims in the frantic, shark-infested waters of the book trade. They document specific moments in America's mercantile history, with implications for America's reading habits and how consumers will opt to amuse and entertain themselves in the 21st century."

During the footage he shot from within and near his booths at BEA 2010 and 2011, Mr. Prince was directed by Polish-born Piotr Kajstura, winner of several filmmaking awards and grants for his work with, among others, the tourism board of South Carolina.

BOOK EXPO 2010, BLOOD MOON'S VIEW FROM THE FLOOR.
AND BOOK EXPO 2011, BLOOD MOON'S VIEW FROM THE FLOOR 2
© Blood Moon Productions, Ltd. Available now, electronically and without charge,
from the home page of **BloodMoonProductions.com.**

## *What Book-Industry Critics Said About the 2010 Installment of this Film:*

"**Blood Moon Productions**, which specializes in books about Hollywood celebrity scandals of the past—many of which were hushed up at the time—offers a feature-length video on BookExpo America 2010, which aims to give "nonprofessional book people an insight into book fairs" while highlighting some Blood Moon titles. The narrator is Blood Moon president Danforth Prince, who interviews, among others, Carole Stuart of Barricade Books, Philip Rafshoon, owner of Outwrite Bookstore and Coffeehouse, Atlanta, Ga., Graeme Aitkin of the Bookshop in Sydney, Australia, Eugene Schwartz of ForeWord Reviews, and a what seems like half of the staff of National Book Network, Blood Moon's distributor."
**Shelf-Awareness.com** August 3, 2010 (volume 2, issue #1247)

DIVING BACK INTO THE SHARK-INFESTED WATERS OF THE BOOK TRADES!

Book Expo 2011
Blood Moon's VIEW FROM THE FLOOR ❷
SEE IT NOW

*Blood Moon's View from the Floor 2.*
An updated installment filmed at Book Expo 2011
Viewable and downloadable now, without charge, from
*www.BloodMoonProductions.com*

**BLOOD**
**MOON**
Productions, Ltd.